# VOTERS, PATRONS, AND PARTIES

# Voters, Patrons, and Parties

*The Unreformed Electoral System of
Hanoverian England 1734–1832*

FRANK O'GORMAN

CLARENDON PRESS · OXFORD
1989

Oxford University Press, Walton Street, Oxford OX2 6DP
Oxford New York Toronto
Delhi Bombay Calcutta Madras Karachi
Petaling Jaya Singapore Hong Kong Tokyo
Nairobi Dar es Salaam Cape Town
Melbourne Auckland
and associated companies in
Berlin Ibadan

Oxford is a trade mark of Oxford University Press

Published in the United States
by Oxford University Press, New York

British Library Cataloguing in Publication Data
O'Gorman, Frank, 1940–
Voters, patrons and parties: the unreformed
electorate of Hanoverian England 1734–1832.
1. England. Electoral systems, 1734–1832
I. Title
323.6' 3' 0941
ISBN 0-19-820056-0

Library of Congress Cataloging-in-Publication Data
O'Gorman, Frank.
Voters, patrons, and parties: the unreformed electoral system of
Hanoverian England, 1734–1832/Frank O'Gorman.
Bibliography: p.    Includes index.
1. Elections—Great Britain—History. 2. Political parties—Great
Britain—History. 3. Political culture—Great Britain—History.
4. Great Britain—Politics and government—1714–1837. I. Title.
JN951.046  1989    324.241' 009–dc19    88-30304
ISBN 0-19-820056-0

Set by Dobbie Typesetting Limited, Plymouth, Devon
Printed in Great Britain by
Courier International Ltd
Tiptree, Essex

# PREFACE

The preparation of this book has profited enormously from the generosity of institutions and the kindness of individuals. I should like to acknowledge here the financial assistance I received from both the Wolfson Foundation and the British Academy. I have been pursuing the research on which this book was based for a number of years: that number would have been much greater without their support. The University of Manchester Regional Computing Centre gave inordinately in terms of facilities and advice. In particular, the unique programming skills of Mr John Lloyd-Jones were indispensable to the construction of Chapter 4. Furthermore, his kind and tolerant treatment of a historian who was struggling to come to grips with the computer revolution was as compassionate as it was invaluable. Professor Harry Dickinson of Edinburgh University and Dr Theo Hoppen of Hull University read part of the book in manuscript, and I should like to acknowledge their help and criticism while absolving them of any responsibility for what follows.

Earlier versions of parts of the argument in Chapters 2 and 4 appeared in the *Journal of Modern History*, 56 (1984) and *Social History*, (1986). I am grateful to those journals for permission to reprint material from my articles. The theme of the third section of Chapter 5, was set out in pilot form as 'Popular Constitutionalism in the Eighteenth Century', in Raphael Samuel (ed.), *Patriotism: Ideology and Myth in the Making of the English National Identity*.

Over the years I have developed a very considerable debt to the staff of a number of institutions who have made this book possible. The British Library, the National Register of Archives, and the Institute of Historical Research provide the indispensable foundations for research into electoral history. Thereafter, I found it necessary to resort to the following institutions and their staffs: Bedfordshire Record Office; Berkshire Record Office; Birmingham Public Library; Birmingham University Library; Bristol Archives Office; Bristol Public Library; Buckinghamshire Archaeological Society; Cambridgeshire Record Office; Cheshire Record Office; Chester Public Library; Cirencester Public Library; Colchester Public Library; Cornwall Record

Office; the Royal Institute of Cornwall; Coventry Public Library; Cumbria County Record Office; Derbyshire Record Office; Devon Record Office; Dorset Record Office; Durham County Record Office; Dyfed County Record Office; Essex Record Office; Gateshead Public Library; Glamorgan Record Office; Gloucester Public Library; Gloucester County Record Office; Grimsby Public Library; Guildford Museum; Gwynedd Record Office; Hampshire Record Office; Hereford County Record Office; Hereford Public Library; Hertfordshire Record Office; Hull University Library; Huntingdonshire Record Office; Humberside Record Office; Kent Record Office; Lancashire Record Office; Leeds City Library; Leicester Museum; Leicester County Record Office; Lincoln Archives Office; Lincoln Public Library; Greater London Record Office; House of Lords Record Office; City of Manchester Record Office; Newark Public Library; Newcastle-upon-Tyne Record Office; Norfolk Record Office; Northamptonshire Record Office; Northumberland Record Office; Nottinghamshire Record Office; Nottingham University Library; Oxford Public Library; Oxfordshire County Record Office; Plymouth Public Library; Reading University Library; Reading Public Library; St Albans Public Library; Sheffield Public Library; Shrewsbury Public Library; Shropshire Record Office; William Salt Library, Stafford; Southampton Public Library; Staffordshire Record Office; Suffolk Record Offices; Surrey Record Office; Sussex Record Office; Warwickshire Record Office; Wigan Public Library; Wiltshire Record Office; and York Public Library.

I am grateful to owners of manuscripts for access to and permission to quote from their collections, notably the Trustees of the Wentworth Woodhouse Estate, the Duke of Devonshire, the Duke of Portland, the Duke of Grafton, the Lord Spencer, the Lord Bathurst, the Marquis of Bath, and the Glynn and Strutt families.

Any investigation of the unreformed electoral system owes an enormous debt to the wonderful volumes issued by the History of Parliament Trust: R. R. Sedgwick (ed.), *The House of Commons, 1715–1754*, L. B. Namier and J. Brooke (eds.) *The House of Commons, 1754–1790*, and R. G. Thorne (ed.), *The House of Commons, 1790–1820*. The five volumes of the latter appeared in print during the very latest stages in the preparation of this book. Fortunately, I had been permitted pre-publication access to the Introductory volume, for which I am enormously grateful to Mr Thorne. In particular, I was gratified to see that my views on Independency were, to some extent, at least, shared by one other historian. Thanks to the patience of Oxford University Press, I was able to read the published volumes of *The House of Commons,*

*1790–1820* and, where desirable, to make specific reference to its contents in the following pages.

I should also like to express my thanks publicly to Mr Brian Kelly who worked as my research assistant, preparing over 30 parliamentary poll books for computer input. I am pleased to take this opportunity of paying tribute to his patience, accuracy, and unfailing good sense.

It is platitudinous to remark that no scholar works in isolation from his colleagues and contemporaries. Nevertheless, I am very much aware how much I have learned from Professors Geoffrey Holmes, John Phillips, and William Speck. I do not share, and cannot endorse, all their opinions and judgements on all aspects of electoral and political history before 1832. On some matters, indeed, I have had the temerity even to dissent from their views. Nevertheless, I could not have written this book without their example and their inspiration. Notwithstanding this acknowledgement, the interpretation of electoral politics which follows, and the treatment of specific issues in the political and electoral history of England in the century before the Reform Act of 1832, is solely my own responsibility.

FRANK O'GORMAN

*University of Manchester*
*September 1987*

# CONTENTS

# TABLES AND FIGURES

# ABBREVIATIONS

| | |
|---|---|
| Ag. Hist. Rev. | Agricultural History Review |
| Am. Hist. Rev. | American History Review |
| Bucks. Records | Records of Buckinghamshire |
| Bull. Inst. Hist. Res. | Bulletin of the Institute of Historical Research |
| Business Hist. | Business History |
| Cirencester Archaeol. Hist. Soc. | Annual Report and Newsletter of the Cirencester Archaeological and Historical Society |
| CJ | Commons Journals |
| Durham Univ. J. | Durham University Journal |
| Econ. Hist. Rev. | Economic History Review |
| Eng. Hist. Rev. | English Historical Review |
| Guildhall Misc. | Guildhall Miscellany |
| Guildhall Studies | Guildhall Studies in London History |
| Hist. J. | Historical Journal |
| Hist. Stud. ANZ | Historical Studies, Australia and New Zealand |
| Int. Rev. Soc. Hist. | International Review of Social History |
| J. Brit. Studies | Journal of British Studies |
| J. Chester Archaeol. Soc. | Journal of the Chester Archaeological Society |
| J. Econ. Hist. | Journal of Economic History |
| J. Interdiscip. Hist. | Journal of Interdisciplinary Historical Research |
| J. Merioneth | Journal of the Merioneth Historical and Record Society |
| J. Mod. Hist. | Journal of Modern History |
| J. Soc. Hist. | Journal of Social History |
| J. Stats. Soc. | Journal of the Statistical Society |
| Libraries Bulletin | Libraries, Museums, and Arts Committee Bulletin |
| Liverpool Dioc. Review | Liverpool Diocesan Review |

| | |
|---|---|
| *Midland Hist.* | *Midland History* |
| *Northern Hist.* | *Northern History* |
| *Parl. Affairs* | *Parliamentary Affairs* |
| *Parl. Hist. Yrbk.* | *Parliamentary History Yearbook* |
| *Records of Bucks.* | *Records of Buckinghamshire* |
| *RO* | *Record Office* |
| *Social Hist.* | *Social History* |
| *Studies in Burke* | *Studies in Burke and His Time* |
| *Trans. Bristol and Gloucs. Archaeol. Soc.* | *Transactions of the Bristol and Gloucestershire Archaeological Society* |
| *Trans. Hist. Soc. Lancs. and Cheshire* | *Transactions of the Historical Society of Lancashire and Cheshire* |
| *Trans. Inst. Brit. Geog.* | *Transactions of the Institute of British Geographers* |
| *Trans. Royal Hist. Soc.* | *Transactions of the Royal Historical Society* |
| *Trans. Salop. Archaeol. Soc.* | *Transactions of the Shropshire Archaeological Society* |
| *Trans. Worcs. Archaeol. Soc.* | *Transactions of the Worcestershire Archaeological Society* |
| *VCH* | *Victoria County History* |
| *Welsh Hist. Rev.* | *Welsh Historical Review* |
| *Wilts. Archaeol. Mag.* | *Wiltshire Archaeological Magazine* |

# 1

# *The Electoral System in Hanoverian England*

HISTORIOGRAPHY

In the century before the Reform Act of 1832, British society underwent profound changes. These can be characterized in a variety of ways but they are normally considered to have been 'revolutions' in agriculture, industry, commerce, and communications. They were still incomplete in 1832, but the old obstacles to material growth and economic expansion were being rapidly overcome. These changes amounted to the replacement of one economic and social order by another. In trying to understand them the historian needs constantly to remind himself of the fact that these developments made their initial impact upon local life and local men and women in a local environment. Upheavals in economic organization led naturally to unprecedented transformations in the pattern of local society and in the nature of institutions and practices within local communities. The exercise of authority—and concomitant habits of deference towards that authority—had therefore to be reconstituted at the local level.

The political and electoral aspects of these tremendous upheavals in local life have never been seriously investigated by historians. The present volume, therefore, requires explanation rather than apology. This is especially the case because many of the favourite themes of political historians of the period—the decline of the monarchy, the rise of parties, the growth of cabinet government, and the emergence of a non-political civil service—seem to bear little immediate relationship to many of the major social changes of the times. Even those who have ventured beyond the purely political sphere and into the cultures of reformers, radicals, evangelicals, proletarians, and bourgeoisies, have necessarily focused their attention upon selected aspects of Hanoverian society. Common to almost all of these historians has been a remarkable indifference to, and consequently massive ignorance of, the electoral foundations of the Hanoverian political and social order.

This book has been written in the conviction that a balanced and fully rounded understanding of Hanoverian society requires the incorporation of an electoral dimension into the familiar chronicles of social and political history. The exercise of political and social control, and indeed the maintenance of political and social stability, occurred primarily at the local level and, frequently, within a constituency framework. The complicated mechanisms of that control, therefore, yield an understanding not merely of electoral matters but of much larger themes besides. As the great national parties at Westminster groped downwards into the constituencies for support— for men, money and morale—in the early nineteenth century, they encountered pre-existing, organized political groups inhabiting a political culture of their own. The interaction of these two political forms needs to be grasped if the rise of party is to be understood in its constituency context. Yet it is just as important to realize the significance of the political culture of the constituency for its own sake, too. Hundreds of thousands of men—voters and non-voters alike—experienced politics at this level. 'Public opinion' existed largely within this framework. Attitudes to authority, and indeed patterns of resistance to authority, were fashioned within this structure. Many forms of political organization conformed to its requirements.[1] The constituency was in many ways the fundamental unit in the Hanoverian body politic.

Historians, however, have ignored and neglected the constituency, preferring to denounce the system of electoral politics which prevailed. Ever since the radical critique of the electoral system in the later eighteenth century, a critique which passed silently but securely into the Whig historiography of the nineteenth, historians have been morbidly preoccupied with the unsavoury aspects of 'pre-reform' electoral politics. Even in the twentieth century Sir Lewis Namier viewed electoral politics from the standpoint of the landed interest; indeed, he tended to represent electoral politics simply as a projection of the economic power of landlords, proprietors, and patrons.[2]

---

[1] Nevertheless, there is an unmistakable extension of political activity outside traditional authority networks in this period commencing, perhaps, with certain aspects of the Wilkite movement. Even more impressive, however, are the crusading politics of the Abolitionist movement in the 1780s.

[2] See, for example, L. B. Namier, *The Structure of Politics at the Accession of George III* 2nd edn. (London, 1967). It is surprising how *little* the electorate figures in Namier's work, which is, after all, a portrait of how the local oligarchy controlled the political system. It is significant that almost all his research on constituencies concentrated upon small and anachronistic strongholds of electoral malpractice. With the exception of a few large boroughs he discusses in *Structure of Politics*, most of his constituency analysis concerns Shropshire and Cornwall. His apparent aversion to the politics of larger constituencies may also be seen in L. B. Namier and J. Brooke (eds.), *The House of Commons, 1754–1790*, 3 vols. (London, 1964). Even since Namier, most work on elections still concentrates on the operation of patronage and the management of the electorate. The accounts of the system in *House of Commons* offer biographies of MPs and brief narratives of constituency control. In very few instances is the electorate thought worthy of discussion in other than stereotyped terms.

Professor Holmes, reflecting the general opinion of an impressive orthodoxy of late Stuart and early Hanoverian scholarship, writes dismissively of the unreformed electorate. Compared to the virile and active electorates of the early eighteenth century, its successor was weak and apathetic. Indeed, in the counties, he diagnoses 'a prolonged electoral coma' and pronounced that 'the franchise was largely academic'. As for the borough electorates, they were 'all but wholly anaesthetised'.[3] The most recent authority on Hanoverian politics, like many other writers, has preferred to expose the 'glaring anomalies' in the electoral system rather than to explain the circumstances which gave rise to their widespread adoption and acceptance.[4] This remarkably unfavourable historiographical treatment of the unreformed electoral system surely needs to be scrutinized.

*First*, it is assumed that very few of the voters were free to vote as they wished. Professor Namier believed that 'not one voter in twenty could freely exercise his statutory right'.[5] Far from expressing their antecedent political, religious, or social preferences, the voters 'followed at election time the instructions of their social superiors'.[6] Yet exactly how over 95% of the electorate could be kept in bondage for so long has never been convincingly explained. *Second*, historians have assumed that the electors 'regarded their franchises, as indeed did the Court, as a kind of personal property on which they expected to make a profit at least once every seven years'.[7] This venal conception of the electorate has had remarkable influence although it rests upon an anecdotal rather than upon a quantifiable basis. Of course, examples of venality are by no means uncommon, but exactly how typical were they? *Third*, elections and the determination of election contests was an exclusive rather than a participatory proceeding, and one which rested upon the political activities of 'the educated and politically alert class of landed proprietors, with a sprinkling from the upper fringe of various professional groups'.[8] How large numbers of electors—somewhere between 250,000 and 300,000—could be excluded from political life is no doubt explained by the *fourth* point—that because

---

[3] G. Holmes, *The Electorate and the National Will in the First Age of Party* (Kendal, 1976), 30, 31.
[4] See I. R. Christie, *Wars and Revolutions: Britain, 1760–1815* (London, 1982), 27–8.
[5] Namier, *Structure of Politics*, 87
[6] I. R. Christie, *The End of North's Ministry, 1780–1782* (London, 1958), 48. Brooke, however, is careful to qualify such assertions: 'the assumption that tenants voted as their landlords wished from fear of being dispossessed is a caricature of the real state of affairs . . . The gentry were the leaders of the county, not its masters'. see Namier and Brooke *House of Commons*, i. 2–3.
[7] J. Owen, *The Eighteenth Century: 1714–1815* (London, 1974), 101.
[8] Christie, *North's Ministry*, 155.

the great majority of electors were politically unaware, politics and political issues were unimportant to the resolution of election contests. Thus we read that 'political considerations in the modern sense did not normally enter a great deal into all this'.[9] Furthermore, the electors 'paid little or no heed to the way their members were likely to vote in the Commons'.[10] Elections are thus assumed to have been a conflict of material and personal pressures rather than a conflict of values and ideology.

Most students of the period are familiar with this kind of historiography. They should realize that it owes more to the radical writers of the late eighteenth and early nineteenth century and to the Whigs of the reign of Victoria than it does to modern scholarship. Consequently, anecdotes and examples—usually of a singular character—are adduced to demonstrate how electors behaved and what the electoral system was like in the dark age before 1832. In fact, the unreformed electorate has yet to be rescued from the Whig interpretation of modern British history.

In the present state of knowledge we cannot answer some of the most basic and straightforward questions which it is possible to ask. Was the electorate growing in size, and if so, at what rate? If it was growing in size, was it becoming harder to influence and to control? How amenable to control, in fact, *was* the electorate? Was it in any degree politically conscious, and was that consciousness sharpening? If so, what forms did this consciousness take? To what extent did the electorate identify itself with Whig and Tory parties? How was the electorate organized, and with what degree of efficiency? Was it really the case that some crude combination of corruption, intimidation, and treating usually made the electors behave as 'the patrons' wished? (If so, why was the election campaign such a highly refined ritual?) Indeed, could the campaign influence the outcome of an electoral contest? The collection of unverified assumptions which passes for a 'model' or 'interpretation' of the unreformed electoral system will allow us to answer hardly any of these questions. The trouble with the existing model is not that it is 'wrong'—indeed, it is just sufficiently credible to enable us to relax our critical instincts—but that it is unhelpful to us. These deficiencies damagingly reverberate on to much larger issues. The control of the electorate by an 'oligarchy' has always—and perhaps

[9] M. R. Brock, *The Great Reform Act* (London, 1973), 17. See also his comment on p. 16: 'Few people outside aristocratic and parliamentary circles understood politics, or took a continuous interest in them. The shams of the system symbolized and facilitated the ascendancy of these few.'

[10] Owen, *The Eighteenth Century*, 101; see also Christie, *North's Ministry*, 131-2.

unthinkingly—been taken to be one of the essential components in the achievement of political and social stability in Hanoverian Britain, though it is, of course, by no means the only one. Because the forms of the electoral system do not change very much in the century before reform, historians have assumed that political stability was in some ways an outgrowth of electoral paralysis. What justification is there for such an assessment? In the face of so much evidence of increasing literacy, the growth of informal educational provision, the persistence of popular Toryism, the inflammability of religious issues, the rise of radicalism, and of course the growth both of party and political consciousness, is it conceivable that the electorate should have been the only sector in Hanoverian Britain to remain untouched by the march of the mind? What should we make of the surprisingly numerous anti-patronage revolts in the constituencies which, disappointingly, appear to have little or nothing to do either with the rise of party or the growth of radicalism?

There is no shortage of problems for historians of the electorate to busy themselves with. Naturally, the central—though not the exclusive—focus of his or her enquiries must be general elections. By our standards, elections in the Hanoverian period seem to have had very limited functions. Only a minority of constituencies went to the polls at successive elections. The nature of the franchise and the power of patrons restricted the free expression of opinion. The abiding strength of local considerations precluded the expression of any kind of 'national' sentiment. Consequently, it was unusual for elections to have much impact upon questions of national policy. Elections had little effect upon the balance of power between government and opposition at Westminster. Before the mid-nineteenth century elections did not create governments, although a ministry almost always won elections and usually by considerable majorities. It is true that the elections of 1784 and 1831 confirmed existing governments in office in the most controversial of circumstances, but this was most unusual. A general election was not normally an occasion for consulting the sentiments of the people.

This is emphatically not to argue that the sentiments of the people were of no importance in elections. On certain issues, especially those with an immediate and local significance, they could exert a decisive influence over the outcome—even over the existence—of a contest. In many places, the Westminster model of a (usually strong) political establishment confronted by a (normally weak and fragmented) opposition was unconsciously imitated by the intermittent resistance of standing local oppositions to established structures of patronage and influence.[11]

This was the essence of electoral conflict, the base upon which regional and national issues were from time to time superimposed. Elections consequently afforded an opportunity either for the local balance of social and political power to be reaffirmed or, in certain circumstances, for it to be challenged. On such issues as these, local opinion might reasonably be expected to express itself.

From this standpoint, then, the importance of elections is that they provide a periodic opportunity for a public check and report on the assiduousness of the local élite in fulfilling its responsibilities, affording an opportunity for the neglected to complain and for the grateful to mark their appreciation. At the very least, the imminence of elections must have concentrated the paternalist minds of those individuals and families who entertained parliamentary and electoral ambitions. These ambitions depended upon a wide variety of local circumstances for their fulfilment. For it goes without saying that these were *local* relationships involving *local* élites with *local* ambitions and obligations. The stability of the Hanoverian regime rested, in the last analysis, upon the smooth and successful functioning of *local* deference structures. The counterpoint between the ideals of paternalism and of deference together with the tension generated between them constitutes the essential thematic key to electoral politics in the unreformed period.

The investigation of these local structures of power requires, among many other things, extensive use of quantitative techniques; electoral analysis inevitably involves the observation of fairly large numbers of individuals. Fortunately, the survival of poll books, poll lists, canvassing books, committee books, payment lists, expense accounts, rate books, and directories enables the electoral historian to make some assessments about the quality of electoral behaviour. When the computations have been completed, however, the problem still remains of establishing an appropriate interpretive structure in which to accommodate them.[12]

[11] Plumb has argued that because of the neglect of this dimension 'the history of party is in the sorry mess that it is'. For an earlier period, he has contended that there could be no political stability while there were 'two groups of men fighting for the control of the franchise in the Parliamentary boroughs' (J. Plumb, *The Growth of Political Stability in England, 1675–1725* (London, 1967), 35). For my own detailed assessment of traditional divisions within constituencies see chs. 5 and 6 below.

[12] Scholarly research on the unreformed electorate may be found in two excellent dissertations: John A. Phillips, 'Electoral Behavior in Pre-reform England', Ph.D. (Iowa, 1976) which is a study of Lewes, Maidstone, Northampton, and Norwich between 1760 and 1800, and D. Stoker, 'Elections and Voting Behaviour: A Study of Elections in Northumberland, Durham, Cumberland and Westmorland, 1760–1832', Ph.D. (Manchester, 1980). Happily, Phillips's dissertation was published in 1982 by Princeton University Press. Subsequent references are to the published version. Phillips has also published 'The Structure of Electoral Politics in Unreformed England', *J. Brit. Studies* (1979), 76–100, and 'Popular Politics in Unreformed

Consequently, fundamental problems—of political control, of electoral organization, of patronage, of voter deference, of party, and of 'corruption'—have been reassessed through more traditional methods of analysis and the use of non-quantifiable sources. These include some of the customary source material of the eighteenth-century historian, such as letters between patrons and the families of patrons. It was, however, possible to go a little further than is usual in this direction and to consult sources which electoral structures and electoral conflicts themselves generated. These include reports by agents, canvassers and committee men, letters to—and also from—the voters themselves, the proceedings of clubs and committees, reports in the press and, not least, accounts of the complex rituals of the election campaign.

This book does not purport to be the definitive work on every constituency. Indeed, because of the specific situations of Scotland and Ireland, I have confined this study to electoral politics in England and Wales. Electoral history must, of course, be rooted in local history. But it seemed to me that what was most urgently needed was a solid basis for electoral history, a foundation upon which future work could be built, and yet an interim synthesis or model which might not only guide the student but promote fresh thinking among scholars. One of the curses of electoral history is the trading of instances—often of a spectacular nature—to illustrate a position held, as it were, *a priori*. Because it would be equally misleading to generalize from the study of a few large freeman boroughs as from the examination of a handful of corporation boroughs I have based this study upon a fairly large number of constituencies with different franchisal arrangements and, of course, with a broad geographical spread. (See Table 1.1.)

If this book may be said to be informed by an overriding idea or thesis, it is that electoral system was controlled by local families and connections whose influence was exercised conditionally amidst habits of widespread political involvement. This central idea may be further elaborated.

*First*, the electoral system was controlled by local élites with no little difficulty. The 'oligarchy' which fastened itself upon the boroughs and

England', *J. Mod. Hist.* 52 (1980), 599–625. Glimpses of the electorate may be obtained from certain standard works, including J. A. Cannon, *Parliamentary Reform, 1640–1832* (Cambridge, 1972; 2nd edn. 1980); R. W. Davis, *Political Change and Continuity, 1760–1885: A Buckinghamshire Study* (Newton Abbot, 1972); E. G. Forrester, *Northamptonshire County Electioneering, 1695–1832* (London, 1941); D. E. Ginter, *Whig Organization in the General Election of 1790* (Berkeley–Los Angeles, 1967); P. Jupp, *British and Irish Elections, 1784–1831* (Newton Abbot, 1973); J. H. Philbin, *Parliamentary Representation, 1832: England and Wales* (New Haven, Conn., 1965); R. J. Robson, *The Oxfordshire Election of 1754* (Oxford, 1949). There is further material on particular localities and on specific topics, and these will be introduced in the appropriate chapters. It may fairly be said, however, that no modern synthesis of even the little work that exists has yet been attempted and no general survey of that work hazarded.

TABLE 1.1    *Principal Constituencies Analysed, by Region*

| | N | NW | E | S | SW | W | Midlands | Wales |
|---|---|---|---|---|---|---|---|---|
| **Large freeman boroughs[a]** | | | | | | | | |
| Chester | | + | | | | | | |
| Colchester | | | + | | | | | |
| Coventry | | | | | | | + | |
| Hull | + | | | | | | | |
| Leicester | | | | | | | + | |
| Liverpool | | + | | | | | | |
| Worcester | | | | | | + | | |
| York | + | | | | | | | |
| **Medium freeman boroughs[b]** | | | | | | | | |
| Derby | | | | | | | + | |
| Newcastle-under-Lyme | | | | | | | + | |
| St Albans | | | + | | | | | |
| Southampton | | | | + | | + | | |
| Wenlock | | | | | | | | |
| **Small freeman boroughs[c]** | | | | | | | | |
| Grimsby | + | | | | | | | |
| Hedon | + | | | | | | | |
| Shrewsbury | | | | | | + | | |
| Wigan | | + | | | | | | |
| **Householder boroughs** | | | | | | | | |
| Cirencester[d] | | | | | | + | | |
| Minehead[c] | | | | | + | | | |
| Preston[b] | | + | | | | | | |
| **Scot and lot boroughs** | | | | | | | | |
| Great Marlow[g] | | | | + | | | | |
| Reading[h] | | | | + | | | | |
| **Burgage borough** | | | | | | | | |
| Boroughbridge | + | | | | | | | |
| **Counties** | | | | | | | | |
| Glamorganshire | | | | | | | | + |
| Hampshire | | | | + | | | | |
| Lincolnshire | + | | + | | | | | |
| Yorkshire | | | | | | | | |

| | |
|---|---|
| [a] Voters 1754–1790: 1,000+ | [e] Voters 1754–1790: 250. |
| [b] Voters 1754–1790: 200–1,000. | [f] Voters 1754–1790: 600. |
| [c] Voters 1754–1790: less than 200. | [g] Voters 1754–1790: 250. |
| [d] Voters 1754–1790: 800. | [h] Voters 1754–1790: 600. |

counties in the age of Walpole by and large continued to control it down to the 1832 Reform Act but they did so at considerable cost to themselves in terms of men, money, and organization. Furthermore, the problems of sustaining such political and social control involved them in formidable exertions of a paternalist character designed to satisfy the expectations of the community. Peterborough had only gone to the polls twice in over 60 years when its patron, Lord Fitzwilliam, boasted that it was 'a place where we have no trouble', but he added, significantly, that it was a place 'where we always pay great attention'.[13] Every election contest took place in a highly specific social situation, its proceedings fuelled by ideas of reciprocal obligation.

*Second*, in spite of some of its more antiquated and unrepresentative features, the electoral system was never closed. Indeed, electoral politics became an increasingly active and participatory experience. Electoral life was not as open and as formalized institutionally as it became later in the nineteenth century, but it was not noticeably less bracing. Indeed, such informality led to problems of control. Control by the landed élite did not necessarily mean control by a small élite. The landed interest could not have controlled the electoral system without the collusion of literally tens, even hundreds, of thousands of members of the middle and professional ranks who identified their fortunes and their interests with those of their social superiors. Such widespread support for and participation in the prevailing electoral and political systems did much both to legitimate them and to procure public endorsement of them at a time when both were meeting rising criticism. In the same way, the politics of resistance to landed control cannot be confined to the personally or economically disaffected. Traditions of popular independence struck a chord in the hearts of thousands, voters and non-voters alike. As the period advanced, of course, developments in communications, notably the rise of the press and the growth of an educated and articulate public opinion, steadily raised political consciousness. The tendency of government and opposition to vie with each other in seeking public approval also did something to educate the constituencies in questions of national concern. Furthermore, increasing sophistication in the techniques of political agitation, deriving from radical sources, enabled groups to organize their activities with energy and efficiency.

*Third*, the source of electoral activity was overwhelmingly local, the election contest the expression of—not the solution to—local conflict. The study of electoral politics becomes the study of local

[13] R. G. Thorne (ed.), *The House of Commons, 1790–1820*, 5 vols. (London, 1986), ii. 302.

communities. I found that the plunge into their electoral history was as refreshing as it was stimulating, bringing me face to face with political cultures whose energy and sophistication were a revelation to me. Much of this book is concerned to describe the world of electoral politics and to relate it to the world of the 'political nation' and its parliamentary concerns. The objective of the book, however, is mildly polemical. It is to offer a revisionist interpretation of the unreformed electoral system and of unreformed electoral politics. I wish to rescue the unreformed electorate from the Whig interpretation of English history and from the neglect, contempt, and ignorance of generations of historians and propagandists. It is not my concern to exaggerate such sterling qualities as it may have had nor to defend the occasionally indefensible. I do however wish to draw attention to a layer of political existence and political activity not normally acknowledged and not at all well understood. I wish to offer my own re-creation of the world of electoral politics in the century before the 1832 Reform Act. In doing so I am only too painfully aware of the limitations which accompany the attempts of one person to achieve such an objective and I do not believe that I have been able to do justice to every topic with which I deal. However, after many years of preparation and justifiable prevarication, I nevertheless, launch my findings upon the seas of academic debate.

In the great tide of radical opinion which ebbed so dramatically in the early 1830s, the political nation came overwhelmingly to demand the thoroughgoing transformation of the existing electoral system. Such a demand had been welling, albeit intermittently, ever since the days of Wilkes. There can be no question that a growing awareness of serious flaws in the electoral structure yielded a rising demand for its renovation. Radical propaganda, of course, much of it wildly extravagant, noisly drew attention to every manifestation of bribery and corruption practised in the name of aristocratic control and gravely weakened the confidence of those who might have defended the system. There is a sense, too, in which the House of Commons seemed seriously to be out of step with public opinion, after 1815 at least. The repeal of the Test and Corporation Acts in 1828 and the passing of Catholic emancipation in 1829 inflamed such sentiments. By this time the serious underrepresentation of the new industrial centres and the lack of representation of some of the largest industrial towns could no longer be defended with any conviction.

No doubt these long-term developments would in time have led inexorably to a new electoral system. Nevertheless, it is worth remembering that the demand for change came from within the existing electoral system as well as without. The remarkable eruption of electoral sentiment seen in 1831 was in many ways a projection of traditional electoral values, an extension of customary ideals of independence, a display of distaste for aristocratic control. These were, in short, integral elements of the unreformed electoral system. In normal times, they could be kept in check, but in 1831 those who normally kept them in check abandoned the existing electoral system. They did so because they perceived that to fight for it might bring the entire political and social order crashing down around them. The formidable difficulties which normally attended the control of the electorate had suddenly grown to terrifying proportions. The restraints which normally conditioned and constrained the electors seemed to have disappeared. The unreformed electorate was the victim of the great political crisis of 1831. Ironically, however, if the new electoral system was to endure it must necessarily incorporate sufficient elements of the old to ensure continuity and to promote stability. These objectives were attained largely because the Reform Act was created by the type of men who presided over the old system. It was, of course, no accident that the new electoral system was to be, in so many respects, similar to the old, and no surprise that continuity rather than change was to be the watchword of 1832.


## THE EXTENT OF ELECTORAL OLIGARCHY

The unreformed electoral system was fashioned in the age of Walpole and it endured until the age of Grey. It owed its existence to the oligarchical tendencies which shaped British society in the eighteenth century. In the 1720s the executive was tightening its grip upon the legislature, the court over the country, the aristocracy over the gentry and the Whigs over the Tories. Indeed, this Whiggish, aristocratic oligarchy extended beyond politics and into the church, the law, the economy, the services, and even into the world of ideas. The unreformed electorate was the product of these tendencies—and of the reaction which they bred.

After the Hanoverian succession the Whigs at once took steps to consolidate their power by destroying that of their opponents. Indeed, the writing was on the wall as early as the general election of 1715 when the Whigs returned 358 MPs to the Tories' 200. They proceeded to exploit their majority by attacking the electoral base of the Tories and Jacobites. The Septennial Act of 1716 substituted a seven-year maximum duration of Parliament in place of the three-year maximum laid down by the Triennial Act of 1694.[14] These frequent Parliaments, stated the Septennial Act, had caused 'more violent and lasting heats and animosities among the subjects of this realm, than were ever known before the said clause was enacted'. The Septennial Act gave the Whigs the time and the opportunity to hasten the discomfiture of the Jacobites after the failure of the 1715 insurrection. More importantly, it enabled them to proceed with a vigorous purge of the Tories. By 1722, when the delayed general election was finally held, the Whigs were able to defeat the Tories by about 380 to 180 seats. If this were not enough, the Whigs proceeded to attack the Tories' popular base in the City of London with the City Elections Act of 1725. Although the partisan intent of the Act may have been exaggerated by historians, it was unquestionably directed against the power of the Tories in the wards of the City.[15] It had the effect of disfranchising thousands of poorer freemen.

However, the coping stone of Whig control of the electoral system was laid by the conscious regulation of the electorate by the Whig Parliaments of the early eighteenth century. In many places there had been considerable confusion over the definition and extent of the franchise in the second half of the seventeenth century. It was common for the defeated side in an election to petition Parliament against the return, complaining that bribery had taken place or that the electorate had been unduly restricted. Between 1660 and 1688, Parliament had adopted a fairly even-handed approach to such cases. Out of 51 determinations in these years it found in favour of a restricted as opposed to a wide determination of the franchise in 28 cases (55%). After 1688, however, parliamentary opinion began to harden. From 1688 to 1727 it favoured the restricted determination in 78 out of 106 cases (74%). In 1715, 87 petitions were heard. The 46 Tory petitions were uniformly unsuccessful but the 41 Whig petitions resulted in the unseating of 31 Tories.[16] Such existing tendencies were

---

[14] It could have been much worse. Both Walpole and Newcastle considered the desirability of returning to the 17th-cent. practice of Parliaments without any time limit. During the debates on the Septennial Act it was strongly argued that 'Animosities and divisions [were] continued by Triennial Elections', but it was conceded that even private quarrels could become unduly inflated by the 'unreasonable Resentments, Avarice and Ambition of some and the Folly and Madness of *others*'; see Copies of Speeches on the Repeal of the Triennial Act, 1715–16, D/DA 62/3, fo. 7, Notts. RO.

[15] As well as being a ruthless assault upon the Tories, the Act was 'a sensible and in large measure even-handed attempt to deal with some long-standing abuses and difficulties' (I. G. Doolittle, 'Walpole's City Elections Act (1725)' *Eng. Hist. Rev.* 98 (1982), 505): See also N. Rogers, 'The City Elections Act Reconsidered', *ibid.* 200 (1985), 604–17.

[16] Cannon, *Parliamentary Reform*, 33–4; R. R. Sedgwick, *The House of Commons, 1715–1754* 2 vols. (London, 1970), i. 23. No less than 70% of petitions sponsored by the Opposition between 1715 and 1754 were simply not heard (*ibid.* 14). For further discussion of petitions see below, pp. 164–8.

significantly enhanced by the Last Determinations Act of 1696, reinforced by the more notorious amending Act of 1729. These Acts purported to be 'for all the more effectual preventing of bribery and corruption in the election of members to serve in Parliament'. Their real intention was to lay down the principles for determining the legality of the franchise in a constituency. The Act of 1696 had laid it down that the most recent decision should stand. In 1729, however, an amendment declared final and binding the previous, or last, determination 'all usages to the contrary notwithstanding'.[17] In other words, Parliament could for all time decide and determine the nature of the franchise in a constituency after a disputed return, whatever evidence existed. The way was now completely open to establish Whig control of the electorate.[18] Last Determinations succeeded in deciding the issue of electoral participation in favour of a restricted franchise. As Professor Plumb has remarked:

There can be very little doubt that many of the boroughs that came into the category of narrow constituencies were created by the decision of the Commons between 1689 and 1729. It was only to be expected. Twenty four votes were easier to control than three hundred, three hundred easier than three thousand. And those voters who survived the restricting process were always the influential members of the corporation, usually the mayor, alderman, and common councillors; and, of course, they gained, too, as there was less dilution of profit.[19]

The consequences of all this legislation were to be felt for a century. By guaranteeing a longer period between elections, and often a reduced electorate as well, the security of a Member of Parliament was vastly enhanced and the value of his seat in Parliament markedly increased. In the early eighteenth century it had still been possible to purchase a seat in a small borough for under £1,000. By the end of the century the going rate was probably nearing £5,000. The costs of electioneering were correspondingly increased. Fewer families and individuals were able to afford election expenses, and the frequency of election contests declined. As we shall see in later chapters, uncontested elections normally outnumbered contested elections by as much as 2 : 1 ratio.

---

[17] E. and A. Porritt, *The Unreformed House of Commons*, 2 vols. (Cambridge, 1909), 8–9. However, the Porritts do not mention that the Commons agreed the amendment by only 91–89 votes; see W. Cobbett (ed.), *The Parliamentary History of England*, 36 vols. (London, 1806–20), vii. 753–4.

[18] It cannot be emphasized too often that the growth of oligarchy in the boroughs was under way long before 1729. By that date many boroughs had already fallen under the control of a local family; see e.g. W. A. Speck, 'Brackley: A Study in the Growth of Oligarchy', *Midland Hist.* 3 (1975), 30–41. What Last Determinations did was to accelerate and render permanent a trend already well in evidence. It was impossible to open up the boroughs after 1729.

[19] Plumb, *Political Stability*, 95.

One of the key characteristics of the unreformed electoral system is the marked absence of elections.

The electoral system which is the subject of this book had thus been created as a response to Whig party interests and the need to settle the country in the interests of the new dynasty. The perpetuation of that electoral system owed much to Whig suspicion—even fear—of public opinion and popular tumult. Most of the indicators we possess—the press, popular literature, theatre, and recreation, to say nothing of riots, petitions, and meetings—suggest that the Whig oligarchy was widely disliked. In spite of the fact that the Tories only returned around 130 MPs at the general elections of 1722, 1734, and 1741, more voters actually voted Tory than voted Whig.[20] In the large, open constituencies, which are the best guides to public opinion, the Tories did exceptionally well. It was in the boroughs with small electorates that Whig money and Whig manipulation enabled oligarchy to triumph.

The establishment of an oligarchical electoral system, it need hardly be said, is much more than a purely political phenomenon. The economic and social context of politics needs to be taken into consideration. Indeed, when that context *is* taken into consideration, it becomes at once apparent that the economic and social origins of Walpolean 'stability' are to be found in the second half of the seventeenth century. Professor Holmes, noting the growing cohesion of different groups and interests in provincial towns, inclines to the view that 'the fabric of social stability in England from the late 1680s onwards was basically strong and growing steadily more secure'. A combination of demographic stability, steady economic and commercial development, and the growth of the professions were all quietly taking the sting out of political and party divisions in the boroughs, preparing the way for the acceptance of Whig oligarchy in the eighteenth century.[21] Social stability, therefore, permitted the conflict of parties to rage in the reigns of William and Anne without serious or permanent damage to the social fabric. As we have noted, the electoral system was already closing up. Already, by the reign of Anne, 35% of constituencies were 'safe' seats.[22] In some places,

---

[20] L. Colley, *In Defiance of Oligarchy: The Tory Party 1714–1760* (Cambridge, 1982), 122.

[21] G. Holmes, 'The Achievement of Stability: The Social context of Politics from the 1680s to the Age of Walpole', in J. A. Cannon (ed.), *The Whig Ascendancy: Colloquies on Hanoverian England* (London, 1981), 21–2.

[22] Between 1701 and 1715, 114 Tory and 74 Whig MPs sat for 'safe' seats in England, Wales, and Scotland; see W. A. Speck, *Tory and Whig: The Struggle in the Constituencies, 1701–1715* (London, 1970), 121–2. Colley notes that 'more than one quarter of England's 203 boroughs were not contested or were contested only once between 1700 and 1713'; Colley, *In Defiance of Oligarchy*, 118. For a case study in the process of oligarchy before 1715 see Speck, 'Brackley', 30–41.

indeed, the process by which local families and interests came to control constituencies and corporations can be traced back almost as far as the Restoration. These developments were accelerated by the Qualifications Act of 1710. The Act required county MPs to possess landed property worth £600 per annum and borough MPs £300 per annum. It needed only the withering away of serious party tumult at Westminster and the imposition of a Whig regime to enable the constituencies to leave the rage of party behind and to settle down to less immediately divisive activities. The regularity of contested elections declined sharply in all types of constituencies by the middle of the eighteenth century.

The precise combination of forces which went to effect the achievement of electoral stability varied from place to place. Three types of processes may be discerned. *First*, some boroughs found an oligarchy thrust upon them by political device, through purchase, stratagem, take-over, and, most of all, via Last Determination. Calne was a householder borough experiencing regular contested elections until 1724 when the Commons decided on petition that only members of the corporation were allowed to vote. Calne was contested only once more, in 1734, in its history.[23] *Second*, short- and medium-term considerations weakened the impetus behind regular election contests. The lapse—or, at least, the decline—in religious antagonisms, the decline of party fervour, the political ambitions of the constituency élite in the Whig polity which emerged after the Hanoverian succession, the failure of the '15, and the purge of the Tories in the early 1720s all reduced the pressure from above. The desire for peace and security on the part of electors and non-electors alike and their anxiety to participate in the expansion of wealth and jobs as well as material goods probably weakened the pressure from below. *Third*, long-term social and economic movements contributed something to electoral stability. Some historians have been keen to associate political stability, 'the triumph of the Venetian Oligarchy', with the decline of the gentry and the consolidation of aristocratic élites.[24] The greater wealth of the aristocracy and the increase in the number of dependent tenant farmers undoubtedly enabled the aristocracy to dominate local life in the provinces in many areas. Furthermore, their continued

---

[23] For other examples see ch. 2.

[24] Most prominently Plumb, who in *Growth of Political Stability*, 9–10, makes very influential use of Habbakuk's work on aristocratic estates: H. J. Habbakuk, 'English Landownership, 1680–1740', *Econ. Hist. Rev.* 10 (1940), 2–17; id., 'Marriage Settlements in the Eighteenth Century', *Trans. Royal Hist. Soc.* 4th ser., 32 (1950), 15–30. There was a slight restatement of his position in 'The Rise and Fall of English Landed Families, 1600–1800', ibid. 5th ser., 29 (1979), 187–207.

predominance was facilitated by a cluster of further considerations: by enclosures, by the persistence of low rates of interest, by the ready availability (to some) of profits from office-holding in central government and (to others) of status, influence, and power deriving from their involvement in formal and informal aspects of local administration. There can be little question that large landowners were better equipped to survive and prosper in an age of reckless conspicuous consumption than small ones.

To what extent does political 'stability', and indeed electoral 'oligarchy', relate to the enlargement and consolidation of landed estates? In some of the central and southern counties of *England*, there does appear to be some connection. But it must be confessed that most works of a local character have queried or qualified such a conclusion or, at least, greatly complicated it.[25] The period 1720–40 witnessed an economic recession, and one which the aristocracy found it as difficult to survive as the gentry. Once the consolidation of aristocratic estates began in earnest thereafter, the establishment of electoral oligarchy had in most places already been accomplished. Even then, we should not be too ready to consign the gentry to oblivion in an aristocratically dominated country. In many counties, as Dr Beckett has recently argued, especially on the periphery of the central part of England, the gentry survived up until the end of the eighteenth century and even beyond.[26] My impression is that these areas—Cumberland, Durham, Westmorland, Lancashire, Cheshire, Shropshire, Monmouthshire, Devon, and Cornwall—do not, on the whole, display patterns of electoral control markedly different from those which prevailed elsewhere. In short, electoral oligarchy is far more complicated than a cursory glance at the 'consolidation' thesis might suggest.

Indeed, the very term 'oligarchy' may appear to be a pejorative description, used to deplore the narrow and corrupt character of British political and electoral life in the eighteenth century. To the twentieth-century mind there appears to be overwhelming justification for such a view. The restriction of electorates, the reduction of election contests, and the closing up of boroughs all point in the same direction. On the other hand, we should recognize that in some ways electoral politics possibly tended to broaden the basis of oligarchic rule. It offered

---

[25] See e.g. C. Clay, 'Marriage, Inheritance and the Rise of Large Estates in England, 1660–1815', *Econ. Hist. Rev.* 21 (1968), 503–18; B. A. Holderness, 'The English Land Market in the Eighteenth Century: The Case of Lincolnshire', ibid. 27 (1974), 557–76; Philip Jenkins, *The Making of a Ruling Class: The Glamorgan Gentry, 1640–1790* (Cambridge, 1983).

[26] J. V. Beckett, 'The Decline of the Small Landowner in Eighteenth Century and Nineteenth Century England: Some Regional Considerations', *Ag. Hist. Rev.* 30 (1982), 97–111.

relatives, friends, clients, and dependants of the landed order access to power and profits which promised to enable them to maintain—and improve—their social positions. Electoral politics furnished legitimacy and participation as well as patronage. The investment of the Hanoverian oligarchy in the electoral system of the age—an investment represented not only in the purchase price of a borough but in the continuing costs of favours and services—was an appropriate means of serving its own interests: to doubt this or to expect, somehow, the contrary to prevail seems both nonsensical and irrelevant. To rest the case at this point in the argument, however, would be dangerously misconceived. For it is also the case that the preoccupation of the Hanoverian ruling classes in the electoral system involved them in a permanent commitment to Parliament, and thus to parliamentary and representative forms and processes. The strength of this commitment may not have been particularly profound in the 1720s but it should not be underestimated. By the 1760s, however, it had assumed an almost hallowed ideological status.

Nevertheless, patrons and candidates were prepared to invest larger and larger sums in the regime in the form of election costs because they anticipated concrete returns of one kind or another for their money. The most spectacular of these was, of course, to control the parliamentary representation of one or more constituencies and thus acquire power and influence in the House of Commons. Others might aspire to more realistic ambitions: to obtain legislation for their family or estate or constituency. The vast majority of patrons could not afford to aim so high. They would rest content with the creation of an electoral interest which would, at very least, make them of some real consequence in the constituency. Even at this relatively humble level, participation in electoral processes brought recognizable dividends: contacts with the upper classes, the personal and social rewards of political involvement, such as status and recognition, and, not least, a sense of social duty.

The investment of the Hanoverian élite in the electoral system increasingly assumed the appearance of a well-hedged bet. As both political excitement and the frequency of election contests declined—in 1761 only 18 out of 201 English and Welsh boroughs with electorates of less than 500 went to the polls—so patrons and candidates had more regular recourse to careful protection of their investments through the negotiation of compromises.[27] Even where this was not possible, the

---

[27] Almost all the English seats were two-member constituencies. Accordingly, a compromise enabled the seat to be shared between two rival interests or families or parties without the cost and inconvenience of a contested election.

edge of voter resentment might be blunted through the generous distribution of favours, treats, and offices and, in general, the judicious provision of paternalist services.

Consequently, just as the representative system was never really endangered in the mid-eighteenth century, so the needs of voters and non-voters were never absolutely neglected. To notice these somewhat reciprocal elements in Hanoverian electioneering is not, however, to advance a comfortable, consensual theory of Hanoverian social relationships. It is a matter of record, nevertheless, that the Hanoverian patronal classes were keen to honour at least the forms of public accountability, willing at least to talk the language of service to the community, and anxious to be seen to be advancing the needs of the constituency. And to flatter and to woo the voters in an age of rising political consciousness was to go far towards guaranteeing that in spite of the attack upon its formal structure, the unreformed electoral system was never entirely without life and energy.

To what extent, it must be asked, *was* the unreformed electoral system closed and exclusive? Furthermore, was it becoming more or less so? Radical writers of the half century before the 1832 Reform Act were in no doubt whatsoever. The famous and influential *Report of the Society of the Friends of the People on the State of the Representation* published in February 1793 announced that 308 out of the 513 MPs for England and Wales were 'said to be returned by patronage'. A year later, Thomas Oldfield, in his *History of the Boroughs*, raised the figure to 359 and then added in 39 of the 45 Scottish seats to give a grand total of no less than 398 out of 558 seats. In 1797 his *History of the Original Constitution of Parliaments* raised the total still further, to 415. Finally, in his *Representative History of Great Britain and Ireland* (1816), he rested his total at 416.[28] These estimates were to prove remarkably influential. They were to be mindlessly and uncritically repeated on countless occasions.[29] Although Oldfield was careful to maintain the distinction between nomination and influence, his successors were not so scrupulous, even at a time when the behaviour of MPs was becoming subjected to more

---

[28] These estimates are conveniently assembled in full in A. Aspinall and F. A. Smith (eds.), *English Historical Documents* (1959), 216–36. The 1793 estimate was written up by George Tierney on the basis of evidence supplied by Oldfield; see E. C. Black, *The Association: British Extra-Parliamentary Political Organization* (Cambridge, Mass., 1963), 283–7.

[29] One of the earliest of the early 19th-cent. publications which I have found uses directly the estimate made by the Friends and 'calculates' that 310 MPs were 'dependent', 348 not; *A Ready and Sure Way to Obtain a Reform in Parliament*, London, 1819 W. G. Lewis's *A Peep at the Commons* (London, 1820) uses the same material without attempting any calculations. His work is a romantic essay in radical thought, dependent (like so many of these works) upon Oldfield.

detailed scrutiny than ever before.[30] Oldfield's figures for 1816, for example, distinguish 244 MPs returned by 'nomination' from '158' returned by 'influence'. George Wade's enormously influential *Black Book* of 1820 lumped the two together, added a few score for good measure, and announced that 487 out of 658 MPs were 'returned by nomination'.[31] Within the next few years, radical writers waxed almost hysterical in their yet more exaggerated estimates.[32] How much truth was there in these computations? How extensive was the electoral oligarchy of Hanoverian Britain? Could it really have been the case that two-thirds, even three-quarters, of MPs were returned by nomination? If so, then electoral life in the unreformed period must have been little more than a formality. To what extent has modern scholarship vindicated such an interpretation?

At first glance, it seems to have done so. Recent research has established beyond any doubt that the number of seats under nomination and influence increased steadily from the early eighteenth century to the early nineteenth century. In the reign of Anne not many more than 100 MPs were returned in this way.[33] During the Parliament of 1741 the number was between 210 and 235.[34] This estimate was confirmed by Professor Namier for the Parliament

---

[30] The fashion of publishing systematic biographies of MPs seems to have originated with Joshua Wilson's *Biographical Index to the Present House of Commons* published in London in 1806. This volume includes a few division lists for the parliament dissolved in that year. *A Biographical Index to the Present House of Lords* also by Wilson, appeared in 1808, listing peers and their family connections and histories. By the early 1820s the parliamentary behaviour of MPs was being subjected to constant scrutiny. John Marshall's *An Alphabetical List of the Members of the Commons* (London, 1822) reprinted in *The Pamphleteer*, 21 (1823), 293–316, lists how MPs voted on 14 major divisions in the 1821 and 1822 sessions of Parliament. Other such publications include *The Electors' Remembrancer* (London, 1822), also published in *The Pamphleteer* 20 (1822).

[31] George Wade, *The Extraordinary Black Book*, 2 vols. (London, 1820). According to Wade, these 487 MPs were returned by 87 peers and 90 commoners (i. 417, 423). His list of MPs makes no attempt to validate these assertions. It contains data concerning their *connections* and says very little about their electoral backgrounds (*ibid.* 425–45). Thus, he computes that the MPs related to peers (228), and the MPs who were lawyers (25), navy officers (15), army officers (80), or 'placemen and pensioners' (126) were 'dependent'. (His total of 474 fails to square with his earlier assertions.)

[32] *The Extraordinary Black Book* gave rise to a number of fairly pale but no less sensational imitations. These include *A Full View of the British Commons* (London, 1821) and *Links of the Lower House* (London, 1821). Both are alphabetically arranged biographies of MPs that stress their connections rather than their electoral backgrounds. It is amazing what a substantial degree of obloquy could be cast upon the unreformed electoral system without any significant evidence. As was, perhaps, to be expected, this genre continued unabated down to the end of the unreformed era. *The Workings of the Borough System* (London, 1830) estimated that no fewer than 586 out of 658 MPs were 'dependent'.

[33] Speck, *Tory and Whig*, 72.

[34] Owen's estimate for the Parliament of 1741; see J. B. Owen, 'Political Patronage in Eighteenth-century England', in P. Fritz and D. Williams (eds.), in *The Triumph of Culture* (Toronto, 1972), 369–87.

of 1761.[35] By 1780 the figure had advanced to 240.[36] The estimate used by the Friends of the People in 1793 is regarded by Professor Cannon as a serious underestimate. He believes that at least 30 MPs should be added to the estimate of 308.[37] Furthermore, there is no reversal of the trend thereafter. Computations for the elections of 1806 and 1807 place the figure at well over 300.[38] Could it be that the radicals were right after all? Might not this inexorable increase in electoral control be a damning characteristic of the unreformed electoral system?

Of course, it depends what we choose to mean by 'control'. As I have already noted, Thomas Oldfield was careful to distinguish between 'nomination' and 'influence'. The Friends of the People report in 1793 spelled out exactly what these meant. Nomination was 'that absolute authority in a borough which enables the patron to command the return'. Nomination boroughs 'are under undoubted control': 'These, in general, are the private property of the patrons, or have the right of voting vested in a small corporate body, the majority of whom are his immediate dependents.' Indeed, such boroughs could be and were bought and sold on the open market like any other commodity until such sales were rendered illegal by Curwen's Act of 1809. 'Influence' was by no means so tangible. The 1793 report described it as

that degree of weight acquired in a particular county, city, or borough, which accustoms the electors on all vacancies to expect the recommendation of a candidate by the patron, and induces them, either from fear, from private interest, or from incapacity to oppose, because he is so recommended, to adopt him.

This definition, taken over and used by Sir Lewis Namier,[39] calls for a little comment. Old Sarum, with seven voters in the second half of the eighteenth century and with no property, people, or community worth representing, was unquestionably a nomination borough. Chester, on the other hand, for all the exertions of the powerful Grosvenor influence upon all aspects of its life, remained a proud city, capable of expressing its independence but in normal times prepared

[35] Namier put the figure at 224 for 1761; *The Structure of Politics*, 176–82. Cannon would increase Namier's figure by 20; see his *Parliamentary Reform*, 50 n.

[36] Christie, *North's Ministry*, 52–3.

[37] J. Cannon, *Aristocratic Century: The Peerage of Eighteenth-century England* (Cambridge, 1984), 111–12. The drift of Cannon's calculations of the electoral influence of peers bears out the expansion of electoral influence indicated above, doubling from just over 100 in 1715 to 200 at the end of the century (ibid. 106–7).

[38] Hinton's figures for the 1806 and 1807 elections are 446 and 448 respectively, but these totals include 100 new Irish MPs who sat after the Act of Union in 1801; M. Hinton, 'The General Elections of 1806 and 1807', Ph.D., (Reading 1959), 660–5.

[39] Namier, *Structure of Politics*, 143.

to give due credit to the weight of property, rank, and money. Influence, in short, was the natural expression of the rights of property in the electoral arena, a mechanism for exerting power and control. It can clearly be distinguished from 'nomination' at the conceptual level, even if it is frequently very difficult to distinguish them in practice. In a proprietorial electoral system influence, far from being an 'abuse', was absolutely inevitable. To what extent electors chose to submit to influence is an extremely complex problem and one to which we shall have good reason to return.

The key issue, therefore, is the extent of nomination. By 1747 there were 64 nomination boroughs yielding 121 MPs.[40] At the end of the century the number of MPs sitting for nomination boroughs was rather less than 200.[41] For the early nineteenth century, contemporary estimates as well as modern scholarship place the figure at about 200 out of 658 MPs;[42] in short, about 30% of MPs sat for nomination boroughs. Earlier the figure would have been smaller.

Not all these boroughs were completely safe. Even here, electors had to be wooed and money had to be spent. Few boroughs were as closed as Boroughbridge, last contested in 1715 and appearing on every list of nomination boroughs. Yet it was snatched from under the nose of the great Newcastle interest in 1818 and was contested at the elections of 1820, 1826, and 1830. Even in these seats work had to be done, voters satisfied, and services provided. The effectiveness of patronage, moreover, can easily be exaggerated. Many boroughs which may be classified as 'under patronage' might have been held tenuously, passed from one insecure patron to another. An exhaustive modern analysis of the influence of peers over the House of Commons has revealed that between 1802 and 1832 only 81 out of 319 electoral interests (25.4%) survived intact. The remaining 238 had an average life of 10.4 years.[43] Furthermore, radical writers often equated a tiny electorate with corrupt nomination. One of the most knowledgeable

[40] Owen, 'Political Patronage'.

[41] Tierney's (low) estimate of 1793 was 172. Oldfield estimated the figure at 194 and 167 respectively out of 513 English and Welsh MPs in 1794 and 1797. John Robinson estimated the number of close boroughs at 89 in 1784; W. Laprade (ed.) *The Parliamentary Papers of John Robinson, 1774–1784*, Camden Society, 3rd ser., 33 (London, 1922), 82.

[42] Oldfield's estimate of 223 in 1816 is markedly higher than that of John Marshall in *The Analysis of the British House of Commons as at Present Constituted* (London, 1823), who put it at 203. (Oldfield's estimate does not include Scotland, however.) Two modern, independent calculations put the number of English and Welsh MPs under nomination at 180 in 1806/7 and 179 in 1818; Hinton, 'General Elections of 1806 and 1807', Ph.D., 693–4; L. V. Sumner, 'The General Election of 1818', Ph.D. (Manchester 1969), 178. Thorne finds 89 English close boroughs in 1790 *House of Commons*, i. 113.

[43] James J. Sack 'The House of Lords and Parliamentary Patronage in Great Britain 1802–1832', *Hist. J.* 23 4 (1980), 931–7.

and sophisticated radical writers was John Marshall, author of the *Analysis of the British House of Commons as at Present Constituted* 1823). Yet his list of nomination boroughs includes three perfectly respectable corporation boroughs,[44] three others which were undergoing prolonged periods of uncontrollability,[45] nine in which the control of the patron was by no means complete,[46] and a further nine which were being regularly contested in the early nineteenth century.[47] At the same time, he fails to include at least eight boroughs which seem to exhibit all the characteristics of a nomination borough: a tiny electorate, a lack of contests, and an absence of internal opposition.[48] Even the best and most detailed radical classification of nomination boroughs turns out on close inspection to be seriously flawed.

The distribution of electoral interests was highly diverse. Relatively few interests dominated even a single seat, and complex alliances and informal coalitions abounded. Even the greatest borough patrons like Edward Eliot or Sir James Lowther, could rarely aspire realistically to the control of more than a handful of seats. To attempt to build even such a modest electoral empire could cost a fortune. Few private individuals could afford to attempt it.

The biggest patron of all, of course, was the government. Indeed, the extent of government influence over the electoral system struck fear and alarm into contemporaries. After all, governments won every single general election in the century before Reform. Nevertheless, they did so less through their own direct control of constituencies than through an intricate, informal web of contacts, relationships, and friendships with well-disposed private patrons. There were few government boroughs. In 1754 only 13 boroughs yielding 25 seats were controlled directly by the government.[49] In the following half century there was little change. 'In 1780 only 24 seats in 15 boroughs

[44] Bath and Salisbury, proud and dignified cities and Winchester—a small freeman borough but in most respects similar.

[45] Malmesbury, Scarborough and Totnes. For details of the difficulties of managing these tiny constituencies see Thorne, *House of Commons*, ii. 127–9, 423–4, 458–60.

[46] Bury St Edmunds, Cambridge, Dartmouth, Dorchester, Minehead, Plymouth, Portsmouth, Wigan, and Wycombe.

[47] Bossiney, Callington, Camelford, Helston, Queenborough, Petersfield, Seaford, Truro, and Wooton Basset.

[48] I do not see how the following can possibly be omitted: Bishops Castle, New Woodstock, Northallerton, Richmond, and Wenlock. The other three are Welsh boroughs (Beaumaris, Brecon, and Monmouth) which are classified separately by Marshall but without comment.

[49] These included six Treasury boroughs (Harwich, Hastings, Oxford, Rye, Seaford, and Winchelsea), six Admiralty boroughs (Dartmouth, Plymouth, Portsmouth, Rochester, Saltash, and Sandwich), and one controlled jointly by the Admiralty and the Ordnance (Queenborough); see Namier and Brooke, *House of Commons*, i. 54.

could be classified as under government control.'[50] At the general elections of 1806 and 1807 the government was still able to return between 25 and 30 MPs.[51] Thereafter the government interest seems to have rapidly declined. Even Oldfield could only drag up 11 constituencies yielding 18 MPs in his estimates of 1816, strikingly similar to a modern assessment of 17 seats in 10 constituencies for the general election of 1818.[52] By 1823 only three seats could be described as secure and government interest remained at this level for many years after the first Reform Act.[53]

There were, of course, many other constituencies, perhaps as many as 50 or 60, where the government could directly influence a minority of voters.[54] The most notable of these include Berwick, Bristol, Carlisle, Colchester, Gloucester, Grimsby, Hampshire, Hull, Westminster, and York. Too much should not be made of this. At Carlisle in 1768 only 61 out of about 1,000 voters were under government influence (6%), and at Berwick in 1786 only 52 out of 950 (5.5%).[55] Only in the closest of contests could such support prove decisive. And while there is evidence of the strict exercise of discipline upon government voters, there are also numerous examples of bungling and inefficiency, giving rise to frequent laments by government sympathizers that its influence was in danger of collapse. The history of electioneering in Hampshire is a significant commentary upon the inability of successive generations of government agents to exploit the potential of 'the dockyards at Gosport and Portsea, the numerous ports, the Crown tenants in the New Forest, and the ports in the Isle of Wight'.[56] To be successful, government influence had to be wielded by local men and without doing violence to local feeling and local issues. In the last analysis, governments simply did not have sufficient control of local situations to capitalize effectively upon the potential electoral strength available to it. As a result, government influence was rarely decisive in these boroughs.

---

[50] Christie, *North's Ministry*, 65.

[51] Hinton, 'General Elections of 1806 and 1807', Ph.D., 163, 376-7.

[52] Sumner, 'The General Election of 1818', Ph.D., 185-9.

[53] P. Fraser, 'The Conduct of Public Business in the House of Commons, 1812-1827', Ph.D., (London, 1957), 174-6. The seats are Harwich, Plymouth, and Queenborough. Gash lists Chatham, Davenport, and Sandwich as being always obedient to the government of the day. At Harwich and Hastings private interests were asserting themselves. Queenborough disappeared in 1832. See Gash, *Politics in the Age of Peel* (London, 1953), 323-41.

[54] This is very difficult to measure because the potential influence of the government was not always mobilized on account of lack of pressure from London. In 1754, however, the Treasury was 'actively concerned' in 35 constituencies assisting 65 candidates. See Namier and Brooke, *House of Commons*, i. 58. In 1806 the government directly intervened in 58 constituencies, in 1807 in 39; see Hinton, 'General Elections of 1806 and 1807', Ph.D., 664-5.

[55] D. Stoker, 'Elections and Voting Behaviour: A Study of Elections in Northumberland, Durham, Cumberland and Westmorland, 1760-1832', Ph.D. (Manchester, 1980), 30-2.

[56] Namier and Brooke, *House of Commons*, i. 293.

Government influence could assume other, less direct forms. From time to time private patrons could be prevailed on to place their seats unreservedly at the disposal of ministers. It is difficult to give precise estimates of the extent of this practice but it appears to have been surprisingly uncommon. At the general election of 1780 North found seats for 31 MPs in boroughs belonging to private patrons.[57] At the general election of 1826 Croker spotted 12 seats thus available to the government.[58] It was entirely feasible for such interest to be deployed in favour of ministerially inclined candidates but such informal support cannot be quantified. Government, of course, was usually willing to reward such sympathetic patrons. As the Duke of Bedford grumbled in 1761, 'I am too frequently obliged to apply to the Treasury for favours to People in Boroughs in which I am immediately concerned myself.'[59]

While it is impossible to quantify favours and the promise of favours, it is perfectly possible to make some sort of estimate of the amount of money spent by Hanoverian governments on elections. In the first half of the eighteenth century such payments were made from the Secret Service fund. In 1754, for example, around £25,000 was spent in 35 seats.[60] George III refused to authorize such payments from Secret Service funds, and for some time they were no longer made from this source. Nevertheless, he was quite willing to pay similar sums out of his privy purse. For the general election of 1780, around £62,000 was 'paid to government candidates . . . to enable them to defray the necessary legal and concomitant expenses which arose from the different canvasses, Polls and Trials before the Committees'.[61] For the general election of 1784, however, just over £30,000 was spent from the Secret Service fund on 19 seats, 14 fewer than in 1780.[62] Six years later the Pitt ministry spent a total of around £40,000 from Secret Service and other sources on 15 seats.[63] These amounts, of course, represent little more than a few drops in the vast, almost limitless, ocean of election expense. In the last analysis, Hanoverian governments did not rely upon direct financial subventions for their electoral support.

[57] Namier and Brooke, *House of Commons*, i. 82.

[58] *Correspondence and Diaries of John Wilson Croker*, ed. L. J. Jennings (2 vols., London, 1884), i. 367–72.

[59] Duke of Bedford to Denys Rolle, n.d. 1761, Woburn MSS 36, fo. 202, Bedford Estate Office.

[60] Namier and Brooke, *House of Commons*, i. 57–8, 84, 95.

[61] Lord North to George III, 18 Apr. 1782, see Sir John Fortescue (ed.), *The Correspondence of George III*, 6 vols. (London, 1928), vol. v, no. 3668; Christie, *North's Ministry*, 102.

[62] A. Aspinall, *The Later Correspondence of George III*, 5 vols. (Cambridge, 1962–70) i. 116–18.

[63] Thorne, *House of Commons*, i. 118–19.

The convention of issuing such payments, and the social and political morality which lay behind them, was never popular. There was always considerable public sensitivity about the question of government interference in elections, a sensitivity which steadily increased as the eighteenth century wore on. After the passage of Curwen's Act in 1809, which made the buying and selling of seats illegal, the government became uneasy at the prospect of financial relations with patrons.

We are placed in considerable difficulties in consequence of Curwen's Bill, and it will be absolutely necessary that we should so conduct ourselves, both in Great Great Britain, and Ireland, as to be able *distinctively to state* that we have been no parties to any money transactions whatever, between those who may have influence in boroughs and the persons who may be elected to represent them. . . . It cannot be either safe or proper for Government to embark on any transaction which could be considered as a violation of an Act of Parliament, and an Act of Parliament so recently passed.[64]

The operation of government influence was a risky and delicate affair. Electors were particularly sensitive to any instances of government arrogance, but they were likely to entertain high expectations of the rewards of government patronage. It is no accident that most boroughs with a sizeable government interest developed powerful independence parties. For example, the government interest in Southampton, in spite of many years of devoted cultivation by the Rose family, became increasingly unpopular in the early years of the nineteenth century. It did not survive the death of George Rose senior in January 1818 by more than a few months. At the general election of that year, Southampton became an opposition borough.[65]

By this time party politics was once more beginning to influence the character of electoral politics.[66] After the victory of Whigs over Tories had decisively settled the party struggles of the early eighteenth century, a lengthy period in which elections were mediated by essentially local concerns followed. However, during the reign of George III a new party duality began slowly to emerge which turned upon the conflict between successive governments and the opposition of first the Rockingham, then the Portland, then the Foxite Whigs, and then, in the early nineteenth century when the language of party was returning to the political vocabulary, the Whigs of Lord Grey. By this time elections were being strongly influenced by party considerations. The influence of the government, therefore, may be seen as an organizational agency of party, providing a permanent, structural foundation for the party of successive administrations.

---

[64] Sir Robert Peel to Lord Liverpool. BL (Add. MS) 40181 fos. 5–6, Peel Papers.
[65] *Hampshire Chronicle*, 13 Apr., 8 and 22 June 1818.          [66] See ch. 6.

Although the period with which this book deals witnesses the fall of one party system and the rise of another, it is nevertheless a distinct epoch in electoral history. For one thing, the forms and procedures of the electoral system undergo very little change. Only one constituency in the century of unreformed politics—Grampound—lost the franchise, and only four others were subjected to statutory regulation.[67] The conventions and legalities of electoral politics suffered no major upheavals. Although the size of the electorate began to increase in the later eighteenth century, there were no significant changes in either the social composition of the electorate or in the distribution of the franchise. Indeed, the techniques employed to control the electorate throughout this period underwent little alteration. It may therefore be as well to commence this investigation of electoral politics by concentrating upon some of these less dynamic aspects of constituency control and leaving to later chapters some consideration of the emergence of political issues and the development of opposition to an oligarchic electoral system.

[67] Grampound was disfranchised in 1821, its seats going to the county of Yorkshire. In 1770 the corrupt borough of New Shoreham in Sussex had its scot and lot franchise thrown into the Rape of Bramber, a remedy which vastly improved its electoral morality. Much the same pattern can be observed at Cricklade in 1782, when a bill extended the franchise of freeholders in the nearby hundreds. In 1804 bribery at Aylesbury was punished with a similar extension of the franchise into the neighbouring hundreds, and at East Retford in 1828 the franchise was extended into the hundred of Bassetlaw.

# 2

# *The Structure of Electoral Politics*

## THE CONTROL OF CONSTITUENCIES

The pattern of electoral control varied with the social and economic make-up of each constituency. In most of them a settled regime of control by the landed interest prevailed. In others rapid social changes were consigning some communities to obsolesence while pointing others towards a future of demographic and economic expansion. These changes seriously complicated a set of problems which always afflicted the Hanoverian ruling order, those concerning political stability and the possibility of establishing political unanimity. That ruling order was not fixed and settled. Viewed close up, its constituent families, institutions, and interests were rarely at peace. Their interminable personal, family, social, and political enmities not infrequently found expression at the electoral level. These conflicts did something to prise open and to keep open a dangerously oligarchic electoral system. How the ruling order nevertheless retained its control provokes issues which take us into the inner workings of the electoral system.

Historians usually find it sufficient to affirm that the control of the 269 English and Welsh constituencies—never, admittedly, an altogether straightforward affair—was successfully accomplished through some combination of 'patronage', 'influence', and 'corruption'. The circumstances of electoral control are so specific, however, that such 'explanations' do little to illuminate the electoral politics of any one constituency or group of constituencies. What is needed is a somewhat more sensitive tool of analysis which effectively describes the nature of electoral politics in a group of constituencies and which yet distinguishes that group from others. This can best be provided not by categorizing the constituencies according to the four main types of franchise, since each type (corporation, burgage, scot and lot, and freeman) embraces a wide range of electoral situations, but by distinguishing the basic elements of control which both outweigh others and yet which determine the character of electoral relationships in a group of constituencies. A typology of electoral behaviour organized in this fashion will offer not only a factual description of the varying quality of electoral politics in different types of constituencies, but provide a means of analysing these central features of electoral behaviour.

*Venal boroughs*

We may distinguish a group of just 20 constituencies in which electoral politics had been reduced to the status of a purely financial transaction, in which electoral support was forthcoming as a response to pecuniary persuasions and in which political issues played little or no part. Of course, making payments to electors was a widespread practice before—and long after—the Reform Act of 1832. As we shall see in Chapter 3 other services and other persuasions had to supplement these payments, which were, in any case, a well-nigh universal lubricant of the electoral engine. In the constituencies in this first category, however, financial persuasions had obliterated other types of political and social relationship to create a fresh set of simple, direct obligations. These are constituencies where quite spectacular patterns of venality were exhibited and where many of the electors were very well paid for their votes. Consequently we are not concerned here with customary or special payments made to sustain an acknowledged social bond, but with payments which replaced such bonds. These constituencies include some of the smaller boroughs with a scot and lot type of franchise,[1] together with a few of the smaller freeman boroughs.[2] In these boroughs, outsiders with heavy purses could buy up electoral support by purchasing houses and then by allowing the voters to live in them rent-free or at reduced rates. Electoral support could be further sought by distributing 5, 10, 20, or even as much as 30 pounds or guineas to the voters. At Shaftesbury in 1774, one candidate made 4,000 guineas available for distribution to the 300 voters.[3] The procedures for the promise and transmission of such money became consciously ritualized. At Cricklade in 1782 one candidate tapped once on the floor with his stick for each pound promised. The going rate

[1] In this type of borough franchise the occupation rather than the ownership of property is involved, and an interest could be readily established through the simple procedure of buying up houses. Within this category there are three distinct franchisal types: the 38 scot and lot boroughs (in which the franchise attached to resident householders paying the poor rate) the 12 householder boroughs (in which inhabitant householders receiving neither alms nor poor relief could vote), and the 6 freeholder boroughs (in which the vote belonged to owners of freeholds). In all of them the franchise was extremely ambiguous. For example, to attack the common abuse of occasional residence an Act of 1786 imposed a six-month residence qualification but it was very unevenly observed.

[2] In freeman boroughs, only 'free men' of the borough could vote. This franchise was therefore not a property qualification but a somewhat haphazard function of the ancient municipal constitution. Its precise definition varied from place to place. In some of the 92 freeman boroughs the freedom could be obtained by inheritance, in others by marriage to the daughter of a freeman, in others by membership of a guild, and in others by purchase.

[3] *Report of the Committee on the Shaftesbury Election Petition* (London, 1775), 113. 'Every general election was contested at Shaftesbury between 1761 and 1812, as a succession of would-be-patrons were overthrown by the expense and corruption of the borough.' See R. G. Thorne (ed.) *The House of Commons, 1790–1820*, 5 vols. (London, 1986), ii. 139.

was 20 taps.[4] At Stockbridge, apparently, 'Stockbridge language' automatically added three noughts to a figure when an aspiring outsider was calculating his election costs.[5]

No two historians will agree on a final list of venal boroughs. Those where financial considerations appear by the middle of the eighteenth century to have displaced all others include, in my opinion, 15 boroughs of the scot and lot variety and 5 of the smaller freeman boroughs. Few of them, however, were effectively controlled for long in this manner. Since there were many rich and ambitious men wishing to enter Parliament quickly, there was likely to be keen competition for the representation of these boroughs. Their electorates were on the whole small enough to attract such men, but large enough to render precarious any control which they might establish. The electorates of many of the scot and lot boroughs, furthermore, were increasing in size as time passed, as population increased, as more houses were built and as techniques of persuasion developed.[6] Nevertheless, these boroughs included the most corrupt of all the constituencies, those whose practices had disgraced the unreformed electorate for two centuries. It is these boroughs which have given a wholly undeserved reputation for venality and corruption to the electoral system as a whole. Most of these boroughs lost one, or both, seats in 1832 (see Table 2.1).[7]

The control of these constituencies was unstable and short-lived because the relationships established by exclusively financial mechanisms were inevitably short-term. Attempts were made to strengthen them by the practice of lending money to voters but such sums were rarely repaid.[8] In other places annual payments to voters were probably intended to achieve the same objective, but it is

---

[4] *Report of the Committee on the Cricklade Election Petition* (London, 1782), 358–9.

[5] *Report of the Committee on the Stockbridge Election Petition* (London, 1790), 22. At Stockbridge the customary forms for the transmission of money payments were so widely understood that it was not uncommon to send children for the money.

[6] At Ilchester the standard payment for a vote rose from 2 guineas in 1702 to £30 in 1784; see *V C H Somerset*, iii 195–6. Similar inflation can be seen at Tregony, where votes could be obtained for £5 early in the 18th cent. By 1790 they cost £20. See D. Ginter, *Whig Organization at the General Election of 1790* (Berkeley–Los Angeles, 1967), 189–91.

[7] As will be seen from Table 2.1, the size of the electorate was *increasing* in most of the scot and lot constituencies. Although Hindon steadily closed up, Arundel increasingly came to resemble an open borough; see Thorne, *House of Commons*, ii. 421, 390–1). Financial excess, however, in the cases of Aylesbury, Cricklade, and New Shoreham led to the restructuring of the constituency and, in each case, its conversion into a replica of a county seat. Grampound was disfranchised in 1821 for bribery and corruption. As Thorne aptly comments 'Grampound's crime was the freelance bid by its small electorate to turn the tables on their patron and use the system to their own advantage' (ibid. ii. 61). The moral that there was one law for the patrons and yet quite another for the voters seems irresistible.

[8] The interest, however, might be paid by the voter, sometimes in the shape of goods and produce.

*The Structure of Electoral Politics*

TABLE 2.1    *Effect of the 1832 Reform Act in Venal Boroughs*

| Constituency | Electorate | | Effect of 1832 Reform Act |
| | Mid 18th cent. | 1831 | |
| --- | --- | --- | --- |
| *Scot and lot* | | | |
| Arundel | 200 | 460 | Lost one |
| Callington | 100 | 225 | Lost both |
| Mitchell | 50 | 70 | Lost both |
| New Shoreham | 100/800[a] | 1,000 | Kept both |
| St Ives | 200 | 300 | Lost one |
| Shaftesbury | 300 | 360 | Lost one |
| Stockbridge | 100 | 150 | Lost both |
| Wallingford | 200 | 300 | Lost one |
| Wooton Bassett | 250 | 300 | Lost both |
| *Householder* | | | |
| Aylesbury[b] | 500[a] | 1,000 | Kept both |
| Hindon | 20 | 170 | Lost both |
| Honiton | 700 | 450 | Kept both |
| Ilchester | 200 | 60 | Lost both |
| Tregony | 150 | 280 | Lost both |
| *Freeholder* | | | |
| Cricklade[c] | 1,200[a] | 1,150 | Kept both |
| TOTAL | 4,670 | 6,755 | |
| *Freeman-type* | | | |
| Bishops Castle | 150 | 60 | Lost both |
| Bossiney | 30 | 25 | Lost both |
| Dunwich | 40 | 32 | Lost both |
| Grampound | 50 | —[d] | — |
| Launceston | 30 | 17 | Lost one |

[a] Boundaries extended in 1771.
[b] Boundaries extended in 1804.
[c] Boundaries extended in 1782.
[d] Grampound was disfranchised in 1821 for bribery and corruption.

extremely doubtful if they ever did more than temporarily satisfy the greed of venal electors. There are a few traces of voters signing bonds of loyalty, promising their votes as a condition for becoming freemen or for taking out a lease.[9] More common in the endeavour to establish

---

[9] At Dunwich the bond could be for as much as £600; see A. Childs, 'Politics and Elections in Suffolk Boroughs in the Late Eighteenth and Early Nineteenth Century', M. Phil., (Reading, 1973), 13–14.

more durable electoral relationships was the patron's payment of the poor rates or his provision of services to and favours for voters and their families.

For their part, the voters were willing to enter into the spirit of things. There are instances of voters clubbing and banding together in an attempt to maintain their independence of patrons and to keep up the value of their votes. A Commons Committee discovered in 1781 that the members of the Malt House Club at Arundel had sold their votes for £30 each at the general election of 1780.[10] This was rivalled by the Christian Club of New Shoreham, an association of voters who organized themselves at the by-election of 1770, ostensibly for charitable purposes but really to sell the seat to the highest bidder, the profits to be divided between them. They extracted £50 for a vote and demanded other services from the candidates. It was this corruption which led to the disfranchisement of the 81 voters concerned and the extension of the boundaries of the borough into the Rape of Bramber.[11] More widely, voters would not only pocket any money offered to them and accept the conventional election treats of dinners and ale but they would seek to lay the candidates under as much further expense as possible. This they would do by charging exorbitant sums for election tasks like erecting the hustings or providing ribbons and music. Furthermore, experienced voters in venal boroughs knew when to commit themselves: as late as possible, when the price of votes had risen. The last thing these voters wanted was the closing of their borough. They throve and prospered on contested elections and upon the uncertainty of electoral instability. Paradoxically, therefore, these boroughs were difficult to control, and some of them were frequently contested. However, it is difficult to detect any trend or development in patterns of contested elections in the venal boroughs. As can be seen from Table 2.2, there was a slightly less than 40% chance of an election being contested in the scot and lot or householder type of constituency, considerably less in the freeman boroughs.

## Proprietorial Boroughs

A second group of boroughs may be recognized in which the vote was treated as a form of property and the voting process as a transaction

---

[10] T. H. B. Oldfield, The *History of the Boroughs of Great Britain*, 2 vols. (London, 1794), i. 168.

[11] L. B. Namier and J. Brooke (eds.), *The House of Commons, 1754–1790*, 3 vols. (London, 1964), i. 368. At Aylesbury in 1804 some of the electors signed a petition for a Third man in order to provoke a contest. They hoped to gain £10 each and proceeded to establish a Benefit Club to control the fund; see *Report from the Select Committee on the Aylesbury Petition* (London, 1804), 55.

TABLE 2.2 *Contested Elections in Venal Boroughs, 1741–1831*

| Constituency | 1741–74 (6 elections) | 1780–1806 (6 elections) | 1807–31 (7 elections) |
|---|---|---|---|
| *Scot and lot/householder* | | | |
| Arundel | 3 | 1 | 3 |
| Aylesbury | 2 | 3 | 3 |
| Callington | 3 | 1 | 3 |
| Cricklade | 4 | 5 | 2 |
| Hindon | 3 | 2 | 1 |
| Honiton | 4 | 4 | 3 |
| Ilchester | 2 | 5 | 4 |
| Mitchell | 3 | 1 | 1 |
| New Shoreham | 1 | 2 | 3 |
| St Ives | 2 | 1 | 6 |
| Shaftesbury | 3 | 6 | 4 |
| Stockbridge | 1 | 3 | 2 |
| Tregony | 1 | 4 | 5 |
| Wallingford | 3 | 0 | 3 |
| Wooton Bassett | 3 | 3 | 3 |
| TOTAL | 39 | 41 | 46 |
| MEAN | 1.9 | 2.1 | 2.3 |
| | (32%) | (34%) | (33%) |
| *Freeman* | | | |
| Bishops Castle | 2 | 1 | 2 |
| Bossiney | 1 | 0 | 2 |
| Dunwich | 0 | 0 | 0 |
| Grampound | 2 | 0 | 3 |
| Launceston | 1 | 1 | 0 |
| TOTAL | 6 | 2 | 7 |
| MEAN | 1.0 | 0.3 | 1.2 |
| | (16.6%) | (3.6%) | (16.6%) |

in property relationships. This group comprises the burgage boroughs and some of the scot and lot and freeholder boroughs. In the 31 burgage boroughs, the right to vote depended upon the ownership of burgages, i.e. specific properties to which the franchise had customarily been attached. If a prospective patron could purchase a majority of these burgages, he had control of the seat.[12] In 15 scot and lot boroughs

[12] The burgage boroughs were Appleby, Ashburton, Bere Alston, Bletchingley, Borough-bridge, Bramber, Castle Rising, Chippenham, Clitheroe, Cockermouth, Downton, East Grinstead, Great Bedwyn, Heytesbury, Horsham, Knaresborough, Malton, Midhurst, Newport,

of a related kind it was possible for patrons to buy up a majority of the properties in which residence conveyed the vote.[13] Electoral control in these 46 boroughs depended overwhelmingly upon the possession of property.

Not surprisingly it is in these constituencies that some of the worst abuses of the unreformed electoral system are to be found. Twenty-six of them lost both their seats in 1832.[14] Another 11 lost one.[15] Only nine were deemed worthy of retaining both their seats.[16] By the late eighteenth century most of these places had been closed up. As a consequence they were rarely contested. Seventeen of the 31 burgage boroughs and 5 of the 13 scot and lot boroughs considered here did not experience a contested election after 1774.[17]

The possession, retention, and extension of property for personal, family, or financial reasons provided a potent motive for electoral involvement. Property was carefully bought to advance the borough interest of ambitious patrons. As the historian of Buckinghamshire put it, writing of Wendover: 'There was no political question for the independent electors to settle: the electors had nothing whatsoever to do with the matter, only to vote as they were directed by the proprietors of the property they occupied.'[18] And Oldfield described the town of

Newton, Newtown (Isle of Wight), Northallerton, Old Sarum, Petersfield, Pontefract, Richmond, Ripon, Thirsk, Weobley, Westbury, and Whitchurch. Definitive allocations are almost impossible to determine. For the record, I choose to include Castle Rising, Malton, and Newton here, aware that their confused franchises render disputable any such allocation. It is not just allocations which are difficult and confusing. 'Pontefract had ceased to belong to this category since 1783, but Saltash joined it in 1787' (Thorne, *House of Commons*, i. 38). I have therefore allowed the number of burgage boroughs to remain stable.

[13] Aldborough, Amersham, Corfe Castle, Eye, Gatton, Great Marlow, Haslemere, Ludgershall, Reigate, St Germans, Stamford, Steyning, Tavistock, Wendover, and Weymouth and Melcombe Regis.

[14] Seventeen burgage boroughs lost both seats in 1832: Appleby, Bere Alston, Bletchingley, Boroughbridge, Bramber, Downton, East Grinstead, Great Bedwyn, Heytesbury, Newport (Cornwall), Newtown (Isle of Wight), Newton, Old Sarum, Castle Rising, Saltash, Weobley, and Whitchurch. Six scot and lot boroughs lost both seats: Aldborough, Amersham, Corfe Castle, Gatton, St Germans, and Steyning. Three freeholder boroughs—Haslemere, Wendover, and Ludgershall—also lost both seats.

[15] Eight burgage boroughs lost one member: Ashburton, Clitheroe, Horsham, Midhurst, Northallerton, Petersfield, Thirsk, and Westbury. Two scot and lot boroughs lost one: Eye and Reigate. In addition, I include Weymouth and Melcombe Regis here, which lost two of its four members.

[16] Six burgage boroughs: Chippenham, Cockermouth, Knaresborough, Malton, Richmond, and Ripon. Oldfield favourably contrasted the three scot and lot boroughs (Great Marlow, Stamford and Tavistock) with these corrupt burgage boroughs; see Oldfield, *History of the Boroughs*, i. 536.

[17] Of the burgage boroughs, Appleby, Bere Alston, Bletchingley, Bramber, Castle Rising, Great Bedwyn, Heytesbury, Newton, Newtown (Isle of Wight), Northallerton, Old Sarum, Richmond, Ripon, Thirsk, Weobley, Westbury, and Whitchurch. To these must be added the scot and lot boroughs of Amersham, Corfe Castle, Reigate, St Germans, and Tavistock.

[18] R. Gibbs, *Buckinghamshire: Records of Local Occurrences*, 3 vols. (Aylesbury, 1879–85), iii. 208.

Amersham, 'where no political will is enjoyed and where privilege of franchise is only a necessity of obedience'.[19]

Elections were determined, therefore, by property transactions rather than by political conflicts. The representation of Great Marlow at the general election of 1790 was determined several years earlier when Sir William Lee of Hartwell, who owned the second largest interest there, was informed 'that Mr Clayton intended to sell all his houses in Great Marlow and that he wished to make the first offer of them to Mr Lee in case he inclined to increase his property and interest there, that they procured so many votes for the borough as gave Mr Clayton a seat in the House'.[20] Clayton sold, the Lees bought, and the election was decided. In such circumstances, as the petition of the Association of Friends of the People put it in 1793, elections were 'notoriously a mere matter of form'.[21] Boroughs and their representation could, in effect, be bought, sold, and inherited just like any other piece of property. With the rising cost of boroughs, such a piece of property could be an excellent investment. In the middle of the eighteenth century the Montagu interest began to buy up burgages and buy out rival patrons at Midhurst in Sussex. When it was sold in 1787 it was worth £40,000.[22]

The ease of controlling these boroughs should not be exaggerated. They could be expensive to manage, especially where a residential qualification survived. In some of them the electorate ran into several hundreds and coalitions of patrons—always a risky, personal, and transient business—were required to control them. At Reigate the Hardwicke and Somers families controlled 197 out of the 213 voters between them. Most of the 15 independents were copyholders, a rarity in these boroughs. Friction could arise between the two sides over the most trifling affair. In the 1780s a public meeting to elect new trustees for the local library ended in the dual nomination of rival sets of trustees. It was this that led to the engagement of 1786 which divided the borough thereafter.[23] No wonder that patrons attempted to squeeze every advantage they could out of their property by splitting burgages, dividing houses, and manipulating the court and burgage

---

[19] Oldfield, *History of the Boroughs*, i. 38.

[20] John Fiott to Sir William Lee, 11 Nov. 1786. D/LED/3/50, Lee MSS., Bucks RO. The best published account of the politics of a burgage borough is J. V. Beckett, 'The Making of a Pocket Borough: Cockermouth, 1722–1756', *J. Brit. Studies* 20/1 (1980), 140–57.

[21] See above, p. 18.

[22] Namier and Brooke, *House of Commons*, i. 396. According to Albery, the Duke of Norfolk bought out the Irwin electoral interest at Horsham for the staggering figure of £91,475; see W. Albery, *Parliamentary History of Horsham* (Horsham, 1947), 47.

[23] Material on Reigate is particularly copious. See the 'State of Reigate' and the 'Agreement of 1786' in D/ECd/E.160, Herts. RO.

rolls where titles were registered. At Wendover the Verney interest strove to make its properties yield as many votes as possible:

Several of the Houses belonging to the Earl Verney are empty and in some of them there are widows. And, in order to get the more voters, his Agents pretend that he will fill all these Houses with new inhabitants and make them parisheners by letting them much land at Claydon or in some distant part of the County as will make up the several rents of the houses he shall place them in . . . if the widows shall not take in such new inhabitants, they are turned out and it is insisted that if such inhabitants live in such Houses forty days before the election they will have the right to vote.[24]

The loyalty of burgage holders in burgage boroughs could be secured by leasing the freeholds to them on very long leases at peppercorn rents. This happened at Horsham and at Westbury, but it could render the voter dangerously independent of the patron. Patrons in these boroughs preferred to restrict the size of the electorate whenever they could in order to secure their interests.

Successful electioneering in these boroughs demanded the closest attention to local, customary practices whose precedents collectively amounted to electoral law. Legal authority arose, as the Boroughbridge petition of 1820 put it, 'from practices long as old persons can recollect, and what they may have heard from persons who are dead'.[25] Burgage houses could be distinguished from others by a varied mixture of personal reminiscence and old rental rolls. Properties once designated as burgages remained so, and the land on which they stood might retain the franchise even when the property was demolished. It was not merely at Old Sarum where features of the natural countryside found to their astonishment that they enjoyed a vote. At Horsham, it was not only barns and stables but also some fields which had the vote, burgages once having been situated there. Indeed, it was difficult to know just which features of the place did carry a vote, and which did not. Little plots of land at the side of streets at Horsham were found to have a vote. A steward, Meredrew, traversed the town, desperately seeking out burgages, but having found 66 confessed: 'My Lord Henry Youst[*sic*] to make 85 but I cannot find any more.'[26]

[24] Case with Counsel's Opinion as to the Franchise in Wendover, 27 Nov. 1753. D/MH/40/37, Earl of Buckingham's MSS, Bucks. RO.

[25] C. Bradley, 'The Parliamentary Representation of the Boroughs of Pontefract, Newark and East Retford, 1754–1768', MA (Manchester, 1953), 48–9.

[26] Albery, *Parliamentary History of Horsham*, 93–7. The contested election at Downton in 1784 resulted in a petition. During the subsequent committee hearing it was established that one of the burgages which conveyed the vote lay under a stream which flowed through the village. Because of sound precedents, however, its right to vote was vindicated. See J. A. Cannon, 'The Parliamentary Representation of the Boroughs of Chippenham, Cricklade, Downton, Hindon, Westbury and Wooton Bassett in Wiltshire, 1754–1790', Ph.D. (Bristol, 1958), 160–2.

And Oldfield describes the extraordinary franchise at Northallerton in the later eighteenth century:

Some of the burgages are merely stables, outhouses or cow houses in which the preservation of a chimney is both the sole remnant of humanity and of the right to vote. Others are let to poor persons at a small annual rent on condition of them keeping them in good repair. Many are totally ruinous or uninhabited. In some instances the vote is separated from the house by the practice of granting a lease for 999 years, subject to an annual peppercorn.[27]

Inevitably, legal ambiguities constituted the very stuff of electoral politics in such places. Could franchise-bearing properties be created or divided? Such practices, although technically illegal, were widespread. Was residence a necessary qualification for the franchise and, if so, for what length of time? What fixtures (e.g. a chimney) proved that the house was a genuine domicile and not a temporary residence for the period of the election? Even in Old Sarum, with its handful of electors, MPs and agents could manifest neurotic anxieties about these legal niceties.[28] In the scot and lot boroughs considered here a six-month residence qualification was imposed in 1786, but it was patchily observed.[29] In any case, was it necessary in such a borough to occupy all of the house? All that was clear was that a voter must occupy a 'distinct tenement' with a separate staircase. In most cases someone who rented such a tenement could vote but not in all, and he would certainly need to fulfil the residence requirements.

To overcome these potential uncertainties patrons indulged in a number of practices designed to render their seats as impregnable as possible. By far the most common was that of conveyancing. In the majority of boroughs of this type, the burgage houses were not normally inhabited. Just before an election, a patron would convey the house to a nominated dependant, friend, supporter, or relative, who would live in the house for a locally defined period, perhaps a day, just before the election. The deed of conveyance would be granted to the voter just before the election by the patron's agent and returned to him immediately after the poll. In that way the ownership of the precious burgage house never came into question. Agents had to be

---

[27] Oldfield, *History of the Boroughs*, i. 283–4.
[28] There is a remarkable series of letters in the Caledon MSS in the PRO (Northern Ireland) between Porcher, MP for Old Sarum, and his agent, W. Boucher, between 1807 and 1818. Clearly Porcher was constantly anxious about the legal safety of his enormous investment in the borough (£43,000.) D.2433/B/4/1/5, C/7/12, C/8/8.
[29] Porritt and Porritt, *Unreformed House of Commons*, 31, 35–7. Such a bill had been introduced in 1739 but had failed to pass. Significantly, it exempted the burgage boroughs from its provisions.

very careful about conveyancing. The conveyance had to be correctly made out and the title proved beyond doubt. Much documentation was necessary. Each burgage was conveyed by an indenture of lease and release, which conveyed the freehold, and therefore the right to vote, for one year. These 'transfers' of property as they were known were accomplished by 'snatch papers', which were given to the voter as evidence of his credentials. These rarely stated anything about the vote. They merely affirmed the tenant's occupation of the burgage. For this the voters rarely paid any 'rent'. On the contrary, they received a reward for the modest yet necessary service they did for the patron. These occasional voters were sometimes borrowed from a local landowner when they could not be hired in the constituency itself. At Pontefract in 1768 Lord Galway needed to find no fewer than 150 obliging voters. At least 30 came from the Pontefract tradesmen, and another 30 from the local Galway estates. Others had to be drawn from the family's estates in Nottinghamshire.[30]

Sometimes the real obstacle to controlling constituencies of this character was not so much the electors as the petition which a defeated candidate might lodge against the return, a very common occurrence. To pay the litigation costs and the costs of transporting and accommodating witnesses could double the expense of a contest. It was sometimes impossible for a committee of the House of Commons to reach an informed decision amidst the legal quagmires which accompanied elections of this type. Sometimes a party vote in the House of Commons was the only means of deciding who should sit. Such a disaster could destroy the most secure of interests. After more than three decades of fairly stable control of Bramber, Sir Harry Gough lost everything when the House of Commons voted on 14 February 1769 to unseat his members.[31] To avoid such a circumstance it was advisable to invest in a certain amount of local good-will. The usual rituals of canvassing, treating, and speeches, together with flags, parades, and chairings, helped to entertain the voters. Indeed, in some of these boroughs the patrons appear to have gone much further in order to protect their investment. Sir William Drake's control of Amersham could not have been challenged. Namier and Brooke pay him the compliment of not wasting more than three lines on the borough.[32] Drake, however, was a studious benefactor of the town.

[30] There is a mass of detail on this election, especially in the Hothfield MSS (WD/H, box 39, Westmorland RO). See also the MSS at D/Cu/1/13 in the Curwen MSS, Carlisle RO.

[31] M. Cramp, 'The Parliamentary Representation of Five Sussex Boroughs, 1754–1768', MA, (Manchester, 1953), 40.

[32] Namier and Brooke, *House of Commons*, i. 214. Thorne gives the same borough four lines (*House of Commons*, ii. 18).

Voters and non-voters all received his bounty. An 'Address from the Electors of Amersham' in 1784 thanked him for his 'generous and liberal benefactions to the Poor in this Parish, in the course of the last and preceding winter'.[33] Similarly, Eye is described as 'a pocket borough of the Cornwallis family' in *The History of Parliament*, but it required regular financial and other benefactions to keep the small scot and lot constituency happy—activities which had to be carefully channeled through the Eye Corporation if the touchy voters were not to be ruffled.[34] It is not clear how much these acts of generosity contributed to an election victory but they probably did something to reduce the risk of disaffected burgage-holders and other residents providing awkward testimony in the event of a petition. Even in this somewhat unlikely area of the unreformed electoral system, therefore, some echoes of paternalism are frequently to be heard.

## Corporation Boroughs

A third category of seats is those in which the corporation directly or indirectly controlled the representation. In the 27 corporation boroughs,[35] members of the corporations were themselves the electorate. Whoever controlled the corporation thus controlled the representation. Buckingham was a tiny corporation borough whose electorate consisted of the bailiff and the 12 burgesses of the borough. The municipal corporation's Report stated in 1835 that the Marquis of Buckingham had a commanding influence in the town where the corporation 'for a long time served as an instrument for enabling the patron of the borough to return two members, and nothing more'.[36]

To these corporation boroughs must be added 9 freeman boroughs.[37] It is almost impossible to distinguish these from the corporation boroughs because here too a patron controlled the

---

[33] Electors' Address, 2 Apr. 1784. D/DP/12/46, Drake MSS, Bucks. RO.

[34] On the mode of distributing annual sums to the citizens, see Sir Miles Nightingale to Charles Bumpstead, 9 Feb. 1824, (item 13 1/01/21, East Suffolk RO; see also Namier and Brooke, *House of Commons*, i. 380.

[35] One in Wales and 26 corporation boroughs in England: Andover, Banbury, Bath, Bodmin, Brackley, Buckingham, Bury St Edmunds, Calne, Christchurch, Devizes, Droitwich, Harwich, Helston, Lostwithiel, Malmesbury, Marlborough, Newport (Isle of Wight), New Romney (up to 1787) Salisbury, Saltash, Scarborough, Thetford, Tiverton, Truro, Wilton, Yarmouth (Isle of Wight). Beaumaris in Wales, was a corporation borough under the control of the Bulkeley family.

[36] T. A. Hume, 'Buckinghamshire and Parliament', *Records of Buckinghamshire*, 16 (1960), 97.

[37] The 9 freeman boroughs included here are: Cambridge (by the end of the 18th cent.), Chipping Wycombe, Liskeard, Lyme Regis, Lymington, Orford, Poole, Rye, and Tewkesbury. Of these only Tewkesbury had an electorate above 200.

corporation, which in turn controlled the representation. To these must also be added two boroughs with a scot and lot franchise, where control of the corporation effectively permitted control of the representation.[38] Few of these boroughs were greatly decayed; many were rich and thriving small towns. There were, of course, other boroughs where the role of the corporation in electoral politics was of some account. In many other freeman and scot and lot boroughs they were an important element. Nevertheless, in those places the electorate was too large or too independent (or both) to submit tamely to corporation control. Other techniques and influences were required to discipline—and control—those electorates. In the boroughs at present under consideration, however, the pattern of electoral politics, and not just the control of the representation, was entirely determined by the activities of the corporation.

Because of their small electorates and because most of these boroughs had fallen under patronage during the early part of the eighteenth century, if not before, contested elections were rare. On average only 5 of the 27 corporation boroughs were contested at each general election between 1741 and 1774, and the rate fell to under 4 thereafter. Individual cases provide some startling examples of electoral expiry. Andover did not go to the polls after 1796, Brackley after 1754, Lostwithiel after 1722, Buckingham after 1715, Wilton after 1710. Once the tentacles of oligarchy had fastened themselves around these boroughs there was little prospect of their escape. The same holds for the freeman and scot and lot boroughs in this category where contests were even rarer.

In what ways precisely was the corporation such a critical factor in the management of these 38 constituencies? During the eighteenth century the poverty of many corporations led to them placing themselves voluntarily under the patronage of rich, local families anxious to control the representation. Given the self-electing nature of corporate bodies it was not long before many corporations were dominated numerically by the family, friends and dependants of landed patrons. This was, moreover, a situation which was impossible to reverse. (Only three corporation boroughs—Bath, Devizes, and Salisbury—remained independent; because of the wealth and property of their corporations, and because of the civic pride and self-conscious dignity which consequently characterized these towns, they never succumbed to local, landed patronage.) Control of the corporation,

[38] Penryn, where according to Oldfield the borough was a manor belonging to the See of Exeter, of which it was held by the corporation (Oldfield, *History of the Boroughs*, i. 96), and Seaford, one of the Cinque Ports, where control of the corporation was indispensable for controlling the representation.

furthermore, led directly to influence over the electoral process itself, in particular the nomination of the returning officer, whether mayor or bailiff. At Christchurch,

the Mayors however whose Principles have been doubtful, or whose Circumstances have been low, have generally, I believe, but privately, received . . . a Present of 20 or 30 Guineas by way of Retainer. This Donation is funded in good Policy, for on the Conduct of the Mayor the whole Interest of the Borough depends.[39]

Patrons would not normally risk their own personal reputations at this level. They usually employed stewards or agents whose abilities and personalities could be of the first importance.[40] These men were particularly active in rendering their patron's political authority financially attractive, either by direct bribery or by the custom of 'lending' money to members of the corporation, of which repayment was rarely demanded.[41] If Oldfield is to be believed, the sale of votes had become so sophisticated in Andover, Devizes, and Malmesbury that the voters employed an agent to sell their seat to the highest bidder.[42] Elsewhere, the distribution of offices was a cheap and effective method of control. At Harwich and Saltash most members of the corporation were provided for by the government and remained loyal so long as comparable inducements were not offered from other quarters.[43] At Tiverton the sons of members of the corporation obtained the benefits of their father's influence in the shape of military

---

[39] Undated memorandum, 'Particulars of the Borough of Christchurch'. 2M30/361, Hants. RO.

[40] At Marlborough, the Marquis of Aylesbury's estate agent was himself a member of the corporation. At Harwich, where the control of government was somewhat more distant than that of local patrons in most corporation boroughs, the services of local managers was crucial, and on occasion threatened to become hereditary. At Malmesbury, MPs were returned on the direct nomination of the high steward, who was 'elected' annually by the corporation. Here, as at Newton, the patron, as lord of the manor, appointed the officers, steward and bailiff, who were usually the returning officers. Helston was run by a clergyman for the Duke of Leeds in the later 18th cent. Devizes was managed by a recorder on behalf of rich London merchants.

[41] At Malmesbury, the Wilkins family until 1804 paid members of the corporation £30 p.a. in return for a bond of allegiance of £500. In 1757, however, the corporation revolted and obtained an extra £50 per man. Lord Mount Edgecumbe regularly paid the debts of Lostwithiel Corporation and advanced further sums of money. At Helston, the Duke of Leeds subsidized the public entertainments of the corporation (BM Add. MSS, 33110, fos. 48–9, Newcastle Papers). At Marlborough the members of the corporation were receiving £50 p.a. in election years in the 1740s. The Marquis of Aylesbury controlled the Marlborough Corporation through individual and collective benefactions; see Namier and Brooke *House of Commons*, i. 410.

[42] T. H. B. Oldfield, *Representative History of Great Britain and Ireland*, 6 vols. (London, 1816), v. 179.

[43] There was an occasion in the 1760s when, for example, a rival interest arranged for a ship to be built at Harwich, thus providing prosperity as well as employment; see L. B. Namier, The *Structure of Politics at the Accession of George III* (London, 1929), 441–69.

and naval commissions at one extreme, and the much more modest posts of land- or tide-waiterships, at the other.[44]

The control of the small freeman boroughs required little more than an extension of these methods. Consequently, the corporation was packed with compliant individuals, and the resources of the corporation were used for flagrantly political purposes. At Liskeard, Edward Eliot had built up a position of near supremacy in the 1770s. To render him secure,

he was allowed to nominate from his friends, the non-resident Freemen, whom he could bring in to vote in case of any opposition to his wishes within the Corporation. According to the universal practice by both parties then prevalent the Patron had, no doubt, to make it worth while for the Corporation to be thus subservient to his wishes. The Patron, for some years at any rate, paid large sums every year to the Corporation (in 1799 it was £850), and probably found Government places and situations for the sons and relatives of the Corporation. He paid the school-master at the Castle School and so forth.[45]

The primary electoral function of the corporation in freeman boroughs was to admit new freemen and to determine technical questions concerning the freedom in general. One device was to safeguard a position of established strength by restricting carefully the number of new creations. The most startling example was the savage restriction placed upon the creation of new freemen by John Mortlock at Cambridge in the 1780s. By 1826 the electorate numbered just 26.[46] Elsewhere it might be tactically advisable to admit a mass of new creations in order to swamp the freemen of a hostile interest or simply to render a strong position impregnable. At Lymington in 1774 Sir Harry Burrard attempted this latter by creating 36 new freemen before having the corporation pass a resolution restricting its own size to 50, no new freemen to be chosen until the number had fallen below 20. Not surprisingly, the borough was secure in his family until the Reform Act.[47] Such ruthlessness had its dangers. To create new freemen might offend the old, jealously guarding their status. To keep the number

---

[44] There is a fascinating and comprehensive account of the faction, intrigue, and political culture of corporation boroughs in the correspondence of Beavis Wood, town clerk of Tiverton between 1765 and 1806 (John Bourne (ed.), *Georgian Tiverton: The Political Memoranda of Beavis Wood, 1768–1798*, Devon and Cornwall Record Society, NS 29 (1986), esp. pp. 8, 16, 21, 27, 30, 34–5, 47, 106, 123.

[45] A. de C. Glubb, *When Cornwall Had 44 MPs* (Truro, 1945), 19. On Liskeard, see also G. S. Veitch, 'William Huskisson and the Controverted Elections at Liskeard, 1802 and 1804', *Trans. Royal Hist. Soc.* 4th ser., 13 (1930), 205–28.

[46] D. Cook, 'The Representative History of the County, Town and University of Cambridge, 1689–1832', London, 170.

[47] *VCH Hampshire*, iv. 462.

small tended sometimes to make the freedom hereditary in certain families.[48] Normally, however, patrons were able to have their way so long as they were careful to oblige and to flatter the freemen and to provide for the needs of the borough.

The control of scot and lot boroughs of this type required a rather more direct exploitation of the political and economic resources of the corporation. Its ownership of land and houses could be exercised with partiality. Preference could be shown in the letting of wastelands, the charging of rents for the encroachment of buildings on to pavements and streets and the issue of licences for markets and to inn-keepers. Finally, appointments to local offices of all kinds, the administration of the Poor Law, and, not least, the use made of local charitable institutions, bequests, and funds were other spheres where favours to political friends might help to control the constituency.

The whole community could benefit directly or indirectly from electoral control through the corporation. Continuity of employment for local tradespeople might be secured in some places. In others an imposing array of public buildings might be erected, as at Helston. Successive patrons of Tiverton provided money for the declining economic base of the town, especially after it had been half ruined by the Revolutionary and Napoleonic wars. Loans to bankrupt firms enabled them to set up trade again.[49] Where there was more than a single patron, the town might do well from their attempts to outdo the other. Bury St Edmunds, enjoying a system of joint patronage between the Grafton and Hervey families, profited well from this arrangement.[50] Consequently, these well—if partially—managed boroughs were able to avoid many of the worst features of electoral degradation. Although they had tiny electorates, they were surprisingly well treated in 1832. Fifteen of the 26 corporation boroughs in England kept both seats, 6 kept one, and only 4 lost both.[51] Of the remaining 11 boroughs dealt with here, 5 kept both seats, 4 lost one, and 2 lost both.[52]

---

[48] As happened at Orford in the mid-18th cent., see Childs, 'Politics and Elections in Suffolk Boroughs', M.Phil., 12.

[49] E. S. Chalk, 'Tiverton Letters and Papers, 1724–1843', *Notes and Queries*, 170 (1936), 22–4.

[50] Childs, 'Politics and Elections in Suffolk Boroughs', M.Phil., 259–60.

[51] Those that kept both seats were Andover, Banbury, Bath, Bodmin, Buckingham, Bury St Edmunds, Devizes, Harwich, Marlborough, Newport, Salisbury, Scarborough, Thetford, Tiverton, and Truro. Those that kept one seat were Calne, Christchurch, Droitwich, Helston, Malmesbury, and Wilton. Those that lost both seats were Brackley, Lostwithiel, New Romney, and Yarmouth. Beaumaris kept its only seat. Saltash can no longer be regarded as a corporation borough after 1787.

[52] Cambridge, Lymington, Penryn, Poole, and Tewkesbury kept both seats. Chipping Wycombe, Liskeard, Lyme Regis, and Rye kept one. Only Orford, and Seaford lost both.

Nevertheless, both in law and in practice, corporations treated the representation as they treated their corporate funds and offices—as a piece of property which itself had no rights and privileges.[53] Such a state of affairs could not possibly endure indefinitely. The ruthless partisanship with which corporations were used by one side or another to control the representation and the well-publicized abuses which disgusted an increasingly sensitive public opinion were among the most vulnerable aspects of the unreformed electoral system.[54]

## Patronage Boroughs

The fourth—and largest—group of constituencies may best be termed patronage boroughs. These are boroughs in which settled, natural interests dominated, based, as Brooke has aptly remarked, on the solid foundations of landed property, services to the constituency, and the goodwill of the electors.[55] These elements serve to distinguish them from constituencies where the vote was little more than a financial transaction, a property investment, or a simple and direct consequence of corporation control. Although the electoral politics of patronage boroughs reveal plenty of evidence of these baser features, they nevertheless exist within a qualitatively different political environment. The control of the representation in these constituencies is part of a wider system of clientage structures which in their all-embracing manner ordered the society of town and country into hierarchies of dependence and obligation. In a world of anticipated deference, however, electoral support was as much a personal as a political action, and opposition to a local family carried with it overtones of personal hostility. So long as the patron fulfilled his paternalistic obligations, it was expected that the voter would reciprocate by tendering his electoral loyalty to him. The abiding strength of this idea of paternalistic leadership and control is only partly to be understood by attributing it to a 'quasi-feudal' tradition.[56] After all, the idea that power should not be exercised arbitrarily was not exactly old-fashioned, the notion that the possession of great power carried with it obligations and responsibilities by no means outdated. A critical handbill rhetorically advised Lord Richard Grosvenor of Eaton Hall,

---

[53] As the lord chancellor told the House of Lords in July 1828, corporations 'held property not in trust, and over such property the corporation exercised the same right as individuals did over their property' (*Parliamentary Debates*, NS, 19 (1745-6)), quoted in M. Brock, *The Great Reform Act* (London, 1973), 27.

[54] Brock, *The Great Reform Act*, 24-8.

[55] Namier and Brooke, *House of Commons*, i. 46.

[56] As Namier was apt to do in dealing with Chester and similar places; see *Structure of Politics*, 105-8.

near Chester, to reassess his performance of his duties and ask himself; 'When I took possession of my good living . . . in the County of Chester . . . did I not enter into a contract with the inhabitants thereof, to take care of the soul of every individual, high and low, rich and poor, without distinction.'[57] The fact that the Grosvenors had enjoyed both Chester seats for many decades laid even greater obligations upon them because they had clearly prospered from public service.[58] How far paternalists lived up to their own standards is impossible to determine but because these standards were constantly being cited, their currency cannot be doubted. In practice, it is perhaps no accident that most of the patronage boroughs knew little of the worst excesses of venality and corruption. The exercise of paternalist responsibilities went far towards providing a stable yet flexible framework for political and social life, and one which endured down to the Reform Act of 1832—and in many places, beyond that.

There were over 80 patronage boroughs, and for the most part they enjoyed credible and fairly respectable electoral regimes. They included 20 scot and lot type boroughs and 61 freeman boroughs of various sizes.[59] The electorates of the small and medium-sized freeman

[57]   Handbill, 1786, in the Grosvenor MSS, Chester RO.

[58]   As a letter from 'CANDIS' to the *Chester Chronicle*, n.d. Sept. 1811, roundly affirmed (copy in the Grosvenor MSS, ibid.)

[59]   *The scot and lot patronage boroughs* were: Abingdon, Bridgewater, Bridport, Chichester, Dorchester, Fowey, Lewes, Milborne Port, Newark, New Windsor, Peterborough, Pontefract, Reading, Tamworth, Wareham, and Warwick. Four householder boroughs may also be included here: Cirencester, Minehead, Preston, and Taunton.

There were 27 *small freeman boroughs* (i.e. less than 200 voters) in 1754: Aldeburgh, Barnstaple, Bewdley, Camelford, Dartmouth, East Looe, East Retford, Grimsby, Hastings, Hedon, Higham Ferrers, Huntingdon, Hythe, Morpeth, New Woodstock, Plymouth, Plympton Earle, Portsmouth, Queenborough, St Mawes, Stafford, Totnes, Wells, West Looe, Wigan, Winchelsea, Winchester.

To these should be added *20 medium-sized freeman boroughs* (i.e. 200–1,000 voters c.1754): Berwick, Boston, Derby, Great Yarmouth, Grantham, Guildford, Ipswich, Kings Lynn, Lichfield, Ludlow, Maldon, Monmouth, Newcastle-under-Lyme, Okehampton, Rochester, St Albans, Sandwich, Southampton, Sudbury, Wenlock.

Finally, there were *14 large freeman boroughs* (i.e. 1,000 + voters in 1754): Bedford, Beverley, Bridgnorth, Carlisle, Chester, Dover, Durham, Exeter, Hull, Lancaster, Maidstone, Oxford, Worcester, York.

In the text there seems little point in observing this distinction between types of constituencies. By the early 19th cent., for example, the interesting constituency of Great Yarmouth, listed above as a medium-sized borough, had 1,400 voters, thus illustrating how constituencies can move with facility between a typology of constituencies distinguished by the size of their electorates. Similarly, constituencies experienced considerable changes over time. By the early 19th cent., St Albans, for example, clearly a patronage borough under the influence of the Spencer family until 1784, had become very like a venal borough, and Barnstaple had become so corrupt as almost to warrant inclusion in the same category, while the number of voters at Winchester had fallen so low (down to 7 at one point) as to have made it effectively a proprietorial borough; see Thorne, *House of Commons*, ii. 101–5, 480. Nevertheless, some generalizations must be made in spite of these complexities.

boroughs increased slightly from a mid-eighteenth-century low point back to and above early eighteenth-century levels.[60] The electorates of scot and lot and large freeman boroughs increased much more rapidly.[61] Contested elections in the small freeman boroughs were quite rare. Only about one-third were contested at any general election, a rate which suggests a high level of electoral stability. Other types of patronage borough could not be so thoroughly stabilized. One half of the scot and lot boroughs were contested at each general election, two-thirds of the medium and larger freeman boroughs. Clearly, opposition could express itself with some facility in these places where the electors were numerous and exceptionally mobile, and consequently difficult to control.[62]

The structure of patronage in these boroughs was both infinitely varied and constantly changing. In some of them, a single patron—the Duke of Marlborough at Oxford, for example, or the Duke of Devonshire at Derby—exercised a preponderant influence. The electoral politics of the borough were thus largely determined by this simple fact. But control of the larger of these boroughs could not be secured without lavish generosity to the voters and without consulting the interests of the town. In most of them local candidates were preferred. In the larger boroughs, especially, outsiders were not welcome. In others, however, a much more complicated situation existed. In many boroughs two families shared the representation (e.g. John Page and the Duke of Richmond at Chichester in the second half of the eighteenth century, Lord Aylesford and Lord Romney at Maidstone, or the Walpoles and Townshends at Great Yarmouth). At New Windsor the corporation was for many years in the interest of the Earl of Beaulieu, although 'a very great personage', as Oldfield called him, could not be ignored.[63] In yet others electoral politics turned upon the conflict between the corporation and an independent party (e.g. Plymouth, Chester). Elsewhere the role of the church was a factor to complicate matters (e.g. Exeter and Worcester). In others, loose and fluctuating confederations of local families might vie for

---

[60] The medium freeman boroughs considered here (200–1,000 electors in 1754), for example, have a total of electorate of 14,175 in the early 18th cent. (R. R. Sedgwick, *The House of Commons, 1715–1754*, 2 vols. (London, 1970), 12,780 in the second half of the 18th cent. (Namier and Brooke, *House of Commons*), 14050 in the early 19th cent. (Thorne, *House of Commons*), and 15,165 on the eve of the 1832 Reform Act. (J. H. Philbin, *Parliamentary Representation, 1832, England and Wales* (New Haven, 1965).)

[61] The large freeman boroughs considered here have a total electorate of 15,710 in the early 18th cent. and 19,700 in the second half of the 18th cent. 19,900 in the early 19th cent., and 25,554 on the eve of reform.

[62] On the mobility of the electorate see pp. 192–98. On contests see pp. 106–16.

[63] Oldfield, *Representative History*, i. 11.

predominance but without significant continuity, a situation which permitted the voters to assert themselves and demand extra financial benefits.

Up to a certain point the tactics and methods used to control other types of borough may be found in the patronage boroughs. As we shall see, however, what was needed for the settled and successful management of these boroughs was a much more thoroughgoing attention to local economic interests, a greater willingness to take heed of local opinion, and, in general, a more generous provision of municipal services, facilities, and welfare than we have yet encountered. Certainly, financial payments to electors—sometimes euphemistically termed 'loans'—were common. Normally, however, this signified nothing more than the customary displays of generosity which afforded treats to the electors and which were expected of all candidates. Where natural interest was healthy, the normal operations of deference usually rendered superfluous any extravagant expenditure of money. At Abingdon, for example, E. L. Loveden was returned for £300 in 1784.[64] Where intense competition between interests unsettled these relationships, the price could climb steeply,[65] but outright bribery was quite rare. Although contemporaries were morbidly afflicted with visions of rising tides of corruption, in this as in other areas of national life, the extravagant use of money alone appears to have been confined to certain constituencies, and then usually to a minority of the voters (e.g. Newark). Even in the worst and most notorious constituencies, most voters never came under suspicion. In other cases, references to 'bribery' might mean nothing more than payments to voters.[66] Financial inducements, then, were a universal and indispensable feature of unreformed electioneering, but they could very quickly backfire. A candidate who depended on his purse alone won little respect in these boroughs. One candidate at Wigan found that it ruined his chances in 1753 and he had to withdraw.[67] Nevertheless, voters could quickly develop the habit of expecting more. The managers of Portland's interest there lamented that they were plagued 'by the lower class of burgesses who are continually wanting some trifle or other and that they may not be displeased [we are] frequently obliged to advanced small sums'.[68] The true foundation of Portland's interest at

---

[64] D/ELv./190, Loveden MSS, Berks. RO.

[65] At Tamworth in 1765, for example, 42 electors received 'loans' of over £800 from the Townshed interest, a transaction which may have secured the allegiance of 22 'new' voters; see D. Stuart, 'The Parliamentary History of Tamworth', MA (London 1958), 103–5.

[66] In Abingdon, for example, in 1796, 70 out of 240 voters were 'bribed', whatever that may mean (*VCH Berkshire*, ii. 166).

[67] A broadsheet entitled, *To the Burgesses of Wigan* (4 May 1753) pilloried Sir John Searle's somewhat extravagant promises (Wigan Pub. Lib.).

[68] A. Radcliffe to Duke of Portland, 5 June 1764. PWF 9675, Portland MSS, Nottingham Univ. Lib.

Wigan was not the systematic corruption of the electorate, but the solid support of a majority of the burgesses earned by a combination of favours, treats, offices, and service and, of course, of customary payments. Yet financial inducements alone were an ineffective means of establishing a secure and lasting interest in a patronage borough.

Control of the corporation was, similarly, a totally necessary but not a sufficient means of maintaining control of these boroughs. During the course of the eighteenth century most corporations became self-selecting bodies, steadily departing from the more popular election which had been widespread earlier in the century. In spite of the determined opposition of local independence parties, it proved impossible to stem the tide. In scot and lot boroughs power over—or in—the corporation was necessary because the corporation itself might own large numbers of houses, residence in which conveyed the vote. In freeman boroughs it was even more necessary because only the corporation could bestow the freedom on individuals and thus, quite literally, create voters. The temptation to put this power to partisan use was to prove irresistible in two-thirds of the freeman boroughs. In 1761 the Derby corporation created 257 tenants of the House of Cavendish, 'Bastard Burgesses to swamp the chartered and independent burgesses of the borough'.[69] Similar examples could be multiplied indefinitely. These honorary freemen, or 'faggots' as they were called, sometimes had little or nothing to do with the borough. In 1743 the Mayor of St Albans created 459 honorary freemen, many of them resident in London.[70] After a particularly unsavoury case at Durham in 1762 Parliament passed the Durham Act of 1763, which withheld the vote from honorary freemen created within the 12 months prior to an election. It was easy, however, to get round the Act by ensuring that honorary freemen were created in good time, not normally a tactic requiring unusual perspicacity. Occasionally Parliament toyed with the idea of providing a remedy for this abuse but nothing was done until the Reform Act of 1832 gave the suffrage to resident, registered £10 householders.[71] Similarly, bills to reform other practices came to nothing. A bill to establish a residential qualification for freemen failed in 1773; another to prevent the creation of honorary freemen reached its second reading in 1779 but got no further. Finally, a bill to prevent occasional freemen from voting was withdrawn in 1789. In none of these areas were abuses cured before 1832.

[69] Handbill issued by Sir Charles Robert Colville, Collection of Squibs and Broadsides, Derby Borough Lib.
[70] H. F. Lansberry, 'Politics and Government in St Albans, 1688–1835', Ph.D. (London, 1964), 224.
[71] Porritt and Porritt, *Unreformed House of Commons*, i. 65–8.

There were many other ways in which the corporation could influence elections. As we have seen, it could administer the rights, property, and offices under its control in a partial manner. These could be, in a local context, substantial, and could include municipal buildings, schools, shops, houses, farms, and other properties. There might, in addition, be a whole range of specific trusts administered by the corporation endowed with funds, appointments, land, and property. Here was an enormous source of political power, wealth, and office which could be used for political and electoral purposes. The administration of charities was a frequent abuse. The charity commissioners concluded in 1836 that lands, houses, and monies had been vested in certain of the corporations as trustees, for charitable uses, but that their administration had been both inefficient and partial.[72] Furthermore, the mayor or the bailiff was usually the returning officer, whose ability to influence the course of an election was considerable. No wonder that the first thing the Duke of Portland did to consolidate his influence at Wigan in 1765 was to elect his own mayor and burgesses.[73]

Even in large freeman boroughs the advantage gained by such methods might very well tip the balance in a close contest, although by themselves they would rarely be decisive. Patrons, however, had to be careful because public opinion became more sensitive to corporation abuses. Reconstituting his electoral strategy after the loss of one of the two Chester seats in 1812, Lord Grosvenor dropped his earlier tactic of creating honorary freemen in favour of a systematic policy of creating resident freemen free of charge. Such a policy would, he hoped, be less liable to public disapproval.[74]

As we might expect, the possession of private property in these boroughs could be an invaluable asset in electioneering, but it had to be exerted with discretion. Even in the mid-eighteenth century there were limits to its usefulness. At the scot and lot borough of Tamworth in 1761 George Townshend owned houses which had 25 tenants yielding 36 votes in his interest. During the next few years he spent £17,000 on additional houses. By the end of 1765 he had 43 voters, but at the canvass of that year before a by-election 2 were described as 'uncertain' and 9 as 'opposed'. Similarly, the Weymouth interest at Tamworth in 1769 possessed 90 tenements in the town, with 72

[72] *Report of the Commissioners appointed to inquire concerning Charities and Education of the Poor in England and Wales* (London, 1836).

[73] Portland to Pennington, 21 Sept. 1765, D/DX. TA Box 33/21A, Pennington MSS, Wigan RO; Ollerhead to Portland, 28 Oct. 1765, PWF 7266, Portland MSS, Nottingham Univ. Lib.

[74] John Fletcher to Lord Grosvenor, [n.d.] 1812, Grosvenor MSS, 252. Chester RO.

voting tenants. These promised 58 'certain', 4 'uncertain', and 9 'opposed', with 1 'not voting'. (It was, in fact, the prospect that these two interests might buy up yet further properties that led to the emergence of an independent party at Tamworth before the general election of 1774.)[75] The point is, however, that out of 115 votes secured for these two interests by the ownership of property, no fewer than 25 of them were unreliable.

Even the most careful management of borough properties was incapable of guaranteeing the future behaviour of electors. The Duke of Newcastle decided to reorganize his management of the scot and lot borough of Lewes after a closely run election in 1734. Here are his new tactical plans, dated 19 August 1739, for the general election of 1741:[76]

To have a proper person settled at Lewes, to have the care, and conduct of the interest there.

To appoint persons in the several parishes, to take care of that parish, and to make their returns to the person, who has the care of the whole.

To lay out the work to be undertaken at Lewes, and at Bishopstone.

To consider the several artificers, that can be appointed, and the works, where they can be employ'd.

To take the names of all the empty houses in the interest, and to fill them forthwith; and to propose persons for that purpose.

To see, what more houses can be got, either by building, repairing, or hiring.

To consider, what houses can be taken in lease, or bought.

To consider, what women are in houses, that can be removed for voters.

To agree upon proper parish officers, for the next two years, in the several parishes.

Constables, for the two years.

To take a list, of all the sure voters;

— of all the doubtful ones;

— of the proper persons, to apply to those doubtful voters; and the means of getting them.

To see, what persons can be got off from the other side; and by what means.

The living of St. Michael's now held by sequestration. What establishment can be made for a minister.

Whether we should do anything about the organ; and the putting it up.

Whether any country gentlemen, our friends, should come, and settle at Lewes; and where they can get houses.

In spite of all this, Lewes remained an extremely troublesome borough, and opposition was never eliminated. The fact that the borough had

---

[75] Stuart, 'Parliamentary History of Tamworth', MA, 96–101.
[76] '*Considerations Relating to the Town of Lewes*', BL Add. MSS, 32058, fos. 389–90, Newcastle Papers.

agreed to accept Newcastle's patronage was no guarantee of its future servility. The electors would not accept just any candidate that Newcastle chose to foist upon them, and the borough became increasingly difficult to manage. After his death in 1768 the Pelham interest could only hold one seat at Lewes, and that not without difficulties. In short, the possession of property was only one ingredient in the recipe for establishing an interest in a patronage borough. As a friend of Luttrell's remarked about the representation and electorate of Minehead: 'I'm informed that if you put your application for the choice but even of one single member on the footing of hereditary right, in your property, it will not go down with them.'[77]

What would unquestionably go down well was the willingness of the great local families and interests to place their economic resources at the service of the voters. This meant, for one thing, that the purchasing power of the leading families of the interest concerned had to be placed at the disposal of the craftsmen, shopkeepers, and inn-keepers friendly to that interest. To withhold such custom was a certain means of committing electoral suicide. After all, the *continuity* of such custom could ensure the prosperity of the borough. One enthusiastic patron at Grimsby ordered no fewer than 2,000 pairs of shoes, which were smartly shipped to London for sale.[78] No less important, perhaps, was the further custom generated by the election itself. This, too, had to be shared among loyal supporters: the transportation of non-resident voters meant extra custom for carters and coaches; the accommodation of the same voters meant extra custom for inn-keepers and hoteliers; the eating and drinking comforts of all voters brought days, possibly even weeks, of vital extra custom to butchers, shop-keepers, bakers, vintners, inn-keepers, and others. The ceremonial aspects of elections presented further opportunities for others to seek employment: agents, musicians, printers, sign-makers, carpenters. It was exactly this sort of custom which converted sympathetic and prospective supporters into reasoably enthusiastic partisans. Elections bought excitement and activity, energy and purpose, but also well-paid employment and custom to potential friends of an interest.

[77] John St Aubyn to H. F. Luttrell, 16 May 1747, DD/L Ms 2/43/6, Dunster Castle MSS, Som. RO.

[78] E. Gillett, *History of Grimsby* (Oxford, 1970), 148–50. Another expedient for the protection of the trade of the borough was the lending of money to local traders when trade was bad. As a friend advised Portland about Wigan: 'If you take your Interest in the manufactures they make, or the goods the shopkeepers deal in, you would not lose £20 a year out of the loan of £2,500 which is more than is necessary. By these contrivances Ld. Barrymore kept his Seat at a trifling expense for fifty years, and his Son lost it by recalling the money' (Sir William Meredith to Duke of Portland, 24 Aug. 1765, PWF 6711, Portland MSS, Nottingham Univ. Lib.).

Similarly, a successful patron or patrons had to ensure that their constituents enjoyed a reasonable share in the distribution of local offices. These included government posts and contracts; legal offices and promotions; army commissions, discharges, and transfers; local places, favours, and requests; appointments to postmasterships, tide-waiterships, and positions in the Excise among many others. Such patronage constituted an enormous slice of material and social advancement to which the ambitious and the optimistic might aspire. An electoral interest was just as much an agency for the allocation of local power and office as it was a means of cultivating electoral support. Certainly, those patrons sympathetic to government must have had a greater prospect of satisfying the requests of their constituency than those who were left in the political wilderness. The voters of Sandwich had every reason for remaining faithful to Philip Stephens throughout seven general elections (although there is no evidence that he actually spoke in the House of Commons). As Oldfield puts it, 'the voters were bound to this gentleman by every tie of gratitude, as there is scarcely a single family connected with Sandwich, which has not been provided for by him in the admiralty, navy or monies'.[79]

These patronage mechanisms by themselves could not secure a seat. There were always far more applicants than there were places to satisfy them, and for every successful applicant there were several who were disgruntled at their failure. Not surprisingly, the ability to nurse bruised egos and to revive flagging spirits was a prime requirement of electoral management. For such reasons the role of personality was all-important. Even the mighty interest of the Lord Warden of the Cinque Ports at Hythe was notoriously lethargic unless he took these matters seriously.[80] Personal attention and local knowledge were the key requirements. (The combination of the two made the Sandwich interest at Huntingdon, for example, far more secure than most seats controlled simply by the distribution of money or the ownership of property.) Non-resident patrons were consequently always in a difficult position. Those who did not live locally had to rely on indirect control through an agent, a situation which bristled with problems and uncertainties.

It was only local men with long-term connections with the borough who were likely to fulfil a yet further demand made on patrons: the provision of public and municipal buildings for the borough which it otherwise might have gone without: town halls, law courts, exchanges, schools, hospitals, libraries, gaols. These all had to be

---

[79] T. H. B. Oldfield, *Key to the House of Commons* (London, 1819), 247.
[80] A. Newman, 'Elections in Kent and its Parliamentary Representation, 1715–1754', (D.Phil.), (Oxford, 1957), 315.

staffed, maintained, repaired, and decorated. In addition the streets had to be paved or widened. At St Albans, the Spencers went so far as to install a water supply.[81] The Grosvenor interest in Chester was particularly prominent in promoting public works, building schools, hospitals, and even the North Gate of the city—all in the early nineteenth century when the family's control of the city was beginning to encounter opposition. At Minehead a fire swept through the town in July 1791, burning over 70 properties and rendering 400–500 people destitute overnight. Most of the property destroyed belonged to the Luttrell family, who enjoyed the greatest natural interest in the town. Its failure to rebuild the properties provoked an angry, contested election in 1796, and the family lost one of the two seats. After this disaster 23 leading members of Luttrell's interest—gentry, gentlemen, and prosperous tradespeople—met to draft a plan to restore the fortunes of the family's interest through restoring the burned properties and generally embarking upon a programme of civic reform, municipal rebuilding, and community development,[82] a programme that would not have been out of place for a New Town Development Corporation in the second half of the twentieth century.

Election imperatives did not only dictate the honouring of custom, the distribution of offices, the building of municipal amenities, and the provision of local services. It entailed the provision of welfare, the administration of charity, and the labour of works of Christian mercy. Very many voters and their families must have experienced some improvement in their economic situation during an election. At Grimsby, for example, the two parties, the Blues and the Reds, provided a range of services for electors on what looks like a competitive basis, vying with each other to distribute corn, meat, and coal for the freemen.[83] Many patrons—like Lord Carlisle at Morpeth—allowed voters to use common land and permitted them informal access to game on his estates.[84] In many cases, of course, such charitable inclinations were less a sign of Christian goodness than a calculated desire to establish the dependence of the voter upon the charitable benefactor. The Grosvenors made annual payments to the poor but, more significantly, mainly to the poor freemen, of the city of Chester. Furthermore, on two other occasions they used their political machine to dispense famine relief: in 1799–1800 when no

---

[81] Lansberry, 'Politics and Government in St Albans', 186–8.

[82] The *West Somerset Free Press*, 9 July 1791, box 11, 1/60/13, 16–17, Dunster Castle MSS, Som. RO.

[83] Gillett, *History of Grimsby*, 177.

[84] J. Fewster, 'Politics and Administration of Morpeth in the Later Eighteenth Century', Ph.D. (Newcastle, 1960), 73.

fewer than 8,000 of the population of Chester were applying to the parish,[85] and in 1812 when a scarcity of corn and potatoes led to such distress that the Grosvenors intervened to release supplies onto the market, thus lowering prices.[86] Other benefactions from patrons were carefully designed to create the maximum degree of public goodwill: an organ for a church, premises for a Sunday school, and the like. The creation of dependence and the careful establishment of goodwill over many decades established a type of loyalty which was not easily set aside and which was the hallmark of a patronage borough.

Such loyalty could be severely strained if the representation of the borough was disposed of without reference to local opinion. Sharing the representation of Derby with the Devonshires, the Stanhope family decided without consulting the freemen to run Thomas Stanhope in a by-election in 1748, after the death of John Stanhope. There is evidence that the Devonshires were party to this plan. Stanhope was humiliatingly defeated by an independent, Thomas Rivett. The Stanhope interest was doomed and the Devonshire interest was endangered.[87] As the eighteenth century wore on, such considerations of municipal pride were complicated by great political and moral questions. The opinions and feelings of the voters had, in the last analysis, to be consulted—as the general elections of 1784 and 1807 demonstrated in many constituencies, and as particular, long-term issues, such as the war in America, Catholic emancipation, slavery, the Corn Laws, and parliamentary reform demonstrated constantly. To offend the voters by ignoring their sensitivities was no way to hold on to a seat. To notice the extent to which patrons and MPs had to reflect and to convey the sentiments of voters—and, to some extent non-voters—in patronage boroughs is not to indulge in romantic exaggeration of the political sophistication of the unreformed electorate but to acknowledge its ability to pursue its own interests and to articulate its own prejudices. To ignore either was electoral suicide.[88]

Eleven of the 12 Welsh boroughs conform generally to the characteristics of patronage boroughs but their regional distinctiveness calls for separate treatment. (Beaumaris, the twelfth, was a corporation borough). All 11 were freeman boroughs with fairly large electorates (500 to 4,000). Seven of the 11 were, in fact, groups of boroughs in

---

[85]   Mayor of Chester to Lord Grosvenor, 24 Dec. 1800, Grosvenor MSS, 215, Chester RO.

[86]   'A Firm Friend' to Lord Grosvenor, 17 May 1812, Grosvenor MSS, 251, ibid.

[87]   Indeed, Thomas Gisborne, the Duke of Devonshire's agent, wrote to him: 'I am sorry to say I am afraid the affair is desperate . . . Your friends have disposed me to add that they think this is the beginning of the loss of your interest in this town.' 15 Dec. 1747, Devonshire MSS, Chatsworth.

[88]   For further discussion of electoral paternalism see ch. 5.

which a shire town was united with its contributory boroughs: Caernarvon, Cardiff, Cardigan, Denbigh, Flint, New Radnor, and Pembroke. Montgomery had freed itself of its contributory boroughs in 1728. The remaining boroughs were Brecon, Carmarthen, and Haverfordwest. All the Welsh boroughs were single-member constituencies.

Most of these boroughs seem to have avoided the worst excesses of bribery and corruption. The Marquess of Anglesey, on the very eve of the Reform Act, wrote of Caernarvon: 'Most of the town is mine, and lies in the very midst of my property; but I repeat that I have not the slightest desire for it, if it is not perfectly within range of propriety.'[89] There were some few notorious excesses. The right to create honorary burgesses was auctioned at New Radnor in 1776.[90] One man was killed in an election fracas in Flint in 1734.[91] But the worst excesses of English electoral life were avoided partly because of the size of the Welsh borough electorates and partly, as the Porritts argue, because municipal and parliamentary politics were not so closely interwoven in Wales.[92]

Nevertheless, the control of Welsh freeman boroughs was principally exercised through their corporations. The lavish creation of freemen ensured that election contests would be a rarity. In most of these boroughs the burgesses were enrolled in a special court of record or meeting of the governing body of the town. The link between local landed families and such bodies was inevitably close. At Cardigan, with its 4,000 voters, cruder techniques, such as possession of the Writ and the co-operation of the returning officer, were needed. In the seven multiple Welsh seats it was necessary to have influence over offices in the contributory boroughs. At Caernarvon, for example, the predominance of the Glynllivon interest was secured through their holding not only the post of constable of Caernarvon Castle, but also the mayoralty of Nevin and Pwllheli. Where borough property was limited (as at Cardigan), the representation was easily monopolized by a single, local family. Where it was considerable (as at Swansea, a contributory borough of Cardiff), a group of powerful burgesses could stubbornly resist landed, oligarchical control.[93]

Nevertheless, the presence in all the Welsh constituencies of landed families exercising their natural interests not only inhibited contests

---

[89] Lord Anglesey to Lord Holland, 2 May 1831, D.619/27, Anglesey Papers, PRO Northern Ireland.

[90] *CJ* xxvii. 399.

[91] P. D. G. Thomas, 'Government and Society', in D. Moore (ed.), *Wales in the Eighteenth Century*, (Swansea, 1976), 23.

[92] Porritt and Porritt, *Unreformed House of Commons*, i. 118.

[93] R. Rees, 'Parliamentary Representation of South Wales, 1790–1830', Ph.D. (Reading, 1962), 13.

but provided the services of a paternalist character which marked these boroughs. Although accurate figures are notoriously difficult to establish, the third Marquess of Bute donated 7-8% of his gross annual rental in Glamorgan to charity.[94] His innumerable gifts of clothes, books, food, materials, and shoes are an impressive addition to these contributions.[95] In 1830 the chief agent of the Plas Newydd interest contemplated a likely opposition at Caernarvon and wondered whether the burgesses could possibly 'overlook a faithful discharge of Public Duties in the Representatives whom they have chosen from branches of the Plas Newydd family for nearly half a century: whether they can so far forget the advantages of [sic] their town—their families—and many Individuals have deriv'd from the munificent contribution, and Personal exercise of influence in their favour'.[96] Such flourishes were undoubtedly rhetorical exaggerations; that they could seriously and publicly be made is, however, surely significant.

## Open Boroughs

A further small yet significant fifth category of borough seats contains those which were not controlled by one patron or even by a group of patrons and which were increasingly marked by a strong political consciousness. They include some of the medium and large freeman and scot and lot boroughs.[97] In over 20 constituencies with large electorates, some of them running into several thousands, the voters were both too numerous, and too poor, to expect office. Instead they demanded contested elections, treats, and, above all, excitement. Election contests were thus frequent, rowdy, and potentially very expensive.

Some of these constituencies were open simply because their electorates were too large to be controlled. Pre-bureaucratic forms of political organization could not cope with the 5,000 electors at Bristol, the 7,000 at London, or the 12,000 in the largest borough constituency, Westminster. The gargantuan organizational requirements, to say nothing of the astronomical financial resources, needed to fight

[94] J. Davies, 'The Second Marquess of Bute', in *Glamorgan Historian*, ed. S. Williams, 8 (1972), 14, 20.
[95] Vouchers 92–100, Bundle X/13, Bute MSS, Cardiff Pub. Lib.
[96] J. Sanderson to R. A. Poole, 29 May 1830, Plas Newydd MSS, quoted in L. Jones, 'An Edition of the Correspondence of the First Marquess of Anglesey relating to the General Elections of 1830, 1831 and 1832 in Caernarvonshire and Anglesey', MA (Liverpool, 1956), p. i.
[97] The medium-size freeman boroughs include Hertford, Leominster, and, by the early 19th cent., Shrewsbury. The large freeman boroughs are Bristol, Canterbury, Coventry, Colchester, Evesham, Gloucester, Hereford, Leicester, Lincoln, Liverpool, London, Newcastle-upon-Tyne (just), Norwich, and Nottingham. The large scot and lot boroughs of Southwark and Westminster may also be considered here, as may Northampton, a large householder borough and, after 1806, Preston, a large inhabitant householder borough.

elections tended to inhibit contests in the eighteenth century, leaving partisans to compromise the seats. By the early nineteenth century, however, most of these constituencies were polling with some regularity. Sheer size and the absence of overweening patrons allowed the political (and not so political) tendencies of these constituencies free play.

In some places the pace of political awareness was being forced by social and economic changes. Preston was controlled by an alliance of the Derby (land) and Horrocks (industry) interests in the early nineteenth century.[98] As the industrial revolution changed the occupational structure of the town, opposition to this alliance rapidly spread. Focusing on the largest occupational group within the Preston electorate—the weavers—and concentrating on the issues of unemployment and prices, the radical candidatures of Hunt and Cobbett did much to politicize both the town and the electorate. The same sort of process could be seen at work at Liverpool, where the control of the town by the corporation weakened steadily in the later eighteenth century. Liverpool was the port of the industrial revolution in the North; its wealth was based upon the textile, American, and slave trades. The control of the corporation gave way to a complex amalgam of new interests and ideologies which broke the old chrysalis of electoral control. The eighteenth-century electoral contests between corporation and independents disappeared. The dissolution of old structures of control occurred just as dramatically at Nottingham. In the mid-eighteenth century, Whig and Tory families had compromised the representation of Nottingham. (Namier was content to assert that the town was 'apt to be influenced by the neighbouring big landowners'.[99]) But by the late eighteenth century their control was seriously endangered. Population was rapidly increasing: 12,000 in 1754, 16,000 in 1774, and 18,000 in 1780.[100] The size of the electorate did not itself change very considerably during this period, but economic changes ensured that its structure did. In 1754, according to the poll books, 27% of the voters were framework knitters; in 1774 the figure was 38%, but in 1780 it was a staggering 62%. Their ability to act as a group can be seen in 1780 when almost to a man (97% of them) they voted for Robert Smith, a popular MP who had

---

[98] Interestingly, the Preston franchise had been defined as the inhabitants after a disputed return in 1768. This had enabled the town to be wrested out of the hands of the corporation but only into those of local families.

[99] Namier, *Structure of Politics*, 114.

[100] D. Gray, *Nottingham: Settlement to City* (Nottingham, 1953), 48; J. D. Chambers, 'Population Change in Nottingham, 1700–1800', in L. S. Presnell (ed.), *Studies in the Industrial Revolution* (London, 1960), 122–3.

supported their cause. In constituencies like Preston, Liverpool, and Nottingham, powerful social and economic pressures were forming which were to co-exist with, and sometimes to challenge, the traditional structures of political control.

In a number of these constituencies, however, it was the historical accident of franchisal arrangements which ensured that the representation remained fairly open. Hertford, for example, only had an electorate of around 500, but the stipulation that the number of honorary freemen could not exceed three prevented the influence of the corporation from growing, as it did in so many other places. As a consequence, Hertford, became one of the most respectable, sober, and open boroughs in the country. At Northampton every inhabitant householder had the vote. The consequence was that Northampton had one of the highest electorates in relation to population of any borough. In 1801 the census estimated the population at 7,020. Assuming the electorate to be about 1,000, two-thirds of adult males had the vote. For many decades in the eighteenth century, aristocratic influence had been strong enough to control the town. After the famous election of 1768—essentially, a great tribal contest between three aristocratic families—patrons were either ruined or horrified by the immense sums of money expended. Thereafter the borough steadily shifted out of their control. By 1784 the Spencer interest saw its candidate defeated because they were unable to come to terms with the wide franchise of the town and did not realize that influence and money alone were an inadequate basis of support.[101]

In other boroughs considered here, however, it was essentially the inability of patrons to satisfy the venal instincts of electors which kept the representation open. Coventry is perhaps the best example of this. Down to 1774, its electoral politics turned upon the conflict between the corporation interest and the independent voters. In addition to the creation of non-resident freemen the corporation used the extensive charities in its care to influence the voters. As Table 2.3 shows, the percentage of corporation supporters receiving charity was consistently greater than their share of votes in an election, whether or not they won.[102]

---

[101] The Spencer interest clearly saw that its hour had come. After the failure of Lord Lucan in 1784 the Spencers closed the charity school at Northampton which they had opened in 1769, after they had successfully established their interest there; see J. C. Cox, *Records of the Borough of Northampton*, 2 vols. (Northampton, 1898), ii. 507. There is also a pertinent poem in the Collection of Political Handbills, 1784/1, Northampton Pub. Lib.: 'If we the matter understand,/ The school was build upon the sand, / If that's the case, you'll quickly see, / 'Twas *private* views—not charity'.

[102] S. E. Kerrison, 'Coventry and the Municipal Corporations Act of 1835', MA (Birmingham, 1939), 178.

TABLE 2.3     *Venality of Coventry Voters, 1761–1833*

| | % of corporation voters | |
|---|---|---|
| Year of election | Total poll | Among charity recipients whose votes can be traced |
| 1761 | 76.6 | 92.8 |
| 1775 | 23.4 | 52.0 |
| 1790 | 55.4 | 85.2 |
| 1802 | 50.6 | 85.8 |
| 1820 | 17.6 | 47.3 |
| 1826 | 51.9 | 71.1 |
| 1833 | 43.1 | 70.9 |

*Source*: S. E. Kerrison, 'Coventry and the Municipal Corporations Act of 1835', MA (Birmingham, 1939), 178.

Although the corporation retained a powerful influence into the nineteenth century it was unable to command the borough as it once had. During the regular contests of the late eighteenth century and early nineteenth century (only the elections of 1806 and 1812 were uncontested in Coventry after 1747), the independence of the freemen and the gradual emergence of national issues steadily undermined the power of the corporation.

In other constituencies venality had never corrupted the voters. Here, powerful traditions of political and electoral respectability chimed with customs of popular participation to effect a distinctive type of electoral politics. For example, there were powerful interests at Canterbury— the Anglican Cathedral, the Protestant Dissenters, and several local landed families—but none of them ever obtained a preponderant influence for any time. Similar conditions prevailed at Gloucester, Hereford, and Leominster. Lincoln and Evesham were markedly less respectable but were nevertheless open boroughs where no single interest prevailed. The extent to which these places permitted genuine popular participation will be discussed in Chapters 5 and 6. For the moment, it is enough to note that by the early nineteenth century, personal and local concerns had unquestionably given way to a concern for larger political and moral issues.

### The English and Welsh counties

The English and Welsh counties occupy a self-contained sixth category. The 40 English counties returned two members each, the 12 Welsh returned one. The county franchise combined several of the characteristics of the proprietorial and patronage borough constituencies, but in their electoral politics they were quite distinct. For one thing, the franchise in county constituencies was ambiguous. In theory it was attached to freehold property worth more than 40s. per annum rated to the land tax assessment. Customarily, however, 'freehold' received a generously broad interpretation and included leases, mortgages, offices, and annuities as well as freehold land. County voters were therefore almost as likely to be office-holders, smallholders, artisans, and even tradesmen, as farmers. Consequently, they may be taken to be somewhat more representative of the rapidly changing socio-economic structure of the country than may at first be assumed. Such a franchise gave almost unlimited scope for such devices as the splitting of freeholds and the creation of annuities. The sheer physical size of county constituencies, the number of voters— ranging from the 800 freeholders of Rutland to the 23,000 electors of Yorkshire in the early nineteenth century—and the resulting organizational complexities made contested county elections horrendously expensive. 'No man', wrote one observer very truly, 'ought to engage in such an undertaking who is afraid of his Money.'[103] To reduce these ruinous expenses some attempts were made to place the franchise on a more rational basis. In 1781 it was proposed to make the vote dependent on a charge or assessment to the land tax made within six months prior to an election. The bill failed to pass. In 1788, however, a bill did pass which proposed the establishment of an elaborate system of registering county voters from lists kept by the land tax collectors. The trouble with this proposal was that its expense would have had to be met out of the county rates. When the extent of the cost was realized—in one county, £55,000 per annum for the printing costs alone—adverse opinion made itself felt. Twenty-three petitions protested against the Act; only one defended it.[104] The Act was abandoned in 1789.

This county franchise dated from 1430 and was not significantly altered until 1832. It endured for four centuries partly at least because it was flexible enough to ensure the continued representation of property in general, not landed property in particular. The county electorate was wealthy, propertied, and eminently respectable. But it was not as independent as some contemporary commentators believed. Economic inequalities and economic obligations such as leases and

---

[103] John Lethbridge to Francis Drake, 5 Mar. 1820, D.D/NE/120, Lethbridge MSS, Som. RO.

[104] Porritt and Porritt claim (*Unreformed House of Commons*, 26–7) that there were under 20 petitions, but 23 appear in *CJ* xliv. 660. See also G. M. Ditchfield: 'The House of Lords and Parliamentary Reform in the 1780s', *Bull. Inst. Hist. Res.* 54/130 (1981), 207–25.

rentals resulted in economic dependence. Further, more generalized inequalities inherent in social relationships ensured the social predominance of aristocratic and gentry families over dependent clientage groups within county society. The publication of poll books ensured that a tenant's or dependant's vote would be known. There was thus a sense in which the county representation was a natural consequence of the ownership of land. When the first Lord Hardwicke purchased Wimpole in 1739 it was taken for granted that his family would wish to play a prominent part in the affairs of Cambridgeshire. Yorke's interventions in county politics in the 1740s were those of a family of national significance. By 1747 the family had taken one of the county seats.

It was therefore not merely the expense of county elections which inhibited their frequency but the threatened disruption of normal social relationships. As one handbill from the Lowther interest in Westmorland somewhat desperately put it in 1826, when the county was facing its third contested election at successive elections,

so frail is the gratitude of the populace, that the political quackery of a few speeches and handbills can efface in a day not only the remembrance of former benefits but every principle of morality and religion . . . The contest began in an effort at dissolving not only an old connection between the county and the paramount House of the County. It will succeed in embittering . . . the connection between the gentry and their dependents.[105]

Where the landed interest could maintain its unity in spite of party divisions, successive compromises ensured that the county representation fairly faithfully reflected the ownership of landed property in the counties. In Huntingdonshire, Cambridgeshire, and Nottinghamshire the representation was normally divided between different aristocratic houses. In Cumberland, Derbyshire, Herefordshire, Northumberland, and Staffordshire it was normally divided between the aristocracy and the gentry. In several counties in the West—in Cheshire, Cornwall, Devon, Dorset, Shropshire, Somerset, and Worcestershire—it was normally divided between the houses of the gentry. Through a compromised election the worst financial excesses and social dangers of county elections might be minimized or avoided.

The consequence was a seriously declining frequency of contested county elections until by the mid-eighteenth century only a handful of the English and Welsh county seats experienced contests at a given general election. In the last few decades of the unreformed period,

---

[105] WD/PW Election Bills, 1826, Kendal RO.

however, the rate increased until by the early nineteenth century one-sixth, at least, of county seats in England were being contested. In the early eighteenth century the rate had been one-half.[106] Candidates, however, had to pay even for the privilege of an uncontested return. Voters expected some entertainment as well as food and drink. The uncontested return at Derbyshire in 1774 cost the Devonshire interest no less than £554.[107] This was nothing compared to the costs of a contested election: at least £5,000, and often very much more. That at Oxfordshire in 1754 cost the three candidates £40,000 each. The even more infamous Yorkshire contest of 1807 cost three candidates a total of £250,000. Even though most county contests cost very much less than these enormous sums, country squires would not dare to disturb existing arrangements in these circumstances. By the same token, however, most aristocratic patrons would not involve themselves in such expense. Largely for this reason, the Tory hold on so many English county constituencies remained undisturbed in the mid-eighteenth century for many decades after the effective demise of the parliamentary Tory party.[108]

Similarly, the rarity of election contests in the Welsh counties reflected the stable patronage structures on which electoral control rested. Their smaller electorates, moreover (500–2,000) rendered them more controllable than their English counterparts. Wales did not, for the most part, have an aristocracy as numerous or as wealthy as the English, and until the early nineteenth century there was no commercial or industrial class to challenge the squirearchy. The control of the Welsh counties was, therefore, established more completely, and, in some respects, maintained more unscrupulously, than the English. The proportion of tenants to freeholders was higher in the Welsh than in most English counties. In Pembrokeshire, for example, 2,100 of the 3,000 county voters were leaseholders.[109] There could be exceptions, especially in the industrializing counties. Leaseholders made up only one-quarter of the Glamorgan electorate in the poll book of 1820.[110] Even so, few wholly freehold tenures survived, except in West Wales. Land in Wales was most commonly held leasehold for lives.[111]

---

[106] Thorne, *House of Commons*, i.106.

[107] Ben Granger to Unidentified Recipient, 3 Nov. 1774, Curr's Lists, 86/Compartment I, Devonshire MSS, Chatsworth.

[108] As late as 1741, no fewer than 31 of the 40 English counties had at least one Tory MP. And as late as 1761, no fewer than 47 Tory MPs were returned for county seats. See Colley, *In Defiance of Oligarchy*, 119, 296.

[109] R. G. Thorne, 'The Pembrokeshire Elections of 1807 and 1812', *Pembrokeshire Historian*, 6 (1979), 7.

[110] R. Grant, *The Parliamentary History of Glamorgan, 1542–1976* (Swansea, 1978), 21.

[111] Rees, 'Parliamentary Representation of South Wales', Ph.D., 7.

Threats of eviction were more frequent, as were questionable electoral tactics, such as the preparation of temporary leases. Even so, control of a county by a single family was rare. The great Mansel family in Glamorgan could only influence about 200 of the 1,500 county electorate. Subtle social and psychological ties were much more important than direct coercion in controlling county voters even in Wales. Occasional cries of protest against these family oligarchies made themselves heard—for example, at Flintshire in 1807 and in Pembrokeshire in 1812—but these were lonely voices of protest against the reality of the control of the Welsh county electorate by local landed families.

The fundamental unit of county politics was the electoral interest. At the first whisper of an election, candidates and their agents would write to those landlords, farmers, merchants, and friends presumed to be able to influence a number of voters.[112] Most interests were small, and the relationships within them personal as well as material. They consisted of those who had a direct economic dependence upon a patron, such as a tenant, lessee, or employee, and their families. To these must be added dependants secured by other means, e.g. friendship, office-holding, favours, etc. On the fringe would be voters canvassed through personal contact and possibly the promise of patronage.[113] The soliciting of votes and interests was the main business of a county election. But when an interest was promised it was usually with a severe qualification. Patrons offer 'every support in my power' or 'the disposal of the little interest I possess'.[114] Friends promise 'every means that is in my power', and 'any assistance in my power', but frequently they confess to 'a trifling interest'. The lingering of the old custom that a patron's permission had to be sought before his voters were canvassed suggests that once the permission was given then their approval would be forthcoming. But it was not always so, as one canvasser found to his cost. He reported

that he has got about 60 plumpers [single votes], 20 or 30 doubles, some would consider of it, many were from home but their wife's [sic] promised

---

[112] Such letters are common in the electoral correspondence of the period e.g. the 19 letters written by Sir E. Knatchbull on the death of his father seeking the support of powerful interests in the county of Kent. In all 19 cases he was successful and he peacefully succeeded to his father's county seat; see U951/C4/1–19, Knatchbull MSS, Kent RO. Evidently, the fear of disturbing the peace of the county was an overwhelming consideration. One correspondent confessed, however, 'I am not aware that I have any great interest in the County' (ibid. C4/12).

[113] Namier's definition of 'interest' 'the pressure which they could bring to bear on dependants', (*Structure of Politics*, 87) is unacceptably vague and materialistic.

[114] This and the following examples are taken from the extensive preparations for the Yorkshire election of 1812 in the Wentworth Woodhouse MSS (E.230, nos. 23, 11, 398, 48), Sheffield Pub. Lib. Another fairly representative sample of replies to canvassing letters to those with interest is given in Sir F. Hill, *Georgian Lincoln* (Cambridge, 1966), 32 n. 2, concerning the Lincolnshire by-election of 1779.

as far as they could, many who had freeholds at the last election have sold them—in short I dare say nearly the whole will go the right way.

After all, to promise one's vote or one's interest was no easy matter. Pursuit of interest was a delicate, complex affair, with its overtones of mutual service and, at times, somewhat prickly incomprehension. The Revd William Peter of Mawnan in Cornwall espoused Lord Abercorn's interest in the county in the 1780s but had little to show for it:

When I lived at Liskeard, there was a severe contest for the county of Cornwall. You came to Mrs Peter to entreat her for my vote and interest in favour of Sir John Molesworth and Mr Praed, who informed you she could say nothing about it, as I was gone to Mawnan to secure my votes, and that I should return in a day or two, when you came again and desired my vote and interest in their favour. I then gave you my reasons that I could not give up the interest I was engaged in without greatly injuring myself. You told me I should by no means suffer, and that I ought to keep up the family connections. On that footing I embraced your interest, and afterwards Mrs Peter told me you promised, when in power, the family should always find a friend in you, and never want, though I then greatly suffered for adopting your interest, but without murmuring.[115]

None other than Edmund Burke was invited to support the Temple interest at the Buckinghamshire by-election of 1779. He replied:

My Property in the county is so trifling, and my Interest so very inconsiderable, that I must consider it as a civility to have such an Interest asked for. But such as it is, I cannot handsomely dispose of it without a previous communication with Ld. Verney, to whose friendship I owed a Seat in a manner uncommonly disinterested, in two successive Parliaments. He has therefore the most perfect right to dispose of my Votes.[116]

Of course, the acid test of the electoral effectiveness of interests in delivering blocs of electoral support lies in how voters actually voted. It is much easier to attempt some analysis of the strength of county rather than borough interests because they are usually much better defined and have an identifiable social, economic, and to some extent, legal basis. It is, in fact, quite possible to relate such lists of voters in interests as survive (with all their ambiguities) to lists of voters in the scarce county poll books. One list that does survive suggests an almost overwhelming unanimity of political sentiment among the

---

[115] Revd William Peter to Lord Abercorn, 23 Mar. 1791, T.2541/EL5/8, Abercorn MSS, PRO., Northern Ireland. The Revd Peter had to fall back on Abercorn for pecuniary assistance as he had refused offers of preferment from the other side.

[116] Edmund Burke to Lord Temple, 12 Apr. 1780; see *The Correspondence of Edmund Burke*, Vol. iv, ed. J. Woods (London, 1963), 226–9.

tenants on the Countess of Guildford's estate at Waldershare at the ferociously contested Kent election of 1754. The tenants gave the two Whig candidates 163 and 161 votes each, the Tory only 10.[117] But to what extent was this degree of unanimity typical? No doubt this example represented an almost perfect marriage of interest, sentiment, organization, and money, but not everywhere was there the cohesive paternalism which influenced the Waldershare Park estate voters. Indeed, a nineteenth-century study has found that although the political affiliation of the landlord provides the strongest of all available indications of the tenant's vote, the correlation is not great.[118] Professor Davis, furthermore, has asserted that no Buckinghamshire landlord enjoyed the power to enforce unanimous political obedience upon his tenantry.[119] Such would seem to be the case elsewhere. Although Professor Moore has argued strongly for the capacity of voters to respond collectively and unanimously to the lead given by their patron,[120] a large number of voters, in fact, went their own way. I have calculated from Moore's own figures that around one-quarter of county voters voted against the wishes of their landlords.[121] If we include voters who refused to vote at all—perhaps 20–25% of the county electorate—then *at very least* one-third of the county electorate could not be relied upon. Furthermore, we should recognize that not all voters can be allocated to an interest group. About 10% of the county electorate were non-resident,[122] and most of these voters had little real connection with the county. Moreover, a substantial minority

[117] The Countess of Guildford's Estate Voters, 1754, U.31901, Guildford MSS, Kent RO. Careful investigation revealed why 10 votes had been lost; such reasons were found as 'Says he made a mistake', or 'Both these men were seduced by Rev. Mr. Turney.' A similar document dated 1 June 1796 lists 44 voters on Sir Richard Sutton's Broughton estates in Nottinghamshire. The county was not contested then, nor indeed, since 1722. From the marks and remarks on the list as many as 10 could not be counted on in the event of a contest. The remaining 34 (77%) were assumed to be reliable. See DDM/103/321, Notts. RO.

[118] R. Douglas and R. Sykes, *The Political Sociology of Guildford and West Surrey in the Nineteenth Century*, SRRC Report HR 2611 (London, 1976). The correlation was only 0.33 (N = 61).

[119] R. W. Davis, 'The Mid-19th-century Electoral Structure', 151.

[120] D. C. Moore, *The Politics of Deference* (Hassocks, 1976), 29, 37. See also 60–1: 'In Cambridgeshire, as in Huntingdonshire, the basic political fact was the existence of certain definable groups. Thus in Cambridgeshire, as in Huntingdonshire, the outcome of a contest was largely the function of the size, cohesion, and orientation of these groups. In some years, it was obviously easier to perpetuate the cohesion of those groups which were oriented in one direction, in other years of those which were oriented in another.' Moore also writes that 'the changes in the overall polls from one contest to another which account for the returns of different candidates at different contests were largely the products of changes of orientation and changes in the relative size and cohesion of specific blocs' (ibid. 10).

[121] See the detailed calculations in my 'Electoral Deference in Unreformed England, 1760–1832', *J. Mod. Hist.* 56 (1984), 413–20, 428–9. My analysis of a further seven county constituencies in the 18th cent. reached very similar conclusions (ibid. 418).

[122] For a full discussion of turnout, see ch. 4.

of patrons would for a variety of reasons declare their neutrality in a contest.[123] The point is hardly an academic one. Robson found that in Oxfordshire in 1754, 'the direct interest of the landlords embraced only a minority, if a substantial minority, of the freeholders'.[124] Even Professor Moore, the doyen of deference voting, remains astonishingly vague. He neither defines nor quantifies the 'significant majorities' and 'large majorities' of voters whom he assumes belong to interest groups.[125] In certain places he admits that 'significant numbers of voters were not members of communities or networks which were politically enmeshed'. In others, 'clearly defined block cannot be seen in every parish'.[126] Furthermore, a significant minority of voters in county elections in fact lived in quite large unenfranchised towns, enjoying urban life-styles and urban occupations. In the early nineteenth century over 20% of the county electorate were of this type.[127] (In the eighteenth century, however, the figure was considerably lower.)[128] Interests formed the base and superstructure of county politics, but quite large number of voters—perhaps one-half—did not belong to them or felt able to disregard or otherwise avoid the claim made upon them. It is considerations such as these which explain the high levels of dissident voting.

Political support had to be worked for. It could be won, but it was not an automatic consequence either of group membership or of land ownership, and in the counties it could not be bought. On certain issues, too, the wishes of the voters had to be acknowledged. It is

[123] See e.g. A. Jenkin to A. M. Agar, 29 Nov. 1824, Robartes MSS, Cornwall RO; on Lord Downe's promised neutrality at the (eventually uncontested) Yorkshire election of 1812, see E230, no. 56, Wentworth Woodhouse MSS, Sheffield Pub. Lib. If a prominent interest declared his neutrality—as Lord Upper Ossory did in Bedfordshire in 1794—then other applicants would rush to fill the vacuum; see Lord Hampden to Lady Upper Ossory, 8 Aug. 1794, LL9/10, Beds. RO. Robson calculates that of 'the most considerable landlords in Oxfordshire in 1754, 23 were Whig, 15 Tory, and 5 neutral'; see R. Robson, *The Oxfordshire Election of 1754* (Oxford, 1949), 49.

[124] Robson, *The Oxfordshire Election*, 47. I am reminded of Davis's discovery that in the borough of Aylesbury, only 18% of the 570 electors on the register between 1847 and 1859 were the tenants of great landlords; see Davis, *Political Change and Continuity: 1760–1885 A Buckinghamshire Study* (Newton Abbot, 1972), 173–5. For an earlier period, Speck remarked that 'the number of voters who were also tenants was probably small, and the more important contribution of the political magnates who supported a party interest at election time was to employ their servants to canvass the county.' (W. A. Speck, *Tory and Whig: The Struggle in the Constituencies, 1701–1715* (London, 1970), 38).

[125] Moore, *Politics of Deference*, 29, 30.

[126] Ibid. 42, 87.

[127] J. A. Cannon, *Parliamentary Reform 1640–1832* (Cambridge, 1972), 293–8. The range—from 63% for Middlesex to 7% for Lincolnshire—is enormous.

[128] In Sussex, for example, the figure for 1820 was 1,090 out of 4,114 voters (according to Cannon's rule of thumb, by which 1,090 voters inhabited towns which had 100 + voters), corresponding to a rate of 26.4%. This contrasts with 12.6% in 1774 (493 out of 3,912), and 12.7% in 1734 (485 out of 3,817); ibid.

stretching the imagination too far to imagine that in all changes or swings of opinion only the landlord classes were involved, and that the often literate, cultivated, and affluent county voters were indifferent. Is it seriously contended, for example, that in Derbyshire—a good deference county if ever there was one—the massive swing of opinion in favour of reform in 1831 (to the ratio of 30 : 1, if one canvassing report is to be believed) was the conspiratorial wish of the landed classes?[129]

In the counties and in the boroughs, as this survey demonstrates, the control of constituencies was conditional. The precise combination of conditional factors would vary from place to place and from time to time, but in general the candidate had to be personally acceptable to the electors. (The death of an MP or of the head of an interest was invariably a critical moment in the life of any interest.) The candidate, moreover, had to ensure the provision of a wide variety of paternal services to the constituents and had to behave in a manner which did not offend the political susceptibilities of his constituency. It was the successful fulfilment of these responsibilities which ensured uncontested elections rather than the direct operation of money, property, or fear.

This examination of the control of the electorate reaches by a different route a similar conclusion to that of the last chapter: that about one-third of the constituencies of England and Wales no longer experienced a formal process of representation. In the remaining two-thirds, however, a legitimate form of electoral competition existed. Nevertheless, even in the apparently closed first three categories examined in this chapter—the venal, proprietorial, and corporation boroughs—control was not always complete, and the given proportions perhaps overstate the degree of control to which the electorate was in practice subjected. As Sir Lewis Namier once remarked, 'In fact, there was no absolute certainty where there were any real voters, and there was no keeping them without constant attention, expense, importuning of Ministers in their behalf, entertaining them, pleasing their wives and daughters . . .'[130] The corrupt electorates were among the least reliable of electorates, and interests in venal constituencies usually had a short—and very expensive—life. Interests in corrupt constituencies could be bought and sold but, significantly, they did not last for very long. The voters of corrupt Grampound repudiated the Edgecumbe interest in favour of that of Edward Eliot in 1758.

---

[129] 'Even in Ashbourne and Wirksworth', wrote the Devonshire's agent about what was arguably the most reactionary part of the county, 'nine tenths of the freeholders have declar'd for reform' (W. J. Lockett to Duke of Devonshire, 28 Apr. 1831, Devonshire MSS, Chatsworth). For a more detailed discussion of voter awareness, see ch. 5.

[130] Namier, *Structure of Politics*, 169.

In 1796 they turned out Eliot in favour of Sir Christopher Hawkins. Seven years later a dispute over the franchise led to uproar and some arrests.[131] Even a sleepy and apparently 'closed' corporation borough like Banbury, with its magnificent total of 18 electors, needed careful management. Such a constituency could not be taken for granted, even by a prime minister. Indeed, it was not taken for granted by Lord North while he *was* prime minister. The necessary writing of letters, granting of courtesies, and seeking for offices was frequently undertaken by him personally.[132] Even in such seats, electoral control was a two-way process, involving a reciprocity of service and sentiment in return for loyalty and obedience.

The foregoing sketches in the broad outlines of the electoral system, suggests the variety of constituency types which existed within it, and indicates the methods and processes by which electoral control was effected and local political stability safeguarded. We need now to move a little closer to the operations of electoral politics in order to investigate how such control was transmitted and such stability attained.

## THE ORGANIZATION OF ELECTORAL POLITICS

Most discussions of electoral politics in the Hanoverian period revolve around patterns of electoral control in different kinds of constituency. The men and the agencies which operated the electoral system in the age before reform have gone almost entirely unnoticed by historians. The teeming underworld of electoral politics has never yet been prised open and penetrated, yet this is the level at which 'politics' was most commonly experienced in this period. Consequently, the committees and the agents who made the system work, and the process of canvassing, which was the critical point of contact between the system and the voters, remain lost in obscurity. Many issues concerning these men and those who employed them have scarcely even been discussed, let alone understood. The relative importance to be attached to the politics of influence, on the one hand, and the politics of organization, on the other, cannot now be weighed with any precision. Historians have always tended to assume that organization was little more than a projection of influence. Organizational factors are not allowed to enjoy any independent standing, in spite of the fact that election campaigns became a good deal more complex during the eighteenth century than they had been earlier. It had always been natural for the

[131] R. C. Jasper, 'Edward Eliot and the Acquisition of Grampound', *Eng. Hist. Rev.* 58 (1943), 475–81; BRA/1384/I, Cornwall RO.
[132] See the correspondence between North and his Banbury agent, Matthew Lamb (BL Add. MSS 61, 862, fos. 119–43; North (Sheffield Park MSS).

*ad hoc* exertions of the candidate and his family, friends, and dependants to be supplemented by occasional extra assistance. At first, such help was confined to particular matters: to the administration of accounts, to the legal aspects of the poll, and then, perhaps, the occasional canvass. Steadily, however, it became increasingly common to employ specialized assistance to manage these and other functions. This was particularly the case in view of the social backgrounds of MPs and candidates, and the practice for gentlemen to absent themselves from the constituency for occupational reasons (in the law or the services, for example), or for social reasons (the season, the grand tour, etc.). The most common and the most convenient means of organizing and exploiting such assistance was via the election committee.

### Election Committees

The election committee was unquestionably the most important agency of electoral organization. Quite simply, the committee was responsible for the election of the candidate. From the adoption meeting to the final chairing it organized his election campaign. It rallied supporters and deployed them throughout the constituency. It organized the canvass and supervised the poll. It arranged the composition, publication, and distribution of addresses, squibs, and handbills. It both raised money and spent it. It set up a network of local committees, where appropriate, and endeavoured to superintend their activities. It collected information and advice, influence and assistance, and sought, in general, to harness diverse elements of sympathy and support into a controlled election campaign.

The approach—even the expectation—of a contested election led to the prompt establishment of an election committee. Sir Matthew White Ridley's chief agent wrote to him as soon as the dissolution of 1830 had taken place: 'I have organized a numerous, respectable, and zealous Committee, who will exert themselves to the utmost on your behalf; this is absolutely necessary, as no pains are spared by the other parties.'[133] Indeed, the earlier the committee was established, the better for the weight and momentum of the campaign. Anxious candidates might jump the gun in order to gain a clear advantage. Coke of Norfolk, wracked by the humiliation of his disastrous defeat in the Norfolk county election of 1784, organized his committee two years before the election of 1790.[134] In some places, notably those which polled with some regularity, there is evidence that election committees

---

[133] Amos Donkin to Sir Matthew White Ridley, 7 June 1830, Ridley MSS, Northumb. RO.

[134] B. D. Hayes, 'Politics in Norfolk, 1750–1832', Ph.D. (Cambridge, 1957), 263–5.

enjoyed a fairly continuous existence. The United Interest Committee at Newark seems to have maintained an unbroken existence between 1802 and 1830.[135] This was clearly the practice, too, at Norwich by the late eighteenth century, and at Liverpool by the early nineteenth century.[136] Conversely, an unsuccessful candidate might keep his committee in existence, even in a county constituency, ready to move at the next vacancy or contest.[137]

Such committees were of varying size and status. In general, they were small enough to be efficient rather than formal bodies, and they were respectable enough to impress the community. They most usually consisted of 10 to 15 active men of some wealth and substance. In the larger towns and counties they could be most impressive. Henry Hobart's committee of 12 at Norwich in 1786 included one baronet, one banker, and several wealthy merchants.[138] Roscoe's committee at the Liverpool election of 1807 was led by a banker, Arthur Heywood, who had contributed £500 to the 1806 election fund. It also included a fair sample of merchants, at least two of whom had contributed £50.[139] Where committees were larger—and there are examples of social prestige magically expanding the size of these committees—attendance would normally be confined to a minority of active functionaries.[140] At Coventry in 1780 the 'General Committee' for Edward Yeo and Colonel Holroyd included 24 names, but it was suggested that 'out of the said General Committee a private, and select one, be formed, to which any of the members at large are to have access'.[141] Where these large and formal committees existed they may have been designed to conceal the unedifying aspects of contemporary electioneering behind a front of social respectability.

Whatever their precise composition these committees met regularly, not infrequently on a daily basis, in order to transact the enormous amount of business involved in running an election. Indeed, the

---

[135] J. Moses, 'Elections and Electioneering in Nottinghamshire Constituencies, 1702–1832', Ph.D. (Nottingham, 1965), 285–6. For a standing committee at Berwick in the later 18th cent. see Stoker, 'Elections and Voting Behaviour: A Study of Elections in Northumberland, Durham, Cumberland and Westmorland, 1760–1832', Ph.D. (Manchester, 1980), 114.

[136] J. Day to William Windham, 16 Feb. 1785, 37908 fos. 27–8, BL Add. MSS, Windham Papers; J. Adams, *An Impartial Collection* (Dublin, n.d.), 4, 14.

[137] There is an interesting example from the Wiltshire contest of 1818 and the by-election of 1819. *VCH Wiltshire*, v. 204.

[138] *A Correct Copy of the Evidence on the Norwich Petition* (Norwich, 1807).

[139] *Liverpool Chronicle*, 13 May 1807; Thomas Booth to William Roscoe, n.d., Roscoe Papers, 335, Liverpool City Lib.

[140] See the list of 35 names for the Paget Committee at the 1830 election at Caernarvon, less than half of whom normally attended the meetings, Poole Papers, 5451, Gwynedd County RO, Caernarvon. For the election of 1831 the comparable figures are 13 and 7 (ibid. 5399).

[141] 'Establishment of the Committee for Col. Holroyd', 2 Mar. 1780, Sheffield Papers, Coventry Publ. Lib.

growing complexity of business sometimes led to a greater specialization of function. Canvassing was occasionally supervised by one committee, with another superintending the remaining election business. In large constituencies some minute specialization can be seen. At the contested elections in Westmorland in 1818, 1820, and 1826, the Lowthers had separate subcommittees for receiving outvoters, for canvassing, for arranging for the transport of voters, and for the London voters. At the election of 1820, there was even a subcommittee to organize the chairing of the candidates.[142]

Geography was by far the strongest influence upon the specialization of election work. Especially, but by no means exclusively, at county elections, the central, superintending committee would spawn a number of subcommittees or clubs with responsibility for defined geographical areas. In big counties, such as Yorkshire, such local specialization was absolutely essential to the effective cultivation of the freeholders. A host of local committees was summoned into existence on all sides in readiness for the election of 1807, each answerable to a general committee for each of the three ridings, and another for the town of York.[143] The London committees of each candidate competed for the 500 votes to be found there, a number larger than could have been found in many borough seats.[144] Radicals frequently appear to have been in the vanguard of organizational innovation. As early as 1806 they had streamlined their organization at Middlesex into small districts; by 1830 there were 20 such committees.[145] Some other counties, however, seem by the same period to have achieved a like specialization. Sir Richard Vyvyan fought the by-election in Cornwall of 1824 with a small general committee, a number of 'secretaries of districts', a further number of commisariat managers, and a large number of parish committees.[146] H. T. Liddell's electoral committees at the 1826 elections in Northumberland were, if anything, even more sophisticated. In addition to the general committee there were 13 district committees for areas within the county and a further 4 for areas outside it: 'These Committees will direct the Subdivision of their respective Districts, regulate the Boundaries of each and form in every

---

[142] Stoker, 'Elections and Voting Behaviour', Ph.D., 114–15.

[143] E. A. Smith, 'The Yorkshire Elections of 1806 and 1807', *Northern Hist.* 2 (1967), 74–5.

[144] Such far-flung committees inevitably enjoyed considerable independence in the conduct of their campaign and in the arrangements reached for transporting the voters. F. F. Foljambe to Lord Milton, 2 May 1807, E. 177/11; F. F. Foljambe to Lord Fitzwilliam, 2 May 1807, E. 177/13, Fitzwilliam MSS, Sheffield Pub. Lib.

[145] *Morning Chronicle*, 31 Oct. 1806, 20 Mar. 1830.

[146] W. Elvins, 'The Reform Movement and County Politics in Cornwall, 1809–1852', MA (Birmingham, 1959), 36.

parish another smaller Subdivision according to the state of population and other circumstances thereof, a Local Committee.'[147] It was these local bodies which were to undertake the canvassing of freeholders. Such arrangements were by no means confined to county constituencies. One of the reasons for the continuing influence of the Westminster committee in radical circles between 1780 and the 1820s was its secure base of parochial committees.[148] These seem to have become a regular feature of election arrangements in all of the largest boroughs by the early nineteenth century.

There was some danger that enthusiastic election committees might attempt to centralize election campaigns too thoroughly. It was always infinitely preferable to use existing structures in the first instance, and with them local knowledge and personal familiarity, than to send out agents who might ignore existing social mechanisms. While a central committee was needed, of course, to co-ordinate and to streamline election activity, it should never dictate to local people. Local activity, indeed, could acquire a spontaneous character. At Norfolk in 1817 the central committee of Edmond Woodhouse created a subcommittee which proceeded to canvass the hundreds of Blofield and South Walsham. It began to appoint its own superintendents and other party workers, not unreasonably, but then began to organize its own transport and nominate the time of the arrival of the voters at the poll. This impinged upon the normal responsibilities of the central committee, which was only with difficulty able to incorporate the activities of its enthusiastic offspring.[149] Clearly, electoral activity had to be local to be effective, but it remained necessary for the central committee to co-ordinate well-meaning and spontaneous gestures of support.

The single most important responsibility of election committees was the canvassing of the constituency, an activity which had to be begun at the earliest possible moment. The Cust committee at the Grantham election of 1830 showed just how it ought to be done.

The Committee thus formed did not lose one moment, for on the meeting breaking up, which was a little after 10, they immediately commenced operations, and before one in the morning, had furnished about a dozen select and active canvassers with letters of solicitation and other instructions; and

---

[147] 'Suggestions submitted to the Committee and Friends of the Hon. Mr. Liddell', 14 Mar. 1826, Liddell Papers, Newcastle-upon-Tyne Univ. Lib.

[148] See, e.g., the description of the organization of the Westminster Committee in 1818 to be found in P. Jupp, *British and Irish Elections, 1784-1831* (Newton Abbot, 1973), 127-8. It was also clear from the newspapers in 1818 that separate parish committees were meeting in different inns; see the *Morning Chronicle*, 11 June 1818.

[149] See Jupp, *British and Irish Elections*, 44-5.

appointed each canvasser an appropriate route, embracing together the whole county, and in many instances, far beyond its limits.[150]

All aspects of the canvass had to be co-ordinated. Party colours had to be standardized throughout the constituency and appropriate quantities of ribbons and cockades ordered. Committees attempted to standardize the method of canvassing by defining the information to be solicited and noted. They could also decide upon a second or even a third canvass and issue advice concerning the distribution of second votes. Throughout, it was necessary to monitor the activities of local committees:

Some one from this office will call on you on Wednesday next to ascertain the precise state of your Canvas, by which time we trust it will be finished, and the Returns for your district made up with all possible accuracy & strictly conformable to the printed Instructions. There must be two Copies of the Returns, one of which the person who waits on you will take away, and the other will be retained by You.[151]

The composition and circulation of election propaganda was the next most vital task for these committees. Election campaigns had an insatiable appetite for an unending stream of propaganda: advertisements placed in and letters written to the local press; posters, placards, cartoons and announcements with which to festoon the constituency; broadsides, handbills, songs, and squibs to circulate among the electors. Most of it was composed by themselves or by their clerks, writers, and musicians. Clearly, it was as essential to regulate the content as it was to maximize the flow of this torrent of publicity.[152] The issue of the candidate's election address demanded particular exertions: 'You will be so good to get as many Copies as you may think necessary of the Address immediately and either deliver on your Canvass or send to every Freeholder in the District allotted to you.'[153] Even where no contest was anticipated it was good policy to circulate an address. This was what Lord Milton's committee did in Yorkshire in 1818.[154] Constant vigilance was essential if the

---

[150] *Storr's Impartial Narrative . . . 1830* (Grantham, 1830), ix.

[151] Castleman to Unidentified Recipient, n.d., 1831, KY 90. Bankes MSS, Dorset RO.

[152] These need not be written exclusively by members of the committee. Certain of the more sophisticated types of propaganda—songs, rhymes, etc.—might be delegated to others. It is known that a Collector of Customs, one Silvester Richmond, was employed by the Gascoyne Committee at Liverpool in 1806 and in 1807 for General Tarleton. The squibs of Roscoe's committee, on the other hand, were composed by a Unitarian minister, Revd William Shepherd; see B. Whittingham-Jones, 'The History of Liverpool Politics', 2 vols. (TS), i. 529–30; ii. 667, 674. It has been argued that in the North, at least, the tendency for committees and their staff to write their own material was probably increasing; see Stoker, 'Elections and Voting Behaviour', Ph.D., 109–11.

[153] Castleman to F. Fooks, 29 Apr. 1831, KY 90. Bankes MSS, Dorset RO.

[154] G. I. Fitzwilliam MSS, Sheffield Pub. Lib.

outflow of information was to be relied upon. A tactless candidate might need to have his errors gently corrected by a competent and watchful committee:

The Burgesses are now left to enquire why Sir Charles did not come forward earlier and why he did not openly declare himself at once when there was no existing reason for Silence. There is not always Wisdom in the politics of Counsellors. However, this deficiency will be partly supplied by the Address, which appears in *The Sun and Courier* of last night.[155]

It was important, above all, to influence the opinions of the electors. This might be done by the address and by the canvass, but it could also be done by plastering a constituency with notices and announcements in order to familiarize the voters with the identity and opinions of the candidate.[156] Circular letters might also be sent to every elector: 'I directed Mr. Calcraft's Speeches to be sent to all Parts of the County . . . This Step has been much approved of and has done a great deal of good—I send you more of them as requested.'[157]

Election committees took practical responsibility, in all but the smallest seats, for the raising and spending of money. Thus, they were ready to launch subscriptions and organize funds in a candidate's interest. Committees superintended the treating of the voters, arranged for the opening of the inns, and determined the sums to be allowed to each man. They attempted to control the process of payment through local agents.[158] To entertain the voters liberally and generously while observing some reasonable limitations upon expense was a problem which taxed the most adroit committee. Yet again, local knowledge of the voters and personal familiarity with the inn-keepers were the essential qualities which committees sought in their local agents. Problems often remained, however, with the inn-keepers, whose continued co-operation was obviously necessary to a successful campaign. Whether the amount allowed to each voter should be uniform or whether the amount should bear a direct relationship to

[155] Minutes of the Committee of Sir Charles Paget, 10 July 1830, Poole MSS, Gwynedd Archives Service.

[156] 'The Committee has determined on more vigorous measures in the way of Placards' (Col. Tyrell's Committee to John Cunningham's agent at Braintree, 2 Aug. 1830, D/DO/B5, Cunningham Papers, Essex RO).

[157] Mr Read to Thomas Lowman, 2 May 1831, KY 90, Bankes MSS, Dorset RO.

[158] See e.g. the Minutes of the Committee of Charles Bathurst at the 1806 Bristol Election, 12144, Bristol Archives Office. On this occasion, Bathurst's committee, operating through 'managers' of the parishes of Bristol, set specified amounts for each voter and established procedures for discharging the debts. The committee placed advertisements in the Bristol newspapers inviting voters who had not done so to submit their accounts by a stated date. For further examples of this kind of activity see E. A. Smith, 'The Election Agent 1734–1832', *Eng. Hist. Rev.* 84 (1969), 32–3.

the expenses actually incurred was never easy to decide. Nor was it always easy to decide how to pay inn-keepers: by the day, by the week, by the numbers of voters involved, or by the amount of food and drink actually consumed—assuming, of course, that this could ever be accurately measured.

Furthermore, the time of these committees was also taken up in negotiations with the opposing committees on the question of sharing the conveyance and treating costs of voters who split their votes.[159] So complex and time-consuming could these details become that specialized agencies for dealing with them became increasingly common in the unreformed era. By 1820 the radical committees in Middlesex had even acquired a treasurer for subscriptions.[160] By 1830 there was a finance committee in Essex on Colonel Tyrell's side.[161] How these finance committees operated is revealed in a rare account from the Dorset contest of 1831:

> You will immediately get a few of our friends in your Town to form themselves into a Finance Committee and they should meet daily and examine very closely every Morning the Expenses of the preceding day and sign the Bills and those Bills must be kept by them 'till the conclusion of the Poll and they should appoint some honest persons on whom they can place strict reliance and place one at every public House that is opened in your district and each of those persons must be instructed to let none but our own votes be admitted and each must keep an account of the Expenditure and the names of the Voters who may come to the House, . . .
>
> and the Account of the Expenditure and names of the Voters signed by the person keeping such Account, must be transmitted daily to the Finance Committee.[162]

Whatever the precise mechanism, committes were understandably anxious to keep election expenses as low as possible, an anxiety reflected in the massive survival of financial accounts among their papers.

The ultimate objective of all election committees, however, was to establish a satisfactory basis for an efficient, economical, and peaceful

---

[159] See e.g. the entry for 15 May 1807 on p. 17 in the Book of the Chairman of Lord Milton's Committee at the Yorkshire election of that year. 'It being thought adviseable that a deputation should go from this Committee to the Committees of the other Candidates in order to arrange an Agreement for payment equally of the Expenses of Conveyance to York of Split Vote's . . .' (Battie-Wrightson MSS, Leeds Cent. Lib.).

[160] *Morning Chronicle*, 8 Mar. 1820.

[161] It even established certain rigid criteria for election payments in an attempt to keep election expenses down in a protracted contest. Expenses had to be claimed under certain heads: (*a*) conveyances, (*b*) reasonable refreshment, (*c*) canvassing. See entry for 7 Aug. 1830, Cunningham Papers, D/DO/B.5. Essex RO.

[162] Castleman to Thos. Fooks, n.d., May 1831, KY 79, Bankes MSS, Dorset RO.

Poll. It could be in the interest of none of the candidates to fight an election with uncontrollably rising costs against a background of tumult and violence. This was why formal meetings between deputations from the rival committees in the days before the poll were regular features of election campaigns. On occasion, indeed, such meetings were chaired, and even instigated, by the returning officer, who had just as much reason as the candidates for seeing the peace of the borough maintained.[163] Such meetings discussed a wide variety of topics: the timing of the poll, the policing of the town, the procedure for settling disputes, the size and order of tallies, the positioning of the polling booths, and, not least, the sharing of expenses for voters who divided their votes between two rival parties.

A satisfactory outcome to an election campaign required the most detailed attention to the needs and movements of the voters long before the opening of the poll. The circumstances of individual voters demanded close scrutiny if lengthy and damaging protests were to be avoided. Local agents would be exhorted to canvass voters in their districts. The bringing up of these voters to the poll could not be left to chance or accident. It had to be carefully regulated not merely for the sake of efficiency but for the sake of effect. Instructions to local agents frequently have an anxious, almost peremptory, tone:

The general Committee for conducting Capt. Yorke's Election, considering it absolutely necessary that fifty of the voters in his interest in the Hundred of Ely, and fifty other voters in the Hundred of South Witchford Hundred should be sent early to the Poll on Thursday next (the first day of polling.) I am directed to inform you of this determination and to beg that you will use all possible Exertions in sending them off—and, providing for open Carriages for the journey.[164]

Such voters required entertainment, refreshment, and possibly a bed for the night.[165] It was the duty of the general committee to

---

[163] Or indeed of the county. The Sheriff of Yorkshire brought all the committees together before the great contest of 1807 'to settle the Regulations respecting the Poll', particularly those concerning the procedure for settling disputed qualifications for for reimbursing the extraordinary expenditure of officials (fos. 8–10, Book of the Chairman of Lord Milton's Committee, Battie-Wrightson MSS, Leeds Cent. Lib.).

[164] J. Nicholls, Secretary of the Conveyance Committee, to H. R. Evans, 23 Oct. 1831, Evans MSS, Cambs. RO. Candidates occasionally admitted their failings in this respect. At the Northumberland election of 1826 Liddell, behind on the first day's poll, admitted 'the badness of the arrangements for receiving the poll, which had prevented his voters getting up'. Bell, on the second day, admitted 'the difficulties he had in procuring conveyances, and some of his voters being capsized on the road' (*A Collection of the Authentic Papers, Speeches etc.* (Alnwick, 1826), 219–20).

[165] In county elections such a sudden migration of the freeholders could place an enormous strain not merely upon the supply of horses and carriages but also upon the supplies of knives and forks. At the Devon election of 1818 the thoughtful men of Lord Ebrington's Committee

co-ordinate and provide for these requirements, whether they organized the voters directly or, as frequently happened at county elections, encouraged patrons to bring up their own voters. Voters coming individually, on the other hand, might require a ticket to obtain refreshment and hospitality.[166] However they came, voters needed to arrive at the poll at times convenient to them, so that, for example, their trades were not unduly interrupted; and their arrival had to be scheduled such that local fairs and market days were respected.

Committees had to organize the poll so that a sufficient number of voters appeared each day to complete the number of tallies that could be anticipated. This required ready communication with local agents, and sometimes a continuous supply of money, or the promise of it, as well. Even in borough elections, the bringing of voters to the poll could hardly be random. Voters from different interests, parishes, trades, and even streets had to be brought up in some pre-arranged order. They had to be primed and prompted as well as wined and dined, and then they had to be returned to their homes again in one piece.

The committee needed to achieve the maximum impact with its polling arrangements. Certainly, a healthy stream of well-disciplined voters in the early days of the poll was highly regarded. 'It is almost unnecessary for us to add, that in selecting the Voters to be first sent, it will be desirable to forward Plumpers.'[167] Such a stream could only be ensured by the careful protection and organization of voters. They might be conducted to a particular inn while messengers shuttled to and from the poll. At the appropriate time a 'superintendent' or 'captain' would lead the voters to the poll. Through such organization and such persuasions the competitive tempo of the poll might be influenced. The committee might decide that it must accelerate its rate of polling, perhaps to demoralize the opposition, and organization would be correspondingly tightened.[168] All of this obviously demanded a full

---

transported 407 knives and forks from Exeter, 364 and 378 of which respectively were returned. See 'A List of Knives and Forks brought from Exeter, 10 August 1818', Papers and Correspondence of Lord Ebrington's Committee, Ebrington MSS, Devon RO.

[166] *The Norfolk Election Budget* (1817), 47–8. The Committee in such a situation was anxious to restrain the expenses incurred and would do so by placing checks at inns to note expenditure.

[167] Persuading voters to plump (i.e. to use one vote only in the service of a preferred candidate) was a necessary tactic in three-cornered contests. Papers and Correspondence of Lord Ebrington's Committee, n.d., June 1818, Ebrington MSS, Devon RO.

[168] For example: 'The Majority obtained by our Opponent yesterday, great as it may appear, was I can assure you less than we anticipated, and considering the efforts made, and the election tricks and manœuvres used to obtain this majority, it is no proof of our opponents strength. A few days strenuous exertions on forwarding voters, which the Committee earnestly press on you, will put Col. Tyrell in a very different situation on the Poll. Let this hope stimulate you and all friends to the cause' (Richard Bartlett to John Cunningham, 7 Aug. 1830, Cunningham MSS, D/DO/B.5, Essex RO).

complement of reliable, informed, and sober poll agents to guide and control, to shepherd and protect the voters, defend their qualifications, record their votes, and return them to their homes or inns.

In any case, the committee and its agents had the responsibility of ensuring that their voters possessed the appropriate qualifications, and that they could answer the questions of hostile attorneys. Bailiffs, constables, and friendly agents had to be stationed in appropriately helpful places to keep order, to give advice, and to set an example.[169] At the end of each day's polling the agents might be asked to check the accuracy of the names polled during the day and assist with final calculations. A sound committee, however, would work its agents even harder. Bankes' committee at the 1831 Dorset election asked its agents to furnish the committee 'every morning by 8 o'Clock with a statement of the Votes remaining unpolled in his Division, specifying those that are for, against, doubtful, neuter'.[170]

From the first breath of a dissolution of Parliament, then, until the chairing ceremony, the committee was responsible for all arrangements affecting the poll, acting as the mainspring of all election activity. Candidates, inevitably, had to leave to their committees the major responsibility for their election. Indeed, possessing the local knowledge that alone permitted any possibility of electoral success and commanding the organization that could ensure it, they could advise the candidate to abandon a hopeless campaign or to take such measures as might revive it. Sometimes, committees behaved as though the candidates did not exist. So far as election expenses were concerned, a candidate was almost completely in the hands of his committee. One of them wrote to his chief agent:

With respect to the Bills for eating and drinking previous to the election I really must be very much guided by the opinion of my friends. I am very much disposed to refuse payment altogether; but on the other hand I do not wish to place the Committee or the respectable part of the Managers in an unpleasant situation . . . I can only say that I shall cheerfully pay what you think right.[171]

A sitting member might well find that his absences on parliamentary duty left him even more dependent upon his committee. Sir John Egerton's

---

[169] 'Northumberland Election, Stations of Bailiffs and Constables' (19 June 1826), Newcastle-upon-Tyne Univ. Lib. 'All the Bailiffs and Constables above named are employed on this occasion upon the express condition, that such of them as may appear intoxicated, during the proceedings shall not only immediately be discharged, but they shall also forfeit all claim to any Remuneration which they would otherwise be entitled to for their attendance; and such of them as shall quit their respective Stations, or otherwise neglect their Duty, will be fined.'

[170] KY 90, Bankes MSS, Dorset RO.

[171] John Courtenay to Unidentified Recipient, 68/30/5, Courtenay MSS, Devon RO.

absences at Westminster left him dependent upon the independent committee that protected his interests in Chester. Key decisions respecting his canvass in 1812 were left to the chairman of his committee.[172] During the campaign the candidate might be told when and where to appear, what to do, whom to meet, and, to some extent, what to say. There are examples of committees tinkering with the speeches and addresses of candidates, writing their letters for them, and even deciding to whom to address them.[173]

In an age when national party institutions had not yet come to dominate local electoral life, the election committee was the central focus of all activity, the mainspring of policy, the source of campaigning energy. After the 1832 Reform Act the registration societies and constituency parties gradually acquired these functions. The need to register the voters in a party cause significantly altered the situation. The election committees of the unreformed period may be distinguished from their party successors in that they frequently lacked a permanent existence and a defined ideological purpose. They did not establish a general allegiance to a party on the basis of one or more national issues nor acceptance of the leadership of a party in Parliament. Even after 1832, however, the gentlemen of the Whig and Tory parties were pleased to delegate the common routine of electoral persuasion to professional committee men who knew and understood the voters and who lived in their world. Consequently, the work of election committees continued unabated after 1832, only slowly to be taken over by the political parties.

### Election Agents

If election committees took the vast majority of campaign decisions, they were largely executed by election agents. Many of them were practising attornies and had some formal, legal qualifications. Their widespread employment marks the growing professionalization of electoral politics in the eighteenth century. It was to the legal profession that the Hanoverian ruling order entrusted the safeguarding of its property and the protection of its electoral interests. The increasingly complex nature of election business and the need for informed local knowledge and advice necessitated this.

Most election committees were chaired by a chief agent who, depending upon his own experience and upon his relationship with

---

[172] *Chester Poll Book* (Chester, 1812), 93. The chairman, however, was Roger Barnston, an old campaigner who had contested the city in 1784.

[173] Amos Donkin to Sir Matthew White Ridley, 15 and 28 June 1830, Ridley MSS, Northumb. RO.

the candidate, might establish a predominant influence over it. Under such a chief agent, a number of lesser agents would perform the routine drudgery of electioneering. Their functions were quite clear. It was to protect an electoral interest and to advance its fortunes by identifying and canvassing voters, organizing supporters, arranging inducements, and generally representing the interests of the candidate. Towards these objectives the agent might find himself involved in a range of activities—raising funds, liaising between voters and candidates, distributing largesse, and seeking patronage. In the end, it came down to one very simple precept: 'It must be his business to promote the interest of his employer to the utmost of his power, and get him all the votes he can.'[174] Their ruthless single-mindedness in pursuit of these objectives rendered election agents one of the most hated subgroups in Hanoverian society, a sure sign of their very special importance. For one thing, attornies could and did prosper from the active land and property market of the Hanoverian period. Agents could and did accept retainers from both sides, sell blocs of votes to the highest bidder on occasion, exploit the law for their own purposes, and make profits out of electioneering. In an electoral system which imposed few formal controls upon electoral morality, the temptations in the way of the individuals who had to operate the system were enormous. But the contemporary hostility towards election agents probably reflects less upon their morality than upon their ubiquitous presence and their meddlesome indispensability. It also reflects the uncomfortable dependence—both material and psychological—which the Hanoverian political élite placed upon election agents, and, just possibly, a pang of guilt for the excesses of which agents were occasionally guilty.[175] The agent was consequently a figure of enormous importance. He was only a representative of the local patron, but he carried responsibility for enforcing electoral discipline in the community. Detailed examination of this critically important figure requires no apology.

Most election committees were led and directed by a chief agent, normally the driving force of the campaign and its organization. Such men owed their positions to the absence of the patron or candidate and the high regard which the patrons had for them. Men like George Latham at Wigan for the Duke of Portland (1768–81), Richard Sykes at Hull and Robert Sinclair at York for Lord Fitzwilliam in the late eighteenth century and early nineteenth century, and Charles Clarke

---

[174] G. Bowyer to Mr Sellwood, 5 Oct. 1795, Abingdon Borough MSS A/EE/p. 11, Berks. RO.

[175] For example, the ruthless restriction upon the privileges of freemen at Morpeth in the late 1750s. See Fewster, 'Politics and Administration of Morpeth', Ph.D., 75–9.

at Orford for the Marquis of Hertford stood closer to the patrons than to the committees they led, and indeed exerted considerable personal authority over them.[176] In the smaller proprietorial boroughs, indeed, the committee might be reduced to purely routine tasks and to a vastly subordinate status. (In a very few it might not even need to exist.) In the larger seats and in the counties, where the structure of electoral interests was more complex, the chief agent would assume a less dictatorial character as his, and his patron's, position depended to a greater extent upon the activity and the support of others. In either case the efficiency of the committee depended heavily upon his exertions:

Through such a man, when found, the ostensible conduct and direction of everything must pass; and he must also have a competent knowledge of the county and not only be ready to enter upon business the moment necessity requires, but be in the meantime casting about for proper assistance and conferring with intelligent friends to the cause. He should be a man of resources and expedients, for it is inconceivable what a spirit things go on with under such exertions.[177]

Such a man was completely indispensable. The third Duke of Portland, not a man to fawn or to exaggerate, wrote to Latham:

There is no body that can supply your Place and let me beg you to do so much justice to yourself as to believe what I am sure every impartial man who is a friend to the borough will tell you that the salvation of our Common Interest depends upon your keeping the lead you have so justly acquired.[178]

No wonder patrons were anxious to obtain and to secure the services of these valuable men. One of the reasons for Lascelles' failure to win in Yorkshire in 1807 was the inferiority of his chief agent, Edward Wolley, compared to his counterparts, and his concurrent employment as an agent at York.[179] To have an unreliable agent was completely disastrous. Henry Bankes wrote to Lord Uxbridge to tell him of the collapse of his campaign at Dorset in 1806:

At the same time that I thank you for your kind intentions of support, I must regret that they have been absolutely ineffectual; your Lordship's Steward, Mr. James, having permitted all your tenants to vote against me, on the first day of the election, without waiting for your directions. I am also informed, as I think upon good authority, that he was not inactive in canvassing against

---

[176] Excellent MS series illustrating these relationships survive for Wigan, 1768–81, in the Portland MSS (PWF 9955–9996, Nottingham Univ. Lib.) and the Cullum MSS for Orford, 1760–83 (E.2./42/4, Suffolk (West) RO).

[177] J. Dring to Fitzwilliam, 18 Aug. 1785, Fitzwilliam MSS, Northants. RO.

[178] 5 Dec. 1776, PWF 9960, Portland MSS, Nottingham Univ. Lib.

[179] *York Herald*, 25 Oct. 1806.

me, tho' I know that he thinks proper to deny it now. This is not the only instance in which I have experienced the opposition of the Stewards, and the support of their Masters, and I am sorry to say that the influence and power of the former have prevailed.[180]

Indeed, chief agents were not always trusted by the candidates. Some of them liked to have a relative or friend to support them in taking overall charge of the campaign. J. G. Lambton acted in this capacity for his brother-in-law Lord Howick at the Northumberland contest of 1826.[181]

Many of these chief agents had in the eighteenth century been the estate steward or estate agent to an aristocratic or gentry family. Between 1750 and 1782, the Grosvenors' chief agent at Chester was Henry Vigars, their estate steward. His supervision of Chester elections was little more than a projection of his estate responsibilities.[182] By the later eighteenth century a more professional approach was becoming evident. Not a single estate steward or estate agent was used as chief agent in any of the 13 Hampshire constituencies after 1774. Thereafter, the Whig agents in the county, William Faithfull and his successor, Samuel Deverell, were both prominent Winchester lawyers. The Tory agent, Harry Green, had solicitors' practices in both Winchester and Basingstoke.[183] The increasingly legalistic aspect of election business, its involvement with titles to property, with precedent, and, of course, with election petitions, no doubt had much to do with this tendency.

It was this command of the proper ordering of things which enabled chief agents to enjoy enormous power. If it was their patrons who in the last analysis possessed the power, it was the chief agents who in practice wielded it. There are, indeed, several famous examples of agents actually stealing seats from their patrons. After years of election service and local knowledge it was perhaps a natural progression for an agent to contest the seat. The government was particularly

---

[180] 13 Nov. 1806, D.20/23, Bankes MSS, Dorset RO.

[181] Stoker, 'Elections and Voting Behaviour', Ph.D., 95–6.

[182] Letters of Henry Vigars to Richard Grosvenor, Grosvenor MSS, Chester RO. For the estate steward, see G. E. Mingay, 'The Eighteenth-century Land Steward', in E. L. Jones and G. E. Mingay (eds.), *Land, Labour and Population in the Industrial Revolution* (1967); E. Hughes, 'The Eighteenth-century Estate Agent', in H. A. Cronne, T. W. Moody, and D. B. Quinn (eds.), *Essays in British and Irish History* (London, 1949). The most recent addition to this literature is D. P. Gunstone, 'Stewardship and Landed Society: A Study of the Stewards of the Longleat Estate', MA (Essex, 1972), esp. pp. 128–33. For a later period, see E. Richard, 'The Land Agent', in G. Mingay (ed.), *The Victorian Countryside*, 2 vols. (London, 1981), vol. ii; D. Spring, *The English Landed Estate in the Nineteenth Century* (Baltimore, 1963); id., 'The English Landed Estate in the Age of Coal and Iron' *J. Econ. Hist.* 11 (1951), 3–24.

[183] S. Lowe, 'Hampshire Elections and Electioneering, 1734–1830', M.Phil. (Southampton, 1972), 213.

vulnerable to its own ambitious agents. Dartmouth, Hedon, and Yarmouth (Isle of Wight) were taken over by their managing families. Even private patrons were not entirely safe from their agents. The Wilkinson family tried to seize the representation of Aldborough and Boroughbridge from the Duke of Newcastle in the mid-eighteenth century, and by the end of the eighteenth century the Phillips family had actually taken over at Camelford and the Luxmoores at Okehampton.[184] In the years immediately before the 1832 Reform Act it was the Marquess of Anglesey's chief agent, John Sanderson, who commanded his electoral interest. Minor agents and solicitors went in great awe of him. Indeed, he 'virtually controlled the Paget's affairs'.[185] This was not merely the achievement of an efficient servant, but the consequence of the fact that the public reputation of the patron—indeed, his level of prestige within the community—had come by now to depend almost entirely upon his chief agent. Sir Matthew White Ridley's agent was determined to improve his unflattering public image at Newcastle-upon-Tyne. Sir Matthew was unpopular, he told him roundly, because he was too mean with his money, too aloof with all classes; he employed outside labour and appeared to have little interest in the town and its affairs. Worse still, he allowed family celebrations—birthdays, anniversaries, and so on— to pass without offering a friendly treat to the voters.[186] A detailed programme of image-refurbishing was politely but fearlessly set forward.

The moral was clear. It was the consistent and the constant attention to little things which aroused gratitude and merited respect, not the crude and obvious wielding of large sums of money. The accounts of William Pearson, T. B. Lennard's chief agent at Ipswich in the 1820s,

---

[184] For these examples, see E. A. Smith, 'The Election Agent', 19; Namier and Brooke, *House of Commons*, i. 48–9, 227, 254–7, 432–3; I. R. Christie, *Myth and Reality in Late Eighteenth-century British Politics* (London, 1970), 240–3.

[185] Jones, '1st Marquess of Anglesey', MA, p. xxxix.

[186] Amos Donkin to Sir Matthew White Ridley, 14 and 19 June 1830, Ridley MSS, RO. In a remarkable burst of candour, Donkin told Ridley: 'I have ventured to collect all the information in my power as to the unpopularity you mention, (which certainly does exist *particularly* among the lower classes) to a considerable extent. It's not however entirely confined to the lower Classes & I shall therefore begin with the better classes first, & with regard to them the whole charge seems to be comprised in the word "Hauteur" which is given as description of the *manner* in which you receive people . . . the very persons however who repeat these stories *support you* upon public grounds . . . All this is very contemptible—but we must take the world as we find it . . . I have heard some stories (but not lately) about your getting into a passion with people when taking the diversion of hunting . . . I now come to the clamours of the lower orders, & though their charges are utterly contemptible, yet they are enforced with astonishing perseverance & malignity . . . The cause of all this is the Idea which exists among them that you are too careful of your money—or in other words, that you do not occasionally give them a "blow-out"—or pay them some occasional marks of attention to keep them in humour . . .'

nicely illustrate the point. They are full of small sums for small services, including a £21 annual subscription to the Members' Plate at the Ipswich Races, an £8. 8s. annual donation to the Ipswich Bell Ringers, £4. 4s. annually to the 'Christmas Box to the town's Servants', £2. 2s. annually to the Town Band, and £1.1s. annual subscriptions to the Ipswich Female Benefit Society, the Ipswich Education Society, the Red Sleeve Charity School, the Charity for the Relief of the Widows and Orphans of the Clergy, and the Lancastrian School.[187] Such attentions were clearly the attractive face which patrons and candidates liked to show to the community.

The indispensability of their services was reflected in the payments made to chief agents. William Faithfull received £665 for six months' work in Hampshire in 1790, although slightly less than half of this for the considerably shorter poll at the by-election of 1779.[188] This may have been exceptional. In general, their remuneration seems to have been on a level with that received by land stewards, perhaps £100–200 per annum in the mid-eighteenth century, rising fairly steadily thereafter. Such sums seem trifling to the modern mind but, as has been sensibly pointed out, were comparable to the remuneration of the incumbents of the Chairs of modern history newly created at Oxford and Cambridge.[189] The value of such men to the Hanoverian élite is reflected in their acceptance into the gentry ranks of society which they occasionally attained. They dined and sometimes hunted with their social superiors, bought a farm—perhaps a small estate— and soon became of great consequence in the community. 'His master's voice' and representative was a gentleman and possibly a friend, although not an equal. Not surprisingly, several acquired quite respectable small fortunes with their country estates.

Most agents in elections, however, were sub-agents, responsible for a district, a group of parishes, or even a few streets. Their numbers varied widely, depending upon the size and complexity of the constituency. There are instances in the counties of one side hiring 30 agents, as happened in Hampshire in 1807.[190] The Bankes campaign in Dorset was in the hands of no fewer than 26 agents in 1806–7 and of 34 in 1831,[191] while Milton's extraordinary campaign in Yorkshire in 1807 may have required as many as

[187] 'Expenses of Nursing Ipswich Constituency, 1821–26', D/DL. 0. 41. 3, Lennard MSS, Essex RO.
[188] Lowe, 'Hampshire Elections', M.Phil., 214–15.
[189] Hughes, 'The Eighteenth-century Estate Agent', 192.
[190] Lowe, 'Hampshire Elections', M.Phil., 210.
[191] KY 90/0, 92/7, Bankes MSS, Dorset RO. There were 40 agents at the 1807 contest in Bedfordshire; see RV. 11. I.C., Wells MSS. Beds. RO.

100 agents.[192] The side which could retain the most agents had an immediate advantage in a contested election as much as in a preliminary canvass. Such an advantage might be so overwhelming as to leave the opposition helpless.

The retention of agents, like most aspects of electioneering, was somewhat less arbitrary than it might at first glance appear. To appoint an unpopular agent would displease the voters. It was better to appoint someone they knew and could trust. There are also signs that on particular occasions agents needed to know something of the candidate's platform before accepting the retainer. Captain C. P. Yorke, a candidate at the Cambridgeshire county contest in 1831, instructed his committee to mention to agents solicited: 'The Captain avows himself friendly to a moderate Reform in the Representative System, but opposed to the dangerous measure contemplated by the Bill introduced into Parliament by the present ministry.'[193] Agents might refuse the retainer because 'the generality of my friends differ quite contrary to his Lordship', or because 'my Health and political Sentiments' would not allow it.[194] And although money might, in the last instance, attract a sufficiently large swarm of agents to strengthen a cause, it could be counter-productive. At the Glamorgan election of 1818 Edward Edwards's lavish expenditure of £15,000 won over most of the attorneys, and he threatened to do the same in 1820. A hostile pamphleteer protested against the candidature of a man who

is again attempted to be foisted on us, by a phalanx of attorneys and attorneys only . . . I should submit that the land-holder, the man of independent fortune, . . . most of whom are ornaments to the magistracy, and the great links which for ages have held society together in peaceful succession, are entitled to stand forth in the front ranks of the county. These men have the least interest to misuse power . . . These are the men we ought to look up to for protection to preserve us from that worst of despotism, the tyranny of attorneys.[195]

Once agents and attorneys had been retained, a candidate had the outlines of an electoral organization which could swing into action whenever desired. Chief agents usually had the discretion to hire sub-agents, and it was these latter who did the work. They undertook the critical business of canvassing. Indeed, they are often termed 'canvassing agents', although their functions were wider than this. They

[192] E. A. Smith, 'The Election Agent', 28.
[193] Cambridgeshire Election Committee Correspondence, 1831, Evans MSS Cambs. RO.
[194] W. Benson to C. Bowns, 24 Sept. 1812; H. Bell to C. Bowns, 2 Oct. 1812, E.213(b), Letters declining the agency for Milton, Fitzwilliam MSS, Sheffield Pub. Lib.
[195] *A Letter to the Freeholders of the County of Glamorgan on the importance of selecting a proper person to represent them in the ensuing Parliament*, 19 Feb. 1820. From a collection of old election bills and ballads, 1800–1840, MS.6.16, Glam. RO.

distributed publicity of all kinds throughout the constituency and they were responsible for the practical details of conveying voters to the poll. The detailed election expenses of sub-agent John Cunningham at Braintree, Essex, in 1830 and 1831 reveal numerous items of expenditure: preparing lists of freeholders; obtaining duplicates of the land tax assessments; corresponding with patrons and landlords requesting permission to canvass tenants; forming local election committees; canvassing expenses; drawing up canvass returns and communicating the same to the central committee; arranging for the transportation, accommodation, and entertainment of the freeholders; and paying the costs of the orchestra which serenaded them.[196] Consequently, there can be no question of their indispensability. One observer at the Huntingdonshire county election of 1807 believed that the want of an agent in one hundred would cost the Hinchingbrooke interest a hundred votes or more.[197] There was some prospect, too, that repeated enlistment might itself breed and encourage party loyalty: 'The only use I can see in Retaining Agents, now all is so quiet, is that in the event of a contest at any future period all those Agents who now accept Retainers would be considered as enlisted in our Cause.'[198] And so, although there *are* instances of venal agents, of agents willing to sell their services to the highest bidder and even willing to change sides,[199] not all agents were so contemptible. One of Hinchingbrooke's agents in 1807 refused a bribe to support Lord Proby because he considered himself wedded to the Hinchingbrooke interest.[200] Indeed, unsolicited offers of support from local agents are not an uncommon feature of the election correspondence of the time.[201]

Most election agents were local attornies about whose political motivations it is impossible to generalize with much confidence. In so far as they may have had political ambitions at all, their horizons were probably limited to the corporation or the town hall. Their increasingly frequent employment by the electoral patrons of the Hanoverian oligarchy marks not merely the professionalization of electoral politics, however, but, to some extent, a necessary abdication of responsibility over the mechanisms of electoral control on the part

---

[196] 1830, D/DO. B.5. Essex RO.
[197] 8/133/5, Hinchingbrooke MSS, Hunts. RO.
[198] Joseph Cummings to Lord Ilchester, D.124, box 337, Ilchester MSS, Dorset RO.
[199] See E. A. Smith, 'The Election Agent', 29.
[200] Edward Greene to Lord Hinchingbrooke, 8/134, Hinchingbrooke MSS, Hunts. RO.
[201] e.g. Lord Burford to Lord Fitzwilliam, 3 July 1789, Fitzwilliam MSS, X 1603, Northants. RO; Edward Greene to John Richards, n.d., Apr. 1807, 8/134, Hinchingbrooke MSS, Hunts. RO. 'I now trouble you with this to say I shall be happy to render you or your party any Service in my Neighbourhood without Fee or Reward.'

of the upper crust. In terms of running, organizing, and thus determining the outcome of election campaigns, the Hanoverian oligarchy maintained a distant and ultimate control. This tendency is seen in the employment of the same firm of solicitors and attornies time after time to run elections in a constituency, and, moreover, for the same sub-agents to be employed time after time, even those from particularly humble backgrounds.[202]

The church, which had supplied many an election agent in the early eighteenth century, similarly began to relax its hold upon the electoral system as the century wore on. Although there can be no doubt that individual members of the churches could and did play an important role in electioneering, especially if they owned land and could thus establish an electoral interest, there is some doubt about their activity as agents.[203] Much of the evidence concerning clerical involvement in elections focuses upon activities other than agency: upon preaching, exhortation, publicity, and pamphleteering.[204] There is no evidence of widespread clerical involvement in election agency. The Porritts' account, for example, includes almost every form of election activity *except* agency.[205] By the early nineteenth century the church, like the upper classes of Hanoverian Britain, was no longer in day-to-day control of electoral organizations in most constituencies.

These local agents, nevertheless, were the local representatives of the candidate and his committee. Once retained they would be requested to canvass voters in their districts. Sometimes lists of voters were sent to them but usually they were left to compile their own. They might be sent details of voting qualifications in the constituency and left to their own initiative to exploit them. They would be expected to report to the committee the results of their canvass and to specify particular circumstances or problems affecting individual voters. During the days before the poll they would be active in circulating addresses and other forms of propaganda. Where relevant, they would co-operate in the raising of money, but more usually they would simply record expenses and submit receipts to the committee. In county elections they would be expected to arrange for transporting the voters to the poll, where possible at reasonable expense, for example by persuading friendly gentlemen to loan their carriages for a few days.

---

[202] For dramatic examples see the use of a watchmaker at St Albans in canvassing and preparing lists for £50, and even the casual £5 paid to a tripeman in 1780 for rounding up country voters on his outride; Lansberry, 'Politics and Government in St Albans', Ph.D., 161, 162–3.

[203] For some examples of the Anglican clergy acting as agents see E. G. Forrester, *Northamptonshire County Electioneering, 1695–1832* (London, 1941), in Northants. in 1806.

[204] Lowe, 'Hampshire Elections', M.Phil., 221–2.

[205] Porritt and Porritt, *Unreformed House of Commons*, 296–9, 307–8.

They would also be responsible for the booking of inns, arrangements for the organization, protection, and observation of the voters—and of their expenses—*en route*, and frequently the provision of ribbons and colours etc. Finally, local agents were expected to submit accounts for the expenses of their voters and of the inns at which they stayed. The following circular to agents was typical of county election arrangements:

One Agent or his Clerk in every district of your Division to meet at Sherborne on Monday next at ten in the Morning to make the necessary Arrangements for the Conveyance of the Voters from the whole of your Division and to take care that about twenty are sent daily to Dorchester so as to arrive there at Eleven on Tuesday next and every other Morning at half past nine and to call at the Antelope Inn when proper persons will attend to accompany them to the Poll. It is not wished that more than 20 should attend from each Division *daily* therefore you will only convey as many voters as will make up the Number 20 with those who may find Conveyances for themselves. You will particularly attend to getting all the doubtful votes as early to the Poll as possible and let one or more of our firmest Voters accompany each Party. It is also wished that the votes for Banks and Portman should be polled first and the Plumpers to Banks be reserved to the last . . .

Some Confidential Friends of Mr. Banks must be requested to make all the necessary arrangements with respect to the Engagement of the Public Houses and to the appointment of the persons to check the Expenditure at each.[206]

The agent was a critically important point of contact with the voters. As Curwen told the House of Commons: 'He is the person immediately known to and connected with the electors in small boroughs; he manages all their affairs; he assists them amidst all their wants and necessities.'[207] The agent moved among the voters, familiar not merely with their political inclinations but with their circumstances, their families, and their lives. Any change in those circumstances which was likely to affect their title to the vote or in other ways to impinge upon an election campaign was of interest to him. Henry Fowles, Luttrell's agent at Minehead, John St Aubyn, recorded in his canvass books not merely the usual canvassing information but also detailed comments on personal circumstances, those of non-voters as well as voters.[208] Agents would normally go to any reasonable length to

---

[206] Instructions to Agents in the Interest of Mr Banks, 7 May 1831, KY 93, Bankes MSS, Dorset RO.

[207] 19 May 1809, *Parliamentary Debates*, xiv. 666.

[208] Canvass books, 1767–69, box 110, 1/59/7. D.D/L., Dunster Castle MSS, Som. RO.

please or satisfy a voter in order to obtain or maintain his political support.[209] For an agent to offend a voter personally was to sacrifice his vote, as one candidate found to his cost:

I have no hesitation in acknowledging that as well in County as in General Politics I perfectly agree with your Sentiments, but the same obstacle that stood between me and the Interest you supported at the late County Election still remains and that is, (I frankly tell you) Mr. Platt one of the Duke of Bedford's Agents, by whom I was insulted and from whom I have not even had an attempt to Explain. I therefore can't (with pleasure) join that Man in Public or Private Concerns.[210]

Such a sad, and probably unnecessary, electoral vendetta obviously persisted for many years, an apt commentary on the sensitivity of the relationship between electors and agents.

So inextricable was the mutual dependence between candidates and agents that relations between them could quickly become unsettled. Agents, in particular, felt that they were in an exposed, public position and they frequently manifest a touchy prickliness. Candidates sometimes had to go out of their way to humour them. R. S. Milnes, MP for York between 1784 and 1802, unwittingly upset an agent at Pontefract in 1784, and his chief agent, Smithson, had carefully to smooth the agent's ruffled feathers.[211] Candidates and patrons could be just as touchy. Delaval so mistrusted his agents at Berwick in the 1780s that he set a representative, Robert Pearson, to spy on them all.[212]

One of the reasons for agents to feel less than complete loyalty towards their employers was their distinctly modest levels of payment. Dr Smith has stated that the remuneration of canvassing agents ranged from 1½ to 3 guineas per day, that of poll agents being slightly greater.[213] In addition, he would, of course receive his retainer, which seems universally to have been 5 guineas. This meant that a typical agent may have received over £50 for his exertions in a particular election campaign.[214] Here is one typical agent's statement of account:

---

[209] Agents not uncommonly lent voters their horse and carriage in order to facilitate their progress to the polls; see, for example, n.d. 1810, D/DQ/19/2, Burgoyne MSS, Essex RO. For examples of an agent sponsoring a legal opinion in order to preserve an elector's suffrage see the correspondence in BS 1459/1-3, Beds. RO.

[210] J. Beverley to Lord Hinchingbrooke, 1807, 8/133/32, Hinchingbrooke MSS, Hunts. RO.

[211] Bundle 13, Harewood MSS, Leeds Cent. Lib.

[212] Stoker, 'Elections and Voting Behaviour', Ph.D., 95-6.

[213] E. A. Smith, 'The Election Agent', 33-5.

[214] At the 1812 Staffordshire contest, for example, £2,000 was shared among 33 attornies; 188, Hatherton MSS, Staffs. RO.

| | |
|---|---|
| Retainer . . . prepatory to the Election | 5. 5s. 0d. |
| Canvassing previous to the election | 20. 7s. 0d. |
| Attended the poll as Inspector, 6 days | 31. 10s. 0d. |
| Attended the whole of Sunday (15 May) Made up lists of voters who had polled and those remaining unpolled. | 7. 19s. 9d. |
| [Other.] | 0. 9s. 8d. |

$$65. 11s. 8d.^{215}$$

These are not unreasonable rates for professional men who, as they frequently made a point of emphasizing, had to abandon entirely their normal routine of work and remuneration while an election contest lasted. Although most accepted without murmur the going rate, it cannot have been solely the expectation of making money which led men to become agents time after time. Their motivation must also be sought in the area of social emulation, the desire to rub shoulders with the great, to assume a position of responsibility for affairs, and, not least, to be seen to be doing so. Many men of humble background and uncertain educational status found a place for themselves in the informal electoral organizations in the century before reform. The need to be at the centre of events, to participate in the excitement of the campaign, and to play a leading role in one of the great community activities of the age—these ambitions, not financial reward alone, motivated election agents.

In an age which knew little of the parliamentary parties, election agents were the men who worked the electoral system. It was they who acted as the officer corps in the battles between electoral interests, orchestrating the movements of the mass of the voters. Of course, the registration clauses of the 1832 legislation led to the establishment of more permanent, party officials. This race of men, however, bore distinct and striking resemblances to the election agents of the unreformed period. They were essentially local men who had little routine contact with the great local representatives of the parliamentary parties. The hard slog of election work was still the concern of men who stood some distance apart from the fashionable world of parliamentary parties. The ultimate disappearance of their political culture was to be the consequence of two developments: the steady

---

[215] Thomas Lowman to Henry Bankes, n.d. 1831, KY 90, Bankes MSS, Dorset RO.

growth and development of parties with local organizations and the drafting of effective 'corrupt practices' legislation. Significantly, these two developments culminated simultaneously in the 1880s. The ending of the old regime in electoral politics, in this as in other areas, was to be a slow and subtle transformation.

## Canvassing

In a modern electoral system the principal purpose of canvassing is to identify and mobilize support, to publicize the candidate, and to draw attention to key issues. In the unreformed electoral system, and indeed for long afterwards, these functions were supplemented by other objectives which were arguably of even greater importance. The most prominent of these was to enable candidates and their organizations to decide whether to stand a poll. Fitzwilliam's candidates at the Yorkshire county contest in 1784 withdrew when the canvass showed that they stood at a 4 : 1 disadvantage among the voters.[216] To stand a poll, with its financial demands and its organizational requirements, would have been an expensive waste of time and effort. Furthermore, the information thrown up by the canvass might itself bear heavily upon the nature of the contest and provide striking indications of the scale of the task that lay ahead. The canvass for the Leveson–Gower interest at Newcastle-under-Lyme in 1790 yielded 41 plumpers and 555 double votes. Of these latter the Leveson–Gower interest had only 252. The deficit, therefore, 'must be made up by the Young Men who are intituled to their freedom'.[217] In the Welsh boroughs, with their more complex system of contributory boroughs, such information was even more indispensable to election committees. 'By your statement of votes, it appears that the result of a Poll would depend upon the 50 Nevin voters', wrote the agent for the Paget interest in 1830 about the borough of Caernarvon, which had over 1,000 voters.[218] Poor canvass returns could lead a candidate to redouble his efforts, as Sir Sampson Gideon, a poor third on the canvass at Cambridgeshire in 1780, was forced to admit.[219] There was, therefore, an experimental aspect to very many canvasses. As Dr Rees has shown

[216] N. C. Phillips, *Yorkshire and English National Politics, 1783–1784* (Christchurch, New Zealand, 1961), 50. Much more remarkable was the outcome of the Staffordshire canvass in 1820, when the Trentham interest, which had represented the county unopposed for 73 years, surrendered the seat after a canvass but without a contest. See E. Richards; 'Social and Electoral Influence of the House of Trentham', *Midland Hist.* 3 (1975), 135–7.

[217] Parcel 2, bundle i, D. 1788, Aqualate MSS, William Salt Lib., Staffs. RO.

[218] J. Sanderson to Unidentified Recipient, 13 July 1830, 5480, Poole MSS, Gwynedd RO, Caernarvon.

[219] D. Cook, 'Representative History of Cambridge', Ph.D., 49–51.

in his work on South Wales between 1790 and 1830, no fewer than 28 canvasses did not conclude in a contest. Of these, 12 were undoubtedly 'serious attempts to sound opinion in the hope of support', 12 went as far as drawing up lists of agents retained and patrons to be approached, while only 4 were political gestures.[220]

The initial canvass, therefore, decided whether an election would be contested and, if so, determined the character of the contest to a very considerable extent. This central feature of electioneering has been all but ignored by historians. Professor Smith's study of canvassing in Yorkshire neglects many of the issues to be dealt with in this chapter for the sake of a chronological account. Professor Cannon's study of Wiltshire raises the issue of how far tenants actually followed the instructions of their landlords but omits many other considerations.[221] What follows, therefore, attempts to establish both a framework of information and a structure of interpretation for this indispensable aspect of electoral organization.

Canvassing was an important preliminary to an election contest, but it was much more than a political event. The conventions and the forms of canvassing rituals suggest further possible constructions. The lavish gestures of respect paid by candidates and their agents to the voters, even when there was little or no likelihood of a contest, suggest that public competition for electoral support was in progress, softened, even concealed, by rituals of social inversion. These somewhat theatrical gestures were intended to flatter voters, who were presumed to be intelligent, independent, and capable of making balanced and informed electoral choices.

Some contemporaries saw through all this. One writer, 'Impartial' of Shrewsbury, wondering whether 'the approaching ceremony of the *General Canvass* be not more for ostentation than out of any respect for you', told the voters in 1796:

The Gentlemen who are to walk the Canvass be your superiors in rank and fortune and should be treated with respect. When they *pull off* their hats, be sure you do the same; and when they do *bow*, do you *bow* also . . . Be as *grave* as possible, Gentlemen, while the canvass procession goes forward.

---

[220] Rees, 'Parliamentary Representation of South Wales', Ph.D., 23. See also R. W. Smith, 'Political Organization and Canvassing: Yorkshire Elections before the Reform Bill', *Am. Hist. Rev.* 74 (1968–69). Smith shows that in the century before reform, 12 canvasses occurred at the 25 general elections but only 3 contests (in 1734, 1741, and 1807). In the light of this, and, indeed, much other evidence, I find Moore's opinion—'In the pre-reform period canvassing was rarely if ever undertaken except when a contest was in prospect', *Politics of Deference*, 302—inexplicable.

[221] R. W. Smith, 'Political Organization'; J. A. Cannon, 'The Wiltshire Election of 1772: An Interpretation', *Wilts. Arch. Mag.* 58 (1960).

I acknowledge it is a public FARCE, and were *Democritus* alive, he would burst his sides with laughter to see such a scene of aristocratic pageantry.[222]

It is not hard to understand his cynicism. Whatever the prevailing social conventions, the fact remains that for an elector to resist a personal canvass for his vote meant a direct, personal refusal, one which was rendered more difficult by the social pressures so manifestly on display. The large and intimidating numbers of social grandees served powerfully to legitimate the candidate's claim on the support of the elector. To disregard it required a countervailing legitimacy which most electors simply could not command. In the last analysis, then, the appearance of MPs and peers as waiters, serving dinner to the electors of Westminster in 1784, may have been an intensely dramatic example of social inversion, but it left the electors substantially unaffected— although it just possibly made their ultimate political inferiority slightly easier to swallow.

There can be no question, however, that the electors enjoyed being courted in this manner. When the Earl of Sefton set out to canvass Liverpool in 1806 he received the following instructions: 'Be indefatiguable in your canvass, and solicit as many votes as possible personally; you have no conception how great a personage every Freeman conceives himself to be on the eve of a contest.'[223] Innumerable accounts of canvasses stress the high proportion of gentlemen of status, wealth, and respectability: peers, knights, gentlemen, magistrates, members of corporations, etc.[224] Indeed, one of the first objectives was to establish canvassing parties of both numbers and social respectability. Such parties could make an impact upon the community and convey to the individual elector an impression of impending victory. In some constituencies, the canvassing party might be of moderate size, perhaps a dozen or two.[225] In others, the party might be larger and somewhat less distinguished. It might, for example, include several members of a candidate's committee.[226] But in both counties and boroughs, the objective was the same: the larger the party of gentlemen, the better. It was better not to canvass at all than to canvass in small numbers. Walter Spencer Stanhope simply refused to canvass Hull in 1790 when

---

[222] *Five Minutes Good Advice, to the Freemen and Freemen Burgesses of Shrewsbury Before a General Canvass*, Shropshire RO.

[223] Whittingham-Jones, 'Liverpool Politics,' i. 417.

[224] At the Abingdon canvass of 1809, Sir George Bowyer 'was attended by a dozen or more of the leading people of both parties' (A/AEp/11, Abingdon Borough MSS, Berks. RO). For King George III's canvass of Windsor in 1780 see Namier and Brooke, *House of Commons*, i. 211.

[225] For some canvassing parties in the north of England see Stoker, 'Elections and Voting Behaviour', Ph.D., 62–3.

[226] J. Adams, *An Impartial Collection* (Dublin, n.d.), 24, 30, 34.

he found that he had disappointingly few people to canvass with him.[227] Much, therefore, depended upon the friendly and voluntary co-operation of important local families. Once their co-operation had been established it could be frequently and flagrantly exploited, for example by the use of aristocratic, female canvassers and their public flaunting of fairly innocent sexual and sartorial behaviour. A kiss, a smile, a wave, and a dress of flamboyant party colours were common features of the general canvass.[228]

The timing of the canvass was influenced by powerful customary considerations. There was much to be said in favour of an early, pre-emptive strike. Thomas Lethbridge reflected on his defeat at the East Somerset county election of 1832, 'I certainly blame myself for not coming forward earlier, & I fear not canvassing the 3 previous days to the *Nomination* & this was the cause of my losing the Election . . .'[229] A full county canvass required 6 to 10 weeks, depending, of course, upon the size of the county and the number of agents available. A small borough required only a couple of days. Consequently, to delay a canvass by only a day or two could prove fatal in a borough contest. A late canvass was a hopeless cause.[230] By then, voters, had pledged their support and they disliked breaking their pledges. One agent in the Yorke interest at Cambridgeshire in 1831 put it very plainly:

I received your Letter . . . Yesterday and am sorry to Inform you: I shall be able to render very little service to the cause of Capt. Yorke as Mr. Payton & etc. having canvassed round our Neighbourhood and engaged nearly all the Voters even before I had heard the election was likely to take place.

[227] Hammond to Fitzwilliam, 14 June 1790, Fitzwilliam MSS, Northnts. RO.

[228] The activities of Georgiana, Duchess of Devonshire, at the Westminster election of 1784 have become legendary, but they were by no means unusual. For the much more effective contribution of Mrs Jane Osbaldeston in Yorkshire, see E. A. Smith, 'Yorkshire Elections', 80. There are many other examples. At Nottingham in 1820 a toast was drunk to 'Our Female Friends to whom we were so much indebted on our Canvass in Nottingham' (*A Short Review of Proceedings* (Nottingham, 1820), 12). A candidate at Boston in 1830 raised a glass 'for my *Female Advocates*, so good, so fair, so strenuous, so decided' (*A Sketch of the Boston Election* (Boston, 1830), 13). In the early 19th-cent. novel, set in Ireland, *Canvassing*, written by 'the O'Hara family', 'Lord Warringden was accompanied by the young ladies as well as by their father', their function being to engage the electors in slight conversation as a means of relaxing them.

[229] Lethbridge to Francis Drake, DD/NE/12, Lethbridge MSS, Som. RO. This did not prevent all forms of activity. Newspaper announcements sometimes appeared prior to the announcement of the dissolution.

[230] The lateness of the canvass was a perennial explanation for an unsuccessful campaign. The failure of the Foxite candidates at Surrey in 1812 was attributed to this cause; see the *Morning Chronicle*, 26 Oct. 1812. Similarly, the Earl of Thanet blamed Brougham's defeat at Westmorland in 1820 on a late canvass; see Earl of Thanet to Brougham, 3 Mar. 1820, J. 986, Brougham MSS, London Univ.

You may depend upon myself and anything else I can do but am fearfull we are very much too late.[231]

The timing of an early canvass, like that of the declarations of a candidature, was absolutely vital to success. An early canvass at York in 1802 gave the Fitzwilliam interest a clear advantage. One agent reported that two-thirds of the voters had given 'positive engagements'. The early start had given real impetus: 'We wish to make our Impressions as deep as we can, in the first Instance, without foreign Interference. And I begin to think we could do without it.'[232]

Yet there was much more to the tactics of canvassing than a quick start. Sometimes voters liked to reserve their position to the last possible moment. To do so not merely safeguarded the financial value of their vote. It allowed them the freest possible disposal of their votes between candidates whose identities and, to some extent, political stance might be far from evident early in the campaign. Furthermore, an over-hasty canvass risked the damaging imputation of threatening the peace of the borough or county.[233] The Paget interest advised the voters of Caernarvon 'to pause before they lend their aid towards plunging their hitherto peaceable Towns and Neighbourhoods into the inconveniences, mischiefs and miseries of a premature Contest'.[234] Certainly, in county constituencies the idea that voters should not be approached until after the nomination had taken place was still very strong, although the convention was frequently breached. Another

---

[231] Thomas Richards to H. R. Evans, 13 Oct. 1831, Committee Papers and Correspondence, Evans, MSS, Cambs. RO. At the Grimsby election of 1826 a late candidate addressed the voters as follows. 'I perceive many of you consider yourselves bound by the promises which you made to Mr. Wood and Heneage in their first Canvass, and which promises were extorted from you by their (or their agents) assertion that there would be no Opposition. I can assure you that you are not bound by any such promises, because they were given CONDITIONALLY. The true intent and meaning of your promise was this, "IF NO OTHER Candidate comes and there is no opposition, I will give you my Vote." Another Candidate has appeared, and that leaves you at full liberty to vote which way you please. For the word "IF" prevents your promise from being binding, unless the condition on which you granted your Vote is Fulfilled' ('To the Much Injured Electors of the Ancient Borough of Great Grimsby', *Poll for the Borough* (Grimsby, 1826), p. i).

[232] R. Sinclair to Fitzwilliam, 17 May 1802, F.35g, Fitzwilliam MSS, Sheffield Pub. Lib.

[233] For example, Sir Richard Worsley began his canvass at Hampshire in 1779 even before the county meeting has been announced. He personally canvassed the close and college of Winchester to the annoyance of the freeholders of the city, who were indignant at the implied assumption that they were 'either dependent on those two bodies or obliged to vote as ordered' (*A Collection of Handbills, Squibs etc. published during the late Contested Election* (Winchester, 1780), quoted in Lowe, 'Hampshire Elections', M.Phil., 78). An early start could sometimes be used as an excuse for *not* canvassing. J. H. Loft explained that his failure to canvass arose from his fear that it might create 'a state of confusion and drunkenness to prevent the industrious from following their usual occupations and injuring their families' (DD/T.35, Tallents MSS, Notts. RO).

[234] 25 June 1830, Paget MSS, Gwynedd Archives Service.

convention spared the delicacy of friends and relatives of sick and dying MPs: it was not thought legitimate to canvass during such a period.[235] Similarly, to canvass on Sunday was a gross breach of courtesy; tradition had it that a 'Sunday canvass' yielded only untrustworthy promises.[236] Finally, there existed a very strong convention that a promise once given could not lightly be broken. A voter would not lightly release himself from such a pledge; he had to be released from it by the candidate himself. A vote was in fact promised to a person, not an interest. Such a relationship, once established, ought not to be casually broken, and a gentlemanly candidate would endeavour not to. At the Dorset election of 1807, W. M. Pitt affirmed 'that it has been my constant practice, to abstain from soliciting any vote, which I knew to be already promised, and that I have always given instructions to that effect to those who act for me'.[237]

In a hierarchical society the business of canvassing was inevitably influenced by social and economic considerations. In such a society, those with influence over others on the basis of property, employment, custom, and family or personal connection could be expected to use it. In county elections, of course, landed proprietors were presumed to have legitimate influence over their tenants and dependants. Hopeful candidates and their agents attempted to secure the support of landlords long before the election was due to be held. In certain counties where landed influence was particularly strong, canvassing can appear as a projection of estate ownership. The first votes in an estate, and sometimes the second votes, too, were disposed of almost as a job-lot.[238] The first vote was usually reserved to the landlord, the second being at the disposal of the voter himself. The voters, therefore, even on an estate, would expect to be canvassed, at least for their second vote. However, such a voter could not be canvassed from outside the estate without the agreement of his landlord. The rights of the proprietor over his tenants and dependents were inviolable. This does not imply that such rights were inevitably total and oppressive. Rather,

---

[235] See. for example, the reluctance to canvass too quickly after the death of an MP at Northumberland in 1826; see *A Collection of the Authentic Papers, Speeches etc.* (Alnwick, 1826), 211. Robert Ongley lost much public credit for canvassing too soon after the death of a Member at Bedfordshire in 1767; see Namier and Brooke, *House of Commons*, i. 205.

[236] *An Account of Proceedings at Berkshire, 1818, Speeches at the Nomination* (Windsor, 1818), 34.

[237] *To the Gentlemen, Clergy and Freeholders of the County of Dorset, 1807* KY. 79/45, Dorset RO.

[238] See e.g. the account of proceedings at Northamptonshire in 1806 in Forrester, *Northamptonshire County Electioneering*, 96–101. Certainly, canvassing agents liked to give the impression that a parish had gone entirely in the patron's favour, e.g. Robert Stewart to Lord Hinchingbrooke, n.d. 1806, 8/133/6, Hinchingbrooke MSS, Hunts. RO: 'At the two former places . . . all are secured for your Lordship.'

they were primary and presumptive. The proprietor had first, and very powerful, call upon the electoral loyalty of his people. This was clearly understood and almost universally accepted; hence the instinctive willingness of voters to refuse to promise their votes until they had learned of their master's instructions. One vote might thus be relied on. But the disposal of the second vote was a very different matter. Sometimes it was left entirely to the voters to decide.[239] More commonly, some combination of personal, tactical, and political considerations would influence its disposal.

There were no universally respected canvassing times, but in view of the work to be done it is not surprising that canvassing parties liked to make an early start. At Lincoln in 1820 the canvass began at 8.00 a.m. each day.[240] At Bedford in 1830 'the canvass was resumed at an early hour'.[241] Sir Robert Peel himself stated: 'After travelling all night I began a personal canvass on foot yesterday at half past nine in the morning, and concluded it at half past nine in the evening without a moment's Intermission.'[242] It was hard and long work. The day's proceedings would be terminated with a stirring speech from the candidate, underlining his surprise at the warm and friendly reception he had encountered during the day.

The demands of the poll and the timing of the tallies imposed a particular set of priorities upon canvassers. Urban areas with sizeable concentrations of voters would, all things being equal, be canvassed first. The less familiar, geographically less inviting, and politically more apathetic rural areas would be left until later.[243] Common sense and electoral experience established a rough set of priorities. The more respectable voters would expect to be canvassed first, and in view both of the influence which they could exert over other voters and of the example they could set, it was necessary to respect their wishes.[244] An effective canvass, moreover, depended upon the care with which the candidates had chosen the route and order of their general canvass. They needed to travel through the most densely populated areas of the county or borough, where they would meet their supporters, committee members, and agents. Later in the day the canvass would

---

[239] e.g., 'My Lord Middleton, I understand, has written to Mr. Hodgkinson to say that he wishes his Tenants to give one vote to Mr. Hawdley and *to do as they please* with the other' (Edward Tallents to the Duke of Newcastle, NcC 529, Newcastle (Clumber) MSS, Nottingham Univ. Lib.).

[240] Lincoln Poll Book, 1820, p. 37.

[241] R. Muggeridge, *History of the Late Contest* (Bedford, 1830), 12.

[242] Sir Robert Peel to Thomas Paget, 29 July 1820, DG 24/985/13, Leics. RO.

[243] J. Andrews, 'Political Issues in the County of Kent', M.Phil. (London, 1967), 20-1.

[244] Amos Donkin to Sir Matthew White Ridley, 29 June 1830, 25/29, Ridley MSS, Northumb. RO.

end with a dinner or other celebration of the cause and candidature. The timing and organization of these events and the extent to which they were backed up by the continuous exertions of professional agents, were critical elements in canvassing. Agents had to get supporters and friends on to the streets, whether voters or not, to give the canvassing party a rousing welcome. The main business of the day, however, was to meet the voters. Little was left to chance. Second and third visits might be necessary to raise the voters who were out when canvassed. Behind the show and the spectacle, a lot of hard work was being done. The canvass was nothing if not thorough.

Indeed, the canvass required much more than hard work. It demanded a keen sense of tactical skill. The first priority was to canvass early and get to the voters before the other side did. Even a well-established interest could take fright at an exploratory canvass from another quarter.[245] The Fitzwilliam interest lost Malton in 1807 because of poor canvassing. They started late, they did not know for whom they were canvassing, and their canvassing tactics were far inferior to those of their opponents.[246] Further, a familiar canvassing tactic was to neutralize the canvass of the opposition by visiting houses immediately after they had been canvassed by the opposite side. Occasionally, this could result in simultaneous canvassing. At Bedford in 1830, 'the Canvass commenced on each side the following morning, the rival Candidates opening hostilities in the High Street, on one side of which were Mr. Polhill and his friends canvassing'.[247] Usually, however, candidates strove to keep out of each other's way and sought to gain an advantage by other methods. One of these was to have a large sprinkling of local worthies in the canvassing party for particular localities; thus the composition of a canvassing party might well be constantly changing, a second, and different, canvass, might increase the number of promises. At York in 1802 the Fitzwilliam candidate, Laurence Dundas was decidedly short of promises after the first canvass. A second canvass shook out some absentees.[248] Another common trick was for a slightly weak candidate to effect a partnership with a more popular candidate in an attempt to capitalize on the latter's reputation.[249] Such putative alliances were fraught with difficulty and

---

[245] See e.g. the shocked reaction of the Bedford interest to some exploratory canvassing from its opponents; C. Vickry to D. MacNamara, 5 Jan. 1790, R.3/883, Bedford MSS, Beds. RO.

[246] As one Fitzwilliam agent readily admitted; John Cleaver to Fitzwilliam, 12 May 1807, F.72-16, Fitzwilliam MSS, Wentworth Woodhouse MSS, Sheffield Pub. Lib.

[247] Muggeridge, *History of the Late Contest*, 10.

[248] D. Sykes to Fitzwilliam, 20 May 1802, F.35-96, Fitzwilliam MSS, Sheffield Pub. Lib.

[249] At the Essex County election of 1830 the Committee of the District of Braintree in Colonel Tyrell's interest resolved to deny reports that their agents 'have been stating that their object is to obtain votes as well on behalf of Col. Tyrell as of Mr. Western, they being "one

with danger, not least because the friends and supporters of one candidate, to say nothing of his agent, might not share his enthusiasm. But it might be even more dangerous to repudiate such a coalition entirely. Henry Bankes weighed up his relationship with Thomas Pitt at the Dorset county election of 1807:

It appears to me that Mr. Pitt & some of his Friends are a little unreasonable with regard to me: they profess to afford me no kind of assistance, while they expect everything from me. It has been and is my earnest wish to join Mr. Pitt, but how can it be in my power to form a junction, if he continues to refuse it. I naturally expected that . . . Gentlemen in Mr. Pitt's Interest & my own, would canvass jointly for us both, & where only a single Vote was at liberty I hoped that my Agents would endeavour to secure that second Vote for me.[250]

Where such a junction was not forthcoming, however, a rumour was better than nothing. One favourite tactic was to circulate reports that a particular candidate was likely to win with ease, thus reducing his need for further support from the voters. At the same election, Thomas Pitt's agent wrote:

We find that every manœuvre is practising to obtain votes which have been promised to Mr. Pitt under the false pretences that he is already secured. It has therefore been thought proper to send out hand bills and I shall be obliged to you to circulate [them] in your Neighbourhood.[251]

Like so many aspects of electioneering in the eighteenth and nineteenth centuries, canvassing was accompanied by highly refined celebrations. Flags and colours would make a visual impact upon the electors, advertising the candidate and identifying him with a local party or tradition. There was no point in sparing the expense. 'The Colours of our Ribbons must be the same as the last. As many Favours should be ordered in your District as will exceed by 1/3rd the number of my votes.'[252]

Election canvasses were great community occasions but their ultimate objective remained the establishment of personal relationships between the voters and the candidate. Personal meetings were undertaken whenever possible, but where larger electorates were involved they were not always feasible. Personal letters to the voters from the candidate were a common substitute for personal encounters. At the Cambridgeshire contest of 1780, for example, Philip Yorke sent

and the same"' (Papers of J. Cunningham, agent for Col. Tyrell's Braintree Committee at Essex, 1830–1, Essex RO).

[250] Henry Bankes to F. Fookes, 23 Apr. 1807, KY 79/51, Bankes MSS, Dorset RO.
[251] Thomas Salisbury to Thomas Fookes, 4 May 1807, KY 79/46, ibid.
[252] Henry Bankes to Mr Castleman, n.d. 1807, KY 67/37, ibid.

personal letters to the outlying voters whom he could not reach in person.[253] Canvassing cards, sometimes of an impressively ornate and elaborate character, were a common substitute for letters.[254] But such stratagems were no substitute for the personal encounter. As one agent remarked, 'a personal canvass everywhere will decide a very large portion of freeholders'.[255] It was not enough just to send round canvassing agents to places which the candidate could not reach. If he could not go himself, then he had to send respectable gentlemen on his behalf wherever possible. This was particularly common in county elections, where independent freeholders could be prickly to the point of rebellious. The amateurish canvasses of gentlemen with influence had to be added, therefore, to those of the professional agents.[256] In Dorset in 1806 the chief agent for the Bankes interest noted: 'There are many Gentlemen in the different Districts who have undertaken to canvass on Mr. Bankes' behalf. The Agents in these districts will of course insert in their Canvass lists the result of the Canvass of these Gentlemen as well as their own.'[257] And in Huntingdonshire, one agent told Lord Hinchingbrooke: 'I think you will find a journey to Gaxby answer very well as there are several Persons in this Neighbourhood who expect to be called upon.' Another agent reported that if both Lord Hinchingbrooke and his candidate 'intend to visit our quarter, it will be of great use to confirm some dubious Voters'.[258]

To judge from the canvassing papers which survive, everything was done to make the canvass as thorough as possible. One intrepid canvasser at the general election at Hedon in Yorkshire, with an electorate of around 150, canvassed Beverley, Bridlington, Hornsea,

[253] Cook, 'Representative History of Cambridge', Ph.D., 55.

[254] One of the best collections of these cards known to me is in the Bristol Archives Office (21503(1)) and relates to the Bristol election of 1812.

[255] Robert Harvey to Edmund Wodehouse, 13 May 1807, Wodehouse MSS, quoted in Jupp, *British and Irish Elections*, 46–7.

[256] e.g., at the Yorkshire election of 1807 the chairman of Milton's interest wrote to propertied men of the county: 'Relying upon your kind anxiety to forward Lord Milton's Interest, I beg leave to suggest to you that you will materially assist it by communicating with the professional Agent in your Neighbourhood, and by canvassing such voters as have not yet been seen, and by employing your Influence wherever it may be most effectual, both until and after the Commencement of the Poll.' In other counties, however, the role of the patron sometimes outweighed and clearly predominated over that of the agents. At the Devon contest of 1818 the following instruction was sent to friends in the interest of Lord Ebrington: 'Although I should by no means advise at present the renewal of a general Canvass, unless that step should be taken by either of the other Parties, yet it is very desirable that you should take every opportunity of quietly sounding the Freeholders in your Hundred.' No mention of agents is made. Ebrington MSS, Devon RO.

[257] Mr Castleman to F. Fookes, 7 Nov. 1806, KY 79/23, Bankes MSS, Dorset RO.

[258] Robert Stewart to Lord Hinchingbrooke, n.d. 1807, 8/133/6; K. Sellars to Mr Fellowes, 3 May 1807, 8/133/14; Hinchingbrooke MSS, Hunts. RO.

and Hull in search of a few outvoters.[259] In counties, district canvassing agents had the wearying task of tracing every freeholder on the land tax assessments. It was essential that they did their job properly. The possibilities of the opposition party lodging successful protests against the credentials of friendly voters had to be minimized.[260] The trouble was that canvassing of this minute and intensive character could become counter-productive. Voters were always sensitive but they could become sick of being pestered by tiresome canvassing agents. One agent frankly admitted: 'I found today in Sherborne that many of my *Local Soldiers* are so annoyed at my endeavours for Mr. Bankes that, I am told, many mean to resign. This to say the least speaks volumes for their disappointment and the speedy evaporation of their loyalty.'[261]

Canvassing was often accompanied not merely by social festivities but by treating and the promise of further treating. Voters expected the candidates to be generous, and while immediate gratification of their wishes was not always practicable it was, on the other hand, by no means impossible to associate the canvass with some gestures of generosity. One common technique was for the candidate to arrange to meet parties of voters at a local inn.[262] Another was to hold breakfast parties every morning. Sir William Milner boasted to Fitzwilliam that his canvassing breakfasts attracted 400 people each morning.[263] The canvass could thus serve to effect or, more usually, to promise to effect, such examples of a candidate's generosity as would not offend the electors' sensibilities.

As we saw earlier, canvassing agents received a retainer of around 5 guineas, and for each day of canvassing a further payment of around 1½ to 3 guineas. There is evidence in some places of extremely sophisticated scales of payment. In the counties especially, where the time spent in canvassing could be so vital, payment was sometimes calculated on an hourly basis. In a large borough like Coventry this was also done. In 1780 canvassers were paid by the hour, and it was possible to compute the number of hours spent canvassing particular districts.[264] Depending on the size of their districts, canvassers

[259] J. Markham, *The 1820 Parliamentary Election at Hedon* (York, 1821), 37.

[260] See e.g., Instructions for Mr Bankes' Agents, 1831, KY 90, Bankes MSS, Dorset RO.

[261] Sherborne Agent to F. Fookes, 'Wednesday Evening', 1831, KY 93, ibid.

[262] This happened, for example, at the Glamorgan county election of 1831. Enid Ball, 'Glamorgan: a Study of the Concerns of the County and the work of its MPs 1825–1835', Ph.D. (London, 1965), 71.

[263] Sir William Milner to Fitzwilliam, 23 June 1790, box 40, Fitzwilliam MSS, Northants. RO.

[264] 1119/1, Sheffield MSS, Coventry RO. It appears to have taken 538 man-hours to canvass around 2,500 freemen, slightly under five per hour, a rate which compares extremely well with the speedy rush of 20th-cent. canvassers.

received from £20 to £100 plus expenses. These expenses did not normally amount to much: accommodation, stationery, and perhaps the use of a clerk. All of this usually brought the cost of a day's canvassing up to £15 or even more per day.

So horrific were these figures that chief agents sometimes queried the account. A strenuous negotiation, and sometimes a slightly adjusted figure, followed.[265] An agent in the Yorke interest in 1831 in Cambridgeshire had to give a full account of his campaign:

I trust this Statement will be a satisfactory Assurance to the Committee that my time was fully employed . . . You will see that I had but 8½ days for my Canvass of the twelve Parishes within my District, in all of which except Littlefort, I was obliged to canvass three times, and in many of them a fourth.[266]

Only through such vigilance could election expenses be contained; and, moreover, it promoted thorough and effective canvassing of the voters.

In all this, what of the candidate? After all, it was on his behalf that all of this activity was undertaken. There is no doubt at all that much about the candidate was of crucial significance: his family, his residence, his wealth, his opinions, and his personality. All candidates had to know something of the constituency and to be alert to the needs and expectations of the electorate. The candidate had to canvass the voters and mingle with them. He had to be visible. For example, the entry of the candidate into the town at the start of a campaign was frequently marked by processions and parades, festivities and speeches. For these purposes public and civic buildings would be employed: town halls, churches, inns, fairs, and markets. In these situations, it did not matter much what a candidate said or did so long as he was there and so long as he displayed himself to the largest possible number of voters.[267] At the same time, voters did not expect candidates to behave like frenzied partisans. They were, in a sense, expected to remain above the mundane battle waged so ferociously on their behalf

---

[265] For example, after the Dorset contest of 1831 one agent submitted a bill for £74. 13s. 6d. but in the end he had to accept a downward revision to £65; see KY 86/11, Bankes MSS, Dorset RO.

[266] H. R. Evans to C. P. Harris, 25 Jan. 1832, Papers of H. R. Evans, Committee Papers and Correspondence, Cambs. RO.

[267] A candidate's absence damagingly raised central questions about his candidature. No wonder a Peterborough agent was worried. 'Benyon's absence is deplorable and allows his opposition to spread rumours about him' (G. Cowhill to Fitzwilliam, 27 Feb. 1802, F. 38/18, Fitzwilliam MSS, Sheffield Pub. Lib.). Such an absence could dominate a canvass. One sarcastic Welsh canvassing agent commented: 'I think it's a princely and proper Step to take to Canvass the Boroughs because it will enable you to explain the causes which make it impossible for Sir Charles Paget to make his immediate appearance' (J. Sanders to R. Poole, 6 July 1830, Poole MSS, Gwynedd RO).

by their agents. Little more could be expected of a candidate than that he appear early, remain visible, open his purse, and behave agreeably and attentively towards the voters. Not all could attain the heights of ideal candidature scaled by Sir William Milner at Hull in 1790, who reportedly canvassed the home of every single freeman. Hull had an electorate of around 2,000.[268]

Because canvassing was one of the principal components in electioneering before 1832 it is scarcely irrelevant to enquire how accurate and reliable it was. Because final canvassing lists do not survive in copious quantities it is impossible to do more than compare those that do survive with the results of the contests. These are, in fact, more than 80% reliable, sometimes 90% or more, results which are not entirely surprising in view of the care and thoroughness with which the canvass was undertaken. The figures we have for the counties are particularly creditable, in view of the problems of geographical distance and electoral size. Dr Stoker's study of the north of England provides invaluable data on Cumberland in 1768 and County Durham in 1760.[269] Data from other counties confirm his picture of over 90% reliability. Data on particular voters in the parishes show a rather lower degree of canvassing reliability and a greater degree of voter independence. Very detailed data from the Essex contest of 1831 (Table 2.4) compare canvass promises and actual votes in parishes. Here a rate of 83% reliability in an apparently random survey of parishes speaks for itself. A rather fuller survey for Wiltshire in 1772 (Table 2.5) gives a slightly higher average (87.1%).

In the boroughs, canvassing could be even more precise. Dr Stoker found correlations between canvassing and the poll at Carlisle in 1768 as high as 99% and 91% for the two parties.[270] Voters elsewhere were slightly less predictable. Professor Phillips noted a somewhat lower correlation at Lewes in 1774 (81.5%).[271] At Shrewsbury in 1830 Corbett received 607 promises, but only 440 (72.5%) were actually kept.[272] No doubt instances of very high canvassing correlations can be traded with those of substantially lower figures, but one thing should

[268] F. 35(i) 84–1, Fitzwilliam MSS, Sheffield Pub. Lib.

[269] In Cumberland in 1768, 92% of voters voted as canvassed; in Durham in 1760 Clavering obtained 1,383 votes after he had obtained 1370 canvass promises. However, as Stoker points out, the canvass gave him 839 singles and 531 splits, while the poll gave him 945 singles and 437 splits, a difference of +11% and −18%, respectively. See Stoker, 'Elections and Voting Behaviour', Ph.D., 79–80, 82.

[270] Ibid. 84–5, 87–8.

[271] J. A. Phillips, *Electoral Behavior in Unreformed England, 1761–1802* (Princeton, 1982), 130 n. 40.

[272] T. Phillips, *History and Antiquities of Shrewsbury* (Shrewsbury, 2 vols. 1837), i. 202.

TABLE 2.4   *Canvass Promises and Votes at Essex, 1831*

|  | Promises | Polled | |
|---|---|---|---|
|  |  | No. | % |
| Black Votley | 6 | 3 | 50 |
| Bocking | 20 | 17 | 85 |
| Bradwell | 3 | 2 | 66 |
| Braintree | 34 | 30 | 88 |
| Cressing | 5 | 5 | 100 |
| Garfield | 5 | 3 | 60 |
| Great Saling | 8 | 7 | 88 |
| Panfields | 5 | 4 | 80 |
| Shalford | 2 | 2 | 100 |
| Stisted | 18 | 17 | 95 |
| Weatherfield | 9 | 8 | 89 |
| White Votley | 3 | 0 | 0 |
| TOTAL | 118 | 98 | 84 |

*Source*: D/DO/B5, Cunningham MSS, Essex RO.

TABLE 2.5   *Canvass Promises and Votes at Wiltshire, 1772*

|  | Canvass | | Goddard votes | | Herbert votes | |
|---|---|---|---|---|---|---|
|  | Goddard | Herbert | No. | Accuracy (%) | No. (%) | Accuracy |
| Bradford | 55 | 16 | 71 |  | 6 | 37 |
| Calne | 63 | 3 | 54 | 86 | 0 | 0 |
| Melksham | 21 | 22 | 19 | 90 | 16 | 73 |
| Salisbury | 98 | 248 | 88 | 90 | 240 | 97 |
| Trowbridge | 48 | 53 | 21 | 44 | 36 | 68 |
| TOTAL | 285 | 342 | 253 | 88.7 | 298 | 87.1 |

*Source*: VCH *Wiltshire*, v. 203.

be made clear: the figures quoted are often for the total number of promises given matched with the final vote, which can be rather misleading. For example, at Cirencester in 1802 an astonishingly high correlation can be claimed:[273]

| Canvass | | | | Voted | | |
|---|---|---|---|---|---|---|
| Preston | Beach | Howell | | Preston | Beach | Howell |
| 46 | 62 | 26 | | 46 | 62 | 27 |

[273] *Cirencester Poll Book* (1802).

However, further examination of individual voters' behavior reveals that of the 72 voters in this sample, only 44 of them, in fact behaved exactly as promised, while 28 of them (39%) voted differently in some way. At Shrewsbury in 1830, 228 out of 800 voters voted unpredictably (28%).[274] The figures therefore conceal a much higher degree of unpredictability than might at first appear. The fact that a process of self-cancellation tends to raise the overall correlation should not conceal the surprisingly high figure for dissidence, fluctuation, and unpredictability. When to this figure is added the number of voters which the canvass did not reach, the electorate appears to be even less predictable than a concentration upon canvassing may suggest. Outvoters were difficult to reach; the lack of an official register made records unreliable; and when a constituency had not been contested for some years, the right to the franchise became a matter of recollection rather than record. In 1768 Cumberland had not been contested since 1722. No wonder the canvass reached only 80% of the freeholders, with only 69% of the electorate behaving predictably.[275] Abingdon, however, was contested at almost every election between 1768 and 1830. Even so, the canvass of 1802 yielded no fewer than 49 'neutral' or 'doubtful' voters out of 233 (22%).[276] Things could get even worse. Lambton canvassed a particularly problematic area of Durham in 1820. Of 148 voters, 31 were out, 17 refused, 18 split, and only 82 actually supported him (55%).[277]

The evidence of canvassing therefore presents a clear picture of an electorate which contains a substantial minority of unpredictable voters. But when the 'neuters' are added to the 'outs', and then to the 'doubtfuls', and these to the large number of uncanvassed voters, we have an electorate well over one-quarter of which was *not* being successfully mobilized. It is a reasonable hypothesis that these problems of management mounted as the electorate increased in numbers and as political issues became more potent as influences bearing upon elections. Political parties had not yet fashioned the organizational mechanisms with which to confront and control this electorate. This golden age of the independent voter was to end after 1832 when party and registration began to discipline the electorate. It is astonishing to read Professor Moore's comments on the electorate of this period. His verdict that 'the proportions of the doubtful voters would have to be small' and that 'most voters would have to behave as members of

---

[274] T. Phillips, *History and Antiquities of Shrewsbury*, i. 202.
[275] Stoker, 'Elections and Voting Behaviour', Ph.D., 79, 87.
[276] A/AEp 11, Abingdon Borough MSS, Berks. RO.
[277] *Durham Chronicle*, 7 Mar. 1820.

definable groups' could not be more wrong.[278] It was the high proportion of doubtful voters and the failure of many voters to behave as members of definable groups which constitute the essential characteristics of the unreformed electorate.

[278] Moore, *Politics of Deference*, 314.

# 3

# *The Processes of Electoral Politics*

CONTESTS, CANDIDATES, AND CAMPAIGNS

In the last chapter we investigated patterns of constituency control and electoral organization. We now wish to move in a little closer to observe the men and the processes that enabled the electoral system to work in the way that it did for as long as it did. In subjecting to analysis the frequency of contested elections and the conditions for their ocurrence, in endeavouring to appreciate the types of men who became parliamentary candidates and the type of behaviour which was expected of them, and in trying to make sense of the peculiar electioneering processes that accompanied elections to the unreformed Parliament, we constantly remind ourselves that, whatever its representative deficiencies, the electoral system of this period was an organic growth, a political and social system with its own norms and values. It is the purpose of this chapter to open up that system to our understanding.

## Contests

In the history of the British Parliament the method for producing Members of Parliament has necessarily been of the very greatest importance. As Professor Mark Kishlansky has remarked, 'the greatest transformation in the process of parliamentary selection was its dominance by contested elections'. That transformation occurred in the second half of the seventeenth century. Contests had been very rare in the sixteenth and early seventeenth centuries: 'Communities avoided division over parliamentary selections for all the obvious reasons—cost, trouble, fear of riot, challenge to magisterial authority—and for one other: the refusal to assent to the choice of an M.P. was an explicit statement of dishonour.' When they did occur, contested elections were hardly ever caused by political differences. They tended to be bitter personal disputes and family vendettas, as well as the result of accident, suspicion, fear, and breakdowns in communication. Contemporaries detested the prospect of a contested election. 'By counting each man as one, the meanest freeholder equal to the worthiest gentleman, the community violated every other social norm by which it operated. 'In the later seventeenth century the number of contested elections rose sharply. Religious disputes, parliamentary conflicts, and, not least, party differences divided the country: 'Competition among the gentry for social distinction, for patronage, and for influence at court mixed with the emerging ideological divisions over politics and religion.'[1] By the early eighteenth century, between one-third and one-half of all elections were being contested.

These decades were tumultuous, unusually tumultuous, perhaps, and it was both inevitable and natural that such a high frequency of contested elections would decline when the 'rage of party' began to die down. As Table 3.1 reveals, the rate declined to around one-fifth at the general elections of 1747, 1754, and 1761. Thereafter, however, the rate began to recover slightly, and for the next 50 years it hovered between one-quarter and one-third. At the last five elections to the unreformed Parliament it settled at around one-third. Although this represents a marked decline from the peak period of 1705 to 1734, the lower rate hardly deserves the strictures which have been passed upon it.[2] The general tendency towards contested elections was maintained and, in the English boroughs, at least, as Table 3.2 indicates, the contest rates for the early eighteenth century had been almost regained by the early nineteenth. Such a degree of recovery was remarkable in view of the weighty factors inhibiting election contests in the later eighteenth and early nineteenth centuries: the absence of nationally organized party competition, the broad and general agreement at most elections on fundamental religious and constitutional issues, the horrendous expense of elections, the perennial impetus towards compromise rather than competition in two-member seats, and that general reluctance to engage, and encourage others to engage, in political and social conflict which characterized the Hanoverian upper classes.

The number of contests at each general election is not the only guide to the frequency with which electors were called upon to exercise their political choices. Almost as relevant is the frequency with which general elections were held. Professor Holmes has chosen to contrast his 'first age of party' between 1679 and 1722, when there occurred the 'astonishing' number of 17 general elections in 43 years, a rate of one every 2½ years, with what happened later. 'In the next forty-three years', he comments, 'there were six, an average of one every

---

[1] M. Kishlansky, *Parliamentary Selection:Social and Political Choice in Early Modern England* (Cambridge, 1986), 134, 17, 61, 190.
[2] J. A. Cannon, *Parliamentary Reform, 1640–1832* (Cambridge, 1972), 36–7; see also 30–1.

TABLE 3.1   *Contested Elections in English and Welsh Constituencies,*
*1701–1831*

| General election | English counties N = (40) | English boroughs N = (203) | Welsh counties N = (12) | Welsh boroughs N = (12) | Total (N = 267) | |
|---|---|---|---|---|---|---|
| | | | | | No. | % |
| 1701 | 18 | 71 | 1 | 1 | 91 | 34 |
| 1702 | 18 | 67 | 2 | 0 | 87 | 33 |
| 1705 | 26 | 82 | 1 | 1 | 110 | 41 |
| 1708 | 14 | 78 | 3 | 2 | 97 | 36 |
| 1710 | 23 | 104 | 3 | 1 | 131 | 49 |
| 1713 | 12 | 85 | 1 | 2 | 100 | 37 |
| 1715 | 14 | 88 | 4 | 4 | 110 | 41 |
| 1722 | 17 | 107 | 5 | 4 | 133 | 50 |
| 1727 | 12 | 79 | 6 | 7 | 104 | 39 |
| 1734 | 13 | 91 | 3 | 5 | 112 | 42 |
| 1741 | 4 | 61 | 5 | 6 | 76 | 28 |
| 1747 | 3 | 50 | 2 | 0 | 55 | 21 |
| 1754 | 5 | 51 | 3 | 1 | 60 | 22 |
| 1761 | 4 | 41 | 1 | 1 | 47 | 18 |
| 1768 | 8 | 60 | 3 | 2 | 73 | 27 |
| 1774 | 11 | 69 | 4 | 2 | 86 | 32 |
| 1780 | 2 | 64 | 1 | 1 | 68 | 26 |
| 1784 | 7 | 65 | 1 | 1 | 74 | 28 |
| 1790 | 8 | 66 | 0 | 1 | 75 | 28 |
| 1796 | 4 | 55 | 2 | 1 | 62 | 23 |
| 1802 | 6 | 66 | 2 | 1 | 75 | 28 |
| 1806 | 7 | 54 | 0 | 1 | 62 | 23 |
| 1807 | 11 | 58 | 2 | 1 | 72 | 27 |
| 1812 | 4 | 53 | 1 | 6 | 64 | 24 |
| 1818 | 11 | 81 | 1 | 3 | 96 | 36 |
| 1820 | 10 | 63 | 1 | 3 | 77 | 29 |
| 1826 | 11 | 77 | 0 | 1 | 89 | 33 |
| 1830 | 10 | 74 | 0 | 1 | 85 | 32 |
| 1831 | 11 | 63 | 2 | 2 | 78 | 29 |

*Sources*: W. A. Speck, *Tory and Whig: The Struggle in the Constituencies 1701–1715* (London, 1970), App. E; R. R. Sedgwick, *The House of Commons, 1715–1754*, 2 vols. (London, 1970), i, App. 1; J. A. Cannon, *Parliamentary Reform, 1640–1832* (Cambridge, 1972), App. 3; L. B. Namier and J. Brooke (eds.), *The House of Commons, 1754–1790*, 3 vols. (London, 1964), i. App. 1; R. G. Thorne, *The House of Commons, 1790–1920*, 5 vols. (London, 1986), i. App. 1.

seven years.'[3] To extend the comparison would be even more illuminating, however, and not a little surprising. Between 1780 and 1831 there were 13 elections, one in slightly less than every four years. And if, like Professor Holmes, we wish to give the figures the best

[3] G. Holmes, *The Electorate and the National Will in the First Age of Party* (Kendal, 1976), 2.

possible gloss, we might single out the period 1802–31, which contained nine elections, or just over one every three years, a rate that compares well with that for 'the first age of party'.

Election contests, moreover, were tending to occur most commonly in constituencies with the largest electorates. In the early eighteenth century, contests had been distributed fairly indiscriminately among all constituency types. After the mid-eighteenth century this was no

TABLE 3.2    *Contested Elections in English Constituencies, 1701–1831*

| General election | Counties (N = 40) | | Boroughs (N = 203) | | Total (N = 243) | |
|---|---|---|---|---|---|---|
| | No. | % | No. | % | No. | % |
| 1701 | 18 | 45 | 71 | 35 | 82 | 34 |
| 1702 | 18 | 45 | 67 | 33 | 85 | 35 |
| 1705 | 26 | 65 | 82 | 40 | 108 | 44 |
| 1708 | 14 | 35 | 78 | 38 | 92 | 38 |
| 1710 | 23 | 57 | 104 | 51 | 127 | 52 |
| 1713 | 12 | 30 | 85 | 42 | 97 | 40 |
| 1715 | 17 | 42 | 94 | 46 | 111 | 46 |
| 1722 | 17 | 42 | 112 | 55 | 129 | 53 |
| 1727 | 12 | 30 | 85 | 42 | 97 | 40 |
| 1734 | 13 | 32 | 94 | 46 | 107 | 44 |
| 1741 | 4 | 10 | 62 | 30 | 66 | 27 |
| 1747 | 3 | 7 | 48 | 24 | 51 | 21 |
| 1754 | 5 | 12 | 55 | 27 | 60 | 25 |
| 1761 | 4 | 10 | 42 | 20 | 46 | 19 |
| 1768 | 8 | 20 | 62 | 30 | 70 | 29 |
| 1774 | 11 | 27 | 70 | 34 | 81 | 33 |
| 1780 | 2 | 5 | 67 | 33 | 69 | 28 |
| 1784 | 7 | 17 | 69 | 34 | 76 | 31 |
| 1790 | 8 | 20 | 66 | 33 | 74 | 30 |
| 1796 | 4 | 10 | 55 | 27 | 59 | 25 |
| 1802 | 6 | 15 | 66 | 32 | 72 | 30 |
| 1806 | 7 | 17 | 54 | 27 | 61 | 25 |
| 1807 | 11 | 27 | 58 | 29 | 69 | 28 |
| 1812 | 4 | 10 | 53 | 26 | 57 | 24 |
| 1818 | 11 | 27 | 81 | 40 | 92 | 38 |
| 1820 | 10 | 25 | 63 | 31 | 74 | 30 |
| 1826 | 11 | 27 | 77 | 38 | 88 | 36 |
| 1830 | 10 | 25 | 74 | 36 | 84 | 35 |
| 1831 | 11 | 27 | 63 | 31 | 74 | 30 |

*Source*: See Table 3.1.

TABLE 3.3   *Contested Elections: English and Welsh Constituencies, 1701–1831, by Constituency Type*

| Constituency type | No. | 1701–34 (10 elections) | | | 1741–74 (6 elections) | | | 1780–1831 (13 elections) | | |
|---|---|---|---|---|---|---|---|---|---|---|
| | | Total | Average No. | % | Total | Average No. | % | Total | Average No. | % |
| Counties | 40 | 170 | 17.0 | 42 | 35 | 5.8 | 14 | 102 | 7.8 | 19 |
| Corporation | 27 | 91 | 9.1 | 34 | 29 | 4.8 | 18 | 47 | 3.6 | 13 |
| Burgage | 31 | 91 | 9.1 | 31 | 20 | 3.3 | 12 | 42 | 3.2 | 11 |
| Scot and lot | 53 | 262 | 26.2 | 48 | 128 | 21.3 | 39 | 269 | 20.7 | 38 |
| Small freeman (<200) | 34 | 132 | 13.2 | 39 | 44 | 7.3 | 21 | 138 | 10.6 | 31 |
| Medium (200–1,000) freeman | 30 | 113 | 11.3 | 38 | 40 | 6.7 | 22 | 147 | 11.3 | 38 |
| Large freeman (>1,000) | 28 | 176 | 17.6 | 63 | 87 | 14.5 | 52 | 235 | 18.3 | 65 |
| Welsh | 24 | 22 | 2.2 | 9 | 12 | 2.0 | 8 | 20 | 1.5 | 6 |
| TOTAL | 267 | 1,057 | 105.7 | 40 | 395 | 65.3 | 25 | 1,000 | 77.0 | 29 |

*Source:* See Table 3.1.

longer the case. Table 3.3 attempts to assess rates of recovery in different types of constituency. Clustering elections together in defined periods from 1701 to 1832, it is clear that in certain types of constituency the rates of contested elections which had been common between 1701 and 1734 were never regained. This was so not only in the county constituencies but also in the corporation and burgage boroughs, which normally had small electorates and where, as Professor Phillips remarks, 'the restricted nature of their franchises and their greater susceptibility to manipulation or control' lowered the rate.[4] Similarly, in the (usually tiny) Welsh seats, rates of recovery were limited. As the size of the electorate in borough seats increases, however, so the rate of contest recovers. In the small freeman boroughs the rate of recovery (comparing 1741–74 with 1780–1831) is already marked. In the medium freeman boroughs the recovery (comparing 1701–34 with 1780–1831) is complete, and in the large freeman boroughs the new rate actually surpasses the rate for the early eighteenth century. Even in the very variously constituted scot and lot boroughs and others with similar residential qualifications, the rate of contests remains high. In the borough constituencies, at least, contests tended to be confined to those constituencies with the largest and most open electorates.[5]

Furthermore, the number of elections actually and formally contested does not exhaust the extent of electoral activity. Preliminary canvassing, frequently of an extensive and competitive nature, together with other forms of electoral campaigning, might occur in a constituency which was not, in the event, formally contested. If the outcome of the campaign could be predicted with some certainty, then the side likely to be defeated might withdraw and cut its financial losses.[6] It is difficult to estimate the incidence of 'aborted' contests of this type. In 1780, for example, there were two contested county elections—in Cambridgeshire and Surrey—but there were aborted contests at Bedfordshire, Cumberland, Warwickshire, and, most spectacularly, at Yorkshire.[7] In 1784 there were seven contested county elections—

---

[4] J. A. Phillips, *Electoral Behavior in Unreformed England 1761–1802* (Princeton, 1982), 68–70.

[5] Phillips reaches similar conclusions (ibid. 70–2). The 33 largest boroughs (of *all* franchisal types) contested more regularly than any others, and moreover they included two-thirds of the borough electorate. The corporation and burgage boroughs—31% of the parliamentary boroughs—had only 6% of the borough electorate and, of course, the lowest rate of contests.

[6] On the possibility of aborted contests see also R. W. Smith, 'Political Organization and Canvassing: Yorkshire Elections before the Great Reform Bill', *Am. Hist. Rev.* 74 (1969), 1538–60.

[7] I. R. Christie, *The End of North's Ministry* (London, 1958), 73–9; L. B. Namier and J. Brooke (eds.), *House of Commons 1754–1790*, 3 vols. (London, 1964), i. 82–5.

in Bedfordshire, Berkshire, Buckinghamshire, Gloucestershire, Hertfordshire, Middlesex, and Suffolk—but there was much activity at the aborted contests in Derbyshire, Dorset, Lancashire, Norfolk, Somerset, Staffordshire, Surrey, and, once again, Yorkshire.[8] Precise estimates for the general elections of 1806 and 1807 suggest that the total figure for contested elections needs to be supplemented by 50–75% to reach the number of contests both formal and aborted.[9] (Were we to do this, incidentally, then the number of election contests would approximate quite closely to the figures estimated for 'the first age of party'.) Nor is there any reason for thinking that such aborted contests were negligible skirmishes. A student of South Wales boroughs between 1790 and 1830 has added to the 19 formally contested elections no fewer than 28 aborted ones. Of the 28, 12 went as far as drawing up lists, engaging agents, and canvassing for promises. Another dozen were 'serious attempts to sound opinion in hope of support'. Only four were of negligible importance.[10]

What did election contests signify? Most people with political inclinations were almost neurotically reluctant to push their political differences to the point of formally contesting an election. At one level, electoral patrons may have been concerned about the cost of contests and the possible incidence of disorder and even violence. But there was more to their reluctance to take a political disagreement as far as an election contest than that. An election contest might threaten to disturb settled social relationships upon which the life of the community depended. A pamphlet of 1806 defined the meaning of 'the peace of the county' in the context of the Northamptonshire contest of that year. It is one of the most frank and open statements to be found anywhere about the constant yearning to avoid contested elections:[11]

By the peace of the county, I understand, the uninterruptedness of the present state of society,—leaving where they were before, old family connections and friendships,—tenants without the risque of offending their landlords,—and tradesmen of losing valuable customers in opposite interests,—leaving the general order of men engaged in their accustomed occupations and pursuits without temptation to idleness, intoxication, licentiousness and possibly

---

[8] M. D. George, 'Fox's Martyrs: The General Election of 1784', *Trans. Royal Hist. Soc.* 4th ser., 21 (1939), 133–68. Namier and Brooke, *House of Commons*, i. 91–3.

[9] For the 1806 and 1807 estimates, see M. Hinton, 'The General Elections of 1806 and 1807', Ph.D (Reading, 1959), 446. For further copious examples of aborted contests, see D. A. Wager, 'Welsh Politics and Parliamentary Reform', Ph.D. (Wales, 1972), 132–4, 135–41, 158, 240.

[10] R. D. Rees, 'The Parliamentary Representation of South Wales, 1790–1830', Ph.D. (Reading, 1962), 23–4. See above, 91.

[11] E. G. Forrester, *Northamptonshire County Electioneering, 1695–1832* (London, 1941), 106.

perjury. By disturbing the peace of the county, I mean the converse of the proposition. And when we consider how many evil passions are stimulated to unbounded action in the course of a contested election in a large county,—how much rancour and discord are produced,—how much ruin,—how many excesses,—and how many crimes, I hope I shall not be accused of another cant, viz., that of fanaticism in warning the electioneering Candidates, how they lightly and rashly incur the guilt of such consequences, merely upon an opportunity afforded them without an expediency.

What lies behind this mentality is some distant recollection of the Civil War, the Protectorate, the Popish Plot, and 'the rage of party' of the late seventeenth century and early eighteenth century. Some contemporaries were very frightened indeed of the social consequences of contested elections. One observer went so far as to pronounce that 'A Contested Election is a remaining proof of the Existence of Original Sin.'[12] This may have been going a little far. Nevertheless, there was a pronounced tendency for constituencies to change their politics *without* recourse to a contest whenever possible. At the general election of 1818, for example, 153 seats changed hands between different parties, but in as many as 56 of them (37%) there was no contest.[13] What a contested election indicates, then, is the breakdown of one or more of the conditions for containing differences within the community and for minimizing the impact of personal and political disagreements. The underlying unity of the local political nation could be disrupted and election contests ensue in a number of ways.

*First*, personal or family considerations might disrupt the unity of the local political élite. The Shrewsbury contest of 1796 is a dramatic instance of the collapse of the unity of the ruling electoral order. John Hill was the sitting MP for Shrewsbury and he shared the distaste of his brother, Sir Richard Hill, MP for Shropshire and the head of the Hawkestone branch of the Hill family, for the Attingham branch, with its glorious mansion and its extensive estates. The head of the Attingham branch, William Hill, was determined to take advantage of his cousin, John Hill's, unpopularity with the Shrewsbury voters, and this he did by beating him into second place at the contest of 1796. Without these dynastic rivalries it is extremely unlikely that a contest would have occurred in 1796, to say nothing of the eight subsequent

[12] This was Rowland Hunt, who tried desperately to keep the electoral peace at Shrewsbury in 1796. See *An Account of the Mandamus Clause* (Shrewsbury, 1806), 665/3/13, Eyton Hall MSS, Shropshire RO.

[13] L. V. Sumner, 'The General Election of 1818', Ph.D. (Manchester, 1969), 88–121. This continued to happen long into the 19th cent. As Moore has demonstrated, between 1835 and 1847, 41% of county seats changed hands between the parties without a contest; See D. C. Moore, 'The Matter of the Missing Contests: Towards a Theory of the Mid-19th Century Political System', *Albion*, 6 (1974), 93–119.

contests to which the borough was subjected before 1832. In these, however, issues of local and even national concern proceeded to agitate the electorate.

*Second*, for a variety of reasons, a patron might prove to be incapable of providing effective leadership for clients, friends, and dependants in the constituency and, of course, the voters. In the late 1770s the Duke of Portland decided both for political and financial reasons to reduce his electoral commitments to Wigan. He was thus prepared to share the seat with the Bridgeman family. This caused consternation within his interest. In the confusion of loyalties which followed, Sir Richard Clayton attempted to use Portland's interest to obtain a seat in Parliament. When Portland's agreement was not forthcoming, Clayton, none the less, endeavoured to take advantage of the un-certainty in Portland's interest by putting pressure on some of its leading members. In the end he was not elected at the general election of 1780, but his ability to force a contest is significant.[14] Electoral patronage could be an expensive and exhausting business, and occasional collapses of electoral will-power should not occasion surprise.

*Third*, the voters might for any one of innumerable reasons repudiate their earlier loyalty to a patron, family, or candidate. There might be powerful political reasons for this relating to the past conduct—or future promise—of a candidate. David Hartley's opposition to the American War unquestionably provoked a contest at Hull in 1780 and cost him his seat.[15] Elsewhere, an entrepreneurial candidate with both nerve and money could always exploit latent grievances. In the political excitement of 1784, John Crewe, a local gentleman with a modest estate, tried to capitalize on the independent sentiment which was never far beneath the surface of eighteenth-century Chester and which normally found something to complain about in the thoroughgoing influence over the town exerted by the Grosvenor family. On this occasion, however, the Grosvenors were able to exploit their friendship with Pitt and their support of the monarchy in a traditional constituency.[16] It should not be thought that voters were always dependent upon a social superior to precipitate election contests. There were constituencies where they were accomplished at running third candidates in order to procure financial advantages. Morpeth

---

[14] Clayton obtained 24 votes against 58 for Bridgeman's candidate and 53 for Portland's.

[15] 'My father always brought in one member, and we could have brought in any Man except Hartley, we have now done with him for ever' (R. Sykes to Fitzwilliam, 3 May 1784, box x 1603, Fitzwilliam MSS, Northants. RO).

[16] The two Grosvenor candidates, Thomas Grosvenor and Richard Wilbraham Bootle, polled 713 and 626 respectively. Crewe polled 480.

and Reading are good examples to set beside the usually quoted cases of Amersham and New Shoreham.

*Fourth*, in a large number of constituencies the presence of rival organizations, associations, or clubs of voters enshrined and perpetuated electoral conflict. Such associations were of various types. Some recalled the party conflict of an earlier era, the Blues and Yellows of Ipswich and the Blues and Orange of Norwich, for example. In others, associations of independent voters grimly, if not always effectively, pursued their hereditary vendettas against those who controlled their constituencies and the restrictions they placed upon the numbers of voters and the freedom of election. The corporation at Coventry was a closed and corrupt body whose dubious methods of controlling both the town and its reputation not surprisingly caused considerable offence in an electorate which numbered over 2,500. The conflict between oligarchy and exclusive politics, on the one hand, and between independence and participation, on the other, was the essential theme of electoral politics at Coventry during a century of regularly contested elections. A similar central issue may be discerned at Worcester where in the 1770s the independence of one side developed into a sturdy radicalism. In such places fissures of this kind rendered it all but impossible to establish the conditions for compromise and consensus which might have prevented election contests. Where such conflict was institutionalized, moreover, a steady stream of contested elections often occurred.

*Fifth*, the resignation, retirement, or death of a long-sitting or particularly popular MP was particularly dangerous. Electoral loyalty had a strong personal quality. It could not be casually inherited. The only way that the Mostyn family found that they could retain the county seat of Flintshire which Sir Roger Mostyn had held for 38 years was by bringing forward his heir at the by-election in 1797. Only a Mostyn could hold the county seat for the interest.[17] Particular families might find their generations of service thus rewarded by the goodwill of the constituency, but goodwill alone did not win elections. The loyalty that could win a seat had to be worked for from the start. The Delaval interest was usually strong enough to control one seat at Berwick, and between 1765 and 1774 and again from 1780 to 1786 John Hussey Delaval, the head of the Delaval family, represented it. In spite of his political ability, his endeavours on the town's behalf, and, not least, his careful management and organization of his electoral

---

[17] This one, however, was too young. He was thrown out on petition on the grounds that he was a minor. The incident is still instructive. See Wager, 'Welsh Politics and Parliamentary Reform', Ph.D., 122–5.

resources, he was spectacularly incapable of passing his interest on to another. His attempt to have John Hiley Addington returned on his interest after his resignation in 1786 failed by 361 to 316 votes. So much for the gratitude of the Berwick voters. In some parts of the country such personal considerations outweighed all others. In South Wales, 'The death of a member without an heir, or the coming of age of an heir in another family, more readily gave rise to a contest than did any disagreement over national policy.'[18]

*Finally*, the electoral ambitions of families and individuals frequently precipitated contests. There are many examples of aristocratic families attempting to add a second county seat to their undisputed possession of a first.[19] In boroughs, too, there was a seemingly inevitable tendency for powerful interests to make attempts upon the second seat. The politics of many a freeman borough turned upon such considerations. In other places, outsiders with money to spend and ambitions to satisfy might readily invade a borough and provoke a contested election, especially where the number of voters was fairly small and where settled patterns of natural influence did not exist. Frequent contests at Grampound, Penryn, and other tiny constituencies in the West Country fall into this category.

The exact combination of circumstances which provoked electoral conflict differed from place to place and from election to election. What is certain is that so long as the function of elections remained of local rather than national political significance, then their immediate reference was to the status and balance of power within the constituency. So long as the power of central party machines remained weak, elections would be determined by local issues, local men, and local organization. The doubling of the rate of contested elections which was such a noteworthy feature of the early impact of the Reform Act of 1832 owed much to the operations of the new franchise and to the registration clauses of the Act. It owed something, however, to the fact that the rate of election contests was ceasing to have a purely local reference. The intrusion of national issues in elections, especially those of a party character, made it even more difficult than it already was to establish a stable, enduring balance of local political power. When the intensity of such issues weakened in the middle years of the nineteenth century, the rate of contests similarly relaxed.[20]

[18] Rees, 'Parliamentary Representation of South Wales', Ph.D., 25.
[19] See Namier and Brooke, *House of Commons*, i. 6–9.
[20] In 1835, 227 seats were contested (57%), 174 (43%) uncontested. In 1837, 251 seats (63%) were contested, leaving 150 (37%) uncontested see D. Close, 'The General Elections of 1835 and 1837 in England and Wales', D.Phil. (Oxford, 1964), 227–8, 486–7. Thereafter the number of contests dropped fairly sharply. At the general elections of 1841 and 1847 the

*Candidates*

In the somewhat parochial electoral world which existed before 1832, the identity, personality, and activities of the candidates were bound to be of paramount importance in elections. A candidate had to fulfil two sets of requirements: a formal set of statutory requirements and an informal set of social requirements. Although complete and meticulous observance of both sets of requirements was not necessary, the inability of a candidate to observe the essential elements of at least one was a certain recipe for electoral disaster. The former may quickly be dealt with. In law a candidate had to be of the age of 21 years to stand. An Act of 1695 forbade minors to serve in Parliament and imposed penalties if they took their seats and voted. Moreover, the operations of the Septennial Act meant that the aspirations of a likely candidate, perhaps the eldest son of a local patronal family, might have to be shelved for up to six or seven years. Short of bringing in a candidate to keep the seat warm for him—a risky business, since such MPs could develop ambitions of their own—there was little alternative but to turn a blind eye to breaches of the law. These, however, were very few, less than a handful in each Parliament.[21] The constituency was not likely to object if the candidate in other ways showed his mettle and if he forebore from voting in the House until he was of age, a convention which seems in the main to have been observed. Charles James Fox, for example, was only 19 on his return for Midhurst but he was careful not to vote until his 21st birthday, although his speeches created an immediate impression. The House of Commons, none the less, was a young assembly. One-quarter of the members who sat between 1734 and 1832 entered the House below the age of 25, and a further quarter entered between 25 and 33 years of age.[22] A candidate had, in addition, to attain certain property

figure dropped below 50%. It rose to 60% in 1852, only to slump below 50% at each of the next two elections (1857, 1859) amidst the stability of the electoral balance of power characteristic of those years. The beginning of the end of that political world was foreshadowed at the general election of 1865 (53%) and, of course, in 1868, when almost 70% of constituencies fought a contest on the new franchise. Thereafter the rate of contested elections never dropped below 70%.

[21] For the early 18th cent. see Cannon, *Parliamentary Reform*, 36. For the later period see H. E. Witmer, *The Property Qualifications of Members of Parliament*, (New York, 1943). Porritt and Porritt argue (*The Unreformed House of Commons* (Cambridge, 1909), i. 231–4) that the practice of inserting a *locum tenens* became established in the later 18th cent. They offer a few anecdotal instances but these seem to be exceptional cases.

[22] Twenty-one MPs under the age of 21 were returned in the six Parliaments between 1715 and 1754, 13 in the six Parliaments between 1754 and 1790. R. R. Sedgwick, *The House of Commons, 1715–54*, 2 vols. (London, 1970), i. 137; Namier and Brooke, *House of Commons*, i. 101; G. P. Judd, *Members of Parliament, 1734–1832*, (Yale University Press, 1955), 23. Brooke notes that at each general election about 15% of the House was below 30; Namier and Brooke, *House of Commons*, i. 97). Between 1790 and 1820 the figure hovered between 13% and 17% (R. G. Thorne, *The House of Commons, 1790–1820*, 5 vols. (London, 1986), i. 278).

qualifications, £600 per annum in freehold land for a county seat, £300 per annum for a borough seat. Significantly, the property qualification was first introduced in 1710. The Act, amended in 1760, required the candidate, if elected, to submit a description of his property to the returning officer and a statement that it had not been acquired specifically to earn the qualification. The insistence on landed property of some substance—and the double weighting of the county representation—speaks for itself. Clearly, the original intention was to establish a House of Commons composed of landed men of substance and such independent standing as could preserve the constitution from the moneyed interest. After 1714, however, there arose a more general conviction that the landed interest, as the bulwark of the political system, had an automatic right to such singular preference. Among Tories and country MPs, moreover, there existed a belief that only propertied MPs could resist the blandishments of ministerialists. In practice, the letter of the law was flouted and fictitious and temporary qualifications seem to have been common. That there was widespread collusion in flouting the provisions of the Act is reflected in the tiny number of exclusions during the period of its operation—10 between 1710 and 1858.[23] Even more significantly, the qualification did not apply to 'the eldest son, or heir apparent of any peer, or lord of Parliament, or of any person qualified by this act to serve as knight of a shire'. The exclusion was intended to operate against the humble, not the great.

Behind these legal qualifications lies the assumption or expectation that a parliamentary candidate would have landed property of sufficient substance to earn a natural interest in the constituency in which he wished to stand. No residential qualification existed, of course, since no one wished to exclude the representation of property from outside the constituency. There existed, however, a powerful presumption in favour of the representation of settled, landed, local property as opposed to the representation of mercantile, financial, or professional property whose permanent stake in the constituency might be less fixed than that of land.[24]

This becomes more evident when we consider the backgrounds of parliamentary candidates. *First*, the younger sons, or other heirs, of aristocratic families comprised a substantial and growing proportion of parliamentary candidates. For one thing, Members of Parliament themselves were becoming steadily more aristocratic in character.

[23] Porritt and Porritt, i. 170–81.
[24] Such presumptions operated with phenomenal success, in Wales at least. Between 1780 and 1835, all but 5 of the 137 Welsh MPs derived their main income from land. Wager, 'Welsh Politics and Parliamentary Reform', Ph.D., 12.

Professor Cannon has demonstrated that although only 8% of MPs were the sons of English and Irish peers in 1713, the figure doubled by the mid-eighteenth century and trebled by the early nineteenth.[25] In view of the natural advantages of aristocratic candidates, the ratio of aristocratic MPs to MPs as a whole was probably greater than that of aristocratic candidates to candidates as a whole. Nevertheless, the percentage of aristocratic candidates increased from around 15% in the mid-eighteenth century to over 20% in the early nineteenth. Such aristocratic candidates might be found in all types of constituencies, but two may be singled out. They might be commonly encountered in borough seats located near to the family estate, such as Bedford, Carlisle, Chester, Durham, Oxford, and York, and they would be found in county constituencies, where aristocratic families normally occupied one, and sometimes both, seats, such as Bedfordshire, Buckinghamshire, Cumberland, Derbyshire, Gloucestershire, Lincolnshire, Northumberland, Oxfordshire, Rutland, Westmorland, and Yorkshire.[26] *Second*, perhaps the next largest group of candidates was supplied by the families of the local gentry, especially for constituencies situated close to the residence of the family concerned. Although it is very difficult to offer a precise estimate, at least one-quarter of candidates were of this type. About 15% of all MPs were baronets, a rough and approximate guide,[27] and when to these are added the large number of other candidates from this stratum a total of 25% is quite attainable.

After this, it becomes increasingly difficult to estimate the origins of candidates with any precision. This is notoriously the case with the *third* category, those candidates with professional backgrounds, particularly those in the army, navy, and the law, because of the problem of double-counting. Nevertheless, there is a very strong probability that the percentage of Members of Parliament with professional backgrounds rose steadily from around one-quarter early

[25] J. A. Cannon, *Aristocratic Century: The Peerage of Eighteenth-century England* (Cambridge, 1984), 112–13. Cannon's conclusions for the later 18th cent. are confirmed by Namier and Brooke's claim that 15% of MPs between 1754 and 1790 were from aristocratic backgrounds (*House of Commons*, i. 99). In the early 19th cent. the figure climbed to over one-fifth; Thorne, (*House of Commons*, i. 282–4).

[26] Judd's figures for sitting MPs show that out of 5,034 MPs between 1734 and 1832, 883 were sons of peers or peeresses and 64 were Irish peers (19%). The overall figure for aristocratic *candidates*, however, is likely to be higher (*Members of Parliament*, 31).

[27] Judd shows that 787 of the 5,034 MPs were or became baronets (16%). The figure for gentry *candidates*, of course, is likely to be considerably higher because many contests were between gentry families or in other ways involved them. Thorne's estimate for baronetcies is 14% (*House of Commons*, i. 286–7).

in the eighteenth century to over one-third in the early nineteenth century.[28] Another steadily expanding (*fourth*) group which supplied a growing number of candidates was that which included merchants, industrialists, and commercial men. This had supplied only about 7% of Members of Parliament in the early eighteenth century. By the early nineteenth, however, the percentage had increased to between 15% and 20%.[29]

Universal statistics for all candidates who contested parliamentary elections over a century do not exist. The profile of candidates no doubt resembles that for elected MPs, with the essential proviso that unsuccessful candidates were almost certainly less rich and of slightly lower social status than those who were successful. In the counties, moreover, the proportions of candidates from the second of the above categories would be particularly pronounced. It is almost certainly the case, moreover, that representatives of new forms of wealth were steadily increasing in number as the eighteenth century advanced. After all, no less than one-quarter of all *borough* MPs have been described as having commercial involvements.[30]

The ambitions of men in seeking to enter Parliament present little difficulty to the historian when we bear in mind not merely the central role played by the House of Commons in the politics of the Hanoverian period but also its unique social context. Quite simply, the House of Commons was the gateway to careers of all types. The retention or enhancement of social prestige—those most powerful of all social pursuits—seem sooner or later to have involved membership of the House of Commons. Members of the aristocratic ruling class looked to Parliament to preserve their status, to protect their interests, and to provide for and to advance the careers of its members. The country gentry class regarded a seat in Parliament as the pinnacle of its ambitions, the sure seal of local approval for family merit and achievement. Men with new wealth were sometimes goaded into electoral opposition by the social exclusiveness of the county set. George Medley was a wine merchant in the Portugese trade who bought an estate in Sussex to live the life of a country gentleman. He launched an opposition in 1768 to the established interests at Seaford (as well as at Lewes and in the county) of the Duke of Newcastle:

[28] Sedwick, *House of Commons*, i. 141–6, 155; Namier and Brooke, *House of Commons*, i. 126, 138, 143; Thorne, *House of Commons*, i. 300, 306, 313; Judd, *Members of Parliament*, 49.
[29] Sedgwick, *House of Commons*, i. 148–52; Thorne, *House of Commons*, i. 318; Judd, *Members of Parliament*, 56.
[30] Judd, *Members of Parliament*, 56–7.

He desired no more than common civility, and not any obligations to anybody; but he found that they thought he either had no money or no spirit to spend it, but should find themselves mistaken in both; he particularly mentioned the never having been sent to when the county address was presented, and then sent to the next day to excuse the neglect, which was worse than the neglect itself . . .[31]

Others regarded a parliamentary career as a means to advancement in other spheres—in the law, the armed services, and the civil service— and as a means of seeking political office and the profits and honours that could be gained from it.

The supply of candidates could in certain places and in certain circumstances be governed by conventions whose origins can now be only dimly perceived. In Lincolnshire, for example, a powerful tradition demanded that candidates should come equally from the north and south of the county. Similar geographical conventions persisted in East and West Kent, East and West Somerset, East and West Sussex, and North and South Wiltshire.[32] In these—and in other—constituencies, of course, informal contacts between different individuals, families, interests, and organizations would govern the emergence of a candidate. In Wiltshire, candidatures were regulated and approved at the Deptford Club, an association of country gentlemen and peers which arranged candidatures from 1729 to 1812 and possibly even later. In the counties the formality of a county meeting usually ratified and approved the arrangements made informally by its social leaders. In some places this echo of popular approval of candidatures was more loudly maintained. In Tewkesbury at the general election of 1754 a group of voters resolved to support only candidates who would contribute towards the repair of the roads.[33] Even in the counties the freeholders might on occasion repudiate the choice of their superiors.[34] Their sensibilities were always a factor to be reckoned with. Fitzwilliam, for all his property and popularity in Yorkshire, made an ostentatious display of refusing even to suggest a replacement for Lascelles in 1812, preferring to leave all such decisions to the

---

[31] William Poole to Duke of Newcastle, 12 Feb. 1761, BL Add. MSS. 32918 fo. 487, Newcastle Papers. Other sections of this interesting letter are cited in Namier and Brooke, *House of Commons*, iii. 127, in the biography of Medley.

[32] *Thoughts of a Lincolnshire Freeholder* (Lincoln, 1795), 26–7. George Grenville wrote to Lord Hyde on 29 Sept. 1763 that the death of Knatchbull left a vacancy for the county of Kent 'which must be supplied with an East Kent man'. *Additional Grenville Papers, 1763–65* (Manchester, 1962), 45. See also 53–4. See also Thorne, *House of Commons*, i. 14.

[33] Namier and Brooke, *House of Commons*, i. 292.

[34] For a rare instance see B. Bonsall, *Sir James Lowther and Cumberland and Westmorland Elections, 1754–1775* (Manchester, 1960), 76.

freeholders.[35] As for the boroughs, it was by no means unknown for voters in the more venal constituencies like Hull and Northampton to run their own candidate, thus asserting their influence and advertising the competitive nature of electioneering. In 1784 a voters' candidate emerged, opposed to the candidate of the dominant Spencer interest at Northampton, 'supported by a few of the malcontents of the Compton interest and all that description of people who are always desirous of a third man'.[36] Even in more respectable constituencies, the voters themselves were perfectly capable of acting in a wholly non-venal manner in an endeavour to influence the choice of candidates. At York at the election of 1784 frequent meetings of voters were held in an attempt to find someone to run against Henry Duncombe, the parliamentary reformer.[37] Elsewhere, candidates frequently refer to the popular pressures which accompanied their agreement to run, a ploy which no doubt served to excuse their presumption in disturbing the peace of the county or borough.[38] At Liverpool, apparently, both the corporation and anti-corporation interests selected their candidates at public adoption meetings to which all electors were invited. The favourable reception attending William Roscoe's meeting persuaded many to support him in 1806.[39] The extent of such 'popular', if sometimes venal, candidatures cannot now be exactly measured. Their existence serves to remind us, however, that there were well-established and well-understood conventions governing candidatures which inhibited the arbitrary imposition of an unpopular candidate upon a sullen and resentful constituency.

Indeed, there were unwritten, informal conventions concerning the characteristics to be sought in parliamentary candidates. In the late nineteenth century and twentieth century, a parliamentary candidate has become the local representative of a national political organization. Before that date, particular significance still attached to the personal

[35] After his success in seeing his son, Lord Milton, elected in 1807, Fitzwilliam was sensibly cautious. 'Respecting the selection of the Person, we can have nothing to say, nor to advise. Milton feels too much the extent of favour he solicits for himself, to presume to think either Who shall be his colleague, or to have in contemplation the making of a joint and common cause with any Gentleman, by whatever respectable Party he may be brought forward, or however much the Gentleman himself might be respected and beloved by him,' (Fitzwilliam to Mr Dixon, 27 Sept. 1812, F. 42*b*, Fitzwilliam MSS, Sheffield Pub. Lib.).
[36] Earl Spencer to the Dowager Lady Spencer, 29 Mar. 1784, Althorp MSS, Althorp Hall, Northants.
[37] J. Fountayne to Fitzwilliam, 9 Nov. 1783, F. 35*e*, Fitzwilliam MSS, Sheffield Pub. Lib.
[38] Such references are to be found in the Lincolnshire constituencies, e.g. at Boston in 1830 (*Sketch of the Boston Election* (Boston, 1830), 45, 61–3; *Poll for the County of Lincoln* (Lincoln, 1807), 4; *A Collection of the Addresses . . . Great Grimsby* (T. Squire, 1820), 19, 22–3.
[39] B. Whittingham-Jones, '*The History of Liverpool Politics, 1761–1835*', 2 vols., ii.555; Thomas Booth to William Roscoe, n.d., Roscoe MSS, 335, Liverpool Pub. Lib.

qualities of the candidate. The ideal candidate should be accessible, approachable, and sensitive to the wishes of the constituency. This meant that he should be a local man, of honour, reputation, and integrity, known to everybody. He should be a gentleman but he should be cordial with all classes. He should command the platform, silence the heckler, and amuse the crowd. He should be a representative of a long-established local family, possessing a settled estate in or near the constituency. In Wales, indeed, candidates for the county were not above claiming descent from the princes, chieftains, or noble families of Wales.[40] The ownership of property was almost always a necessity in the counties. One sitting member was hounded out of his Kent county seat in 1830 for his want of it.[41] In borough seats, too, local landed families were more than welcome. As one aspiring candidate for the City of Exeter put it: 'The City of Exeter ought to be represented by Old families of the County.'[42] There were good reasons for this. Independent wealth and solid local standing were cardinal virtues in a candidate for a proud city. The tradition and experience of local service which such families had accumulated were always relevant electoral considerations. Some towns might have more specific requirements—Liverpool, for example, demanded a representative who could further the trade and international commerce of the town[43]—but the moral was the same: the interests of the constituency must be advanced.

Traditions of local service founded upon intimate knowledge of the needs of the constituency, together with the bonds of gratitude forged by generosity and protection for the needy and the infirm, powerfully boosted a candidate's prospects. This was a big issue at Malton in 1807 when Fitzwilliam's agents were worried about the record of their own interest. Leatham, their opponent, was hospitable and generous to the poor, 'and his behaviour to the poor during that year of dreadful scarcity [1799–1800] is remembered greatly to his advantage on the present occasion'. Leatham, in fact, had sent wagon-loads of barley to the market in a successful attempt to lower market prices. The

[40] Rees, 'Parliamentary Representation of South Wales', ch. 3; id., 'Electioneering Ideals Current in South Wales, 1790–1832', *Welsh Hist. Rev.* 2 (1965), 233–4.

[41] J. H. Andrews, 'Political Issues in the County of Kent, 1820–1846', M.Phil. (London, 1967), 14.

[42] W. Courtenay to the Mayor of Exeter, 8 June 1802, 58/30/5, Courtenay MSS, Devon RO.

[43] For example, the extensive election literature for the contest of 1761 concentrated exclusively upon the likely competence of the three candidates at furthering the commerce of Liverpool. The new candidate, Sir William Meredith, was a country gentleman and therefore roundly attacked for his ignorance of commerce. See the Williamson Collection of election literature at Liverpool Pub. Lib. 97, 99, 100, 103–5, 108–9, 114–15.

Fitzwilliam interest, on the other hand, had hoarded scarce food, especially fish and potatoes.[44] Substantial reserves of wealth were an irresistible advantage in electioneering, especially if they were liberally bestowed upon the constituency, its inhabitants and, of course, its voters. In particular, displays of paternalism were well designed not merely to attract favourable publicity and comment but also to silence the protests of Tory, radical, or independent critics of proprietorial politics. (An outsider was starting from a severe disadvantage in all but the most closed and most venal constituencies.) A successful candidate, moreover, would be keen to reward his supporters for their efforts and his friends for their loyalty by making available to them local offices, favours, and licences, as well as making his own intercessions on their behalf. Local patronage must be readily forthcoming and must be available to local men. It caused great offence if local places found their way into the hands of outsiders.[45] At the parliamentary level, he would be expected to attend regularly, to promote the needs and interests of the constituency, to represent local sentiment on the great issues of the day, and, in most places, to demonstrate loyalty to the constitution, the monarchy, and the established church.

Not surprisingly, the origins and personalities of the candidates could themselves become important issues at elections simply because they impinged upon profoundly important issues of electoral morality. Details concerning the background, family, residence, opinion, and personality of the candidate and of his relationship with the constituency and its electors were of the first importance. Indeed, their prominence has much to do with that characteristic of the unreformed electorate which has puzzled generations of historians—its alleged indifference to the great national issues which were increasingly coming to influence parliamentary politics. Such indifference is to be accounted for neither by corruption on the part of the electorate, nor by any inability on its part to think politically. Questions of political significance to Westminster politicians seemed much less real to voters than critically important issues concerning the welfare and prosperity of the constituency at a time of rapid social and economic change, the status and activities of those in authority over them, and the treatment of its institutions.

---

[44] John Cleaver to Lord Fitzwilliam, 5 May 1807, F.72–10, Fitzwilliam Papers, Wentworth Woodhouse MSS, Sheffield Pub. Lib.

[45] See the indignant letter protesting 'that yr. Friends at Hull are much offended that you and yr. Friend Mr Hartley should be so Slighting as to suffer such a Paltry Inland Town as Haddon, that pays not a Thousand Part of the Duty to the King as Doth this Corporation, notwithstanding they are suffered to Interfere with it as for Example, when any Place or Imployment is Vacant'. W. Willson to Sir George Savile (24 Feb. 1779), D/EHy/1047, (Hartley-Russell MSS, Berks. RO).

It was the right attitudes rather than the right policies that were required. To avoid giving offence to some sections within the electorate, candidates usually said as little as possible about policy. E. J. Walhouse, attempting in 1812 to succeed his recently deceased father in the Staffordshire county seat, affected a posture of awesome modesty: 'When I reflect upon my age, and the little opportunity that has presented itself to me of cultivating your acquaintance, I feel a degree of diffidence in thus offering myself to your attention.' Confessing his ignorance of the 'Manufacturing Interests of this great County', he pledged himself nevertheless to pursue the 'freedom, happiness and prosperity of the County'.[46] Elections were thus about personalities as much as politics. Not all contests, however, would have been quite as consensual as the Berkshire county contest of 1812, when all three candidates were pledged to parliamentary reform.[47] Even candidates who were not short of political courage usually refrained from stirring up the electorate with dramatic expositions of their opinions. The two MPs for Nottingham had controversially come out against the American War in the 1770s but their election addresses in 1780 were silent on the issue. Daniel Parker Coke blandly declared: 'It is my determined Resolution, faithfully to attend my duty in Parliament, where the welfare of the Kingdom in general, and that of this opulent town in particular, shall be (my) constant Care and Study.' Robert Smith was only slightly more forthcoming, believing, 'that my past Conduct in Parliament, has convinced you, that, I have always considered your delegation as a sacred Trust, and should I now, be so highly distinguished, as to be re-chosen your REPRESENTATIVE, I shall continue to make my Public Duty, the first object of my Life with an especial Attention to the Dignity, Welfare and Happiness of this great Commercial Town'.[48] That summed it up. Since elections focused essentially upon the candidate, his suitability for the constituency, and the likelihood of his being of service to its inhabitants, it followed that the election campaign would agitate issues of parliamentary and national concern only in so far as they impinged upon these primary, local concerns. The conclusion is inescapable that there existed highly developed, if informal, criteria for parliamentary candidates to observe. This is, in my view, a conceptual half-way house between Professor Kishlansky's somewhat exaggerated contrast

---

[46] Handbill declaring candidature, vol. 2 of bound volumes in the Hatherton MSS on the 1812 Staffordshire Election, Staffs. RO.

[47] *Poll of the Freeholders* (Abingdon, 1812), 1–14. Things could change very rapidly, however. The contest of 1818 in Berkshire was something of an ideological epic, with almost daily discussion of national issues.

[48] M.479/107–8, Smith-Godfrey Notts. RO.

between personal and political influences in the selection of parliamentary candidates ('the diminution of the social side of selection in favor of the political one depersonalised selections').[49] In some ways, personal qualities became *more*, not less, demanding when political and ideological considerations agitated the electorate. It does not seem to me to be particularly rewarding to argue that the former gave way to the latter as the eighteenth century advanced. What seems to have happened is that personal considerations remained of all-consuming relevance to elections, but that political issues were always capable of accompanying them. Depending for their exact balance upon local circumstances, we can only conclude that elections might turn upon some combination of both personal and political circumstances.

## Campaigns

An election campaign began formally with the dissolution of the old Parliament and the issues of the writ of summons for the holding of elections to the new. The writs were despatched from the clerk of the crown in Chancery to the sheriffs, who, in turn, despatched a precept to the returning officers of all seats within each county. No formal directions existed concerning these communications. Not before 1813 was it made compulsory for the writs to be carried by the Post Office. No time was fixed by law for their delivery. Consequently, government supporters could establish an advantage over their opponents if they had advance notice of a dissolution. The two days' notice they enjoyed in 1807 is the most significant example in this period, but it is not the only one.[50] Such an advantage enabled them to begin to seek support, to procure agents, to generate publicity, to begin fund-raising, and to book conveyances. An early start might, in fact, give one side such an advantage as to decide its potential opponents against a contest. It was not merely advance notice of a dissolution which might convey such an advantage. Interference with the writs, causing their sudden appearance or their inexplicable delay, was fairly common. The House of Commons was notoriously unwilling to attend to partisan interference with the timing and communication of the writs.[51] Sometimes, however, it was merely general inefficiency and natural confusion which delayed the communication of the writ, and special measures might need to be taken to speed its arrival.

[49] Kishlansky, *Parliamentary Selection*, 193; see also 21, 111.
[50] Hinton, 'General Elections of 1806 and 1807', Ph.D., 488.
[51] S. Heywood, *A Digest of the Law Respecting Borough Elections* (London, 1798), 88. 'The House seems not till of late years, to have been strict in enquiring after or severe in punishing delays.'

Once the writ reached the returning officer, normally the mayor or bailiff in the boroughs and the sheriff in the counties, there was further possibility of malpractice. Although an Act of 1696 had checked the earlier abuse of witholding notice of the arrival of the writ, it was still up to the returning officer to decide the date of the election. Although the election had to be held within eight days of the receipt of the precept—and public notice of the time and place of the election had to be issued—it was still possible to give one or other side a few days' advantage.[52]

The returning officer was obviously in a position of very great potential influence. Not only could he decide the date, time, and place of the election, he was also responsible for its conduct and the maintenance of order. It was his responsibility to secure the attendance of the appropriate number of clerks and officials and to settle with those contesting the election who should attend on their behalf. Even more important, the determination of disputed franchise credentials lay in his hands. In county elections he would engage the services of an assessor, normally a solicitor or barrister, to advise him. He might well need such assistance, because after the Act of 1745 each hundred had its own booth, and each booth its own clerks to take the poll. The possibilities of error and partiality are evident. To tighten up the system, an Act of 1780 required the clerk of the peace or his deputy to attend county polls with copies of the land tax assessments to facilitate the determination of franchise questions.[53] In borough elections the returning officer might discharge such responsibility personally. In burgage boroughs, in particular, where legal wrangles over the ownership of property and over the franchises attributed to them were endemic, these responsibilities were of critical importance. They could also be decisive in freeman boroughs, where the rights of non-resident, temporary freemen might be in dispute. The Durham Act of 1763 restricted the vote to freemen of one year's standing and required the returning officer to maintain a book (the first hint of a register) listing those entitled to vote. No guidance and no penalties accompanied these provisions, however, and much was left to the discretion of the returning officer.

The possibilities of returning officers abusing their authority were limitless. For example, at the Coventry election of 1780, the polling

---

[52] A further Act of 1746 required the returning officer to give three days notice of the election.

[53] The Act itself caused confusion. It was not immediately clear whether the clerk or his deputy should attend in person (they should) or whether their attendance needed to be invited by the candidates (it did). See a copy of the Act and an interesting counsel's opinion, CD5/4/858, Smith Godfrey MSS, Notts. RO.

booth was ominously positioned directly in front of the mayor's parlour. Even more ominously, it was connected by a private way to an inn traditionally loyal to the cause of the corporation.[54] A disputed return was the only possible outcome. Contemporaries were understandably sensitive about the role of the returning officer. At the Lincolnshire by-election of 1823 the mere rumour of the appointment of a returning officer whose impartiality was questionable caused an immediate uproar and the withdrawal of the nominee.[55] How common the corruption of returning officers was is difficult to assess. It was probably kept in check by the readiness of an injured party to petition against the return in the case of such official corruption.

The returning officer, furthermore, had the responsibility, sometimes vital, of maintaining public order during elections. It might, for example, be advisable to appoint extra constables from among the substantial and respectable inhabitants of a town. Emergency arrangements were sometimes called for, especially if the two sides had physically to be kept apart. At the 1830 Boston nomination, for example, business was conducted on the balcony of the new Assembly Rooms with the populace beneath. 'The Blues occupied the end adjoining the fish-market, and the Pinks that nearest the bridge.'[56] Thereafter, the returning officer had to ensure that each elector's voting preferences were accurately recorded in the official poll books. The returning officer's final responsibilities related to the declaration of the result and to the closing ceremonies of the election. Nevertheless, every candidate could demand a scrutiny of how the votes were cast, and this the returning officer had to undertake.

Although election campaigns could last for several weeks or even months, it was none the less essential for a candidate to announce his candidature at the earliest possible moment, usually as soon as the returning officer had announced the election date. Declarations made before this announcement were much disliked as betokening a cavalier attitude towards the peace of the borough or county.[57] In the counties

---

[54] T. Whitley, *Parliamentary Representation of the City of Coventry* (Coventry, 1894), 178; *Jopson's Coventry Mercury*, 18 Sept. 1780. A similar trick was tried at the election of 1804 at Aylesbury where a passageway connected the town hall, a nearby public house, and the county jail. See *Report of the Committee on the Aylesbury Petition* (London, 1804), 7.

[55] The friends of Sir W. Amcotts-Ingilby protested at the possibility of Sir John Thorold becoming returning officer. Sir John had already promised his vote to Ingilby's opponent. *Poll for the Election . . . Lincolnshire* (1824), 8.

[56] *A Sketch of the Boston Election* (Boston, 1830), pp. xxi–xxii.

[57] Especially in the counties, where it was considered fatal to a candidacy to make any move before a county meeting. See John Chetwode to M. Walhouse, 25 May 1812, Hatherton MSS, no. 5, Staffs. RO. For the assertion that it was 'unconstitutional' to canvass Leicester county before the county meeting see R. Heathcote, *Memoirs of the Late Contested Election* (Leicester, 1818), 2–3.

a special county meeting, held several months or even a year before an election was expected, might clarify the situation, providing the opportunity for a Member to announce his impending retirement or for county worthies to catechize their representatives on their parliamentary record and to decide on the representation. Precipitate electioneering was usually counter-productive. Of course, rumours of likely candidatures, some of them innocent but some of them no doubt carefully contrived in order to test the electoral water, circulated in the weeks and months prior to an election. These might indicate which way the wind might blow. The real as opposed to the phoney electoral battle commenced, however, with the announcements of candidature and the circulation of the candidates' statements or addresses. Frequently written by election agents and committee men, these addresses were largely platitudinous, complimentary to the electors and to the constituency, rehearsing the candidate's past, present, and future contributions to the life of the constituency in unexceptionably heroic terms.[58] These were publicized through some combination of paid newspaper advertising, circulation by hand, public display, personal letters to the electors, and even by the holding of public dinners. Such early announcement of a candidature was an indispensable means of publicizing a possible candidate's intentions, of forestalling rival candidatures (on one's own as well as on one's opponents' side), of making an early appeal to the electors, and of determining the issues on which the contest was to proceed.

Thereafter, the organizational machines of the rival interests swung into action in a full-scale attempt to procure support for their candidates. While committees met to plot and plan, while agents swarmed all over the constituency, and while the formal canvass proceeded, a veritable torrent of rival publicity—squibs, poems, songs, cartoons, handbills, letters, and advertisements—deluged the constituency. Meanwhile candidates gave optimistic estimates of the state of opinion and the progress of the canvass, along with repeated denials of corruption, coalition, and discourtesy. Daily speeches, celebrations, parades, displays, treats, and dinners fostered and maintained the excitement, enthusiasm, and involvement of the public.

[58]  The standard 19th-cent. guide to electoral organization was Edward W. Cox's *Hints to Solicitors for the Conduct of an Election*, first published in 1868. This guide was obviously directed at the electoral conditions following the 1832 Reform Act, but Cox had been active in elections since 1824 and some of his observations may relate to conditions before 1832. As might be expected, the cynical Cox stressed the inability of candidates to compose these addresses. ('A prudent manager will not permit the candidate to frame an address without his own careful revision.') He further stresses the need for simplicity. ('See that the sentences are short.') Open University edn. (Milton Keynes, 1974), 13–14.

The campaigning and canvassing would continue until polling day. As Cox remarked: 'A canvass is never complete until the poll is closed.'[59] At the appointed time the returning officer, the candidates, their sponsors, friends, and other notable worthies would climb the hustings. The returning officer would then read out the writ. He would then read the oaths of allegiance, supremacy, and abjuration. Next were read Acts of Parliament against bribery and corruption. Finally (in freeman boroughs), the Act of 1763 excluding occasional freemen from voting was read. Each candidate would then be nominated and seconded by eminent and weighty supporters. In their speeches the virtues of the candidate, his local connections, his independence, and his statemanship would be lavishly extolled. The candidate would then enlarge upon his own virtues in a speech which needed to be lofty, gentlemanly, magnanimous, and good-humoured. Personal invective and political vituperation he would leave to his nominators and seconders. Thereafter it was open to members of the public to make their contributions. On the minority of occasions when they *were* forthcoming, they can usually be identified as local party stalwarts or local characters determined to make a point.[60] Nevertheless, such contributions maintained the illusion of popular participation and the tradition of unrestricted expression of opinion. What proportion of the crowds could hear any part of the speeches amidst the lively atmosphere of noise, interruption, and possibly even minor outbreaks of violence cannot be precisely calculated. It was probably not large.

After the nominations were completed and the speeches ended, the returning officer might call for a show of hands. (If there was no opposition then the successful election of the candidates would be announced without a show.[61]) If there was an opposition, a show of hands would follow. Election managers, in fact, went to elaborate lengths to ensure that their candidates came successfully through this first ordeal. One of Lord Milton's agents thought that if Lascelles outperformed Milton at the show of hands in 1807, '*it* will be a prejudice to us in the *popular* opinion, notwithstanding our Declarations to stand

---

[59] Ibid. 15.

[60] The intervention of one Mr Bickeno of Newbury at the Berkshire County nomination meeting of 1818 was such a case. He was anxious to repudiate the parliamentary reform sentiments of one of the candidates who had argued that all taxpayers should have the vote. Bickeno's construction of 'taxpayers' as including indirect taxpayers was singular. *The Poll of the Freeholders* (Windsor, 1818), 42–3.

[61] It should perhaps be stressed that the formalities described above were forthcoming even if there was no opposition. Certainly, in all but the meanest boroughs, the candidates were strongly expected to attend. See the discussion on this point in the correspondence between Henry Welbore and Sir William Pierce Ashe A'Court, 1796, MSS of the Borough of Heytesbury, No. 135, Wilts. RO.

a Poll . . . and I think we should meet the shew of hands with vigour . . . Will it not dismay the House of Harewood. Or at any rate it will shew our Spirit, support our friends and dishearten our adversaries.'[62] Since, however, there was absolutely no possibility of distinguishing between electors and non-electors in the crowd, and since customary practices made no provision for establishing such a distinction, the 'losing' side at the show of hands invariably demanded a poll. This was almost always granted by the returning officer.[63] The clerks were sworn in and the polling of the voters began.

Both sides, of course, would have anticipated the need for a poll. Immense pains would already have been taken to bring to the meeting a large number of reliable voters who had been fully canvassed and whose support could be counted on. Other voters would be in reserve, saved up for later in the poll. While they waited to poll they would receive adequate supplies of food, drink, and possibly even entertainment. They would be housed at inns, at public buildings, in temporary structures, and even in tents and marquees in order to keep them together and to protect them from the attentions of opposition agents as well as the weather. The better the voters were marshalled, the more easily their polling could be organized. Voters polled in tallies, usually of 10, sometimes as many as 20, and the contest lasted until the tallies of one side were exhausted. Between 10 and 20 tallies would poll each day, a total of somewhere between 100 and 400 voters. The length of the contest thus depended upon the number of voters to be polled.

The polling took place at hustings specially erected or converted for the occasion. It was from the hustings, of course, that nominations were made and speeches and declarations of the count during the poll delivered. During the poll the candidates, the returning officer, and the poll clerks would sit on the hustings. In the earlier part of the period, and in tiny constituencies later, the hustings might be little more than a raised, open platform. As time went on and the size of electorates increased, the hustings became more elaborate, vastly enlarged, and sometimes even roofed. The erection of the hustings began as soon as the proclamation fixing the date and time of the election had been read. Perhaps inevitably, 'the operation of the workmen attracting as is wont a crowd of idlers who appeared to look on with deep interest,

---

[62] Thomas Tottie to the Committee of Lord Milton, 16 May 1807, Fc.163/6, Fitzwilliam MSS, Sheffield Pub. Lib.

[63] It was the returning officer's responsibility to decide whether the taking of the poll should be held as a separate convocation to the nomination meeting. My impression is that he was often persuaded to do so if there was a petition from one or both sides signed by a considerable number of people.

in joyous anticipation of the expected scenes of the following week'.[64]
On the hustings would be placed the poll bars. These were tables or
desks at which sat the poll clerks who recorded the votes of each voter.
In most constituencies the hustings would be erected outdoors but in
some central place, such as a market square or outside the town
hall. In some of the tiniest boroughs, however, the hustings might
be erected indoors, inside the town hall, the sessions house, or
even, as in the 1830 contest at Boston, inside a church. Such
assemblies, being hot, congested, and noisy, were invariably
unpopular.

To expedite the lengthy process of polling at county elections and
in some of the larger boroughs, the poll would be taken not at the
hustings but in specially constructed polling booths. These were erected
in front of the hustings.[65] These were enclosed structures. Inside them
a representative of the returning officer, a polling clerk, and agents
and messengers of both sides engaged in the contest would sit around
a table covered in (usually green) baize cloth. The voters would queue
up and shuffle through a complex succession of bars, each guarded
by a constable. The exercise of the suffrage could therefore be a
tolerably private affair. It is certainly not the case that voters had
invariably to vote in front of a jeering multitude. Nevertheless, privacy
was not greatly prized; suspicion of secrecy as betokening collusion
and corruption remained extraordinarily powerful.

The poll was taken in the following manner. The voter approached
the bar, table, or hustings and was asked by the returning officer for
the details of his qualification. At a county election, he would need to
provide his name, address, occupation, and the location of the freehold
which carried the franchise and the name of the occupants.[66] This

---

[64] J. Gore, *The Poll for the Election of 1830* (Liverpool, 1830), p. xiii.

[65] Their precise arrangement, convenience, and accessibility sometimes exercised returning
officers and election committees. See e.g. 'Memorandum of Various Considerations respecting
the Polling Booths', Coventry, n.d. 1780, Sheffield MSS, 122, Coventry RO.

[66] Towards the end of the 18th cent. there were a number of schemes to modernize both
the county franchise and the taking of the poll in county elections. Largely owing to Charles,
3rd Earl Stanhope, a stream of bills dealing with the registration of county voters was presented
in 1785, 1786, and 1788. For details of the unsuccessful fortunes of the first two of these see
G. M. Ditchfield, 'The House of Lords and Parliamentary Reform in the 1780s', *Bull. Inst.
Hist. Res.* 54/130 (1981), esp. 210–13. The bill of 1788 passed, however. Its main features
included the compilation of an official register of freeholders eligible to vote in elections. Stanhope
endeavoured to make the procedure as straightforward as possible and free from bureaucratic
interference. He had underestimated the likely cost of implementing the scheme—£55,000 for
printing costs alone—and reaction in the counties. Eighteen of the 40 English counties petitioned
against it, and a repeal bill was rushed through in 1789 to prevent the scheme being used at
the forthcoming general election. (Ditchfield, 'Parliamentary Reform', 215–16. There is, however,
further evidence of the unpopularity of the act even in places which did not petition; see e.g.
debate of 12 Mar. 1789, *Parliamentary Register*, xxv. 492–3.) For William Pitt's sympathetic

information enabled not only the officials but also the agents on each side to check these details against the land tax returns. At this point the poll agents for each side might question the voter if they could spot a weakness in his qualifications. If the voter's answers failed to resolve the difficulty, the poll agent might enter an objection against the voter. It was then up to the assessor to reach a decision, a process which normally involved an interview with the elector in question and his interrogation by the agent, attorney, or even counsel of both sides. Once his qualifications to the franchise had been approved, the elector would inform the official how he wished his votes to be cast. He would then be dismissed through the back door of the booth. In boroughs, variations in the franchise dictated slight variations of practice. In freeman boroughs a list or roll of qualified freemen, usually in the order of their admission, would be available, and a freeman would need to do little more than establish his identity. In some of the smaller freeman boroughs the roll was read out several times, thus enabling objections to be made against the voters as their names were called.[67] In burgage boroughs, evidence of 'ownership' of the burgages was usually called for, and papers had to be produced. In the boroughs enjoying some kind of residential qualification such evidence was not quite so strictly demanded. In all types of constituency, however, once the vote was cast it was recorded by clerks in lists of the poll. Messengers, runners, and agents for each side noted the vote, calculated the totals, and adjusted their lists of likely supporters accordingly.

At his discretion and depending on the circumstances, the returning officer and his clerks, and, more usually, the poll agents of each side in the election, were free to administer to each voter a number of oaths to swear. These were of two broad types: the loyalty and the bribery oaths. An elector whose loyalty to the crown was even mildly suspected might be required to take either the unexceptionable oath of allegiance, promising 'true allegiance' to the monarch, or the oath of abjuration, affirming the monarch's right to the throne. Those suspected of Roman Catholicism might be required to swear the transubstantiation oath which, of course, acknowledged the doctrines of the Anglican, while repudiating those of the Roman, church. A somewhat more general oath for those thought to be disloyal was the supremacy oath, which fairly thoroughly repudiated the authority and jurisdiction of the church

---

reception of the principle of Stanhope's Act see his speeches in the Commons, 27 Mar. 1789, ibid. xxv. 535–42. For later attempts to (unsuccessfully) establish registers of voters see J. Prest, *Politics in the Age of Cobden* (London, 1979) 5–9. This useful account of the bills of Russell, Althorp, and Nugent in 1828 badly needs to be extended by further research.

[67] This happened at Newcastle-under-Lyme, with its electorate of 600; *A Copy of the Poll* (Newcastle, 1790).

of Rome, the Pretenders, and indeed any other 'foreign prime, person, prelate, state, or potentate'. The bribery oath, on the other hand, required the voter to state that no money, gift, nor reward had come his way, a somewhat implausible assertion. The administration of the bribery oath was usually nothing more than a tactical device to challenge particular voters and classes of voters against whom some irregularity might be demonstrated. Everyone practised treating, and transfers of money were universal. It was therefore extremely dangerous for one side to protest and to petition against electoral practices of which both sides were equally guilty and to which the electors had become indissolubly attached. Indeed, there are instances of both sides in a contest agreeing not to tender the bribery oath.

It is not easy to estimate what proportion of electors were challenged and thus had the oaths tendered to them. At Liverpool, apparently, the bribery oath was only twice administered between 1796 and 1830. In the counties the oaths were tendered more frequently. Nevertheless, the estimate reached by the Select Committee on County Election Polls, 1826–7, that one-third of freeholders were challenged, seems a serious exaggeration.[68]

When the votes had been cast they were recorded in official poll books. An Act of 1696 compelled the returning officer to take down details of the voter's qualifications and the disposal of his votes. A further Act of 1745 permitted each candidate to keep a check on the poll in a cheque book. This provision greatly facilitated the publication of the poll books, the indispensable source for the electoral historian. It was a straightforward matter, therefore, for the returning officer, possibly assisted and checked by a small committee of officials, to count the votes and announce the state of the poll each evening.

What happened at Bedford seems fairly typical of polling under this system:

The first step is to get a Copy of the Books of Freemen and Burgesses from the Town Clerk and particular Care should be taken that you have a true Copy . . . The poll is conducted by the Mayor and 2 Burgesses who have 2 Check Clerks as also has every candidate, and when the Poll closes each day they examine one list, for which are made into 3 (the London, Bedford

---

[68] Whittingham-Jones, 'Liverpool Politics', i. 379; Prest, *Politics in the Age of Cobden*, repeats the claim made by the select committee. See *Parliamentary Papers, 1826–1827*, iv. 1105–6. Stoker ('Elections and Voting Behaviour'. A Study of Elections in Northumberland, Durham, Cumberland, and Westmorland, 1760–1832, Ph.D. (Manchester, 1980) 154–5) has estimated that in the northern counties between 4% and 18% of voters might be challenged. At Yorkshire in 1807, 1,852 voters were refused their credentials out of the 24,215 who applied (7.6%) (*York Herald*, 20 June 1807). At Dorset county election in 1831, 300 out of 3,000 voters had their credentials challenged. See the correspondence of the Ashley interest, item KY 92, 4119, in the Bankes MSS, Dorset RO.

Town, and Country Votes.) With the Poll Books wrote by our Clerks, and check of all that have Voted [sic]. Three Attorneys attend the Hustings each day, one with a list of the London Voters, another Bedford Voters and another the Country Voters, and as soon as a Voter's Name is announced they search in their lists for it and if he is not entered he is no freeman. The Householders are only checked by receiving Alms and when any Account is given during the Canvass and Election it ought to be put in the list against the Name that when the Check Clerk looks at the name whilst the town is polling he may instruct the Counsel to reject him. The Check Clerk who takes the Poll for the Committee should send an account every half hour to the Committee . . . and a Messenger should be stationed for the express purpose of bringing the State of the Poll to the Committee. The Attorney who attends the Committee will check them off as they arrive . . . He should have plenty of Messengers to fetch up Voters towards the Close.

All information respecting Voters should be entered in one book by the Chairman.[69]

The system clearly thrived on claim and counter-claim. Consequently, the worst abuses and excesses were limited by the checks and restraints which accompanied the more competitive elements in the process of polling.

Polling hours varied from place to place but they seem normally to have been from 8.30 a.m. or 9.00 a.m. to 4.00 p.m. or a little later. Earlier closing on market day, or of course on the last day of the poll, was not unknown. Until 1785 the poll could theoretically remain open for as many days as there were electors to poll. It is not clear how stringently the Act of 1696 which imposed a maximum of 40 days was enforced. Nevertheless, the incredible length of the Westminster election of 1784—the polls remained open from 1 April to 17 May—provoked enormous alarm and indignation, which led to the Act of 1785 restricting polls to 15 days, not including Sundays.

The rate of polling could be influenced by a variety of factors, such as the number of booths, the firmness of the returning officer, and the vigilance of the poll agents on each side. This latter could be decisive. As the Select Committee Appointed to Inquire into the Taking of Election Polls in Cities and Boroughs (1827) quickly discovered, a variety of expedients could be adopted. One side might slow down the rate of polling in order to frustrate its opponents, involving them in the additional expense of accommodating voters. Once in the lead, it might be very tempting for a candidate and his advisers to instruct their poll agents to slow down the poll by indulging in near vexatious protests against voters. Accusations of this sort of activity are, however, more easily found than evidence to support them. One of the worst

---

[69] Bedford Town Election, 1790, WG 2654, Beds. RO.

TABLE 3.4 *Rate of Polling at Preston Elections, 1812–1826*

| Year | Total votes | 1st day | 1st 3 days | Duration of poll (days) |
|------|-------------|---------|------------|-------------------------|
| 1812 | 3,474 | 59 | 807 | 8 |
| 1818 | 4,537 | 136 | 1,337 | 7 |
| 1820 | 6,203 | 210 | 874 | 13 |
| 1826 | 7,566 | 114 | 320 | 15 |

*Source:* W. Addison, *An Alphabetical List of the Electors* (Preston, 1812, 1818, 1820); L. Clarke, *An Alphabetical List of Persons . . . 1830* (Preston, 1831).

examples of slow voting came at Preston in 1826, when William Cobbett was a candidate. Day after day he justifiably complained that the slow progress of the poll threatened to disfranchise half of the Preston electorate and to damage his own prospects (see Table 3.4). Only when mob violence threatened to get out of hand did the mayor agree to speed up the poll, in this case by abandoning the use of tallies. Other constituencies, however, had a reasonably consistent rate of polling when one contest, or any part of a contest, is compared to another.[70]

To prevent chaos and confusion, polling was almost always conducted in tallies of men of the same interest, usually 10 but sometimes 12, 16, or, at most, 20. There was no legal necessity for this. It was a customary practice and one which was almost universally adopted. Each voter was allocated to a tally and came under the authority of a tally leader or captain, often an influential and respected individual capable of getting his tally from the tally room, tent, or inn to the poll and back. The tally captain might even be a small patron and the tally his interest. The progress of a tally to the poll was a splendid event. Wearing the local party colours, and possibly carrying a banner or ribbons, the tally would be accompanied by a band and would march in a procession. The pomp and excitement of the occasion was the individual elector's great moment. Secure in his tally, and with the protection of his own well-marshalled party, he could enjoy his moment of public recognition. The candidates polled their tallies in turn. The reason for this was that an equality or near-equality on the poll prevented disruption and violence breaking out from a

[70] e.g. in Chester, where over almost half a century (1784–1826), with an almost 50% increase in voters (from 1,095 to 1,503), the average number of votes cast per day remained remarkably steady, ranging from 108 in 1812 to 139 in 1820.

disappointed losing side. In a straight fight, therefore, or where two candidates confronted two others, the excitement over numbers could be very great indeed.

An indispensable key to successful electioneering was a correct grasp of tally tactics. Indeed, many poll books give daily states of the poll, a suggestion of the importance contemporaries attached to the daily accumulation of votes. It was vital for the membership of each tally and the timing of its poll to be clearly understood. Since nothing looked worse than an incomplete tally, a core of reliable supporters would be on hand to make up any deficiency. Election managers agreed upon the virtues of keeping at least some reliable electors in reserve until the last. Normally, gentlemen were required to reserve their votes for the later stages of a poll in order to give the best possible appearance of weight and respectability during the critical last days of a contest. Generally, too, the higher-status voters tended to vote later in the day than the common run of voters for much the same reason. More important, in those constituencies with large numbers of outvoters, the timing of the arrival of these voters was a vital matter. Certainly, those engaged in a contest had to be prepared to bring up the London voters and other outvoters if they could not secure a commanding majority from the voters resident in the constituency. To do so in the last couple of days of a contest could be the mark of inspired electioneering, requiring as it did large numbers of helpers to accompany them. It was a card which was impossible to trump.

At the end of the 15th day—earlier if one side conceded defeat and withdrew from the contest—the returning officer would read each of the three proclamations which together legally terminated the poll. Legal niceties could dog this, as so many other, aspects of the poll. On the tenth day of the Lincolnshire county by-election of 1823:

> The polling went on so slowly this morning that the High Sheriff, in the exercise of the discretion vested in him by law, felt it necessary to issue a proclamation stating that unless the freeholders came forward to vote, the poll should be closed. The proclamation was made a second time within a quarter of an hour, and in a few minutes after, one vote was polled for Sir J. Thorold. The proclamation was of course issued afresh, and in this manner was the polling continued, so as merely to keep within the limits of the law.[71]

After a few hours of this sort of thing, both sides were happy to agree to the closing of the poll at 4.00 p.m. The declaration of the result was announced fairly quickly since little counting now needed to be done. After the crier had made the public announcement of the result

---

[71] *The Poll for the Election* (Lincoln, 1824), 61.

the closing speeches were made. These speeches, both victory and defeat, needed two qualities: magnanimity and—after weeks of exhausting activity—reasonable brevity.

After the declaration of the result and the speeches which accompanied it, the victorious candidates had manfully to reconcile themselves to the ceremony of the chairing. The experience of being carried amidst throngs of cheering—and possibly jeering—electors in decorated chairs around the town was the somewhat painful and embarrassing culmination of the election for the candidates concerned. The chairing was the final, great manifestation of political commitment and political loyalty, on the one hand, and of social prestige on the other. The chair would be gorgeously decorated and was often preceded by a guard of gaudily dressed horsemen. In a minutely defined order of procession, strictly observed 'in order to prevent the Confusion and Irregularity which might otherwise occur',[72] the worthies of the victorious party would accompany the chair, leaving other supporters and helpers to bring up the rear. Flags, colours, and music would lend an air of party conviviality to the celebrations. The restraint and formality of a county election chairing contrasted vividly with the clamour of the borough counterpart.

In the boroughs, fine social gradations were much less in evidence as the crowds milled around the chair, urging the Members to throw money. Even in the boroughs, however, attempts were made to keep order. The entire event was carefully stage-managed, the whole community responding to the festivities with its own customary disciplines. Brinksmanship might be threatened, but boisterousness rarely spilled over into violence and anarchy. In some places mock-chairings of the defeated candidates, or their representatives, have been identified.[73] Clearly, the candidates were not going to be allowed to escape lightly, nor were their supporters to be deprived of their entertainment. At the other extreme, particularly unpopular successful candidates might find it prudent to forego the chairing rather than risk the odium of the crowd.[74] At the end of the chairing the Members would be returned to their hotel, house, or headquarters, whereupon the chair would be torn to pieces by the increasingly inebriated crowd. Nevertheless, the likelihood of serious disorder was probably low.

Even this might not be the end, however. The chairing would be followed later the same evening by a huge treat or dinner for loyal

[72] Newark Handbills, n.d. no. 6, DDT 22. Tallents MSS, Notts. RO.

[73] *A Sketch of the Boston Election* (Boston, 1830), for example, mentions such a mock chairing (p. xxx).

[74] Wager, 'Welsh Politics and Parliamentary Reform', 238–9, relates the inability of John Frederick Campbell to stay for the chairing ceremony at Carmarthen in 1818.

supporters, sometimes supplemented by a rather more decorous affair for the local grandees of the party. In a larger constituency, the supporters might have to be billeted upon more than one inn, the Members having to circulate among them before retreating to their own rather less exhausting celebration.[75] Before they would quit their battle-field and seek out their beds, however, the hour would be late. The electors appeared to have as much stomach for the interminable toasts which punctuated their proceedings as they did for food and ale.

The theme of all this activity is carefully managed participation. Little was left to chance. The smallest details received the careful attention of election committees. Surviving committee books list minute jobs and activities and match these to the names of carefully selected individuals. There was plenty to do. People had to be found to march in parades and processions, to wear the (carefully chosen, designed, manufactured, and distributed) colours, ribbons, cockades, and banners. Cooks were needed to prepare food, servants to serve it, and others to wash up afterwards. There was a continuous need for music: for musicians, singers, writers, and choruses. Burly males had to be found to carry the chair its long and exhausting distance. Then there were the stewards and constables, horsemen and messengers. As Cox remarked, 'although electors cannot be employed, there is nothing to prohibit the employ of the sons and relatives of electors'.[76]

Most of all there was the propaganda. Newspapers were, of course, important but many towns did not have them before 1832, and, in any case, they appeared only weekly. Speedier communication demanded the rapid dissemination of information to convey a message, to develop a theme, to deny—or spread—a rumour, and to encourage supporters. This was achieved through the frequent printing and circulation of election squibs and handbills. Their sheer number is phenomenal. No fewer than 42,000 pieces of election literature circulated at the Carlisle by-election of 1816.[77] At the *aborted* 1812 Nottinghamshire county contest, 500 election addresses were distributed in Nottingham and 2,000 in the county.[78] Even in unexciting campaigns a minimum of 20 to 30 different propaganda sheets would be produced. These usually very undistinguished pieces of election literature were circulated on street corners, in market places,

---

[75] These proceedings were taken extremely seriously by the electors. Indeed, those in Nottingham in 1820 were deemed worthy of publication; see *Account of the Grand Dinner in Celebration of the Final Victory of Independence and the Substance of the Speeches Delivered on that Occasion* (Nottingham, 1820).

[76] Cox, *Hints to Solicitors*, 13–14.

[77] Stoker, 'Elections and Voting Behavior', Ph.D., 134.

[78] CP 5/2/1, no. 9, Smith Godfrey MSS, Notts. RO.

clubs, coffee-houses, and inns. Some would be posted on committee rooms, public buildings, and churches, and displayed in inns, clubs, and shops. The broadsheet ballad was written for those who found the normal run of election literature too exhausting, and in the later eighteenth century an immense outpouring of political verse began. None of this happened by accident or for amusement. The rival election organizations refused to believe that votes were altogether committed by influence and remained convinced that persuasion and argument might convince at least some of the electors of the virtues of rival claims and arguments.

In spite, then, of the degree of management, there can be no mistaking the implied claim to electoral participation. The politics of influence were in effect being merged in the politics of communal involvement. At its simplest, this meant the affirmation of the loyalty of hundreds, and probably thousands, of people to individuals, families, causes, and colours. Deeper themes repeat themselves. In so far as elections were politicizing experiences, they inculcated certain traditional values and extolled certain traditional virtues. These amount to an acceptance of an hierarchic, unequal society, but a society in which electors jealously guard their independence and thus their capacities to negotiate and bargain with their superiors. Elections manifest the electors' proud possession of the liberties and the freedom which guarantee their independence. Even in tiny Liskeard, at the general election of 1806 'almost every individual of the town and neighbourhood who could squeeze himself had insinuated himself there, for the avowed purpose of contending for a right, to which they had been led to suppose themselves entitled viz. that of voting for Member of Parliament'.[79] Election speeches and election literature hammer home certain fundamental lessons. The freedom of electors to espouse a popular cause like the independence of the borough must not lead to licence and to anarchy. Election literature is pervaded with the gospel of restraint, of tolerance of one's opponents, of manly and generous goodwill, of a firm and a willing acceptance of the outcome of the election, however galling it may be. The language of liberty is carefully rehearsed amidst a real awareness of the fragility of social discipline and the need to preserve the social order.

Given the libertarian nature of the environment in which the election occurred, it was necessary for election managers to depend upon the customary disciplines of the community to restrain partisanship and thus to preserve the order of the town or county. Election speeches

---

[79] *Royal Cornwall Gazette*, 18 Apr. 1807, quoted in W. M. Comber, 'The Cornish Boroughs and Parliamentary Reform, 1800–1832', MA (Exeter, 1976), 64.

and election literature ceaselessly reiterate, and thus inculcate, certain principles. Electors may maintain and guard their independence and negotiate and bargain with their political and social superiors but they must know their place and respect their betters. They must, in short, honour the hierarchic conditions which sustained natural interest. Electors should exhibit manly and generous goodwill. They must accept the result of the election with manly resignation, shake the hand of their opponents and return willingly to normality, nursing no grievance, stoking up no resentments. The freedom of electors to support a popular or a political cause must not lead to anarchy. At this level, electoral culture is profoundly traditional and socially conservative. It is, however, nothing if not vibrant, vigorous and, in the last analysis, capable of development and transformation. In the end, election campaigns did something to remind the social and political élite of Hanoverian England of the conditional nature of popular acquiesence in their authority and helped to define the limits within which their social leadership was tolerated.

## CASH AND CORRUPTION

Few topics in the whole of modern British history have aroused such a chorus of unanimous condemnation as the financial reputation of the unreformed electoral system. For almost two centuries the uncritically parroted conclusion of historians has been that before the Reform Act of 1832—that landmark in the history of liberal progress—the electors were 'venal', the electoral system was 'corrupt', and 'bribery' was widespread.

In an attempt to distinguish myth from reality, this chapter will consider the question of election expenses in different types of seats at different times. It will try to explain where the money came from. More importantly, it will consider where the money went (between elections as well as at elections, and at uncontested as well as contested elections). Some of it, of course, went to cover 'official' fees and costs, but this was just a small part. Most of the money went on the voters, but just how significant and effective was the treating and entertainment which occurred? And what is the historian to make of the direct payment of money to these voters?

The financial dimension to electoral behaviour in the century before reform has presumably received such widespread criticism because it has been so poorly understood. It was not only that electoral politics in the eighteenth century were in many respects unlike those of our own day, but also the normative values which accompanied them.

Hanoverian society was paranoically suspicious of 'corruption' when the state was believed to be responsible for it but remarkably tolerant when private groups and individuals practised it. Even radical candidates accepted these values, although many of them had a sensitive understanding of the limits of permissible electoral activity. What explains this remarkably tolerant attitude towards mixing money with electoral politics?

*First*, many of the payments and donations which accompanied electoral activity in the unreformed period were regarded as the legitimate concomitants of natural interest: they were intended to compliment, reward, and flatter the faithful not to change opinions and disturb settled loyalties. There was nothing reprehensible in an elector receiving money from a party which he was going to support anyway. *Second*, contemporaries were able to manifest a greater sense of discrimination between different types of electoral generosity than most historians have been able to. The most widely approved included charitable donations to particular institutions (churches, hospitals, schools) and to needy groups. These could be distinguished from more routine payments of a paternalist character to corporations, guilds, and societies and from particular actions designed to create and maintain electoral goodwill (the provision of jobs, influence, custom, and favours). Different again were displays of culinary and alcoholic generosity so commonly cited by historians. Electors had indeed come to regard these as an inseparable feature of electioneering. Indeed, even in non-election years, annual treats and dinners were held in many places.[80] Intrinsically different again were payments for votes to electors. These, however questionable, were often nothing more than compensation for loss of wages, produce, or custom incurred on account of the election.

None of these activities necessarily represents a genuine corruption of the individual elector or of his conscience (although taken to extremes and divorced from natural interests, of course, they sometimes could). Rather, they signify the natural operation of influence and paternalism in an electoral context. Money can thus be regarded as a means of exchange by which patrons attempted to exert their influence over the electors and by which electors endeavoured to negotiate with their patrons. Both could—and did—transgress the normative limits to electoral activity by crude attempts to replace natural interest either with money or with intimidation. This transgression, however, was an object of criticism and condemnation by contemporaries, not of approval.

---

[80] e.g. at Reading (R. C. Bailly, 'The Parliamentary History of Reading, 1750–1850', MA (Reading, 1944), 37.

The outlay of money on elections depended on a wide range of local factors. A rough equality of local parties might provide the necessary stimulus to the competitive persuasion of the electorate. Similarly, a reasonably small electorate—though not the very smallest—could sometimes tempt patrons into lavish expenditure simply because of its prospective manageability. It is significant that of the Cornish boroughs the most corrupt were Grampound (50 electors in 1754), Penryn (200), and Tregony (150), not Bodmin, Bossiney, Callington, Camelford, Helston, and Launceston (all with under 50 electors). The presence of a corrupt corporation accompanied by an experienced number of hardened electors was further calculated to optimize election expenditure. The final requisite for expensive electioneering was a disputed local franchise. This would serve to pour money into the pockets of attorneys as well as electors and might very well lead to a petition disputing the return.[81]

Where did the money come from? Social realities naturally ensured that patrons and candidates provided most of it, and this they normally did. Wealthy patrons liked to pay expenses themselves in order to maintain the candidate's dependence upon them and prevent him from establishing an interest of his own, but it was not always quite so straightforward. The patron and his friends, family, and supporters might raise quite large sums, leaving the candidate to find the rest. There are even some quite famous examples of candidates relying on voluntary subscriptions to fund the costs of an election. Middle-class dissenters from all over the country contributed to the Yorkshire subscription of 1807 which paid Wilberforce's expenses. Altogether, a sum in excess of £64,000 was subscribed.[82] Radical reform candidates at Westminster in the early nineteenth century like Burdett and Hobhouse almost always had their expenses paid by subscription. Subscriptions were not uncommon in the reform landslide of 1831: 'Our returns exceeded by some hundreds those of 1830, and funds have flowed in upon us in such super-abundance that some of us must make a good thing of it, or be necessitated to send the over-flowings to your Pitt Club.'[83] Similarly, famous and successful MPs sometimes

---

[81] For the most part these ingredients were absent from electioneering in the Welsh constituencies, which were thus saved from some of the worst abuses to be found in England. On this point modern research has borne out Oldfield's original assessment. Wager, 'Welsh Politics and Parliamentary Reform', Ph.D. 14; T. H. B. Oldfield, *The History of the Boroughs of Great Britain*, 2 vols. (London, 1794), ii. 1–2.

[82] R. I. Wilberforce and S. Wilberforce, *Life of William Wilberforce*, 5 vols. (London, 1839) ii. 149. A subscription of £43,944 was raised in Yorkshire alone. Over 2,500 subscriptions were paid in, but as many represented churches and societies the number of contributors was far greater.

[83] W. W. Nash to John Parkinson, 3 Nov. 1831, concerning the Cambridge election. D2433/D/5/188, Caledon MSS, PRO Northern Ireland.

discovered that a grateful constituency expressed its thanks by funding the election expenses of their next return. Henry Brougham found his election as MP for Liverpool in 1812 easy on his pocket.[84] Other large trading towns like Bristol and London seem also to have regarded their MPs as agents whom they paid to protect their economic interests.[85]

Yet subscriptions are also to be found in less exalted circumstances, especially in county elections. Oldfield relates how Ralph Caesar was promised a subscription to fund his expenses at the by-election of 1736 at Hertfordshire.[86] The Wiltshire by-election of 1772 cost Ambrose Goddard £20,000, of which £8,250 was raised through a subscription.[87] The Rockingham party in Yorkshire raised no less than £15,000 for the election of 1784, £9,000 of which they returned to the subscribers when a contest failed to materialize.[88] Even where William Adam's central Whig party fund contributed money to a local election campaign it does not seem to have equalled what was available from other sources. In 1784 Lord Sheffield and William Seymour Conway contributed £300 as candidates to Coventry's election expenses, Adam gave only £100, while a further £500 came from other sources.[89]

Subscriptions were a common method of spreading the expense of inordinately costly elections. By the early nineteenth century they seem to have become very common indeed. Although they do not seem to have been used in all parts of the country,[90] their function in broadening the basis of support for local electoral parties outside the charmed circle of aristocratic and county society should not be underestimated.[91] Although the lists of subscribers which survive are

[84] Henry Brougham to Lord Grey, 16 Oct. 1812. Memoirs of Lord Brougham (1872) ii. 61–5, printed in P. Jupp, *British and Irish Elections, 1784–1831* (Newton Abbot, 1973), 124–6.

[85] The Bristol elections of 1774 cost the government side £2,000. £7,200 was found by subscription. In 1780 all the £8,100 spent on the government side was raised by subscription. Lord North to George III, 18 Apr. 1782, Sir J. Fortescue, The *Correspondence of George III*, 6 vols. (London, 1928), v. 465–74.

[86] Oldfield, *History of the Boroughs*, v. 260.

[87] Namier and Brooke, *House of Commons*, i. 408.

[88] Yorkshire County Election Papers 1784, X1603, Fitzwilliam MSS, Northants. RO. Over £20,000 was subscribed on the other side, but all except £4,000 of it was returned. R. W. Smith, 'Political Organization', 1546–7.

[89] List of Receipts of Money for Election Campaign, Sheffield MSS, i. 128, Coventry RO. For subscription receipts see ibid. 127.

[90] In the four northern counties Stoker has encountered little evidence of their existence. 'Rank and file voters expected to receive money not give it. Prior to the 1831 and 1832 elections the only attempt to raise money from the public was in Westmorland when the Blues opened a subscription to defray £6,000 of debts still outstanding from the 1820 election. It raised only a few hundred pounds.' Stoker, 'Elections and Voting Behaviour', Ph.D., 314. I have encountered no subscriptions in the Welsh constituencies.

[91] It is important to notice that subscriptions also served to *prolong* partisanship when they were used to fund petitions against election returns. This is known to have happened, for example, at the Gloucestershire by-election of 1776 (see List of 39 Subscribers, DIL, XXIV/17, Oxon. RO) and at the Berkshire election of 1784 (see Namier and Brooke, *House of Commons*, i. 206).

often dominated by a small number of large subscriptions, the lists also contain small sums from quite small men. A Leicester election subscription of 1762 raised £1,140. Only four subscriptions exceeded £100, the remaining 24 ranging from £10 to £50.[92] Similarly, few of the 39 subscribers to the Gloucestershire election fund of 1776 exceeded £100, most of them ranging from £10 to £60.[93] In 1831 the Fitzwilliam interest at Northamptonshire opened a subscription for sums ranging from £50 to as little as 1s. It raised £406 within a few days.[94] Where detailed lists of such subscriptions survive, it is possible to ascertain how far down the social hierarchy the contributors originated. The subscription for William Thornton, who came in for the Rockingham interest at York at the by-election of 1758, included 41 names funding over £12,000. The list naturally includes Rockingham, Thornton, several members of the York Rockingham Club, and several clergymen, but it also includes the names of several tradesmen contributing £10 to £25 each.[95] Such a fund could have immediate electoral significance. The £30 to £50 subscription announced by the Paget interest at Leicestershire in 1830 was regarded as a weather-vane. If 'the voluntary exertions of the freeholders' were not forthcoming then the contest might be abandoned.[96] They were, and it was not.

Given the wide variations in local circumstances—the physical size of constituencies, the number of electors, the nature of the franchise, and the availability of money—it is extremely difficult to generalize about election expenditure. At the beginning of the eighteenth century it was still perfectly possible to contest a borough seat for £1,000 to £1,500. By 1800 these costs had perhaps tripled.[97] A county seat cost between £5,000 and £10,000. These are minimum figures. In the seats with larger electorates the costs could be very much greater. As Fitzwilliam once remarked, with feeling gained by experience: 'an

---

[92] DE 575, Leics. RO. 'I and many of my neighbours have given £10 each' to a subscription at Newark in 1831, wrote one of his agents (F. Tallents to Duke of Newcastle, n.d. 1831, Ne 4,526, Newcastle (Clumber) MSS, Nottingham Univ. Lib.).

[93] See sources cited in n. 91.

[94] Letters to Milton, G8, May–June 1831, Fitzwilliam MSS, Northants. RO.

[95] F. C. Price, 'The Parliamentary Elections in York City, 1754–1790', MA (Manchester, 1958), 108–12.

[96] The Chairman of Paget's Committee to an unidentified recipient, 10 Aug. 1830, 301 Paget MSS, Leics. RO.

[97] Of course, where circumstances permitted, costs could be very much lower. According to Oldfield (*History of the Boroughs*, i. 192) Bridport could be contested for £1,500–£2,000 late in the 18th cent. Charles James Fox's expenses for Westminster in 1802 cost him nothing; the £800 expenses were paid by Whig peers (Fitzwilliam MSS, F115E, Wentworth Woodhouse MSS, Sheffield Pub. Lib.).

election, to be carried on without expense, is a forlorn case and had better never be attempted'.[98]

The counties were the most expensive constituencies, on account of their geographical area and their large number of electors. The great Oxfordshire contest of 1754 horrified contemporaries with its astronomical expenses, at least £40,000 for each side,[99] but this sum was frequently exceeded in subsequent decades. Although the normal run of contested county elections may have cost something in the region of £5,000 to £10,000 for each electoral interest involved,[100] there are many much more expensive examples. The Essex by-election of 1763 cost its two opposing interests £30,000 each, that at Sussex in 1807 up to £20,000 per side, that at Northumberland in 1826 over £20,000 per side.[101] But some contests vastly exceeded even these enormous figures. The great Yorkshire county contests of 1807—the most expensive county election to the unreformed Parliament—cost the three sides a whopping £250,000.[102]

The larger boroughs (with over 1,000 electors) could come near to equalling the expenses of county elections. The financial trends are the same. The expenses of such a seat in the early eighteenth century did not usually exceed £1,000. After the Septennial Act (1716) placed a greater value on these seats, however, their costs began to rise steadily. By the early nineteenth century the figure had reached £5,000–10,000. In some places costs were kept within bounds, especially where frequent contests inhibited enormous increases in costs and where the popularity of a person or family imparted a greater

---

[98] Fitzwilliam to Milton, 30 June 1818, G.I.,Fitzwilliam MSS, ibid.

[99] R. Robson, *The Oxfordshire Election of 1754* (Oxford, 1949); Namier and Brooke, *House of Commons*, i. 4, 356.

[100] The Northamptonshire by-election of 1748 cost the Cartwright interest over £4,000; see Forrester, *Northamptonshire County Electioneering*, 68. The Kent contests of 1802 and 1818 cost the Honeywood interest £6,474 and £3,589 respectively; see Andrews, 'Political Issues in Kent', M.Phil., 16–17. The Huntingdonshire election of 1826 cost the Mandeville interest £13,000 (Jupp, *British and Irish Elections*, 60). An extremely detailed set of a candidate's expenses has survived for an unidentified Gloucestershire election. Their presence in the Abingdon Borough MSS (200, Berks. RO) strongly suggests the election of 1784. The infrequent contests in Welsh counties seem to have been slightly less expensive. That for Caernarvonshire in 1826 cost about £3,000 each side (R. G. Thomas, 'Politics in Anglesey and Caernarvonshire, 1826–1852', MA (Wales, 1970), Appendix O). There could be exceptions, however; the Edwards interest spent £18,000 at the 1818 Glamorgan contest (Wager, 'Welsh Politics and Parliamentary Reform', 204).

[101] Namier and Brooke, *House of Commons*, 4, 276; Hinton, 'General Elections of 1806 and 1807', Ph.D., 500; Stoker, 'Elections and Voting Behaviour', Ph.D., 310–11. In the same vein, the three Westmorland contests of 1818, 1820, and 1826 cost the Lowther interest around £25,000, £21,000, and £30,000 respectively (ibid. 311–12).

[102] Bundle 14, Lascelles Account book, 1807, Harewood MSS, Leeds Public Library; F.48b., Fitzwilliam MSS., Sheffield Pub. Lib. Even the uncontested election of 1826 caused £150,000 to be spent; see R. W. Ram, 'The Political Activity of Dissenters in the East and West Riding of Yorkshire, 1815–1850', MA (Hull, 1964), 73.

degree of electoral stability than might exist elsewhere. The most outstanding example is the record of Sir Matthew Ridley and his son at Newcastle-upon-Tyne, who between 1796 and 1830 only twice exceeded £1,000 in election expenditure.[103] Furthermore, the large Kent boroughs of Canterbury, Dover, and Maidstone could still be contested in the early nineteenth century for under £5,000.[104] William Windham's return for Norwich in 1790 cost as little as £1,267. Twelve years later, however, his election cost him four times as much.[105] The same pattern may be detected at Lincoln, where the Lumley interest paid £2,800 in 1774 (when it won) and £1,100 in 1780 (when it lost). By 1812 it was costing £12,000 to fight a seat at Lincoln.[106] In other constituencies the inflation of election expenses had set in earlier. At the general election of 1774 it was already costing candidates over £10,000 to fight Worcester.[107] The process may be seen most spectacularly at work in Chester. The contest of 1747 cost each of the three interests involved around £2,500 each. In 1784 when Chester was next contested the Grosvenors paid over £24,000 for the return of their two candidates. The loser, John Crewe, who had spent well over £10,000, was forced to sell his home, Bolesworth Castle. To win a seat at Chester the opposition to the Grosvenors had to pay out comparable amounts of money. This was the key to Sir John Egerton's success in 1812, when his return cost him over £20,000. (The Grosvenors spent £23,000.) This was the limit. Thereafter the Grosvenors *reduced* their election costs to £15,000.[108] It is rare to find election expenses much higher than this. The general election of 1826, however, elicted a few outstanding examples. One candidate at Leicester spent over £22,000 on his return.[109] Perhaps the record for a single interest at a by-election is the £50,000 which the Whig candidate, Lord John Townshend, spent at the Westminster by-election of 1788.[110] Finally, the record for a single borough election must still

---

[103] Stoker, 'Elections and Voting Behaviour', Ph.D., 308.

[104] Andrews, 'Political Issues in Kent', M.Phil., 17–19.

[105] For 1802 see J. A. Phillips, *Electoral Behavior*, 78 and n. For 1790 see BL Add. MSS 37908, fos. 48–55, Windham Papers.

[106] T. W. Beastall, *A North Country Estate The Lumleys and Sandersons as Landowners, 1600–1900* (London, 1975), 89–90; Sir F. Hill, *Georgian Lincoln* (Cambridge, 1966), 224–5.

[107] Namier and Brooke, *House of Commons*, i. 426.

[108] See my article 'The Chester Election of 1784', *J. Chester Archaeol. Soc.* 57 (1970–1), 41–50. See also G. Huxley, *Lady Elizabeth and the Grosvenors* (Oxford, 1965), 86–7; Edmund Holt to Lord Grosvenor, 18–26 Apr. 1812, Grosvenor MSS 252, Chester RO.; J. Hemingway, *History of the City of Chester* 2 vols. (Chester, 1831), ii. 411.

[109] A. Temple Patterson, *Radical Leicester* (Leicester, 1954), 154.

[110] See F. O'Gorman, *The Whig Party and the French Revolution* (London, 1967), 14–15; D. E. Ginter, 'The Financing of the Whig Party Opposition, 1783–1793', *Am. Hist. Rev.* 71 2 (1966), 421–40.

be the 'Election of the Three Earls' at Northampton in 1768, when
the Earls of Halifax, Northampton, and Spencer between them spent
over £100,000.[111]

The borough seats with slightly smaller electorates did not experience
the extravagance associated with some of the larger seats, but they
could still be surprisingly expensive. Shrewsbury in 1796 is alleged
to have cost £100,000.[112] In the middle of the eighteenth century,
£3,000 would be the lower limit for a freeman or scot and lot borough
with an electorate of 500 to 1,000 voters.[113] By the early nineteenth
century costs had risen steeply.[114] At the freeman borough of Ipswich
a candidate had to spend £10,000 in 1807, rising to £12,000 by
1820.[115] Reading, a scot and lot borough with approximately the
same number of voters, cost the same.[116] The smaller scot and lot
boroughs—those with a couple of hundred voters—were not so
expensive. Wooton Bassett, a Wiltshire scot and lot borough with about
250 voters, cost about £3,000 per seat in 1754.[117] Seats in small
freeman boroughs were worth slightly more by this time.[118] To
compare election costs in burgage boroughs is slightly misleading
because the initial costs involved in the purchase of burgages was a
significant element in the future security of an interest. Even though
these seats were rarely contested, the burgesses expected to be treated
and entertained and thus rewarded for their 'loyalty' while conveyances
were being exchanged. All this cost money. Costs amounted to over
£500 at Northallerton in 1812. At Ashburton they amounted to over
£700 in 1790, and as much as £1,000 in 1830.[119] In the corporation
boroughs such costs were rather less. At the Marlborough by-election
of 1762 they amounted to just over £350, and at the general election

---

[111] J. C. Cox, *Records of the Borough of Northampton*, 2 vols. (Northampton, 1898), ii.
501–6.

[112] J. R. McQuiston, 'Sir Richard Hill, Shropshire Evangelist', *Trans. Salop Archaeol. Soc.*
58/2 (1961), 170–1. Cf. Thorne, *House of Commons*, i. 60.

[113] A seat at Derby in 1734 cost around £3,000 (D/F, Bv/0.11, Berks. RO).

[114] The sum of £3,000 was mentioned, however, as an absolute minimum for Lichfield in
1807. Leach to Dyott, 18 May 1807, D.661/10/1/5. Dyott MSS, Staffs. RO. For further
examples see Thorne, *House of Commons*, i. 60–1.

[115] M. Childs, 'Politics and Elections in Suffolk Burroughs During the Late Eighteenth
Century and Early Nineteenth Century', M.Phil. (Reading, 1973), 92, 101.

[116] A. Aspinall, *Reading Through Seven Centuries* (Reading, 1962), 80.

[117] *VCH Wiltshire*, v. 226.

[118] A seat at East Retford cost almost £4,500 in 1830 (Nec. 4522/14, Newcastle (Clumber)
MSS, Nottingham Univ. Lib.). At the same election a seat at Barnstaple cost £5,000
(A. de C. Glubb, *When Cornwall Had 44 MPs* (Truro, 1945), 54–5). The case cited
by Thorne—£17,000 at Shaftesbury in 1796—seems atypical (*House of Commons*,
i. 60).

[119] Bundle 14, Harewood MSS, Leeds Cent. Lib.; Ashburton, Election Indentures, 58/9 box
117/14 and box 135/8/1, Devon RO.

of 1768 just under £800.[120] Costs of *contested* elections in burgage
and corporation boroughs, however, could rise just as high as those
for medium-sized freeman or scot and lot boroughs.[121]

The costs of fighting a contested election could be so enormous that
it might be both cheaper, and safer, in the long run, to contemplate
the purchase of a seat. This might be done in two ways: for the term
of a Parliament or in perpetuity. In the case of the former, a large
number of seats changed hands at each general election for a fixed
term. Over 40 were sold in 1806, for example.[122] Such a seat would
cost about £3,000 for a Parliament in the later eighteenth century,
rising to £5-6,000 in the early nineteenth.[123] To purchase a seat
outright would cost very much more. A controlling interest in a burgage
borough seems to have cost around £60,000 in the early nineteenth
century.[124] A tiny freeman borough with only a handful of electors
might cost about the same. Camelford in Cornwall was sold by the
Duke of Bedford for £32,000 in 1812, but a decade later the third
Earl of Darlington paid £58,000 for it.[125] Most sensational of all,
Gatton, which was worth £90,000 in the early years of the nineteenth
century, was worth an incredible £180,000 on the eve of the Reform
Act.[126] It was not so much the size of the electorate which determined
the price of a seat as the security of the investment, and the certainty
of control, which purchase could acquire.

Historians have not normally incorporated into their understanding
of election expenses the notion of annual maintenance expenditure.
Without constant care and attention the control of, or an interest in,
a borough would weaken and decline. Consequently, money needed
to be spent in the years between elections and not merely in the period
immediately before elections. Generalizations about this maintenance

---

[120] List of Marlborough Burgesses, 1762; 588/0.20, 0.29; James Day to the Marquis of
Granby and Sir John Hynde Cotton, n.d. 1768, 588/023; Cotton MSS, Cambs. RO.

[121] The cost of the contested by-election of 1744 and the contested general election of 1747
at Scarborough together cost the Lascelles interest £7,000, but in these cases there was a strong
government–opposition complexion (E. Lascelles to Marquis of Rockingham, 22 Dec. 1760,
Rockingham MSS, Wentworth Woodhouse MSS, Sheffield Pub. Lib).

[122] Twenty-three were sold through the government, 10 through friends of the government
and 7 among the opposition. Hinton, 'General Elections of 1806 and 1807', Ph.D., 103–5.

[123] Cannon, *Parliamentary Reform*, 35; Thorne, *House of Commons*, i. 195.

[124] This figure does seem to recur. A controlling interest in Cockermouth cost the Lowthers
£58,000 in 1756 (Bonsall, *Sir James Lowther*, 40–2). Similarly, the purchase of Bletchingley
cost Matthew Russell £60,000 in the early 19th cent. (*The Farington Diary*, ii. 94.) In the same
period Old Sarum cost the 2nd Earl of Caledon £60,000 (James J. Sack, 'The House of Lords
and Parliamentary Patronage in Great Britain, 1802–1832', *Hist. J.* 23/4 (1980), 914. In 1810,
however, Westbury cost £75,000. Thorne, *House of Commons*, i. 52.

[125] Comber, 'The Cornish Boroughs', MA, 20; Sack, 'The House of Lords', 914.

[126] *The Farington Diary*, ii. 94; W. Carpenter, *Peerage for the People* (London, 1841),
524.

expenditure are very difficult indeed. A settled and secure borough would certainly require the spending of several hundred pounds a year at least. Between 1790 and 1818 the Forester interest at Wenlock, a medium-sized Shropshire freeman borough, cost an average of £400 per annum in a period when there were no contested elections. Wenlock was not a particularly difficult borough.[127] Others were more expensive. Morpeth had a more persistent independent tradition and required more careful nursing. It cost double the expenditure which the Foresters devoted to Wenlock. A larger freeman borough, Carlisle, was even more expensive. The Curwen interest spent over £1,000 per annum in the protracted war against the Lonsdale family on annual maintenance expenditure. This level of expenditure approached the ceiling which some patrons could afford. Even the Duke of Bedford found the £1,500 per annum which he was constrained to spend on the two dozen voters of Camelford in the early nineteenth century too much for his taste. He was relieved to sell his interest in the place and cut his losses.[128]

As will be obvious by now, even an *uncontested* election cost money and involved patrons in some expenditure. In most corporation and burgage boroughs this would not be very heavy in view of the firm levels of electoral control normally established. Not all corporation boroughs were as cheap as Harwich, where the two successful candidates at the uncontested election of 1807 had only to share election costs of £250.[129] Election costs could similarly be negligible in secure burgage boroughs, the Lowthers rarely spending more than £30 for uncontested elections at Cockermouth in the early nineteenth century.[130] Well-tended medium-sized boroughs rarely cost more than a few hundred pounds. In 1768 Ludlow cost the first Earl of Powis no more than £230.[131] Wenlock had an electorate of almost indentical size but uncontested election formalities cost considerably more, as Table 3.5 indicates. Surprisingly, uncontested returns in large boroughs and even in the counties were scarcely more expensive than in the smaller boroughs. The uncontested Nottingham by-election of 1779 cost Robert Smith a trifling £481. 16s. 6d., presumably because of the overwhelming goodwill which existed towards him and his family in the town and the conformity of his opinions on America with

---

[127] Bundle 336, Forester MSS, Shropshire RO.
[128] Stoker, 'Elections and Voting Behaviour', Ph.D., 314–16; Thorne, *House of Commons*, i. 60.
[129] Hinton, 'General Elections of 1806 and 1807', Ph.D., 498.
[130] Stoker, 'Elections and Voting Behaviour,' Ph.D., 310 n. 1.
[131] H. T. Weyman, 'Ludlow Members of Parliament', *Trans. Salop. Archaeol. Soc.* 2nd ser. 7 (1895), 43.

TABLE 3.5    *Election Expenses at Wenlock:*
*Forester Interest, 1790–1818*

| Year | Outlay (£) |
|------|------------|
| 1790 | 665 |
| 1796 | 923 |
| 1802 | 1,000 |
| 1806 | 834 |
| 1807 | 400 |
| 1812 | 730 |
| 1818 | 532 |

*Source*: Bundle 336, Forester MSS, Shropshire RO.

those of the electors. Again, the size of the electorate—Nottingham had over 2,000 voters—was not the overriding factor in determining election expenses.[132] Similarly, well-tended county seats could be defended without a contest for modest amounts. The two Derbyshire seats cost the Devonshire interest no more than £554 in 1774, the two Cambridgeshire seats cost £400 in 1784, and the two Surrey seats just over £1,500 in 1796.[133]

How was election money spent? Professor Plumb has remarked that the bulk of the expenditure in the early eighteenth century went less on direct bribery of the voters than upon entertainments, fees, and donations.[134] As the century wore on, the proportion of outgoings directed towards 'fees' (i.e. formal and statutory expenses) sharply declined, while the amounts expended upon entertainments and donations steadily increased. Entertainments may be taken to include all types of social 'treating' designed by candidates and their agents to establish and maintain goodwill between themselves and the electors.

---

[132] Smith's expenses are complete and unusually detailed. The originals are to be found in the Nottingham City Library, SMT 249 (formerly M.479 fos. 121–3) 'An Account of Expenses paid at Mr. Robt. Smiths Election'. They have been printed by the *Thoroton Society Record Series* in 'A Nottinghamshire Miscellany', 21 (Nottingham 1962).

[133] Ben Granger to Unidentified Recipient, 3 Nov. 1774, Currey's Lists, 86/Compartment I, Devonshire MSS, Chatsworth; 'Election Expenses of Philip Yorke and Sir Henry Peyton', 22 Apr. 1784, BL Add. MSS 35382 fo. 73, Hardwicke Papers: John Frederick's 'Account of my Election Expenses when chosen for Surrey 1794 and again 1796', 183/35/39, Frederick MSS, Surrey RO.

[134] J. Plumb, *The Growth of Political Stability in England, 1675–1725* (London, 1967), 88–9. For donations see my account of paternalism, pp. 229–37.

Thus may be included the 32 dinners and other assemblies held by Whigs and Tories for the Kent freeholders in the six months before the Kent county election of 1734 and the innumerable further such assemblies held during the period of the campaign itself. These range from relatively small parish dinners to enormous occasions providing for as many as 800 freeholders.[135] Although treating in the boroughs was usually less lavish, one thing was certain: to refuse to treat the voters was an insult to men who viewed themselves as privileged individuals meriting the candidates' attention and generosity. In exactly the same way that MPs expected to profit from their seat in Parliament,so did electors expect some public recognition of their privileged status as electors. To ignore this could create the threat of violence and the prospect of vandalism and insubordination.[136] To maintain an electoral interest required that voters were at very least accommodated in a generous manner during the dangers and inconveniences of an election.[137] All sides were agreed that the best antidote to licence and disorder at election times was well-regulated treating to humour the voters and to reward the faithful.

The most common type of electoral treating was the provision of alcohol, food, and accommodation at inns and other public houses. In the best regulated campaigns, tickets would be issued to declared, proven, or promised *bona fide* supporters, entitling them to claim a fixed amount of drink and food, and possibly a bed, at a named inn. After the election the inn-keeper would deliver up the tickets to claim his recompense. Such a system was vastly preferable to the indiscriminate issue of money to all and sundry because it established some control over the behaviour of the electors by concentrating supporters in particular places. Their movements could be effectively marshalled and controlled by a system of patrols and their persons protected from unwelcome external attentions. Indeed, in some large boroughs (e.g. Leicester in 1754) over one-half the inns had 'inspectors' billeted on them to ensure that this system worked successfully.

Every tavern in every town would be commissioned by one side or the other, the appropriate lists appearing in the press and distributed in handbills. As soon as candidatures were declared, the inns for the

[135] A. Newman, 'Elections in Kent and Its Parliamentary Representation, 1715–1754', D.Phil. (Oxford, 1957), 64–6. See also the details of similar treats at the Oxfordshire county election of 1754. Robson, *The Oxfordshire Election*, 57–60.

[136] See e.g. the worried letters about the prospect of violence at Leicester at the election of 1790: R. Wilson to Mr Porter, 26 June 1790 and Mr Pochin to Sir Thomas Cave, 26 June 1790 (3438, 3439, Braye MSS, Leicester City Museum).

[137] See the remarkably direct statement of this philosophy from Richard Lowndes to Lord Gower, n.d. 1788, D.593, D/1788/2. 6.ii. Leveson-Gower MSS, Staffs. RO.

rival interests would be opened. The first essential would be to reach the outvoters, who would naturally be accommodated free of charge, but the same inns could provide daily treats for local voters. Consequently, the inn played a central role in election campaigns. It is significant how many election rhymes and songs are, in effect, an invitation to *toast* a candidate, a cause, or a constituency. Indeed, in 1761 Sir William Meredith's victory at Liverpool was marked by a souvenir drinking mug.[138] The amount of alcohol permitted was generous. The treating limit per individual varied with the contest, of course, and the constituency. Towards the end of the period, 7s. 6d. to 10s. was a typical amount.[139] The records of a particular inn can be both interesting and instructive. The Sun Tavern in Mitre Street, Shrewsbury, sent the following account for the ten days of the poll in 1796:

|  |  | £ | s. | d. |
|---|---|---|---|---|
| 443 | Breakfasts | 14 | 5 | 4 |
| 572 | Bread and Cheese | 8 | 16 | 4 |
| 1,265 | Dinners | 89 | 1 | 0 |
| 1,164 | gallons of Cider | 117 | 8 | 6 |
| 1,875 | gallons of Ale | 162 | 6 | 3 |
|  | Rum | 1 | 6 | 4 |
|  | Tobacco | 6 | 12 | 3 |
|  | Gin 'for Constables' |  | 5 | 6 |
|  | Miscellaneous expenses |  | 19 | 10 |
|  | TOTAL | £401 | 1s. | 4d. |

Shrewsbury had about 500 voters in 1796 and about a dozen inns. It is likely that the Sun Tavern was catering for no more than 100 voters, each of whom must have consumed at least 3 gallons of ale or cider during the ten days of the election.[140] Whether such copious quantities of alcohol were actually consumed is very doubtful. Publicans customarily exaggerated the amount of ale and cider consumed or, alternatively, charged inflated prices for it. Indeed, before the bills were actually paid, a lengthy process of negotiation was required to reach a satisfactory compromise figure. As the Duke of Norfolk remarked after the contested election at Leominster in 1796: 'I believe in all transactions of expenditure *a reasonable time is allowed that each party*

---

[138] K. Boney, 'Liverpool Plumper Mug', *Libraries Bulletin* (Liverpool), 3/3 (1954), 39–40.

[139] For the extensive documentation of the drinking accounts of the contested election of 1790 in Newcastle-under-Lyme see D593/S/16/10/7–8 in the Leveson-Gower MSS, Staffs. RO. Most tickets seem to have been worth 7s. 6d. Those at the Leicestershire county election of 1830 were worth 10s.; see (DE/41/1/163, Paget MSS., Leics. RO).

[140] Attingham MSS, 74, Shropshire RO.

*may be satisfied no mistake has been made.*'[141] Sometimes years passed before accounts were settled. Even when they were they gave no pleasure to either side, the publicans deploring the meanness and neglect of the upper crust, the patrons deploring the blatant overcharging of the publicans.[142] In some places, of course, both sides would acquiesce in a deliberately inflated figure, a sort of concealed bribe to electors, but such a proceeding could itself generate demands for further displays of generosity.

Treating was just as necessary when an election was uncontested as when a contest threatened. The election of 1802 at Newark was uncontested, but 42 public houses were open for customary election treats.[143] The Ashburton accounts of 1790 also reveal the payment of over one-third of the total expenses of around £700 to inns.[144] In Wenlock at the uncontested election of 1790 it was two-thirds.[145] Similarly, at the uncontested Maldon election of 1830, T. B. Lennard spent £352. 13s. 0d. at 15 inns out of a total expenditure of £585. 10s. 6d.[146] Nor is there any case for believing that the proceedings at an uncontested election were any less lively and festive than at contested elections. At Minehead in 1747:

In the afternoon it happened that Mr Leigh, agent for O'Brien came to town, and while the others were at the key, firing guns and displaying colours, got a great number of friends with himself at the 'Feathers', where he elegantly treated them, and when the others returned from the key and were crying up their friend Whitworth, they came out of the Inn and cryed their friend O'Brien, and by throwing up their hats happened to hit one of the other party in the face, which caused a fray, that might have set the town alight but for the mob being pretty sober, remained quiet and it was soon quelled.[147]

Treating was no less essential between elections, whether contested or not. The Forester accounts for 1801 show that £272. 9s. 8d. was

[141] Duke of Norfolk to Mr Lewellyn, 4 May 1696, Pilley MSS, Hereford and Worcs. RO.
[142] The Grosvenors faced a set of publicans' bills for over £14,000 in 1784 but succeeded in negotiating them down to £8,500 after checking the innkeepers' bills against the receipts of ale and wine merchants. Even after this, the Grosvenors paid for 1,187 barrels of ale, 3,756 gallons of rum and brandy, and over 27,000 bottles of wine. There were 1,500 electors in a town whose population was 16,700. The election lasted two weeks, see Huxley, *Lady Elizabeth*, 86–7. Nevertheless, 21 out of the 23 innkeepers listed in the Poll Book voted the Grosvenor ticket, and 16 of the 18 wine merchants. A similar reduction was negotiated in 1812, from £34,000 down to £24,000 (Edmund Holt to Lord Grosvenor, 18 and 26 April 1812, Grosvenor MSS 252, Chester RO).
[143] QDE/3/4 and DD.T.22/77, Tallents MSS, Notts. RO.
[144] £244. 8s. 9d. out of £697. 0s. 9d. to be exact; 58/9/Box 117/14, Palk MSS, Devon RO.
[145] £457. 3s. 4d. out of £665. 12s. 10d. in 1790; Bundle 336, Forester MSS, Shropshire RO.
[146] D/DL.042/4, Essex RO.
[147] W. Hayman to H. F. Luttrell, n.d. 1747, DD/L., Letters, 1732–47, Dunster Castle MSS, Soms. RO.

spent on Wenlock constituency, £40 of it on 'Bailiff's Wine', £17. 9s. 4d. on 'Expenses for a Treat to Burgesses at Bilstone', £5. 5s. 0d. on 'Usual Treat to Jurors'.[148] Slightly more generous was the MP for St Albans who in 1810 sent his agent £300 for the treating of his supporters.[149]

Elections, whether contested or not, provided candidates and their patrons with further opportunities of displaying their generosity towards the community. The employment of local people and the purchase of local produce, goods, crafts, and wares were integral elements in any successful election campaign. During the months prior to the election, the normal pattern of purchase of groceries, linen, meat, and many other commodities mysteriously accelerated.[150] Furthermore, election festivities created a demand for specific types of expertise. Musicians were in great demand. No election occasion, whether the entry of the candidates into the town, the canvass, parades, treats, or dinners, was complete without music. One band earned almost £700 during the great Yorkshire contest of 1807.[151] Other substantial sums found their way into the hands of 'ringers'. At the uncontested Newark election of 1802 ringers of bells were paid 2 guineas a day (2½ on election day) and enjoyed a liquor allowance of 3 guineas.[152] In other places ringers received a fixed sum for the duration of the campaign.[153] Carpenters were also in great demand. The cost of erecting the hustings was always substantial—up to £100 or even more by the late eighteenth century. Then there were the costs of making the chair (whether or not there was a contest the chairing and other ceremonies were still held), of covering it, of dressing it, of making, covering, and decorating the chairstand, and, of course, of bearing it before and during the chairing. Then there were the rosettes and ribbons to be made and distributed among likely friends. Sir Charles Turner paid 37 different bills for ribbons, rosettes, and sashes at the uncontested election at Hull in 1796. Significantly, he

---

[148] Bundle 336, Forester MSS, Shropshire RO.

[149] Mr Hart to Unidentified Recipient, 30 Jan. 1810, Halsey MSS, Herts. RO.

[150] There are some excellent examples in the Sheffield Papers for the general elections of 1780 and 1784 at Coventry in the Coventry Pub. Lib. Sir George Savile once wrote of elections at Lincoln in terms 'not only of the guineas given but of the tradesmen employed (a more decent and well covered kind of bribery indeed and shading off into what one calls *natural interest* and fair influence of neighbourhood and property)' (Sir George Savile to R. L. Saunderson, 12 Jan. 1783, Savile MSS) Notts. RO.

[151] E.179/230, 232, Fitzwilliam MSS, Sheffield Pub. Lib. At the contested Essex county election of 1830 the band earned £184. See the account of one of J. T. Tyrell's agents, D/DWe.A.1, Essex RO.

[152] Bundle 7, 'Minute Book of the United Interest Committee', 1802, Tallents MSS, Notts. RO.

[153] Seven guineas in the case of Maldon in 1830. D/DL 042/4, Essex RO.

paid another 38 bills for the same items during the next two (non-election) years.[154]

The extent of these services could affect the result of the election. At Chester in 1784 no fewer than 85 tradesmen and inn-keepers were specifically commissioned by the Grosvenors to provide some sort of election service (out of a total electorate of 1,500). Of these, 67 voted: 63 for the Grosvenor ticket, 1 split, and only 3 against. The Grosvenor candidates, therefore, can be shown to have received around 10% of their votes from this source alone (the two candidates received 713 and 626 votes).[155] In constituencies with smaller electorates the proportion may have been very much higher.

Almost every conceivable activity which could be construed as bearing upon the election could be used to establish or to maintain the goodwill and gratitude of the voters and their families and their friends. Little jobs could be found for those lacking particular skills. They could carry flags or banners, distribute election literature or information, act as porters or checkers at an inn, or perform one of the many small services around the committee rooms or poll. The careful perusal of surviving election accounts bears witness to the large number of individuals who in one way or another were dragged, willingly or unwillingly, into the world of electoral politics. Many of those who could not be profitably employed by ingenious committee men still make their appearance in election accounts under headings like 'gifts to poor freemen', 'money to the poor'. If even these categories would not suffice, then injuries, or alleged injuries, received during the election might cover the case in hand. Lord Milton's carriage appears to have been so carelessly driven around Yorkshire during the election of 1807 that a large number of people received fairly serious injuries, for which they had to be suitably compensated.[156]

Such a game had its rules and its conventions. It could be played with skill and thus with profit. One ambitious voter submitted the following 'True Account' of his expenses to the Committee of Lord Ashley after the contested Dorset election of 1831:

[154] 13100–36, 13241–75, Hull Election Accounts, Kirkleatham MSS, Northallerton RO. Similarly, the mercers and milliners of Chester did very well out of the 1784 contest in Chester, charging the Grosvenors £1,300 and £2,500 respectively. (Account Book of Bills . . . 1784, Grosvenor MSS, Chester RO.) At the Northamptonshire election of 1806 an agent for the Cartwright interest noted: 'Be pleased to inform Mr. Cartwright's Committee that I am afraid they must follow the Example of the other Candidates, and send down a Parcel of Cockades for our Voters, otherwise our humbler Friends will be, I apprehend, very much offended' (10 Nov. 1806, Cartwright MSS, Northants. RO, quoted in Forrester, *Northamptonshire County Electioneering*, 117).

[155] Account Book of Bills, Grosvenor MSS, Chester RO.

[156] Numerous such strange and amusing instances are listed in Bowns' Account, E.92, Fitzwilliam MSS, Sheffield Pub. Lib.

|  | £ | s. | d. |
|---|---|---|---|
| CHAISE FROM LAVINGTON TO SARUM: 18 MILES | 1 | 7 | 0 |
| Driver |  | 3 | 0 |
| Refreshment at Sarum: Dinner |  | 6 | 6 |
| 'Magnet' Coach to Dorchester |  | 18 | 0 |
| Driver |  | 1 | 0 |
| Biscuits for Supper |  | 1 | 0 |
| Private bed at Mr Davies, a Clergyman | – | – | – |
| Breakfast at the King's Arms |  | 2 | 0 |
| Saturday morning |  |  |  |
| Dinner at the King's Arms |  | 5 | 6 |
| 'My Lord Ashley's Success' in a Pint of Wine |  | 3 | 0 |
| By the Mail Coach back to Salisbury | 1 | 1 | 0 |
| Sandwich for Supper at Sarum |  |  | 9 |
| At the White Hart: |  |  |  |
| Beer |  | 1 | 0 |
| Light |  |  | 6 |
| Bed |  | 2 | 0 |
| Breakfast |  | 2 | 0 |
| Black Horse: Dinner, Beer, Wine |  | 5 | 10 |
| By the Devizes Mail Homeward |  | 8 | 0 |
| Driver |  | 1 | 0 |
|  | 5 | 9 | 9 |

Whether exaggerated or not—the likelihood is that most of these charges are not unduly high—such an account underlines the physical inconvenience of participating in a county election, as well as the possibilities of maximizing one's opportunities in so doing.[157]

Quite separate from payments for treating, entertainments, and services were the fees for official, formal, and statutory services. These sums went to defray the services of local officials: the returning officer and possibly his deputy for the conduct of the election, the poll clerks for the compilation of the poll book, the clerk of the peace for attending at county polls with copies of the land tax assessments, and to cover the expenses of erecting the hustings and of hiring sergeants to maintain law and order. In the early eighteenth century such services cost £50–100.[158] In all such cases the principle adopted was that the charges were thrown upon the candidates, who divided them among

---

[157] J. Williams to Mr Green, 16 Oct. 1831, 4119, Tinney MSS Dorset RO. Not all applicants received the expenses they felt entitled to. At the contested Yorkshire election of 1807 one voter came across the Pennines from Manchester to plump for Lord Milton. He sacrificed a week's wages (£2. 2s.), incurred costs of over £3, but received only £1. 1s. 5d. See Fowler to Bowns, 3 Nov. 1807, E.179/147, Fitzwilliam MSS, Sheffield Pub. Lib.

[158] Plumb, *Growth of Political Stability*, 91.

themselves.[159] By the early nineteenth century they had risen considerably. The great Yorkshire contest of 1807 produced costs of almost £3,700 for the expenses of the sheriff and other local officials, the services of lawyers, bailiffs, poll clerks, and undersheriffs.[160] In a small constituency, these costs were negligible, especially if the election was uncontested. The formalities at the by-election at Marlborough in 1762 cost one candidate only 22 guineas of £359. 16s. 6d; at Ashburton in 1790 £14. 3s. 0d. out of £697. 0s. 9d; at Wenlock in 1790 £70. 18s. 7d. out of £665 12s. 10d.[161] Even the contested Maldon election of 1830 cost one candidate only a little over £100 (out of £585).[162] In this aspect of electioneering, therefore, it does not seem that the bribery of local officials can have proceeded very far. It may well be the case that overcharging occurred and that candidates paid more than might strictly be justified, but the sums are small and represent a relatively tiny proportion of total outgoings.[163]

One of the most seriously misunderstood aspects of election expenditure is that of the alleged bribing of voters. Exaggerated incidents and spectacular scandals are recycled by historians in order to 'prove' that the electorate was corrupt. Several observations need to be made about this possibility. It is extraordinary, in fact, just how few fully validated cases of bribery there are. Certainly, relatively few voters were actually charged with bribery.[164] In spite of numerous contemporary allusions to bribery in South Wales, for example, between 1790 and 1832, only in Cardigan was it common, and only in Carmarthen did the cost of votes rise as high as £20–30, i.e. considerably beyond the limit of normal complimentary payments.[165] Indeed, there are several reasons for believing that widespread bribery

---

[159] An Act of 1745 clearly threw upon the candidates the obligation of paying for the erection of polling booths at county polls and for the services of a poll clerk in each booth. This principle was extended to boroughs with under 600 electors in 1791, but to all boroughs only in 1828 when it was enacted that the legal costs for administering the oaths should fall upon the candidates. Porritt and Porritt, *Unreformed House of Commons*, 185–95.

[160] Election Expenses, 1807 Yorkshire, Harewood MSS, Leeds Cent. Lib. The less spectacular county poll at Essex in 1830 cost one side about £600 out of a total expenditure of £4,294. 3s. 7d. See D/DWe.A1, Essex RO.

[161] 588/020, Cotton MSS, Cambs. RO; 58/9, box 117/3b, Palk MSS, Devon RO; Forester MSS, Shropshire RO.

[162] D/DL. 042/4, Essex RO.

[163] Gash's figures in *Politics in the Age of Peel* (London, 1953, 113–15, seem curiously high and give a misleading impression. They are taken from the Parliamentary Paper of 1834 which was critical of inflated expenses and, as Gash himself notes, 'the greatest expenses usually occurred in the larger constituencies' (ibid. 116).

[164] J. A. Phillips, (*Electoral Behavior*, 78) has noted that of 262 voters at Norwich in 1786 challenged by petition, only 33 were charged with bribery.

[165] 'Parliamentary Representation of South Wales', Ph.D., 36–7.

was *a priori* unlikely. Many of the voters were of sufficient substance and respectability to be insulted by the prospect of a bribe, especially if the transaction was likely to become public knowledge. Furthermore, many of the frequently quoted stories do not survive close examination. They are inherently unlikely when they are not factually incredible. For example, Porritt's statement that Lord Penrhyn spent £30,000 on his return at Liverpool in 1790 is inherently unlikely since he retired on the second day. Similarly Muir's statement that a vote was worth £20 is impossible because only at one election, that of 1806, did election expenses even approach this figure. With electorates of this size (Liverpool had 3,000 electors in the early nineteenth century), bribery on any scale becomes unlikely. Even at the notorious Liverpool contest of 1830, electors received only £15 on average, in addition to treats, although a few individuals were given significantly more. It was the scale rather than the nature of the payments which horrified contemporaries (3,500 freemen received payments, often in a nauseating and publicly vaunted manner).[166] One of the most proletarian, and thus most vulnerable, electorates was to be found at Preston, where 2,500 people had the vote in the early nineteenth century. The largest outlay of money on record at Preston occurred at the contest of 1812, when the coalition spent over £5,000. About £3,500 went on the electors themselves, a princely sum of less than £1. 10s. for each individual.[167] Such payments to voters were unquestionably made, but this does not mean that the electors were 'corrupted' as a consequence.

Payment of money to voters, in fact was carefully designed to achieve specific objectives. At the Leicester election of 1754, the Halford interest spent about £3,000. Well over £2,000 was spent on treating. The money that went into the pockets of voters, by comparison, was trivial. About 50 outvoters from London received three guineas each 'for their trouble and Expenses'—not, as we have seen, a sum likely to compromise a weary traveller's conscience—and about 360 Leicester voters had the costs (usually one guinea) of taking up the freedom paid for them. It is hard to see much evidence of bribery here.[168] Nor was

---

[166] F. F. Sanderson, 'The Structure of Politics in Liverpool, 1780–1807', *Trans. Hist. Soc. of Lancs. and Cheshire* 127 (1978) 76–7 and the references there cited; Porritt and Porritt, *Unreformed House of Commons*, 76; B. Whittingham-Jones, 'Some Unreformed Elections at Liverpool', *Liverpool Dioc. Rev.* 8 (1933).

[167] *Expenses of Horrocks and Hornby, Elections 1812, 1818, 1820*, Lancs. RO.

[168] Election Accounts, 1754, Halford MSS, Leics. RO. Flat rates for outvoters were sometimes modified into a graduated scale according to distance travelled. At the East Retford election of 1830 voters travelling over 100 miles received 1s. per mile, those travelling 50 to 100 miles 6d. per mile see NeC. 4520, Captain A. Duncombe's Election for Retford and Bassetlaw in 1830, Newcastle (Clumber) MSS, Nottingham Univ. Lib.

there much of it in evidence at Waldeshare Park, Kent, where the Countess of Guildford's estate included 169 voters in the Kent county election of the same year. Here 120 voters received a sum of between 7s. 6d. and 1 guinea, but 49 were given nothing at all. Hence the estate spent the magnificient sum of £135. 12s. 2d. on these voters.[169] It is true that much higher payments can be found. Many borough electors might have expected more than the Leicester freemen did, but in most boroughs the voters were not bribed. Although a pamphleteer of 1831 observed that £5 could amount to two months' wages for a farm labourer, very few farm labourers had the vote before 1884.[170] What is so striking about the vast majority of payments to voters, however, is their harmlessness. Voters did benefit from elections. They might enjoy some hospitality and convivial treating, and they might, as we have seen, have the costs of taking their freedom paid on their behalf. On top of this they might receive whatever expenses were due to them.[171] But outright bribery—the deliberate purchase of a vote—is something quite different. On the vast majority of occasions, the transfer of money to voters confirmed rather than undermined the relationships arising out of natural interest, paternalism, and deference.

It is impossible to compute average payments of electors for the privilege of their votes. What is certain is the universal belief among voters that these *douceurs* were a birthright to which they were automatically entitled.[172] Voters might not vote *for* their interest without such attention, but it was very doubtful if they would vote against it whatever sum was offered. The demand for rewards, and support for, as well as participation in, the system which produced them, came from below. To remove these rewards and supports would have been dangerous as well as unpopular. Since all parties offered money for votes, they tended to offer like amounts. If one side made

[169] Election Expenses of Voters on the Countess of Guildford's Estates, Guildford MSS, Kent RO. Similarly at Boston in 1820 at least 46 voters were unpaid out of an electorate of 250–300 see 3/9/14/1–57, Ancaster MSS, Lincs. RO.

[170] *Full Report of the Proceedings at the Town Hall 1831* (New Windsor, Berks. 1831), 24–7.

[171] This could, of course, be a cover for illegal payments. The voters of the venal borough of Barnstaple customarily received £6–£10 for travelling expenses, whether or not they travelled. *Cornwall*, 54–5.

[172] The term 'birthright', in fact, is Oldfield's, used in his description of the Hull voters. 'For upwards of thirty years the candidates have paid the poorer order of voters two guineas for each vote. The number who took money was commonly two-thirds of the votes. So established is this species of corruption, that the voters regard it as a sort of birth-right' (Oldfield, *History of the Boroughs*, ii. 269). The modern historian of Hull discounts the effectiveness of 'bribery', however: 'the most that the political leaders could hope for was willing support, for meaningful bribery was out of the question' (Gordon Jackson, *Hull in the Eighteenth Century* (London, 1972), 303).

a bid to increase the sum paid to each voter, the other would be sure to respond. The elector was not 'selling' his vote in the sense that he was doing violence to his conscience. Nor was he selling it in any sense to the highest bidder (although the price of votes did sometimes rise towards the end of an unusually close contest).[173]

There are, of course, clear examples of open and intended bribery in smaller boroughs. It is difficult to place any other construction upon what happened at Wendover in 1740–1. In February 1740, John Hardinge wrote to Mr Hampden about the distribution of benefits to the voters within the borough of Wendover:

The Gentlemen of Wendover . . . thought it best to give notice that all the Poor and needy Housekeepers within the Borough, except those that did receive alms, that thought fit to come to the Market Hall should receive five guineas a piece . . . and three pounds more they have given to the Poor Widows.

Concerning the opposition, he went on,

there have been several letters sent and great correspondence between Gibbons and the town; and the poor men expect that Gibbons will lend them five or six Guineas a man, and some say ten, otherwise he could not be so positive of carrying his point; so that now to avoid coming under the penalty of the Act of Parliament for bribery they now borrow money and never pay it again.

Such bidding for electoral support ran entirely against contemporary electoral standards and was confined to 20–30 seats, as we have seen.[174]

Particularly unedifying to contemporaries—no doubt because of the conspiratorial activities of lower-class voters—were the much publicized cases of voters forming associations to sell themselves, and thus their constituencies, to the highest bidder. The Malt House Club at Arundel and the Christian Club at New Shoreham are frequently cited instances of lower-class voter self-help. Less notoriety attached to the euphemistically named 'Association for the Purity of Elections' which appeared in Reading in 1820. Ostensibly formed to expose abuses and to recompense voters victimized and intimidated by the corporation, it was probably a Whig association for distributing money to Whig voters in a patronage borough. Like many such societies it soon disappeared. By 1830 all trace of it was lost.[175] The point about such associations is how self-defeating their activities usually were.

---

[173] The best example known to me occurred at Reading in 1754 when £30–£40 was being offered for votes at the end of a very close contest won, in the end, by one vote. Namier and Brooke, *House of Commons*, i. 212.

[174] John Hardinge to Mr Hampden, 21 Sept. 1740, D/MH/39/28, Earl of Buckinghamshire MSS, Bucks. RO. See above, pp. 28–31, for a discussion of 'venal' boroughs.

[175] Bailly, 'Parliamentary History of Reading', MA, 45–7; for Arundel and New Shoreham see above, p. 31.

At Arundel in 1784 and at New Shoreham in 1770 the victorious candidates were unseated on petition. In the case of New Shoreham, indeed, the constituency was remodelled by taking in the Rape of Bramber. A further example of counter-productive electoral bribery occurred at Shaftesbury in 1774, when the 'lending' of money to electors—up to 20 guineas—again led to the unseating of the victorious candidates.[176] Such instances prove what *could* happen in the unreformed electoral system. They do not prove what was typical, still less do they prove what was needed for the establishment and maintenance of a stable electoral interest.

Nevertheless, there can be no denying that a ready supply of money was absolutely indispensable in electioneering. Indeed, the weight of election expenses was a constant source of anxiety to the landed orders of Hanoverian Britain. Even the fourth Duke of Newcastle, congratulating the new mayor of Newark on his election to office in 1812, begged him to keep the cost of elections in the borough as low as possible.[177] As Professor Cannon has remarked: 'The one measure of reform that was always guaranteed a hearing in the House of Commons was a proposal to curb election expenses and eliminate bribery.'[178] But it was guaranteed little more than that. Throughout the eighteenth and early nineteenth century, Parliament refused to take any vigorous action either to curb election expenses or to eliminate 'bribery'.

Until the end of the seventeenth century, treating and bribery were Common Law offences. The first statute to attempt to control them was passed in 1696. The Treating Act threatened MPs with the loss of their seats if they or their agents gave or even promised money, gifts, treats, or rewards. Although the Treating Act of 1696, as Seymour affirms, remained 'the basis of all efforts that were later made to prevent bribery until 1854',[179] it was unwieldy and expensive to invoke and time-consuming in its operations. Parliament therefore attempted to tackle these abuses by penalizing the electors. In 1729 the Bribery Act provided an oath for all electors to swear, and laid down a fine of up to £500 for electors against whom bribery could be proved. Prosecutions under this act were infrequent. The law required that for bribery to be established, either money or the promise of money must be proved to have been given *before* the poll; this

---

[176] Oldfield, *History of the Boroughs*, ii. 168; Namier and Brooke, *House of Commons*, i. 271, 389, 396–7.

[177] Duke of Newcastle to Mayor of Newark, 29 Sept. 1812, NeC, 4525 33/54, Newcastle (Clumber) MSS, Nottingham Univ. Lib.

[178] Cannon, *Parliamentary Reform*, 35.

[179] C. Seymour, *Electoral Reform in England and Wales* (New Haven, 1915) 168.

evidence, moreover, had to be forthcoming within 14 days of the conclusion of the poll. It was easy for experienced agents and canvassers to mind their language and to await the expiry of the critical 14 days before issuing payments to voters. There were always ways round the Bribery Act. Every constituency had its own methods. At Sudbury, for example, the *children* of voters were lavishly treated, the freemen were paid for attending a monthly club, and the wares of the voters were purchased for outrageous prices. In short, the freemen received their treats and their money but the Bribery Act was not violated.[180]

In the early nineteenth century there was a steady stream of reform proposals and although none became law they offer interesting insights into contemporary attitudes. In 1806 Tierney moved a bill to reduce election expenses by limiting payments to outvoters, always a significant slice of an election account. It was reasonable, Tierney asserted, for the outvoter to be paid his travelling expenses 'and some little allowance made for junketting with his friends at a time of election', but the bill failed its second reading when it was pointed out that it would effectively disfranchise the poorer, distantly residing, county voters.[181] In 1826 Russell was astoundingly successful in bringing forward a Bribery Act which passed the Commons. This extended the retrospective period for which petitions could be introduced to six years and enabled enquiries to investigate the borough itself, not merely the candidate and his activities. If found to be corrupt the constituency could be disfranchised. Although time overtook the bill before it reached the Lords it is very doubtful if it could have passed the second chamber.[182] The more realistic and potentially effective the measure, the less its ultimate chance of success. However well intentioned, such reform proposals foundered on the rock of prevailing electoral opinion and, it must be admitted, existing electoral realities. Gifts to voters and election treats were regarded as legitimate social benefits. Elections were occasions which stimulated local trade and employment and enabled the less well off to earn, or at least receive, a few shillings. To stop all this would be unpopular, dangerously so if it left intact at the same time the aristocratic system of contacts and perquisites. Not only would any significant reform of the system have been unpopular with the voters, but it would also have been stoutly resisted by people in other capacities. Many occupational and professional groups—attornies, lawyers, officials, printers, milliners, inn-keepers, carpenters, victuallers, and many others—made a very healthy profit out of elections.

---

[180] Childs, 'Politics and Election in Suffolk Boroughs', M.Phil., 178.
[181] *Parliamentary Debates*, 10 and 21 Mar. 1806, vi. 371–3, 425, 505.
[182] Ibid., NS, xiv. 1003–6; xv. 1401–3; xvi. 99–110.

There was a limit, however, to what contemporaries would tolerate. Allegations of bribery and corruption were certainly common enough and, in certain circumstances, they could even influence the outcome of a contested election. Certainly, if a losing candidate were unwilling to accept the outcome of an election he might prolong election excitement by demanding a scrutiny. And if this did not lead to the unseating of his opponent, it was still open to him to petition the House of Commons against the result.

If a candidate's request for a scrutiny was accepted, the returning officer would withhold making a return. He would scrutinize the credentials of the voters and pronounce upon the complaint. Scrutinies were little more than a ploy in the electoral battle, an extension of the election campaign, an attempt to unsettle a victorious side with the threat of a petition. They had to be launched quickly. The returning officer was bound to make a return before the new Parliament met, so speed was absolutely vital. Herein lay the intrinsic weakness of a scrutiny. There simply was not enough time to examine the voting credentials of several hundred—to say nothing of several thousand—electors in the few weeks between the termination of a poll and the meeting of Parliament. Scrutinies rarely succeeded in seating defeated candidates. By the mid-eighteenth century, petitions to Parliament had become the accepted mode of protesting against the results of contested elections.

A petition had to be lodged within 14 days of the start of the new Parliament. Until then none of the victorious candidates of contested elections could feel safe. Before 1770 an election petition was tried by a majority in the House of Commons. Election petitions were read at the bar of the House, and might even be heard there, but most were heard before the Committee of Privileges and Elections. This was a large committee, effectively a Committee of the Whole, which reflected the balance of numbers between government and opposition. In fact, most petitions sponsored or likely to be supported by the opposition were never heard. In practice, the process of dealing with election petitions was likely to reinforce the government's majority in the House.[183] In 1741, however, when Walpole's opponents secured a majority, the boot was on the other foot and election petitions were determined against him. Whatever the balance of partisanship, election petitions were rarely decided on their merits and even more rarely with reference to the interests of the electors.

---

[183] Between 1715 and 1754, 70% of petitions sympathetic to the opposition were not heard. 'This was done by giving priority to petitions from government supporters, as far as possible deciding them in favour of the petitioners, and closing the election committee before any opposition petitions had been heard' (Sedgwick, *House of Commons*, 14).

With the relaxation of party conflict in the middle of the eighteenth century, election petitions lost their party function. The proceedings on these petitions, stripped of their former purpose, now seemed even more futile and indefensible than ever. Most Members detested the tedious hours of parochial detail which election petitions involved. There was consequently little opposition in the Commons when George Grenville proposed in 1770 that election petitions be heard before an impartial Select Committee.[184] This was appointed from a minimum quorum of 100 MPs. The sitting MPs and the petitioners struck out names alternately until only 13 remained. These 13 MPs, to whom were added 1 MP by each side in the dispute, formed the committee. Thus outright partisanship was minimized. Complex stipulations were included in the bill in an attempt to force the committee to give prompt and speedy attention to petitions. The committee's terms of reference included franchisal questions and the conduct of returning officers. Nothing of substance was precluded from their competence. These Select Committees were far from ideal for the hearing of election petitions. Members of Parliament were not particularly well-qualified to pronounce upon the complex obscurities of election law and precedent. They were slow, cumbersome, and therefore expensive.[185] Nor were they immune from displays of partisanship, lobbying, and canvassing. In spite of these drawbacks the Grenville system lasted for very nearly a hundred years, until 1868 in fact, when disputed election returns were referred to the Common Law courts.

There were three major issues of substance in election petitions. The first concerned the franchise and thus the make-up of the local political nation. The Last Determinations Act of 1696, together with that of 1729, placed beyond the competence of either the House of Commons or the Select Committees established by Grenville's Act any changes in the franchise of the boroughs. In 1788 an Act was passed relaxing the operation of Last Determinations, and it became legal to contest them. Only a handful of places seem to have taken advantage of this relaxation, yet there remained ample grounds for dispute over the franchise. Especially in those constituencies which rarely experienced a contested election, ambiguities over the right to the franchise could

---

[184] For Grenville's motives and for the passage of the Grenville Act see P. Lawson, 'Grenville's Election Act, 1770', *Bull. Inst. Hist. Res.* 53/128 (1980), 218–28.

[185] Most cases took between 30 to 40 days at an approximate cost of £100 per day. (*CJ*, 48 (1792–3), 741). Some county petitions could be more expensive. The Buckinghamshire petition of 1784 cost the Verney interest over £200 per day (Marquis of Buckingham to W. W. Grenville, 10 Apr. 1715, *H. M. C. Dropmore*, i. 250).

occur.[186] All too often, however, they were aggravated by examples of electoral sharp practice when a returning officer sympathetic to one party might either admit to the franchise persons of a particular description who could be relied upon to be friendly or to exclude voters likely to be hostile. A second frequent complaint among petitioners related to the bribery and corruption of the voters. Immediately after the passing of Grenville's Act there seemed some likelihood that a sterner line on bribery might be forthcoming. In 1771 and 1782, corruption among the voters of New Shoreham and Cricklade respectively led to the disfranchisement of the voters in question and the extension of the constituency to the freeholders of adjacent rural areas, both seats becoming, in effect, like county seats. These were exceptional cases, however. There was to be no concerted attack on bribery, and there was to be no resumption of the hunt for delinquent boroughs until after the general election of 1818.[187] The third and most frequent focus of complaint was the role of the returning officer. His power to admit or refuse voters, to control the manner, place, and timing of the poll, and his responsibility for maintaining law and order could be exercised in a partial manner and with serious electoral consequence. Earlier in the eighteenth century, governments would ensure through the annual appointment of sheriffs the existence of returning officers favourable to themselves.[188] This they continued to do down to the Reform Act of 1832. It was, however, local partiality—to local patrons or to a corporation, for example—which fuelled the fires of most petitions complaining of the actions of returning officers.

The rate of petitioning was traditionally a high one. In the later seventeenth century, petitioning had been a regular means of prolonging electoral conflict in an age of party strife. Professor Plumb calculated that 'about 75% of contested elections went to the House of Commons for a final decision'.[189] The figure remained high during the years of Walpole's supremacy, when petitioning was used as a means of unseating enemies of the Whig ascendancy. (See Table 3.6) The rate of petitioning remained high in the late eighteenth century and only began to decline after the epic contest of 1784 (see Table 3.7). Although contemporaries were apt to exaggerate the number

---

[186] e.g. the rebellion at Liskeard, uncontested for over a century, by the inhabitant householders in 1802 and 1804 against the restricted freeman franchise and the control of Edward Eliot. See G. S. Veitch, 'William Huskisson and the Controverted Elections at Liskeard, 1802 and 1804', *Trans. Royal Hist. Soc.*, 4th ser., 13 (1930), 205–28.

[187] For which see Cannon, *Parliamentary Reform*, 177–80.

[188] Sedgwick, *House of Commons*, i. 20–1.

[189] Plumb, *Growth of Political Stability*, 86.

TABLE 3.6    *Petitioning in the First Half of the Eighteenth Century*

| Date of election | No. contests | No. petitions | % contested results petitioned |
|---|---|---|---|
| 1715 | 111 | 87 | 78 |
| 1722 | 129 | 99 | 77 |
| 1727 | 97 | 61 | 63 |
| 1734 | 107 | 69 | 64 |
| 1741 | 66 | 43 | 65 |

*Source*: Data on petitions from Sedgwick, *The House of Commons*, 14. Data on contests from Cannon, *Parliamentary Reform*, 278–9.

of petitions, and historians to believe them, of the fact of decline there can be no doubt.[190]

What explains this decline? The steadily rising cost of bringing and defending petitions must have been an inhibiting consideration, especially when the more frequent occurrence of general elections in the early nineteenth century is recalled. In fact, the Grenville committees probably had some impact upon this process. Their impartiality may have done something to dissuade government supporters, in particular, from bringing petitions to the House where formerly they might have relied upon the government's majority. It is possible, too, that the somewhat sharper moral sensitivity of the early nineteenth century, or, at least, the ability of the press and public to work themselves up over notoriously delinquent boroughs like Cricklade, Grampound, and Penryn, may have further diminished the enthusiasm for those acts of rigorous electioneering which had formerly invited petitions.

The major reason for the declining rate of petitions, however, was their immense cost. As Sir George Savile once said, 'Whether your petition would cost you £1,000 or £10,000 I would not say, but I know your success would be very doubtful to say the least of it.'[191] The costs of retaining counsel, of procuring evidence, of accommodating witnesses for weeks, months, and even years could be enormous. Whatever else may be said about election committees, they did endeavour to be as thorough as circumstances permitted. Quite

[190] The Porritts, for example, regard 60–70 petitions per general election as the normal figure (*Unreformed House of Commons*, 539). Only once after 1784 was that figure reached. A good example of contemporary exaggeration occurred when Sir George Johnstone told the House of Commons in 1809 that 80 petitions had followed the general election of 1807 (*Hansard*, xiv. 658, 19 May 1809); in fact, there had not been that many contests in 1807. What Johnstone was probably doing was conflating the figures for 1806 and 1807 and, even then, adding in the number of special reports of cases of bribery, the rights of election, and the conduct of returning officers. Only thus can the figure of 80 possibly be reached.

[191] Sir George Savile to Richard Lumley Saunderson, 12 Jan. 1783, Savile MSS, Notts. RO.

TABLE 3.7    *Petitioning in the Late Eighteenth Century and Early Nineteenth Century*

| Date of election | No. contests | No. petitions | % contested results petitioned |
|---|---|---|---|
| 1774 | 81 | 64 | 79 |
| 1780 | 69 | 56 | 81 |
| 1784 | 76 | 69 | 91 |
| 1790 | 76 | 39 | 51 |
| 1796 | 59 | 23 | 39 |
| 1802 | 72 | 51 | 71 |
| 1806 | 65 | 42 | 61 |
| 1807 | 71 | 37 | 52 |
| 1812 | 57 | 26 | 46 |
| 1818 | 93 | 40 | 43 |
| 1820 | 73 | 50 | 68 |
| 1826 | 88 | 37 | 42 |
| 1830 | 84 | 41 | 49 |
| 1831 | 74 | 17 | 23 |

*Source*: Data on petitions from Sedgwick, *The House of Commons*, 14; Namier and Brooke, *The House of Commons*, 1; Thorne, *The House of Commons*. Data on contests calculated from the general indexes of the *Commons Journals*.

a large number of electors and other local residents were called and questioned and thus had to be available. How to entertain them could indeed be a problem:

As to the cheapest Mode of keeping your Witnesses it cannot be determined without knowing the Line of Life they are in. I think keeping them at an Inn if they are low people where there is an Ordinary with a Man to keep them together will be cheapest. At the George and Blue Boar, Holborn, there is an Ordinary every day at half past two o'clock for sixteen pence per head, Beds at one Shilling each and there is a Coffee Room to read the Newspaper in; they should from breakfast to dinner be amused by seeing London, the Lyons at the Tower, Westminster Abbey and other Sights, in the Evening sent to the One Shilling Gallery at the playhouses, that will prevent them spending more Money in getting Drunk and keep them in their Senses.[192]

After the outlay of so much money on a contest it was vital to be able to afford the costs of a petition. A county petition could be so expensive that subscriptions among the major figures of the county would be raised to meet it. Indeed, the cost of petitions could equal the cost of the contested election itself.[193]

[192] John Beardsworth to Thomas Fletcher, 8 Nov. 1790, D/1788/2/5ᵛ, Staffs. RO.
[193] The Buckinghamshire petition of 1784 was to be funded on the side of the Verney interest by a subscription 'raised towards defraying the expense of the Petition by sending circular letters

Finally, perhaps the most indestructable assumptions underlying the allegedly 'corrupt' aspects of the unreformed electoral system relate to the activities of corporations. In corporation and in very many freeman boroughs, in all in perhaps half the total number of borough seats of England and Wales, the activities of corporations have been depicted, by radicals and by reformers, as squalid, venal, intimidatory, and devoid of all political or social merit or value. Formal vindication of the truth of these charges was apparently bestowed by *The Report of the Commission on Municipal Corporations* of 1835, which levelled the most damaging charge of all: that through their manipulation of the freemen rolls, the corporations actually created voters. As Professor Phillips has wisely remarked, however, such creations are evidence of the mobilization of voters, not of the specific influences imposed upon them.[194] Further, it might be added, if both sides were at it, their actions might well have cancelled each other out. In this way, the creation of freemen marked the determination of rival parties to sponsor new voters, not the determination of 'the corporation' to reduce its citizens to slavery.[195] Any such attempts would simply have invited hostile publicity, and probably a petition, from the injured interests.[196]

to the Different Gentlemen connected with the County. The Gentlemen present agreed to contribute towards it in the same manner as they had to the election' (Lord George Cavendish to Sir William Lee, 21 Feb. 1785, D/LE/D/2/31, Lee MSS. Bucks. RO). On this occasion about £7,000 was raised, a sum which equalled the cost of the election (*Morning Chronicle*, 4 May 1784). Similarly, the petition which followed the vigorously contested Gloucestershire county by-election of 1776 was funded on the side of the Berkeley interest by a subscription launched at an impressive meeting of gentlemen at the Bell Inn, Gloucester. For the resolutions, the subscription, and the list of 27 gentlemen see DIL/xxiv/176, Oxon. RO.

[194] Phillips notes that such creations in Norwich and Maidstone divide fairly equally between local parties. (*Electoral Behavior*, 75.) He also cites evidence for Colchester and Liverpool. See also M. E. Speight, 'Politics in the Borough of Colchester, 1812–1847', Ph.D. (London, 1969), p. 144 but cf. 70–73, 139–42; E. M. Menzies, 'The Freeman Voter in Liverpool, 1802–1835, *Hist. Soc. Lancs. and Cheshire*, 124 (1973), 85. Further evidence may be produced. The average rate of admitting new freemen in Chester was 69.9 between 1700 and 1750 and 42.6 from 1750 to 1800. However, in the years before contested elections, the rate rose sharply: to 412 in 1746–7 and 422 in 1783–4. In 1784, however, from 422 new freemen the two Grosvenor candidates attracted the votes of 168 and 154 respectively, the one serious opposition candidate of 160; O'Gorman, 'The Chester Election', 41–50.

[195] Lord Grosvenor confided to a memo written on the third day of the campaign of 1812 that his own interest had created 173 freemen while the opposition led by Sir John Egerton had created 177 (Grosvenor MSS, Chester RO). Such claims can be checked by reference to *The Alphabetical Register of Chester Freemen, 1784, 1812, 1818, 1820 and 1826* in the Grosvenor MSS, ibid.

[196] Lord Carlisle's tampering with the admission of freemen at Morpeth led to expensive litigation as well as to a petition. See Joseph M. Fewster, 'The Politics and Administration of the Borough of Morpeth in the Later Eighteenth Century', Ph.D. (Newcastle, 1960), 136–52, 250–78. Whenever corporations acted in a quasi-coercive manner there was a burst of criticism. *Berrow's Worcester Journal*, 18 Nov. 1773, has some interesting illustrative detail concerning the practice at the by-election of 1773. The publicity aroused public sensitivity and attempts

The problem with the corporations was less their incipient authoritarianism than their sheer inefficiency. On the whole, corporations were content with administration, with collecting payments, rents, and fines, and with circulating money and offices to family, friends, and dependants. They enjoyed only a shadow of their former power, and they hid their impotence in their civic ceremonial. Whether their activities promoted or inhibited the prosperity of their communities is a complex, and possibly unanswerable, question. There are examples on both sides. The York corporation mishandled the question of the Ouse navigation, but the corporation of Worcester was active in promoting civic development and economic growth.[197] These municipal patronage structures, it is safe to say, probably bestowed stable but unimaginative urban government on the corporate towns and enabled landed interests to involve themselves in urban life. They promoted and facilitated the control of constituencies by landed families and thus they occupied a vitally important link in the chains which kept the unreformed electoral system in being.

In this chapter I have dealt with a variety of practices and institutions and throughout I have argued against adopting a moralistic attitude towards them. This is done in no sense to make excuses for original sin nor to exculpate men from electoral misdemeanour. Nor is it a case of arguing that we should allow contemporaries to be judged by their own standard. In an age which did not know of central party discipline, and when honours, office, and favours were distributed informally, the tighter and more measurable values of later generations were unattainable. For example, in the absence of conventions of party discipline, political persuasions had to be informal and thus susceptible to social and economic influences. Electoral behaviour, therefore, inevitably reflected the hierarchical and paternalist society of the day. It was these realities which imposed their own morality upon electoral practices. When the discipline of paternalism was removed or the legitimate interests of voters forgotten, then financial and material considerations alone might come to prevail, as in some of the worst of the venal boroughs like Cricklade, Shaftesbury, and Stockbridge. Yet these were violations against contemporary standards; historians should not mistake them for the standards themselves. Electoral 'corruption' was a means of controlling electors who were increasing

---

to repeat the practice in 1774 caused a petition. The committee hearings were dominated by arguments and evidence concerning the practice of employing freemen as constables (ibid. 4 Mar. 1776).

[197] A. Armstrong, *Stability and Change in an English County Town* (Cambridge, 1974), 23.

both in numbers and in political awareness. Electoral 'corruption' thus played an absolutely indispensable part in retaining aristocratic control, indeed, any control, of the electoral system. This is why it was not and could not be dismantled until the establishment of bureaucratically organized, mass political parties.

# 4

# *The Unreformed Electorate*

This chapter subjects the unreformed electorate to empirical and statistical investigation. In doing so, two principal objectives will be pursued. *Firstly*, the impressions about the electorate and electoral behaviour which have already been generated need to be considerably refined before they can be confidently unleashed upon the world of scholarship. Not everything that has been argued in the first three chapters of this book lends itself to precise investigations employing the calculator and the computer, but some of it does. Consequently, this fourth chapter may be able to say something about the size of the electorate and the extent to which it might be deemed representative, about the location of the electorate, its physical stability and continuity, and the extent of its participation in electoral politics. *Secondly*, we need to pursue more intensively than has hitherto been possible in this study the problem of what determined voting behaviour. To this end we need to consider the social and economic composition of the electorate and the extent to which occupation, more specifically the *type* of occupation, determined voting behaviour. Such an approach may add a socio-economic reference to an activity normally described in political, partisan, or financial terms. We may consequently be able to offer a more balanced explanation for the sources of electoral behaviour than is usually offered by political historians.

In order to approach issues of this order traditional methodologies must be supplemented with more modern technologies. The exchange of anecdotes and the trading of instances are quite insufficient for the quantitative aspects of electoral history. There is, however, a danger that excessive attention to one or just a few constituencies might produce an unbalanced picture. We need, in short, a survey of sufficient generality to provide a reasonable, relevant, and reliable working model of electoral behaviour in the unreformed period, but one which, at the same time, avoids the dangers of superficiality. The almost insoluble problem is to decide which constituencies to choose as the basis of one's research and as the source of one's data.

Indeed, one of the greatest difficulties in the field of electoral history before 1832 is to obtain some grasp of what is typical and general when local situations were so different, when the size of electorates varied so enormously, when the franchise varied so widely, and when, in some cases, electoral processes bordered on farce. What is needed is a viable typology of constituencies.[1] To acquire significant generality, such a typology must satisfy five basic conditions. *First*, it must represent the prevailing varieties of franchise. Generalizations based on the study of a handful of freeman boroughs would be as dangerous as those arising exclusively from a study of Welsh counties. Because the nature of the franchise did much to determine the pattern of electoral politics, the personnel of the electors and their social relationships, as well as the issues and objectives of electoral politics, it is obvious that a satisfactory typology of constituencies must stretch as widely as possible.[2] *Second*, it must include constituencies of different sizes. The population of the town or borough is less immediately significant than the number of those entitled, or potentially entitled, to vote. Nevertheless, the question of size bears so heavily upon the organizational structure of electoral politics that the small as well as the large must find a place in any study of the unreformed electoral system. *Third*, a satisfactory categorization of constituencies must include those under different degrees of control. These degrees of control may be difficult to specify but it is certainly possible to distinguish those which were closed, those under patronage, and those which were open. Inevitably, closed boroughs never, or at most rarely, went to the polls. Examples must therefore be drawn from contested constituencies which were either open or under patronage. *Fourth*, a reasonable geographical spread of constituencies will enhance the general significance of conclusions reached from the analysis of electoral data. The dangers of making general statements from a study of the south-western constituencies would unduly reflect the distribution of rotten boroughs, while a study of the eastern counties would exaggerate the importance of Protestant Nonconformity. Constituencies need to be drawn from all over the country. *Fifth*, and irrespective of any previous considerations, an adequate typology of borough constituencies must accommodate different types of urban situation. At the very simplest level of analysis, three may be distinguished. First, the category of provincial metropolis is by now well established.[3] Such

[1] The need for such a typology was first expressed by H. Hanham 'Some Recent Studies of Voting', *Political Studies*, 4 (1955–6), 150–2, and repeated by J. R. Vincent (*Pollbooks: How Victorians Voted* (Cambridge, 1967), 5), but none has yet been forthcoming.

[2] The point may be an obvious one but it has not always been observed. Even Plumb thought it sufficient to divide constituencies into counties, large boroughs (above 500) and small boroughs (about 150); see J. H. Plumb *The Growth of Political Stability in England, 1675–1725* (London, 1967).

[3] Vincent employs such a category (*Pollbooks*, 14) but does not delineate the characteristics of such towns.

towns as Bristol, Exeter, Liverpool, Norwich, and York, among others, derived their wealth and their authority from a variety of sources, including their positions as administrative, ecclesiastical, maritime, and political centres. Second, the general category of market/ cathedral/county towns may appear unduly wide and diffuse but it includes a large number of represented boroughs. Although such places as Gloucester, Hereford, and Shrewsbury were political, ecclesiastical, and administrative centres, they maintained largely, although by no means exclusively, local patterns of commerce, and, consequently, introverted and parochial patterns of politics. Finally, there were the large number of small towns with populations of a few thousand or less. Such boroughs had fallen on hard times since their seventeenth-century prosperity. They had since failed to develop themselves commercially, usually through their inability to develop adequate communication links. It was of course with this category of borough that the worst of the abuses of the unreformed electoral system are associated.[4]

The major statistical and empirical feature of this particular enquiry has been the systematic establishment of a computerized database, at present located in a Prime 9955 at the Regional Computer Centre at the University of Manchester. The six constituencies which are represented on this database, and the 33 election contests which are analysed on it are summarized in Table 4.1. The data for the voters were organized hierarchically using the SIR (scientific information retrieval) scheme. The database included over 22,000 cases (voters) engaged in almost 40,000 voting selections. Each case included the name of the voter, his occupation, his residence, and information concerning the distribution of his two votes, as well as other, varied material which the poll books contained. This amounted to a computer representation of the poll book.

The six constituencies which are the subject of the database, and thus of the present electoral enquiry, to some extent meet the demands of the constituency typology outlined above. *First*, they represent some of the franchisal types (given the restrictions of time and resources, it is simply not possible for one individual to cover them all). The most obvious omission is that of the county seats. However, because county poll books do not include the occupation of voters, they are much less useful than their borough counterparts. What we have here, then, are representatives of the 92 freeman and 49 scot and lot/householder

---

[4] For this last category see C. W. Chalkin, *The Provincial Towns of Georgian England* (London, 1974), 5. Many of these towns prospered in the 17th cent. and declined in the 18th cent. See G. Holmes, *The Electorate and the National Will in the First Age of Party* (Kendal, 1976), 24–8.

TABLE 4.1    *Elections Database*

| Constituency | Franchise | Contests |
|---|---|---|
| Chester | Freeman | 1812, 1818, 1826 |
| Cirencester | Householder | 1768, 1780, 1807 |
| Colchester | Freeman | 1790, 1796, 1806, 1807, 1812, 1818, 1820 |
| St Albans | Freeman | 1820, 1821, 1830, 1831 |
| Shrewsbury | Freeman | 1806, 1807, 1812, 1814, 1819, 1826, 1830, 1831 |
| Southampton | Freeman | 1774, 1790, 1794, 1806, 1812, 1818, 1820, 1831 |

types, 141 of 203 English boroughs (69%). We have no representatives of English and Welsh counties, freeholder, burgage, and corporation boroughs, or Welsh boroughs, although Shrewsbury may to some extent be regarded as a Welsh constituency. Burgage boroughs were not included, because of the obvious pressures under which voters were put, corporation boroughs were not included because of the paucity of voters. *Second*, these constituencies range in size from one small freeman borough (Shrewsbury) to two large freeman boroughs (Chester and Colchester). Electorates range, therefore, from a few hundred to a few thousand. Clearly, it was advisable to avoid the extremes: the few giant boroughs with over 3,000 voters and the rotten boroughs with farcically few. Most constituencies fall within this middle range of sizes of the electorate, as adopted here. *Three*, although we have here constituencies under varying degrees of control, it has not been thought desirable to attempt to mirror the patterns of patronage evident throughout the electoral system. Southampton was a relatively open borough, in spite of the government interest there, in which religious issues could make themselves felt. Colchester was rather similar, perhaps more independent, more expensive, and more boisterous. The politics of Chester were more decorous, perhaps, but certainly no less partisan, the paternalist regime of the Grosvenor family meeting increasing hostility in the early nineteenth century. Similarly, the oligarchic politics of Shrewsbury in the early nineteenth century met increasing opposition and, consequently, a run of contested elections.

(The increase of the Shrewsbury electorate, from 300 in the later eighteenth century to 1200 on the eve of the 1832 Reform Act, is particularly noteworthy.) Patronage and frequent contests were factors at St Albans, too, slightly less so at Cirencester. All this is exactly typical of electoral politics throughout the political system; the power of local families over constituencies was ever present, even if rarely complete. *Fourth*, these constituencies are geographically spread from north to south and from west to east. *Fifth*, different types of urban situation are evident here. Chester was a great regional centre, an economic, ecclesiastical, and administrative capital for Cheshire and North Wales. Colchester was an important market town in a primarily (and, increasingly exclusively) agricultural area. Shrewsbury was a county town. Southampton was, of course, a maritime town, Cirencester and St Albans market towns. Again, it is not claimed that the constituencies included here reflected the entire spectrum of varying urban situations in England. Rather, it is fairly representative of those *types* which were prominent within the electoral system.

The selection of constituencies accommodates the main requirements of the typology outlined above. There are, however, as there are bound to be with any such selection, certain weaknesses. These include the absence of county constituencies, the over-weighting of freeman boroughs (although there were over twice as many freeman boroughs as any other kind of borough in the electoral system), the absence of very large boroughs, and the absence of what may be termed 'industrial revolution' towns. I have endeavoured to supply these deficiencies by manually analysing data from carefully selected additional constituencies. These may be categorized as follows: *county constituency*: Lincolnshire (1818, 1823); *non-freeman boroughs*: Abingdon (1802), Minehead (1768, 1796, 1802), Preston (1818, 1820); *large boroughs*; Canterbury (1830), Leicester (1826), Liverpool (1780, 1784, 1790, 1802, 1818), Oxford (1820), Rochester (1830); *'industrial revolution' towns*: Preston (1818, 1820), Nottingham (1830), Wigan (1830). If these do not balance against the bias inevitable in any selection of constituencies, then there are further additional contested elections in particular sections of what follows to attempt to eliminate that bias altogether. Altogether I have employed data from 22 constituencies at 59 contests.[5]

In doing so, I was well aware of the limitations of a quantifying approach to electoral history. Poll books say little or nothing about

[5] In addition to the 33 contests at my 6 'selected' constituencies and the 21 contests at 12 listed above I have deployed data from the small freeman boroughs of Boston (1826), Grantham (1820), and Grimsby (1826), from the medium-sized freeman borough of Newcastle-under-Lyme (1790), and the large freeman borough of Lincoln (1826).

the campaign, its crises, accidents, and dramas. They divulge nothing about personalities and corruption, and little about religious and political issues. Poll books and complementary sources only exist on account of the calculations made by jobbing printers about the economies of an edition of a poll book rather than the needs of the twentieth-century scholar. They may even have been published only in unusual circumstances of electoral excitement.[6] Furthermore, historians have to make an act of faith in assuming the reliability of poll books although in reality their accuracy can be questioned. Some of them are prefaced with earnest apologies by publishers, acknowledging the occasional errors which the hectic circumstances of their compilation inevitably incurred. The books were compiled at the hustings. Not only the clerk taking the official poll but rival party agents also would be striving to hear the complexities of the data called out by the voter amidst the noise and hubbub. This might be complex information: his address, occupation and his qualification. The opportunities for error—misidentification, omission, or phonetic spelling—were legion. Human error could also intervene if the poll book was published, both at the the copying and printing stages. We do not know how extensive such errors were.[7]

There is also, in this minute examination of voting records, a danger of taking it all too seriously, of imagining that voting in parliamentary elections was the only measure of political behaviour, to the neglect of popular agitation and crowd behaviour, on the one hand, and to the neglect of municipal (or county) politics and the world of petitioning and public meetings, on the other. We have to recall constantly the context within which votes were given, a context mediated and conditioned over the years in very complicated and sensitive processes. It goes without saying that we should avoid anachronism and eschew the transposing into this period of the assumptions and the results of research relating to others. To assume, for example, that electoral politics pre-1832 was similar to, inferior to, or even an anticipation of, electoral politics after 1832 is methodologically unacceptable.[8] We may, then, lift the analysis of the unreformed electorate on to a secure empirical basis of sufficient generality if we can address appropriate enquiries consistently across a broad selection of constituency types over time. To that endeavour we now turn.

---

[6] Vincent remarks, for example, that there tend to be more poll books for periods of political excitement (*Pollbooks*, 1). I have not noticed such a phenomenon before 1832, however.

[7] One ingenious estimate puts the error at about 1%. At the county election at Kent (7,000 voters) in 1734, the printed poll book omitted 64 names given in the MS poll book and added several others. See K. Von den Steinen, 'The Fabric of an Interest. The First Duke of Dorset and Kentish and Sussex Politics, 1705–1765', Ph.D. (UCLA, 1969), 57.

[8] The eight hypotheses advanced by Vincent (*Pollbooks*, 14), for example, seem, on the whole, irrelevant to the pre-1832 situation.

THE NATURE OF THE ELECTORATE

The unreformed electorate has always been viewed in an unfavourable and condescending light, not least because it seems to compare badly with what came before and with what came after. Every historian who has written about the 1832 Reform Act, for example, has assumed that the post-1832 electorate was superior *both qualitatively and quantitatively* to its unreformed predecessor. Consequently the Reform Act is still seen as 'a great and benficient feat of statesmanship' which made a powerful contribution to 'peaceful political evolution'.[9] Yet the unreformed electorate, as we have seen, was capable of impressive political sophistication in its organization and, as we shall see, its capacity to express political issues and ideologies. It was, perhaps, not so different from the post-1832 electorate in all this. On the issue of numbers, however, it is worth examining the evidence again in order to understand the extent to which the 1832 reform did increase the number of electors within the electorate.

There is an overwhelming consensus of opinion in favour of the traditional view that the 1832 Reform Act significantly enhanced the size of the electorate. Table 4.2 summarizes the existing historiography on this point. As many commentators have noted, although the electorate did increase steadily in size in the century before the Reform Act of 1832 it failed completely to keep pace with population growth. Between 1754 and 1831, for example, the population almost doubled but the electorate increased in size by only 20%.[10]

Two remarks need to be made about Table 4.2. The first is that the figures for 1689, 1715, 1754–1790, and 1831 do not allow for turnout: that for 1832 does. In other words, the registered electorate in 1832 comprises all males entitled to vote. The figures for the earlier dates show only electors *who actually voted*, and should therefore be adjusted upwards to allow for those who failed to vote.[11] It is almost incredible that such a basic methodological error has been perpetrated by decade after decade of historians.[12] The figures for the pre-1832

[9] M. Brock, *The Great Reform Act* (London, 1973), 335–6. See also J. A. Cannon, *Parliamentary Reform, 1640–1832* (Cambridge, 1972), esp. ch. 11; N. Gash, *Aristocracy and People: Britain 1815–1865* (London, 1979), 145, for assumptions about 'anomalies and abuses'; see also ibid. 49, 150–5.

[10] Cannon, *Parliamentary Reform*, 42

[11] Speck has already realized this, his assessment for 1715 is now 300,000, an increase of 20%; see W. A. Speck, *Stability and Strife: England 1714–1760* (London, 1977), 16. For my estimates of turnout see below, 182–91.

[12] Cannon has now generously acknowledged the error; J. A. Cannon, *The Historian at Work* (London, 1982), 16.

TABLE 4.2    *Size of the English and Welsh Electorates, 1689–1832*

|  | 1689 | 1715 | 1754–1790 | 1831 | 1832 |
|---|---|---|---|---|---|
| Electorate | 200,000 | 250,000 | 282,000 | 366,000 | 656,000[a] |
| Population (million) | 5.4 | 5.8 | 8.5[b] | 13.9 | 13.9 |
| Electorate as % of population | 3.7 | 4.3 | 3.3 | 2.5 | 4.7 |
| Electorate as % of adult males[c] | 17.2 | 19.9 | 14.3 | 12.2 | 18.4 |

*Sources*: J. Plumb, 'The Growth of the Electorate in England 1660–1715', *Past and Present* 45 (1969), 111; W. A. Speck, *Tory and Whig: The Struggle in the Constituencies* (London, 1977), 16–17; J. A. Cannon, *Parliamentary Reform 1640–1832* (Cambridge, 1972), 40–3, 258–9, 290; M. Brock, *The Great Reform Act* (London, 1973), 312. The scattered estimates in Thorne, *House of Commons* I, 4,20, 23,29, 34,38, 42,63, suggest an electorate of 325–330,000 in the early nineteenth century.

[a] Taken as the number of registered electors eligible to vote before the election of 1832, according to the Report of the Committee of the House of Commons on Election Expenses, 1833.

[b] For 1801.

[c] Assuming adult males to be 21.5% of the population in 1695, 23% in the later eighteenth century, and 25.5% in the early nineteenth century. See J. G. Phillips, *Electoral Behavior in Unreformed England, 1761–1802* (Princeton, 1982), 202–3.

TABLE 4.3    *Adjusted Estimate of Size of the English and Welsh Electorates, 1689–1832*

|  | 1689 | 1715 | 1754–1790 | 1831 | 1832 |
|---|---|---|---|---|---|
| Electorate | 240,000 | 300,000 | 338,000 | 439,200 | 656,000[a] |
| Population (million) | 5.4 | 5.8 | 8.5 | 13.9 | 13.9 |
| Electorate as % of population | 4.6 | 5.2 | 4.0 | 3.2 | 4.7 |
| Electorate as % of adult males[b] | 20.6 | 23.9 | 17.2 | 14.4 | 18.4 |

[a,b] See Table 4.2

electorate need to be increased by at least 20%. Table 4.3 incorporates these adjusted figures.

Secondly, there is a further reason why this higher estimate should be accepted. The figure for 1831 which is commonly accepted today is that calculated by Professor Cannon. His estimate of 366,000 is given, subject to adjustment for turnout. Cannon, however, repudiates the estimate reached by the nineteenth-century author J. Lambert, of just over 435,000. Cannon's repudiation of the figures on which Lambert presumably relied, those provided by the returning officers during the great inquest on the constituencies in 1831–2, strongly suggests that he underestimated the accuracy of those figures. They apparently do allow for turnout. If we accept Lambert's figure for the English boroughs (435,391), and then, like Cannon, add 20,000 for the Welsh boroughs, we achieve a total electorate of just over 455,000 in 1831. That figure corresponds very closely with my estimate of 439,000 for the English and Welsh electorate in 1831. The Reform Act of 1832 added about 200,000 voters to an electorate of around 440,000, an increase of about 45%. This, of course, is significant, undeniably so, but it is considerably less than the 80% argued by Professor Cannon.[13]

Blanket calculations of this type, however, conceal the wide variety of electoral situations involved. Some types of constituency experienced little or no increase in their electorates from the mid-eighteenth century to 1831: the counties, the small freeman boroughs, the corporation and burgage boroughs.[14] Their combined effect in depressing the impact on the overall total of those types of constituency whose electorates did increase is self-evident: the scot and lot boroughs and the medium and large freeman boroughs (see Table 4.4).

After a period of marked stability in the size of these electorates, a period of dramatic increase began in the later eighteenth century which was continued by the 1832 Reform Act. The electorate was already rapidly increasing in size long before the Act of 1832. That increase, moreover, was taking place where the electorate was already most open and most vociferous, where contests were taking place and where party formation was most highly developed. In some places, the electoral system was remarkably representative. There were the Old Sarums and the Gattons, but in many of the larger freeman boroughs around 25% of adult males had the vote.[15] In a medium

---

[13] Id., *Parliamentary Reform*, 259, 290–2. Interestingly, some recent authorities do accept Lambert's figures. See e.g. C. Cook, *British Historical Facts* (London, 1975), 115–17; D. Butler and J. Cornford, *International Guide to Electoral Statistics* (London, 1968), 333. For the reliability of the returning officer's figures see D. Stoker, 'Elections and Voting Behaviour: A Study of Elections in Northumberland, Durham, Cumberland, and Westmorland, 1760–1832', Ph.D. (Manchester, 1980), 182.

[14] The total electorate in the small freeman boroughs (under 200 voters) increased from 4,115 to 4,792 between the mid-18th cent. and 1831. Cannon estimates that the electorate in the counties increased by only 6% between 1754 and 1831. *Parliamentary Reform*, 42. The burgage boroughs hardly increased their electorates, the corporation boroughs not at all. See also R. G. Thorne (ed.), *The House of Commons, 1790–1820*, 5 vols. (London, 1986), i. 34, 38.

[15] e.g. Coventry, Chester, Nottingham, and Leicester in the 1820s. We have even more precise figures in the Norwich poll books for 1830. Out of an electorate of 4,202, there were 3,153 resident—20–25% of an adult (20 + years) male population of 15,403.

TABLE 4.4  *Size of the Electorate in Larger Boroughs, Mid-Eighteenth Century to 1831*

| Constituency | Mid-18th cent. | Later 18th cent. | 1831 |
|---|---|---|---|
| Scot and lot | 10,553 | 11,432 | 21,670 |
| Medium freeman | 14,675 | 12,780 | 15,165 |
| Large freeman | 47,360 | 54,700 | 70,945 |

to largish scot and lot borough like Reading, one-quarter of adult males had the vote in 1826. In certain of the potwalloper boroughs, moreover, universal male suffrage had all but arrived. At Honiton and Cirencester over 75% had the right to vote, while even at Northampton over 50% did.[16] Even in the medium freeman boroughs between one-quarter and one-third of adult males had the vote,[17] in the medium scot and lot boroughs over 40%.[18]

The small size of the electorate in many boroughs has caused much amusement in the past,[19] and in some of the very tiniest, and closed, boroughs the amusement is probably justified; none the less, such numbers need to be treated extremely carefully. Tiny Appleby (100 electors in the early nineteenth century), Morpeth (212), and Cockermouth (300) look unimpressive, but their electorates as a percentage of adult males—22%, 26%, and 23%, respectively—are, in fact, higher than the percentage for many counties with their huge electorates. The Oxfordshire contest of 1820 found 3,115 electors able to vote out of a population of 16,446 of adult males, yielding 18.9%. Just occasionally, too, a relatively small electorate conceals something approaching universal male suffrage. The Minehead elections of 1768,

[16] As many as 60%, according to J. A. Phillips, *Electoral Behavior in Unreformed England, 1761–1802* (Princeton, 1982), 42.

[17] e.g. Southampton, where the electorates of 769 (8.0% of a population of 9,617) in 1812, 1,012 (7.6% of a population of 13,353) in 1820, and 1,403 (7.3% of a population of 19,324) in 1831 yield percentages of adult males of 31.4%, 29.8%, and 28.6% respectively. Similarly at St Albans, electorates of 575 (9.9% of a population of 5,733) in 1821, and 656 (10% of a population of 6,582) in 1831 yield percentages of adult males of 38.8% and 39.2% respectively.

[18] The Warwick electorate of 1,060 was 16.3% of a population of 9,109: 63.9% of adult males had the vote. These figures are of those *actually voting*; the figure for the electorate *as a whole* would be even higher if allowance were made for turnout. However, the figures used do not allow for the non-residence of a certain percentage of voters. As this is roughly the same as the number of non-voters (see below, pp. 191–3), the two are likely to have cancelled each other out; see E. Heathcore, *Poll of the Burgesses* (Warwick, 1831).

[19] Once again, generations of historians have waxed strong and cynical. Namier was one of the worst. 'Thus in the whole of England only 112 out of 405 borough representatives (i.e. almost 28%) were returned by electorates of 500 or above' (L. B. Namier, *The Structure of Politics at the Accession of George III* (London, 1929), 101–2).

1796, 1802, and 1807 occurred among an electorate of around 300, over 80% of adult males. The astonishing growth of some of the unenfranchised industrial towns should not cause us to forget how relatively slowly, by comparison, others were growing. Cambridge, for example, had a population of only 6,422 in 1728. By 1794 it was still under 10,000. In 1801 Northampton still had a population of only 7,000 souls, Hull had 30,000, Newcastle 28,000, and Nottingham 29,000. Their electorates of 1,000, 1,500, 3,000, and 3,300, were nothing to be ashamed of, yielding percentages of adult males of 56%, 19.6%, 42%, and 44.6% respectively.[20]

Professor Cannon has argued that between 1754 and 1832 'there was a sharp decline in the proportion of people who had even a formal share in the political life of the nation'.[21] In view of the increase in the size of the electorate, and in view of the foregoing consideration of the representativeness of the electorate, I do not believe that such a view can be sustained. Nevertheless, there can be no doubt at all that the Reform Act of 1832 *did* make a difference. As we saw from Tables 4.2 and 4.3, the electorate increased as a percentage of adult males from about 14% to about 18%, a discernible and significant difference but scarcely the stuff of which political revolutions are made. Between 1689 and 1832 the electorate as a percentage of adult males wavered between 14% and 25%. The increase effected by the 1832 Reform Act was well within these limits. It remained in that proportion to population right up to the eve of the Reform Act of 1867, when it more than doubled. In 1868 no fewer than 12% of the population, or 54% of adult males, were entitled to vote, a sudden and dramatic increase in the percentage. From this perspective, at least, it is continuity rather than disruptive change which characterizes the period 1689 to 1866. The tendencies within the unreformed electorate to increase its numbers in response to demographic and social change were accelerated, not created, by the Reform Act of 1832.

It is a continuity, none the less, which contains one perceptible development: the tendency for turnout at contested elections to increase between 1689 and 1832. The miserably small turnouts of the early eighteenth century were, on the whole, to be exceeded later in the eighteenth century and in the early nineteenth. These, in their turn, tended to be overtaken by the spectacularly high turnouts of the years after 1832.

---

[20] I must leave to another occasion an estimate of the percentage of households in such towns which had a voter. Working on the assumption that a household may be estimated at 4 to 5 persons, a very high percentage of the total households in the boroughs mentioned here must have had a voter.

[21] Cannon, *Parliamentary Reform*, 42.

In making such statements we must, of course, be extremely cautious. Only after 1832 when an 'objective' definition of turnout exists—the percentage of registered electors who vote—can figures be assembled with any certainty.[22] The historian of the unreformed electorate has no such convenient yardstick to employ. In freeman boroughs some attempt may be made to calculate the size of the potential electorate by examining freeman rolls, directories, and, of course, poll books for earlier elections. In the case of the scot and lot boroughs, rate books might yield a corresponding figure, in the counties, the land tax returns. Sometimes, election literature, and even the poll books themselves, attempt to estimate the size of the potential electorate. It was difficult enough for contemporary election managers to trace the voters, their movements, their residence, their qualifications, their occupations, their wealth, their legal status, and, of course, their deaths. What chance, then, does the historian have, in this complex, wearing, and hazardous area, of making accurate assessments of the numbers of those who did not vote?

In the early eighteenth century that number was extremely high. Professor Holmes's examples of turnout range from 55% to a maximum of 75% between 1689 and 1722.[23] From the mid-eighteenth century onwards a significantly higher rate of turnout is in evidence. Estimates for turnout at 110 contests in 32 constituencies are given in Table 4.5. For what it is worth, the overall average of these turnout figures is 80.6%.

The astonishingly high rates of turnout in the scot and lot householder constituencies are obviously to be explained by the residential nature of the qualification. Turnouts in the larger freeman boroughs tend, on the whole, to be lower because of the relatively high number of non-resident voters who qualified for the franchise but who might not be able to travel to vote.[24] Occasionally they dip alarmingly, usually on account of the nature of the contest. At Colchester in 1818, for example, the contested by-election ended on the third day, when the radical candidate declined to prolong the poll. At 274–182, almost 100 behind, he calculated that he could not win. Such cases, however, were quite rare. Most contests were fights to

---

[22] It is well known that the registered electorate after 1832 was never complete, i.e. it did not contain all those who met the voting qualification. The extent of this shortfall is not often realized. Thus, at the Ipswich election of 1832, 77.25% of the registered electorate voted—apparently quite a decent turnout figure, but in fact only 51.5% of those who met the qualification; see *Pollbook for Members, 1832*, John Rylands Univ. Lib. Manchester. At Nottingham in 1832 the registered electorate of 5,166 was only about 60% of those entitled to vote; see *Alphabetical List of the Burgesses* (Nottingham, 1832).

[23] Holmes, *The Electorate and the National Will*, 23.

[24] For outvoters see below, pp. 191–3.

TABLE 4.5　Turnout in 32 Constituencies: Mid-Eighteenth Century to 1831 (%)

| | 1741 | 1747 | 1754 | 1761 | 1768 | 1774 | 1780 | 1784 | 1790 | 1796 | 1802 | 1806 | 1807 | 1812 | 1818 | 1820 | 1826 | 1830 | 1831 |
|---|---|---|---|---|---|---|---|---|---|---|---|---|---|---|---|---|---|---|---|
| *Large freeman boroughs* | | | | | | | | | | | | | | | | | | | |
| Bristol | | | | | | | | | | | | | | 66 | | | | | |
| Canterbury | | | | | | | | | | 91 | | | | | | | 86 | | |
| Chester | | | | | | | | 70 | | | | | | 78 | 88 | 88 | | | |
| Colchester | | | | | | | | | 83 | 49 | | 83 | 59 | 88 | 30 | 92 | | | 70 |
| Dover | | | | | | | | | | | | | | | | 96 | | | |
| Durham | | | | | | | | | | | | | | | | | | 83 | |
| Gloucester | 69 | 55 | | | | | | 56 | | | | | | | | | | | 53 |
| Hereford | | | | | | | | | | | | | | | 57 | 66 | 89 | | |
| Leicester | | | | | | | | | | | | | | | | | 88 | | |
| Liverpool | | | | | 86 | | | | | | | | | 77 | | | 76 | 87 | 80 |
| Maidstone[a] | | | | | | | 59 | 90 | | | | | | | 82 | | | 84 | 92 |
| Norwich | | | | | | | | | | | 82 | 83 | 67 | 75 | 82 | | | | |
| Nottingham | | | | | | 90 | 81 | 85 | | | | | | | | | | | |
| Oxford | | | | | | | | | | | 81 | 90 | | | | | | | |
| Worcester | | | | | | | | | | | | | | | | | | | 87 |
| *Medium freeman boroughs* | | | | | | | | | | | | | | | | | | | |
| Derby | | | | | | 97 | | | | | 71 | 88 | 71 | | | | | | |
| Rochester | | | | | | | | | | | | | | | | | 82 | 73 | |
| St Albans | | | | | | | | | | | | | | | | 62 | 76 | 50 | 82 |

| | | | | | | | | |
|---|---|---|---|---|---|---|---|---|
| Sandwich | | | | | | | | 75 |
| Southampton[b] | 76 | 92 | 89 | 87 | 91 | 89 | 93 | 85 |
| *Small freeman boroughs* | | | | | | | | |
| Boston | | | | | | 68 | | |
| Shrewsbury | | 92 | 72 | 67 | | | 56 | 78 | 25 |
| *Scot and lot/ householder boroughs* | | | | | | | | |
| Cirencester | 82 | 92 | 95 | | | 85 | | |
| Lewes[a] | 94 | 99 | 87 | 74 | 93 | 95 | 95 | 97 | 80 | 94 | 93 |
| Minehead | | 68 | 89 | 99 | 91 | | | |
| New Windsor | | 95 | 91 | 92 | | | | |
| Northampton | 90 | | | | | 73 | 71 | |
| Reading | 86 | 93 | 81 | | 90 | 73 | 96 | |
| Warwick | 93 | 81 | | | | | 80 | |
| *Counties* | | | | | | | | |
| Essex | 81 | 68 | | | | | | |
| Lincolnshire | | | 97 | 86 | | | | |
| Oxfordshire | 96 | | | | | | | |

*Sources*: As for Table 4.2.
[a] Figures taken from J. G. Phillips, *Electoral Behavior in Unreformed England*, 88–9.
[b] Becomes large freeman borough in early nineteenth century.

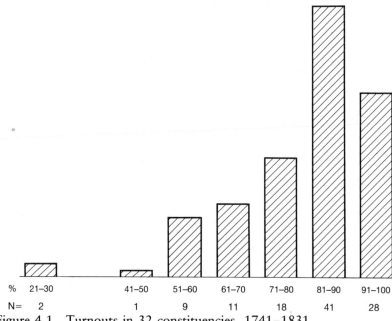

Figure 4.1   Turnouts in 32 constituencies, 1741–1831

the finish; even in the freeman boroughs, the turnouts reflected the fact. It is, perhaps, invidious to offer averages for a phenomenon like turnout. Fig. 4.1 indicates the frequency of different levels of turnout between 1741 and 1831. Significantly, *almost twice as many* turnouts were above 80% than were below it. With some exceptions, the low turnouts of the early eighteenth century were thus a thing of the past. Remarkably, some constituencies were actually coming close to polling out.

What explains these higher turnouts? Improvements in communications must have made it easier for outvoters to travel and for news and information to spread. Such considerations would affect all types of constituencies, but especially the counties and the freeman boroughs. Patrons and voters alike, moreover, would feel an enhanced sense of participation in the less frequently contested elections which were such a feature of the unreformed electoral system. Certainly, more sophisticated organizational techniques did much to mobilize the electorate. It was less the voluntary and spontaneous enthusiasm of voters which made for high turnouts than the ability of election committees to get the vote out. Community excitement and involvement should not, however, be excluded from all this. As we have seen, elections generated massive local interest and excitement. Many electors would willingly involve themselves in the election, particularly if they regarded the suffrage as a trust and even if they regarded it as a means to personal profit. It follows that many of those who did not were in fact deliberately withholding the vote, even though it would have made them a profit and allowed them to participate. Abstention, therefore, must in many cases be regarded as a positive act of political will.

Many of those who chose not to involve themselves in the election were drawn from the upper classes of local society. Professor Holmes has shown that in the early eighteenth century less than 50% of the gentry would vote at a particular election.[25] They did not do much better later in the eighteenth century. The participation of the 'Gentlemen of Hampshire' in elections varied from 50% in 1734, 75% in 1779, and 60% in 1806.[26] In the boroughs, things were not much better. At Rochester only 34% of gentlemen and their social superiors participated in 1826, 53% in 1830. In most cases the gentlemen constituted a much higher percentage of abstainers than they did of the electorate as a whole: 21% as opposed to 14.8% in Rochester in 1807, 20% as opposed to 16.3% in 1830, 20% as opposed to 16% in Sandwich in 1831, 34% as opposed to 12% at Warwick in 1792, 18% as opposed to 13% at Oxford in 1802.[27] The reasons are not far to seek. Members of the upper classes of society appear to have wished to steer clear of political excitement, to avoid controversy, and to prevent trouble. They did not wish to give offence and had no desire to agitate the sort of contentious issues within a community which might have endangered their social leadership. Folk memories of the first age of party and an awareness of the fragility of social discipline and political order inhibited many gentlemen from throwing themselves wholeheartedly into the game of electoral politics. Among the many unpleasant aspects of a contested election, 'the animosities that it leaves are not the least, and that it is allmost impossible for those who have been considered as leading persons not to be so implicated that their appearance at least for some time after, rather tended to keep them alive than otherwise'.[28] Consequently, many of the higher status electors exhibit an attitude of studied withdrawal, which is not to be mistaken for political indifference.

After the Reform Act of 1832, turnout increased to a slightly higher statistical plateau, aided, indisputably, by the registration clauses of

[25] Holmes, *The Electorate and the National Will*, 21–2.
[26] S. Lowe, 'Hampshire Elections and Electioneering, 1734–1830', M.Phil. (Southampton, 1972), 215–19.
[27] The poll books for these contested elections are among the few to describe the non-voters as well as voters.
[28] Duke of Norfolk to Dr Pilley, 23 Feb. 1796, Pilley MSS, Hereford and Worcs. RO.

the Act, the tighter definition of the franchise, the elimination of outvoting, and the provision of more polling booths and centres. Nevertheless, most calculations of turnout in the reformed electoral system go no higher than 80–85%.[29] This is not very much higher than the rates of turnout that prevailed before 1832. The difference, in truth, is not great. When we examine rates of turnout for 25 years before and after the 1832 Reform Act in particular constituencies, such difference as there is in most cases almost dissolves (see Table 4.6). The Reform Act did not inaugurate dramatically different levels of electoral turnout and mobilization. These were already exceptionally high. The participation record of the unreformed electorate clearly compares very creditably with that of its more favoured successor.

What specific factors explain different levels of turnout? In the present state of knowledge it is difficult to be sure. I do not believe that medium term trends over time are discernible. Professor Phillips trembles on the verge of such Whiggishness when he argues 'for heavy, and perhaps even increasing, voter turnout' in his work on Lewes and Maidstone.[30] It is very difficult to detect such medium-term trends in the cases of those constituencies of which we have fairly extensive runs of turnout data (see Table 4.7). Turnouts in most cases were likely to be over 80% unless special circumstances intervened (e.g. a short poll, a hopeless contest). There are signs, too, that some constituencies tended to have lower turnouts than others.

The relatively low turnouts at Shrewsbury, for example, are undoubtedly a consequence of the exclusion of outvoters, after the victory of the independent candidate, Thomas Jones, in 1806, and his protest against the unscrupulous manipulation of the outvoters by his opponents. Furthermore, there can be little doubt that the type of franchise had some influence over turnout. From Table 4.5 it is clear that the scot and lot freeholder franchise seemed to attract spectacularly high turnouts. Turnout, moreover, relates to the development of party organizations. It is interesting that high turnouts are frequently registered in those constituencies which are acknowledged to be in the forefront of party formation (Leicester, Maidstone, Norwich, Nottingham, Oxford, Rochester, Southampton, and Reading), while those constituencies in our lists to which party

---

[29] Nossiter, *Influence, Opinion and Political Idioms in Reformed England: Case Studies from the North-east* (Brighton, 1975), presents evidence of turnout from 52 boroughs in the six northern counties at each election between 1832 and 1886. The average figure is 84.6%. Newmarch estimated turnout at the 1852 election at 82% (W. Newmarch, 'On the Electoral Statistics of the Counties and Boroughs of England and Wales, 1832–1857', *J. Stats. Soc.* 20 (1857), 169–234).

[30] J. A. Phillips, *Electoral Behavior*, 88.

TABLE 4.6 *Comparison of Turnout for 25 Years Before and After the 1832 Reform Act (%)*

| | 1807 | 1812 | 1818 | 1820 | 1826 | 1830 | 1831 | 1832 | 1835 | 1837 | 1841 | 1847 | 1852 | 1857 |
|---|---|---|---|---|---|---|---|---|---|---|---|---|---|---|
| Bristol | | 66 | | | | | | | | | 64 | 75 | | |
| Canterbury | | 78 | 88 | | | 86 | | | | | 91 | 90 | 85 | 89 |
| Chester | | 88 | 90 | 92 | 88 | | | | | 64 | | | | |
| Colchester | 59 | 53 | 30 | | | | 70 | 90 | | 63 | | | | |
| Gloucester | | | 57 | | | 53 | | 92 | 96 | 94 | 90 | | | |
| Hereford | | | 66 | | 89 | | | 66 | 90 | 90 | 80 | | | |
| Leicester | | | | | 88 | | | 91 | 92 | 77 | | | | |
| Liverpool | | 77 | | | | 87 | 80 | 78 | 72 | 81 | | | | |
| Maidstone | | | | | 76 | 84 | 92 | 79 | 73 | | | | | |
| Norwich | | | 82 | | | | 90 | 90 | 82 | 87 | | | | |
| Rochester | 71 | | | | 82 | 73 | | 65 | 87 | 88 | | | | |

TABLE 4.7    *Turnout in Six Constituencies, 1774–1831*

| | Voters | Electorate | Turnout (%) |
|---|---|---|---|
| Chester[a] | | | |
| 1812 | 1,175 | 1,500 | 78 |
| 1818 | 1,347 | 1,500 | 90 |
| 1826 | 1,501 | 1,700 | 88 |
| Cirencester[b] | | | |
| 1768 | 652 | 800 | 82 |
| 1790 | 461 | 500 | 92 |
| 1802 | 428 | 500 | 86 |
| Colchester[a] | | | |
| 1790 | 1,241 | 1,500 | 83 |
| 1796 | 737 | 1,500 | 49 |
| 1806 | 1,125 | 1,500 | 83 |
| 1807 | 887 | 1,500 | 59 |
| 1812 | 1,322 | 1,500 | 88 |
| 1818 | 456 | 1,500 | 30 |
| 1820 | 1,383 | 1,500 | 92 |
| St. Albans[c] | | | |
| 1820 | 462 | 750 | 62 |
| 1821 | 574 | 750 | 76 |
| 1830 | 402 | 800 | 50 |
| 1831 | 657 | 800 | 82 |
| Shrewsbury[d] | | | |
| 1806 | 723 | 1,000 | 72 |
| 1807 | 674 | 1,000 | 67 |
| 1814 | 837 | 1,200 | 70 |
| 1819 | 671 | 1,200 | 56 |
| 1826 | 670 | 1,200 | 56 |
| Southampton[c] | | | |
| 1774 | 380 | 500 | 76 |
| 1790 | 460 | 500 | 92 |
| 1794 | 490 | 550 | 89 |
| 1806 | 611 | 700 | 87 |
| 1812 | 638 | 700 | 91 |
| 1818 | 667 | 750 | 89 |
| 1820 | 839 | 900 | 93 |
| 1831 | 1,018 | 1,200 | 85 |

*Note*: Size of electorate is calculated from poll books, canvassing lists, and published sources, in particular L. B. Namier and J. Brooke, *The House of Commons, 1754–1790*, 3 vols. (London, 1964), vol. i; J. H. Philbin, *Parliamentary Representation, 1832: England and Wales* (New Haven, 1965); and R. G. Thorne, (ed), *The House of Commons, 1790–1820*, 5 vols. (London, 1986), vol. i. Figures in these published sources are however unreliable, often reflecting *voting* figures.

[a] Large freeman borough.
[b] Householder borough.
[c] Medium freeman borough
[d] Small to medium freeman borough.

development came a little later show slightly lower turnouts (Gloucester, Hereford, St Albans, Boston). A further contributory influence may be the size of the constituency. In some of the very biggest (Bristol and Liverpool), relatively low levels of turnout are registered, perhaps a consequence of the inability of committees and canvassers to exhaust the possibilities open to them. Interestingly, there is little evidence in these tables that particular issues or specific personalities stimulated higher turnouts. There is little indication that turnouts were higher at those elections normally taken to be excitingly partisan (1784, 1807, 1818, 1831) than those which took place in quiet years (1790, 1802, 1812). This is surprising, because election committees certainly behaved as though voters could be persuaded of the rights and wrongs of particular issues through canvassing and propaganda. It might have been true early in the eighteenth century that the function of propaganda was 'to rouse the élite to exert their influence in aid of the party they already favoured, and so ensure the appearance of those supporting their party at the polls',[31] but later in the century such appeals were directed at the voters themselves.

It was a constant complaint of radicals and reformers, none the less, that large numbers of voters did not reside in the constituency in which they voted. Given the nature of the franchise, and the propertied and occupational attributes which conferred the right to vote, this was, of course, perfectly possible. Towards the end of the eighteenth century the Society of the Friends of the People claimed that in some of the larger freeman boroughs the outvoters, as they were called, constituted a proportion of the electorate ranging from 25% to a staggering 70% in the case of Lancaster.[32] These estimates were taken from contemporary poll books, and their accuracy can readily be confirmed.[33] They can be matched from other large freeman boroughs,[34] and, indeed, from other types of constituency as

[31] N. Landau, 'Independence, Deference and Voter Participation: The Behaviour of the Electorate in Early 18th-century Kent', *Hist. J.* 22/3 (1979), 581.

[32] The petition of 1793 included Coventry (25%), Bedford (37%), Canterbury (38%), Bristol (40%), Newcastle-upon-Tyne (50%), Lincoln (55%), Colchester (60%), and Lancaster (70%).

[33] Namier, for example, calculated that outvoters at the Newcastle-upon-Tyne election of 1780 were 1,097 out of 2,245 voters (49%) (*Structure of Politics*, 95).

[34] Manual analysis of poll books yields the following percentages of outvoters: Chester 1747, 31%; Dover 1770, 30%; Leicester 1766, 40%; Nottingham 1818, 41%; 1826 38%; Colchester 1812–31, 66%; see M. Speight, 'Politics in the Borough of Colchester, 1812–1847', Ph.D. (London, 1969), 110. Outvoters at York at the elections of 1754, 1774, and 1784 were about 25% of the electorate; (F. C. Price, 'Parliamentary Elections in York City 1754–1790', M.A. (Manchester, 1958), 256–61); Durham 1831, 64% (Stoker, 'Elections and Voting Behaviour, Ph.D., 326); Exeter 1802, 25%; Norwich 1802, 31%; 1806, 28%; 1807, 21%; 1812, 23%; 1818, 28%; 1830, 28%; Newcastle-upon-Tyne 1774, 30%; 1777, 31%; 1780, 33% (T. R. Knox, 'Popular Politics and Provincial Radicalism: Newcastle-upon-Tyne, 1769–1785', *Albion*, ii (1979), 238).

well.[35] Even the counties had up to one-quarter of their voters travelling in from outside.[36] Even when we have made allowance for the fact that these percentages relate to those who actually voted at particular elections and not to the potential electorate, there is no doubt at all that a significant minority of voters in the unreformed electoral system did not reside in the places in which they voted.

What was responsible for non-residence, on such a massive scale? In many cases, the non-residence may have been technical, a consequence of urban sprawl beyond old boundaries.[37] Many outvoters were freemen or freeholders who had properly qualified for the franchise in a borough before moving to reside elsewhere. As the examples cited above suggest, non-residence was worsening as the unreformed era drew to its close. The redrawing of the constituency boundaries which was such an important element in the legislation of 1832 was long overdue. Nevertheless, the blatant creation of non-residents as freemen in freeman boroughs had nothing to do with population movements. It became a customary practice on the part of patrons intent upon preserving or establishing their influence in a town.[38] It is no accident that some of the very highest levels of non-residence occur in the lesser, and more corrupt, of the freeman boroughs. Finally, the mobility of labour and crafts rendered outvoting a natural phenomenon in this unusually mobile society.

Voters, then, travelled to vote. They travelled from nearby villages and they travelled from all over Europe. (Most elections in a reasonably large constituency boasted at least one such heroic voter.) Most important, and most homogeneous of all, however, were the London voters. They were numerically significant. The magnetic social and economic pull of the capital is reflected in the tendency for London

---

[35] Medium freeman boroughs: Ipswich 1784, 50% (A. R. Childs, 'Politics and Elections in Suffolk Boroughs During the Late Eighteenth Century and Early Nineteenth Century', M.Phil. (Reading, 1973), 75); Berwick 1765, 43% (Stoker, Elections and Voting Behaviour, Ph.D., 326). Great Yarmouth 1818, 53%; 1820, 55%; 1830, 45%; Rochester 1830, 63%; small freeman boroughs: Hythe 1790, 84%; Hedon 1802, 70%; 1826, 74%; householder boroughs: Preston 1768, 33%. See relevant poll books for Great Yarmouth, Rochester, and Hedon; for Hythe see H. Stooks-Smith, *Register of Parliamentary Contested Elections* (London, 1842), 47; for Preston see Oldfield, *History of the Boroughs*, i. 341.

[36] Namier estimated the outvoters as 16% of the Surrey electorate in 1742 (*Structure of Politics*, 66 n. 1). Newman found that outvoters were 9% and 10% respectively of the electorate of Kent in 1734 and 1754 (A. Newman, 'Elections in Kent and Its Parliamentary Representation, 1715–1754', D.Phil (Oxford, 1957),Table H). In 1818 outvoters were 25% of the Westmorland electorate (Stoker, 'Elections and Voting Behaviour', Ph.D., 326). The Northamptonshire poll book for 1831 has 13% outvoters.

[37] At Durham in 1831, 778 of the 1,185 freemen were outvoters, but 558 of them lived within seven miles; see J. H. Philbin, *Parliamentary Representation 1832: England and Wales* (New Haven, 1965), 68.

[38] See above, pp. 41–2, 47–8, 169.

voters to represent around 10% of all voters.[39] Their indispensability is demonstrated by the numerous advertisements which appeared in the newspapers before each general election summoning the London voters for the largest constituencies to separate meetings. Attempts to woo these voters consumed much time and money. Their existence and their eagerly anticipated arrival arguably did something to mitigate the parochialism of elections. More than anyone, the London voters may have been alive to national and parliamentary considerations. Their intervention could decide a contest. The Nottingham election of 1818 was won by a margin of only 33 votes out of 6,403, of which total 396 were furnished by the London voters. Roscoe's victory at Liverpool in 1806 by 13 votes depended upon his superior appeal to the London voters.[40] On some occasions, the behaviour of the outvoters as a whole could transform a fairly comfortable win into a clear defeat. At the Dover by-election of 1770, John Trevanion's lead among the resident voters by 360–307 was turned around by his poor performance among the outvoters by the margin of 176–96 to achieve his defeat by 483–456.

The moral is obvious. Elections could be won and lost by the efficient organization of the outvoters in general, and the London voters in particular. After all, the fact of a contested election was itself a recognition of the near-impossibility of determining which side had superiority. The task, not merely of locating, influencing, transporting, protecting, and wining and dining the outvoters but of returning them in one piece, stretched the resources of any interest to breaking point. Because outvoters normally resided beyond the limits of deference and paternalism, they could only be won through superior organization. Nevertheless, the fact that some, at least, of the electors were not absolutely dependable retainers of the leaders of either local side may have done something to politicize election contests.

It is of course natural to discuss 'the electorate' or 'the voters' in this rather static manner, but to do so can be misleading. 'The electorate' was not a fixed and unchanging entity. Its personnel varied from election to election. This phenomenon of electoral turnover may be described as the process by which electors who had voted at one

---

[39] In the cases cited by the petition of the Friends of the People in 1793 the London outvoters range from 18% in Colchester, 14% in Coventry, 13% in both Bedford and Lincoln, 11% in Bristol, 9% in Newcastle-upon-Tyne, to 8% in Lancaster. These figures are confirmed by other contemporary evidence. The 275 Oxford outvoters in London constituted 12% of the Oxford electorate (Letters of J. Brooks from J. L. Wilkinson on the Oxford election of 1802, especially that of 10 Apr. 1802, D/E.Su (M). B.14.16 Berks. RO). At the Norwich elections of 1802 and 1806, the London voters were 10% and 9% of all voters; at Great Yarmouth in 1831 they were 12%.

[40] *Liverpool Chronicle*, 12 Nov. 1806.

election and who did not vote at the next contested election in the same constituency were replaced by electors who did. Electors may not have voted at the succeeding election for a variety of reasons, including death, the loss of the franchisal qualification, and a simple disinclination or inability to vote. 'New' electors might appear through the acquisition of the franchise, coming of age, or by deciding to use the vote they had hitherto refrained from using. Although the real size of the electorate may not have increased (or reduced) much, if at all, between two general elections the internal composition of that electorate might vary considerably. The question is, by how much?

From the evidence available (see Table 4.8), around one-fifth to one-third of the electorate at any election would be new, and thus inexperienced, unless the period between elections was very short, such as the one year separating the contests of 1806 and 1807, and 1830 and 1831, at Shrewsbury. Of course, much turned upon the particular circumstances of an election contest and the nature of the constituency, but the number of inexperienced voters was by any measure quite

TABLE 4.8    *Experienced Voters as Percentage of Total Electorate, Selected Constituencies, 1784–1831*

| Constituency | Year | Previous election | % experienced voters from preceding election |
|---|---|---|---|
| *Large freeman* | | | |
| Chester | 1826 | 1820 | 70.2 |
| Liverpool | 1784 | 1780 | 65.5 |
| Liverpool | 1790 | 1784 | 77.4 |
| Norwich | 1818 | 1812 | 61.4 |
| *Householder* | | | |
| Preston | 1812 | 1807 | 50.4 |
| *Medium freeman* | | | |
| Rochester | 1830 | 1826 | 83.2 |
| Southampton | 1820 | 1812 | 72.1 |
| *Small freeman* | | | |
| Shrewsbury | 1807 | 1806 | 91.1 |
| Shrewsbury | 1812 | 1807 | 54.2 |
| Shrewsbury | 1814 | 1812 | 76.0 |
| Shrewsbury | 1819 | 1814 | 86.2 |
| Shrewsbury | 1826 | 1819 | 66.9 |
| Shrewsbury | 1830 | 1826 | 64.2 |
| Shrewsbury | 1831 | 1830 | 94.4 |

TABLE 4.9 *Turnover of Voters in General Elections in Liverpool, 1780–1790*

| Election date | Voters who also voted in 1780 | |
|---|---|---|
| | No.[a] | %[b] |
| 1784 | 745 | 64.6 |
| 1790 | 527 | 45.7 |
| 1802 | 238 | 20.6 |
| 1818 | 133 | 11.5 |

[a] 1154 in 1780.
[b] 100% in 1780.

large.[41] Where contests were separated by an uncontested election, the percentage of experienced electors naturally fell even if the period between the two contested elections was not long.[42] At a contested election in a constituency *not* contested at the previous general election, about half the voters would be new.[43] This type of electorate, then, with large numbers of new voters flooding the polls at contested elections, must have been difficult to know, and thus to control, in view of its relative anonymity. The irregularity of contested elections together with the operations of electoral turnover weakened the tendencies to continuity of voting within the electorate. Table 4.9 summarizes the subsequent history of the Liverpool electorate of 1780. Slightly over one-third of these voters did not return to vote on a

[41] There is in the Whitbread MSS in the Beds. RO a survey dated 1812, clearly part of preparations for a contest in Bedfordshire (which did not, in fact, take place). Of an electorate of about 3,000 at the general election of 1807, 297 had since surrendered or sold their property, 627 new voters were regularly assessed, 27 voters rejected in 1807 were now assessed, and another 90 were likely to come forward. Consequently only 69% of the potential voters in 1812 were likely to be 'experienced'.

[42] To 48%, for example, at St Albans at 1831 (from 1826, the election of 1830 being uncontested) and 46% at Oxford at 1812 (from 1806, the election of 1807 being uncontested).

[43] My findings coincide fairly closely with Phillips's results (*Electoral Behaviour*, 98. His calculations of the number of experienced voters at successive elections in Norwich range from 51% to 65% and, for the period between the contests of 1768 and 1780, 46%. His calculation for successive elections at Maidstone ranges from 51% to 65%. His calculation for successive elections at Northampton ranges from 60% to 62%, and his figure for the period between the contested elections of 1774 and 1784 is 50%. His figure for successive elections at Lewes ranges from 51% to 82% and for the period between the contested elections of 1780 and 1790 is 37%. Stoker's figures ('Elections and Voting Behaviour'; Ph.D., 205) for successive elections at Westmorland are 69% (1768), 70% (1774), 58% (1820), and 45% (1826), and for Northumberland (between the two contested elections of Feb. and June 1826) 69%. For Newcastle he notes a figure of 80% for 1777 (from 1774), 77% for 1780 (from 1777). For Carlisle the figures are 76% (between the two elections of Apr. and Nov. 1786) and 87% (for 1790 from 1786). Bristol was not contested between 1756 and 1774. After thus missing two general elections, in 1774 only 20% of voters were experienced, 50% at the by-election of 1781, and 67% in 1784.

subsequent occasion. Slightly less, therefore, than two-thirds of those voters voted on at least two occasions. Indeed, almost one-half participated in the electoral process on at least three occasions, and just over 10% on five.[44]

A comprehensive survey of the 1975 electors who voted at the six general and two by-elections at Shrewsbury between 1806 and 1831 confirms these rough indications. Table 4.10 shows the extent to which these voters, as they came to the polls for the first time at successive elections, took advantage of the voting occasions open to them. It should be stressed that the figures are on the severe side. They do not make allowance for the deaths of voters, nor for such other personal, familial, or occupational circumstances which might have made it impossible for them to vote. Still, for what they are worth, these figures are summarized in Table 4.11. Exactly 30% of electors vote once only, 70% vote at least twice. No less than 43% of the electors vote three or more times, 29.4% four or more times, and a very creditable 18.7% five or more times.

What explains the shifting, changing composition of the electorate? At one level, tactical devices were responsible. The artificial creation of voters through such contrivances as the splitting of freeholds and the arbitrary creation of honorary freemen may have been at work in some places. A low turnout of voters, especially one occasioned by the early abandonment of a hopeless poll, could sharply affect the composition of the electorate. More importantly, however, electoral turnover was a consequence of natural process—death, coming of age, the inheritance of property to which the franchise was attached, occupational advancement, and so on. Finally, however, and perhaps most central of all, turnover was a reflection of the astonishing mobility of people in pre-industrial and early industrial society. With migration rates out of parishes reaching 10% a year, the degree of electoral turnover falls into context.[45] In the new industrial towns that were enfranchised (Preston is a good example), a high degree of occupational mobility resulted from the decline of the old craft trades, the expansion of factory employment, and, not least, the intense vulnerability of the cotton industry to cyclical slump. Even outside the industrial areas, however, high turnover rates were maintained by the varieties of

[44] J. A. Phillips also found that the figures tend to move sharply from election to election (*Electoral Behavior*, 99). The proportion of voters voting for the *third* time between 1780 and 1802 varied at Norwich from 27% to 40%, at Maidstone from 30% to 42%, at Northampton from 19% to 30%, and at Lewes from 22% to 34%.

[45] T. H. Hollingsworth, 'Historical Studies of Migration', *Annales de démographie historique*, 2 (1970), 87–96. The census of Cardington, Beds. revealed that 64% of boys and 57% of girls moved out of the village before they were 15, one-quarter of them out of the county; see Speck, *Stability and Strife*, 67.

TABLE 4.10   *Voting Experience in Shrewsbury: New Voters at Each Election, 1806–1831, and Total Number of Elections at which They Voted*

| No. elections voted at | 1806 No. | % | 1807 No. | % | 1812 No. | % | 1814 No. | % | 1819 No. | % | 1816 No. | % | 1830 No. | % | 1831 No. | % |
|---|---|---|---|---|---|---|---|---|---|---|---|---|---|---|---|---|
| 1 | 58 | 8.0 | 16 | 26.7 | 53 | 18.1 | 82 | 37.6 | 45 | 48.4 | 62 | 27.9 | 259 | 74.2 | 17 | 100.0 |
| 2 | 182 | 25.2 | 10 | 16.7 | 68 | 23.2 | 57 | 26.1 | 25 | 26.9 | 101 | 45.5 | 90 | 25.8 | | |
| 3 | 96 | 13.3 | 9 | 15.0 | 58 | 19.8 | 30 | 13.8 | 18 | 19.4 | 59 | 26.6 | | | | |
| 4 | 116 | 16.0 | 7 | 11.7 | 44 | 15.0 | 39 | 17.9 | 5 | 5.4 | | | | | | |
| 5 | 99 | 13.7 | 8 | 13.3 | 53 | 18.1 | 10 | 4.6 | | | | | | | | |
| 6 | 83 | 11.5 | 8 | 13.3 | 17 | 5.8 | | | | | | | | | | |
| 7 | 69 | 9.5 | 2 | 3.3 | | | | | | | | | | | | |
| TOTAL | 723 | 100.0 | 60 | 100.0 | 293 | 100.0 | 218 | 100.0 | 93 | 100.0 | 222 | 100.0 | 349 | 100.0 | 17 | 100.0 |

TABLE 4.11   *Voting Experience in Shrewsbury: Summary of Number of Voting Occasions, 1806–1831*

|              | Electors |       |              |
| ------------ | -------- | ----- | ------------ |
| No. elections | No.     | %     | Cumulative % |
| 1            | 592      | 30.0  | 30.0         |
| 2            | 533      | 27.0  | 57.0         |
| 3            | 270      | 13.6  | 70.6         |
| 4            | 211      | 10.7  | 81.3         |
| 5            | 170      | 8.6   | 89.9         |
| 6            | 108      | 5.5   | 95.4         |
| 7            | 71       | 3.6   | 99.0         |
| 8            | 20       | 1.0   | 100.0        |
| TOTAL        | 1,975    | 100.0 | 100.0        |

occupational mobility resulting from patterns of apprenticeships, the practise of itinerant crafts, and the custom of primogeniture. Finally, the growth in the size of the electorate, especially in the late eighteenth and early nineteenth centuries, together with the rising political awareness of the time, did something to hoist the figure. Obviously, local circumstances would determine the precise combination of these contributory factors.[46]

Most electors, then, voted on only a few occasions in their life-times. The total size of the electoral pool (the numbers of people who at one time or another had voted or who had the right to vote) must at any one time in the early nineteenth century have amounted to over one million, vastly in excess of the measured size of the electorate.[47] This may be better illustrated from one constituency. Shrewsbury was contested infrequently until 1806. Contests in 1806, 1807, 1812, and 1814 attracted turnouts of between 670 and 840. By 1814, however, no fewer than 1,300 people had voted in the previous eight years, an electoral pool almost double the usual voting electorate. By the eve of the 1832 Reform Act it must have easily exceeded that figure. In

[46] Of the Chester electorate of 1820, 405 were not available to vote in 1826. One-quarter had died and the rest had moved: 69 to Liverpool and 51 to London. It is difficult to estimate precisely the death rate of electors. Around, or slightly less than, 2% per annum has been suggested (Stoker, 'Elections and Voting Behaviour', Ph.D., 201). This would roughly accommodate the Chester figure.

[47] It is hard to see how it can be less. Using a similar approach, Holmes reached the 'very conservative estimate' of 700,000–800,000 for the early 18th cent. (Holmes, *The Electorate and the National Will*, 24). His estimates, however, although they allow for turnover and turnout, do not take account of the number of times individual electors voted. The agreed increase in the electorate from 1715 to 1831, whatever the base, is usually taken to be about 50%. Using Holmes's figures as a base, there can be no doubt that the pool must have reached one million (about 30% of adult males) by 1831.

the event, there are grounds for thinking that the impact of the 1832 Act was perhaps to increase the size of the electorate but to diminish the size of the electoral pool.[48]

We have seen from this chapter that the unreformed electorate was significantly larger than has hitherto been estimated. Its levels of participation easily exceeded those current in the early eighteenth century and approached those which prevailed after 1832. Electors were highly mobile and the electorate was a shifting, nebulous body of (often non-resident) individuals. What sort of people these were, how they earned their living, and what values they professed we must now examine.

## THE STRUCTURE OF THE ELECTORATE

In the first section of this chapter I established a number of physical characteristics of electoral behaviour in the century before reform concerning participation (turnout), residence, and renewal (turnover). In this section I hope to describe the social and economic structure of the electorate. This can most readily, though not exclusively, be accomplished through approaching its occupational composition. Electoral behaviour cannot be understood unless it is related to the social and occupational environments within which electors existed and to which such ideologies as they might profess referred. Investigations into these environments in the post-1832 period have significantly illuminated our understanding of early Victorian society.[49] To acquire such a perspective for the decades immediately before the Reform Act of 1832 is an urgent necessity if political change in the first half of the nineteenth century is to be understood and the stability of the political system clarified. The purpose, then, of what follows is to endeavour to explicate electoral behaviour not only by reference to attitudes stated and professed but by investigating the environments of work and life as much as those of status and class.

Rather surprisingly, historians of the later seventeenth and early eighteenth centuries have not shown much interest in this central aspect of electoral history. Professor Speck summarizes the contents of two

---

[48] This is because electors after 1832 appear to have voted more regularly than their unreformed counterparts. As many as half the electors voted three times or more, (one-third before 1832), only one-quarter on one occasion (one-half before 1832). See M. Drake, 'The Mid-Victorian Voter', *J. Interdiscip. Hist.* 1/3 (1971), 473–90.

[49] Nossiter, *Influence, Opinion and Political Idioms* and Vincent, *Pollbooks*, blazed this particular trail. Rather alarmingly, however, few historians have consolidated their achievement. Vincent's work appeared in 1968, Nossiter's in 1975. There is scope for further work in this area of post-Reform electoral politics.

poll books without comment,[50] while Professor Holmes prefers to explore 'the more sensitive question of the places that were represented'.[51] Meanwhile, the social identities of the voters remain unknown.[52] It is strange that this should be so. The research of the last 20 years has established beyond doubt the development of occupational specialization and variation in the towns of Georgian England as the eighteenth century proceeded.[53] The subdivision of existing trades and crafts, the appearance of new ones, and the emergence of new professions alike reflected a climate of ingenuity, inventiveness, and resourcefulness which was both a cause and a consequence of the remarkable economic growth of the period. The adaptation of the occupational structure of Hanoverian society to that economic growth, to the quickening of agricultural and industrial change, and, of course, to demographic expansion may be seen in the poll books.

Poll books record the occupational descriptions given by the voter himself. These self-ascribed occupational descriptions could be a fanciful and exaggerated statement of the voter's status and skill but there are two grounds for accepting them as fairly reliable units of evidence. First, in all but the largest constituencies, the resident voters, at least, would be known, their credentials could be checked and exaggeration of the wilder sort eliminated. Second, it is possible, if exhausting, to check an individual's poll book description with other evidence, especially rate books and directories.[54] Such sampling reveals a large number of inconsistencies of terminology but nothing more serious. For example, if we compare the Preston voters who voted both in 1807 and 1812, one-third of the voters give a slightly different occupational description. Thus, joiners become confused with carpenters, hairdressers with barbers, bricklayers with bricksetters, and, inevitably, smiths with blacksmiths, gunsmiths, and whitesmiths. On the whole, however, these inconsistencies do not distort the occupational *categories* into which it is necessary to distribute the electors.

---

[50] W. A. Speck, *Tory and Whig: The Struggle in the Constituencies, 1701–1715* (London, 1970), 118–20.

[51] Holmes, *The Electorate and the National Will*, 25.

[52] It would be dangerous to attempt to apply Hirst's conclusions for the early 17th cent. to a later period. Hirst's freemen are often poor, unable to pay their rating assessments, and painfully vulnerable to economic conditions. See D. Hirst, *The Representative of the People?* (London, 1975), 93–6.

[53] See the important paper by A. Everitt, 'Country, County and Town: Patterns of Regional Evolution in England', *Trans. Royal Hist. Soc.* 5th ser., 29 (1979), 79–108, esp. 91–94, 98–104, and the authorities there cited.

[54] Only those who have undertaken such surveys can appreciate the problems of identifying the voters in directories and other supplementary sources. Changes of address, ambiguities of spelling, differences in initialling, and the incomplete nature of many sources render the process painfully slow and sometimes futile.

The occupational descriptions which voters ascribe to themselves are so finely detailed and so numerous that some scheme of classification *must* be applied to them or analysis becomes impossible. For the larger boroughs, poll books might contain over a hundred specific occupational descriptions, some of which might only contain a few examples. Such data need to be organized into larger categories. The stiffest problem facing the electoral historian is to establish categories which facilitate and clarify the meaning to be derived from the data while avoiding the dangers of transposing late-twentieth-century social concepts to a society which did not acknowledge them. As Professor Katz has memorably remarked, to impose categories upon the bewildering and specific variety of occupations 'bristles with ambushes'.[55] For present concerns, we need to establish a structural classification of occupations; we are much less interested in the mobility of individual electors *between* occupations. The critical problem is to decide by which criteria to group occupations. (My own set of allocations is to be found in Appendix 1.) In the following classification, occupations are related not only by their functions but also by their shared life-styles:

1. Gentlemen/professionals/respectables
2. Manufacturers/merchants
3. Retailers
4. Skilled craftsmen
5. Semi-/unskilled men/labourers
6. Agricultural occupations.

Consequently, craftsmen are grouped together not simply because of the physical similarity of their work (which can often be exaggerated) but because craftsmen *as craftsmen* had many social values in common.

The occupational categories adopted here contain two manifest disadvantages. The first is that the lines of distinction between the third and fourth, and sometimes even the fifth, are not as clear as may be desired. Is a baker, for example, being both producer and vendor, best assigned to category 3 or category 4? I have sought, where appropriate, to follow the allocations of earlier writers, usually applying Nossiter's dictum that it is craftsmen who make a product, retailers who sell it.[56] Moreover, a craftsman has usually been taken to be a

[55] M. B. Katz, 'Occupational Classification in History', *J. Interdiscip. Hist.* 3/1 (1972), 63. There have been a number of attempts to classify occupations, usually derived from 19th-cent. census data, frequently stressing industrial occupations of the 19th cent. rather than craft occupations of the pre-1832 period. See also A. Armstrong, 'The Interpretation of the Census Enumerators' Books for Victorian Towns', in H. J. Dyos (ed.), *The Study of Urban History* (London, 1968), 78–9. Armstrong merely employs the categories used by the census enumerators.
[56] Nossiter, *Influence, Opinion and Political Idioms*, 145.

man following a trade for which a period of apprenticeship was required or for which special skills were necessary, as distinct from an unskilled or semi-skilled worker who could assume his occupation without such legal inhibition. There are, nevertheless, a number of grey areas in which, as Professor Phillips has remarked, groupings of occupations 'continue the long tradition of idiosyncracy'.[57] The second is that the occupational terms used are sometimes too generic. Within the fourth category, for example, they do not distinguish between masters and journeymen. Professor Neale some years ago drew attention to the problems of poll book analysis when it was not clear whether a particular voter was a large employer or a small employee.[58] The problem is a very real one, but there are perhaps two responses to it. The first is to note that it has been raised in a post-reform context in an urban situation. It has less applicability to the market towns of eighteenth-century England. Second, it relates to relatively few occupations. It is not a characteristic difficulty relating to typical occupations.

Indeed, in a haphazard but pragmatic manner, historians are independently coming to agree upon relevant criteria for categorizing occupations. There is, in practice, massive common ground between the classifications of Dr Nossiter and Professor Phillips and those which I have employed.[59] Thus the groupings and allocations are far from arbitrary. They were, to some extent, recognized by contemporaries. References to 'shopkeepers', 'artisans', 'craftsmen', 'professional men', and 'the landed interest' are legion. We should not claim too much for them. They are not self-conscious social groups, they are not status groups, and they are not social classes. They are groupings of occupations which display recognizably similar functional and social qualities which illuminate the study of electoral behaviour. Whatever deficiencies these groupings possess, they do enable comparisons to be made of the electoral behaviour of similarly defined groups between constituencies and across time, even across the great divide of 1832. Table 4.12 describes the occupational structure of the unreformed

---

[57] J. A. Phillips, *Electoral Behavior in Unreformed England*, 178. What does one do with a bird stuffer, or a billiard room keeper?

[58] R. S. Neale, 'Class and Class Consciousness in Early Nineteenth-century England; Three Classes or Five?', *Victorian Studies*, 12 (1968), 5–32.

[59] Nossiter was the real pioneer of this type of enquiry. Although Vincent 'discovered' poll books his scheme of occupational classification (in some cases 'selected categories', in others, simple listing) was most unsatisfactory. For tabulations of occupation see Nossiter, *Influence, Opinion and Political Idioms*, 211–12; J. A. Phillips, *Electoral Behavior*, 321–2. The most comprehensive listing is that provided by Stoker ('Elections and Voting Behaviour', 391–401). My own listing of over 600 occupations (App. 1) consistently profits from these earlier classifications which are summarized in App. 2.

TABLE 4.12   *Occupational Structure of the Electorate in Six Constituencies, 1768–1831 individual years (%)*

|  | 1 | 2 | 3 | 4 | 5 | 6 |
|---|---|---|---|---|---|---|
| **Chester (large freeman constituency)** | | | | | | |
| 1812 | 11.2 | 4.5 | 26.2 | 53.1 | 3.4 | 1.6 |
| 1818 | 9.4 | 4.7 | 24.7 | 56.0 | 3.6 | 1.6 |
| 1826 | 7.9 | 4.2 | 26.4 | 55.2 | 4.7 | 1.6 |
| **Cirencester (Householder constituency)** | | | | | | |
| 1768 | 3.0 | 8.6 | 17.0 | 47.4 | 22.8 | 1.2 |
| 1790 | 5.4 | 5.2 | 21.7 | 39.0 | 26.7 | 2.0 |
| 1802 | 9.0 | 5.9 | 19.7 | 33.3 | 31.9 | 0.2 |
| **Colchester (large freeman constituency)** | | | | | | |
| 1790 | 8.6 | 4.0 | 14.0 | 46.4 | 20.6 | 6.4 |
| 1806 | 8.7 | 5.1 | 12.9 | 36.6 | 28.0 | 8.7 |
| 1807 | 8.8 | 4.3 | 12.4 | 34.4 | 31.2 | 8.9 |
| 1812 | 9.6 | 5.7 | 13.5 | 34.8 | 25.7 | 10.7 |
| 1818 | 9.9 | 2.6 | 15.1 | 42.8 | 25.4 | 4.2 |
| 1820 | 12.1 | 5.5 | 14.9 | 35.1 | 26.4 | 6.0 |
| **St Albans (medium freeman constituency)** | | | | | | |
| 1820 | 12.8 | 3.7 | 19.3 | 29.2 | 32.8 | 2.2 |
| 1821 | 17.2 | 3.5 | 21.4 | 28.1 | 27.4 | 2.4 |
| 1830 | 15.7 | 3.7 | 25.9 | 29.6 | 22.9 | 2.2 |
| 1831 | 14.2 | 3.7 | 23.3 | 29.7 | 26.5 | 2.6 |
| **Shrewsbury (small freeman constituency)** | | | | | | |
| 1806 | 16.4 | 4.0 | 25.8 | 43.4 | 7.5 | 2.9 |
| 1807 | 14.6 | 5.5 | 27.2 | 43.4 | 8.3 | 1.0 |
| 1812 | 9.2 | 3.1 | 22.2 | 53.7 | 11.0 | 0.8 |
| 1814 | 11.5 | 3.7 | 22.4 | 50.2 | 11.0 | 1.2 |
| 1819 | 12.4 | 6.4 | 24.4 | 45.9 | 10.0 | 0.9 |
| 1826 | 11.2 | 4.0 | 25.6 | 50.5 | 7.8 | 0.9 |
| 1830 | 11.0 | 6.2 | 24.2 | 49.0 | 9.0 | 0.6 |
| 1831 | 9.6 | 6.9 | 26.1 | 50.5 | 5.9 | 1.0 |
| **Southampton (medium freeman constituency)** | | | | | | |
| 1774 | 31.6 | 2.2 | 19.7 | 30.5 | 13.9 | 2.1 |
| 1790 | 31.5 | 5.7 | 25.2 | 25.2 | 10.9 | 1.5 |
| 1794 | 30.4 | 6.3 | 24.9 | 26.3 | 10.8 | 1.3 |
| 1806 | 31.4 | 10.0 | 22.4 | 24.1 | 10.5 | 1.6 |
| 1812 | 28.8 | 8.6 | 23.8 | 24.6 | 12.2 | 2.0 |
| 1818 | 28.0 | 8.2 | 25.6 | 24.1 | 12.6 | 1.5 |
| 1820 | 25.1 | 8.1 | 24.3 | 24.1 | 14.8 | 3.6 |
| 1831 | 19.3 | 7.6 | 25.1 | 30.6 | 14.2 | 3.2 |

*Note*: For summary of occupational categories, see pp. 207–15; a full listing is given in App. 1.

TABLE 4.13    *Occupational Structure of the Electorate in Six Constituencies, 1768–1831, Mean for the Period (%)*

| Constituency[a] | Period | 1 | 2 | 3 | 4 | 5 | 6 |
|---|---|---|---|---|---|---|---|
| Chester | 1812–26 | 9.5 | 4.5 | 25.7 | 54.8 | 3.9 | 1.6 |
| Cirencester | 1768–1802 | 5.8 | 6.6 | 19.5 | 39.9 | 27.1 | 1.1 |
| Colchester | 1790–1820 | 9.5 | 3.9 | 13.8 | 38.4 | 26.9 | 7.5 |
| St Albans | 1820–31 | 15.0 | 3.6 | 22.5 | 29.1 | 27.4 | 2.4 |
| Shrewsbury | 1806–1831 | 11.9 | 5.0 | 24.7 | 48.3 | 8.8 | 1.3 |
| Southampton | 1774–1831 | 28.3 | 7.0 | 23.9 | 26.2 | 12.5 | 2.1 |

*Note*: For summary of occupational categories, see p. 207–15; a full listing is given in App. 1.
[a] For constituency type see Table 4.12.

electorate in the designated constituencies for which data were collected and assembled on the computerized database (Chester, Cirencester, Colchester, St Albans, Shrewsbury, and Southampton). These data are summarized in Table 4.13. In four of the six cases a remarkable structural similarity appears. In Chester, Colchester, St Albans, and Shrewsbury, category 1 (gentlemen and professionals) constitutes around 10%, stretching up to 15% of the electorate, about twice as much as the category 2 (merchants and manufacturers). At fashionable naval, and hierarchical, Southampton, the figure for category 1 is vastly in excess of this, although it fell steadily in the last three decades of the unreformed period. In Cirencester, on account of the representative nature of the franchise, it is, unsurprisingly, considerably less. The most numerous types of occupational category within the electorates of these six constituencies, however, are category 3 (retailers) and 4 (craftsmen). The craftsmen are undoubtedly the more numerous. At Colchester they outnumber the retailers by three to one, at Chester, Circencester, and Shrewsbury by about two to one. At St Albans and at Southampton they are roughly equal. The numbers of electors in the category 5 (semi- and unskilled labourers) would obviously depend upon the wealth of the town as well as its occupational structure and franchise. The householder franchise of Cirencester was responsible for the relatively large number of electors in this category, while at Colchester it was the structure of marine occupations which was responsible.[60] In the case of St Albans it is not at all as easy to understand the large number of electors in this category, other than an unusual preference among those who compiled the poll books for

---

[60] The large number of marine occupations at Colchester is evident from a glance at the poll books. Weaving as a trade had disappeared in the town in the later 18th cent. See Speight, 'Politics in Colchester', Ph.D., 6–7.

the description 'labourer', a term rather more sparingly employed elsewhere. In fact, the decline of the silk and cotton industries in the town in the early nineteenth century and the dependence of the inhabitants upon the coaching trade and attendant services such as the brewing industry left many inhabitants and electors dependent upon unskilled and casual work. In more affluent and more fashionable Chester, the numbers of voters in this category were much smaller. The number of voters in the category 6 (agricultural occupations) was necessarily tiny in borough seats, but something of the agricultural nature of Colchester life can be seen in the figures for that constituency. It is worth pointing out that although the relative distribution of different occupational categories varies between the six constituencies in question, within each constituency the distribution is fairly fixed. Thus, the Southampton and Shrewsbury electorates differ fairly markedly in some key aspects (the size of category 1 is much bigger at Southampton, that of category 4 much bigger at Shrewsbury), yet there is not very much sign of change in the electorates of these two constituencies during the period studied. The only exception lies in the diminishing size of category 1.

To what extent may the structure of the electorate in these constituencies be regarded as typical? Table 4.14 assembles further comparable data, manually worked, from types of constituency similar to those already examined and from some constituency types not previously examined. Within the freeman and scot and lot/householder boroughs there are few surprises. The figures for Minehead interestingly reflect the decline of the port (see category 2) and the rise of the town as a resort (see category 1) as well as its continuing dependence upon the rural economy (many voters actually lived outside the town).[61] The figures for Preston and Grimsby are unique, accurately reflecting the socio-economic realities of the constituencies concerned; the occupational structure of these rapidly industrializing constituencies is inevitably going to be different from that of more settled freeman and scot and lot boroughs. In the case of the analysis of a county electorate, it is, if anything, surprising that the percentages achieved by occupational category 6 is so low, although the percentages achieved in categories 3, 4, and 5 are no doubt linked into the activities of the farming community. (Urban penetration of the county electorate had not gone far in Lincolnshire in the early nineteenth century.) With some fairly predictable variations, then, the data in Table 4.14 appear

[61] DD/L.Ms.Box 110 1/59/8,21, Dunster Castle MSS, Som. RO.

TABLE 4.14    *Occupational Structure of the Electorate in Constituencies of Different Franchisal Types, 1747–1830 (%)*

| | Date | 1 | 2 | 3 | 4 | 5 | 6 |
|---|---|---|---|---|---|---|---|
| **Large freeman** | | | | | | | |
| Canterbury | 1830 | 16 | 1 | 23 | 40 | 8 | 12 |
| Chester | 1747 | 17 | 2 | 15 | 21 | 39 | 6 |
| Chester | 1784 | 25 | 2 | 6 | 29 | 34 | 4 |
| Great Yarmouth | 1754 | 22 | 7 | 11 | 42 | 17 | 1 |
| Great Yarmouth | 1795 | 14 | 3 | 11 | 41 | 26 | 5 |
| Great Yarmouth | 1820 | 20 | 6 | 12 | 42 | 12 | 8 |
| Leicester | 1820 | 13 | 9 | 17 | 51 | 6 | 4 |
| Lincoln | 1826 | 7 | 2 | 14 | 38 | 27 | 12 |
| Liverpool | 1780 | 4 | 4 | 18 | 67 | 6 | 1 |
| Liverpool | 1784 | 7 | 8 | 16 | 63 | 5 | 1 |
| Liverpool | 1790 | 7 | 8 | 12 | 66 | 6 | 1 |
| Liverpool | 1802 | 7 | 8 | 13 | 67 | 4 | 1 |
| Liverpool | 1818 | 9 | 7 | 9 | 69 | 5 | 1 |
| Nottingham | 1830 | 8 | 6 | 15 | 65 | 4 | 2 |
| Norwich | 1818 | 17 | 8 | 16 | 48 | 7 | 4 |
| Oxford | 1820 | 13 | 2 | 26 | 44 | 12 | 3 |
| **Medium freeman** | | | | | | | |
| Ipswich | 1820 | 16 | 9 | 31 | 28 | 10 | 6 |
| Newcastle-under-Lyme | 1790 | 6 | 1 | 13 | 62 | 16 | 2 |
| Rochester | 1830 | 16 | 3 | 18 | 38 | 23 | 2 |
| **Small freeman** | | | | | | | |
| Boston | 1826 | 6 | 2 | 18 | 57 | 16 | 1 |
| Grantham | 1820 | 12 | 1 | 15 | 48 | 23 | 1 |
| Grimsby | 1826 | 1 | — | 17 | 30 | 51 | 1 |
| Wigan | 1830 | 21 | 10 | 20 | 40 | 7 | 2 |
| **Scot and lot/householder** | | | | | | | |
| Abingdon | 1802 | 16 | 17 | 29 | 38 | — | — |
| Minehead | 1768 | 13 | 8 | 9 | 21 | 12 | 37 |
| Minehead | 1796 | 19 | 3 | 7 | 20 | 12 | 39 |
| Minehead | 1802 | 18 | 2 | 9 | 20 | 13 | 38 |
| Preston | 1818 | 6 | 5 | 12 | 22 | 53 | 2 |
| Preston | 1820 | 6 | 3 | 9 | 30 | 50 | 2 |
| Northampton | 1820 | 7 | 6 | 19 | 49 | 16 | 3 |
| **County** | | | | | | | |
| Lincolnshire | 1818 | 14 | 1 | 8 | 14 | 14 | 49 |
| Lincolnshire | 1823 | 16 | 1 | 9 | 15 | 14 | 45 |

*Note*: For summary of occupational categories, see pp. 207–15; a full listing is given in App. 1.

to vindicate the general applicability of the data assembled in Tables 4.12 and 4.13.[62]

What explains the levels of occupational representation contained in these tables? It is only possible to approach this problem through moving a little closer to each of the six occupational categories in turn.

*Category 1* consists of the gentry and the professional classes. This loose coalition of closely integrated élites was not only occupationally heterogeneous but, as we shall see, also exhibited fairly uniform social values. Averaged from the examples in Tables 4.12 to 4.14, it comprised 13.6% of the entire electorate. This is a very high figure indeed. As might have been expected, some of the smaller freeman boroughs considerably exceed this figure, but by no means all. The householder boroughs, predictably, consistently failed to meet this figure, the smaller scot and lot boroughs comfortably exceeded it.

This category includes the main body of great and middling rural landlords whose political weight and importance were out of all proportion to their numbers. The gentry were clearly distinguished by wealth, rank, and status from the yeomanry, who had their own values and a well-developed sense of their own identity. Closely linked with them, however, were the greater tenant farmers of the land and the 'gentlemen' of town and country. In a small and humble borough, electors described as 'gentlemen' might include men from a significantly lower social stratum than the landed gentry of the counties, but in other boroughs the category might include the great urban aristocratic and patrician classes. All these men had in common a fairly uniform educational background, and thus common cultural, and increasingly, leisure interests. They had a sensitive appreciation of the value of money and the exploitation of assets, property, and talents. Ironically, they displayed an intensifying hostility to 'trade' in its more vulgar manifestations, a sure sign of the growing exclusiveness of the upper classes in a period of dramatic social change.[63]

[62] Although my figures are taken from a much more diverse and representative run of constituencies, they largely bear out J. A. Phillips's findings for 1761–1802 in *Electoral Behaviour*, 321–2 (summarized in App. 2). Such variations as appear may arise from our different classification of occupations; his list of occupations is surprisingly brief so it is not possible to be certain how all occupations have been classified. In the same way, Stoker had his own criteria for classifying occupations ('Elections and Voting Behaviour', Ph.D., 218–21), but his findings (see App. 2) also resemble those of Phillips and myself.

[63] There is no solid evidence that new 'bourgeois' elements were able to penetrate the landed interest. In 1974 Lang discovered that very few successful London merchants in the early 17th cent. sought to acquire a stake in the country; see R. G. Lang, 'Social Origins and Social Aspirations of Jacobean London', *Econ. Hist. Rev.* 27 (1974), 28–47. More recently, Rogers has reached identical conclusions about certain London merchants in the 18th cent.; see N. Rogers, 'Money, Land and Lineage: The Big Bourgeoisie of Hanoverian London', *Social Hist.* 4/3 (1979), 437–54.

Swelling the ranks of this category are thousands of professional men, their increasing number and importance such a prominent though much neglected feature of Hanoverian society. Only five professions had been known to mid-eighteenth-century society: the church, law, medicine, army, and navy. Thereafter, bankers, attornies, schoolmasters, and hosts of others followed. It is important to be clear what these men were. They served in non-manual occupations whose status was objectively as well as subjectively ascribed. Almost all of these offered services in specialized fields, expertise which required lengthy periods of training and education. Thus, the values of professional men—expertise, merit, ability, respect for authority, personal concern, and community service—sharply reinforced their status. Their rewards were not merely pecuniary but those of skill, service, status, and prestige.[64] Interestingly, these overlap with the more traditional and socially recognized attributes of the 'gentleman': 'morality, selflessness, courage, self-control, independence, responsi- bility'.[65] More importantly, these values link naturally into the values of landed society. They assume the existence of hierarchy, the maintenance of social norms, obedience to authority, and the possibility of social mobility both upwards and downwards. Indeed, it may be remarked that the professions made downward mobility respectable and even legitimate for a society which was built around the custom and practice of primogeniture. Thus the professional men, while depending on the upper crust for their livelihood, nevertheless performed invaluable services for them. Consequently, they enjoyed considerable and increasing prestige and status. Indeed, it was perfectly natural for professional men to call themselves 'gentlemen'.[66] In the last analysis there was nothing derogatory about a gentleman pursuing a professional career.

One of the most noticeable features about the English 'élite' or 'upper class' is not its exclusiveness but its sheer size. For example, in 1792, Chester had no fewer than 222 families headed by a gentleman or better, roughly comparable to this category.[67] This group contributed over one-tenth of Chester's electorate. Their increasing wealth and

---

[64] For the development of some of these themes see G. Holmes, *Augustan England: Professions, State and Society, 1680–1730* (London, 1982), esp. 11–18.

[65] G. Best, *Mid-Victorian Britain, 1851–1870* (London, 1971), 269.

[66] 'The lawyers organized themselves into the Society of Gentlemen Practisers in the Courts of Law and Equity while the leading clothiers in Leeds called themselves gentlemen merchants. Defoe insisted that the appellation "gentlemen-tradesmen" was not an absurdity. In 1746 Lillo's *The London Merchant* was put on at Southwark at the "desire of the united body of gentlemen salesmen". *The Gentleman's Magazine*, launched in 1731, sought to cater for this aspirant clientele' (Speck, *Stability and Strife*, 41).

[67] P. Barfoot and J. Wilkes, *The Universal British Directory* (London, 1792), 703.

growing number linked them with others in Cheshire and throughout the North-west and Wales. They were a significant agency of social control, value transmission, and, not least, purchasing power. They ensured élite control of the middling orders and their institutions, and, through them, society at large in Chester. It is not in the slightest degree surprising that patrons and their dependants continued up to and beyond 1832 to have such an influence over the electorate because they constituted a large percentage of that electorate. Table 4.12 shows that this group represented no less than 30% of Southampton's electorate until the early nineteenth century, when a decline set in due to the relative slump in the importance of the port. Elsewhere, it rarely fell below 10% except at Cirencester, a householder borough. It was not, of course, an entirely cohesive unit. As we shall see later, however, it was usually able to marshall its extensive numbers with some decision. In the country as a whole, according to Patrick Colquohoun in 1803, there were over one-third of a million persons in this category.[68]

*The second category* comprises merchants and manufacturers, a polyglot collection of pre-industrial and early industrial capitalist occupations. Electorally, it was a tiny group, but its influence was far greater than its share of the electorate—an average of 5.8%—suggests. Men in this group would employ others, perhaps two or three servants and a number of employees. It was a distinct and tiny group. Gregory King distinguished 2,000 'eminent merchants' families from 8,000 'lesser merchants' families, while Joseph Massie analysed the annual income of 13,000 merchants, ranging from £200 to £600 per annum. Patrick Colquohoun in 1803 still distinguished 2,000 'Eminent merchants, bankers &c' from the families of 13,000 'Lesser merchants trading by sea'.[69] Their occupational and financial pull is indisputable. It is hard, before 1832 at least, to view these men as a Marxist 'bourgeoisie' or as exponents of an autonomous bourgeois culture. No doubt they all subscribed through their actions to certain assumptions about individualism, achievement, secularism, and professionalism. No doubt, too, their numbers, their wealth, and their impact upon society were increasing rapidly. It is perfectly reasonable

[68] This figure includes 'Temporal peers, Bishops, Baronets, Knights, Esquires, Gentlemen and Ladies living on incomes, Persons in higher civil offices, Persons of the Law, Eminent clergymen and Lesser clergymen' (estimates of Patrick Colquohoun, based on the census returns of 1801 and the pauper returns of 1803; see R. Porter, *English Society in the Eighteenth Century* (London, 1982), 388–9).

[69] Gregory King, *Scheme of the income and expense of the several families of England . . . for 1688*; Joseph Massie, *Estimate of the social structure and income, 1759–60*; Patrick Colquohoun, *Estimates Based on the Census Returns of 1801 and the Pauper Returns of 1803*; see Porter, *English Society*, 386–9.

to argue, moreover, that by the early years of the nineteenth century such men were beginning to feel a sense of common identity and interest which they did not shrink from articulating (over the Corn Law of 1815, for example). In these ways, such men manifestly constitute a coherent category. Yet they were not necessarily inimical to the prevailing establishment in country, county, and town. Although their relations with the gentry remain unclear, it does appear that for most of this period they felt that their fortunes, their status, and their livelihoods depended upon coexistence with traditional groups, with whose patterns of consumption and styles of life their own patterns of production were inextricably intertwined, rather than hostility towards them.

*The third category*, and distinctly lower in the social structure, comprised the retailers, normally termed 'tradesmen' in the eighteenth century. They average 20.5% of the electorate. In spite of the limited range of goods sold by these small, independent retailers, there can be no doubting their social importance. Their numbers were rapidly increasing: from 225,000 in King (for 1668) to 376,000 in Colquohoun (1801–3). As early as 1726 Defoe tried to define them:

In the north of Britain and likewise in Ireland, when you say a tradesman you are understood to mean a mechanic, such as a smith, a carpenter, a shoemaker, and the like.

But in England, and especially in London and the south part of Britain, shopkeepers, whether wholesalers or retailers of goods, are called tradesmen; such are our grocers, mercers, linen and woollen, drapers, tobacconists, haberdashers (whether of hats or small wares), glovers, hosiers, milliners, booksellers, stationers, and all other shopkeepers who do not actually work upon, make or manufacture the goods they sell. In the other hand, those who make the goods they sell, though they do keep shops to sell them, are not called tradesmen but handicraftsmen, such as smiths, shoemakers, founders, joiners, carpenters, carvers, turners, and the like. Others who only make, or cause to be made, goods for other people to sell, are called manufacturers.

As there are several degrees of people employed in trade below these, such as workmen, labourers and servants, so there is a degree of traders above them, whom we call merchants; where it is needful to observe, that in other countries, and even in the north of Britain and Ireland, the shopkeepers are called merchants. But in England the word merchant is understood of none but such as carry on foreign correspondences, importing the goods and growth of other countries and exporting the growth and manufactures of England to other countries or, to use a vulgar expression, because I am speaking to and of those that use that expression, such as trade beyond sea. In England these, and these only, are called merchants.[70]

---

[70] Daniel Defoe, *The Complete English Tradesman* (London, 1726), 1838 ed., 6.

It was not always as simple as that. In some trades it was common for the maker to keep a shop as well. Bakers and cabinet-makers are the most notorious of these marginal cases, many of which can only be allocated to a category with secure local knowledge.

In spite of technological innovations elsewhere in the economy, retailing techniques did not change much until the middle of the nineteenth century.[71] The size of the units, the kind of people employed in them, and patterns of buying and selling underwent no startling changes in the eighteenth century.[72] They retained considerable pride in their social status and sharply distinguished themselves from the craftsmen, emphasizing their strong sense of independence and the unusual degree of economic security and personal freedom which their occupation endowed them with.[73] They were somewhat less dependent upon their social superiors than other social groups and orders, and their contacts with them were almost invariably impersonal and pecuniary. They did not identify themselves with the social élite and felt a cool deference towards them which was the consequence of social distance. They had little or no capital, no patrons, no national, regional, or even local organizations to protect their interests and further their pretensions. Some of them were full of resentment against aristocratic extravagance, nepotism, and corruption, believing that such misapplication of resources impoverished themselves. They hated the established habits of the landed interest of taking credit and failing to pay bills promptly. 'No grievance was felt more strongly than this hidden subsidy to aristocratic wealth.'[74] As a consequence they tended to talk the language of individual rights as well as that of the rights of property. Such hostility to the upper classes stamps the retailers with a certain common set of assumptions and attitudes but, in truth, they were too singular to be a class, too individualistic ever to even envisage the remote possibility of co-operating in group activity. Of their political awareness and their literary and organizational skills there can be no doubt. But it was their individualism which was in large part responsible for the failure

---

[71] See e.g. M. J. Winstanley, *The Shopkeepers' World* (London, 1982), 2–8. For the traditional mentality of the shopkeeper's existence see D. Vaisey (ed.), *The Diary of Thomas Turner 1754–65* (London, 1984).

[72] M. T. Wild and G. Shaw, 'Locational Behaviour of Urban Retailing during the Nineteenth Century', *Trans. Inst. Brit. Geog.* 61 (1974), 101–18.

[73] J. Blackman, 'The Development of the Retail Grocery Trade in the Nineteenth Century', *Business Hist.* 9 (1967), 110–12; S. I. Mitchell, 'Retailing in Eighteenth-century and Early Nineteenth-century Cheshire', *Trans. Hist. Soc. Lancs. and Cheshire*, 130 (1981), 37–9; R. Porter, 'The Marketing of Agricultural Produce in Cheshire During the Nineteenth Century', ibid. 126 (1977), 139–55.

[74] J. Brewer, 'Commercialization and Politics', in N. McKendrick (ed.), *The Birth of a Consumer Society* (London, 1982), 198.

of the various independence and radical movements of the later eighteenth and early nineteenth centuries to endure and to prosper. It was the dilemma for retailers to be excluded from the establishment of local society but yet to be incapable of organizing themselves sufficiently menacingly to threaten or to weaken it. At the same time, they were painfully aware of the threats to their status from social groups beneath them; above all, they were anxious to separate themselves from the growing numbers of plebeian workers of mine and factory. Their essentially *local* interests narrowed their horizons and did much to enable politics to retain its local character for so long.

   *The fourth category* of voters is that of the craftsmen. They are the largest single group, comprising 39.5% of the electorate in the constituencies from which data are available, ranging from around 50% in some of the freeman boroughs to the significantly smaller proportions in scot and lot and householder boroughs. The structure and terminology of work in particular environments, together with the vagaries of descriptions in the poll books, are responsible for some of the more extravagant results in Table 4.14 (Liverpool, Nottingham, and Newcastle-under-Lyme), but even these seem very fair reflections of realities of life in those towns. Although the term 'craftsman' is so elastic that it can accommodate an almost infinite variety of crafts and subcrafts, the skilled artisan normally owned his own tools and materials, worked in a shop which he frequently owned, employed one or two apprentices, and possibly several day-workers or journeymen. In addition, he might put out work to other men in the same trade. Craftsmen normally had less to do with the public than the retailers. They would take orders from customers, from retailers, or from trading masters, but most of their outside contacts were with members of the same or similar trades. In spite of increasing specialization and the tendency of many crafts to subdivide further in apparently never-ending fragmentation, there persisted a powerful awareness of craft traditions:

Given the high mobility of the journeymen, this . . . solidarity extended beyond the workshop to the trade in general in the area. Pride and interest in their work, the fact that they could often talk during work that did not entail the 'thunder of machines', the spare time consequent on the irregularity of work, the freedom during work, all reinforced the social bonds between members of the trade that were continued in leisure time. But whereas in France this still had some religious focus, in Britain it centred wholly on that great secular institution, the public house, source of drink, food, lodging, employment, entertainment and company. Here in the public house to which members of a particular trade resorted, was strengthened the occupational community and the particularism so concerned with the honour and reputation of the trade and here were reproduced workshop practices and concerns![75]

Such awareness of common traditions was most formally expressed, of course, in the enduring institution of the guilds, which retained significant, if declining, functional and ceremonial roles. In 1814 Parliament repealed the clauses of the Elizabethan Statute of Artificers which had given legal sanction to their customary attempts to control recruitment and to regulate apprenticeships. This did not, however, put an end to feelings of craft solidarity. After all, members of the same craft usually experienced strikingly similar economic and social problems—wage rates, unemployment, technological rivalry, and fluctuations of demand. Although their reactions to these problems might differ from time to time, from place to place, and from trade to trade, there can be no question that craftsmen were a coherent social group. A common awareness of the traditional functions and privileges of their labour, a customary pride in the skill of their crafts, the ubiquity of guilds, friendly benefit societies, charitable institutions, and apprenticeship regulations typify most crafts. Furthermore, there persisted a strong tradition that in times of distress remedies should be sought through the law to defend the rights and privileges of craftsmen: 'They had the same concerns with status distinctions and the honour of their trade, similar values of respectability and aversion to charity, emphases on traditional privileges, the tendency to envisage their appropriate reward in traditional terms, the same guild-like ideals of regulation.'[76] The craftsmen constitute, in the last analysis, a status group separated from the lower strata, and even the retailers, by a wide range of social, economic, occupational, and ideological features.

There are, furthermore, grounds for thinking that this craftsman stratum of the electorate was thriving and prospering during the period under review. It is, of course, true that the dismantling of traditional regulations together with the undeniably piteous conditions of certain crafts has suggested a picture of decline and impoverishment. But the destruction of the privileges and livelihoods of certain craftsmen in the textile industry, memorably depicted by the Hammonds and by E. P. Thompson, was scarcely typical. For one thing, the textile industry employed fewer craftsmen than others, notably the building, the shoe-making, tailoring, cabinet-making, and printing trades. In other cases, technological change scarcely touched many crafts. The possession of rare and unusual skills, in an age of economic growth,

[75] I. Prothero, *Artisans and Politics in Early Nineteenth-century London: John Gast and His Times* (Folkestone, 1978), 35.
[76] Ibid. 28, 337.

population explosion, urbanization, and building, provided many craftsmen with plentiful work and reasonably well paid employment:

When one turns to examine the craft-economy of any particular place, what one finds is certainly not a static or hidebound structure. On the contrary, new branches of established crafts were developing all the time, new skills were arising in response to new needs as if by spontaneous generation, and old skills were continually splitting up and splaying out into new specialisms.[77]

It cannot be said too often that one of the most important consequences of the Industrial Revolution was less the growth of factory employment than the dramatic expansion in the numbers of small shops and tiny units of production. It was from this group that the largest section of the electorate was drawn.

*The fifth group* in the structure of the electorate comprises unskilled men, workers, and labourers. Of the poll books in which an analysis of this category could proceed, they averaged 14.2% of the total. Within the freeman boroughs the proportion tended to increase as the size of the electorate decreased, a significant reflection of Everitt's hypothesis that craftsmen formed a distinctly higher proportion of the population in the larger freeman boroughs.[78] In the householder boroughs, they formed a very large percentage of the electorate, almost one-half, an expected finding because of the very wide electorates in those boroughs. Elsewhere, their figures approximated much more closely to those of the freeman boroughs. It can scarcely be denied that this category is, in many ways, the least satisfactory and the least homogeneous, of the six. It hardly needs to be said that these were not proletarian men, that they were heterogeneous, and may even have included a few self-employed men of quite an independent stamp. Most men in this category did not work in factories, and many did not work in industry. There are foundrymen and miners, to be sure, but this category is dominated by the carters, the cleaners, the mariners, the sailors, and the wagoners. These are the lower orders of a pre-industrial type, except perhaps in rapidly industrializing Preston, although even there most men employed in textiles worked in small units. (It is necessary to remember, however, that as the 1831 census showed, those adult males employed in manufacturing industry were only half the number employed in agriculture.) They had little in common. It

---

[77] Everitt, 'Country, County and Town', 100. The same point has been noticed from a later period: 'The conditions which favoured the craftsman were really much more those of the period just before the industrial revolution than those of the nineteenth century' (H. Pelling, *Popular Politics and Society in Late Victorian England* (London, 1968), 421–43).

[78] Everitt, 'Country, County and Town', 99.

would be difficult to claim that they were marked by any sense of shared experience or expectations. They felt themselves distinct from those craftsmen who served apprenticeships and whose pattern of behaviour publicly displayed their attachment to certain status forms, and they were frequently, although not always, less financially and occupationally secure. Consequently, it tended to be voters from this category whose voting credentials were most frequently challenged and who were those with the least resistance, economically and ideologically, to bribery and intimidation. Although there is little to suggest that these men were either apathetic or unwilling to further their own interests, it is doubtful if they possessed the capacity for corporate action which could overtake sections of the other categories.

*The sixth and final category* considered, the agriculturalists, was certainly capable of defending its interest, 'the landed interest'. Understandably, they dominate the county electorates and figure largely in one or two small, rural boroughs. In most boroughs, however, they were very sparsely represented. (They average only 6.4%.) In the counties they have been designated as 'deferential' voters, but, as we shall see, the extent to which this is true can easily be exaggerated.[79] What is surely beyond dispute is the common ground between the voters in this category and the dominating rural élite which appears in the first category. In other words, its political values were deferentially derived, and there is a clear *prima facie* case for assuming a considerable similarity between the voting behaviour of this group and that of its patrons. Nevertheless, these electors must have actually participated in elections less frequently than any other category, given the low rate of contested county elections.

The structure of the electorate was surprisingly stable. When measured over time in the same constituency there is little sign of change or development. It is clear from Table 4.12 and from the case of Liverpool in Table 4.14 that the different categories maintained much the same relative balance between each other down to 1832.[80] Within any one constituency, the slight changes which might appear may be attributed to inconsistencies of terminology, to variations in turnout, especially of the outvoters, and to 'artificial' contrivances such as the arbitrary creation of freemen. In the few industrial towns to be represented before 1832 changes may be observed. Table 4.15 summarizes the shifting composition of the Preston electorate, highlighting the number of textile workers. The increasing number of textile workers can, of course, be discerned here, but the general

[79] See below, pp. 237-44.
[80] J. A. Phillips found exactly the same phenomenon, see *Electoral Behavior*, 195-7.

TABLE 4.15        *Structure of the Preston Electorate, 1807–1837 (%)*

|                                    | 1807  | 1818 | 1820 | 1830 | 1837  |
|------------------------------------|-------|------|------|------|-------|
| 1. Gentlemen and professionals     | 4     | 9    | 6    | 6    | 9     |
| 2. Merchants and manufacturers     | 3     | 1    | 3    | 2    | 4     |
| 3. Retailers                       | 16    | 13   | 12   | 12   | 15    |
| 4. Craftsmen                       | 64    | 29   | 25   | 22   | 65    |
| 5. Semi/unskilled labourers        | 12    | 15   | 16   | 15   | 7     |
| (Textile workers)                  | —[a]  | 31   | 37   | 42   | —[a]  |
| 6. Agriculturalists                | 1     | 2    | 1    | 1    | —     |

[a] In 1807 and 1837, textile workers were included in group 4.

occupational structure of the Preston electorate was not severely unbalanced by this development, nor indeed by the impact of the 1832 Reform Act.

This is not to imply that the electorate was fixed and unchanging. Occupations, crafts, and trades were coming and going, and the poll books were capable of registering these changes. Indeed, the composition of the electorate was capable of reflecting several of the most important social and economic realities of the period: the presence of a large, rurally dominated civilian élite, the existence of a numerous and influential professional sector, the subdivision of crafts and the existence of a numerically strong retailing sector.[81] The electorate was clearly quite representative of some of the groups that were increasing in wealth and numbers in Hanoverian England. The unreformed electorate, moreover, reached quite far down the social scale, beneath the artisanate and into the labouring classes to an extent that the Great Reform Act could not emulate.[82] In the places that were enfranchised it is possible that the structure of the electorate was not, in fact, a bad representation of the social structure in general.[83] We should avoid the view that a new world of urban industry was consigning

[81] Everitt, 'Country, County and Town', 99. In Chester in 1811, 391 families (10% of the total) relied on agriculture, 2,296 (61%) on handicrafts and manufactures; see J. M. Pigot, *History of the City of Chester* (Chester, 1815), 89. This compares with the 53.1% of the electorate who can be allocated to the 'craftsmen' category at the 1812 general election and the 4.5% to 'merchants and manufacturers'. The 1.6% 'agriculturalists' in the poll book is not such a good fit, but some portion of the 11.2% in the 'Gentlemen and Professionals' category must be added.

[82] At least, over 14% of the electorate can be assigned to category 5. See Tables 4.12 to 4.14.

[83] J. A. Phillips, *Electoral Behavior*, 190–3.

the unreformed electorate and the places it represented to the scrapheaps of irrelevance. The eighteenth-century town melted social barriers and promoted social mobility and assimilation. Something at least, of that world may be seen in the poll books.

That world did not suddenly pass away in 1832. As Table 4.16 reveals, there are differences in the occupational composition of the electorate before and after 1832, but they are not dramatic differences. There is no sign of a reduction in the proportionate size of the 'gentlemen and professionals' group and, even, a distinct increase in the size of the 'merchants and manufacturers' group. Retailers advance at the expense of craftsmen, but it is difficult to see a departure in the direction of democracy in 1832. There seems no escape from the conclusion that the 1832 Reform Act diminished the penetration of the electorate down the social scale.[84]

TABLE 4.16 *Structure of the Electorate in Two-member English Boroughs, pre-1832 and 1832–1866 (Average of 32 constituencies, %)*

|  | Pre-1832 | 1832–66 |
|---|---|---|
| 1. Gentlemen and professionals | 14 | 17 |
| 2. Merchants and manufacturers | 6 | 10 |
| 3. Retailers | 20 | 26 |
| 4. Craftsmen | 40 | 30 |
| 5. Semi/unskilled labourers | 14 | — |
| 6. Agriculturalists | 6 | 2 |
| 7. Drink | — | 9 |
| 8. Other | — | 6 |

*Source*: Data for 1832–66 are from T. J. Nossiter, *Influence, Opinion and Political Idioms in Reformed England: Case Studies from the North-east* (Brighton, 1975), 166. Pre-1832 data are from Tables 4.12–4.14.

The unreformed electorate was structured rather like a blunted diamond: a substantial 'upper class' of gentlemen and professionals swelled into the more numerous groups of retailers and, still more, craftsmen, before relaxing into the less numerous unskilled and labouring occupations. Perhaps the strongest impression remains

[84] These conclusions are clearly borne out by comparing the freeman voters, who were, of course, retained in 1832, and the £10 householder voters; see e.g. the figures assembled by Stoker ('Elections and Voting Behavior', Ph.D., 220–1) for Berwick, Newcastle-upon-Tyne, and Durham in 1832.

that of the large number of petty capitalists, small, independent producers and retailers, enmeshed in an urban social system whose universally acknowledged superiors merged neatly into county society. Few electors were in a totally dependent and vulnerable situation. By the same token, however, few would have been beyond the reach of influence *of some kind*, from below as well as above. Tensions within the electorate might be of a tangible, often economic, kind: custom, patronage, supply, subsidies, payments. But they might also be the product of social pressures: emulation, conformity, status, fear of disorder.

Indeed, electors *as electors* exhibit certain definable social qualities. In spite of their occupational, economic, and political differences, their collective participation in elections conveys a certain social meaning. Electors, of course, accepted the prevailing social and economic system, the existence of hierarchy and subordination, the principles of economic and social advancement, and the sacrosanctity of property. Electors were prepared to defend and advance their interests within the existing social order. In view of these realities, the moderate performance of electoral radicalism comes to seem less surprising (see Ch. 5).

Nevertheless, there were divisions within the electorate, and to these we shall now turn. The simplest and most common of these divisions is that between support for and opposition towards established interests and sitting members. Why did electors make the choices that they did on this fairly simple issue? In the present state of research it is not possible to offer definite conclusions as to why people voted in a particular manner. The voter himself may not have clearly grasped his own compulsions. If he did it is more than likely that he did not articulate them, still less conveniently note them for the benefit of the academic researcher. Because we do not possess and therefore because we do not employ a language which enables us to weigh competing pressures upon an individual it is not possible to present a ranking order of likely causes of voting behaviour. There is a danger that with increasingly sophisticated techniques for measurement there may emerge an excessive confidence in what can be measured. The historian must always remain alive to the possibility that what really provokes voting behaviour is that which is least sensitive to scales of measurement.

However inadequate it may be at the definitional level, there is something to be said for persevering with the sixfold scheme of occupational classification adopted earlier. I venture to disagree with Professor Phillips's assumption that these groupings 'are poor substitutes for some more realistically complex definition of groups in society that might constitute social classes'.[85] They ought, at least, to be permitted to show the respective political choices which they made over several decades. Starting with the 33 contested elections in my six chosen constituencies, I selected 24 in which voters were faced with a fairly straightforward choice between support for and opposition to established interests, i.e. candidates who represented a dominant local family (such as the Grosvenors at Chester), or alliance of such families, or alliance of such families with the local corporation. (In the rest, established interests were divided against each other.) Adopting this very simple distinction between candidates who supported and opposed established interests, certain tentative conclusions may be outlined.

First, there is an overwhelming tendency for voters in category 1 to support established interests. There can be no mistaking the message conveyed by Table 4.17. By margins of 3 and even 4 to 1, upper class voters flocked to support established candidates. There is, of course, not the slightest reason to be surprised at these tendencies. The common adoption of social, political, and family interests among the local élite of Hanoverian England is only to be expected. At St Albans in 1831, however, when two opposition Whigs defeated a Conservative, the percentage of voters from this category who supported established interests came close to falling below one-half. At Southampton, which returned independent members in 1818 and 1820, moreover, these voters willingly jumped on the independent band-wagon, deserting the Rose interest to which they had always been faithful, an interesting warning against gradualism in voting behaviour. In no fewer than 18 of the 24 cases, the category 1 voters supporting established candidates exceeded the percentage of their party's average vote at an election. What is just a little more significant is the very similar set of electoral choices made by voters from category 2, the merchants and manufacturers. As remarked earlier, they seem to have identified their fortunes and their aspirations with this traditional élite. As Table 4.17 reveals, they voted by very considerable majorities in its support. In the 24 cases in question, however, the percentage of voters supporting established candidates from this category was lower than the party's

---

[85] J. A. Phillips, *Electoral Behavior*, 259. Phillips believes that 'Social strata may, in fact, closely approximate social classes but . . . supplementary evidence is so sorely lacking . . . that serious obstacles impede the definition of social strata'! Adopting a slightly artificial three-tiered division of the electorate ('that has been shown to convey economic inequalities in addition to differences of status'), he abandons his earlier functional categories of occupation (ibid. 260). I think this regrettable. After a sophisticated series of tests he is forced to conclude that 'the total political impact of these socio-economic variables tended to be negligible' (ibid. 277). As I hope I demonstrate in the rest of this chapter, the functional categories can yield fruitful hypotheses.

TABLE 4.17 *Voting for Established Candidates at Five Constituencies, 1768–1831, by Occupational Category (%)*

|  | 1 | 2 | 3 | 4 | 5 | Overall |
|---|---|---|---|---|---|---|
| *Chester* | | | | | | |
| 1812 | 63 | 55 | 49 | 48 | 53 | 51 |
| 1818 | 72 | 56 | 54 | 56 | 71 | 58 |
| 1820 | 74 | 52 | 45 | 54 | 64 | 53 |
| *Colchester* | | | | | | |
| 1790 | 70 | 74 | 73 | 72 | 72 | 73 |
| 1806 | 81 | 84 | 75 | 67 | 71 | 76 |
| 1807 | 91 | 66 | 87 | 87 | 93 | 90 |
| 1812 | 85 | 74 | 68 | 61 | 70 | 69 |
| 1818 | 73 | 58 | 52 | 57 | 66 | 60 |
| 1820 | 75 | 63 | 57 | 56 | 61 | 62 |
| *St Albans* | | | | | | |
| 1820 | 78 | 73 | 78 | 85 | 59 | 81 |
| 1821 | 70 | 65 | 70 | 53 | 53 | 62 |
| 1831 | 52 | 23 | 30 | 27 | 37 | 26 |
| *Shrewsbury* | | | | | | |
| 1806 | 62 | 66 | 77 | 73 | 73 | 72 |
| 1807 | 64 | 74 | 77 | 75 | 75 | 74 |
| 1812 | 85 | 66 | 77 | 69 | 73 | 73 |
| 1814 | 94 | 62 | 75 | 56 | 63 | 70 |
| 1819 | 30 | 61 | 69 | 58 | 63 | 58 |
| *Southampton* | | | | | | |
| 1774 | 58 | 57 | 65 | 60 | 59 | 60 |
| 1790 | 84 | 80 | 76 | 78 | 78 | 79 |
| 1794 | 73 | 48 | 48 | 43 | 53 | 54 |
| 1806 | 84 | 76 | 70 | 70 | 78 | 76 |
| 1812 | 84 | 74 | 73 | 65 | 79 | 74 |
| 1818 | 26 | 21 | 24 | 20 | 23 | 24 |
| 1820 | 35 | 30 | 30 | 30 | 28 | 31 |

*Note*: For summary of occupational categories, see p. 207–15; a full listing is given in App. 1.

average in 13 cases, higher in 8, and the same in 3. Here and there—at Colchester, Chester, and Shrewsbury—there are just a few signs of a declining attachment. At St Albans at the very significant contest of 1831 and at Southampton in 1818 and 1820 they largely abandon it altogether. These were not the only voters massively to sustain the local electoral interests of the Hanoverian élite. Many voters from category 5 did so, refuting any suggestion that a class war within the electorate was brewing. These were the voters lowest down the social and occupational scale. Their vulnerability to influence, intimidation, and bribery was probably a more powerful cause of their fidelity to local élites than any innate deference. Nevertheless, an instinctive and even unthinking willingness to obey social disciplines must have sustained them. In exactly half of the 24 contests considered here, the percentage of voters from category 5 supporting established candidates exceeded its party's share of the poll, in 11 it was less, and in 1 it was the same. Lower class voters were not, for the most part, radical: the 'Labourers' *opposed* Orator Hunt at Preston in 1830 by a ratio of 2 to 1.[86]

Perhaps surprisingly, established candidates did not fare much worse among categories 3 and 4, the retailers and craftsmen. These voters were, perhaps, marginally, more inclined to local opposition than those with whom we have dealt hitherto, but there was sometimes very little in it. Only at Chester, and in 1818–20 at Colchester, did voters from these categories oppose local patrons in any significant numbers. At Chester, traditions of local independency and, indeed, its more emphatic organization, prevailed more than in any of the other constituencies dealt with here. By 1818 and 1820 such patterns of local opposition had become entrenched at Colchester too. As might be expected, at St Albans in 1831, these voters also deserted established candidates in large numbers. They seem, however, little more inclined to do so than other categories dealt with here. Voters from these categories tend to support established interests only slightly less enthusiastically than the three categories we have examined so far. Among the retailers only in 8 of the 24 contests did their votes exceed the percentage party vote, in 14 it was less, and in 2 it was the same. Among the craftsmen, the average party voting percentage was exceeded 5 times, in 17 it was less, and in 2 it was the same. With the benefit of hindsight, and perhaps with the exercise of anachronism, it is possible to detect a number of excellent social and economic reasons why the retailers and craftsmen should exhibit independent patterns of political behaviour at elections to the unreformed parliament. 'Bourgeois consumerism, the democratization of taste, the emergence of a more broadly based market for goods and services' have been cited as the basis of the retailers' challenge to an economy dominated by landed patricians and their adherents.[87] Nevertheless, the abiding strength of the patrician economy helps to explain the ability of large minorities of retailers and craftsmen to *support* that economy. They were imprisoned within it. They were open to influence

---

[86] The count was 77–38. In 1818 the same group had *opposed* the radical Whig candidate, Crompton, by 31–13.

[87] Brewer, 'Commercialization and Politics', 199–200.

from above as well as below, especially when their custom was drawn from genteel and opulent families. Consequently, many retailers and craftsmen supported established candidates. These tensions can occasionally be reflected in the interests of the publishers of poll books; not for nothing did they extract the voting behaviour of particular retailing trades and craft occupations for the edification of their readers.[88]

Voting behaviour among producers and retailers within the pre-industrial economy was determined according to their perspective upon the clientage economy of the patrician classes. What the foregoing tables reveal is the overwhelming proportion of electoral support for established interests and local élites among all categories of occupation. Nevertheless, when essentially political and ideological conflicts occurred—over local independency, radicalism or party issues—these proportions of support could rapidly be reversed, endangering the seemingly unassailable positions of local patrons. At most contested elections, however, established interests were successful, and the figures in Table 4.17 must therefore be regarded as in some ways thoroughly predictable. What may occasion more surprise, however, is the ability of candidates of established interests to attract roughly equal support from all five of the occupational categories dealt with here. (Category 6, the agriculturalists, was too small for figures to be meaningful.) Both support for, and opposition to, these candidates is broadly spread across occupational categories rather than narrowly based and concentrated in any one (or few) social and occupational groupings. As Professor Phillips remarked after the most thorough analysis of the partisan choices of his electors 'the total political impact of [these] socio-economic variables tended to be negligible'.[89] There is no *prima facie* indication that voters from different occupational categories voted differently. Conflicts within the unreformed electorate, then, appear to have had political, ideological, and, possibly, personal causes rather than simple socio-economic origins.[90] Consequently, we need to

---

[88] *The Burgesses' Poll at the Late Election* (Newcastle, 1774) compared voting by trade and craft occupation at the 1741 and 1774 elections. Compilers of many Liverpool poll books liked to undertake similar enquiries, as in 1812 and 1818.

[89] J. A. Phillips, *Electoral Behavior*, 277.

[90] This question is, of course, a horrifyingly difficult one which historians are only now coming to consider empirically. Evidence from *occupational category* does not so far seem to suggest a socio-economic conflict within the electorate, although, as we shall see later (pp. 259–85), the structure of independent parties was by no means identical with that of support for established interests. This does not preclude the possibility that other measures of social differentiation might yield evidence of such divisions. There is evidence, for example, that at the Westminster elections of 1784 and 1788 the highest rate-payers tended to support government candidates and the lowest tended to support opposition candidates (I am very grateful to Mr Edmund Green of Royal Holloway and Bedford New College of the University of London for allowing me to benefit from his knowledge of the Westminster constituency.)

examine the type of issue, local as well as national, political as well as personal, which tended to unsettle these fundamental patterns of electoral support. As we have seen, the successful (and nearly successful) independence revolts at Chester and Southampton and the radical tide of 1831 at St Albans were just such instances. How typical these were and how widespread opposition was to the electoral oligarchy of Hanoverian England deserves attention. To what extent was such opposition on the increase? What type of language and aspirations sustained it? What combination of circumstances fostered it? For the next part of this enquiry it will be necessary to turn to the world of issues and ideals, to examine the mental worlds of both patrons and voters, before attempting to reconstruct the political universe of independents and radicals.

# 5
# *Ideological Aspects of Electoral Behaviour*

Historians have been reluctant to attribute much significance to the role of ideas and opinion in elections to the unreformed House of Commons. Simply because many elections went uncontested it is assumed that serious differences of opinion in the electorate cannot have existed. Even when elections were contested, issues are usually regarded with considerable suspicion: 'During elections all discussion was naturally dominated by the rival candidates, and for this reason was generally kept within the confines of personalities and local rivalries.'[1] The electorate, it is assumed, were indifferent to anything other than material persuasions until they were 'politicized' at some future date, a nice example of anachronism in electoral history. It may, of course, be perfectly true that for much of the unreformed period the mass of the electorate remained unaware of formal political philosophy and, in many constituencies, unfamiliar with issues of national significance. Even within this context, however, electors could display considerable interest in local affairs, in the leadership of local communities, in the allocation of power and authority over them, in the exercise of that power and authority, and in the discussion of alternatives to them. The education and the reading matter of the middling orders remained traditional until the nineteenth century, but such a diet only nourished the prevailing concern for customary usages, rights, and liberties.[2] There can be no mistaking the informal political consciousness of the English voter classes.[3]

Formal politicization—through the press, through clubs, and through party organization—was to come slowly and at differing rates of progress in different places. For the moment it is enough to underline the intense, if informal, politicization of the Hanoverian electorate. And if we remember the deliberate involvement of non-electors in the

---

[1] A. D. Harvey, *Britain in the Early Nineteenth Century* (London, 1978), 48.

[2] It is the gradual rather than the dramatic contact of voters (who were, of course, largely a literate group) with the new print culture which needs emphasis. As Neuberg argues, not only the education but also the reading material of the voter classes was very traditional; V. E. Neuberg, *Popular Education in Eighteenth Century England* (London, 1971), *passim*.

[3] Not surprisingly, it was regularly noticed by foreign visitors; see H. Lockett, *The Relations of French and English Society, 1763–1793* (London, 1920), 32–7; J. A. Kelly, *England and Englishmen in German Literature in the Eighteenth Century* (New York, 1921), 13, 129–30.

routine and ritual of election campaigns, as participants in parades, processions, and demonstrations, as employees and helpers of one of the candidates' organizations, as listeners of speeches, toasts, and addresses, or simply as consumers of the *largesse* of the candidates and their agents, then we can readily endorse Professor Plumb's view that here, at the electoral and subelectoral level, existed 'a political nation whom Namier and his followers have almost entirely ignored'.[4] The ability of political, economic, and religious pressure groups to mobilize this latent opinion has, moreover, been carefully chronicled by scholars more recently. They have shown that on a series of political issues ('Wilkes and Liberty', Pitt and Fox in 1782–84, the French Revolution), economic issues ('The War of Jenkins Ear', the American War, the Corn Laws), and religious issues (the Jew Bill of 1753, the abolition of the slave trade, the repeal of the Test and Corporation Acts, and Catholic emancipation), voters could respond powerfully, if (given the rhythm of political conflict), only intermittently.

The fact of political awareness among the electorate will be explored in considerable detail in the rest of this chapter. What we must first examine, however, are the origins of that political awareness. Such an awareness is not imposed by some exterior agency, nor does an individual voter grow into it after being exposed to 'politicization'. Political awareness arises from the social and political environments in which the voter exists, from the social, economic, and political relationships in which he is enmeshed, from the images of himself and others which he perceives, from the ideals and expectations he entertains, and, not least, from the objective realities of the situations he experiences. Electoral behaviour arises out of such powerfully held social, political, and even moral, standards and beliefs. Once these are understood then the motivations of electoral behaviour can be dissected.

## PATERNALISM AND DEFERENCE

Electoral relationships were one manifestation of a set of broad social relationships which were embedded in the theory and practice of both paternalism and deference. The paternalism of the patron or class of patrons towards the constituency and its inhabitants *in general* elicited the deference of the voter or class of voters. In this sense, the voters demanded, indeed, anticipated, paternalist services of many kinds in

---

[4] J. Plumb, 'Political Man', in J. Clifford (ed.), *Man versus Society in the Eighteenth Century* (Cambridge, 1968), 12.

return for their loyalty and, it followed, as a continuous reward for their continuing social and political subordination. These were not simply the relationships of individuals. Although relationships between patrons and voters were technically private, they were, of course, of very great public interest to contemporaries, and thus of central significance to any exploration of the world of electoral politics. How the expectations which governed these relationships were sustained for so long, and in a period of unprecedented social change, is one of the most difficult, but yet most neglected, questions in Hanoverian electoral history.

Professor Pocock has recently discussed the reciprocal capacities in such relationships, where both parties had obligations as well as rights: 'The ideal of deference was not to reduce a man to helpless and imbecilic servility but to treat him in such a way as to acknowledge his essential independence and self-respect on both sides in differing capacities and situation.'[5] Pocock's evidence is derived overwhelmingly from Harrington and the theorists of the seventeenth century, but such attitudes were no less current a century later. One of their most popular late-eighteenth century exponents was Thomas Gisborne. Gisborne stressed that all social institutions, indeed, social behaviour itself, were informed with the rules of natural justice, the violation of which, however, would impair and retard the prosperity of the state. Gisborne is anxious to educate the Hanoverian élite into these responsibilities. Discussing the duties of landowners not merely over their families and tenants but even over persons who are not their immediate dependants, for example, he writes:

To encourage a race of upright, skilful and industrious tenants is one of the first duties of a private gentleman . . . Let him unite the votes of his tenants to his own by argument and honest persuasion. (If his conduct towards them has been as it ought, even those means will scarcely ever be necessary.) But let him not force their compliance by menaces of expulsion from their farms, or forfeiture of his favour.[6]

Such homilies, of course, were rooted in economic advantage, and their currency was not at all surprising in a period of economic expansion. The oppression of individuals would lead to confusion,

---

[5] J. C. A. Pocock, 'The Classical Theory of Deference', *Am. Hist. Rev.* 81 (1976). Significantly, Pocock's definition of deference is 'the voluntary acceptance of a leadership elite by persons not belonging to that elite, but sufficiently free as political actors to render deference not only a voluntary but also a political act'. Deference precludes inferiors from leadership 'but not from an intelligently critical attitude towards those who possess that capacity' (ibid. 517, 519).

[6] T. Gisborne, *An Enquiry into the Duties of Men in the Higher and Middle Classes of Society in Great Britain Resulting from their Respective Stations*, 2 vols. (London, 1798) i. 18; ii. 400–1, 426.

conflict, and contraction. To encourage them, however, would enhance productivity, profit, and employment. Consequently, these ideas had a wide circulation and a general application. Even the radical critics of the political and electoral system accepted the existence of political and electoral deference—so long, of course, as voters were not corrupted by bribery and dependency.

One common derivation from these deferential assumptions was the universal belief that property gave a 'natural interest' in the political, social, and electoral life of the community in which it was held. Wilberforce caught the attitude perfectly: 'That a good landlord should, and must, have some influence over his tenant, independent of political merit, was a proposition he could not but admit; but the nearer we approached to selection upon distinct and independent principles, the nearer we approached to perfection.'[7] The rights of the landlord or patron in these matters was scarcely ever questioned, especially by the landlords. In the Reform Act debates, that remarkable inquest upon the expiring electoral order, Lord John Russell declared: 'Wherever the aristocracy reside, receiving large incomes, performing important duties, relieving the poor by charity, and evincing private worth and public virtue, it is not in human nature that they should not possess a great influence upon public opinion.'[8] Indeed not, but to be fair to the proprietors they recognized that property alone was an inadequate means of forging an electoral interest. Property usually conveyed influence for a patron, 'but that influence would depend upon his popularity in some degree'.[9] That popularity, or, as Croker put it, those 'feelings of gratitude for the benefits which have been conferred upon them' was a natural consequence of munificence, charity, and paternalism.[10] For electoral influence was not simply a right of property. It amounted to a moral trust, involving distinct obligations of service not merely to the voters but to the community as a whole.[11]

---

[7] 26 May 1809, *Parliamentary Debates*, xiv. 753.

[8] 19 Feb. 1831, *Parliamentary Debates*, 3rd ser. ii. 1086.

[9] Lord Althorp, 13 Aug. 1831, ibid. v. 1371.

[10] 4 Mar. 1831, ibid. iii. 102.

[11] See, for example, Lord Grey on 2 Oct. 1831, ibid. vii. 946. (See also a most interesting discussion of this idea of electoral influence as a moral trust by Sir Hames Mackintosh, 4 July 1831, ibid. iv. 684. There is an interesting letter 'To the freemen of Boston, worthy or unworthy' (*Boston Poll Book*, 1830, 32–3) deploring the corruption of electors as a denial of the voters' trust: 'It is true that the voters are a body set apart from the rest of their fellow-townsmen, for the performance to their country, of a service upon which its vital interests depend. They are trustees for the society to which they belong; and in a trust, importing the greatest good or evil to a vast majority of their countrymen. Can there be a more sacred obligation? Is there, in the strictest sense, any thing binding on the conscience of a man, if this is not considered binding? Is it not an act of virtue to be faithful to this trust? Is it not an act of the greatest vice to be unfaithful to it? Is there, indeed, in any act of treachery, anything to render it odious,

These sentiments need to be taken with a certain reserve. They were, no doubt, expressions of an idealized, blissfully harmonious order in which consideration and kindness informed all social relationships. They should not be taken as exact descriptions of contemporary practice. The currency of paternalists' ideas and their constant reiteration should not therefore be underestimated. After all, electoral influence was not confined to the aristocracy. Since the possession of small property or the employment of small offices could bestow a natural interest, the possession of an electoral interest was enmeshed into society at large. It was a function of property and power *per se*, not merely of aristocratic property and power. Unless there was a universal conspiracy to deceive, the currency of such ideas must have represented a certain ideal type or preferred objective in social and electoral behaviour. They must, therefore, have been of considerable ideological force. Acting as a criterion or yardstick against which to judge and to measure the exercise of paternalism, these normative statements must have gone some way, at least, towards inhibiting the Hanoverian propertied classes from governing by force and fraud alone. As William Paley remarked of electors and elections:

The assiduity with which their favour is sought upon these occasions, serves to generate settled habits of condescension and respect; and as human life is more embittered by affronts than injuries, whatever contributes to procure mildness and civility of manners towards those who are most liable to suffer from a contrary behaviour, corrects with the pride in a great measure, the evil of inequality, and deserves to be accounted among the most generous institutions of social life.[12]

No doubt, in the last instance, patrons were capable of enforcing their will. Certainly, their capacity for taking political decisions on behalf

which is not in this act? Is not the consciousness of having been, and being now a villain, with the intention of continuing to be so, a complete perversion of the moral faculty? Is not such a man completely degraded from the rank of a moral being? The opulent man applies to the voting man all the means in his power, to make him commit an act in the highest degree criminal; to betray a trust of unspeakable importance, committed to him by his country. The voters, we are told, ought not to be guilty of such criminal compliance. True:—so say I. They ought to perish, rather. But acknowledging, as I do fully the criminality of such voters; deeply sensible of the degree to which they are demoralized and degraded, by the part they act in returning to Parliament, men whom they must in conscience disapprove; let us look at the still greater guilt of those who influence their voting. What is the nature of an act where a man attains the base end he has in view, by being the cause of the criminal act of another person? To render the obligation of voting more binding still, the sanction of an oath is added.—The voter solemnly swears that he will not betray, but faithfully execute, his trust. —Consider, then, my fellow-townsmen, the important, the solemn trust with which ye are intrusted, should you have an opportunity of performing it.'

[12] E. Paley (ed.), *The Works of William Paley*, 4 vols. (1838), iii. 258, quoted by I. R. Christie, *Stress and Stability in Late Eighteenth-century Britain* (Oxford, 1984), 54.

of those beneath them and their confidence in interpreting the best political interests of their subordinates remained enormous. Nevertheless, in the last analysis, coercion and intimidation amounted to serious departures from conventional standards and customary practices.

Such perceptions of the Hanoverian ruling élite encounter enormous problems of validation—one of the reasons, no doubt, for the uncertainty and confusion which seem to accompany historical excursions into this vexed area. E. P. Thompson, for example, likes to dismiss deference and paternalism as empty gestures, the former as an insincere posture used to purchase the latter, the latter condescendingly proferred as an intermittent, theatrical, and symbolic illusion to satisfy the plebeians.[13] Such instrumentalities maintained a grossly unequal set of class and social relationships. Professor Plumb regards the robust pursuit of political power as the motivating force of the landed interest.[14] For Sir Lewis Namier the preservation of patrimonial inheritance and the advancement of family and local interests were paramount.[15] Others point simply to their avaricious desire to maintain and extend their social hegemony.[16] Because it is not clear by what criteria an entire ruling élite is being judged, it is by no means easy to treat such assessments. We might do well to note, with Dr Colley, how many of these hostile assessments, together with the 'evidence' which supports them, are taken from the contemporary enemies of that ruling order.[17] Further, whatever the generalized indictments of certain scholars might suggest, the 'paternalists' themselves have not, in fact, had a bad press from historians. No doubt the extent to which practice matched precept varied hugely, as it always will, but those historians who have actually studied individual paternalists have reached conclusions vastly different from those who have generalized about them as a class.[18]

[13] See E. P. Thompson, 'Patrician Society and Plebeian Culture', *J. Soc. Hist.* 7/4 (1974), 383-405, id., 'Eighteenth-century English Society: Class Struggle Without Class', *Soc. Hist.* 3/2 (1978) 133-65.

[14] J. Plumb, *The Growth of Political Stability in England, 1675-1725* (London, 1967), 189; Roy Porter, *English Society in the Eighteenth Century* (London, 1982), 121 ff.

[15] L. B. Namier, *The Structure of Politics at the Accession of George III* (London, 1929), 1-76.

[16] T. Beastall, *A North Country Estate: The Lumleys and Saundersons as Landowners, 1600-1900* (London, 1975), ch. 4.

[17] L. Colley, *In Defiance of Oligarchy: The Tory Party, 1714-1760* (Cambridge, 1982), 146-51.

[18] See e.g. G. Mee, *Aristocratic Enterprise: The Fitzwilliam Industrial Undertakings* (Glasgow-London, 1975), *passim*, but esp. 16-22, 131-8, 147-56, 186-90, 201-18; J. Golby, 'A Great Electioneer and His Motives', *Hist. J.* 8/2 (1965); Beastall, *North Country Estate*, ch. 4. Even the sceptical Roberts, always ready to spot humbug and backsliding among his

Deference, therefore, must be carefully distinguished from dependence. The mindless respect which a common servant displayed towards his social superiors cannot be compared with the more balanced relationship which existed between a substantial tenant farmer and an aristocratic superior, or between a respectable shop-keeper and his social superiors. In this situation, both sides concerned had socially approved roles to play and were usually willing to moderate and restrain their partially conflicting interests for the sake of local stability and social and political equilibrium. Both sides had an interest in maintaining the unwritten rules which regulated their relationships. The common servant, for one thing, could be replaced much more readily than the tenant farmer or shop-keeper, whose independence, moreover, might make him a substantial figure in the community, one who could not be treated anything like as arbitrarily as the servant. Intermittent, theatrical gestures would have been noticed by him for the insulting condescension that they were. In any case, they would have been hopelessly inadequate to sustain the economic and social expectations which were particularly current during election campaigns. Indeed, there is some evidence that at the turn of the century such expectations were being more readily acknowledged by the upper crust. From Paley and Burke onwards, the efflorescence of paternalist literature, sustained by the loyalist reaction of the 1790s, the Evangelical movement and, not least, the agricultural prosperity of most of the war years ensured a ready audience for the renewed currents of paternalist ideology.

The pressures upon patrons to make a reality of their paternalist professions were thus enormous. The universality of paternalist values provided an ideological imperative to the Hanoverian élite which underlay their remarkable self-confidence. But how paternalistic were the paternalists? Given the absence of agreed and measurable criteria, and in view of the impossibility of pontificating with any certainty upon the lofty topic of human motivation, it is impossible to reach a conclusion which could satisfy everybody. Obviously, paternalism is an élitist and hierarchical principle which protects the property and justifies the social position of paternalists. As an authoritarian social

paternalists concludes that, on the whole, they made a real attempt to put their ideals into practice. In so far as they failed to match practice to precept, circumstances outside their control are often to blame, especially 'the obstruction they met within the community, and especially from tenant farmers' (D. Roberts, op. cit., 114, 122). Even in 'feudal' Wales the record of paternalism is very respectable indeed; see I. G. Jones, 'Merioneth Politics in the Mid-nineteenth Century: The Politics of a Rural Economy', *J. Merioneth* 5/4 (1968), 286–7. Even more remarkable was the massive scale of local services provided in Cornwall, the county which more than any other was littered with tiny electorates. See W. Comber, 'The Cornish Boroughs and Parliamentary Reform, 1800–1832', MA (Exeter, 1976), 23.

ethic it precludes power- and property-sharing and presupposes an indefinite continuation of the social and political arrangements which exist. Down to the late nineteenth century there continued to exist both in church and state a haphazard but rigidly defended structure of offices, pensions, services, appointments, and reversions which was largely reserved for a few thousand landed and commercial families. The grotesquely inegalitarian distribution of wealth and property in eighteenth-century England cannot be denied by any historian.

What may be said on the opposite side? For one thing, paternalists were prepared to tax themselves, as well as the rest of the nation.[19] For another, they provided the personnel of an unpaid local magistracy which provided the essential bulwarks of order in a violent and exuberant society. They were, inevitably, quick to defend their own persons, positions, and property, but they were not reluctant to defend the persons, positions, and property of others. As Professor Stone has remarked: 'If the elite used the law to defend property, as they did, it was property in the broader sense of life, liberty, and estate . . . not only their own property but also that of the expanding mass of lower-middle class shopkeepers, artisans, small manufacturers and smallholders.'[20] The paternalism of electoral patrons provides one significant test area for the exercise of paternalism in general. What does 'paternalism' mean in practice, and what benefits flowed from it?

To what extent families like the Grosvenors in a proud city such as Chester or the Luttrells in a dependent community such as Minehead lived up to paternalist standards cannot be measured exactly. Agreed criteria do not exist, for such questions are at bottom dependent upon subjective judgements about ethical issues. What, perhaps, cannot be gainsaid about such places is not only the extent of the services provided by patrons but also the fact that few aspects of the life of Chester or of Minehead can have remained untouched by them. The provision of civic amenities—town halls, museums, exchanges,—might be involved. The establishment of schools, hospitals, almshouses almost certainly would be. The provision of necessities in time of want necessarily had to be. It has been estimated that in the famine of 1794–5 over £6 million was contributed to the relief of the poor, in that of 1800–3 over £3 million. Even in smaller places, perhaps entirely for

---

[19] L. Stone, *An Open Élite? England 1540–1880* (Oxford, 1984), 413. In war-time they raised the land tax to 4s. in the pound (20%), and in the French Revolutionary wars they were prepared to tax luxuries. Cannon's discussion of taxation policy refers only to the aristocracy; see J. A. Cannon, *The Aristocratic Century: The Peerage of Eighteenth-century England* (Cambridge, 1984), 141–7). His critical judgement of the aristocracy's ability to avoid paying taxes should be balanced by some calculation of the outgoing necessary to maintain their position.

[20] Stone, *An Open Élite*, 414.

electoral reasons, the extent of patronal *largesse* could even become embarrassing. The influence of the Duke of Leeds over the tiny Cornish corporation borough of Helston, according to one observer, 'appears to have been kept up at a monstrous expense, not only by erecting, repairing and ornamenting public buildings belonging to the borough but by liberal and sometimes extravagant provisions made for and by patronage exerted on behalf of, those individual members of it, who possessed the greatest Influence in the Corporation'. If this were not enough, the duke even paid the poor and church rates, a further £700–1,000 per year. Even then, concluded the survey, 'his Grace's influence in the Borough is of so precarious a nature that he may continue these expenses, and the exertion of his patronage on behalf of the Corporators to the very Eve of another Election; and that even then, he may not be able to secure the Return of a single Member'.[21] The expectation of quite lavish displays of paternalism was the starting and end point for election campaigns. When Sir John Simeon became MP for Reading in 1796 he made gifts of clothes to the poor, donated plum cake to the children, offered cheap loans to tradesmen, provided market facilities for the craftsmen, and obtained financial support for the business activities of the manufacturers.[22] There seems no end to the type of favour, aid, and disbursement demanded and received. Generous donations of private charity were consequently of immense significance. Professor Mingay's estimate that a wealthy gentleman might spend 5% of his income on charitable donations might seem reasonable, but it is likely to underestimate the amount actually spent.[23] This is because charity was often given in kind rather than in money. Furthermore, considerable portions of charitable gifts were bequests after death and thus difficult to square with income during life. The widely differing proportions of income spent upon charity from place to place or even within the same family from generation to generation are enormous.[24]

This merely serves to underline that such activities and such relationships depended very much upon the personal characters of those

---

[21] Report respecting the Borough of Helston, 20 Oct. 1802, BL Add. MSS 33110, fos. 48–9, Newcastle Papers.

[22] R. C. Bailly, 'The Parliamentary History of Reading, 1750–1850', MA (Reading, 1944), 38.

[23] G. E. Mingay, *The Gentry: Rise and Fall of a Ruling Class* (London, 1976), 140; J. R. Poynter, *Society and Pauperism: English Ideas on Poor Relief, 1715–1834* (London, 1969), 114, 203.

[24] J. Davies has worked out that between 1821 and 1848 the Second Marquess of Bute donated 7%–8% of his gross annual rental to charities; see 'The Second Marquess of Bute', *Glamorgan Historian*, 8 (1972), 20. The first marquis, who held the estate in Glamorgan from 1766 to 1814, spent practically nothing on this.

involved. Deference, in particular, was an overwhelmingly *personal* quality, directed towards a particular type of individual and arising from personal familiarity. Although this latter point should not be overdone—the frequency of personal contacts between the classes should not be exaggerated—candidates usually made some real efforts to become personally accessible to the electors. It was the ideal of all patrons to attract the voluntary loyalty of the voters. The Earl of Radnor described his interest in the tiny corporation borough of Salisbury (electorate of 54) as 'an Interest neither begun, nor kept up by the gross Mode of Corruption, nor the common Mode of obtaining favours from Government. It has . . . been preserved by individual attentions, and general upright and fair conduct.'[25] Paternalism of this kind needed to be reinforced by appeals to loyalty to a particular *family* in the locality. When the Marquis of Harrowby looked back on a century's connection between his family and the borough of Tiverton in 1831 he may have indulged in nostalgic exaggeration but his words are instructive:

During the whole of this period, neither myself, nor any member of my family, has owned a house or an acre of land within 100 miles; nor is there a single elector who owes me a single shilling, or whose vote I can in any sense command. Indeed, money is quite out of the question, and I should have heard without the slightest degree of alarm, that two Nabobs from India had gone down to canvass Tiverton, even though they had each £10,000 in his pocket.[26]

The observance of electoral loyalties was, furthermore, profoundly *ritualistic*, and the codes of behaviour which affirmed them strongly reinforced distinctions of rank and position. Such rituals operated at different levels. The impact of the official rituals of the hunt, the assizes, and the season would be limited. Celebrations of local, especially familial, significance, such as births, christenings, comings of age, marriages, and deaths, would be more effective in directing local loyalties towards a particular group within the élite. These would be reinforced by the various celebrations enjoined by the calendar (Harvest, Christmas, Easter, etc.) and occasionally by national events (coronations, naval and military victories, etc.). Most immediately, the impact of election campaign rituals would serve to confirm (or to establish) a loyalty towards a paternalistic figure or his

---

[25] Earl of Radnor to Earl of Folkestone, 18 Aug. 1812, D/EPb O.28. f. 766. Berks. RO. Things were very different in Ireland, at least after the 1832 Reform Act. See K. Theodore Hoppen, *Elections, Politics and Society in Ireland 1832–1885* (Oxford, 1984), 31–8.
[26] 4 Oct. 1831, *Parliamentary Debates*, 3rd ser., vii. 1148.

representative.[27] In normal times, however, the customary processes by which patrons and landlords sought to provide for those with some claim upon them—by bestowing favours, by seeking places and promotion on their behalf, by giving custom and employment, by personal attentions, and by activities of a philanthropic and charitable character—comprise a paternalism of service which should not be lightly dismissed.

The ubiquity of paternalist services and deferential relationships ensure that they fulfilled critical functions in eighteenth- and early nineteenth-century society. They served, at a high level of generality, to incorporate the many of inferior position within a social and economic system which consigned them to indefinite subordination. Paternalism went far towards softening the hidden insults of such social and economic subordination. Consequently, the minute distinctions of social differentiation were maintained almost as a condition of preserving social harmony. Those at the summit of society, exercising their authority within the context of widely recognized paternalistic values, were able thereby to secure the endorsement of their power and thus the legitimacy of their authority. More particularly, elections legitimated the power of the élite by securing public endorsement of its representatives and by procuring public participation in politics, especially that of the middling orders, who manned its election committees, conducted its extensive campaigns and canvasses, and undertook the weary work of political manipulation. Elections afforded an opportunity, rarely foregone, for the élite to renew its public commitment to paternalistic and community responsibilities. The acquiescence of voters and non-voters alike was procured within a normative framework to which all sections of the community subscribed. Namier, Thompson, and others are perfectly justified in pointing out what they take to be the hopelessly one-sided *consequences* of paternalism and deference, expressed in electoral terms, but they ignore the values and the strategies which attained those consequences. In other words, deferential relationships, and the values which accompanied them, not merely legitimated the social and political authority of the élite but defined and limited that authority. From this standpoint, the importance of elections is that they provide a periodic opportunity for public accountability of the local governing class to the community, affording an opportunity for the neglected to complain and for the grateful to repay a kindness with loyalty. The stability of the Hanoverian political order rested, in the last analysis, on the satisfactory functioning of local deference structures. When these did

[27] See above, pp. 138–40.

not function smoothly electoral dissidence, or, in the last resort, a contested election, might occur.

This counterpoint between paternalism and deference lies at the core of electoral politics. In some way, most election issues ultimately relate back to it. It is vital to emphasize that normative values like paternalism and deference were not simply theoretical constructs. They arose directly out of the hard realities of social and electoral circumstance. One of the most important of these realities was the personal character of electoral interests. In the large majority of cases the patron lived in or near the constituency.[28] He was, or wished to be, the acknowledged leader of the community. Consequently, he took an interest in its affairs and endeavoured to stand well with its inhabitants. Foremost among his responsibilities were the peace and tranquillity of the life of the community and the prosperity of the village or town. Consequently, co-operation was preferred to coercion in electoral as well as other affairs. Those with interests did all they could to co-operate with each other, bending over backwards to accommodate each other's pretensions, leaving no stone unturned to know each other's mind, and taking great care to implore each other's influence. Even where dependence existed there was good reason to pretend otherwise. 'It is true that . . . many of them are oblig'd to vote as their employers direct, but still it is worth while to be popular with them, to deter other Candidates from coming forward.'[29] The landed interest hated contested elections. They cost money, they caused trouble, and they unsettled the community. The Duke of Norfolk dared not set foot in Leominster for years after the election of 1790 in case his appearance kept alive the bitter animosities then generated.[30]

For electoral influence to be effective, then, it had to be wielded circumspectly and in accordance with custom and practice. After all, it took some political will and determination to exercise electoral influence not merely over tenants, employees, and other direct dependents, but over shopkeepers, customers, and even friends. In 1780 the third Duke of Portland possessed overwhelming influence

---

[28] This is a strong impression, although I have no statistical evidence on the point. The patron, however, cannot win. 'He was often an absentee', notes Michael Brock, on the strength of a couple of instances (M. R. Brock, *The Great Reform Act* (London, 1973), 26). For E. P. Thompson, however, patrons are very much on the spot, albeit 'withdrawn so much within their parks and mansions' ('Patrician Society', 390). Stone argues that professional careers took 'more and more of the landed élite away from their country seats for longer and longer periods of the year'. He offers, however, no evidence and he fails to make clear the precise period of which he writes (Stone, *An Open Élite?*, 228).

[29] Amos Donkin to Sir Matthew White Ridley, 14 June 1830, ZR1 25/59, Ridley MSS, Northumb. RO.

[30] Duke of Norfolk to Mr Llewellyn, 23 Feb. 1796, Pilley MSS, Hereford and Worcs. RO.

at Wigan but he had to stomach the desire of several of his best friends there to associate themselves in county politics with Sir Thomas Egerton, of whom Portland wrote that 'no man was ever a more subservient or dispicable tool of a Vile Courtly system than he is'.[31] The deployment of electoral influence was thus depersonalized into elaborate customs of courtesy and convention which it was essential to observe, insulting to ignore.[32] A candidate or his agent might approach the tenants, employees, or other dependants only with the express permission of the patron. The patron would normally request his dependants to reserve their votes in his interest while he was determining his advice to them. Once he had made up his mind, he would communicate his decision to them through his steward or agent, through handbills, through leaving cards, or, best of all, by direct intimation. Failure to attend to this would leave the voter free to make up his own mind. As the election approached, it might be necessary to issue a timely reminder to the voters, a nice tactic to appeal nostalgically to 'the old interest'.[33] Finally, it was necessary for a patron to issue some expression of his public appreciation to those who had obeyed his wishes. One of Milton's agents reminded him in 1818 that if Yorkshire were contested his friends 'will be looking with longing eyes for your thanks'.[34] The fiction would be maintained throughout that the patron was simply inviting the friendly co-operation of his dependants in a common enterprise. The elaborate and formal conventions attending the exercise of electoral influence are, no doubt, intended to conceal the obvious inequalities inherent in these relationships, to foster the myth of independence. What they signify, nevertheless, is no less instructive: the unity of the landed classes, the common interest which all shared in an estate or a business and even in the public interest of a county or borough. Most candidates would have agreed with Henry Bankes at the Dorset election of 1806:

In the course of our contest, it is much to be lamented that insidious attempts have been made to separate [sic] the interests of the lesser Freeholders, from

[31] Duke of Portland to Latham, 24 Apr. 1780, PWF 9967, Portland MSS, Nottingham Univ. Lib.

[32] Even in 'feudal' Wales, if the language of one patron is closely inspected. 'Gentlemen, though I am very sensible it is too late to solicit your Votes yet I think it proper to make some Apology for not taking those Advantages of an Earlier Application which I might very justly have done' (Sir John Glynne to the Tenants of Bodryddon, 6 Dec. 1733, D/HE/464, Rhual (Add. MSS), Clwyd RO).

[33] Thomas Cave to Mrs Smith, 30 Nov. 1774, 23, D.57/3378, Braye MSS, Leicester City Museum.

[34] Unidentified Correspondent to Lord Milton, 25 June 1818, Fitzwilliam MSS, Sheffield Pub. Lib. Milton was ill so Fitzwilliam wrote some paragraphs and told the agent to remember to send both to the town and county papers.

that of the larger proprietors: but the Constitution admits of no such distinction: the whole landed interest is essentially connected together, and those who endeavour to draw lines of division are not less the enemies of the lower order, than of the higher. Their doctrines tend to advance that pernicious, and dreadful engine by which the foundations of civilized society have been shaken, and the peace of the world has been subverted, under the specious name of Freedom.[35]

The conventions and forms of electioneering left the voters with appreciable independence. In most circumstances the normal operations of deference and social control would effect social and political conformity. Of their two votes, only one was formally required by the patron. The voter had free disposal of the second. If the patron wished to secure that second vote, he had necessarily to flatter and to woo the voter and to persuade rather than to antagonize him.[36] Even in small boroughs the strongest patron would hesitate to force second votes. Buckingham, a corporation borough with only 13 electors, is described as 'a pocket borough of the Grenville family', but the Marquis of Buckingham confessed that it was 'necessary for me to abide by the rule which I have always steadily observed of never interfering, directly or indirectly, in the choice of a second member'.[37] Most patrons were reluctant to force second votes from their dependants. To intimidate voters into giving their support was a sure— and public—sign that the legitimate means of persuasion approved by contemporaries had been unsuccessful. Contemporaries certainly evince a remarkable sensitivity to intimidation and to threats of intimidation alike—a sensitivity, moreover, which seems to have been intensifying.[38] Although generations of historians have provided

---

[35] To the Gentlemen, Clergy and Freeholders of the County of Dorset, 13 Nov. 1806, KY 79/49, Bankes MSS, Dorset RO. The Lowthers charged Brougham *c.*1818 with 'dissolving not only an old connection between the county and the paramount House of the County', but 'embittering the connection between the gentry and their dependents' (W.D./P.W. Election Bills, Kendal RO). For mid-19th cent. evidence of this idea of an 'agricultural community' see J. R. Fisher, 'The Limits of Deference: Agricultural Communities in a Mid-nineteenth-cent. Election Campaign', *J. Brit. Studies*, 20 (1981), 90–105.

[36] There is evident throughout the assumption that second votes have to be separately canvassed. To read the estate and electoral correspondence of any of the great estates is an interesting corrective to the idea that the power of the greatest members of the landed interest over the electoral system was arbitrary. It had to be exercised with great care and always had to respect the independence of the tenants. See e.g. Robert Mitchell of Sawtry to Lord Hinchingbrooke, 18 Feb. 1768, Hinchingbrooke MSS 8/103, Hunts. RO.

[37] Marquis of Buckingham to Sir William Lee, 27 May 1796, D/LE/D/1/50, Hartwell MSS, Bucks. RO; see L. B. Namier and J. Brooke, *The House of Commons, 1754–90*, 3 vols. (London, 1964), i. 216.

[38] In 1790 the Duke of Newcastle issued no fewer than 60 eviction notices at Newark and met with comparatively little uproar. In 1829 the issue of 37 such notices caused both a public outcry and parliamentary discussion. J. Golby, 'The Political and Electioneering Influence of the Fourth Duke of Newcastle', MA (Nottingham, 1961), 116, 119, 184–5.

examples of the intimidation of voters and the eviction of dependants in their endeavour to establish that control of the electorate was harsh and coercive, such anecdotal evidence strongly suggests that the very opposite was the case: that the publicity and notoriety which accompanied such practices indicate that they were regarded as illegitimate departures from conventional standards, the last resort of a desperate patron rather than the customary method of political control. We must not, of course, underestimate the abiding *threat* of intimidation and eviction, nor should we ignore the occasional resort to these measures by patrons whose relationship with their voters had broken down. Underlying these, however, is a more basic reality. Such relationships were not exclusively private concerns; they involved the general interest of the whole community. Perhaps because of this, eviction and formal intimidation were remarkably rare. A recent study of the four northern counties between 1760 and 1832 has unearthed just one instance of a landlord evicting a tenant. Even more remarkably, the most ruthless of all ruthless exponents of electioneering, Sir James Lowther, was not guilty of such an offence.[39] There were good reasons for this: eviction simply created martyrs, intensified partisanship, and attracted public attention into the private world of the electoral interest. It might be better to permit the occasional example of back-sliding with gentlemanly magnanimity rather than to become a notorious electioneering tyrant.[40]

Patrons had to treat their voters with courtesy and consideration. They did assume that voters could be influenced, but they set about the task of influencing them with enormous diplomacy and infinite care. Although voters might be dependent upon patrons in a variety of compelling ways, through the renting of their homes, through their holding of employment, through the supply of materials, through the purchase of produce, or through the availability of both short-term

---

[39] D. Stoker, 'Elections and Voting Behaviour: A Study of Elections in Northumberland, Durham, Cumberland, and Westmorland, 1760–1832', Ph.D. (Manchester, 1980), 247–8, 339. Much more frequent than these are the quiet and unspectacular instances of paternalism, e.g. 'Tenants to be provided for' STG Election Box 4, 1802–1806, fo. 10, Stowe MSS, Huntington Lib. San Marino, Calif. (about Bucks.).

[40] There may, in fact, have been a slight *revival* in evictions after the First Reform Act. Certainly the press gleefully seized upon many possible instances both in the counties, where the Chandos clause in the Act of 1832 had brought tenants-at-will into the electorate, and in the new industrial boroughs, where in some cases factory owners could direct the votes of their workmen. Of course, accusations of intimidation were a common excuse for defeat and frequently surfaced on the day when a candidate's tally slumped dramatically or when he resigned the contest. See e.g. the resignation of Edward Hanson from the Preston contest of 1812. Hanson was an independent candidate whose defeat at the hands of the extremely well organized Stanley (land) and Horrocks (industry) interests could plausibly be put down to the intimidation of his supporters, see *Preston Chronicle*, 17 Oct. 1812.

loans and long-term capital, the expressed ideal relationship between them was one of interdependence and mutual gain, not one of servility and humiliation. The ideal objective for a patron involved in electioneering was to be able to boast that he had received the voluntary and uncoerced support of those with whom he had an interest. In 1800 Lord Moira wrote that if he bullied his tenants, 'I should revolt those who on other occasions give me real weight by following my influence'.[41] The mobilization of the influence not merely of the patron but of that of his family and friends could be a complicated and intricate proceeding.[42] The anxiety which election managers exhibited about the need to inform and advise their voters scarcely suggests an automatic and instinctive obedience. Even during the long years between contested elections in a safe seat the voters had to be watched. Portland's agent at Wigan once reassured him that 'Our friends are all very steady to all appearances. Be assured, if I perceive any secret combinations I will inform you as I am by nature suspicious. I hope to see into any secret intrigues.'[43] Such a borough agent was indispensable. Even in rural areas, however, voters were carefully watched, their relationships noted, opportunities of humouring them taken, and their opinions recorded.[44] Thomas Coke of Holkham, of all people, should have been assured of the loyalty of his tenantry, but his steward still found it necessary to direct his agents, 'never lose

---

[41] Lord Moira to Col. McMahon, 5 Dec. 1800, printed in A. Aspinall (ed.), *The Correspondence of George, Prince of Wales*, 8 vols. (Cambridge, 1963–71), 170–1.

[42] An interesting example of the tracking down of minor patrons is to be found in the Memorandum for the Duke [of Newcastle] about Interests in Cumberland in the Eighteenth Century, DD4P. 68/1, Notts. RO. Even in a small country like Huntingdonshire at an uncontested election, considerable activity was required to safeguard a seat. Lord Hinchingbrooke, at least, received no fewer than 103 letters pledging support to his interest. 1761, Hinchingbrooke MSS, 8/55, Hunts. RO.

[43] G. Latham to the 3rd Duke of Portland, 4 Feb. 1781, PWF. 9981, Portland MSS, Nottingham Univ. Lib.

[44] Even in these rural areas, by no means all voters could be counted on. At the Bedford election of 1780 reports from the agent Wynne to Butcher, the steward on the Whitbread estate, should be carefully studied by those who regard the 18th-cent. electorate as little better than fodder for polling tallies. They evince remarkable discrimination, considerable awareness, and significant political consciousness. By no means all of them accept the Duke of Bedford's instructions, some offer one vote, some 'Won't Engage' or 'will not promise at present'. Others completely refuse their support. Another 'does not choose to make an absolute promise'—this in a highly deferential county. Furthermore, the excellent collection of election and estate records in the Hinchingbrooke MSS similarly reveal a class of tenant voters capable of making bargains, reserving their positions, and willing to support their landlord on terms and when it suits them. Canvassers found that few tenants were willing to touch their forelocks. 'Thos. Chadwell will vote for L & H if he has the Militia money returned, Thos. Magish gives reasons to think he will stand *neuter*, Barson will not promise till the day of Election, Jacobs will not promise, Maynard not at home . . .' (Observations . . ., Hinchingbrooke MSS 8/57, Hunts. RO). See the letters of Wynne to Butcher, 29 Sept. 1769, 2 Oct., R3/505, R3/507, Whitbread MSS, Beds. RO.

sight of them from the time of leaving their homes until they are polled'.[45]

To cope with the stringent demands of electioneering demanded resources of men and money which might daunt all but the most reckless. Even more important, electioneering required certain qualities of social assertiveness that some patrons lacked. Men who commanded a few voters were likely to ally their interests with more ambitious souls. None other than Sir James Lowther declared: 'Until one has actually seen it, it is hardly to be believed the little influence a country squire possesses . . . Very few control above four or five votes, and there are generally as many in the Parish who would go to the other side, whatever it may be, from the squire.'[46] Personal relationships in such tiny interests sometimes inhibited patrons from allowing politics to intrude into private life. Furthermore, it was by no means uncommon for some patrons to declare their neutrality. Understandably, not every generation of every family had the political desire to involve itself in the expensive world of electioneering. When a current of opinion flowed strongly among the voters, the patrons had to adjust to it and lead their voters, as it were, from behind.

In all this we should not lose sight of the legislative outputs of the system. A precise cost–benefit analysis of these outputs seems impossible to mount. Nevertheless, it is far too simplistic to argue that MPs only passed legislation for their own personal benefit. An analysis of legislation affecting Glamorgan in the early nineteenth century finds evidence of improvements to markets, canals, lighthouses, ports, railways, and even to the administrative system. All this is hardly consistent with a picture of selfish landowners feathering their nests.[47] Where such selfishness was in evidence the interest concerned was doomed. The suggestion that St Albans should be linked to the Grand Union Canal was strongly opposed by the Spencer interest and by their turnpike trust supporters, anxious to defend their revenues. The canal was never cut, and in the late eighteenth century the Spencer interest gradually declined.[48]

These everyday realities of electoral politics weakened the power and authority of patrons and allowed the voters some freedom of manœuvre. Even in the counties, ostensibly dependent voters had far

[45] Circular letter of Francis Blaikie, steward on the Holkham estate, 12 May 1817, Holkham Letter Books, Bodleian Lib.

[46] Sir James Lowther to Lord Lonsdale, 10 Sept. 1820, box 2/12, Lonsdale MSS, Cumbria RO.

[47] E. Ball, 'Glamorgan: A Study of the Concerns of the County and the Work of its Members in the House of Commons, 1825–1835', Ph.D. (London, 1965), chs. 3, 6.

[48] H. F. C. Lansberry, 'Politics and Government in St Albans 1688–1835', Ph.D. (London, 1964), 182–98.

more freedom of action than they are frequently allowed. Only a limited number of patrons would have derived much political benefit from the consolidation of landed estates which is such a marked feature of the period. Even assuming that many did, the benefit was mixed: 'A large proportion of their land was of inferior quality or remote from markets, so that it could not bear high rents until the growth of towns and communications, especially in Northern England, made it worth developing. In the Midlands much of the land was still worked by the small farmers on the inefficient Open Field system; and in upland areas the thin soils made the land suitable only for rough grazing.'[49] Indeed, many aristocratic families were becoming increasingly indebted, hung around with debts and mortgages and imprisoned within a pattern of extravagent building and conspicuous consumption which kept family fortunes on a knife edge. We should remember, too, that the ill-fortunes of the yeoman farmer have been much exaggerated. Holdings of 200–400 acres had been rare early in the eighteenth century; by 1830 they were the most typical size of holding.[50] 'In the late eighteenth and early nineteenth century the aim of most landlords was to build up a large estate. The size of the farms on the estate tended to be an incidental feature of policy, but it was generally advantageous to have a small number of tenants on large farms rather than a large number of tenants on small farms'.[51] In other words, large numbers of county voters were quite substantial, prosperous farmers.[52] For electoral purposes the 40s. freeholder qualification included leases for lives, annuities, and rent charges. The fortunes of county voters were closely tied up with those of their landlords, but few of them were absolutely dependent upon them either politically or economically.

The relationship between a tenant and a landlord was, however, less influenced by the size of holdings than by their tenurial agreement. In the early eighteenth century the form of lease varied with the region.

---

[49] G. E. Mingay, *English Landed Society in the Eighteenth Century* (London, 1963), 53, 87.

[50] J. A. Wordie, 'Social Change on the Leveson–Gower Estates, 1714–1832', *Midland Hist.* 4 (1977), 593–607. 'The rise of the large tenant farm is one aspect of the changing social structure within the estate' (ibid. 597).

[51] D. B. Grigg, 'Small and Large Farms in England and Wales: Their size and Distribution', *Geography*, 48 (1963), 272. Grigg proceeds to argue that the linking of the development to the growth of large farms is mistaken; however, his definition of a large farm (500 acres or more) seems extraordinarily lavish.

[52] e.g. according to Mingay, freeholders as well as leaseholders for lives, owners of rent charges, mortgages, and annuities were both numerous and wealthy enough to form a substantial independent class of voters; see Mingay, *English Landed Society*, 60–1. For a similar conclusion, see F. M. L. Thompson, 'Landownership and Economic Growth in England in the Eighteenth Century', in E. L. Jones and S. Woolf (eds.), *Agrarian Change and Economic Development* (London, 1969), 58–60; J. D. Chambers and G. E. Mingay, *The Agricultural Revolution* (London, 1966), 93.

In the East and in the Midlands, leases for years (21 or less) were common. In the West, South and South-west, leases were normally for lives. In other areas, the north-west and on ecclesiastical estates, leases were for three lives or 99 years or smaller multiples. Once again, economic realities conspired to effect an outcome of mutual advantage. Although there were exceptions,[53] in most places the lease, whether for lives or years, was gradually being replaced by 'tenancy-at-will' or 'from year to year', to the extent that by 1850 the former was the exception throughout England.[54] It was inevitable that long leases would decline in a period of price fluctuation: a long lease would be unfavourable to the landlord if prices rose, to the tenant if they fell. The classic early eighteenth century three-life lease was, in such a period, an ideal recipe for allowing a farm to rot and decay. Yet, there is little evidence either that tenants resented this development or that they were any worse off for the change. There were sound economic reasons why they should acquiesce in the disappearances of long leases: 'The main attribute of the long lease, namely security of tenure and pecuniary reward for improvement, were better provided for under the system of tenancy-at-will by the normal relationship existing between landlord and tenant, and by the development of tenant right systems to compensate the outgoing tenant for unexhausted improvements.'[55]

Furthermore, both the practical and normative restraints upon a landlord to treat his tenants with consideration were enormous. It was,

---

[53] D. Berry, 'The Social and Economic Development and Organisation of the Lake District', MA (Manchester, 1955), 120, 322, 327–8. Berry argues that the estates of none other than Sir James Lowther witnessed the improving of leases as tenancy-at-will agreements were dropped after 1800. Improving tenants were given leases for seven to nine years. On the Holkham estates, 21-year leases continued into the 19th cent.; see R. A. C. Parker, *Coke of Norfolk* (Oxford, 1975), 100, 145–7.

[54] There were many reasons for this. The dramatic rise in agricultural prices in the late 18th and early 19th cent. gave landlords second thoughts about long leases while the general increase in price levels seriously eroded the value of fixed rents. The rapid conversion of waste land to tillage and the general process of enclosure sharply increased the yield of an estate and thus the pressure on a landlord to shorten his leases or to transfer to tenancy-at-will agreements. Although the long lease was in other respects preferable for a landlord—e.g. it enabled him to throw the burden of maintenance upon the tenant—he was also aware that it might encourage carelessness and neglect on the part of the tenantry. See J. A. Perkins, 'Tenure, Tenant-Right and Agricultural Progress in Lindsay, 1780–1850', *Ag. Hist. Rev.* 23 (1975), 13; also F. M. L. Thompson, *English Landed Society in the Nineteenth Century* (London, 1963), 203–6.

[55] Perkins, 'Tenure, Tenant-Right, and Agricultural Progress', 5. He concludes, 'Although the Lincolnshire custom of tenant right was unrecognised by laws, the instances are rare of landlords refusing to accept its provisions as binding upon them' (ibid. 20); Christopher Clay, 'Lifeleaseholds in the Western Counties of England, 1650–1750', *Ag. Hist. Rev.* 29 (1981) 83–96. I am indebted to Christopher Clay of the University of Bristol for his help and advice on the technical questions relating to leases. See also id., 'Landlords and Estate Management', in J. Thirsk (ed.), *The Agrarian History of England and Wales*, v. ii (Cambridge, 1985).

no doubt, his willingness to do so which minimized resentment at the disappearance of leases and thus contributed to the stability of life among the landed interest during this period. When times were bad, the community expected him to provide them with assistance, such as abatement of rents, help with repairs, purchase of produce, and the like. This was just as much a recognition of economic reality as the fulfilment of paternalist ideals. In practice, most tenants and almost all freeholders had effective security of tenure. A copyholder would normally be safe for his lifetime. Consequently, threats of intimidation can have been significant where tenants held on the most insecure of tenures, those held 'at suffrance'. Only these tenants were liable to instant eviction. But eviction was a rare and often an uneconomic occurrence: 'There is no evidence to indicate that the *raison d'être* of annual tenancies on the Trentham properties was electoral influence. The tenurial arrangements were strictly economic devices. There is no sign that the threat of ejection was used to control votes.'[56] To a landlord, farms without tenants were a wasting asset. Furthermore, a reputation for cruelty, negligence, and intimidation was unlikely to encourage efficient farming on his estate, whereas a willingness to accept a temporary financial loss might be an effective guarantee of its long-term economic stability. Similarly, the custom that tenancies should not be interfered with, the tradition that farms should almost of right pass to the son if the family had a long connection with the estate, the belief that tenants should be protected and encouraged rather than exploited reinforced the powerful habits and expectations of the paternalism of the landlord.[57] Any infringements of these conventions was an explosive issue. Allegations of such infringement could become serious issues at county elections. At the Wiltshire election of 1818, for example, the question of the termination of a lease became the subject of a series of broadsides, charges, and counter-charges.[58] Although tenurial relationships were a jumble of local rights and customs, there are some grounds for thinking that the tenant was far from having the worst of the bargain.

[56] J. Perkins, 'Social and Electoral Influence of the Trentham Interest, 1800–1860', *Midland Hist.* 3 (1975–6), 142.

[57] Clay has demonstrated that, of all people, ecclesiastical landlords permitted preferential leases, low rents, and loans at low rates of interest. See C. Clay, 'The Greed of Whig Bishops: Church Landlords and their Lessees', *Past and Present*, 87 (1980).

[58] A landlord, John Bennett, was accused of terminating the lease of one of his tenants, John Fisher, in a prejudicial manner. It was less the substance of the dispute than the assumptions which it depicts which are of interest. Bennett declared that he was always ready 'to submit to take such a rent . . . as should be agreed by two persons mutually chosen to value the estate.' There can be no question from the popular furore that the tenants possessed a highly developed sense of justice and independence. See *Survey of Wiltshire during the Election* (Trowbridge, 1818), 100–1 and *passim*. (Guildhall Lib.)

Even in the rarely contested counties, then, stable electoral relationships were more likely to arise from common interests than from conflicting ones. The mid-Victorians were the heirs of a political system dominated by the landed élite in which deference and paternalism prevailed and in which coercion and intimidation were despised.[59]

This was so, of course, in borough as well as in county elections. As we have seen, the occupational structure of the borough electorate itself precluded absolute control by patrons. Although the Hanoverian political élite was supported by a large and powerful class of dependent and professional men, the electorate was dominated by the retailers and craftsmen—small, independent men who, while tightly enmeshed in the purchasing nexus of the landed interest and its clients, were still sufficiently responsive to communal values as to repudiate abject dependence. They were not immune to influence, but they were sufficiently sturdy to be able to resist it, or at least to negotiate and to compromise with it.

There are at least two further distinctions to be made between the borough and the county electorates. Firstly, in boroughs, electoral influence was frequently exercised by or through local institutions. This 'depersonalization' of influence enormously strengthened the position of the voter. It was considerably easier for a freeman of the city of Bedford to resist the pressure of the corporation of Bedford than it might have been to ignore the personal persuasions of a member of the Russell family. The inefficiency and unpopularity of corporations did not assist the exercise of electoral influence on the part of members of the landed interest. So far as this is the case, it is possible to endorse Professor Kishlansky's theory of 'depersonalization' without wishing for a moment to neglect, nor to diminish, the continuing significance of the importance of the personal element in deferential relationships.[60] Secondly, there can be little doubt that, on the whole, the urban electorates of Hanoverian England came to be noticeably more politicized than their rural counterparts. The task of influencing electors was by no means an easy one. It is at this point in the discussion that we must now turn our attention to the electors themselves, the neglected chorus in the historiography of the Hanoverian electoral system.

[59] The most recent discussion of this subject is contained in an article by Dr A. Heesom '"Legitimate" vs. "Illegitimate" Influences: Aristocratic Electioneering in Mid-Victorian Britain', which, at the time of going to press, was due to appear in a forthcoming issue of *Parliamentary History*. I am indebted to him for allowing me to read a pre-publication copy.

[60] M. Kishlansky, *Parliamentary Selection: Social and Political Choice in Early Modern England* (Cambridge, 1986), 21, 1933.

THE VOTERS: IMAGES, EXPECTATIONS, AND ATTITUDES

The dominant contemporary assumptions concerning paternalism and deference left voters with a very definite idea of their own importance. Far from regarding themselves as fodder for polling tallies, they perceived themselves as independent agents with powers of judgement and conscience. They revelled in the rhetoric of popular independence, a traditional image derived from the language of the 'Free Born Englishman'. Likewise, far from being politically passive they had ideas and opinions of their own, voters and non-voters alike: 'The populace eagerly exercised their Saturnalian privileges, and frequent questions were put to the Candidates and their friends, respecting Shop Boards, turn coats and Trinidad.'[61] As Jephson acknowledges, by the early nineteenth century it was becoming increasingly common for candidates publicly to concede their responsibility to their constituents for an account of their stewardship and to rest their claims for re-election on their past conduct.[62] Voters were not reluctant to make their opinions of a Member emphatically plain. Beilby Thompson found that his association with Fox severely disadvantaged him with the electors in his tiny constituency of Hedon in 1784. Harassed beyond endurance he expostulated: 'I am this moment returned from Hedon— and from the most ungrateful usage and worst treatment every poor Mortal experienced. I have given up all thoughts of standing the poll— or being elected—and am *determined* to retire from the World, and never more interfere with *any* contested Elections.'[63] Voters, of course, were not always so assertive, and their disagreement with a candidate or patron might simply result in a quiet refusal to poll for him rather than a positive vote against. After all, one-fifth of the electorate normally abstained from voting. Nevertheless, voters were touchy about the constituency and its needs, to say nothing of their own vanity. Sir Matthew White-Ridley's agent wrote to him about his unpopularity at Newcastle-upon-Tyne in 1830 and listed its causes. All of the seven grounds he details concern courtesies (e.g. 'You did

[61] *Morning Chronicle*, 7 Nov. 1806, referring somewhat idealistically to the electors of Westminster.

[62] H. Jephson, *The Platform: Its Rise and Progress* (London, 1892), 456.

[63] B. Thompson to Lord Fitzwilliam, 28 Mar. 1784, fos. 34 f., Fitzwilliam Papers, Sheffield Pub. Lib. Exactly the same sort of reception awaited Thomas Powys, a supporter of Fox, who retained his seat at the 1784 election at Northamptonshire, but only after enduring severe questioning by indignant freeholders; see (E. Forrester, *Northamptonshire County Elections and Electioneering, 1695–1832* (London, 1965), 87. Sir William Molesworth wrote to his wife that he was one of Cornwall's leading reformers. If he were not 'I would not command a single vote among my tenantry' (9 Apr. 1831); see W. B. Elvins, 'The Reform Movement and County Politics in Cornwall, 1809–1852', MA (Birmingham, 1959), ch. 5 n. 76).

not give the Burgesses a drink when your eldest son came of age'), the employment of local labour, and minor pieces of patronage.[64] If a sitting member neglected his seat or his constituents he was as good as finished.

There is some evidence to indicate that the individual voter exercised the franchise with the greatest seriousness and after considerable deliberation. Not all voters would have gone as far as the unfortunate shoemaker William Brett at the Newcastle-under-Lyme election of 1807, who was 'in a state of mental derangement, said to be in consequence of being persuaded to vote contrary to his conscience'.[65] Nevertheless, the disposal of the vote was a serious business. An important contested election usually elicited shoals of correspondence from anxious voters, explaining in much detail the intended disposal of their votes to their patrons or his agent and the precise personal, family, and political considerations which lay behind that disposal.[66] Furthermore whenever opinion was agitated, as in 1784 or 1831, voters could be extremely difficult to handle. At the Dorset canvass of 1831 the voters made it perfectly clear that they were aware of the candidates and aware of the issues. They preferred to keep their own counsel and certainly regarded the disposal of their second votes as nobody's business but their own.[67] Even in normal times, the voters had their own ways of negotiating the hazards of electioneering. An astounding number continued to be absent when candidates or canvassers called, yet others had not decided finally, others needed to consult a third party or had already done so. None of this suggests an automatic compliance with the will of the patron. A tenant or dependant would normally wait for the patron to indicate his preferences. If the personal relationship between patron and voter was intact, if the patron had fulfilled the expectations of his position, and if the patron, or the candidate he supported, appeared to consult both the general interest of the constituency and the particular (or occupational) interests of the voter, then the satisfactory operations of deference would deliver at least one, and very possibly two, votes in the patron's interest. This did not always happen. A tenant on the Duke of Bedford's estate, William Arthur, called on Butcher, the duke's steward, to explain in great detail why had and his son regretfully could not support one

---

[64] Amos Donkin to Sir Matthew White Ridley, 14 June 1830, Ridley MSS. Northumb. RO.

[65] Newcastle-under-Lyme Poll Book, 1807.

[66] For some excellent batches of correspondence of this type see the letters to local agents at the uncontested Yorkshire county election of 1780 in the Rockingham Papers, R39 in the Wentworth Woodhouse MSS, Sheffield Pub. Lib. For similar correspondence at the contested Yorkshire election of 1807 see E.209 in the Fitzwilliam MSS, ibid.

[67] Letters in KY 90, Bankes MSS, Dorset RO.

of the duke's candidates at the election of 1768.[68] This sage weighing of the issues was epitomized in the ritual of canvassing. In 1818 Lord Milton reassured his Yorkshire constituents: 'I do not consider the personal intercourse between the Electors and the Candidates on the occasion of an Election as mere form and ceremony but as affording a desirable opportunity of making them mutually acquainted with each other's sentiments and of identifying as far as their respective Independence will permit it parties which ought always to move in unison.'[69] He was capable of going even further. Elections, he had remarked during the 1807 canvass, 'teach the rich not to despise the poor, and they shew the poor that they are not altogether dependent on their more opulent neighbours'.[70] In some ways the canvass was the most interesting point of contact between voters and the candidates (or their representatives), and it was at this point that not only election enthusiasm but also political issues might be generated. The canvass was more than a means of collecting support and counting heads: it was intended to rally supporters, capture the public imagination, and dispel apathy.[71] At the most mundane level, the canvass reminded the voter of his voting rights and served to inform him of the candidate's opinion, however platitudinously this might be presented. On occasion the canvass could become a real exchange of information and ideas. At Morpeth in 1774, apparently, some voters were extremely bitter about the recent high-handed behaviour of the Earl of Carlisle and told his canvassers so in no uncertain terms.[72] So disappointed was one candidate at the Northamptonshire county election of 1806 at the negative reaction to his canvass that he begged for help in drafting a proper canvassing letter and advice on how to canvass[73] Just occasionally the patrons can be found lamenting their dependence upon the good favour of the voters. Lord Anglesea confided to a friend in 1825: 'The representative must act on all publick questions upon his own judgement. If that judgement coincides with the opinion of the electors, then all is smooth and as it should be. But when the reverse

[68] Butcher to Wynne, 29 Sept. 1767, R3, 505, Whitbread MSS, Beds. RO. The document contains numerous other such cases.

[69] Address to the Gentlemen, Clergy's Freeholders of Yorkshire, 1818, Fitzwilliam MS Sheffield Pub. Lib.

[70] *Halifax Journal*, 16 May 1807.

[71] Careful reading of newspaper reports of canvasses suggests this hypothesis, e.g. the detailed reporting of the Whig canvass at the election of 1790 constantly stresses the public and popular aspects of canvassing. See e.g. the *Hampshire Chronicle*, 22 Feb., 1 Mar. 1790.

[72] J. M. Fewster, 'The Politics and Administration of the Borough of Morpeth in the later Eighteenth Century', Ph.D. (Newcastle, 1969), 383–4.

[73] Sir William to James Langham, 24 July 1806, L(C) 125, Langham MSS, Northants. RO.

is the case the Member is bound to withdraw.'[74] Such statements were fairly common by the early nineteenth century. When Sir John Nicholl nominated Sir Christopher Cole at the Glamorgan county by-election in 1817 he declared: 'I know the honest and attached feelings of the yeomanry, their independent spirit, their good sense and sound judgement . . . They well know that the representation of a great and opulent county is widely different from that of an insignificant borough.'[75] This type of language, this talking up to the voters, no doubt, suggests a superficial and flattering intent.[76] Its consequence, nevertheless, is important. It tended to promote that remarkable capacity of the voters to lord it—for a day, at least—over their social superiors.[77] It marks the eagerness of the electors to flex their political muscles by asserting their electoral independence. Electoral patrons were thus willing to tolerate expressions of voter opinion—so long, of course, as it was socially constrained, and so long as it did not attack the property structures of rule by the landed élite.

One of the ways in which electors did flex their muscles was by making use of their influence to gain favours and protection from the

[74] Lord Anglesey to Sir Robert Williams, 2 Sept. 1825, Plas Newydd MSS Univ. College of North Wales, Bangor.

[75] 'A Report of the Proceedings of the County Meeting held at Pyle on 22 August 1817', Traherne Scrapbook, P.3 MSS 6575E, National Lib. of Wales.

[76] Socially inverted rituals are a little noticed aspect of electioneering. Voters loved to go to the poll in a chaise, especially if the weather was bad. The early booking of available chaises was an important, minor aspect of electoral organization. 'Unless I send them in a Chaise one of them declines coming', wrote G. Kingsley to George Burgoyne, 8 Feb. 1810, D/DQ/19/2, Burgoyne MSS, Essex RO. See also examples from Northants. in 1806 (Forester, *Northamptonshire County Electioneering*, 119. It would be interesting to learn what the humble radical wanted who addressed the following peremptory request to Lord Fitzwilliam in 1807: 'My Dear Sir, I wish to see You as soon has your Lordship as Dind.' (G.8. Fitzwilliam MSS, Sheffield Pub. Lib.).

[77] Such an attitude could be taken to extremes and readily satirized, as the following poem in *The Gentleman's Magazine*, 38 (Mar. 1768) demonstrates:

> BALLAD on the GENERAL ELECTION
> Hail, glorious time,
> (Fit fubject for rhyme,
> That ev'ry diftinction can level,
> When the gentleman greets,
> Each blackguard he meets,
> And Pride muft defcend to be civil.
>
> The Elegant peer
> Muft guzzle ftrong beer,
> With freemen to gain their protection;
> And all who afpire
> To be knights of the Shire,
> Gewt drunk to fecure their election.

Such rhymes were not uncommon. *Election Flights to the Freeholders of the County of Cambridge* (1780) included the following doggerel: 'How the Duke, Peer and Baronets, Doctors Divine Deigned with cobblers and Barbers and butchers to dine.'

patrons. This 'moral economy' of electioneering has a number of facets. Voters could use their status as voters to secure an occupational advantage. The Cordwainers of Minehead petitioned Henry Luttrell in 1767:

Sir,
Wee whose names are here under subscribed are *all voters* in Minehead and all cordwainers, Humbly desire that W. Napcott might not have the shop of T. Baker, for wee are all determined that he shant come into the town as there is not work enough to keep us employed. We shall most gratefully acknowledge your response at the forthcoming election.[78]

They might use their influence to secure favours for themselves or their families. An unfortunate voter at Stafford addressed the agent of the Marquis of Gower, Thomas Fletcher:

I shall be obliged to you if you would ask Mr. Cord if he will bild me a shop and Let me have [a] house [next] to hit i shall be oblige to you and him for I have lost possesson of that i had of the Marquis and My Landlord will give me warning for leve at a Ladey day next i shall be Glad of answer as soon as possoble it is all for to spite me.[79]

Others used their influence as voters to secure orders for themselves and their families for produce and commodities, sometimes wildly in excess of their natural social needs. If such orders were not forthcoming considerable offence might be caused, an occupational rebuff which could easily be translated into electoral opposition. The required favours were sometimes of very general concern, as John Dodd, the MP for Reading, noted when he asked the Duke of Newcastle to put pressure on Lord Barrington to remove from the town a regiment of foot quartered there.[80]

Perhaps even more significant than petitioning for favours was petitioning for offices and jobs. Such petitioning was entirely appropriate to an age which knew nothing of competitive examination as a criterion for appointment to offices. Some landlords and patrons had access to an informal system of contacts and recommendations. Others had immediate access to the gift of offices. These latter involved the highly prestigious offices of places in the lieutenantcy and militia,

---

[78] DD/L MS box 110. 1/59/13, Dunster Castle MSS, Som. RO.

[79] John Cockersole to Thomas Fletcher, D/1788/2, Aqualate MSS, Staffs. RO. From numerous further examples may be singled out the readiness of the voters of Boirton to offer their votes to Lord Lichfield so long as he continued the family tradition of paying £10 per year to the poor of the village. 'A Letter from the Boirton Men Offering their votes . . .', DIL XVI/C/I, Oxon. RO.

[80] John Dodd to the Duke of Newcastle, 4 Nov. 1760, BL Add. MSS 32914 fo. 96, Newcastle Papers.

on the bench as JPs, and as coroners and as custom and excise officers. (In the boroughs the mayoralty and town clerkship could be worth £1,000 per annum, the recordership several hundred.) Beneath this layer of patronage was a further layer consisting of hundreds of lesser offices.[81] Then there was ecclesiastical patronage of all types. Next came places and promotions in the professions and in civil administration. In government boroughs the prizes were yet more numerous: places in the admiralty, the excise, and in the tax offices, and at a lower level offices as porters, tide-waiters and customs men abounded. The lord lieutenant of the county had no direct political influence but as the post was usually held by local aristocratic families its patronage became a direct force in county elections. The lord lieutenant recommended names for the bench to the lord chancellor, he appointed to offices, especially commissions in the militia and to the land tax office, and he had influence over a wide variety of other offices and services in the gift of the crown. Partisanship frequently motivated sensitive legal appointments: as *custos rotulorum,* as clerk of the peace, as coroner (about a dozen per county) and, of course, as JP (several hundred per county). In this sense, electoral patronage

---

[81] T. H. Oldfield, *History of the Boroughs of Great Britain*, 2 vols. (London, 1794), ii. 137–9, prints a list of the Tiverton Corporation, showing their offices and relationships with the patron. Similarly, the list of the Lyme Regis freemen (ibid. 182–3) shows their relationship to the Earl of Westmorland. Every one of them was either his relative or his appointee. Clearly, the patron's access to office was of the first importance in electioneering. 'In Hull the chief favours at the candidate's disposal were jobs in the Customs, which were usually applied for around election time' (Gordon Jackson, *Hull in the Eighteenth Century* (London 1972), 303). A survey of the borough of Honiton (55/6/31/7, Devon RO) contained this breakdown of the political influence of the lord of the Manor: '1. The Lord's right to appoint to the office of Portreeve, Bailiff and to aletasters. 2. The two principal inns are let from year to year and thus the Lord can influence not only the votes of his tenants but also those of the tradespeople who sell there as well as many of the domestics. 3. The present bailiff is a cordwainer and employs eighteen cordwainers and they are influenced. 4. The right to graze over meadow and pasture land round the town.' This sort of thing was quite common. The Lord Warden of the Cinque Ports appointed over 60 pilots as well as having the appointment of 'Many Persons at Dover to different obsolete offices', about 30 in number ('Arguments against the Pilot's Bill', W1/1910, Whitbread MSS, Beds. RO). There is also an interesting document concerning Callington in 1779, and 'the services which it is in your Lordship's power to render to some of the electors there', including the provision of employment and promotion (Hinchingbrooke MSS 9/238/3, Hunts. RO). See also the interesting examples of voters' expectations and their willingness to negotiate their support 'on condition of having a cornmill upon a fair rent either in the County of Anglesey or Carnarvon' (P. Jupp, *British and Irish Elections 1784–1831* (Newton Abbot, 1973), 62). Lowther's 'Office Book' notes 22 Carlisle freemen as holding places in the Customs; 20 actually voted in 1768 (15 for Lowther's candidates and only 4 for Portland's, the other splitting his votes). Of the 20 freemen marked as exercisemen, 9 were for Lowther, 8 for Portland, and 3 did not attend the election. There were 6 freemen 'holding offices under the Governor of Carlisle', of whom 4 sat in the corporation, one voted for Elliot and Johnstone, and the sixth, an alderman, for Bentinck and Musgrave. These posts, which were practically sinecures, were 'an inexpensive means of securing influential supporters' (B. Bonsall, *Sir James Lowther and Cumberland and Westmorland Elections 1754–1775* (Manchester, 1960), 88).

was an indispensable method for distributing office and allocating power. In this massive process of distribution and allocation, the position of the MPs and candidates, their families and contacts, was absolutely central.

Voters were ruthlessly determined to use electoral levers on behalf of themselves and more important, perhaps, to procure favours and advantages for members of their families. It was quite normal for an MP to receive a steady stream of requests from his voters, and he would endeavour, often in vain, to act upon them. Thus, five Hull voters wrote to Sir Christopher Sykes in 1784 promising him their votes if he would promise to recommend their brother-in-law to a vacancy in the Hull customs house.[82] In the same manner, Lord Milton had the promise of a vote from a local attorney if Fitzwilliam promised to recommend him as a JP.[83] At Grimsby in 1820 an anonymous supporter of Charles Tennyson asserted: 'in the prosperity of the Port, his interest and yours go hand in hand, his local knowledge in all applications to the Government Offices in behalf of any of you, or of your friends, or for the Port in general, give him an advantage superior to all other men'.[84] It is important to note that votes are not being exchanged for offices. The power of the vote is being used to secure *recommendations* to office.

It is very difficult to estimate the incidence of these requests. Sir John Delaval, at least, received on average one per week at Berwick-on-Tweed, over 300 between elections, an incidence which, ignoring the very real possibility of repeated applications, amounts to something approaching half the number of the electorate.[85] It seems, moreover, to have been a favourite indulgence of electoral patrons to lament the time it was necessary to devote to this particular aspect of electioneering. In most instances, no doubt, this was a private undertaking, but there are many examples of voters exerting their strength in numbers. In 1770 Henry Luttrell received a petition from 42 voters seeking his influence over the appointment of a tide-waiter. Such a petition, signed by over 10% of the electorate, was impossible to ignore.[86] Finally, Coker remarked of the voters of Lord de Dunstanville in 1820 at the corporation constituency of Bodmin: 'Their patron is rather their agent than their master; he had no other hold over them

---

[82] Garner and Bos to Sir 'Charles' Sykes, 13 May 1784, DD/SY/101/14, Sykes MSS, Hull Univ. Lib.

[83] Henry Vernon to Lord Milton, 30 Sept. 1812, F. 42-18, Fitzwilliam MSS, Sheffield Pub. Lib.

[84] *Collection of the Addresses* (Great Grimsby, 1820), 18.

[85] Stoker, 'Elections and Voting Behaviour', Ph.D. 33–4.

[86] DD/L MS box 110, 1/59/7, Dunster Castle MSS, Som. RO.

than good offices and good-will; they jealously elect their own fellow corporators who must be residents, so that the patron can never get his own private friends into the corporation.'[87]

Here, surely, is one massively important reason for the keen participation of voters in elections. Voters were aware of the leverage they might be able to exert over their patrons and they were prepared to behave accordingly. Thus, far from acting as the passive recipients of authority, influence, and corruption, voters enjoyed the capacity to profit materially from an election contest. Indeed, they frequently manifest a striking awareness of the progress of the campaign, its personalities and its issues. Some electors could set themselves up very nicely. One voter who has been very well taken care of by the Plas Newydd interest wrote to Lord Anglesey identifying himself:

I am the poor Harbour Master of Caernarvon, the Crier of the General Quarter Sessions for the County of Caernarvon, the Clerk of the Market Hall of Caernarvon, the Inspector of Weights and Measures for the Town and Liberties of Caernarvon and a Burgess for the Borough of Caernarvon . . .

I will forfeit all my places, and give my vote as long as the blood runs in my Veins to the Ancestors of the Most Honourable Hero that fought and Bled for his King and Country—and if I should be turned out of all my situations I acknowledge that I have done nothing but justice.[88]

But then he had much to be grateful for.

These were not the only considerations which might arouse the participation of voters and non-voters alike in elections. Local issues involving legislation or the parliamentary performance of sitting members inevitably attracted considerable attention. As is well known, most eighteenth century legislation was local in character and effected by petition or other request from the locality concerned. Local acts either granted special powers to prevailing organs of local government to meet local needs or constituted *ad hoc* bodies to perform functions either badly performed hitherto or not performed at all (commissioners of sewers, turnpike trusts, improvement commissioners, etc.). Thus between 1715 and 1760, Parliament passed 80 Acts with particular relevance to Kent; 30 dealt with such matters as changes of name or detail of estate settlement, 22 with road improvements, 14 with harbours and fisheries, and 2 with the poor law and street cleaning.[89]

---

[87] *The Croker Papers*, i. 165, quoted in Comber, 'The Cornish Boroughs', MA, 73, and esp. as quoted in J. J. Sack, 'The House of Lords and Parliamentary Patronage, 1802–1832', *Hist. J.* 23 (1980), 913–37.

[88] Thomas Williams to Lord Anglesey, 5 July 1830, Plas Newydd MSS, Univ. College of North Wales, Bangor.

[89] A. Newman, 'Elections in Kent and Its Parliamentary Representation, 1715–1754', D.Phil. (Oxford, 1957), 387–8.

Among such a list would always be a certain number of contentious proposals. Questions of a local character, as opposed to those of a purely personal or familial nature, would inevitably attract comment. Frequently public meetings would be held to consider the desirability of a particular measure. Proposals which could affect the economic livelihood of a town or area were particularly controversial, as were those affecting local communications.[90] To cut a canal might facilitate the transport of local agriculture and certain industries, but it might also invite outside competition, discriminate against towns not benefitting from the cut, and harm certain vested interests, especially turnpike trustees.[91] There were certainly plenty of controversial issues upon which local opinion might legitimately be sounded.

Consequently there was every good reason why electors should be attentive to the parliamentary conduct of their MPs. Town and county meetings were not infrequent occurrences, and MPs were commonly invited to give an account of themselves. MPs who rarely spoke on the great national and international questions of the time will be found, on reference to the *Commons Journals*, to be assiduous in attending their committees. The protection and advancement of local interests was, after all, what they were there for. There is, furthermore, some possibility that those traditional functions may have intensified rather than weakened as the eighteenth century wore on. As economic development advanced, local improvement bills became more frequent and economic interests more complex. What no constituency could afford was an absentee MP. 'I was much concerned that I was not in town when the Small Debt Bill for Cambridgeshire came before the House', wrote one sympathetic but worried MP who sat for Devizes, 'You may depend on my attending the further progress of it.'[92] In 1831 a Welsh MP with severe reservations about Lord Grey's parliamentary reform proposals nevertheless survived the general election. Even in his victory speech he felt obliged to explain himself: 'I took great pains to consider it; I pondered deeply on all its provisions; I attended, anxiously listening to the nine days' discussions on it; and I at last satisfied myself that, as an honest man, and as an Englishman, I could not give it my support.'[93]

---

[90] See the advertisement for town meetings 'to consider the expediency of soliciting Parliament for an Act to effect a navigation between Bury St Edmunds and Ipswich'. See 586/36, Hertford MSS, West Suffolk RO.

[91] For an excellent example, see Lansberry, 'Politics and Government in St Albans', Ph.D., 189–99; see above, p. 240.

[92] Sir James Tylney Long to Unidentified Recipient, 30 Apr. 1787, 588/028, Cotton MSS, Cambs. RO.

[93] A Report of the Speech Delivered by Lord Granville Somerset, 6 May 1831, p. 5. Evans and Evill MSS (D.25.1401) Monmouth RO.

One of the reasons why the voters could not be ignored was the fact that they were significantly more accustomed to exercising the right of voting than historians have ever imagined. For, to the incidence of election contests at parliamentary elections must be added the substantial number of contested municipal elections for local offices. There was legal provision for the annual election of mayors, aldermen, councillors, and bailiffs. In some places these elections no longer occurred but in many others, especially in the larger freeman boroughs where freeman still enjoyed the chartered right of electing to municipal offices, they seem to have been contested with some frequency.

At Ipswich in the late eighteenth and early nineteenth century, the freeman voted not only in parliamentary and municipal elections but also in elections for the council offices of water bailiffs, hospital guide, town clerk, and town crier. There seems always to have been a close connection between voting in these local elections and in parliamentary elections. Victory in the former was frequently an indication of success in the latter.[94] They were often fought by the same men on the same sides professing the same opinions. At Maidstone there were 8 parliamentary elections between 1761 and 1802 but there were 15 municipal elections. There seems to have been over a 70% correlation of support between municipal and general elections among the voters.[95] Sometimes these contests gave rise to poll books and a voter turnout to equal or even exceed that which prevailed at general elections.[96]

In large freeman boroughs, municipal elections were part of the struggle for control of the parliamentary representation. In 1807 a non-Grosvenor candidate was returned for the city of Chester. Lord Grosvenor responded by nominating himself as mayor in order to consolidate his shaken prestige. His election as mayor in October 1807 intensified the local struggle. In 1809 the anti-Grosvenor party contested the offices of mayor and the popular sheriff.[97] According to the historian of Chester, 'The baneful influence of party now raged in the city with its utmost violence; and was manifested in every

---

[94] See e.g. A. R. Childs, 'Politics and Elections in Suffolk Boroughs During the Late Eighteenth Century and Early Nineteenth Century', M.Phil. (Reading, 1973), 80–1, 101, 104, 108. For the election of bailiff—and even of a school headmaster—in Morpeth see Fewster, 'Politics and Administration of Morpeth', Ph.D., 41 and ch. 10.

[95] J. A. Phillips, *Electoral Behavior in Unreformed England, 1761–1802* (Princeton, 1982), 110–11.

[96] The Exeter mayoral contest of 1735, 1736, 1738, and 1740 gave rise to published poll books (Colley, *In Defiance of Oligarchy*, 134). For turnout see above, pp. 183–91.

[97] According to convention, the corporation nominated one sheriff; the second, 'popular' sheriff was elected. By the end of the 18th cent. both were, in effect, nominated by the corporation. Here, as so often elsewhere, the recollection of alternative, less exclusive, ways of doing things lingered.

transaction, whether of a public or private nature.'[98] This conflict culminated in the election of rival corporations and corporation officials in 1812. Its thorough-going and all-embracing character requires little elaboration. The issues on which municipal elections were fought, however, were not always so grandiose. At the municipal elections of 1795 at Maidstone, a seat for the Common Council was contested over the issue of victualling licences, and over £15 a vote was offered.[99] Such issues could be fought no less keenly than a vital issue of momentous significance. So great was political excitement at Nottingham in 1818 that the nomination of Whigs and Tory candidates for the vacant office of sexton of the parish of St Mary assumed a political complexion and drew 1,278 ratepayers to vote.[100]

The enthusiasm of the voters might be maintained even if parliamentary elections were not contested. Even outside the larger freeman boroughs, voters remained assertive and touchy, sensitive and demanding, ready to involve themselves in contentious issues at the slightest provocation. This unique status of the voters was symbolized by their unrestricted occupation of the constituency during elections. (In the case of counties, the county town.) It was the voters, the agents, and the committees who controlled access to the town and its streets, and who maintained law and order. Just as the customary social order would be suspended, even inverted, for the period of the election, so the voters, and the non-voters, too, would assume a boisterousness and a swagger quite unlike their normal sober character. By law, the army was not allowed within two miles of the place of election until the day after polling was completed. The consequence was that the authorities allowed the election committees to assume responsibility for the preservation of law and order. To the onlooker, election campaigns appeared to tremble constantly on the brink of anarchy and tumult. Excited, partisan crowds, inflamed with alcohol, certainly threatened the peace of the town. Offensive remarks, jokes, and gestures might lead to fairly harmless and casual stone-throwing, even fighting. Jostling, heckling, and verbal intimidation might have the same consequence. This type of rowdyism so common among election crowds seriously discomfited the upper crust. 'The City Meeting . . . was beyond description Tumultuous', one terrified observer of the Exeter nomination in 1761 reported, going on to describe 'a Grand

[98] J. Hemingway, *A History of Chester*, 2 vols. (Chester, 1831), ii. 409.

[99] The election of three councillors in 1822 attracted a turnout of 738 out of 800 freemen, including outvoters from as far afield as Suffolk and Yorkshire. See J. Andrews, 'Political Issues in the County of Kent 1820–1846' (London, 1967), 44–5.

[100] J. Moses, 'Elections and Electioneering in Nottinghamshire Constituencies' 1702–1832', Ph.D. (Nottingham, 1965), 206.

Chorus of Hissing . . . was so loud that Mr. Rolle could meerly begin his intended Speech'.[101] No doubt he lived to tell the tale. Such harmless rowdyism was only to be expected in a situation of ritualised rivalry; rival parades, rival bands of musicians, rival colours, rival clubs, rival politics. What is surprising is how *rarely* serious trouble resulted from all this.[102] The social rituals which did so much to control and discipline the rivalry may have gone some way towards minimizing its consequences. Whatever the explanation, widely shared restraints and natural disciplines usually prevented harmless rowdyism from degenerating into serious violence.

A more threatening form of electoral tumult concerns the selective and deliberate attack upon rival workers, officials, and supporters. There were many variations on this theme. Processions or gangs of supporters might attack the house, hotel, or inn of the candidate or his most prominent supporters. Such violence was often retaliatory. At the bitter Leicester contest of 1754, the anti-corporation Whigs published an advertisement promising violence to the property of their opponents. They fulfilled their promise when a Whig mob pulled down the corporation fences, whereupon the corporation imported into the town 'three hundred colliers . . . from Coleorton Moor armed with bludgeons in which iron spikes had been inserted, to support the Tory cause'. They proceeded to attack the Whig committee-room, causing those who were manning it to flee.[103] Indeed, attacks upon these critically important centres were not uncommon. The canvass was another common target. At Berwick in 1807, the independent mob would not allow the sitting members to canvass the town at all.[104] When the Lowthers began to canvass near Kendal in 1818, reported Lord Lowther, there were 'a hundred and fifty to two hundred gentlemen that met us on horseback and I suppose about twenty

---

[101]  A. Quicke to 'Dear Sister', n.d. 1761, Quicke MSS, 64/12/29/1/59, Devon RO.

[102]  It is not clear how often, in fact, it did but *my own* impression suggests that serious election violence was *infrequent*. In 1831, for example, an unusually unruly election, there were perhaps *nine* major incidents and perhaps a dozen lesser ones in England and Wales, see J. N. Odurkene, 'The British General Elections of 1830 and 1831', B.Litt. (Oxford, 1976), 140–4. Stoker concludes his analysis of the four northern counties over a 72-year period thus: 'Appleby and Cockermouth were, as pocket boroughs, completely untroubled, but the open boroughs of Berwick, Newcastle and Durham also suffered nothing more than boisterousness. Only at Morpeth and Carlisle was there any real trouble. In the counties there was even less disruption, with only Westmoreland being disturbed. The common factor linking these three constituencies that suffered trouble is that the violence erupted only when there was a blatant attempt by one interest to try and take both seats' (Stoker, 'Elections and Voting Behaviour', Ph.D., 334). Overall, there might be serious electoral violence in about half a dozen constituencies at each election and a similar or slightly greater number of less important incidents elsewhere.

[103]  W. Gardiner, *Music and Friends*, 2 vols. (Leicester, 1838), i. 201.

[104]  M. Hinton, 'The General Elections of 1806 and 1807', Ph.D. (Reading, 1959), 488.

carriages; we were all attacked, the carriages broke to pieces'.[105] The candidates themselves stood in particular danger. At York in 1790, Sir William Milner was waylaid by supporters of his opponents concealed in an inn after the chairing: 'The instant I got Opposite they flung Bricks, Bottles, Chamber Potts . . . directly at my head out of the Windows and an astonishing quantity of Tyles from the Top of the House. The arms and back of the Chair were broke and some of my friends close by were hurt.'[106]

These patterns of disorder may be distinguished from the deliberate intimidation of groups of voters by violence or the threat of it. John Tarleton was forced to abandon his candidature at Liverpool in 1768 when his supporters were threatened with blubber knives—long knives on poles used for cutting up whales—and were unable to come forward with their votes.[107] No doubt such activity may have been spontaneous but its timing and organization frequently suggest premeditation. When a mob of Grosvenor supporters went on a two-day rampage against rival voters in Chester in 1812, there may have been a contributory element of sheer enthusiasm amidst the terrifying disorder.[108] But there can be no mistaking the sinister intent of the hired and equipped gangs of bullies who were used to intimidate voters elsewhere. Sometimes the implied threat of violence was enough.[109] Sometimes, however, a reign of terror ensued. An organized and armed mob several hundred strong marched ominously into Pontefract in 1768 in the interest of Sir Rowland Winn:

And after parading the town for some time and terrifying the burgesses and inhabitants there, and insulting many burgesses in the interest of Lord Gallway and Mr. Strachey . . . [they] repaired to the lodgings of Sir Rowland Winn . . . And . . . During the Poll . . . the mob . . . insulted and violently beat a great many burgesses who voted for . . . Lord Gallway and Mr. Strachey, and also others who were in their interest, and endeavouring to go to the poll, but were by those means prevented . . .[110]

The same thing happened at East Retford in 1826 but this time with the dangerous admixture of religious bigotry:[111]

---

[105] Lord Lowther to Lord Lonsdale, 11 Feb. 1818, Lonsdale MSS, quoted in Jupp, *British and Irish Elections*, 47–8.

[106] Sir William Milner to Lord Fitzwilliam, 23 June 1790, box 41, Fitzwilliam MSS, Northants. RO.

[107] *Liverpool Chronicle*, 24 Mar. 1768.

[108] *Chester Pollbook* (1812), p. viii.

[109] See e.g. E. A. Smith, 'The Yorkshire Elections of 1806 and 1807', 81.

[110] G. P. Micklethwaite and Others, Affadavit sworn 2 May 1768, quoted in C. Bradley, 'The Parliamentary Representation of the Boroughs of Pontefract, Newark, and East Retford, 1754–1768', MA (Manchester, 1953), 57.

[111] John Parker to Lord Fitzwilliam, 23 May 1826, box 125, Fitzwilliam MSS, Northants. RO.

Some men have been nearly killed, not by freemen but by a hired mob of the scum of the neighbourhood no doubt hired by our opponents . . . It is expected 20,000 persons will be as spectators at the election from the neighbourhood, and they not only threaten to block up the road to prevent the candidates coming into the hall, but murder the freemen that vote for Roman Catholics . . . The freemen have every reason to expect their lives will be in danger if they go to vote; they cannot now walk the streets (even in day time) without insult . . . Had we only to contend with the freemen it would be nothing, as we could outnumber them, but a hired mob is very alarming. At a general meeting of the freemen on Saturday last they all declared unless some soldiers are not [sic] ordered near the town to support the civil power they dare not go to vote.

Most horrifying of all to contemporaries was the prospect of the complete breakdown of order. Pitched battles between rival mobs were bad enough, but at York in 1768 they became so dangerously uncontrollable that the mayor had to negotiate a truce.[112] Perhaps the most terrifying example of indiscriminate and uncontrollable electoral violence is to be found at Leicester in 1826. Inflamed with an unprecedented combination of religious hatred, social antagonism (many of the voters were very poor), and alcohol, the mob took over the town for several weeks and subjected it to plunder and riot. On the third day of the poll the candidates and the returning officer were attacked. Troops were needed to restore order, and over a hundred arrests were made.[113]

There is no reason to believe that only the largest and most popular towns were involved in rioting of this gravity. Tiny Knaresborough had an astonishing record of vicious, communal rioting because the Duke of Devonshire refused to allow the residents to occupy the burgage houses which carried the vote, thus depriving them of many of the usual fruits of elections. Indeed at the 1804 by-election there the seriousness of the trouble caused the election to be postponed. At the general election of 1806 the duke swore in 300 of his lead miners as constables and sent them into the town. This served to unite the Knaresborough factions, which fell upon the miners and dispersed them. The election was proceeding when a regiment of Scots Greys were drafted into the town to reinforce the miners. The rioting resumed and force was used to subdue the mob. So dangerous was the town that the elected members and their supporters had to confine their celebrations to the safety of Harrogate.[114]

---

[112] F. C. Price, 'Parliamentary Elections in York City, 1754–1790', MA (Manchester, 1958), 103.

[113] R. Reid, *Modern Leicester* (London, 1881) has a chapter on this election; see also A. Temple Patterson, *Radical Leicester* (Leicester, 1954), ch. 8.

[114] Hinton, 'General Elections of 1806 and 1807', Ph.D., 487.

Amidst the excesses to which election disturbances could run in the unreformed period one thing is clear: popular action was determined less by the patrician classes than by the voters and non-voters, whose support and approval they were seeking. There unquestionably existed the autonomy of public opinion at election times over which the Hanoverian élite could exercise only a very limited, and very final, control. Consequently, mobility and action were controlled by the middling and lower orders, not by their social superiors. In this sense, if in no other, an election marked a degree of public endorsement of a patron, a candidate, or an issue on the part of the electors *and those round them*. There was an element of precariousness about public order during elections, but the interest of the majority of the community in reaching a peaceful rather than a violent resolution of local differences remained one of its greatest assets and abiding strengths.

### THE VOTERS: 'INDEPENDENCE' IN THOUGHT AND ACTION

These assertive elements in voter attitudes could in certain circumstances pattern themselves into a primitive layer of political consciousness which may be described as the mentality of electoral independence. This mentality was predicated upon a repudiation of the politics of oligarchy. Independents exerted themselves against attempts to close a borough, to prevent contests or to stifle political activity. They frequently protested against the domination of their constituency—or the threat of domination—by a single interest or a coalition of interests. The political culture of electoral independence was not constantly to the fore in every constituency. It was available as a coherent and legitimate ideological resort when the politics of oligarchy appeared to threaten local independence. This 'restlessness against the local oligarchies', as Professor Cannon has described it,[115] may well have been on the increase in the decades after Robert Walpole had made the world so spectacularly safe for those local oligarchies. Whether it was or not, we should recognize electoral independence as an integral part of the electoral system. This 'restlessness' was the fundamental layer of political consciousness among the non-electors as well as among the electors, the core element upon which other issues were engrafted. The thought and practice of electoral independence prospered in the decades between the decline of the old Whig–Tory distinctions in the middle of the eighteenth century and the emergence of new ones at the end of that century. Even in this latter period, the

[115] J. A. Cannon, 'New Lamps for Old', in his *The Whig Ascendancy*, 210–52.

conflict between oligarchy and independence was the ideological core of electoral activity. The mentality of electoral independence was not motivated primarily by national or party concerns, although they could be superimposed upon it, but local concerns to do with the welfare of the local community, the exercise of power and influence over it, and the structure of social relationships within it. Given the still fairly primitive, albeit vociferous, state of public opinion, the unequal distribution of electoral resources and the chronic inability of independents to unite their efforts across constituencies, the fight was often futile. Nevertheless, the electoral opponents of oligarchy were nothing if not noisy. No wonder that electoral patrons disliked contested elections in view of the embarrassing issues that might be raised in front of a touchy, sensitive, and potentially hostile public opinion.

Electoral independence was most naturally and most spontaneously expressed when the social and political mechanisms which linked the constituency and the electoral patron ceased to function smoothly. If the normative standards of the relationship were violated by the patron, then the electors, often encouraged by the non-electors, might proceed to outright electoral opposition. For example, an apparent lack of generosity might be interpreted as a snub and as a mark of indifference towards the constituency. Fitzwilliam's allegedly ungenerous treatment of Malton during the famine of 1799–1800 sowed the seeds of the revolt of 1806 when he lost control of the seat.[116] Nor was it solely material offences against the electors which might threaten an election contest. To take a constituency for granted could ruffle civic pride or county concern to such an extent that an electoral convulsion could follow.

The most notorious example of how *not* to treat a constituency came in September 1829 when the Duke of Newcastle asked the electors of Newark:

Is it presumed then, that I am not to do what I will with my own? or that I am to surrender my property, and the inherent rights belonging to it, into the hands of those who wish to deprive me of it? This is the simple question; to which I answer, whilst the laws of England exist and are respected, I shall permit no clamour, nor threats, nor even force itself to deter me from doing as I may think fit with my own property.[117]

The burgages may have been Newcastle's property, but this was hardly the way to treat even a burgage borough. Popular independents repudiated such arrogance:

---

[116] E. A. Smith, 'Earl Fitzwilliam and Malton: A Proprietary Borough in the Early Nineteenth Century, 1819–1832', *Eng. Hist. Rev.* 81 (1965), 55.

[117] *Nottingham Review*, 9 Oct. 1829, quoted in J. Golby, 'Fourth Duke of Newcastle', 167.

The times are passing by, when a few men should be able to dictate to the majority of the people. The great mass of the population is gradually becoming more enlightened; this growth of knowledge, this increase of intellect, 'this march of reason, has induced men to enquire into the why and wherefore; men cannot now readily assent to any particular proposition; they now want to know *why* they *must* assent.[118]

Indeed they did. Independents would concede a proper respect to those enjoying natural interest, but they were sensitive to arrogance. The electors of Wigan were quick to spot the Duke of Portland's imperiousness in the 1770s and complained that he treated them 'as a breeder of cattle would do his lean stock, or an African slave-merchant his Negroes'.[119]

Before proceeding to a detailed characterization of electoral independence it is necessary to make two precautionary statements about it. *First*, it is difficult to generalize about an 'ideology' of popular independence because it was essentially the abiding importance of local issues which acted as its focus. In some ways, its importance lies exactly in the fact that it was *not* an ideology to which only the politically educated could aspire and the politically sophisticated articulate. It comprised a wide variety of local responses to a large number of differing local situations, responses which were made by voters and non-voters alike. Its essential character, however, was the elector's sense of liberty, his rejection of patronage, of control, and of servility. It was an assertion of popular liberty. *Second*, it is important to notice that some 'independence' movements were not at all independent in this sense. They were little more than venal association of voters prepared to offer themselves to the highest bidder. In some places, especially in near venal boroughs like Newark, the label 'independent' was used merely to conceal the support of a powerful interest or group of interests. Even in Nottingham in 1814, Admiral Frank proclaimed his 'inviolable independence', but he had the weight and resources of the great Newcastle interest behind him.[120] Such pretensions to independence were bogus. The very fact, however, that covertly political groups employed the language of popular constitutionalism to attract support is a striking testimony to its potency.

One of the recurrent features of independent propaganda links the independence of individuals with that of the House of Commons. Such independence had a natural, historical and philosophical justification.

[118] This was said by the King's Lynn independent, William Ayre; see *The King's Lynn Poll Book* (1826), 27.

[119] Broadsheet Collection MMP25, 'To the Free and Independent Burgesses of Wigan', Wigan Pub. Lib.

[120] Moses, 'Elections in Nottinghamshire', Ph.D., 101–2.

An independent pamphlet published in Liverpool in 1790 affirmed that 'Independence, a blessing primarily bestowed by nature upon all her children, is a barrier in which our ancestors always found themselves invincible; sensible that he only can boast the privileges of a Freeman, who is governed by his own will, they maintained it in the hour of trial against the encroachments of monarchy and aristocracy.' It followed, then, that 'the people are fully secured against the abuses and treachery of their delegates, and the establishment of an House of Commons is only of consequence, when the independence of this branch of the legislature is maintained'.[121] This independent conception of the constitution thus wedded the eighteenth century philosophical commonplace of the balance of the constitution to the reality that the electoral system was composed of paternalist leaders of communities. In the affairs of those communities, independents brooked no outside interference.

The interference of members of the House of Lords in elections to the House of Commons was particularly disliked. A standing order of the House of Commons had in 1701 sought to inhibit such interference. The frequency with which it was cited by outraged independents shows the extent to which it was both ignored by patrons yet remembered by the electors. One of his opponents roundly told Lord Lonsdale in 1816:

It is almost impertinent for me to remind your Lordship, that the better to secure the freedom of elections, no Lord of Parliament, or Lord Lieutenant has any right to interfere in the election of Commoners; this my Lord, is a wise and salutary regulation of the House of Commons and demands your Lordship's serious consideration.[122]

Independent publicists condemned the greed and social ambition of those peers who openly flouted the law:

*The interference of Peers at elections is as contrary to the spirit of the law, as it is dangerous to the liberty of the subject;* and the man who, for an increase of patronage, for himself or family, would break through the sacred barriers of the constitution, *deserves not that his rank or fortune, whatever they may be, should protect him from reprehension;—nor is that subject worthy* of the benefit and protection of salutary laws, who had not virtue or resolution sufficient to defend them[123]

---

[121] *An Address to the Freemen of Liverpool* (1790), pp. 4–5; Williamson Collection, Liverpool Pub. Lib.

[122] William Dobinson to Lord Lonsdale, 18 Mar. 1816, Londsdale MSS, quoted in Jupp in *British and Irish Elections*, 104–6.

[123] *Collection of Papers* . . . (Chester, 1807), 38–9.

It was this issue which provoked such indignation that could not infrequently dominate an election. There was a torrent of propaganda against the influence of the Exeter family at Stamford in 1809 which was summed up in a single sentence: 'Have the inhabitants of Stamford a right to choose their own representatives or have they not?'[124]

Affirmation of freedom of election against aristocratic influence was frequently depicted as yet a further instalment in the unfolding saga of the freeborn Englishman's heroic struggle for liberty. Independents were very conscious of this. It was not uncommon for lists of independent voters to be published, permanent testimony to martyrdom in the cause of freedom.[125] A voter at King's Lynn in 1826, blessed with a sense of personal destiny, stood up and forced himself to declare: 'To preserve the independence of the town is to support the consequence of Parliament—the only means of protecting the Rights and Liberties of the People, and in order to do that, I *will* be Independent myself.'[126] Indeed, radicals such as Oldfield carried through this identification of the freedom of a borough with independence of aristocratic (or corporate, or clerical, or ministerial) domination.[127] The most effective means of maintaining that independence was to keep or make the franchise as broad as possible, a conclusion which independents bequeathed to radicals in the reign of George III.

The independence both of the electors and the constituency had to be defended not only against the aristocracy but against the Church of England. Interference by Anglican clergy in elections was generally resented, not least in over 30 of the larger and more frequently contested constituencies where Protestant Dissenters were active in independence parties.[128] After the York election of 1818 one writer complained:

The interference of several of the Clergy formed too striking a feature in this, as it generally does in all contests of such a kind, to be passed by in this brief account altogether unnoticed. For persons of this description to be seen deeply engaged in party politics, canvassing their parishioners, encouraging

---

[124] *The Stamford Poll Book* (1809), no. 11.

[125] See, for example, the title of the 1790 Southampton Poll Book, '*Independence A Correct List of the Independent Commercial, Gentlemen, Tradesmen who voted for Mr. Dawkins on the 17th and 18th June, 1790 in support of the* Glorious Independence *of the Town of Southampton.*'

[126] *The King's Lynn Pool Book* (1826), 32–3.

[127] Oldfield, *History of the Boroughs*, i. 129.

[128] Such a list would include Abingdon, Aylesbury, Beverley, Bridgwater, Bridport, Bristol, Buckingham, Cambridge, Carmarthen, Cirencester, Coventry, Exeter, Great Yarmouth, Harwich, Hertford, Hull, Ilchester, Ipswich, Leicester, Lewes, Lincoln, Liverpool, London, Maidstone, Maldon, Northampton, Norwich, Nottingham, Portsmouth, Preston, Taunton, Tiverton, Warwick, Worcester, and York. See below, pp. 359–68.

mobs, and frequenting taverns, and, in consequence of these things, to have their names bandied about, and their foibles exposed in electioneering squibs, cannot be esteemed very creditable to themselves, or favourable to the cause of religion. That proper dignity of character, and that moral influence which they ought to possess, are weakened, if not destroyed; whilst the religion which they profess to teach is, amongst the unthinking multitude, brought into contempt, and, with too much plausibility, regarded and spoken of by them, as no other than 'a craft by which men may get their wealth'.[129]

Magistrates were another common target. Those at Norfolk were accused of interfering in the county election of 1806:

Cases were by no means rare, in which publicans had been influenced in the disposal of their votes, by the threats of refusal to grant them a renewal of their licences—persons, too, in a less dependent situation of life, had had the fear of surcharges held over their heads by Commissioners of taxes; and although he had now confined himself to a general notice of what had come to his knowledge on that head, yet he would be bold to pledge himself, that if he should be able to obtain such evidence as was convertible into legal proof, he would bring such disgraceful offences to public exposure and punishment. That, Mr. Windham said, was the mode by which the independence of the County would be best defended?[130]

Corporations were another favourite target of independents. Our independent voter at King's Lynn in 1826 expressed his creed in the following terms:

I was rocked in the cradle of independence, and taught to revere the obligation of an oath, more than the consideration of private interest; I have no particular animosity against any of our opponents; there are many of them whose characters stand high in my estimation; but when a body of men become incorporated, and endeavour by their united influence to dictate who shall be the member of our choice, I feel indignant at the usurpation, and whilst my name exists it will, I trust, ever be found enrolled in the ranks of freedom and independence. If all those who have votes would but act on this principle, if they did but feel as I do on this subject; they would easily and readily free themselves and the Town, from that state of servile dependence and thraldom, in which it is at present placed.[131]

---

    [129] *The York Poll Book* (1818), x.
    [130] *The Norfolk Poll Book* (1806), 22.
    [131] *The King's Lynn Poll Book* (1826), 32–3. A Coventry independent declared in 1777: 'that the Mayor, Sheriffs, Chamberlains and Warden had in former times used to be chosen by the House-keepers at large, and who to this hour, have right to vote for each and every of the above named officer, at the Annual Great Leet.' He hoped that: 'a spirit and resolution becoming good citizens would suffice in overcoming the close Corporation, and that the freemen and householders (who were not necessarily freemen) would regain their rights as laid down in the Charter and Laws of the City.' (The Corporation's right to elect Annual Officers of the City, 1977, A142 MS 1, The Muniment Room, Coventry.)

The prevalence of this mentality, even in formally closed constituencies, indeed, the existence of something like an alternative language of politics, may, in the end, have gone some little way towards inhibiting the expression of aristocratic and patronal power. The political culture of oligarchy had to come to terms with the political culture of independency. Even though the aristocracy and its agents could normally expect to triumph over local independents, they might well be sobered by the experience and might be persuaded to listen to the opinions of the people more attentively in the future.[132] And whatever the outcome of such an election one thing was certain. The mountains of hostile propaganda, sometimes sensationally revealing and exaggerating the material links and the financial rewards of patronage, were an acute embarrassment to a local family or corporation. Such elections always did harm to their reputation and it is no wonder that election contests were hated by them. At best they acted as a safety valve for local resentments; at worst they could be a humiliating, public embarrassment. One unsuccessful candidate at the Grantham election of 1830 commented:

It has been said, gentlemen, that the House of Buckminster is a domineering one; had such been the case, I think it would not have met with the support it has done at this Election. It might have influenced some who were dependent upon it, but so much cannot be said of those Freemen who voted for me and are totally independent. It might, I say, have commanded the votes of some, but it could not have commanded that zeal which has been shown me by others.[133]

The independents saw themselves as the vehicles of a local political regeneration and constantly condemned the corruption of the local political élite. They yearned for a simple, rural body politic in which freemen and freeholders would come forward freely disposing of their votes, unsolicited and uncorrupted: 'Independence is the cause of infant virtue struggling against gigantic oppression.'[134] Independents detested the power of the purse, denounced the spread of commerce, and later in the period, of industrialism. They denounced corruption in Burkean terms, depicting it as a disease which spread from above, numbing every nerve in the body politic until it had destroyed consistency and virtue among the people. The ideal independent candidate was not out for office. When Hungerford was proposed as the independent candidate at Leicestershire in 1774 he promised:

[132] There is an excellent example of this in Monmouth. After the election of 1820 the Worcester family promised to listen to the opinions of the burgesses more closely in future; see Frances McDonnell to J. C. Stanbury, n.d. 1821, Stanbury MSS, DBA 1271, Monmouth RO.

[133] *The Grantham Poll Book* (1830), pp. xxxiv–xxxv.

[134] *Chester Chronicle*, 12 Jan. 1810.

'If I have the honour to be elected by your suffrages as one of your Representatives in Parliament, I shall endeavour to merit your Approbation, by an Honest, Upright, and Independent Conduct [*much applause*]. He then repeated with great emphasis I AM AN INDEPENDENT MAN—and I pledge to you my Honor–that I will never accept of either PLACE OR PENSION under any administration whatever.'[135]

The popular independents were thus sustained by their belief that their local struggle was a crucial element of a national, moral crusade. They denounced parties on both sides, detesting equally the Whigs and the Tories, the government and the opposition, identifying each with the preservation and consolidation of the effete ruling order of the aristocracy and themselves with traditions of sturdy independence and constitutional principle. The great struggle in which they were involved would be lost unless they managed to preserve freedom of election. The Reading Independents of the early nineteenth century roundly asserted:

1.  That Independence of Election consists in every voter exercising his Right, unawed by rank or power, and uninfluenced by hope of reward or Fear of Injury.
2.  That the Voter's Suffrage is his own Property and that those who aim either by Corruption or Intimidation of any Sort to misdirect or Deprive him of it, or resent his using it according to his own will, commit a great crime against Society, are Enemies to the Constitution, and Transgressors of the Laws of their Country.[136]

All of this amounted to a reassertion of the importance of the local community in the face of a hostile and corrupt outside world. A representative ought to be a local man because only a local man with local knowledge could thoroughly endear himself to the people. Only thus could unbreakable ties of mutual regard sufficient to resist external blandishments be established. It followed that only local men, resident, as opposed to outvoters, should vote. Some independent candidates, at least, would have nothing to do with the latter. At Wigan in 1780, the independent Sir Richard Clayton refused to poll the outvoters, and in 1820 the independents there delivered a protest against the acceptance of outvoters.[137] The 1823 Lincolnshire by-election evoked a remarkable expression of independent hostility towards 'an oligarchy composed of what are termed *county families* both Whig and Tory', whose schemes threatened to 'sacrifice or

---

[135] *Leicester and Nottingham Journal*, 19 Nov. 1774.
[136] *Reading Mercury*, 6 Mar. 1820.
[137] *The Poll for the Election of Members of Parliament for the Borough and Corporation of Wigan . . . the Eighth Day of March 1820*, Wigan Pub. Lib.

annihilate almost the only remaining privileges of the middle and lower classes of the freeholders'.[138] The preservation of local community in an age of rapid economic change, the maintenance of the personal relationship between the representative and the electors in an age of keen party rivalry, and a nostalgic backward-looking populism in which the rights of free Englishmen might be preserved—these were among the chief values of the independents. That these values were not spurious is attested by the wide following enjoyed by independents in many constituencies and by the continued existence of independent groups throughout the eighteenth century. There was perhaps something compelling in the notion that all men, and not merely the propertied, had an important political role to play. An independent candidate at Boston asserted as late as 1830: 'I am desirous of the good will of every person; there are none too humble to be without influence, and they all ought to be heard because they contribute to taxation.'[139] To assert and to defend local rights and traditions was an essential first step to preserving national liberty, and many popular independents evinced their consciousness of both aspects of these ideals.

Independence movements were not confined to any particular type or size of constituency; they could be found in the smallest as well as in the largest constituencies. Indeed, in the smallest boroughs, the restriction of the franchise itself kept alive traditions of independency. Even in the corporation boroughs, the most docile and the least rebellious of all constituency types, there were limits to what the corporation, and, indeed, the wider body of citizens, would tolerate. In 1807, after forty years of loyal deference to the Marquis of Lansdowne, the corporation of Calne revolted against his intention to dispense with the services of their MP, Joseph Jekyll, who had represented the town since 1787. He was re-elected against the wishes of his, and their, patron.[140] Elsewhere, too, the corporation could become the focus for independent feeling. At Salisbury, differences between the corporation and their patron, the Earl of Radnor, on

---

[138] *The Lincolnshire Poll Book* (1823), 7.

[139] *The Boston Poll Book* (1830), p. xi. The Independent candidate at the Oxford election of 1812 went out of his way to sneer at the notion that only 'Respectable Persons' should involve themselves in politics and ridiculed the idea that 'None but wealthy and dignified men should have anything to do with politics and are capable of deciding on the fitness or unfitness of candidates'. The same candidate attacked the hereditary possession of seats, repudiated claims to political power based on tradition and ancestry, and asserted that 'the principle of hereditary right is wisely confined to the House of Lords'. ('A Collection of Handbills', 100, 193: G. A. Oxon b.13. Papers relating to the Oxford election of 1812, Bodleian Lib.)

[140] *Morning Chronicle*, 9 May 1807; see also Thorne, *The House of Commons, 1790–1820*, 5 vols. (London, 1986), ii. 414.

national issues led after 1812 to a series of bitter municipal conflicts, including elections for local offices, and even that of mayor. The corporation became the champion not merely of the political independence of the borough but also of its commercial prosperity.[141] In the same county at about the same time, the borough of Marlborough was plunged into uproar by the Marlborough Independent and Constitutional Association, whose secretary, John Woodman, a local solicitor, professed to wish to extend the franchise to the inhabitant householders. They contested the borough in 1826 and again in 1830.[142] It is not clear how much independent activity existed in other corporation boroughs. Resentment against Lord De Dunstanville never did much more than rumble beneath the surface of the politics of Bodmin until he sold the seat to the Marquis of Hertford in 1816. At Truro the independents became active in 1818. In 1820 they took both seats, only to lose them in 1826. At Lostwithiel some rumbles of discontent against Lord Edgecombe were heard in 1830.[143] In Bath and Devizes, too, some occasional rumblings of independent feeling may be discerned. Even in such backwaters of the unreformed electoral system, therefore, independence *was* to be found in the closing decades of the period, but not on a large nor effective scale.

Electoral independence could even be found in at least a handful of the unpromising burgage boroughs. In 1784 and 1805 independent attacks on the Duke of Devonshire's control of Knaresborough were launched on the platform of extending the franchise to resident householders. The independents failed, but the same pattern was repeated in 1807, although no contest then occurred.[144] Similarly, independence was making a fairly consistent mark upon the borough of Chippenham in the late eighteenth century. A declining cloth industry and the hardships of war-time aided the independent cause. In 1802 two independent candidates demanded the extension

---

[141] See Lord Folkestone's Account in D/EP6/027, Pleydell-Bouverie MSS, Berks. RO. A well-wisher ('AMICUS') wrote to Lord Folkestone: 'Your Lordship was doubtless apprised of the formidable Party that was raised inimical to your Interest, and which but for the steady adherence of a few firm friends, might have proved fatal, not only to Your Lordship's Election, but to the Radnor interest altogether' (App. 6).

[142] *VCH Wiltshire*, v. 214.

[143] Comber, 'The Cornish Boroughs', MA, 67–8, 70, 73, 90–4. Thorne, *House of Commons*, ii. 42–5, 87–8.

[144] Namier and Brooke, *House of Commons*, i. 435–6. Lord Fitzwilliam to High Sheriff of Yorkshire, 5 May, Lord G. A. H. Cavendish to Fitzwilliam, 5 May 1807, F.45/123,124, Fitzwilliam MSS, Sheffield Pub. Lib. Thorne, *House of Commons*, ii. 450–2. A rather similar pattern is discernible at Ashburton, where the 1784 contest was the only interruption to the electoral peace which had reigned since 1761.

of the franchise to scot and lot holders. In 1807 they captured a seat.[145]

To show that independents in burgage boroughs were not simply occasional (and usually unsuccessful) armchair critics, the case of Pontefract is most instructive. This was a large borough in which several patrons contested the nomination, but there was a large number of small men owning one or two burgages. In short, Pontefract could not be closed up. Attempts by two patrons in 1767 to strengthen their influence in the borough caused an immediate reaction. The independent burgesses ran their own candidate in 1768 who, amidst ugly popular tumult, topped the poll. The return was voided on petition because of the disturbances. At the by-election the independent candidates stood on the principle of inhabitant householder franchise (the original franchise, down to Commons decisions of 1699 and 1715 in favour of a restricted, burgage, franchise). A succession of contests and petitions was finally resolved in 1783 when a Commons committee affirmed the wider franchise.[146]

Electoral independence in the burgage boroughs, then, was not simply a matter of rhetoric. It constituted a potent and volatile political reaction against neglect and indifference. The classic case is that of Malton in 1807. Rockingham had always been careful to treat the borough gently but his successor, Fitzwilliam, was less scrupulous. He took the loyalty of the town for granted and failed to consult with its leading citizens. Signs of unrest were discernible, but Fitzwilliam was concerned only with the great Yorkshire county contest of 1807. In that year rival candidates emerged at Malton and Fitzwilliam lost a seat. Only after herculean (and quite uncharacteristically ruthless) machinations was the seat recaptured at a by-election in 1808.[147] Independence in Yorkshire next surfaced in the unlikely borough of Boroughbridge, last contested in 1715. The failure of the fourth Duke of Newcastle to countenance the aspirations of the Lawson family led to a contest in 1818 and the loss of a seat.[148]

---

[145] J. A. Cannon, 'The Parliamentary Representation of the Boroughs of Chippenham, Knicklade, Dawnton, Hindon, Westbury and Wooton Basset, 1754–1790', Ph.D. (Bristol, 1958), 29–41.

[146] C. Bradley, 'Parliamentary Representation', MA, 44, 47, 54, 68, 83.

[147] See E. A. Smith, 'Earl Fitzwilliam'. For ambiguities about the definition of the Malton franchise see Namier and Brooke, *House of Commons*, i. 436, Thorne, *House of Commons*, ii. 452.

[148] See the lengthy account of Marmaduke Lawson's speech in Sir Thomas Lawson-Tancred, *Records of a Yorkshire Manor* (Aldborough, 1937), 320–33. A speech of this length and complexity to 65 electors should be essential reading for those who doubt that 'issues' mattered at elections in this period and who question the capacity of electors (especially in burgage boroughs) to comprehend serious issues, national as well as local.

As we might expect, independence movements in the 37 scot and lot, 12 householder, and 6 freeholder boroughs were more conspicuous. They may be found in about half of these constituencies, although we must be careful to distinguish the occasional band of venal voters from an independence movement.

As we have already noticed, such movements may be found in the smaller as well as in the larger boroughs. In the tiny Cornish scot and lot constituencies of Fowey, Penryn, and St Ives, independent sentiment was certainly a factor in promoting a number of contests in the early nineteenth century.[149] At Eye the Cornwallis family had had trouble since at least the 1770s. The voters were touchy, they resented strangers representing the town, and usually had to be very carefully coaxed. A contest nearly occurred in 1790, and the family tried to strengthen its interest by purchasing more property. This did not stop the contest of 1802. In 1811 the town was in revolt, Cornwallis's tenants meeting 'for the purpose of applying to him on the increased rent of land and thythes'. By 1820 the corporation had refused to support the family's nominees. Within three years the Cornwallis interest in this independent-minded borough had been sold.[150]

There were other small boroughs which could be awkward. Seaford was for much of the eighteenth century a fairly safe government borough, but there was a section of the electorate which did not accept this status, which was prepared to support strangers and in so doing to enable themselves and the town to benefit from a school and free medicine.[151] Something similar happened at Stamford in 1809 when a rich London merchant, Joshua Oddy, contested the borough on an independence ticket, promising to consult the interests of the town by cutting a canal from Stamford to the industrial heartland of the Midlands, thus making the town an entrepôt between the agricultural fenlands and the industrial midlands. Oddy deplored the local landlords and the economic stranglehold they had over the town. Losing by a 2 : 1 ratio in 1809, the independent party nevertheless proceeded to establish an interest in Stanford elections. They built houses, opened a newspaper, and kept up a stream of vitriolic criticism of the corporation's administration of charities. Contests were forced

---

[149] Comber, 'The Cornish Boroughs', MA, pp. 83, 90, 109, 119. St Ives was contested at every general election between 1806 and 1830, Penryn at every election between 1802 and 1831, and Fowey in 1818 and 1826. On St Ives, see also Thorne, *House of Commons*, ii. 77–8.

[150] Childs, 'Politics and Elections in Suffolk Boroughs', M.Phil., 300–17.

[151] Namier and Brooke, *House of Commons*, i. 24–5; Thorne, *House of Commons*, ii. 475–80.

in 1812 and 1818, but continued failure ultimately demoralized the independents.[152]

In some of the slightly larger, and perhaps more open, boroughs of this type independence was more regularly and consistently expressed. Dorchester was fairly frequently contested until 1806. Its 400–500 voters, together with the absence of a powerful patron, allowed the independent voice be heard.[153] Perhaps surprisingly, there was a discernible tradition of independency at the royal borough of New Windsor which surfaced with some regularity. In 1780 the king had to canvass personally to suppress it. In 1794 it forced another contest, yet others in 1802 and 1804 until in 1810 the independents forced the crown to divide the borough.[154] At Chichester the independents took both seats in 1790. Thereafter, as Oldfield puts it, the Duke of Richmond was allowed one seat for the sake of the peace of the town.[155] At Aylesbury the Association Movement of 1780 revealed the existence of a considerable body of opinion independent of that of the great landowners. Formed from among the leading tradesmen and lawyers of the town, most of whom had supported Wilkes in 1768, the independents rose to popularity alleging that the Grenville interest had neglected the town and treated it with scant respect. A mixture of venality and independent sentiment stimulated 60–70 electors to invite a third candidate in 1802. Their candidate was elected successfully, but was unseated on a petition in 1804. An Act of that year more than doubled the electorate to 1,000 and enfranchised voters amenable to landed control. Immediately the family interests of Buckingham and Portland were restored. Only thus could Aylesbury's independence be contained.[156] The poll books represent the King's Lynn contests of 1822, 1824, and 1826 as independence crusades. Likewise the Newcastle-under-Lyme poll books in 1812 and 1815. Indeed, that for 1812 celebrates the election as the first victory for 'the independent interest' in a century. Weymouth

---

[152] J. Lee, 'Stamford and the Cecils', B. Litt. (Oxford, 1957), 100–15. These conflicts were, however, the foundation for further divisions over reform in 1830 and 1831 (ibid. 133–64). Other small boroughs of this type which exhibit patterns of independent politics include Abingdon, Arundel, Bridgwater, Bridport, Ilchester, New Shoreham, Wallingford, and Wootton Bassett.

[153] Namier and Brooke, *House of Commons*, i. 265–6.

[154] Ibid. 10–11, 265–6. The New Windsor Poll Books of 1794, 1802, and 1804 contain independent addresses and speeches. See also A. Aspinall (ed.), *The Later Correspondence of George III* (Cambridge, 1962) no. 1496; Thorne, *House of Commons*, ii. 12–13.

[155] Oldfield, *History of the Boroughs* ii. 145–6; Thorne, *House of Commons*, ii. 392–3.

[156] On Aylesbury see R. W. Davis, *Political Change and Continuity, 1760–1885: A Buckinghamshire Study* (Newton Abbot, 1972), chs. 1–2. As early as 1763, John Wilkes had written to his agent, asking him to 'engage every independent you can to dine at the White Hart with me on the election day' (R. Gibbs, *A History of Aylesbury* (Aylesbury, 1885), 222); see Thorne, *House of Commons*, ii. 20–2.

and Melcombe Regis was regularly contested after 1790. As government influence declined, an independent party provoked regular contests which caused much interest in the newspapers because the local independents were in alliance with local patrons *against* the government.[157] Finally a continuous undercurrent of independence may be detected at Lewes, directed from the mid-eighteenth century against the influence of the Pelham family, and, after its overthrow in 1806, against any influence whatever.[158]

In other constituencies of this franchisal type religion was a catalytic factor in perpetuating popular independency. The Warwick Dissenters were the backbone of the independent party which in 1780 revolted against the Earl of Warwick's domination of the town. By 1784 he had lost both seats. The campaign for the Repeal of the Test and Corporation Acts in the late 1780s, however, provoked an Anglican reaction which was consolidated by the loyalist sentiment of the 1790s. This re-establishment of the Warwick interest once more balanced the politics of the borough, even though the two sides were able to resolve their differences with only one contested election, a by-election in 1826. (Warwick is, in fact, an excellent lesson for those who would deduce anything about the electoral politics of a borough from the simple statistics of contested elections.)[159] At Abingdon, the existence of a powerful Dissenting party was a feature of the regular contested elections between 1768 and 1780 and from 1802 to 1807.[160] A similar pattern may be found at Taunton, where a Dissent-led independent party confronted an Anglican corporation.[161]

In some of the largest constituencies of this variety, quite sophisticated patterns of independency could be exhibited. The election of 1754 was the last one in which the old party labels of 'Whig' and 'Tory' were used at Reading. Thereafter the essential cleavage in Reading politics was that between the corporation and the middle-class, independent traders of the town. There is some evidence that, in spite of much evidence of venality, the independents prized the ideal of purity of elections. Francis Annesley, who represented the town from 1774 to 1806, was several times elected without

[157] See e.g. *Morning Chronicle*, 20 and 31 Oct., 1812, 22 June 1818. There is an excellent account of this borough in Thorne, *House of Commons*, ii. 140–7.

[158] See, for example, W. B. Mills, *Parliamentary History of the Borough of Lewes 1795–1885* (London, 1908), 33–5. Mills treats the history of Lewes in the late 18th cent. and early 19th cent. as a conflict between oligarchy and independence, stressing the victory of the independent electors in 1802 and 1812.

[159] *VCH Warwickshire*, viii. 500–3; T. Lloyd, 'Dr Wade and the Working Class', *Midland Hist.* 2 (1974), 64–9.

[160] Oldfield, *History of the Boroughs*, i. 177; Thorne, *House of Commons*, ii. 10.

[161] Namier and Brooke, *House of Commons*, i. 371–2.

expense.[162] Even in a place like Newark independence could thrive. Oppositions were endemic in the early nineteenth century. A writer in 1812 protested against 'certain nobles and their pliant, upstart agents, who are Whigs or Tories as suit their sordid purposes'. In 1829, when Catholic Emancipation was rhetorically screamed at the hustings, the real issue remained the independence of the borough and the real enemy the fourth Duke of Newcastle. The essential axis of electoral politics in Newark down to 1831 was the conflict between aristocratic power and popular independence.[163] Finally, popular independence thrived for a time in the largest borough constituencies of them all. In Westminster and Southwark large numbers of independent electors resented aristocratic or government domination of electoral life; especially in the former, a powerfully independent repudiation of the politics of oligarchy dominated elections in the mid-eighteenth century. Both, however, were caught up in the development of electoral radicalism in the later eighteenth century, a process of transference to which we shall shortly turn.[164]

In the 92 freeman boroughs, independence movements were still more in evidence. In some of the smaller ones—Liskeard is an excellent example—electoral independence could be little more than a somewhat futile and resentful gesture against the closing up of the borough.[165] In others, the rhetoric of independence was little more than a justification for a venal candidature. Berwick-in-Tweed is a case in point, where the venality of 600 electors together with the absence of a dominant patron proved an ideal breeding ground for 'third party' candidatures. In 1785, for example, an Independent Club was established in opposition to the Patriotic Club of the Delaval interest. It successfully promoted the candidature of Sir Gilbert Eliot in 1786. Thereafter there is no trace of it.[166] Such independent clubs were quite

[162] Bailly, 'Parliamentary History of Reading', 36–41, 45, 48, 59, 89–90, 96, 143–5, 243. Aspinall's comment that Reading elections were not concerned with issues before 1807 (*Reading Through Seven Centuries*, 1962, 88) is nonsensical. The American War, for example, was much discussed in 1780 and in 1782.

[163] A letter from 'Moderator' in 1790 offered a damning critique of Newcastle's attempt to suppress the independence of the town. He argued that rank and property must have influence, but should not have absolute predominance (*A Complete Collection of Papers* (1790), 54); see Moses, 'Elections in Nottinghamshire', Ph.D., 283–307.

[164] On Westminster see N. Rogers, 'Aristocratic Clientage, Trade and Independency: Popular Politics in Pre-Radical Westminster', *Past and Present*, 61 (1973), 70–106.

[165] Comber, 'The Cornish Boroughs', MA, 60. The only freeman boroughs in which I *cannot* detect distinct evidence of electoral independence are: Aldeburgh, Bewdley, Bossiney, Camelford, Castle Rising, Chipping, Wycombe, Dartmouth, Grampound, East Looe, Higham Ferrers, Lymington, New Woodstock, Orford, St Mawes, West Looe, Winchelsea.

[166] There is, however, evidence of a plan to persuade a 'third man' to contest Berwick in 1811–12. See J. Gardiner to S. Whitbread, 11 January 1811, W1–1890, Whitbread MSS, Beds. RO. See also Thorne *House of Commons*, ii. 307–10.

common and, on occasion, organized on a sophisticated basis. At Shrewsbury an anti-corporation 'Club of Independents' included by early 1768 over 70 of the 300 voters. Its purpose, however, was less to enhance the cause of Shrewsbury independence than to promote the welfare of these indigent voters. They contributed to a fund for mutual relief but advertised their willingness to give both their votes to any candidate who contributed £500 to the fund.[167]

More commonly, electoral independence was the objective of those who fought a campaign against the oligarchical tendencies of a particular family or individual. Such campaigns could not always be sustained indefinitely. Independence at Cambridge was spawned on Dissent and the American issue. In 1774 it took 40% of the vote. By 1790 it was dead, crushed by the Rutland interest and the organizing genius of John Mortlock.[168] Independents at Morpeth had little more success. In the 1760s the agents of the Earl of Carlisle began to interfere with the ownership of common lands and to admit freemen not elected by the seven guilds of the borough. Led by Francis Eyre, the cause of Morpeth independence triumphed at the general election of 1768 when the cry of 'Eyre and Liberty' was on the lips of the townsmen. The politics of oligarchy were nothing if not resilient. A mixture of bribery, intimidation, patronage, and persuasion wore down the voters. In 1774 the seat was won back, and the cause of independence at Morpeth was destroyed.[169] In other freeman constituencies, the cause of independence had a longer life, even if it did not always determine the content of politics. The folk-memories of electors could be very long. The great revolts of the independents against the Stanhope interest at Derby in the 1740s were still remembered 30 years later.[170] At Grimsby the cause of electoral independence was often to the fore.

---

[167] Namier and Brooke, *House of Commons*, i. 364. Other freeman boroughs exhibiting venal patterns of independency include Hedon, Queenborough, and Stafford. See Thorne, *House of Commons*, ii. 213, 218–19, 363–4.

[168] D. Cook, 'The Representative History of the County, Town and University of Cambridge, 1689–1832', Ph.D. (Cambridge, 1935), 141–84. Mortlock saw that the key to the representation was to reduce the number of eligible freemen and to make them absolutely dependent upon him.

[169] Fewster, 'Politics and Administration of Morpeth', Ph.D., 82–203, 351–404. Other freeman boroughs in which independence was directed against patronal oligarchy include Ludlow and Monmouth. See Thorne, *House of Commons*, ii. 336, 284, 361.

[170] 'A List of the Honorary Burgesses', 7 Sept. 1776, Derby Pub. Lib. There is another nice example at Wigan, when even the *descendants* of the independents of the 1760s and 1770s were praised for the restoration of the borough's 'Rights and Liberties' and for rescuing the town from the enslavement of the Portland–Bridgeman interest; see Broadsheet Collection, MMP25, 675, *To the Free and Independent Burgesses of Wigan* (1820), Wigan Pub. Lib.

The election of 1820 there was described as the culmination of a 30-year struggle 'for the independent exercise of the Elective franchise'.[171]

In perhaps 20 of the larger freeman boroughs, however, elections turned on the conflict between the corporation and its patron(s), on the one hand, and the permanent, standing opposition group, the independents, on the other.[172] The case of Norwich may be taken as fairly typical. The old parties were effectively dead in the 1740s. By then the corporation had ceased its supervisory functions over the economy and began to play a primarily political role. Norwich politics revolved primarily, though not exclusively, around a corporation/anti-corporation axis, until the emergence of national issues and parliamentary alignments as factors in Norwich politics in the 1780s.[173]

Independents opposed both patrons and corporations. The Chester historian, Hemingway, writing in 1831 looked back over a century and wrote:[174]

Although upon every struggle between the two parties, the interest of the corporation in civic, and that of the house of Eaton in parliamentary elections, were constantly predominant, there was still a considerable portion of freemen remaining, who were decidedly opposed to both. The two grounds of opposition were now broad and definite. The first was, the pertinacious obstinacy of the corporate body in continuing to elect their own officers by the select body alone, in opposition to what they believed to be the direct meaning of the charter; and the second, the monopoly of the representation by the Eaton family, which had then uninterruptedly prevailed for the space of nearly three score years, in violation, as was contended, of the freedom of election. These have also been the occasion of our late political struggles;

---

[171] Collection of the Addresses (Great Grimsby, 1820). The independent supporter, Theophilus Levett, observed of the aristocratic dominance of the borough of Lichfield: 'I lament it for the independence of Lichfield and I lament it for the constitution of England' (Theophilus Levett to the Independent Electors of Lichfield, June 1826, D661/19/1/4, Dyott MSS, Staffs. RO).

[172] Namier and Brooke (*House of Commons*, list eight such constituencies (Colchester, Coventry, Exeter, Leicester, Liverpool, Norwich, Nottingham, and Worcester). I cannot understand why Carlisle, Chester, Newcastle-upon-Tyne, and Lancaster were omitted. Furthermore, resistance to the Duke of Marlborough at Oxford and the Whitmores at Bridgnorth surely qualifies these two boroughs. There is also evidence of powerful independent activity at Bedford, where an Independent Club existed at least between 1795 and 1809 (L30/11/132/58, 202/30–31, Beds. RO.) It also surfaced again in the great anti-Russell revolt of 1830 which succeeded by one vote in defeating Lord John Russell.

[173] D. S. O'Sullivan, 'Politics in Norwich, 1701–1835', MA (East Anglia, 1975), 10, 90, 105–10.

[174] J. Hemingway, *History of the City of Chester*, 2 vols. (Chester, 1831), ii. 400–1. An astonishingly constant proportion of the Chester voters were prepared to give the independents at least one vote: 1747, 45.2%; 1784, 43.5%; 1812, 47.6%; 1818, 40.5%; 1820, 48.3%; 1826, 46.4%; and 1830, 38.2%.

with this difference, that in the times I have been speaking of, the head of the house of Eaton sustained the character of a country gentleman, but has since been elevated to the peerage; a circumstance, which, as it provided him a seat in the higher house of parliament, rendered his influence in the return of members more unpopular, as held in contravention of a great constitutional principle.

That was it in a nutshell. It did not much appear to matter whether the principal interest in a town earlier in the century had been a Tory family (the Grosvenors at Chester, the Blacketts at Newcastle-upon-Tyne, for example) or a Tory corporation (the Exeter and Leicester corporations were High Tory). Nor did it matter whether a powerful Whig corporation (as at Coventry and Liverpool) or Whig family (as at Nottingham) tended to dominate. The old party alignments dissolved into the conflict between oligarchy and independence in the middle of the eighteenth century. Such alignments could be sharpened by religious tension (as at Exeter, Leicester, Liverpool, Norwich, and Worcester) or by popular distaste of a ruthless, and often declining, corporation (as particularly at Coventry, but also at Carlisle, Durham, and Lancaster). These independence parties were much more successful than in the smaller freeman boroughs. In some they regularly gained seats. In Liverpool, for example, they controlled one seat after 1761 and after 1774 controlled both. At Coventry, the power of the Corporation was in steady decline after 1768. In most of them, indeed, independents enjoyed considerable success.

This state of affairs can hardly be said to have existed in the counties. Contests were infrequent, and problems of communication weakened county sentiment. Independence, furthermore, could be taken to mean the freedom of the gentry to share in the spoils of county government. A friend of the Duke of Manchester warned him about his control of Huntingdonshire in 1796. People were prepared to concede

all the lead to which it can be reasonably thought your Rank, your Property, and the ancient establishment of your Families in the County may give you a Title. But when you form an alliance and act upon a System which has no object but the absolute exclusion of every other Family . . . from the representation of the County forever, and the Jealousy naturally resulting from such a System if pushed to the length of endeavouring to exclude them also . . . from all share in the public business, and from all the consideration, and attention which is due to their situation as Freeholders and principal Gentlemen in the County, then gentlemen must speak out.[175]

To do so it was occasionally necessary to confront the wealth and power of aristocratic houses with common purpose and unity.

[175] Lord Carysfort to Duke of Manchester, 23 May 1796, 8/118, Hinchingbrooke MSS, Hunts. RO.

Independent associations of the gentry become quite common in the early nineteenth century. The Constitutional Club of Hampshire and the County Club of Devon rallied the gentry of their respective counties.[176] Most famous of all, however, was the Independent Club of Buckinghamshire, which even influenced independent groups in the boroughs of that county.[177]

In all this, of course, the electorate would be exhorted to look to the freedom of the county; such rhetoric no doubt encouraged the electors to look to their own independence. Radical writers like Oldfield almost always present county elections as a struggle between an aristocratic oligarchy and independent electors, even where election contests were rare. There seems to have been a genuine, if latent, resentment against aristocratic control. It flared up sensationally in 1831. Counties which had rarely been contested suddenly witnessed something resembling the class war. In sleepy Shropshire, last contested in 1722, a nervous lady noticed: 'There is no doubt but a strong undercurrent is opposed to the aristocracy in this county as well as others.'[178] Such an undercurrent had, in fact, been sedulously fostered ever since the days of Walpole. A triumphant candidate in Cumberland in 1831 told the voters: 'You have taught the aristocracy that their power is as nothing when put in the balance with your will; that their money is valueless in your eyes and can avail them nothing.'[179]

The best statement of the principles of county independence known to me occurred at the Wiltshire election of 1818. The five resolutions voted at an independent meeting say it all:

*First*, That independence of election consists in every freeholder exercising his right of voting in the choice of a representative in parliament, unawed by rank and power, and uninfluenced by hope of reward, or fear of injury.— *Second*, That the freeholder's suffrage is his own property; and that those who aim, by *intimidation* of any sort, to deprive him of it, or resent his using it according to his own will, commit a great crime against society, are enemies to the constitution, and to the independence of the county, and forfeit all claim to respect from their neighbours and dependants.—*Third*, That it is the right of every man to express his opinion, with freedom and candour,

---

[176] *Morning Chronicle*, 30 June 1818.

[177] Davis, *Political Change and Continuity*, 40 ff. Independent Clubs were, or course, fairly common in the boroughs, especially the larger boroughs. At Oxford, for example, the Blues was the name of an organized Independent Club, consisting of over 400 persons, which met regularly between as well as during elections after 1807. It rallied independent supporters and exercised vigilance over the town's Members. See, for example, *Oxford Journal*, 19 May 1807; and The Diary of Alderman Fletcher, 14 May 1808, 4 and 14 May 1809, C. A. Oxon d. 247, Hughes Hughes MSS, Bodleian Lib.

[178] Mrs Hill to Mrs Kenyon, n.d. 1831, 811/51-2, Hill MSS, Shropshire RO.

[179] *Cumberland Poll Book*, p. lvii.

of the principles, the character, and conduct of every candidate for a seat in Parliament; and, beyond that, we, in our several situations, will use no influence to induce any voter, who may be connected with, or dependent upon us, to prefer one candidate to another.—*Fourth*, That the enormous expense attending contests for the representation of counties, prevents many men of independent minds, who are not trading politicians, from becoming candidates, and not unfrequently leaves the freeholders no choice, or a very bad one; and that it is from the dread of expense alone, and not from a love of independence, nor a want of will to serve their country, that many gentlemen, eminently qualified by fortune and talent to represent us in Parliament, remain in privacy.—*Fifth*, That we will use our influence with, and endeavour to prevail on, freeholders, who are in suitable circumstances, to attend the election at their own expense, considering it a disgrace for such persons to be carried and fed by others; and that we will, in all other respects, endeavour to keep down the expenses of the contest, with a view to induce other gentlemen to come forward on future occasions, as well as to serve those who have declared themselves Candidates on the present.[180]

Independent candidates and parties were very fond indeed of advertising their independent principles in this way. Enormous meetings, punctuated by rituals as well as speeches, by colours, parades, processions, music, songs, even fireworks and gunfire, passed strings of resolutions like those at Wiltshire.[181] There was, in short, some harmony of interest between the gentry, wishing to defend their own interests from aristocratic encroachment and to preserve their influence over the county representation, and the freeholders, wishing to protect both the disposal of their votes, especially their second vote, and their traditional electoral privileges. The infrequency of contested elections, however, often reduced the independence of the freeholders to the level of election rhetoric. It undoubtedly struck a chord, but it did not determine the structure of county politics.

In Wales, the ideal of electoral independence made a late but extremely significant appearance in the early nineteenth century. There were some serious rumbles of discontent which unsettled, but failed to topple, the ascendancy of the Marquis of Bute over the Glamorgan boroughs in 1820.[182] At Monmouth in 1818 there was very nearly a contest to challenge the Beaufort's claim to appoint municipal officers

---

[180] *Survey of Wiltshire during the Election* (Trowbridge, 1818), 183. A comparison of the literature at this election with that produced at the by-election of 1772 concludes that 'the line taken by the champion of independence was much the same' (*VCH Wiltshire*, v. 206).

[181] See e.g. the *Address to the Freeholders of the County of Huntingdon*, 25 Aug. 1812, printed in Jupp, *British and Irish Elections*, 31–5. For details of Brougham's great meetings in Westmorland in 1818 see C. New, *The Life of Henry Brougham to 1830* (Oxford, 1961), 187.

[182] I. W. David, 'Political and Electioneering Activity in South East Wales, 1820–1852', MA (Wales, 1959), 23–5.

and to introduce new burgesses. The Court of King's Bench upheld the burgesses' claim, a decision which in effect was reversed when Beaufort defeated the burgesses at the contested election of 1820.[183] There was also a lot of talk and literature at Newport in 1820 about the local offices the Beauforts obtained out of the system, and a good deal of glorification of the independent burgesses.[184] A protracted struggle at Cardiff between 1817 and 1825 began as a dispute within the corporation but became an unsuccessful attack on the alignment between the Marquis of Bute and the corporation which controlled the borough.[185] On other occasions it required the admixture of a galvanizing issue. Gathering resentment at the domination of the Flint county and borough seats by the Mostyn family had simmered ineffectually for over a decade when in 1807 the issue of Catholic Emancipation caused the defeat of its candidate.[186] The old tranquillity in Welsh electoral affairs was clearly coming to an end in the closing decades of the unreformed system.

How successful were independents in attaining their objectives? At one level, that of reinstating the old charters which embodied a wider franchise, they had little success. The great victory of the independents at Pontefract in 1783, when the burgage franchise gave way to one comprising inhabitant householders was exceptional. Two other victories appear, on closer inspection, to owe little directly to independent forces. The new charter secured at Maldon in 1810, which increased the electorate from 150 to 1,500, owed less to popular clamour than to patronal manœuvering. Similarly, the victorious petition which followed the Preston election of 1768, and which established the franchise there in the inhabitant householders rather than in the freemen alone, was the product of patronal hostility to the Preston corporation. On the whole, the bulwarks of electoral oligarchy remained firmly in place down to 1832. Nevertheless, this more general failure should not conceal the success which increasingly came to accompany their attempts to win seats. Every general election threw up a number of examples of independent parties toppling established interests.[187] Between 1790 and 1820, according to an

[183] Ibid. 29–31.

[184] D. A. Wager, 'Welsh Politics and Parliamentary Reform, 1780–1835', Ph.D. (Wales, 1972), 225–6.

[185] Ibid. 124–7.

[186] R. Rees, 'The Parliamentary Representation of South Wales 1790–1830', Ph.D, 2 vols. (Reading, 1962), i. 224–5.

[187] At the general election of 1802, for example, this was the main issue at Bishop's Castle, Callington, Chippenham, East Grinstead, Eye, Harwich, Hedon, Hythe, Lisheard, Morpeth, New Woodstock, Plympton Earle, and Scarborough. Only in five—Chippenham, Harwich, Hedon, Hythe, and Morpeth—were the independents successful. There was also significant

authoritative assessment, independents made ground in 31 constituencies, made fleeting progress in 9 others, while in at least 30 others the issue of electoral independence was brought to the forefront.[188] The extent to which electoral patrons were being forced on to the defensive by the power of electoral independence in the closing decades of the unreformed period should not be underestimated.

It remained, however, extremely difficult for independents to enjoy complete and total electoral victory. Indeed, the very idea of a permanent victory for the forces of electoral independence is something of a contradiction in terms. They were essentially outsiders in a world of oligarchy. They lacked the contacts, the experience, and the political confidence to consolidate their victories. They lacked the same access to office, patronage, and preferment as other candidates. In most places they failed to build a permanent basis for independent success. Lack of money was a constant source of difficulty. The failure of the independent assault on Gloucestershire in 1811 was deplored by one enthusiast: 'Never was a more glorious cause sacrificed from want of the means to carry it through with effect.' It was the simple things that stung him: 'I am fully persuaded that had any two or three other towns in the County followed the example of the Towns of Stroud and Cheltenham, in raising a fund to convey their Freeholders to Gloucester, we should have had a great majority of votes.' In the end, the moral was clear: 'You must combat the enemy with his own weapons: MONEY.'[189]

Constant failure, lack of resources, hopelessness, political reluctance to fight bred by social deference, and a lack of organizational acumen frequently inhibited the success of independent candidates.

---

independent activity at Abingdon, Penryn, and Wells. For 1818 a similar list would include Aylesbury, Bishop's Castle, Cambridge, Chester, Evesham, Exeter, Fowey, Gloucester, Liverpool, Ilchester, Oxford, Petersfield, Westmorland, and Wooton Bassett. See Thorne, *House of Commons*, i. 163–4, 257–8, 260–2.

[188] Between 1790 and 1820 independents made ground at Great Yarmouth, Guildford, Maldon, Rochester, and Sandwich (1790); Carlisle, Chipping Wycombe, Evesham, New Shoreham, Oxford, and Windsor (1796); Sudbury (1799); Bath (1801); Berwick-upon-Tweed, Beverley, Boston, Chippenham, Grantham, Grimsby, Morpeth, and Warwick (1802); Wallingford (1804); Lewes, Shrewsbury, and Southampton (1806); Chester, St Albans (1807); East Retford, Seaford (1812); Devizes, Weymouth and Melcombe Regis (1818).

The nine constituencies where independents gained fleeting success were Queenborough (1802); Okehampton (1807 and 1812); Abingdon (1809); Chichester, Wooton Bassett (1812); Newcastle-under-Lyme, Tewkesbury, and Totnes (1812 and 1818); and Bishops Castle (1819). Electoral independence was the main issue normally at Abingdon, Barnstaple, Canterbury, Colchester, Coventry, Exeter, Hedon, Hereford, Honiton, Hull, Hythe, Ilchester, Ipswich, Leominster, Lincoln, Liverpool, London, Maidstone, Newcastle-upon-Tyne, Norwich, Nottingham, Pontefract, Poole, Reading, Southwark, Stafford, Taunton, Westminster, Worcester, and York. Ibid. 54, 56.

[189] To the Independent Gentlemen, Clergy and Freeholders of the County of Gloucester, Robert Hughes (Cheltenham), 21 May 1811, D24S/V11/2, Glos. RO.

Nevertheless, they preserved political debate. They continued to mobilize public opinion at the local level, however spasmodically, thus enabling successive assaults on local oligarchies. Although their mentality was traditional they exploited conventional mechanisms of opinion in a lively manner. They used not only the press but also petitions, addresses, and public meetings. If they lost the battle against oligarchy, they never tired of taking their stand against it.

At times it must have appeared quite hopeless. At Minehead, for example, the Luttrell interest went almost unchallenged between 1768 and 1796. Casual neglect, however, provoked contests in 1796 and 1802. In 1796 the Independents gained both seats; in 1802 they lost them. They lacked the patronage and the funds with which to establish a permanent interest. They lacked the access to the law, to the network of contacts, promotions, and offices upon which a healthy interest so much depended. Extravagant propaganda, public meetings, and ominous threats were no substitute for the promise of stability in local affairs.[190]

It is less the inability of independents to establish a permanent regime which needs emphasis, however, than the centrality of independence to constituency politics in the unreformed electoral system. Oligarchy bred independence. Thousands of electors in the eighteenth century embraced independent ideals; thousands of others by their votes repudiated them and adopted the values of oligarchy. Down to the end of the eighteenth century, the conflict between the two was the basis of electoral politics. Independence was a check upon oligarchy and a safety value of opposition to it. The downward diffusion of the values of both bred an intense concern for the local community which was permanent in that it was hereditary. A self-perpetuating cycle of electoral conflict rescued the unreformed electoral system from abject submission to oligarchical control.

There is, moreover, a further layer of explanation for the inability of independents to unsettle the established power of electoral oligarchy. They lacked economic clout. There was a limit to the political capital that could be harvested out of the resentments of the freeholders of the counties against the aristocratic princes of the Hanoverian regime. Similarly, it was only in exceptional circumstances that the hostility of certain sections of the craftsmen within the electorate could seriously threaten the control of established interests. Independent voters were small producers, economically independent, struggling to survive within and to co-exist with the economic, as well as social, monopoly of large landed proprietors and corporations. Their occupational status may

[190] Box 111, 1/60/16–18. DD/L. Dunster Castle MSS. Som. RO.

TABLE 5.1. *Occupational Structure of Independent Voters and the Electorate as a Whole in Five Constituencies, 1774–1831 (%)*

| | 1 | | 2 | | 3 | | 4 | | 5 | | 6 | |
|---|---|---|---|---|---|---|---|---|---|---|---|---|
| | Ind. | Tot. | Ind. | Tot. | Ind. | Tot. | Ind. | Tot. | Ind. | Tot. | Ind. | Tot. |
| CHESTER | | | | | | | | | | | | |
| 1812 | 9 | 11 | 4 | 5 | 28 | 26 | 56 | 53 | 3 | 3 | 0 | 2 |
| 1818 | 6 | 9 | 5 | 5 | 27 | 25 | 59 | 56 | 2 | 4 | 1 | 1 |
| 1826 | 6 | 8 | 4 | 4 | 31 | 26 | 55 | 55 | 4 | 5 | 0 | 2 |
| COLCHESTER | | | | | | | | | | | | |
| 1790 | 9 | 9 | 4 | 4 | 14 | 14 | 48 | 46 | 21 | 21 | 4 | 6 |
| 1806 | 6 | 9 | 3 | 5 | 13 | 13 | 35 | 37 | 33 | 28 | 10 | 8 |
| 1807 | 8 | 9 | 3 | 3 | 11 | 12 | 34 | 34 | 34 | 31 | 10 | 11 |
| 1812 | 5 | 10 | 5 | 6 | 15 | 13 | 44 | 35 | 26 | 26 | 5 | 10 |
| 1818 | 6 | 10 | 3 | 3 | 18 | 15 | 46 | 43 | 25 | 25 | 2 | 4 |
| 1820 | 6 | 12 | 5 | 6 | 16 | 15 | 40 | 35 | 27 | 26 | 6 | 6 |
| ST ALBANS | | | | | | | | | | | | |
| 1820 | 12 | 13 | 5 | 4 | 21 | 19 | 31 | 29 | 26 | 33 | 5 | 2 |
| 1821 | 14 | 17 | 3 | 4 | 17 | 21 | 26 | 28 | 34 | 28 | 6 | 2 |
| 1831 | 10 | 14 | 4 | 4 | 25 | 23 | 33 | 30 | 25 | 26 | 3 | 3 |
| SHREWSBURY | | | | | | | | | | | | |
| 1806 | 23 | 16 | 5 | 4 | 23 | 26 | 40 | 43 | 7 | 8 | 2 | 3 |
| 1807 | 20 | 16 | 6 | 5 | 24 | 27 | 40 | 43 | 8 | 8 | 2 | 1 |
| 1812 | 5 | 9 | 4 | 3 | 20 | 22 | 60 | 54 | 11 | 11 | 0 | 1 |
| 1814 | 2 | 9 | 4 | 4 | 17 | 22 | 65 | 53 | 12 | 11 | 0 | 1 |
| 1819 | 21 | 13 | 6 | 6 | 18 | 24 | 46 | 46 | 9 | 10 | 0 | 1 |
| SOUTHAMPTON | | | | | | | | | | | | |
| 1774 | 33 | 32 | 2 | 2 | 18 | 20 | 30 | 30 | 15 | 14 | 2 | 2 |
| 1790 | 24 | 32 | 5 | 6 | 29 | 25 | 27 | 25 | 12 | 11 | 3 | 1 |
| 1794 | 18 | 31 | 7 | 6 | 29 | 25 | 35 | 26 | 9 | 11 | 2 | 1 |
| 1806 | 19 | 31 | 10 | 10 | 29 | 22 | 31 | 24 | 10 | 11 | 1 | 2 |

*Note*: Ind. = % of Independent vote; Tot. = % of electorate as a whole.

be perceived from Table 5.1, which summarizes the occupational structure of the independent vote in 21 contests in which independence was an issue in five of the six designated constituencies. Some general conclusions can be drawn from the data assembled in Table 5.1. On almost all occasions, category 1, the gentlemen and professional group, is underrepresented among the independents, sometimes by a large margin. Category 3, the retailers, is slightly over-represented, except at Shrewsbury. Although there is some variation in the pattern of support for independents among category 4, the craftsmen, they tend to be overrepresented, sometimes by a considerable amount. They are,

TABLE 5.2  *Occupational Structure of Independent Voters in Newcastle-under-Lyme, 1774–1815 (%)*

| | 1 | | 2 | | 3 | | 4 | | 5 | | 6 | |
|---|---|---|---|---|---|---|---|---|---|---|---|---|
| | Ind. | Tot. | Ind. | Tot. | Ind. | Tot. | Ind. | Tot. | Ind. | Tot. | Ind. | Tot. |
| 1774 | 0 | 3 | 1 | 2 | 10 | 17 | 79 | 66 | 10 | 12 | 0 | 0 |
| 1792 | 2 | 4 | 1 | 2 | 12 | 17 | 83 | 73 | 3 | 3 | 0 | 0 |
| 1793 | 2 | 4 | 1 | 3 | 14 | 16 | 81 | 73 | 3 | 3 | 0 | 0 |
| 1802 | 0 | 5 | 1 | 3 | 18 | 20 | 79 | 71 | 2 | 1 | 0 | 0 |
| 1812 | 1 | 2 | 3 | 4 | 9 | 10 | 86 | 81 | 2 | 2 | 0 | 0 |
| 1815 | 1 | 3 | 1 | 2 | 11 | 12 | 86 | 81 | 1 | 2 | 0 | 0 |

of course, the heart and soul of independence groups. It is at least arguable that the economic individualism of these men underpins the political fragmentation, and to some extent, therefore, the ineffectiveness, of independence movements.

The conflict between independence and oligarchy at the electoral level thus reflects economic and social circumstances. In particular, the position of small, independent producers in an economy increasingly dominated by techniques of mass production and by the purchasing power of great landed proprietors can clearly be seen to be at stake. Declining trades and crafts were a particularly good breeding ground for electoral independence. The textile trades of Chippenham in the early nineteenth century provided numerous recruits for the cause of electoral independence in the town. At Preston, the majority of independent electors were economically suffering weavers. Such men might enjoy the occasional victory—after all, they won a seat at Chippenham in 1807 and in Preston in 1826. But they usually lacked the resources and the expertise to destroy established interests. An analysis of the independent vote at Newcastle-under-Lyme over four decades gives more detailed indications of the dilemma facing independence movements. As Table 5.2 reveals, the occupational structure of the independent vote at Newcastle remained remarkably consistent. Such changes as there are, particularly the increasing representation of category 4, the craftsmen, reflect changes in the structure of the electorate itself, notably the numerical increase in the number of feltmakers. These journeymen hatters resisted attempts by the patron of the borough, the Marquis of Stafford, to restrict the growth of their trade, and consequently the vast majority of them consistently supported independent candidates.[191]

[191] Thorne, *House of Commons*, ii. 360–2.

This type of analysis of the occupational background of electoral independence is indirectly strengthened by the essence of Professor Brewer's discussion of the support enjoyed by John Wilkes. Brewer argues that the Wilkite middling orders were motivated by growing resentment against the aristocracy at their role in a client economy. Just when artisans, and to some extent retailers, were beginning to enjoy some financial independence (deriving, in part, from the greater availability of credit), they felt the enclosing power and restrictive power of the client economy: 'The club member's desire for freedom from economic clientage went, therefore, hand in hand with a desire for political independence.'[192] We must remember, however, that very many members of the middling orders did not resist the tentacles of economic clientage. Many individuals made a living out of it, obtained consistent profits from its operations, sought (and found) economic security and protection therein, and, as a result, identified with established interests while repudiating the beliefs and attitudes of electoral independence. The backbone of independence movements was the craftsmen sector of the electorate. At the same time, as Table 5.1 makes clear, over a fair spread of constituencies, probably more voters from the craftsmen group voted *against* independence candidates than voted for them. If this were not all—and it is worth stressing these matters in the endeavour to avoid caricature and stereotype— over one half of independent voters were drawn from categories *other than* the craftsmen.

In the end, electoral independence could not survive the twin threats of radicalism and national party. As a collection of localized responses to oligarchical tendencies in electoral politics, independence is of the greatest historical importance. In the absence of party polarities after the middle of the eighteenth century, electoral independence was the dominant form of local opposition to those oligarchical developments which threatened to engulf the electoral system. Even when parties revived in the later eighteenth century, many electors found the language of independence more familiar and more immediately attractive than the language of party. The anti-ministerial candidate at Poole in 1807, Joseph Garland, preferred to stand as an independent rather than as a Whig. He believed that with the end of the rivalry between Pitt and Fix the country needed to assert itself, an assertion which could best be accomplished through the cause of independency.[193] And when voters became sick of parties, they could

---

[192] John Brewer, 'Commercialization and Politics', in N. McKendrick (ed.), *The Birth of a Consumer Society* (London, 1982), ch. 5, esp. 232. See also below, pp. 245–59.

[193] D. F. Beamish, 'The Parliamentary and Municipal History of the Borough of Poole, *c*.1740–*c*.1840' (Southampton, 1982), 153–6.

be found receptive to the appeal of independence.[194] When they became sick of the unscrupulous and inconsistent actions of party men they could retreat into the familiar ideology of independency. Infuriated Tories, outraged at the passing of Catholic emancipation in 1829, may be found rallying round independent candidates at the general election of 1830.[195] Independence was certainly widespread and it may have done something to keep boroughs open and to weaken electoral patrons. Yet the Hanoverian oligarchy was still there in the early nineteenth century, and there was little or no sign of it seriously weakening. In 1831–2 it was to be the forces of electoral radicalism and national party which did so much to transform the electoral system, not electoral independence in isolation. Nevertheless, its ultimate disappearance from the historical stage was to be a slow and gradual affair. In some manifestations, electoral independence was still to be found in the electoral system which was established in 1832.[196]

### 'NATIONAL' ISSUES, 1760–1807

The capacity of electors in the eighteenth and early nineteenth centuries to mobilize around issues of parochial concern was matched by their growing sensitivity to issues with a 'national' or parliamentary reference. In a large number of constituencies (but a minority none the less), an exclusive preoccupation with issues concerning local oligarchy and electoral independence began to make room for the great issues of national and parliamentary politics. Local issues did not cease to be important. The range of politics was enlarging. In this process, three causal elements are of the greatest importance. The first of these is the role of the press. The second is the bureaucratization of electoral politics. The third is the phenomenon of petitioning.

---

[194] P. L. Humphreys, 'Kentish Politics and Public Opinion, 1768–1832', D.Phil. (Oxford, 1981), 244.

[195] G. B. Kent, 'Party Politics in the County of Staffordshire, 1830–1847', MA (Birmingham, 1959), ch. 8.

[196] Good old-fashioned contests between independents and oligarchs may be found after 1832 in the proprietory boroughs. There were still about a dozen seats after 1832 where contests were rare and patron control all but complete. But even in a number of larger boroughs (e.g. Peterborough, Stamford, and Ludlow), the axis of electoral conflict was between patron and independents. Upon this could be engrafted the conflict of parties. In Ludlow, for example, the patronal interest merged into the party interest when the Clives assumed responsibility for the formation of the local Conservative Association and for the establishment of a local Conservative newspaper. The same thing happened at Reigate and Dudley. At Totnes, however, the Liberals and Conservatives united to squeeze out the independents. For Totnes see Harold B. Raymond, 'English Political Parties and Electoral organization, 1832–67', Ph.D. (Harvard, 1952), 171–2.

On 31 August 1818 at a meeting in the White Hart Inn in Boston the independents of that town passed a series of resolutions. Two of these were as follows:[197]

UNANIMOUSLY RESOLVED,—That the Press is a most important aid to be employed in the furtherance of the general object; and it is recommended that every possible means be adopted in order to enlighten the minds of the Freeholders, to inform them of their Political Rights, the best means of obtaining the Restoration of them, and the consequent advantages resulting to themselves and their posterity.

UNANIMOUSLY RESOLVED,—That Copies of these Resolutions be forwarded to the Chairmen of the late Committees in the Independent Interest; and that they be advertised in the County Papers.

As a medium for the communication of election business the press was, of course, absolutely indispensable: it carried information, advertisements, opinions, letters, and, increasingly, versions of candidates' speeches. From an early date, election committees had come to understand how the press might be best used for electoral purposes. In Westmorland in 1818 over 200 copies of the London papers were circulated throughout the county because they reported Brougham's parliamentary speeches more extensively than the county weeklies. On the other side, the Lowthers reprinted articles from the *London Courier* in handbill form for distribution.[198] It is well-known that copies of newspapers were to be found in inns and taverns as well as in coffee-houses and libraries. The *Liverpool General Advertiser* of 9 June 1791 affirmed that 'without Newspapers, our coffee-houses, ale-houses and barbers' shops would undergo a change next to depopulation; and our country cottagers, the curate, the exciseman and the blacksmith would lose the self-satisfaction of being as wise as William Pitt'. They were carefully circulated among friends and families, they were kept for reference and information, and they were shared, discussed and valued. What is less well understood is the pattern of the circulation of newspapers. The following description of the exact circulation of newspapers among radicals at Tiverton at the end of the 1790s gives an added dimension to our understanding of these processes:[199]

Next are the weekly papers—*Bell's Messenger*, *Weekly Observer*, and *Recorder*—about which care is taken to get them here by the M. Coach on Tuesday—They go first to Mr. John Dickson, then to Mr. Dickenson, then to Parson Clarke and then they all go to the Phoenix Inn Tavern & Coffee

---

[197] 'The White Hart Inn, Boston, 31 Aug. 1818', handbill in the Lincs. RO.

[198] James Brougham to James Atkinson, 8 Mar. 1818, A.48, Brougham MSS, Univ. College, London; A. Aspinall, *Politics and the Press 1780–1850* (London, 1949), 360.

[199] Extracts from the Harrowby-Tiverton MSS, published in *Notes and Queries*, 170 (1936), *passim*.

House where there are several Clubs till the next Morning—Then the *Observer* goes to Caleb Adam's Ale House, next to Mr. Dickinson, a Taylor's shop, and is then sent into the Country to Sampford Peverell to turn the Minds of the Country Lads. On Wednesday *Bell's* goes to Mr. Acland, Mr. Collard, Hatter, Mr. Cosway, Currier, Mr. Fisher, Mr. Pitts, Staymaker, W. Wood, a Comber and some others to get among the Common people; this paper is much read and others are being subscribed for. *The Recorder* the 2nd day goes to Mr. Parish at a Boarding House, and afterwards to the young ladies at a School.

The *Cambridge Intelligencer*; published by Crab Flower at Cambridge on Saturday, finds its way here on Mondays and goes first to a Comber's Shop— then to a Huckster's and is then circulated among the Common People. Another of these Papers has been taken by Mr. Dennys at the Factory, and was taken by Mr. Follett and Lardner but now dropt. There are several of these papers sent into the Country and it winds much about Wiveliscombe.

The *General Evening Post*, sent to Mr. Thos. Wood and then into the Country at Morebath to Mr. Bere etc.

These appear to me to be the Jacobins' papers chiefly read hereabout;— next I have observed the progress of the Loyal and Orderly Papers to be as follows, first

*The Sun*—only comes here at the Coffee House at the Phoenix—and read no where else—and never shines among the Common people or in Sober families.

The London papers had a national circulation but even the smallest of the provincial papers had a considerable, even regional, circulation. The *Sherborne Mercury* of 5 July 1818 described the pattern of its circulation thus:

THE SHERBORNE MERCURY, contrary to the methods generally made use of, is chiefly distributed by men and horses hired on purpose, in a very regular, expeditious, and expensive manner. Besides the use made of postmen and the mails, thirty men, and more than twenty horses, are employed weekly in its circulation, in every direction, over four counties, extending from the town of Poole, the eastern extremity of Dorsetshire, to Penzance, the land's end, in Cornwall; both which places, as well as very many intermediate districts, are served by men sent for that purpose. The agents for vending it, and receiving advertisements and communications, resident in the towns, exceed eighty.

*The immediate circuit of the Mercury includes upwards of twenty* SEA-PORTS, *served by the newsmen, besides those to which it is forwarded by mails.*

By thus expending a large proportion of the produce of the paper in the means of making it truly respectable, the benefit of a singularly extensive circuit, and a great, constant, and general sale, are secured to advertisers; and the advertisements inserted therein can seldom fail of their proper effect. The public have, indeed, long been convinced of the advantage of advertising in this most established and extensive print, in preference to those which have a confined circuit, and consequently a small and uncertain distribution.

For electoral purposes, the function of such newspapers was to mitigate parochialism by placing election proceedings in a regional, and even a national, context. The wide circulation of provincial newspapers and the dominance of the London press effected these functions.[200] The widespread reprinting of parliamentary news in the London press ensured that a national political community existed even by the middle of the eighteenth century. By the end of the eighteenth century, over one dozen newspapers were being printed in London alone. In addition, evening and Sunday newspapers were in existence. In total, the number of stamps on sheets of newsprint rose from 9.5 million in 1760 to 12.5 million in 1775. By 1801 the number exceeded 16 million. Most large towns of any size had a newspaper before the end of the unreformed Parliament. In 1812 Liverpool had 5, and by the late 1820s an incredible 12.[201] Precise circulation figures for these newspapers are not of critical significance owing to the multiple use made of each copy and the widespread practice of reading aloud. Nevertheless, an edition of a newspaper would run from 500 to 3,000 copies. It is impossible to estimate the exact use made of each copy. It is reasonable to assume that members of a family might either read or hear all or part of the contents. Even so, press circulation usually reached 10–15% of the population of a town. The two Chester papers had a circulation of around 2,000 out of a population of 15,000 in the early nineteenth century. The five Liverpool papers in the same period had a circulation of 10,000 for a population of 78,000. In Newcastle-upon-Tyne in 1832 the three newspapers had a circulation of 6,300 out of a population of 40,000.[202] Long before the end of the unreformed period, newspapers had penetrated deep into the voting

---

[200] The geographical circulation of even the smallest provincial newspaper is impressive. Even a small and not particularly successful paper had an enormously wide circulation area. The *Cirencester Flying Post*, for example, circulated in Berkshire, Dorset, Glamorgan, Gloucestershire, Herefordshire, Monmouthshire, Northamptonshire, Oxfordshire, Radnorshire, Somerset, Warwickshire, Worcestershire, and Wiltshire; see J. Black, 'The *Cirencester Flying Post and Weekly Miscellany*', *Cirencester Arch. Hist. Soc.* 25 (1985), 6. For further details of the circulation of provincial newspapers see R. M. Wiles, *Freshest Advices: Early Provincial Newspapers in England* (Columbus, Ohio, 1965), 96 ff., 113–4.

[201] Estimates of press circulation are based upon I. R. Christie, 'British Newspapers in the Later Georgian Age'; in id. *Myth and Reality in Late Eighteenth century British Politics* (London, 1970); G. A. Cranfield, *The Press and Society: From Caxton to Northcliffe* (London, 1978), 93, 140; R. M. Wiles, 'Provincial Culture in Early Georgian England', in P. Fritz and D. Williams (eds.), *The Triumph of Culture* (Toronto, 1972), 50–1.

[202] Hemingway, *History of Chester*, ii. 223–4; B. Whittingham-Jones, 'Electioneering in Lancashire before the Secret Ballot: ii. Liverpool's Political Clubs 1812–1830', *Trans. Hist. Soc. Lancs and Cheshire*, 3 (1959–60) 117–38. Stoker, 'Elections and Voting Behaviour', Ph.D., 324.

classes and had come to occupy a vital position in local politics. No fewer than 244 separate provincial newspapers were founded in the eighteenth century alone, their total circulation rising from around 50,000 in 1700 to around 400,000 in 1800.

The century of the unreformed electorate is characterized by the acquisition of print culture by the middling orders as they came to establish themselves as a political nation not abjectly dependent for information and ideas upon the parliamentary classes. It is inconceivable that this development and its ideological consequences can have left no impact upon the electorate. The popularization of issues, the communication of political news, the growing facility of electoral organization, the propagation of grievances among the middling orders of craftsmen, retailers, artisans, and apprentices underpin the electoral life of the period, especially after the age of Wilkes and the American Revolution. Nevertheless, there is no reason to believe that the old oral culture suddenly disappeared. Belief in traditional electoral, political, and social values could prosper still in the age of the newspaper. The simplicity, sensationalism, and symbolism of the bulk of election literature appear to bear this out. Here, as elsewhere, there is accumulation, rather than replacement, of ideas and values. In the same way, the emergence of national political movements such as that for the abolition of the Slave Trade did not signify the imminent demise of parochial concerns. Interestingly, in the age of the Industrial Revolution, England still possessed a traditional and highly localized political culture.

Certainly in the larger constituencies, by the 1760s the newspapers were begining to reflect, and thus encourage, a vigorous local political life. This development was extended to almost all urban centres with a population of more than a few thousand, due to the successive impact of the Wilkes, American and radical issues and then, most of all, to the ideological impact of the French Revolution on British society. By the early nineteenth century the press had become the most powerful agency for the communication and agitation of such political issues and social concerns.

The press acted as a general agency of electoral mobilization. More specific in their operations were the activities of election clubs. These organizations performed a variety of functions, tending in two directions. They mobilized electors in the service of interests, groups, and parties. Yet, they could also mobilize electors in defence or furtherance of their own interests. Of the seven major clubs active in Liverpool in the early nineteenth century,[203] the Backbone Club and

---

[203] Whittingham-Jones, 'Electioneering in Lancashire'.

the Canning Club serviced the needs of Tory supporters, the Pitt Club and the True Blue Club mobilized support for corporation candidates, the Liverpool Freeman's Club and the Independent Debating Society and the Concentric Society rallied support to the Whig cause.[204] Most constituencies of a comparable size could provide a comparable list. Such clubs must have been fairly respectable in their clientele. Further down the social ladder, however, hosts of electoral societies and combinations existed. In the early nineteenth century Colchester had about 20 clubs, most of them meeting in inns and ale-houses, their proceedings largely unreported in the local press, sometimes spawning several additional branches in the town.[205] Many constituencies boasted examples of both types of club. Berwick-upon-Tweed with its electorate of 600, had a Patriotic Club which supported the Delaval interest and a Constitutional Club which supported the Lisburne interest, but it also had an Independent Club for unconnected and uncommitted electors.[206] Ipswich had a cluster of clubs swarming around the two rival parties, the Blues and the Yellows.[207] Norwich had a similar proliferation of Independent Clubs which needed in 1784 a candidate of William Windham's stature to weld the cause of independency into a viable electoral machine.[208] Edward Bouverie performed a very similar function for the Northampton independents in the same year.[209] Such clubs existed even in the smaller, slightly less politicized, constituencies. After the mid-eighteenth century, clubs of independent voters are to be found at Lewes, for example,[210] and at Shrewsbury.[211]

Some of these clubs enabled electors to express and preserve their independence. The Blue Club of St Albans, for example, debated long and hard whether Lord Spencer should be allowed to join. Other clubs negotiated preferential terms with tradesmen and professional people for their members. Subscriptions were commonly raised to make available alternative forms of philanthropy and charity and, not least, to protect voters from penalization and victimization. The Yellows

---

[204] Id., 'The History of Liverpool Politics, 1761–1835', 2 vols. TS, n.d., in Liverpool City Lib.

[205] M. E. Speight, 'Politics in the Borough of Colchester 1812–1847', Ph.D. (London, 1969), 167–77, contains the most extensive treatment known to me about this sadly neglected aspect of electoral history.

[206] Stoker, 'Elections and Voting Behaviour', Ph.D., 47.

[207] Childs, 'Politics and Elections in Suffolk Boroughs', M.Phil., 104–6.

[208] D. R. McAdams, 'Politicians and the Electorate in the Later Eighteenth Century', Ph.D. (Duke University, North Carolina, 1967), 75–7.

[209] D. Gray, *Spencer Perceval* (Manchester, 1963), 28 ff.

[210] M. Cramp, 'The Parliamentary Representation of Five Sussex Boroughs', MA (Manchester, 1953), 82, 103.

[211] Namier and Brooke, *House of Commons*, i. 364.

in Ipswich even established a form of contributory health insurance in one of their election clubs in 1790. Such signs of independence frequently caused alarm. Certainly, corporations can be found endeavouring to restrict the growth of such clubs by restricting the issue of licences to inns which would accommodate only friends of the corporation.[212]

These election clubs varied in size, but the most commonly recurring estimate of membership is 150–200. The numbers of people—electors and non-electors alike—involved in these bodies, even when allowance has been made for exaggeration, duplication, and fluctuations of membership, must have been a reasonably high proportion of the adult males of a town, and the numbers of citizens reached by their activities significant. How far their activities impinged directly upon voting behaviour is extremely difficult to assess. Nevertheless, there are examples of these clubs depositing block votes of several dozen, and even several hundred, in favour of a particular candidate.[213]

The third element in the enlargement of political horizons was the phenomenon of petitioning. On issues both local and national it was customary, and increasingly fashionable, to petition Parliament. The *scale* of petitioning has for too long gone unrecognized. In the century between 1750 and 1850 the constituency of Reading sent no fewer than 432 petitions up to Parliament. Each petition was the result of a public meeting, the canvassing of the petition, and, often, considerable local agitation.[214] Many of these were on local matters, but at least one half of them concentrated their fire on humanitarian issues. And all this from a quiet backwater of a constituency in the south of England. Petitions on national issues increased sharply in the later eighteenth century, taking the country as a whole. The campaign against the Jewish Naturalization Act of 1753 elicited no more than a dozen petitions, that against the Cider tax 10 years later 23. The Supporters of the Bill of Rights Society in 1769 mustered 30, the campaign against Catholic relief in 1780 produced 15 and the movement for economical reform a very respectable 38. However, the war of petitions waged between the supporters of Pitt and Fox in 1783–4 provoked over 200, more than the previous six campaigns put together.[215] In this sea of petitions the non-electors as well as the

---

[212] D. R. McAdams, 'Politicians and the Electorate', Ph.D., 178–9; Lansberry, 'Politics and Government in St Albans', Ph.D., 168–73. In addition to Colchester and St Albans, the best example of the diverse electoral, political, and social functions of these election clubs may well be Coventry. See e.g. 113, 270, Sheffield Papers, Coventry RO, for the ward organization and activities of the Independent True Blue Society.

[213] Speight, 'Politics in Colchester', Ph.D., 192.

[214] Bailly, 'Parliamentary History of Reading', MA, 59–60, 93–102.

[215] J. A. Cannon, *The Fox–North Coalition* (London, 1969), 186–7.

electors would be called upon to swim, a timely indication that the 'political nation' could not be confined to those who had a vote.

The extent of the 'political nation' in the later eighteenth century has recently been measured by two scholars who, independently, have reached broadly similar conclusions. Professor Cannon has shown that the war of opinion in 1783–4 elicited petitions signed by as many people as actually voted in the general election of 1784.[216] Professor Phillips, meanwhile, has demonstrated that the size of the electorate in the counties in the age of the American Revolution roughly corresponded with the number of those who signed petitions, while in the boroughs the number of signatories was roughly double the number of electors.[217] The electorate, therefore, was part of a wider audience for political affairs. The 'political nation' was demonstrably larger than the electorate, by at least one-half again and possibly more.

The rapidly increasing importance of the printed media and the increasingly sophisticated organization of electoral politics ensured that electors would become increasingly susceptible to issues external to local patrons and external to the constituency. Electors could thus become willing to respond to issues concerning the welfare of the nation, the defence of popular liberties, the status of the Church of England, and the preservation of the constitution, or, indeed, its reform. When Peel issued the Tamworth Manifesto in 1834, it was the public, formal appeal of a party leader to a developing, homogeneous, national, electoral sentiment. One hundred years before the Tamworth Manifesto local issues were the immediate currency in elections, but national issues were already able to intrude upon electoral parochialism, if intermittently. With gathering and accelerating frequency, however, they came before 1832 to rival and sometimes even to outweigh the importance of local issues. In the earlier part of the period under consideration, 'There is an almost complete divorce between the two, save at the most exceptional times. It would be difficult to discover from local election literature and correspondence that national politics even existed, and there are few direct local reflections of national rivalries or discontents.'[218] This may have been true of the first half of the eighteenth century but as the rest of this section will demonstrate, it has a diminishing relevance for the later part of that century and still less for the first three decades of the next.

In the middle of the eighteenth century, public opinion was occasionally capable of regional and even national expression—against

---

[216] Cannon, *The Fox–North Coalition*, pp. 186–7.

[217] J. A. Phillips, 'Popular Politics in Unreformed England', *J. Mod. Hist.* 52 4 (1980).

[218] Newman, 'Elections in Kent', D.Phil., 387–92. Even this verdict has been sternly repudiated by the latest historian of Kent politics. Humphreys, 'Kentish Politics', D.Phil., 25–6.

the Jew Bill in 1753, in support of Pitt in 1757–8, and against the Cider excise of 1763. None of these successive tides of public sentiment, however, flowed into electoral channels. The Wilkes issue in 1768 came rather too late to have much impact upon the general election of that year. At the next general election, in 1774, there were Wilkite candidates only in Southwark, Middlesex, Surrey, Worcester, Bedford, and Dover. There is other evidence of enthusiasm for the Wilkite cause, however, at Seaford, Cambridge, Southampton, Portsmouth, Peterborough, Bristol, and Newcastle-upon-Tyne. The geographical weighting of these constituencies to the metropolitan and southern regions requires little emphasis.[219] What is more relevant, however, is the fact that agitation in many of these places was not simply a celebration of temporary enthusiasm for the cause of John Wilkes and the slogan, 'Wilkes and Liberty' but a concern for national as well as parochial issues. One of the striking features of the Wilkite phenomenon was the common consciousness felt by radicals and independents throughout the country that they were participating in a common crisis. The press did much to provide encouragement, information, and moral justification for Wilkite opposition to government high-handedness up and down the country. It also embraced local, independent concerns and forged them into a common cause with common enemies. This 'radicalism', moreover, had some endurance. The fact that urban radicalism appeared as an issue in 13 out of 86 contests in England and Wales in 1774 is surely not without significance.[220]

What is even more remarkable for the growing intrusion of 'national' issues into electoral politics is the almost simultaneous appearance upon the electoral scene of the American Revolution and the issues to which it gave rise. In 1774, 'America was mentioned as an issue in not more than ten constituencies, and then always as part of an attack by Opposition candidates against the Government. It was not made an issue by Government candidates and the Government did not ask the electors to endorse their policy.' In 1780 it was an issue in about one-half of the 69 contest in England and Wales.[221]

---

[219] I. R. Christie, 'The Wilkites and the General Election of 1774', *Guildhall Misc.* 11 4 (1962), 155–64 (repr. in id., *Myth and Reality*, 244–59). There were, of course, a large number of places where Wilkite slogans and symbols were in evidence between 1769 and 1774, but where the pressure was not kept up to affect the general election of 1774. See e.g. the Wilkite activity in the tiny freeman borough of Poole in Dorset described in Beamish, 'Parliamentary and Municipal History of Poole', M.Phil., 68.

[220] Brewer, 'Commercialization and Politics', 232–8. See also below, pp. 301–3.

[221] Namier and Brooke, *House of Commons*, i. 75–8. They offer no computation but are inclined to overestimate the power of local issues. For example, they remark that 'In other large constituencies, such as Norwich and Coventry, local issues were probably more important than

Estimates of the mounting currency of the American issue at parliamentary elections, however, are still an inadequate and superficial manner of estimating the political consciousness of the electorate. The working of agencies of politicization, the press, and the clubs, and the proliferation of the consequences of their activity—meetings, addresses, and petitions—are nowhere so well illustrated as in the clear electoral divisions which the American issue provoked. Recent work on public opinion has demonstrated beyond question that in 1775–6 the British public was almost equally divided between coercion and conciliation. Even in constituencies where the issue had not surfaced in 1774, serious divisions appeared within a year.[222] Although only 14 of the 69 boroughs contested in 1774 revealed divisions on the American issue, between autumn 1775 and autumn 1776 no fewer than 52 boroughs addressed the throne for or against coercion. Nor were the numbers involved insignificant. At least one-third and often as many as half the voters were thus involved. Nor was this activity orchestrated by 'patrons' or by the political élite. Supporters of the North government and of the Rockingham opposition are to be found in positions of prominence in some places but usually in a very small minority, probably less than one-quarter. There are striking and coherent continuities to be discerned in the pattern of petitioning. Of the 17 counties and boroughs that supported coercion in 1775, 11 had supported government over the Middlesex election. Two-thirds of those places advocating conciliation had supported the repeal of the Stamp Act, for example. What explains these continuities is the fact that most electors saw the American issue as a constitutional one, involving the indiscriminate use of parliamentary right and power. Those who supported Parliament advocated the enforcement of law and discipline, as did supporters of the Anglican Church, local corporations, and so forth. Those advocating conciliation tended to be those who already opposed corporate power and advocated dissent and opposition. The American issue was thus superimposed upon existing patterns of political activity. By-elections, especially those at Gloucestershire in 1776 and Hampshire in 1779, were fought on the issue. In the latter, for example, America was the main issue. One handbill castigated the North ministry: 'The loss of half of the British

national' (ibid. 86). They most certainly were not; for Norwich see J. A. Phillips, *Electoral Behavior*, 118–19, 124–5; for Coventry, there can be no doubt that national issues, especially that of America, were being strongly ventilated—see the *Coventry Mercury*, 11 and 12 Sept., 1780.

[222] James E. Bradley, *Popular Politics and the American Revolution in England: Petitions, the Crown and Public Opinion* (Macon, Georgia, 1986), 59–90, 121–50. Much of the following paragraph is based on Professor Bradley's researches.

Empire has certainly been owing to the bad policy of absurd plans laid by the folly of pride and rapaciousness, insolence and incapacity.'[223] Indeed, these conflicts over the American issue were by no means confined to open constituencies. They are to be found also in small boroughs, particularly in the south-west, where patrons attempted to impose a governmental view upon dissident electors. The potency of the American issue does not consist only in its capacity as an external issue to aggravate opinion within the electorate but in the ability of local groups, already mobilized, to use the issue in their continuing local battles against patrons and corporations. They could be a further opportunity to exhibit consistency with attitudes already expressed over commercial and American issues, such as the repeal of the Stamp Act, or over issues backing support for or opposition to government, such as the Middlesex election. In this way, a succession of national issues, interacting with local patterns of political alignment, ensured a degree of political consciousness among the electorate which should not be underestimated.

The combined impact of the Wilkes affair and the American issue was to awaken the sensibilities of the electorate to corruption, inefficiency, and even despotism at local as well as at parliamentary level. A sense of spontaneous political curiosity and an enhanced degree of public concern for the exercise of power in the constituencies accompanied the intensification of political hostilities in Parliament. The increasingly clear conflict between the government of Lord North and the Rockinghamite opposition had much to do with this. At the general election of 1780 a clear difference of opinion between government and opposition was evident; it had begun to manifest itself in several constituencies, but as yet only in a small minority.[224] The general election of 1784, however, with its highly personalized confrontation between Charles James Fox and George III, was quite different. In 1784 every one of the seven county contests was a struggle between the followers of Pitt and Fox, and the issues of the East India Bill and of Pitt's minority administration came up in them all.[225] In the borough seats as well, the general election was a verdict on the rival statesmen. Contemporaries interpreted both the elections and their outcome in this way, and historians have quite correctly followed them ever since. Although manipulation, subsidies, and subterfuge played their part, as they always did, political and party considerations need to be taken into account if the general election of 1784 is to be

---

[223] *A Collection of Handbills, Squibs etc. published During the Late Contested Election* (Winchester, 1780), 10.
[224] I. R. Christie, *The End of North's Ministry* (London, 1958), 116–57.
[225] Namier and Brooke, *House of Commons*, 9–10.

understood: 'That the political issues of the day were very widely discussed is apparent from the number of pamphlets, cartoons and broadsheets, as well as from references in national and provincial newspapers and in private correspondence.'[226] Furthermore, the unspectacular number of contests in 1784, 75 in English and Welsh seats, does not take account of those seats where uneven differences of opinion did not issue in a contested election. Yorkshire was, of course, the outstanding example. An agent told Fitzwilliam that

the country in general is in a state of infatuation which will require time to work a cure, it being the received Notion amongst the inferiors in many parts, that Mr. Fox was attempting to dethrone the King and make himself an Oliver Cromwell. The merchants in general have confirm'd them in this Opinion, so that the Name of Fox is enough to make enemies to all who have approved any part of his Conduct.[227]

Yorkshire, like two or three dozen other places, was not contested, although there can be no doubt of the intense local interest in parliamentary affairs.

It is possible to estimate the number of constituencies in which national issues of parliamentary significance, superimposed upon local structures of conflict, had come to play a central role at the general elections of 1780 and 1784. In at least nine counties,[228] and 32 boroughs,[229] according to my estimates, national issues can be seen at work, to judge from election speeches, broadsheets, and election correspondence. Although only 41 constituencies of the 245 in England may seem to be concerned, they are, of course, the type of constituencies where election contests were taking place. Five of these counties were contested in 1784 out of the seven in England contested in that year, and in two, Surrey and Yorkshire, contests were aborted. As for the boroughs, 20 out of the 64 contests in 1780 took place in these 32, and 20 out of the 65 in 1784.

These were, moreover, usually large and fairly open constituencies. The 32 boroughs represent only 15% of the 203 English boroughs, but their combined electorate of 62,400[230] represents almost one-half

---

[226] Cannon, *The Fox–North Coalition*, 224.

[227] R. Parker to Fitzwilliam, 26 Apr. 1784, box 36, Fitzwilliam MSS, Northants. RO.

[228] Beds., Berks., Bucks., Hants., Herts., Middx., Surrey, War., and Yorks.

[229] Bedford, Beverley, Bridgnorth, Bristol, Canterbury, Colchester, Coventry, Dover, Exeter, Gloucester, Hertford, Hull, Ipswich, Leicester, Leominster, Lincoln, Liverpool, London, Maidstone, Northampton, Norwich, Nottingham, Oxford, Reading, Rochester, Southampton, Southwark, Sudbury, Taunton, Westminster, Worcester, and York.

[230] Estimates of the electorate are compiled from Namier and Brooke, *House of Commons*, 1.

of the estimated borough electorate in the late eighteenth century.[231] Other historians (and future research) will amend such a compilation, but it seems to me that in these constituencies, at least, a purely local reference will fail to provide appropriate explanatory categories for electoral politics.

The function of the French Revolution was both to intensify and, ultimately, to extend these patterns of participation. The appearance of an extra-parliamentary radicalism provoked a loyalist counter-reaction which brought ideological questions of national concern to the forefront. Indeed, the encouragement lent by the government and by local political establishments to the progress of loyalist ideas did much to intensify and to institutionalize, and, geographically, to spread, the conflict of issues and of ideas. This is best illustrated, perhaps in the circulation of partisan literature and, in particular, the ready availability in most areas of both a conservative or loyalist newspaper and a radical or reformist one. Liverpool, for example, had two establishment papers, *Gore's General Advertiser* and *Billinge's Liverpool Advertiser*, by the end of the eighteenth century. In 1806 a radical paper, the *Liverpool Chronicle*, was founded. The interaction between these political cultures, of course, did much to define and develop each of them. Consequently, in most sizeable centres, partisanship existed even on the most sensitive of issues, and to some extent the unreformed electoral system was able to reflect it.

The war against revolutionary France was an issue in many constituencies in 1796. Anti-war candidates are known to have stood in at least four counties, two of which were contested, and nine boroughs in England (out of a total of 59 contests).[232] Even in the very quiet election of 1802 anti-war candidates stood in six counties, five of which were contested, and in 15 boroughs.[233] Partisanship on

---

[231] See above, pp. 178–81.

[232] Of the counties, Herts. and Kent were contested. Devon and Middx. were not. All the following boroughs were contested: Bristol, Leicester, Liverpool, London, Norwich, St Albans, Southwark, Westminster, Worcester (D. R. McAdams, 'Politicians and the Electorate', Ph.D., 245–52. See also the *Morning Chronicle*, 24 May and 18, 21, 23 June 1796. The estimate is a conservative one. Thorne, (*House of Commons*, i. 147) for example, includes Dover, but I have not encountered decisive evidence to include it in my estimates.

[233] At Cambs. Hertfs. Kent, Middx. Norfolk (Surrey did not poll) and at Aylesbury, Beverley, Bristol, Canterbury, Hereford, Hull, Liskeard, London, Maidstone, Norwich, Northampton, Nottingham, Southwark, Sudbury, and Westminster. Bristol, Canterbury, Northampton, and Sudbury did not poll. Altogether, there were 66 contests in the boroughs in 1802. The figures above, however, underestimate the extent of anti-war sentiment, to say nothing of resistance to Pitt's repressive legislation. The Two Acts of 1795 provoked 71 petitions to Parliament and 20 addresses to the king. In the war of petitions over the repressive legislation, in fact, its opponents claimed a 4 : 1 preponderance of signatures (130,000 to 30,000). On the petitions see J. Cookson, *The Friends of Peace: Anti-war Liberalism in England, 1793–1815* (Cambridge, 1982), 152.

a national issue could not be more clearly marked. Even on less spectacularly contentious issues, electoral opinion could be mobilized. The issues of the general election of 1807—the treatment of the king by the Ministry of All the Talents (1806–7), the pledge demanded of the ministry by the king and the rise of anti-Catholic sentiment— played some part in 7 of the 11 contested English counties and in 15 of the 58 contested English boroughs.[234]

By the early nineteenth century, then, national issues had come to play a significant role in a further 8 English counties and, at least, a further 8 English boroughs, compared to the estimate for the mid-1780s, giving combined totals of 17 (out of 40) and 40 (out of 203), respectively.[235] Thus, by this time, national issues had arrived on the scene in some 42% of English counties and 19% of the boroughs. These seats contained over 60% of the electorate. Even here, it cannot justifiably be claimed that the position adopted by a candidate on national issues completely overshadowed the position he adopted on local ones. What is claimed is that an appreciation of both is required in order to understand the electoral politics of the later eighteenth and early nineteenth centuries. When candidates pitch their appeal to the electors, however, firmly on a national issue, such as the demand for peace in 1796 or the actions of the king in 1807, there can be no doubt in determining where the balance between national and local issues should be drawn.

The growing centrality of national issues to electoral politics cannot be doubted, but we should not conceive of this as a smooth and steady development. Not every general election fits into this scheme of things. That of 1806 and, especially, that of 1812 were fought mainly on local issues.[236] The newspapers contain few traces of national issues, and election speeches can be searched in vain for their impact. On both occasions the country faced a military and international crisis and was

[234] The counties were Durham, Hants., Hunts., Lincs., Middx., Som., and Yorks. The boroughs were Aylesbury, Cambridge Univ., Canterbury, Colchester, Coventry, Dover, Great Yarmouth, Ipswich, Liverpool, London, Newcastle-under-Lyme, Norwich, Pontefract, St Albans, and York. See Hinton, 'The General Elections of 1806 and 1807', Ph.D., 352–60.

[235] Of the counties, national issues had come to stay in Cambs., Devon, Kent, and Norfolk. In Durham, Hants., Lincs., and Som., local issues remained, on balance, of greater weight. Of the boroughs, national issues came to play a consistent role in Aylesbury, Great Yarmouth, Hereford, Newcastle-under-Lyme, Pontefract, and St Albans. The point is less well established for Cambridge Univ. and Liskeard.

[236] The only type of election literature in 1802 which refers to national issues is the advertisement literature which appeared in the London press.—e.g. the candidates for Sudbury affirming their opposition to the war in the *Morning Chronicle*, 29 June 1802. A report of the Herefordshire county meeting included some animadversions on the nature of Whiggism (ibid. 30 June 1802). For 1812, there are reports of radical candidatures but little else; see The *Morning Chronicle*, 14 Oct. 1812 (for Essex and Kent). See also Thorne, *House of Commons*, i. 228–9.

clearly disinclined to indulge its political differences. With the return of peace, however, these inhibitions vanished. After the election of 1818 a pamphlet entitled *The Late Elections: An Impartial Statement of all proceedings connected with the progress and result of the late elections* was published. *The Late Elections* recorded the opinions of most candidates as expressed during the campaign. Of the constituencies in England and Wales, parliamentary reform was an issue in 24, government repression in 18, the Catholic question in 9, retrenchment in 9, taxation in 7, and the Corn Laws in 4.[237] Both candidates and electors, it seemed, were making up for their recent inhibitions.

Not the least interesting of these developments is the extension of national issues into some of the medium and even smaller provincial towns and the beginning of their penetration into Wales. Until the period of the Revolutionary and Napoleonic Wars, the gentry in Wales were securely in control, the electorate was apathetic and apoliticial, and contested elections were a rarity. At the turn of the century things began to change. The first weekly newspaper in Wales, the *Swansea Cambrian*, was launched in 1804. Public meetings were held and clubs began to organize. Ripples of anti-Catholicism could be felt, especially at the Brecon contest of 1806. The contest at Flint in 1807, too, was fought on the religious issue, in clear contrast to that of 1806 which had been an old-fashioned tussle between independents and oligarchs. At Carmarthenshire, indeed, the principles of English party politics were raised through the candidature of J. G. Phillips, a Foxite Whig.[238] Most elections in Wales, it is true, continued to be fought on local issues, but change was in the air. Decades of electoral torpor were coming to an end, and the political radicalism of the 1820s, to say nothing of the great Nonconformist radicalism of the 1840s, was just around the corner.

In England, however, the day of political radicalism had already dawned. Before the end of the Napoleonic Wars a groundswell of electoral radicalism was beginning to build which was ultimately to play some part in effecting the Reform Act of 1832. Paradoxically, perhaps, the best testament to the ability of the electors to respond to issues with a national rather than a purely local reference lies in their (admittedly qualified) readiness to join enthusiastically in the movement to liquidate the electoral system. In most of the constituencies where the electorate had embraced national issues, at least, part of it was prepared to embrace radicalism. What this

[237] There is a fairly detailed summary of *The Late Elections* in Thorne, *House of Commons*, i. 257–60.

[238] Rees, 'Parliamentary Representation of South Wales', Ph.D., i. 120–2, 180–4; Wager, 'Welsh Politics and Parliamentary Reform', Ph.D., 17–18, 122–7, 141–5.

'radicalism' of the electorate amounted to and how enthusiastically, and on what scale, the electorate responded to it represents a further stage in the politicization of electoral behaviour.


### ELECTORAL RADICALISM

'Radicalism' is one of those concepts much used by historians of Britain in the eighteenth and nineteenth century, especially those of a Whiggish cast of mind. The notion of a 'radical movement' originating with Wilkes and culminating in 1832, or, alternatively, with the Chartists, is a common one which helps to make order and sense of a good deal of agitation. 'Radicalism' at the electoral level, however, has its origins in the mentality of electoral independence. The enormously powerful independent repudiation of corruption and oligarchy and the no less powerful assertions of freedom of election are fundamental elements underpinning the radical critique of the Hanoverian electoral system. Consequently, the rhetoric of independence is frequently interchangeable with that of radicalism, a confusion which baffled even contemporaries.[239] The press, in fact, very commonly refers to radicals as 'the independent interest'. Radical resistance to repressive government legislation both in the 1790s and in the immediate post-war period is frequently represented in independent terms.[240] Burdett was described as the representative of 'the independent interest' in Middlesex in 1802.[241] Even more confusingly, the 'radical tide' in 1831 was occasionally regarded by contemporaries as the high-water mark of independence, too. The issue at the contest at East Retford was stated to be 'local independence and parliamentary reform'.[242] Furthermore, much discussion of parliamentary reform had for its objective the enhancement of the fortunes of local independent parties. An early pamphlet calling for the Secret Ballot aimed at improving

[239] See e.g. the Cumberland contest of 1831, where 'radical' rhetoric condemns aristocratic corruption, vindicates loyalty to the monarchy, and hints at a local 'Norman yoke' mentality. See the *Cumberland Poll Book* for 1831, esp. pp. ix, xiii, xiv–xv, xvii–viii. Similarly James's victory at Carlisle in 1820 was not only regarded as a radical triumph but a vindication of the independent cause; see F. Jollie, *The Political History of Carlisle* (Carlisle, 1820), 19. It is not at all clear to me sometimes where the boundaries between the two are to be drawn. Both in 1802 and at a by-election in 1807, Birch, a radical/independent candidate at Nottingham, almost defies precise categorization. The language of the speeches and other literature printed in the poll books is anti-aristocratic and anti-ministerial; it is both independent and radical.

[240] For example, *The Exeter Poll Book* of 1818, 16–17, 18–19, 27–9.

[241] *Morning Chronicle*, 8 July 1802.

[242] Odurkene, 'The British General Elections', B.Litt., 33–4.

the moral status of the individual voter.[243] Charles James Fox admitted to the House of Commons that the great aim of Charles Grey's reform proposals of 1797 was to increase the number of independent voters.[244] Independent groups had been saying much the same thing for decades.

There was nothing new in attaching local independence groups to national campaigns which focused on parliamentary issues. As Dr Colley has demonstrated, the Tories had been notable exponents of popular politics in the age of Walpole, had for long attacked local oligarchies, and had fairly consistently advocated a redistribution of seats to an appreciative independent audience. The Tories of the first half of the eighteenth century, like some Whigs, had been in favour of more frequent parliaments, but their own Anglican conservatism, their suspicion of Dissent, and the impossibility of disrupting the Whig oligarchy consigned Tory radicalism to the might-have-beens of British history. In much of their propaganda, their contacts with extra-parliamentary groups, and their organizational resources, the Tories pioneered aspects of what we term 'radicalism'.[245] With the dissolution of the old Tory party in the early 1760s, local independent groups were left to their own devices.

The new radicalism of the age of Wilkes was a curious amalgam of metropolitan insolence to the ministers of George III, of old Tory reformism, and of provincial independence. The politics of the new reign seemed provocative enough. The position of Bute, the ending of the Seven Years War, and the authoritarian measures adopted by the Grenville and Grafton ministries towards the figure of John Wilkes were enough to foment political trouble. Against a backcloth of persistent recession, unemployment, and economic insecurity, however, political dissent became something more ominous than the usual local reflexes of disappointed independents. Something resembling a 'radical' movement appears to have been launched which as late as 1774 was still able to field over one dozen radical candidates in the general election of that year.[246] In the 1760s, owing to the activities of radical writers, lawyers, printers, and book-sellers, through the manipulations of radical leaders and the adventures of radical mobs, and, most of all, because of the personal vicissitudes of John Wilkes himself, a radical

---

[243] CW, *The Honest Elector's Proposal for Rendering the Votes of All Constituents Free and Independent* (London, 1767).

[244] W. Cobbett, *The Parliamentary History of England*, 36 vols. (London, 1806–20), xxxiii. 718–9.

[245] Colley, *In Defiance of Oligarchy*, 142–5, 169–73, 291–2.

[246] See above pp. 292–4.

political culture came into existence.[247] In some constituencies, notably Middlesex, Southwark, London, Westminster, Bristol, and Newcastle-upon-Tyne, and possibly Bedford and Worcester, a permanent, institutionalized, and ideologically coherent urban radicalism was forming. This did not only involve a passing interest in 'Wilkes and Liberty', but something more enduring. As a historian of Newcastle-upon-Tyne has written: 'Radical activity centering on national issues was neither isolated nor short-lived. Instead, it persisted throughout this fifteen year period [1769–85].'[248] Sustained, institutionalized electoral radicalism with such stamina had not existed in earlier decades. Electoral independence or Tory radicalism had been at the electoral level an intermittent response to events and personalities, a political and intellectual context whose latent capacities had never been fully realized. At the intellectual level a 'radical' as distinct from an 'independent' position was becoming discernible. Electoral independents had frequently demanded the extension of the franchise in an attempt to reverse the restriction of the electorate which had occurred in the early eighteenth century, a case of revenging themselves on the course of history. In the late 1760s radical writers began to demand altogether a more systematic reconstruction of the electoral system, involving not merely shortening the duration of Parliaments but the ending of rotten boroughs, the redistribution of seats, and, frequently, the secret ballot as well as, ultimately, the extension of the franchise. Often, as in the case of Wilkes himself in his famous speech on parliamentary reform in March 1776, radicals grounded their arguments securely upon the doctrine of the sovereignty of the people.

Independence was giving way to radicalism, but it was giving way to it very slowly. In spite of Professor Brewer's enthusiastic presentation of the case for a radical political culture it would be a mistake to endorse it too readily. There was enthusiasm for Wilkes in hundreds of places but enthusiasm alone does not denote radicalism. By far the most common pattern in the 'Wilkes and Liberty' phenomenon is the transient arousal of local independents from their customary state of torpor and demoralization. In small constituencies such as Bridgnorth, Droitwich, and Wenlock, 'the simple response to Wilkes was modified by long-standing local circumstances'.[249] Even in some of those

---

[247] The classic statement of this case is J. Brewer, *Party Ideology and Popular Politics at the Accession of George III* (Cambridge, 1976), 163–200. See also id., 'Commercialization and Politics', 197–202.

[248] T. R. Knox, 'Popular Politics and Provincial Radicalism: Newcastle-upon-Tyne, 1769–1785', *Albion*, II (1979), 226.

[249] J. Money, *Experience and Identity: Birmingham and the West Midlands 1760–1880* (Manchester, 1977), 170.

constituencies closely involved in the excitement over Wilkes which were contested in 1774, (Dover, Peterborough, Portsmouth, Seaford, and Southampton), it is difficult to sustain the view that radicalism was on the march. In Southampton, for example, the opposition of Lord Charles Montagu to two friends of North's government was more the action of a Rockingham Whig stoking up local independent feeling against the corporation than an episode in the rise of radicalism.[250] Similarly at Portsmouth the contest did not involve radicalism. It was a revolt of the corporation against ministerial influence.[251]

Even where the existence of a radical candidature cannot be denied, the context is worth close examination. There can be no mistaking the fine Wilkite and radical credentials of Sir Watkin Lewes, who contested Worcester on four occasions in the 1770s. Nor can the existence of radical methods be gainsaid. Tumultuous meetings, street crowds, the establishment of radical societies in Worcester, and subsequently in the industrial districts of North Worcestershire and Birmingham, the exaction of pledges and instructions from candidates—all are indicative of a distinctively radical political culture.[252] Lewes himself campaigned on a national radical platform.[253] Yet the electorate was motivated by its desire to restrict the right of the Corporation to create freemen and thus to dilute their own status. The Worcester contests of 1773, 1774, 1776, and 1780 are nice examples of a radical candidate consciously endeavouring to work upon the existing materials of independence and to inject them with a radical spirit. Attempts by the Corporation to exclude pottery workers from the franchise in 1773 enabled him to introduce social tensions into the campaign and to identify himself as the friend of the labouring freemen, a dramatic example of what 'Wilkes and Liberty' might mean in practice.[254] The failure of Sir Watkin Lewes on four separate occasions indicates strongly that he was in advance of electoral opinion.

---

[250] A. Temple Patterson, *A History of Southampton, 1700–1914* (Southampton, 1966), i. 64; see also W. Andrews, *An Address to the Public* (Southampton, 1774), 4–5.

[251] Lake Allen, *A History of Portsmouth* (Portsmouth, 1817), 108; *Hampshire Chronicle*, 26 Sept. 1774.

[252] *Berrow's Worcester Journal*, 8 and 22 Feb. and 14 Mar. 1776. Furthermore, some less significant Wilkite aspects of behaviour were copied by the Worcester crowd, who made a practice of taking the horses from the carriage of Sir Watkin Lewes and drawing it themselves, see *A Circumstantial Account of the Grand Contest for a Member to Serve in Parliament for the City of Worcester* (1774), 9; H. MacDonald, 'Two Eighteenth-century Parliamentary Elections in Worcester', *Trans. Worcs. Archaeol. Soc.* 22 (1943–5), 67.

[253] Namely the programme of economical reform circulated by the Society of the Supporters of the Bill of Rights, which included demands for shorter parliaments and franchise reform; see I. R. Christie, *Wilkes, Wyvill and Reform* (London, 1962), 60.

[254] *Berrow's Worcester Journal*, 14 Oct. 1773.

The spread of electoral radicalism thereafter is a slow and intermittent phenomenon. The Association Movement of 1779–85 excited radical enthusiasm in the provinces but it was a weak force at the 1780 election. Outside the metropolis and Yorkshire very few radicals were elected. Nine of the 12 MPs from the metropolis (London, Middlesex, Westminster, and Surrey) were radicals, and there was every indication that Wilkite political culture had come to stay. Elsewhere, however, radical candidatures were few and far between: Bedford, Plymouth, Nottingham, Newcastle-upon-Tyne, Worcester, and possibly Bristol. This was, perhaps, not much of an advance upon 1774. Yet this does not warrant Professor Christie's conclusion that 'there was little support in the country for programmes of parliamentary reform'.[255] Such support was steadily growing, even though it could not yet determine the outcome of election contests. At Cambridge, for example, a vociferous if ineffective radical group was involved in the politics of the town after 1776.[256] And at Tiverton in the early 1780s local radicals seemed to have been particularly active.[257] But what of the counties, which were, of course, the impetus behind this instalment in the history of electoral radicalism?

The pattern of such contacts may be illustrated from Gloucestershire,[258] one of the first counties to follow the example of Yorkshire. Preliminary meetings in 1780 brought together representatives of local landed families and leaders of the urban professional classes. The Beaufort family, which controlled the office of Sheriff, refused to allow a county meeting. Thereupon a petition was prepared, publicized, and distributed to 30 principal market towns in the county by a committee of 37 men. This committee represented a fair cross-section of Gloucestershire society: landed families great and small and commercial and industrial elements, particularly clothiers. As contacts with Wyvill and the central committee continued and the objectives of the movement became better defined, a more radical pressure group in Gloucester demanded that a full radical programme be supported. Such demands were not accepted, and Gloucestershire decided to go no further than demanding economical reform. This pattern was followed in Buckinghamshire, Dorset, and Hertfordshire. In other counties, too, proposals for more equal

---

[255] Christie, *Wilkes, Wyvill and Reform*, 118–20.

[256] 'whose dissatisfaction with the government was beginning to infect even the tenants of Wimpole' (Cook, 'Representative History of Cambridge', Ph.D., 38.

[257] C. Wyvill, *Political Papers* (London, 1794–1802), xi. 106. J. Bourne (ed.), *Georgian Tiverton: The Political Memoranda of Beavis Wood, 1768–1798*, Devon and Cornwall Record Society, NS 29 (Torquay, 1986), 63, 65, 72, 79.

[258] E. Moir, 'The Gloucestershire Movement for Parliamentary Reform, 1780', *Trans. Bristol and Gloucs. Archaeol. Soc.* 75 (1956), 171–91.

representation and trienial parliaments floundered (Devon, Essex, Huntingdonshire, Kent, Somerset, and Surrey). No wonder, then, that in such counties little permanent *radical* impact upon electoral politics is discernible.[259]

For two decades thereafter, electoral radicalism did little more than mark time. In the 1790s radical groups and individuals were active throughout the country but their endeavours were barely reflected within the electoral system. Indeed, after 1792 the gathering tides of loyalist and patriotic opinion weakened the limited influence which radical ideas had been able to establish among the lower and middling orders. It is significant, for example, that the Association of the Friends of the People was driven to suspend its activities in January 1795, long before the expected dissolution of Parliament. Not that radical activity came to an end in the mid-1790s. There was, for example, massive protest against the Two Acts in 1795–6.[260] Nevertheless, few radicals stood at the general election of 1796. The time was hardly conducive to great radical causes. The biggest issue at the election was the war against France. 'Radical platforms were raised at Bristol, Colchester, London, Norwich, Nottingham and Westminster . . . Boston, Chichester, Derby, Maidstone, Rochester, St Albans and Tewkesbury, to no avail.'[261] Thereafter, radical electoral support began to fall away quite sharply. In the larger freeman boroughs, radical support declined to its very nadir in the mid-late 1790s before staging a revival. In Norwich in 1796 the radical, Gurney, lost to the second-placed candidate, William Windham, by 83 votes. At a by-election in 1799 the margin had widened to 199. In 1802, however, two radical candidates were confortably returned, the second placed now 83 votes ahead of Windham.[262] The same year saw a recovery, albeit slight, elsewhere. A radical candidate stood at Southampton, although he obtained only a derisory share of the vote.[263] Other radical candidatures occurred in 1802: at London, Middlesex, Southwark, Surrey, and Westminster, as might have been predicted, but also at Cambridgeshire, Canterbury, East Grinstead, and Nottingham. More significantly, there was a succession of radical candidates at Leicester in 1800, 1802, and 1807. In 1802 and 1812, in fact, plebeian radical

---

[259] Christie, *Wilkes, Wyvill and Reform*, 110–12.

[260] See J. A. Horne, 'Radicalism in London, 1796–1802: Convergences and Continuities', in J. Stevenson (ed.), *London in the Age of Reform* (Oxford, 1977), 79–102.

[261] Thorne, *House of Commons*, i. 147–8.

[262] The first placed was no less than 476 ahead of him. See B. Aspinwall, 'William Smith, MP, 1756–1835', MA (Manchester, 1962), 86–96.

[263] See Election Speeches of William Scott (*Hampshire Pamphlets* 42 10. Cope Collection, Southampton Univ. Lib.) for his candidature. He obtained only 24 votes, against 411 and 385 for his two opponents.

candidates stood there.[264] Burdett, who had won Middlesex in 1802, lost it in 1804 but regained it in 1806. Nevertheless, the survival, and eventual revival, of moderate parliamentary reform from *within* the electoral system was to be a factor of considerable significance in persuading respectable and propertied opinion up to 1832 to acquiesce in a reform of Parliament.

This remained the pattern for the rest of the war. The only radical condidatures at the general election of 1806 occurred at Boston, where Major Cartwright ran, Honiton, Middlesex, Nottingham, Okehampton, Southwark, and Westminster. At the general election of the following year, radicals contested Boston, Bristol, Grampound, Nottingham, Okehampton, Preston, and Westminster (where Burdett's refusal to treat cost him much freeholder support). Some were a humiliating fiasco. Cartwright received only 8 votes from an electorate of over 300 at Boston. Only Burdett's great victory at Westminster in 1807 (he spent only £780 on his expenses, an enormous tribute to his energy and integrity), looked forward to better days.[265] This was the perfect radical victory. The other successes of 1807 were nothing like as impressive. That at Grampound arose from local antipathy to an unpopular patron. That at Okehampton was really an independent rebellion backed by the patronage of the Prince of Wales. At none of the general elections of these years was there anything resembling a common radical campaign. There was no co-ordination of resources and effort. Everything was left to local initiative. Indeed, radicals were seriously divided. At the general election of 1812 the drive and activity of the metropolitan radicals were, in fact, keenly resented by their provincial counterparts. Radicals of Christopher Wyvill's stamp, terrified by the excesses of Luddism, were sceptical rather than enthusiastic about Burdett's return at Westminster, organized, as it was, through the efforts of a committee of tradesmen which included several old heroes of the London Corresponding Society.[266] Radicals seem to have been quite active in 1812 and, as in 1796, contested about a dozen seats, including, on this occasion, no fewer than four southern counties: Berkshire, Devon, Essex, and Surrey. The borough seats contested by radicals were Berwick, Colchester, Haslemere, Leicester, London, Preston, and

---

[264] Temple Patterson, *Radical Leicester*, 97–9.

[265] Hinton, 'General Elections of 1806 and 1807', Ph.D., 389–407. However, Burdett's election elicited public expression of pleasure from radicals in Bristol, Liverpool, Norwich, and Nottingham. See J. Dinwiddy, 'Sir Francis Burdett and Burdettite Radicalism', *History*, 65 (1980), 20.

[266] On this theme see J. Dinwiddy, *Christopher Wyvill and Reform, 1790–1820*, Borthwick Papers no. 39 (York, 1971), 17–22. See also J. M. Main, 'Radical Westminster, 1807–20', *Hist. Stud. ANZ* 12 (1966), 186–204.

Southwark. This was something of an improvement upon the fortunes of electoral radicalism in 1806–7 but it is not easy to see here much positive benefit from Major Cartwright's famous tours, the second of which in 1813 elicited 130,000 signatures on reform petitions but which came too late to affect the outcome of the election of 1812.[267]

There can be no doubting the rapid rise and fall in the fortunes of radicalism in the period 1815–22, but it is by no means clear that this process had much impact upon parliamentary elections. The high expectations of peace, the excitement generated by campaigns against the Corn Law of 1815 and the Property Tax of 1816, and the unsettled economic situation bred a climate conducive to the spread of radical ideas. The Convention of Delegates of the Hampden Clubs in January 1817 to present reform petitions to the Commons represented a significant harmonization of provincial radical sentiment. This promise was not entirely fulfilled, however, at the general election of 1818, probably because of the suspension of habeas corpus in 1817. The pattern repeated itself after Peterloo, and the impressive display of indignant reformist opinion which it provoked. The Six Acts of late 1819 scarcely encouraged radical successes at the general election of 1820.

Nor were radical breakthroughs to be encouraged by internal splits. Provincial radicalism was at all times closely bound up with local and personal, to say nothing of economic, influences. Even so, the Convention of Delegates manifested serious divisions, especially that between provincial and metropolitan radicals. Superimposed upon this were the splits between the ideological retainers of the great men in the movement—of Burdett, of Cobbett, of Cartwright. The unpleasant and distasteful personal differences between them cannot have done much to mobilize a common national radical effort at the electoral level, especially when there was no unity and no central organization. A tiresome backwardness marked this generation of radical leaders. In some ways they belonged to Wyvill's era, displaying what William Thomas has termed, 'an archaic agrarian radicalism'.[268] Burdett, for example, always believed that the gentry should lead the radical movement,[269] not a sentiment particularly well calculated to appeal to many urban independents. Time seemed to hang heavy over some

---

[267] Thorne, *House of Commons*, i. 232–4. N. Miller, 'John Cartwright and Radical Parliamentary Reform 1808–19', *Eng. Hist. Rev.* 83 (1968), 721. The initial responsibility for founding the Hampden Clubs, however, was not Cartwright's. Only in May 1813, when the idea was already launched, did he abandon his earlier resistance to it. See id., 'Major John Cartwright and the Founding of the Hampden Clubs', *Hist. J.* 17/3 (1974), 191–2.

[268] W. Thomas, 'Whigs and Radicals at the Westminster Election of 1819', *Guildhall Misc.* 3/3 (1970), 174–217.

[269] See Dinwiddy, 'Sir Francis Burdett', 25–6.

aspects of early nineteenth-century radicalism. Much radical rhetoric continued to depict the world of the free born Englishman with an Anglo-Saxon birthright and an independent cast of mind. Few concessions were made to the common man. One pamphlet revelled in the significant title: 'An Exposition of the Striking Conformity of Grievances complained of in the Petitions of the Freeholders of Middlesex in the years 1769 and 1810.'[270]

For all these reasons, radicals failed to make a decisive breakthrough at the general elections of 1818 and 1820. Indeed, at the Westminster elections of 1818 and 1819, fratricidal strife weakened the radical cause. Romilly's success in beating Burdett out of first place at Westminster in 1818 was a huge fillip for Whig morale in the metropolis, repeated when Lamb beat Hobhouse a year later following Romilly's death. No wonder that the metrpolitan radicals were unable to push the Whigs into a firmer commitment to parliamentary reform. Despite all these weaknesses, the cause of electoral radicalism made some very real progess in 1818 and 1820. In at least a score of constituencies in England and Wales, reform opinions were heard on the hustings in 1818 (one-quarter of all contests) and there were rather more radical candidatures than usual.[271] Most speeches reported in the newspapers at these two elections have a Victorian ring to them: they are veritably stuffed with issues, not, admittedly the radical issues alone: the Corn Laws, the Property Tax, and foreign policy are also well to the fore. Lord Egremont was by no means alone in aristocratic circles in grumbling in 1820 that 'this General Election has shown in every part of England, but the Radicals & Revolutionaries are powerful and rising everywhere, & I very much fear that dangerous times are at hand'.[272] At Berkshire in 1818 all three candidates were radicals or, at least, professed radical opinions. Even in an aristocratic backwater of a county, times were clearly changing. Samuel Wells, the county's leading radical, stood for the county seat and obtained a pretty respectable 640 votes (against 1,224 and 1,154 for his two opponents). Encouraged by this magnificent failure, he stood for the borough of Huntingdon in 1820. His moment was evidently past, for he won only seven votes. This was by no means his worst achievement. In 1831, when he stood again for Huntingdon, he obtained only six votes.[273]

---

[270] The (undated) pamphlet may be found in the Guildhall Library. It compares the cases of Wilkes and Burdett.

[271] See the lists in Thorne, *House of Commons*, i. 257–8, 260–1.

[272] Lord Egremont to Lord Ashburnham, 28 Mar. 1820, Ashburnham Papers, quoted by J. McQuiston, 'Sussex Aristocrats in 1820', *Eng. Hist. Rev.* 88 (1973), 553.

[273] *VCH Huntingdonshire*, ii. 49–50.

The return to economic prosperity in the early 1820s, the consolidation of so-called 'liberal' forces within the government of Lord Liverpool, and the exhaustion of radical energies led to a waning of radical support. Beneath the surface, however, a quiet transformation of opinion was taking place among many thousands of members of the middling orders. Opinion was becoming less passive, less deferential. The influence of the press in general, and the attention paid to the actions and speeches of prominent radical leaders in particular, seemed to be working to effect a consciousness favourable to reforming opinions. Social tensions were simmering. Above all, Cobbett and his journalism did much to wrench the old independent mentality out of its parochial context and place it in a national frame of reference. Cobbett's radicalism repudiated oligarchy not merely at the level of the corporation and the country house but at the level of Whitehall and Westminster. Local struggles could thus be seen as part of a national crusade.

The reform of Parliament was no longer a disreputable opinion to hold. To a generation which was beginning to realize the desirability of reform in many spheres—the church, the law, the corporation, the prisons, and the poor law—the reform of Parliament was no longer so shocking. Even in an increasingly agricultural and increasingly Tory town like Colchester there is no doubt that many conversions to parliamentary reform were taking place among the burgesses in the 1820s.[274] The same process can be seen all over the country. Even in a provincial county like Derbyshire, the urban middle classes were joining together with rural, Whig reformers. Reforming opinions were being circulated, reinforced, and popularized by the inevitable newspaper, in this case the *Derby Reporter*, the first copy of which emerged on 2 January 1823. The *Reporter* prospered at the expense of the old Tory *Derby Mercury*. Reformers of all hues got together at town and county meetings to pass petitions. The ground was being laid for the radical tide of 1831.[275] Even Wales was not immune. It was a sign of the times that in 1828 *The Cambrian* began to accept letters for publication that were sympathetic to the reform of Parliament. Before the end of the year the paper had embraced the measure itself.[276] Even that county of rotten boroughs and uncontested seats, Cornwall, began to petition Parliament for the reform of the Cornish electoral system. In the 18 months before the

[274] Speight, 'Politics in Colchester', Ph.D., 231.
[275] E. Fearn, 'Reform Movements in Derby and Derbyshire 1790–1832', MA (Manchester, 1964), 216–20.
[276] R. Rees, 'Electioneering Ideals Current in South Wales, 1790–1830', *Welsh Hist. Rev.* 11 (1965), 233–50.

election of 1826 its farmers underwent a remarkable conversion to the cause of reform. In 1826 they were able to divide the county seat between a Tory and a radical.[277]

Towards the end of the decade the gathering demand for reform outside the electoral system, (especially from the Political Unions, infuriated by Wellington's intransigence and embittered by economic recession), came ultimately to seem invincible. Even in the general election of 1830, powerful surges of local independent feeling and anti-aristocratic sentiment were rocking sitting MPs. Several friends of government, Wellington's government, bent before the wind.[278] During the next few months, British politics witnessed a remarkable frenzy of politicization and participation. Over 1,200 petitions were presented to the House of Commons on the reform issue in the session of 1830–1, 1,200 in the following session, and another 300 early in 1832.[279] A small but cumulatively significant minority of these were signed by over 1,000 signatories. At least 3 of the 58 petitions which poured in from Kent were signed by over 1,000 people.[280] There is no doubt that the electorate shared in the all-consuming interest. Public meetings were all but universal, and attendances were in the hundreds, and even thousands. Subscriptions for reform candidates in 1831 found a ready response. Candidates were quizzed, interest was high, and there were many examples of the electorate's suspicion of timely conversions. *Ad hoc* election committees sprang up in many areas.[281] The highly variegated nature of reform propaganda may have helped. Reformers appealed not merely to theoretical principles but to the practical consequences of the bill: a representation of property would effectively represent the wealth of the country, stimulate industry and commerce as well as agriculture, and secure stability by bringing the middling orders into the electoral system. The overwhelming success of the reformers at the election of 1831—Grey won a majority of 130–40 seats—was not due to influence, to violence, or to mobbery, but to the immense popularity of the bill and the years of persuasion which had preceded it.

[277] E. Jaggard, 'The Parliamentary Reform Movement in Cornwall, 1805–26', *Parl. Hist. Yrbk.* 2 (1983), 124–6.

[278] There were around 20 attempts to open up smaller boroughs. Independents won significant victories at Bedford, Chester, Lichfield, Rye, and Caernarvon. See Odurkene, 'The British General Elections', B.Litt., 34–6.

[279] This number was not, however, particularly great when compared with the great religious struggles over the Repeal of the Test and Corporation Acts in 1828 (5,000 petitions) and Catholic Emancipation in 1829 (20,000 petitions). See Cannon, 'New Lamps for Old', 110.

[280] Andrews, 'Political Issues in Kent', M.Phil. 22, 86–7; Odurkene, 'The British General Elections', B.Litt., 111.

[281] Odurkene, 'The British General Elections', 146–52; Brock, *The Great Reform Act*, 194–201.

The rising radical tide flooded much of the country. At Newark, Edward Tallents wrote gloomily to the Duke of Newcastle of 'a splitting of many of our friends and a certainty of defeat'.[282] According to a Nottingham newspaper, the issue was clear:

It is not a struggle whether Whig or Tory should have power and patronage in their hands, but whether the Country should be governed by a House of Commons, a great part of which is self-nominated or delegated by individual Peers, or by a House of Commons fairly and freely elected as real Representatives of the People.[283]

In Wales, the outburst of reformist sentiment was remarkable. The landed interest had to fight to maintain its position but it lost seats in Glamorgan and even in Monmouth, county and borough. Only in its innermost citadels was oligarchy safe. Even in Breconshire, of all places, where the Beaufort interest seemed impregnable, the radicals forced a contest.[284] In the English counties the freeholders were almost solid for reform. Of the 22 county seats which changed hands, only 2 (Oxfordshire and Huntingdonshire) went to the Tories. When it looked as though the bill might be frustrated in October 1831 after the Lords rejected it, serious rioting broke out in the East Midlands. That at Nottingham seemed particularly dangerous and had a noticeably levelling flavour to it.[285]

Not every voter in every place was radical in 1831, however. In Suffolk there was a distinct lack of enthusiasm for petitions. Many of the freeholders did not like to commit themselves.[286] In Kent many of the freeholders were unenthusiastic, even indifferent. Many of those who did sign petitions did so with reservations. There was no comparing the support for reform with the much greater clamour raised on Catholic emancipation.[287] In Cornwall, many of the great

[282] Edward Tallents to Duke of Newcastle, 27 Apr. 1831, NeC 529, Newcastle (Clumber) MSS, Nottingham Univ. Lib.

[283] *Nottingham Journal*, 30 Apr. 1831, quoted in Moses, 'Elections in Nottinghamshire', Ph.D., 108–9.

[284] David, 'Political Activity in South East Wales', MA, 43–50, 74–80. In the petitioning movement of 1817 only 1 out of over 400 petitions (from Usk, in Monmouthshire) came from Wales see D. Wager, 'Welsh Politics and Parliamentary Reform, 1780–1832', *Welsh Hist. Rev.* 7 (1975), 434. In 1831, however, 'Reform was an issue in at least twenty one constituencies. Nine reformers were elected unopposed, as were eight anti-reformers. In two constituencies, Carmarthenshire and Monmouthshire, anti-reformers declined re-election rather than continue to oppose reform against their constituents' wishes and were replaced by reformers. Only in six constituencies were there contests, and reformers were successful in only one [Caernarvon]' (ibid. 442).

[285] See the dramatic accounts in the Dowson MSS in the Notts. RO. (DD. 523. 1–3). The mob commanded the town, victimized and extorted money from known anti-reformers, and terrorized upper-class Tories until the militia intervened.

[286] See e.g. the letters to Lord Jermyn, 941/11/C, Hervey MSS, Suffolk (West) RO.

[287] Andrews, 'Political Issues in Kent', M.Phil., 88, 100.

interests—lead, mining, industry, commerce—were seriously divided.[288] Many voters, moreover, divided their votes. In 1830 a Tory candidate at Colchester divided no fewer than 35% of his votes with a radical. Even in 1831 he shared 18% of his votes.[289] There were plenty of enemies to reform but they were divided and demoralized. When they did stand to fight they could achieve impressive results. One anti-reform petition from Leicester was signed by 2,200 people.[290] Of the 58 petitions from Kent on the reform issue, 12 were against it, a respectable proportion. What is startling about the 58 petitions, however, is their heavy urban bias: no fewer than 52 originated in the boroughs.[291] One typical anti-reformer in Essex bewailed the run against them in the towns: 'The popular Cry is decidedly against us, and if anything saves us it will be the assistance we shall receive from the County villages. The towns I am afraid will all be against us . . .'[292] For this reason, opponents of reform were so inhibited that they affected to support it. This the Derbyshire Tories conspicuously did.[293]

Of course, the idea of a radical tide can only be sustained so long as it is recalled that 'reform' in 1831 was an umbrella slogan which accommodated reformers of an immense variety of types as well as eternal optimists longing for reduced taxes, the alleviation of distress, and better times in the future. One radical candidate at Wigan disarmingly stood on the slogan: 'Potter and Purity of Election: Food, Knowledge and Justice Without Taxation.'[294] That typifies the spirit of 1831: a new spirit and a kick against the local and national oligarchy of the landed interest. A radical handbill at Harwich bitterly condemned 'the enforcement of Government patronage, in which most of the Corporation, their friends or relatives have long regaled themselves'.[295] The general election of 1831 was a verdict on the unreformed political system, and anybody with an axe to grind was apparently prepared to join in. Not that there was an organized Ultra country party in 1831 for in most places Ultras did not support reform. In rural areas it was the Whig gentry and supporting freeholders and

---

[288] Elvins, 'The Reform Movement in Cornwall', MA, ch. 5.

[289] Speight, 'Politics in Colchester', Ph.D., 116.

[290] Temple Patterson, *Radical Leicester*, 192.

[291] Andrews, 'Political Issues in Kent', M.Phil., 86–7.

[292] John Cunningham to Mr Savill—Only, 1 May 1831. D/DO/B.15, Cunningham MSS, Essex RO.

[293] Fearn, 'Reform Movements in Derby', 254.

[294] Wigan Broadsides Book, 26 July 1830, Wigan Public Library. See also the slogan of E. M. Lloyd Mostyn at Flintshire: 'retrenchment, extensive constitutional reform, civil and religious liberty, and the abolition of slavery' (D/KK/459, Keene and Kelly MSS, Flintshire RO).

[295] *To the Inhabitants of the Loyal Borough of Harwich*, 28 Apr. 1831, Essex RO.

tenants who backed the bill. In the boroughs it was a significant majority of urban trades together with backing from the lower orders.[296]

Not the least interesting feature of the radical tide of 1830-2 is the evidence of working-class and lower-class support for radical objectives. The activities of the political unions went far towards bringing labouring men into politics but these, for the most part, existed outside the structures of the unreformed electoral system. There can be no doubting, however, that distress and economic recession were most important factors in bringing men from the working classes to agitate for reform and in collaboration with members of the middling orders. The nature of class relationships depended largely upon the economic context. At Coventry, industry had an outworker pattern in which deference and paternalism operated to prevent manufacturers and artisans from becoming antagonistic. Coventry radicalism, as a consequence, was coherent, constitutionalist, and reasonably moderate.[297] A very different pattern of economic relationships at Leicester bred an identifiably militant, autonomous, working-class radicalism.[298] In the counties, radical propaganda was just as vitriolic as it was in the boroughs, appealing to the poor and the oppressed to rise against the haughty and the arrogant.[299] The radical tide of 1831 constitutes, therefore, the apotheosis of independence, the culmination and intensification of a century of conflict, however intermittent, between the forces of independency and the forces of oligarchy. There *are* elements of a common 'radical' effort in 1831; some degree of common funding on a national scale and even a radical 'Parliamentary Candidates Society' with 10 provincial offices.[300] Nevertheless, the mobilizing sentiment in the constituencies, at least, was emphatically independent. How else are we to understand the mind of the reformers in 1831? In its simplest form the 'radicalism' of 1831 could be a mild-mannered expression of local independent opinion.

---

[296] D. C. Moore, 'The Other Face of Reform', *Victorian Studies*, 5/1 (1961), 7-34; R. W. Davis, *Political Change and Continuity*; D. C. Moore, 'Is "The Other Face of Reform" in Bucks. an Hallucination?' *J. Brit. Studies*, 15 (1976), 150-6; and R. W. Davis, 'Yes', *J. Brit. Studies*, 15/2 (1976), 159-161; D. C. Moore, 'Some Thoughts on Thoroughness and Carefulness Suggested by Comparing the Reports of the Aylesbury Meeting of 24 February 1830 in *The Times* and the *Bucks. Gazette*', and R. W. Davis, 'Rebuttal', *J. Brit. Studies*, 17/1 (1977), 141-4; E. Jaggard, 'Cornwall Politics, 1826-1832: Another Face of Reform', *J. Brit. Studies*, 22 (1983), 80-97.

[297] Searlby, 'Paternalism, Disturbance and Parliamentary Reform: Society and Politics in Coventry, 1819-1832', *Int. Rev. Soc. Hist.* 22 (1977), 198-208.

[298] Temple Patterson, *Southampton*, 177-8.

[299] See e.g. the anti-landlordism of Herts. radicals. Addresses, etc. Hertfordshire County, 1830-1. D/FcX. 70 z. I, Herts. RO.

[300] Odurkene, 'The British General Elections', B.Litt., 123.

Grimsby independents might have worked themselves up into angrier denunciations of the Yarborough interest and its tendency to enclose common lands than they did in 1831:[301]

We have already expressed our conviction that delusion was practised. That Lord Yarborough has considerable influence we readily admit: and, we as readily say he ought to have it; his property, and his character as a landlord, justify the possession of that influence. We hold a great distinction between *influence* and *control*: the one is legitimate, the other illegitimate; the one a blessing, the other a curse; the one rational, the other irrational. We continue to be as we ever have been, the advocates of the cause of the poor against that of the peer—of the oppressed against the oppressor—of the persecuted against the persecutor: but, our judgment prevents our zeal from running riot.

At the other extreme, the most virulent and inflammatory outbursts of radicalism appear on close inspection to be generalized and politicized statements of essentially independent opinions. The following passage from the harangue of a radical candidate in Grantham in 1831 represents the content of the radical mind and its repudiation of 'Old Corruption' on the eve of the Reform Act of 1832:[302]

First, for . . . the Old System. It has enabled a set of Boroughmongering Peers and Commoners in open defiance of the Constitution, and in direct usurpation of the rights of the people to send more than two hundred members to the Commons House of Parliament, who enact whatever laws their patrons may dictate—no matter how severe, how insulting, how demoralizing—whether corn laws, game laws, laws against the cheap administration of justice; or against economy in any other form; in favour of immense civil and military establishments, of pensions from the treasury to the profligates of both sexes, of profuse grants for the indulgence of courtly prodigality, of sanguinary wars without an object but squandering public money on favourites and jobs, or against the right of petition or the liberty of the press. The power of manufacturing into Members of Parliament unprincipled adventurers having no connection or tie with the people, these Borough-mongers possess and have uniformly and unflinchingly exercised in an unswerving system of self-aggrandisement at the expence of the people; and the consequences are bad laws, a burdensome and terrible form of litigation, an overloaded list of pensioners and place-men, and Eight Hundred Millions of debt. Such are the fruits of Anti-Reform.

To what extent is it possible to identify a 'radical electorate' before 1832? Were 'radicals' different from other voters and, if so, how? It is certainly the case that some radical constituencies had a singular electorate. Westminster, for example, was a huge scot and lot borough

---

[301] *Poll for the Election* (Great Grimsby, 1831), 7.
[302] *Collection of All the Addresses* (Grantham, 1831), 6.

with an electorate of 12,000. London was an enormous freeman borough with over 7,000 electors, rising to 10,000 in the early nineteenth century, its radical voters drawn from 'the mass of smaller merchants, shopkeepers and artisans'.[303] Nevertheless, such a stereotype should not be taken as typical of the radical electorate. As we have seen from the foregoing account, radicalism was just as likely to occur in medium to largish freeman and scot and lot boroughs as it was in the few giant constituencies within the electoral system. In some places, too, there can be no doubt at all that radical candidates received enthusiastic support from a particular occupation. Where would Nottingham radicalism have been without the framework knitters? How much support would Cobbett and Hunt have received at Preston without the weavers?[304] It is by no means clear that such cases were typical. The average radical voter conformed to neither of these stereotypes. In most places, there was little to distinguish the occupational structure of radical electors from the occupational structure of the electorate as a whole. In effect, radical voters were very like other independent, oppositionist voters. It is particularly difficult to test this hypothesis in a series of truly comparable, strictly controlled, circumstances, but Table 5.3 assembles the results of a computerized enquiry into the opposition vote in Colchester at six elections in the early nineteenth century. In the first three of these elections (1790, 1806, and 1807), these voters were suporting an avowedly independent candidate. In the later three, however (1812, 1818, 1820), they were supporting a radical. Yet it is hard to detect anything other than trivial differences between the structure of the independent and the structure of the radical electorate. As Professor Rude discovered some years ago, the radical voter was not a class apart.[305] It is possible occasionally to detect some qualitative differences between independent and radical voters in the same place from time to time,[306] but these are not usually significant. On the whole, independent voters were normally willing to support radical, as well as independent, candidates. In 1831, of course, when supporters of Lord Grey's government appeared to represent a convergence of independency and radicalism, they were willing to support Whig candidates, and did so in their

[303] Namier and Brooke, *House of Commons*, i. 329.

[304] At Preston the textile workers, dominated by the weavers, were by far the largest group in the electorate. In 1830 Hunt received almost 73% of the support of these 305 voters.

[305] G. Rude, *Wilkes and Liberty: A Social Study of 1763 to 1774*, (Oxford, 1962).

[306] There is certainly more of a class cutting edge to Preston radicalism in 1830, compared to Preston independency in 1818. Fewer retailers (25% to 33%) supported the radical in 1830, slightly fewer craftsmen, (40% to 45%) but significantly more of the unskilled/labourer category (62% to 52%).

TABLE 5.3    *Occupational Structure of Independent and Radical Voters at Colchester, 1790–1820 (%)*

|      | 1 | 2 | 3  | 4  | 5  | 6  |
|------|---|---|----|----|----|----|
| 1790 | 9 | 4 | 14 | 48 | 21 | 4  |
| 1806 | 6 | 3 | 13 | 35 | 33 | 10 |
| 1807 | 8 | 3 | 11 | 34 | 34 | 10 |
| 1812 | 5 | 5 | 15 | 44 | 26 | 5  |
| 1818 | 6 | 3 | 18 | 46 | 25 | 2  |
| 1820 | 6 | 5 | 16 | 40 | 27 | 6  |

thousands.[307] Everything depended upon the political colour of the available candidates, the structure of election contests, and the circumstances of the constituency concerned.

In some ways, then, electoral radicalism may be construed as a specific form of electoral independence. It is certainly possible to distinguish between the two but they do have much in common. Independence translates into radicalism under the impact of circumstances external to the constituency: the activities and reputation of a Wilkes or a Wyvill, the ideological impact of the French Revolution in general, or Thomas Paine in particular, the economic and political crises of 1815–16 and 1818–19, and, not least, the great religious and political upheavals of 1828–32. All of these went far towards moulding the potentialities of radicalism. Whether these could be expressed depended upon local feeling, local candidates, and local organization. Perhaps the best means of distinguishing electoral radicalism from electoral independence lies in two qualities of the former. Radicals demanded an extension of the franchise as part of a national crusade against corruption and oligarchy, not merely some local remodelling. Further, radicals moved away from the traditional notions of local rights and privileges and self-consciously adopt a parliamentary-focused ideology with which to vindicate their actions. Electoral radicalism prospered and triumphed in 1830–2 because it benefited from a unique combination of circumstances: the fragmentation of the old Tory party, the death of George IV, the Swing Riots, the activities of the political unions and the establishment of the Whig administration of Lord Grey. It owed more to these fortuitous circumstances than it owed to its own effective strength. It was very doubtful, indeed almost impossible, to imagine that such a combination could ever be repeated.

[307] e.g. the Radical Framework Knitters of Nottingham voted overwhelmingly for Whig candidates at the general election of 1830: 86% voted a Whig party ticket, 12% voted Tory, and 2% split.

# 6
# *The Party Dimension to Electoral Politics*

## PROBLEMS AND INTERPRETATIONS

The historiography of the development of British political parties in the century before the Reform Act has focused almost exclusively upon the parliamentary arena. The constituencies have largely been ignored.[1] Their rich and varied political culture has been neglected. No attempt has been made to relate the world of the constituency to that of the parliamentary politicians. Yet the history of party must surely take account of both. To what extent were the fortunes of parliamentary groups reflected out in the constituencies? Even if they were, what *precisely* was the nature of the link between these two worlds of politics? What is the chronological pattern within which these links may have developed? And in how many constituencies, and of what type, are any such developments discernible?

For too long, historians of party have treated constituency politics in an anachronistic fashion without recognizing the strength and continuity of local political cultures. As we have seen,[2] there is nothing inferior about 'local' issues in a society which was subject to local regulation in so many areas of life. In an age which was entirely sceptical about the desirability—and, indeed, feasibility—of central interference in local affairs, it was inevitable that electoral and party politics would conform to local configurations. Consequently, in the century before the Reform Act, the historian of party must necessarily treat party in its relatively unfamiliar local, as well as in its familiar parliamentary, context.

Not that local electoral structures were ever entirely insulated from the world outside. They were sensitive enough to accommodate matters of parliamentary concern in the seventeenth century and continued to do so thereafter. Although the source and routine substance of electoral conflict remained parochial rather than national, there can be no mistaking the capacity of the unreformed electoral system to respond to successive waves of 'national' excitement, such as those generated

---

[1] I have made some preliminary attempts to relate constituency politics to a model of party development in my *The Emergence of the British Two-party System, 1760–1832* (London, 1982), see esp. 71–80.

[2] See 245–85.

by Sacheverell, by the excise crisis of 1733–4, by John Wilkes, by the American War, and by the great parliamentary conflict of William Pitt and Charles James Fox between 1782 and 1784. These responses could not, however, be maintained. Furthermore, they did not seriously disturb the prevailing structure of patronage and control. The systematic and continuous identification of local men, local structures, and local campaigns with national party alignments, and with perceptions of government and opposition at Westminster, was not finally achieved until the age of Gladstone and Disraeli. Not until then did the constituencies finally submit to the organizational requirements of centralized bureaucratic parties. Even then, this was no breakthrough for progressive forces, no precious victory for modernization. Developments in communications made possible, and an enlarged, and rapidly enlarging, electorate made necessary, the incorporation of local party groups within bureaucratically organized 'national' parties if traditional political élites, in alliance with rising social groups, were to retain their control of political mechanisms.[3]

Until the later nineteenth century local loyalties and local concerns on the whole remained paramount. Parliamentary loyalties were often compartmentalized. Political opponents at Westminster would endeavour to drop their enmities for the sake of preserving local harmony. This explains why there was no automatic extension of partisanship from one arena to the other. Although even the most eminent historians tend still to be puzzled by it, local issues could, and did, cut clean across divisions generated by parliamentary conflict.[4] In the summer of 1826 the freeholders of Northumberland were faced with a clear choice between two local coalitions of interests: it was not immediately clear to them that each side sported both a Whig and Tory candidate, according to the current definitions of national politics. In the same way, candidates of the same political

---

[3] Historians of 18th-cent. England have been extraordinarily anachronistic. Namier, in particular, believed that the historian of 18-cent. parties had simply to clear up problems concerning the antecedents of the parties of the later 19th cent. See *Monarchy and the Party System* (Oxford, 1952), 30. To historians of late 19th-cent. England, not surprisingly, the emergence of mass bureaucratic and centralized parties was a very gradual and incomplete affair. See e.g. H. J. Hanham, *Elections and Party Management: Politics in the Time of Gladstone and Disraeli* (London, 1959), esp. 131–42; T. Lloyd, *The General Election of 1880* (Oxford, 1968); J. A. Garrard, 'Parties, Members and Voters after 1867', *Hist. J.* 20 (1977), 145–63; R. Spence-Watson, *The National Liberal Federation, 1877–1906* (London, 1907); B. McGill, 'Francis Schnadhorst and Liberal Party Organisation', *J. Mod. Hist.* 34 (1962), 19–39; E. J. Feuchtwanger, *Disraeli, Democracy and the Tory Party* (London, 1968); R. E. Quinault, 'Lord Randolph Churchill and Tory Democracy 1880–1885', *Hist. J.* 22 (1979), 141–65.

[4] See e.g. L. B. Namier and J. Brooke (eds.), *The House of Commons, 1754–1790*, 3 vols. (London, 1964), i. 50; A. Harvey, *Britain in the Early Nineteenth Century*, 18.

complexion in national affairs, for or against government, for example, could find themselves locked in mortal electoral combat with each other. More commonly, candidates who were thoroughly partisan at Westminster might well be understandably reluctant to bring their quarrels home with them.[5] Even in the early nineteenth century, 'party politics were not always an issue at elections'.[6]

From this point of view, therefore, the decline in party activity which occurred in the middle decades of the eighteenth century probably had fewer electoral consequences than might at first seem likely. The 'rage of party' at Westminster and in the constituencies gave way after 1714 to the less exciting, and thoroughly one-sided, struggle between the Whigs of Stanhope, Sunderland, and Walpole and the proscribed Tory party. Although there can be absolutely no doubt that an ideologically coherent, and to some extent, an organized, Tory party remained in existence down to the accession of George III in 1760,[7] the declining frequency of election contests[8] marked a significant reduction in political tension. Local élites were prepared to coalesce and to compromise and, of course, to save on election expenses rather than face the social upheaval and organizational exertions which a contested election would involve. This relaxation of party tension enabled a traditional court–country axis to appear in certain constituencies and in certain conditions. As Professor Speck has shown, where a Tory and a country Whig stood against court candidates, 'the elctorate for the most part voted for a pair of candidates, even if this entailed supporting a Tory and a Country Whig'.[9] Indeed, as Dr Cruickshanks has demonstrated, their co-operation at the general election of 1741 reduced Walpole's majority to 16.[10] Dr Rogers has noticed some such coalitions in London and the South-east in a number of large, open boroughs, down to 1741

---

[5] Stroker writes of the four northern countries; 'Party development in the north seems to have lagged behind other areas. Party from the centre made few inroads into northern constituencies. This situation existed [even] when the area was controlled and represented by prominent national politicians. There is a clear paradox with these men acting as party politicians at Westminster but not in the constituencies' (D. Stoker, 'Elections Voting Behaviour: A Study of Elections in Northumberland, Durham, Cumberland, and Westmorland, 1760–1832, (Manchester, 1980), 297–8).

[6] A. D. Harvey, *Britain in the Early Nineteenth Century* (London, 1978), 18.

[7] L. Colley, *In Defiance of Oligarchy: The Tory Party, 1714–1760* (Cambridge, 1982), 53–145.

[8] See pp. 106–11.

[9] J. A. Cannon (ed.), *The Whig Ascendancy; Colloquies on Hanoverian England* (London, 1981), 68.

[10] E. Cruickshanks, *Political Untouchables; The Tories and the 1745* (London, 1979), 26–7.

at least.[11] Nevertheless, there was still plenty of life left in the old party labels. As Dr Clark has argued, although 'Court and Country have some use as descriptions of attitudes or dispositions . . . the tactical units in Parliament and in the country at large were Whig and Tory'.[12] The old party issues still had the force to instigate political and religious sentiment. Dissenters would not vote for Tories, and Tories would not vote for court Whigs. In the last analysis, 'the basic organization of political life continued to focus around the old polarity of Whig and Tory, whose two party denominations continued to evince characteristic sets of principles and policies'.[13] After a detailed analysis of the general election of 1734, Dr Langford has declared that

in Tory dominated boroughs and counties, for example, the Tories who described themselves or were described as being 'in the country interest' would not seriously have contemplated alliance with opposition Whigs. Throughout the West Country, Wales and much of the Midlands, the country seats were controlled by the Anglican country gentry; Whiggism was practically non-existent, so that the introduction of the new party pattern was largely irrelevant. On the other hand, in parts of the country the old Whig and Tory division was so deep that there could be no question of burying the hatchet. In the north, for example the Jacobite crises had left a legacy too bitter for any compromises, and nothing would have induced the Whig families of Northumberland, Cumberland and Westmorland to join their traditional enemies, though many of them were far from being friends of Walpole. The only areas where the new doctrines made some progress were the economically more advanced, and therefore politically more sophisticated, parts of the country, around London and in the south-east generally and to some extent in Yorkshire.[14]

Even in these areas, however, what motivated and mobilized the voters were party pressures and considerations.[15]

---

[11] Rogers has affirmed that in London 'the new opposition to the Court was not, however, strictly Tory . . . Although broad party configurations remained a characteristic feature of London politics, there was nevertheless a growing relaxation of party ties. During the first thirty years of the century, the strictly non-partisan vote more than doubled from around 10% in the years 1710–13 to 24% in 1727' (N. Rogers, 'Resistance to Oligarchy: The City Opposition to Walpole and his Successors, 1725–1747', in J. Stevenson (ed.), *London in the Age of Reform* (Oxford, 1977). It is impossible to resist the observation that, even so, an overwhelming 76% of the vote was 'strictly partisan'.

[12] J. C. D. Clark, *English Society, 1688–1832* (Cambridge, 1985), 31.

[13] S. Baskerville, 'The Management of the Tory Interest Lancashire and Cheshire 1714–1747', D.Phil. (Oxford, 1976), 2, 4.

[14] P. Langford, *The Excise Crisis* (Oxford, 1975), 114–15.

[15] Even in Kent, where Newman has specifically argued that 'after the 1727 election it is difficult to see clearly a distinction between Whig and Tory. The election of 1734 was not one of party, since, as has been shown, the Whigs were split between court and country; in 1741 and 1747 there was no party opposition while in 1754 there was no party issue.' Nevertheless, he concedes elsewhere, 'The pollbooks for 1727, 1734, and 1754 throw some light on the social

It was the recollection and heritage of earlier party conflicts, then, sustained by current party polarities, which effectively divided the political nation in local communities in the mid-eighteenth century. Where these divisions lost their sharpness, old party vendettas were usually diluted into an essentially local preoccupation with oligarchy and independence.[16]

The old Tory party ceased to exist after the accession of George III. Although there is some evidence that its parliamentary cohesion was not at once destroyed,[17] there is no suggestion that the party was able to survive the accession of a king who ended the proscription and isolation that had for almost half a century kept them together. It was not long, however, before a new party polarity appeared: that between successive ministries and the Rockingham Whigs and their successors. The Rockinghams claimed to be the heirs of the Glorious Revolution and the natural guardians of the constitution against the tyrannical schemes of Lord Bute and a sinister, secret cabal of his friends. Declaring systematic opposition to the regime of 'secret influence' and corruption, successive Whig leaders—Rockingham, Portland, Fox, and Grey—carried the mantle of party into the nineteenth century. A continuous and coherent political polarity dominated politics at Westminster between successive ministers, North, Pitt, and Liverpool all pursuing recognizably consistent executive policies towards the empire, the constitution, and the economy, and an opposition which prided itself on its party credentials.

There is an enormous literature on the question of party in the later eighteenth century, although less on the nineteenth, and few would dissent from the view that the politics of party dominated, indeed defined, opposition politics during this period.[18] Furthermore, the

and geographical bases for "party" in Kent. There were three groups, one voting Tory, even in 1754, one Whig, even in 1734, and a "floating" vote. Certain areas voted consistently one way or the other; the Tory areas were largely those where many of the leading Tory gentry lived, and the same is true of the Whigs. The areas which altered in 1734 were largely where those gentry resided who were complained of as apathetic and unwilling to canvass. Thus gentry influence was rather one of example and persuasion than of economic pressure' (A. Newman, 'Elections in Kent and Its Parliamentary Representation, 1715–1754', D.Phil. (Oxford, 1957), iv, 180).

[16] See ch. 5, pp. 267–81.

[17] B. W. Hill, *The Growth of Parliamentary Parties, 1689–1742* (London, 1976); id., *The Growth of Parliamentary Parties, 1782–1832* (London, 1985), 90–102, 121.

[18] See e.g. Frank O'Gorman, *The Rise of Party In England: the Rockingham Whigs 1760–1782* (London, 1975); id., *Emergence of the British Two-Party System*; L. G. Mitchell, *Charles James Fox and the Disintegration of the Whig Party, 1782–1794* (Oxford, 1971); J. A. Cannon, *The Fox–North Coalition: The Crisis of the Constitution 1782–1784* (Cambridge, 1969); Donald E. Ginter, *Whig Party Organization in the General Election of 1790* (Berkeley-Los Angeles, 1967); A. Mitchell, *The Whigs in Opposition, 1815–1830* (Oxford, 1967); A. Beattie, *English Party Politics* (London, 1970); D. Beales, 'The Independent Member', in

tactics and the political contrivances of party were coming strongly to influence the politics of the executive. Although government remained the king's government, a factor which powerfully inhibited its officials from proclaiming their loyalty to a coherent set of party principles, it was universally accused of pursuing 'Tory' policies—on law and order, on radicalism, on religious toleration, and on defence of the monarchy and protection of the constitution—and the term 'Tory' came back into circulation during the first decade of the nineteenth century. In effect, a 'Tory' government pursuing 'Tory' policies was confronted by a Whig party in opposition.

What impact did these tendencies towards party formation have upon the electorate? According to Professor Phillips, a very great deal: 'A substantial, and to a degree identifiable, portion of the electorate experienced a rapid politicization under the activities of both parliamentary and local political bodies.'[19] He proceeds to argue that in Norwich and Maidstone, at least, links were perceived to exist between parliamentary parties and local groups.[20] The evidence of votes actually tendered, moreover, gives some evidence, although it is by no means clear-cut, that partisan voting may have increased.[21] To what extent can these findings be applied more widely? Indeed, how could parliamentary parties induce partisan voting at constituency level (if they may be said to have done so at all?) This, as well as many other issues touching party at the electoral level, requires intensive investigation. In the sections that follow I shall attempt to describe the points of contact between parliamentary and local parties, and the extent of the influence of the former over the latter. I shall then attempt to estimate precisely how many constituencies were influenced by parliamentary parties, the chronological pattern by which this may have occurred, and the conditions which made it possible. I shall proceed to discuss the recently rediscovered relationship between religion and party, and I shall conclude by subjecting partisan voting at constituency level to analysis.

R. Robson (ed.), *Ideas and Institutions of Victorian Britain* (London, 1967). For some lively resistance to this burgeoning orthodoxy see P. Fraser, 'Party Voting in the House of Commons, 1812–1827', *Eng. Hist. Rev.* 93 (1983), 763–84, and J. C. D. Clark, 'A General Theory of Party, Opposition and Government, 1688–1832', *Hist. J.* 23/2 (1980), 295–325. See also my response, 'Party Politics in the Early Nineteenth Century, 1812–1832', *Eng. Hist. Rev.* 102 (1987) 62–83.

[19] J. A Phillips, *Electoral Behaviour in Unreformed England, 1761–1802* (Princeton, 1982), 16.

[20] Ibid. 115–23.

[21] But did it increase as a consequence of these links? It is not possible to be certain, and Phillips is very properly cautious on the point. (See ibid. 212–52.)

## INFLUENCES AND AGENCIES

During the 'rage of party' of the early eighteenth century, the politics of confrontation between Whigs and Tories at Westminster had been both reflected and projected out in the constituencies. In the revival of party politics of the later eighteenth century, exactly the same process occurred. In many places, the same issues which agitated politicians at Westminster and Whitehall agitated patrons and voters in their local communities. Before we attempt to assess the extent to which this process did occur, it is necessary to investigate the agencies through which it *could occur.*

The possible points of contact between parliamentary parties and local political groups are many and varied. Four of them, however, demand special attention: (*a*) the extent to which constituents shared in and/or responded to the issues which agitated parliamentary politicians; (*b*) the degree of sensitivity out in the constituencies to the parliamentary conduct and party allegiances of both patrons and Members of both houses of Parliament; (*c*) the extent to which constituencies were affected by the central organizations of government and opposition; and, finally (*d*), the degree to which the popular subculture of election clubs may have reflected the partisan political values of the political élite of Westminster and Whitehall.

As we observed in the last chapter, in the later eighteenth century the constituencies were coming to respond to political issues generated from Parliament.[22] By the mid-1780s contested elections in at least 40 constituencies were being influenced by partisan national, as opposed to local, issues, a figure which rose to almost 60 by the first decade of the nineteenth century. These constituencies, moreover, housed around one half of the electorate in the 1780s, about two-thirds later. What they had in common, in addition to their relatively large electorates, was a pattern of regular election contests and a high degree of political consciousness. What the political issues that agitated them had in common was a general concern for *constitutional* considerations (e.g. the American Revolution, Pitt versus Fox in 1784, parliamentary reform), their *suspicion of executive power* (e.g. Wilkes, the Two Acts), and their *ability occasionally to mobilize religious sensitivities* (repeal of the Test Act, Catholic emancipation). Such issues might impinge directly upon the populations and predispositions of the inhabitants of local communities, and, given the rapidly improving level of communications and political literacy, it is not at all surprising that

---

[22] See above, pp. 285–300.

parliamentary party issues would meet with some substantial response from the electorate at large.

Frequently, however, the impact of issues would be mediated through the local patron and the sitting Members of Parliament. In this manner, local differences might acquire a more general political significance. For fairly obvious reasons, a majority of electoral patrons tended to support the existing government. 'The majority of borough patrons, both peers and commoners, used their electoral influence in support of ministers, whether because they supported particular men in power, or because they supported all governments, irrespective of personalities and politics, with patronage or reward in view.'[23] Resistance to local patronal influence, then, might well carry with it undertones of hostility to the government and sympathy with the parliamentary opposition. In Norwich in the 1790s, 'identificaton of candidates with party labels and local power blocs was the prevailing custom.'[24]

At another level, however, the electors might have opinions of their own about their members' party allegiance. Certainly, the Abingdon constituents of E. L. Loveden deplored his Foxite politics in the 1780s in general, and during the regency crisis in particular. So great was the current of opinion against him that moves were made, in the end unsuccessful, to unseat him.[25] In some of the larger constituencies a candidate had to conform to the sentiments of local political managers, committee men, and agents. There are instances of these local groups approving, vetoing, selecting, and, of course, influencing candidates of the appropriate political complexion.[26] And as the number of MPs consistently committed to support of government and opposition rose as a proportion of the whole house to around two-thirds by the early nineteenth century, such considerations loomed steadily larger in electoral politics.[27]

Links between Parliament and the constituencies assumed their most concrete form in the growing degree of administrative centralization of government and opposition. Little exists in print on this most important topic, and no apology is needed for detailed examination.

[23] R. G. Thorne (ed.), *The House of Commons, 1790–1820*, 5 vols. (London, 1986), i. 56.

[24] Eugene R. Gaddis, 'William Windham and the Conservative Reaction in England, 1790–1796; The Making of a Conservative Whig and the Norwich Electoral Response', Ph.D. (Pennsylvania, 1979), 366.

[25] See correspondence in the Loveden MSS, D/Elv. 219, Berks. RO.

[26] I note some such instances in the section on canvassing above (pp. 90–101). Phillips argues that election committes at Norwich were capable of exerting considerable influence on candidates. See *Electoral Behaviour in Unreformed England*, 126–7.

[27] See my *Emergence of the British Two-party System*, 63–6. For the most recent discussion of the loyalties of Members of Parliament, see Thorne, *House of Commons*, i. 238–42, 269–73.

Professor Ginter has carefully documented the emergence of organizational developments in the Whig party in the 1780s.[28] These developments are both impressive and extensive, but they require careful scrutiny. Although William Adam's organization intervened in 83 constituencies at the general election of 1790, one-half of these already returned an MP favourable to Fox. Furthermore, in only about one-quarter of the cases cited did party intervention amount to anything more than the writing of a letter. In only eight was even a portion of election expenses paid by the party. In the 1780s, although the existence of party institutions needs recognition in so far as they heralded the emergence, albeit tentative, of a more efficient and bureaucratic principle in the organization of opposition politics, it must be recognized that the local efforts of autonomous agents and activitsts were still of the highest importance. Party institutions of a bureaucratic character were needed to weld together the Fox–North coalition and its various adherents during the great crisis of 1783–4, and again during the regency crisis of 1788–9 and the general election of 1790.[29] These developments unquestionably tended to develop the haphazard and informal organization of the Rockingham party into the experimental and tentative attempts at bureaucratic centralization of the party of Portland and Adam, but it was a development of degree rather than of kind, inspired by political realities rather than by a conscious attempt to replace one ideal of party or party organization by another.[30] Viewed from below, electoral realities remain much the same throughout the 1780s and 1790s. In particular, instinctive dislike of external and centralized interference left little room for effective bureaucratic intervention. At the time of the general election of 1796 almost one half of the 60–70 Foxite Whigs continued to depend upon patrons for their seats. It is doubtful if Adam's party organization alone was responsible for the return of a single member.[31]

[28] D. E. Ginter, 'The Financing of the Whig Party Organisation, 1783–1793', *Am. Hist. Rev.* 71 (1966); id., *Whig Organization*. My own early assessment of these developments may be found in *The Whig Party and the French Revolution* (London, 1967), 12–31.

[29] I argue this point in 'Party in the Later Eighteenth Century', in Cannon (ed.), *The Whig Ascendancy*, 88–9.

[30] To treat the organizational developments of the 1780s as innovations may distort the reality of earlier practice. For evidence that the Rockingham Whigs attempted to augment their numbers by attacking places where they had no or very little natural interest see Cannon (ed.), *The Whig Ascendancy*, 206 n.28. Similarly, Colley has argued that 'tory magnates and MPs in the mid-eighteenth century do seem to have viewed individual electioneering within a wider partisan context' than Ginter would allow (*In Defiance of Oligarchy*, 135). She continues: 'The Foxite Whigs' organization in the 1780s and 1790s marked an increase in scale but only rarely in content on the constituency expedients of their dissident Tory predecessors' (ibid. 141).

[31] T. Price, 'The Foxite Whigs: A Study of Opposition Politics, 1794–1797', MA (Manchester, 1981), 141–2.

What happened, however, to Adam's election machinery after the Portland schism of 1794 when Fox was left with an attenuated rump of a party? Adam retained the role of political manager for the Foxites, but it is doubtful if he played in 1796 the part he had played in 1790. During the election of 1796 he was employed by the Earl of Thanet at Appleby and resided in Westmorland.[32] There was, moreover, much less money for the Foxites to distribute. After Portland and Fitzwilliam had ended their financial support, the party relied upon voluntary and informal subscriptions. These were barely enough to scrape the surface of actual costs incurred during the 1796 election. Thus, while Adam did provide a shadow of his former services, connecting candidates with seats and issuing advice and publicity, the Foxite Whig performance in 1796 was a hand-to-mouth affair. Central co-ordination was lacking. At Tewkesbury and Hertfordshire, for example, one Foxite Whig stood against another.[33] It is hard to judge how extensive Adam's activities were. The party machine certainly intervened at Kent, Canterbury, and Downton, but it entirely deserted Scotland, in marked contrast to the strenuous efforts made there in 1788–90.[34]

Indeed, by this time the Whig Club was inheriting the mantle of party organization. The Whig Club was founded in May 1784 to aid Fox's election to Westminster. It was outshone in importance by the party machine of William Adam during the 1780s but it steadily attracted not merely the professional and commercial men of the metropolis, but men from much further afield as well. From a membership of around 100 in 1785 it grew to have almost 1,000 members by the second half of the 1790s, about one-quarter of them from outside the metropolitan area.[35] In addition to serving as a focal point for the parliamentary activities of the Foxite Whigs, the Whig Club acted as a clearing house for election affairs. The monthly meetings of the Whig Club were the focus of its activities, the toasts and speeches at its dinners the touchstone of Foxite faith and loyalty. The club, in fact, played a vital role in the winter of 1792–3 in fomenting radical opinions.[36] During the campaign against the Two Acts in 1795–6 it played a major role in helping the Foxite Whigs to raise an extra-parliamentary protest movement.[37] Indeed , it may

[32] William Adam to his wife, Blair-Adam MSS, GC1796, Blair-Adam by Kelty, Kinrosshire.
[33] *Morning Chronicle*, 21 May 1796.
[34] Price, 'The Foxite Whigs', MA, 145–8.
[35] Ibid. 120–4, 130–1.
[36] E. C. Black, *The Association: British-parliamentary Political Organization* (Cambridge, Mass., 1963), 290.
[37] Price, 'The Foxite Whigs', MA, ch. 6.

be that the Whig Club became the essential element of institutional and organizational unity in Foxite Whiggism at the turn of the century. Provincial Whig Clubs sprang up, and if several of them wilted before the onslaught of the Loyalist movement, others were still active in the early nineteenth century. After Fox's death in 1806, the Whig Clubs were augmented by numerous metropolitan and provincial Fox Clubs which sprang up and prospered for a quarter of a century. It was institutions such as these, together with the abiding importance of patronage, which provided the cohesion of the Foxite Whig party. Central party institutions played a much less important role. There was, for example, a revival in the activity of central party election funds in 1806–7.[38] This was, no doubt, a natural reaction to the pressures and strains of two general elections. Election subscriptions might be launched for particularly prestigious contests—Broughman's successive campaigns at Westmorland in 1818, 1820, and 1826, Romilly's attempt at Bristol in 1812, Whitbread's assault on Middlesex in 1820, and, of course, the great Westminster contests of 1818 and 1820—but there seems no evidence either of central planning or of electoral co-ordination. Significantly, a flood of money became available for the critical election of 1831. Brooks Club alone voted the party £15,000 for its campaign towards a party election fund which reached £27,000. In addition to this, however, local funds for reform candidates in particular constituencies frequently raised several thousand pounds.[39] It is not unreasonable to estimate that the total Whig party expenditure on the election of 1831 was well in excess of £50,000. In this way, centralization of election activity might occur at particular times and in response to special circumstances. It would be mistaken, however, to exaggerate its importance even when it was in operation, for it did little more than supplement the normal workings of election machinery.

In just the same way, Whig party subsidies to the press were much less important than the voluntary attachment of metropolitan and provincial editors. In spite of William Adam's initiatives in distributing paragraphs and payments to the press throughout the country,[40] the party remained casual and ineffective in its dealings with the press.[41] By the early nineteenth century, indeed, there was less need for

[38] M. Hinton, 'The General Elections of 1806 and 1807', Ph.D. (Reading, 1959), 498–502.
[39] J. N. Odurkene, 'The British General Elections of 1830 and 1831', B.Litt. (Oxford, 1976), 120–8.
[40] D. Ginter, 'The Financing of the Whig Party Organisation', 436; O'Gorman, *The Whig Party and the French Revolution*, 19–20.
[41] I. Asquith, 'James Perry and the Morning Chronicle, 1790–1821', Ph.D. (London, 1973), 96–9.

centralized party publicity. The most famous Whig newspaper was the *Morning Chronicle*, the tribune of Foxite Whig politics since the 1780s, under its editor, James Perry. Perry was personally and socially enmeshed in the world of Whig politics, and, until his death in 1821, it was his abiding commitment to the Whig party which provided the party with its most influential organ. Much the same is true of Daniel Stuart, who bought the *Morning Post* in 1795. His brother-in-law happened to be James Mackintosh, the Whig pamphleteer and writer.[42] Provincial newspapers likewise attached themselves to the Whig party. The *York Herald* was founded with the party's blessing, but without, any party subsidy, in 1789.[43] It was a local initiative and a local inspiration. In the North-east the Lambtons gave their blessing to the *Durham Chronicle* in the 1820s as part of their hereditary feud against the Lowthers, who controlled three newspapers in Cumberland and Westmorland.[44] Local loyalties as well as national allegiances were involved. In many of the larger provincial centres, the existence of a newspaper of one political complexion stimulated the emergence of a newspaper of an opposite political complexion.[45] Indeed, in spite of the unequal struggle between successive governments and the Whig party, a survey of 1811 discovered that out of 53 metropolitan papers, 17 supported and 18 opposed Perceval's government.[46]

The organization of politics on the government side of the House of Commons similarly owed considerably more to local mobilization and to voluntary effort than to centralized initiatives. The government could not and did not mount centrally directed, nation-wide election campaigns. Given its lack of resources and, of course, the spectacularly high cost of electioneering, the government was no more capable than the opposition of orchestrating events from the centre. There are striking similarities between the sort of activities undertaken by both government and opposition. They acted as electoral clearing houses, bringing together candidates and constituencies; they pooled information and contacts, placing informal networks of support and assistance at the disposal of local activists; and they acted as agencies of financial subsidy, placing small, and not so small, sums at the disposal of candidates and agents. On the whole, the government machine did much the same sort of things as its opposition counterpart

[42] A. Aspinall, *Politics and the Press, 1760–1850* (London, 1949), 278–80.
[43] See the correspondence on the founding of the *York Herald* in F. 349, Fitzwilliam MSS, Wentworth Woodhouse MSS, Sheffield Pub. Lib.
[44] Stoker, 'Elections and Voting Behaviour', Ph.D., 322.
[45] See above, pp. 288–9.
[46] D. Gray, *Spencer Perceval* (Manchester, 1963), 133.

but on a somewhat larger scale. Both the Treasury and the opposition employed their own election agents, for example.[47]

The sums known to have been expended and the constituencies upon which they were directed varied considerably from election to election. In 1754 the government spent £25,000 on 65 candidates in 35 constituencies. By 1780 the figure had risen to £62,000, which it spent in about the same number of seats. In 1784, however, no doubt on account of the premature dissolution of Parliament, only £32,000 was spent in half the number of seats.[48] A little more was spent in 1790 on 15 constituencies, but there was no concerted campaign. In 1796 the government had to mediate among the more than 50 supplicants for 13 vacant seats.[49] In many of these elections, especially those of 1790 and 1802, there are several instances of local electoral interests voluntarily offering their support to the government on political grounds.[50] The function of the government campaign was, therefore, twofold: to distribute what money and resources it had, and to act as broker among the various local men, groups, and interests whose energies had to be harmonized for the common cause. Things, moreover, became harder for governments in the early nineteenth century. Curwen's Act of 1809 forbidding the sale of parliamentary seats deprived them of a regular means of support and reinforcement. In 1807 no fewer than 30 seats had been purchased through government agency.[51] Futhermore, the amount of money available to government from the Secret Service fund and from the Privy Purse was steadily diminishing. Arguably, therefore, circumstances were hindering the emergence of co-ordinated, centralized, and interventionist government strategies. In the last analysis, successive governments were dependent upon the voluntary exertions of local families of weight and reputation for the return of friendly candidates.

Government and oppositions were capable of supervising their electoral campaigns even if their capacity to intervene in constituencies was limited. Nevertheless, their activies should not be underestimated in at least bringing together for a common purpose the widely varied electoral activities of local groups and, arguably, in promoting some degree of common identification among the politically conscious class of patrons and wealthier voters. The exertions of local election clubs went

---

[47] For Treasury agents, see D. McAdams, 'Politicians and the Electorate in the Late Eighteenth Century', Ph.D. (Duke University, North Carolina, 1967), 165–6. For opposition agents, see Ginter, *Whig Organization*, Introd.

[48] Namier and Brooke, *House of Commons*, i. 57–8, 84, 95.

[49] Thorne, *House of Commons*, i. 117–9, 144–7.

[50] McAdams, 'Politicians and the Electorate', Ph.D., 155–7.

[51] Thorne, *House of Commons*, i. 195.

some way towards alerting the voters to some consciousness of local party identities and, in turn, in some places, to their parliamentary counterparts.

Of course, we should not be too ready to identify every manifestation of sensible political organization as a sign of party activity. Many election interests liked to organize the voters in election clubs, many of which had absolutely no party significance whatsoever. At Berwick in the 1770s the Patriotic Club supported the Delaval interest, the Constitutional Club supported the Lisburne interest, while independent voters assembled in the Independent Club. These had nothing to do with national party.[52] The Blue Club at St Albans was a sophisticated piece of political machinery but it had very little to do with party. It was founded in the 1760s to support the interest of Lord Spencer. It bore many of the marks of a Friendly Society, the voters and their wives receiving discounted prices from some tradesmen and different forms of preferential treatment from others; it distributed charity and performed works of mercy. By 1776 it had its own committee rooms and a team of people to collect its (very carefully graduated) contributions.[53] The Market House Society which appeared at Taunton in the 1760s was rather similar. It was an association of middle-class, dissenting tradesmen, but dedicated to the cause of independence against the influence of the Wyndham family. By 1784 it had become the most powerful single interest in the borough and was disposing of its representation.[54] Election clubs of this type became quite common, especially after the 1784 general election, and although such clubs were capable of attaching themselves to a pro-government or pro-opposition candidate their motivation was almost always a local rather than a national one.[55]

In some of the larger boroughs, however, the conflict between the governments of North and Pitt, on the one hand, and the Rockinghamite and Foxite oppositions, on the other, was reflected in the conflict of local political clubs. As Nottingham, for example, the old Tory interest formed the White Lion Club in 1774. Its support of the North administration aroused the irritation of local Rockinghamites. In February 1776 in his 'Account of the State of the Parties in this town' Robert Denison told the Duke of Portland that

---

[52] Stoker, 'Elections and Voting Behaviour', Ph.D., 47.

[53] H. C. F. Lansberry, 'Politics and Government in St Albans', Ph.D. 168–72.

[54] Namier and Brooke, *House of Commons*, i. 372.

[55] Brewer tends to exaggerate the potential for radical action in these clubs; see 'Commercialization in Politics' in D. N. McKendrick (ed.), *The Birth of a Consumer Society*, 211, 23, 237–8, 261–2. They may, indeed, represent a stage in the evolution of articulate, political consciousness in 18th-cent. towns but it seems to me that they have a purely electoral, rather than a radical, frame of reference.

'associating upon a broad bottom would be most effectual to the support of the Whig interest here'. Consequently, a Whig Society was born which contested elections on the Rockingham/Portland interest for some years. Like many local party clubs of this type, its name changed to reflect the changing political environment. The White Lion Club gave way to a series of Loyalist clubs at the end of the eighteenth century and they to a Pitt Club early in the new century. Similarly, the Whig Society gave way to a series of successors, though all of them tenaciously retained the name 'Whig' in their titles.[56] The same pattern may be seen at Leicester, where the Leicester Revolution Club, founded in 1784, represented the voluntary attachment of local Whig gentlemen and the anti-corporation interest to the cause of Charles James Fox. Friends to the government organized themselves after the French Revolution into the Constitutional Society.[57] This sharpening polarity was obscured for some years during the revolutionary period when the growth of Leicester radicalism threatened the prevailing structure of local politics, but it rapidly reasserted itself in the early years of the new century, even though radicalism remained a powerful force. It did so, too, of course, at Westminster. During the American War the politics of the great borough came to turn on the struggle between the Foxite Whig Club of Westminster and the Constitutional Club, whose respective colours—buff and blue for the one, blue and scarlet for the other—decorated many an election meeting during the great contests of 1780, 1784, and 1788. Both, in fact, were umbrella organizations for individuals and interests to attach themselves to. The Whig Club, for example, attracted the spontaneous loyalty of a number of parochial clubs sympathetic to the cause of Fox and parliamentary reform.[58]

In other constituencies, the emergence of party clubs which identified themselves with parliamentary parties came a little later. At Liverpool the founding of the Tory Backbone Club just before the general election of 1812 precipitated the establishment of the Canning Club to promote the memory of Pitt. In response to this, the local Whigs organized

[56] M.479/76-7, Smith MSS, Nottingham City RO; Robert Denison to Duke of Portland, 5 Feb. 1776, Portland MSS, Nottingham Univ. Lib.; J. Moses, 'Elections and Electioneering in Nottinghamshire Constituencies, 1702-1832', Ph.D. (Nottingham, 1965), 173, 179-80, 184-5, 211-5; M. Thomis, *Politics and Society in Nottingham 1785-1835* (Oxford, 1969), 159. Although Moses argues that the White Lion Club disappears in the 1790s, there is an (admittedly unsupported) reference in the 1803 poll book to its continued existence. See C. Sutton, *An Alphabetical List of the Burgesses* (Nottingham, 1803).

[57] A. Temple-Patterson, *Radical Leicester* (Leicester, 1954), 65; *Leicester Journal*, 3 Apr. 1784, 13 Nov. 1789.

[58] John Bellamy, *The Whig Club, instituted in May 1784* (London 1792); Sir William Young to Duke of Buckingham, *Courts and Cabinets of the Reign of George III*, 4 vols. (1853-5), i. 416-19.

themselves into the Concentric Club in December 1812.[59] In Chester the old independents of the city organized themselves into the Tory King and Constitution Club in 1817. The old corporation-Grosvenor interest retaliated by forming a Whig Club in 1820. Thus, many years of annual dinners and local conflict were overtaken by a new synthesis of local and national objectives. By this time, Fox and Pitt clubs were spreading through the country until by 1815 most large towns had them or their equivalents, Tory and Whig clubs. Even though these were not election machines they nevertheless brought together those individuals and families who did fight them in a common cause devoted to the memory and principles of their cherished leaders.[60] In such ways could political partisanship be maintained.

Even where the names of local party clubs do not indicate an automatic connection between local and parliamentary politics, supporting evidence may allow us to make that connection. Contemporary writers and compilers like Oldfield occasionally describe the politics of boroughs in terms of their support for or opposition to the ministry, even if the party labels 'Whig' and 'Tory' are not used. Professor Phillips, for example, has been able to discuss the politics of Norwich, Maidstone, and even Northampton in the last two decades of the eighteenth century in 'ministerial' and 'anti-ministerial' terms.[61] At Ipswich, this identification of local loyalties and parliamentary alignments took a little longer. The Blues and the Yellows had traditionally been supported by clusters of local groups and clubs. On the Blue side, at least, these gradually hardened into the Wellington Club in 1825, an avowed Tory association of freemen which influenced the choice of candidates at municipal as well as at parliamentary elections.[62]

Local election clubs in the unreformed parliament may have been a potent factor in generating partisan enthusiasm, but they were informal bodies, most unlike their late nineteenth- and twentieth-century counterparts. They were small, their proceedings were informal—records were very rarely kept of their transactions—and, between elections, almost entirely apolitical. Their existence was rarely continuous. Clubs sprang into existence for a particular purpose, usually to fight an election, and if a seat was badly lost or safely won

---

[59] B. Whittingham-Jones, 'Electioneering in Lancashire, before the Secret Ballot: II. Liverpool's Political Clubs, 1812–1830', *Trans. Hist. Soc. Lancs. Cheshire* (1959–60), 117–38.

[60] The Fox and Pitt clubs could do with a historian. For an initial impression of the Fox clubs, see A. Mitchell, *Whigs in Opposition*, 54–5. For the Whig Club of Cirencester see the materials in the Painswick House Collection, Series F,I no. 5, Gloucester Pub. Libr.

[61] J. A. Phillips, *Electoral Behaviour in Unreformed England*, 121–4, 130–2.

[62] A. R. Childs, 'Politics and Elections in Suffolk Boroughs During the Late Eighteenth Century and Early Nineteenth Century', M.Phil (Reading, 1973), 104–6.

there might be little for the club to do. Even the strongest and most famous of them had no guaranteed existence. There could be no mistaking the political complexion of the Rockingham Club at York. Founded in December 1753, it met monthly, after 1758 quarterly. It was a club of York freemen in the Rockingham interest, numbering between 100 and 200 out of an electorate of 2,000. The club included the upper and professional stratum but, increasingly, came to represent craftsmen and artisans. Membership of, and attitudes towards, the Rockingham Club were the touchstone of local and national loyalties in the politics of York. Henry Duncombe's refusal to become a member in 1783 led Fitzwilliam to refuse to support him. The Rockingham Club directed activity and loyalty to the man who gave his name to the club. After his death in 1782 it was not possible to redirect those sentiments to his heir. Although members of the Rockingham Club accepted Fitzwilliam as his successor, the society languished, torn apart by differences over parliamentary reform. There is no record that it ever met after 1783. It was succeeded by the Yorkshire Club which met fitfully between 1785 and 1794, when Fitzwilliam joined Pitt's government. This was clearly a less personal and more political association than the Rockingham Club had been and was part of the drive to recover Whig strength lost in 1784 throughout Yorkshire, not just in York.[63]

Election clubs served a wide variety of vital functions. They furnished candidates with a steady supply of men, money, and resources. They provided election workers, supporters, and voters. They lent continuity and experience to local political causes. They drew attention to men and issues, generated excitement, and created publicity. They focussed support of an electoral cause upon a common institution, often one with social and charitable connotations. They served to straddle the worlds of local high society and local popular political culture, partisan, vigorous, vibrant, violent, and assertive. Local election clubs, therefore, enabled local opinion to be controlled and influenced by those with the social influence, political will, and economic resources with which to attempt it. Consequently, many election clubs played a part in cultivating local awareness of parliamentary concerns and linking constituency concerns into a wider, national political context. National and parliamentary issues, together with the political values and partisan alignments that went with them, were by no means unfamiliar to large sections of the unreformed electorate. We must now attempt to define

[63] F. C. Price, 'Parliamentary Elections in York City, 1754–1790', 21–2, 187–92, 196–7, and 221–40; E. A. Smith, *Whig Principles and Party Politics* (Manchester, 1975), 49, 65–7, 72–4, 91, 95. Fitzwilliam to H. Zouch, 9 June 1784, E.234, Fitzwilliam MSS, Wentworth Woodhouse MSS, Sheffield Pub. Lib.

more exactly how large that section was, and in which parts of the unreformed electoral system it was to be found.


## THE COUNTIES

In the county constituencies, the historic party distinctions of Whig and Tory died, but they died a slow and lingering death. In some counties, party labels and other forms of party terminology persisted down to the second half of the eighteenth century. In Cumberland, for example, party labels and party colours were employed to highlight the family conflicts between the Curwens and the Lowthers in the 1760s and 1770s.[64] In general, it may be claimed that where Toryism remained strong, then party rivalry and party consciousness tended to linger longest and strongest. It was this which gave such party colouring as there was to the contested county elections in Kent and Oxfordshire in 1754, Derbyshire in 1768, Monmouthshire in 1771, Bedfordshire in 1774, Leicestershire in 1775, and Gloucestershire in 1776. In County Durham, the gentry and squires of the remote valleys in the north of the county remained stubbornly Tory, as did the rank and file of the parochial clergy and, to a lesser extent, the freeman of the towns. No wonder that party labels persisted strongly until the 1760s in this county.[65] The absence of contests in Northamptonshire between 1748 and 1806, moreover, did not mean that party conflict was absent. It was held in check by the practice of dividing the seats in the county: the Whigs took the boroughs, leaving the county seats to the Tories.[66]

Nevertheless, the party identities of the early eighteenth century were dying. For one thing, contested elections in the counties became less frequent. In the 10 general elections in the 40 English counties between 1701 and 1734, an average of 17 counties were contested at each election. Such a frequency could not be maintained. At the six general elections between 1741 and 1774 the figure dropped to less than six. (At the following nine elections between 1780 and 1831 it recovered a little, but only to nine.) For another, the political calculations of Pitt the Elder and the accession of George III ended the proscription of the Tories. The old issues

---

[64] R. S. Ferguson, *The MPs of Cumberland and Westmorland 1660–1867* (London, 1871), 100.

[65] E. Hughes, *North Country Life in the Eighteenth Century*, vol. ii. *Cumberland and Westmorland 1700–1830* (London, 1965), 268–9.

[66] E. G. Forrester, *Northamptonshire County Elections and Electioneering* (London, 1941), 81–2.

that had distinguished the parties—the monarchy, the church, and foreign policy—seemed much less relevant after the Jacobite rebellion of 1745 and the accession of George III. Indeed, about 40% of the old Tories who survived in Parliament after 1761 voted consistently and obediently for the court, and thus for the Hanoverian succession.[67] Although party sentiment in the counties still lingered, the politics of the new reign were not conducted in terms of a Whig–Tory polarity.

Thereafter, county elections tended to be fought on local and familial issues. In some counties in England and Wales, elections turned upon attempts of the great Whig aristocratic houses to extend their enormous power, and the endeavours of the local gentry to stop them. These conflicts between the ruling families occasionally elicited a few old party cries, but these had by now lost their significance. Typical of these were the conflicts between the Yorke (Hardwicke) and Manners families in Cambridgeshire (1784), the Lowther and Curwen families in Cumberland (1768, 1774), and the Manchester and Sandwich families in Huntingdonshire (1768). Further examples of non-party county election contests may be found in Northumberland (1774), in Rutland (1754 and 1761), Sussex (1774) and Westmorland (1761, 1768, and 1774). Similar Welsh county contests include Breconshire (1754), Caernarvonshire (1768, 1774), Pembrokeshire (1768, 1780), and Radnorshire (1774). In the two-member English counties there was a tradition that a powerful aristocratic family was entitled through natural interest to one seat. Considerable resentment, and possibly a contested election, might ensue, however, if it attempted to challenge the second seat. Party considerations were usually lost in all this.

Usually, but not always. There were at least four general elections in the last 50 years of the unreformed period in which issues of parliamentary, and especially of party, significance could accompany these more traditional elements in county contests. This happened in 1784, 1807, 1818, and 1831. In 1784, the parliamentary rivalry between William Pitt and Charles James Fox was an issue in all seven contested county seats in England. The perceptions adopted by the voters towards these issues and personalities were of immediate and overwhelming significance in these contests.[68] Party sensitivities were not aroused to the same extent in 1807, but at least 8 of the 11 county contests in that year reflected the fortunes of the Ministry of all the

---

[67] Not three-quarters, as alleged in B. Hill, *The Growth of Parliamentary Parties*, 39–40, as will be apparent from the evidence there cited.

[68] Beds., Berks., Bucks., Gloucs., Herts., Middx., and Suffolk. In Anglesey, the only one of the Welsh counties to be contested in 1784, national issues were not a factor.

Talents.[69] Lincolnshire may be taken as an example. Uncontested since 1724, it was hardly a politically conscious county like Yorkshire or Middlesex. Yet during the contest of 1807 the voters were left in no doubt where the candidates stood on the parliamentary alignments of the day. Some local worthies like Robert Vyner were clearly on the side of the Talents: 'The last administration had been characterised as men whom it was almost criminal to have had connexions with; but for himself he thought that to have afforded them support was far from being an imputation.' Others, however, warned the freeholders 'that they did not return to Parliament a man whose opinion was recorded as favouring attempts to make the King violate his coronation oath'.[70] Party labels, as such, may not have been used in Lincolnshire in 1807, but the party loyalties of the two sides were not only evident but deliberately employed as a means of attracting electoral support. The general election of 1818 yielded a further series of keenly contested elections in which parliamentary alignments influenced the course and outcome of at least 7 of the 11 contests.[71] Broughman's Whig assault on Lord Lonsdale's Tory redoubt of Westmorland was perhaps the most spectacular of them all. This was nothing less than a symbolic confrontation between the friends of government and the friends of the opposition. As such, it was fought out not only in 1818 but during its further instalments in 1820 and 1826. As Brougham put it: 'Was there ever a case in which *the ministers* as such were more implicated?'[72] For their part, Lonsdale's local supporters were more than ready to accept the challenge to trial by party.[73] Finally, the general election of 1831 was a sensational victory for supporters of parliamentary reform but nowhere more clearly than in the counties. Every single contest turned on party issues, of which reform was the most potent in mobilizing not only electors but patrons, too.[74]

It is not easy to estimate the percentage of English and Welsh counties which were penetrated by party in the last 50 years of the unreformed

[69] Beds., Durham, Hants., Hunts., Lincs., Middx., Som., and Yorks. manifested significant levels of party activity while Dorset, Surrey, and Sussex did not. See the constituency details in Thorne, *House of Commons*, ii. Hinton, 'The General Elections of 1806 and 1807', Ph.D., 306–39.

[70] *The Poll for the County of Lincoln for the Election of Two Knights of the Shire* (1807), 6–7.

[71] Devon, Hunts., Lincs., Som., Sussex, Westmorland, and Wilts. exhibited strong manifestations of party activity, identification, and awareness. Berks. and Leics., on the whole, did not. Herefordshire and Kent were marginal cases. Once again, I have drawn upon the constituency details in Thorne, *House of Commons*, vol. ii.

[72] Brougham to Grey, 22 Feb. 1818, Brougham MSS, Univ. College, London, quoted by A. Mitchell, *Whigs in Opposition*, 49.

[73] Lord Thanet to Brougham, 18 Feb. 1818, J974, Brougham MSS, Univ. College, London.

[74] M. Brock, *The Great Reform Act* (London, 1973), 196.

period, given the wide variety of circumstances in the counties and their propensity to change over time. We may at once eliminate those counties which were not contested in these years or were contested so rarely, and in such a manner, that the notion of party becomes effectively redundant. This at once accounts for Cheshire, Derbyshire, Lancashire, Monmouth, Nottinghamshire, Rutland, and Staffordshire. It is also difficult to see much sign of party life in Shropshire and Worcestershire, both only contested at the eleventh hour, in 1831, as well as in Cumberland, nominally contested in 1820 exhaustively contested in 1831. Consequently, in 10 out of the 40 English counties, party influences may effectively be discounted. Of the 12 Welsh counties, Anglesey, Cardiganshire, Denbighshire, Merionethshire, and Radnorshire may be eliminated on the same criteria.

There were a number of other county constituencies that experienced concentrated outbreaks of party activity which, for a variety of reasons, could not be sustained over time. The flurry of contests at Lincolnshire in 1807, 1816, 1818, and 1823 built up considerable party momentum over 16 years but their significance should not be generalized over the period as a whole. The elemental issues of oligarchy and independence, much canvassed in 1807, nevertheless gave way to thoroughgoing discussion of Catholic emancipation and parliamentary reform.[75] Northumberland was contested twice in 1826. Even on the first of these occasions, and when the county had been uncontested since 1748, party labels and party language were well in evidence. Catholic emancipation and parlimentary reform were thoroughly debated on the hustings, while the candidates and their supporters employed party descriptions of their own principles. ('I am a Tory, Gentlemen, and I glory in the principles of my party.'[76]) The Wiltshire contest of 1818 was the first since 1772. It was fought largely on the same issues of electoral freedom and independence as had been rehearsed on the earlier occasion. The further contest of 1819, however, while recycling this electoral fodder, concentrated much more squarely on national party issues, especially the Corn Laws. Having endured two such contests in two years, the county went to sleep again until the 1832 Reform Act.[77] Ten other counties fall into this category. Norfolk was contested in 1802, 1806, and 1817; Oxfordshire was contested in

---

[75] See the correspondence of Sir Gilbert Heathcote in the Ancaster MSS, 3/7, 9, 13 and that concerning the re-election of William Cust in 1816, in the Tennyson d'Eyncourt MSS, both in the Lincs. Archives Office.

[76] There is an extensive *Collection of the Authentic Papers, Speeches etc. relating to the Northumberland Contested Election, 21 February–7 March, 1826*, in the John Ryland Lib., Univ. of Manchester. The quotation is from p. 232.

[77] VCH *Wiltshire*, v. 200–7.

1826, 1830, and 1831; Somerset was contested in 1807, 1818, and 1826. On the second of these occasions 'The question is whether this County shall send both members to the support of opposition Members, or whether it should offer one, that uniformly opposed, right or wrong, Every measure that is proposed.'[78] Futhermore, Warwickshire was contested in 1820, and Westmorland was contested in 1818, 1820, and 1826. Finally, we should include here several Welsh counties which experienced contested elections: Carmarthenshire in 1796 and 1802, Caernarvonshire and Flintshire in 1796, Radnorshire in 1802, and Glamorgan in 1820. These eight English and five Welsh counties attained quite impressive levels of party activity within certain concentrated periods. Nothing more can be, nor should be, claimed.

A futher category of county seats can be distinguished in which party activity, while discernible, is intermittent. Party sentiment emerges clearly enough at occasional contested elections but it is often difficult to discern what elements of party activity survive between them. It is not clear, for example, what continuities linked the Buckinghamshire contests of 1784 and 1831, although there can be no denying the powerful contribution which party men, issues, and resources made to each of them separately.[79] Similar difficulties confront the Cornwall contests of 1790 and 1831, the Dorset contests of 1806 and 1807, on the one hand, and the two contested elections of 1831, on the other; the Gloucestershire contests of 1784 and 1811; and the interesting Leicestershire contests of 1818 and 1830 (at which latter election the term 'Liberal' makes an early appearance to describe a reforming Whig candidate). At Leicestershire, indeed, contested elections reflected rapidly emerging socio-economic cleavages. In particular, the development of stocking-frame knitting in the industrial villages of the county created a new class of capitalists, bankers, merchants, and manufacturers which looked very early to liberalism, free trade, and dissent. Its attack on the old, landed, county society dominated county politics in the early nineteenth century. The contests of 1818 and 1830 were violent and partisan affairs at which national party issues, especially the Catholic question, came to the fore. By 1831, a radical Whiggism, closely identified with the party of Grey, was confronting a Tory party closely

---

[78] Thomas Lethbridge to Francis Drake, 20 June 1818, DD/NE/12, Lethbridge MSS, Som. RO.

[79] Richard W. Davis, *Political Change and Continuity, 1760–1885: A Buckinghamshire Study* (Newton Abbot, 1972), 33–9, 94–8; D. C. Moore, 'Is the Other Face of Reform in Bucks an Hallucination', *J. Brit. Studies* (1976), 150–61; K. von den Steinen, 'The Fabric of an interest: The Bucks Election of 1784', *Albion* (1972), 206–18.

identified with Wellington and Peel.[80] Nevertheless, it is not always possible to establish such striking continuities, as is well illustrated by the Northamptonshire contests of 1806 and 1831. The first of these contests was a characteristic eighteenth-century county election in which aristocratic influence and voter mobilization were the paramount concerns. That of 1831 was quite different, with its concentration on the reform issue and its heavy and explicit confrontation between the two major parties.[81] The Yorkshire contests of 1807, 1826, and 1830 are rather easier to compare. The copious documentation which survives concerning Yorkshire's electoral politics in the years between these contests reveals continuing political awareness on the part of the patronal and voter classes alike, an awareness that is powerfully penetrated by party issues, party terminology, and party preoccupations. There can be no question that the essential foundation of Yorkshire politics in the early nineteenth century was the ideological division between Whig and Tory.[82] Party consciousness, however, was by no means so thoroughly developed in other counties which may be considered here. Nevertheless, the dispositions of sitting members and candidates towards government and opposition, and to many of the current issues which divided them, were powerful elements in the Durham contests of 1790, 1807, and 1820, the Herefordshire contests of 1790, 1802, 1818, and the Suffolk contests of 1790 and 1830. Finally, two Welsh counties—Breconshire, contested in 1818 and 1831, and Pembrokeshre, contested in 1807, 1812, and 1831—may be included in this category of county seat.

Hampshire is yet another county which experienced several contested elections and which continued to manifest some, admittedly intermittent, party consciousness. It is, however, remarkable for its organizational sophistication, and thus deserves some further attention. Associations of electors in euphemistically titled 'Constitutional' or

[80] See 'Election Letters', Paget MSS 301, Leics. RO ('Our attempt to bring in a Liberal Member of Parliament', 10 Aug. 1830). Leicestershire is a good example of latent party consciousness. A Whig account of the contested election of 1775 condemned 'the old Tory system, originally formed by certain High Church doctrines . . . The Principles on which this system was built were Prerogative, Passive Obedience, Non-Resistance, Slavery'. The author accused William Pochin, the losing candidate in 1775, of trying to destroy distinctions between Whig and Tories. See R. Heathcote, *Memoirs of the Late Contested Election* (1775), L.094, vol. 50; pamphlets printed by Cockshaw and Others, Leicester Pub. Lib. See also *VCH Leicestershire*, ii. 128–9.

[81] Forrester, *Northamptonshire County Electioneering* 92–150. The flavour of the 1831 contest is best captured in *Althorpiana*, a fascinating essay published in Northampton in 1831. The only copy known to me is in the Guildhall Lib.

[82] Even if the structures of the election contests themselves were not always solely determined by party considerations. See Letters to Lord Milton 1812, E.232; Letters Declining the Agency for Milton, 1812, E.213b; Letters to Milton, 1818, Fitzwilliam Papers, Wentworth Woodhouse MSS, Sheffield Pub. Lib.

'Whig' clubs are, as we have seen,[83] by no means unknown. The Devon County Club, for example, was organized to further the electoral interests of the Whig politician, Lord Ebrington, and it remained a force in Devon politics until the Reform Act. What happened in Hampshire, however, was of greater *political* interest. Opposition to the American War in the 1770s made itself felt in the Hampshire Club from 1775 onwards. The club held regular meetings to foment and to harmonize anti-war feeling. After 1780 it began to turn its attention to parliamentary reform. Although it had not originally been committed to either government or opposition it had by 1788 become a Foxit institution and one, furthermore, meshed into that party's institutional network. During the regency crisis the Hampshire Club rallied local support behind Fox and proceeded to support the candidates of his party in 1790. Hampshire Pittites retaliated by establishing the Hampshire County Club. Organized party in Hampshire, however, could not survive continuously the years of wartime sacrifice and patriotism. The Hampshire County Club was wound up in 1796, and the Hampshire Club abandoned its meetings two years later. But this was not the end. When party feeling began to revive, the Hampshire Club resumed its activities, supporting Whig candidates in the contested elections of 1806 and 1807. The functional nature of party institutions, and the intermittent and discontinuous nature of their existence, could not be better illustrated.[84]

There remain 12 county constituencies which exhibited a reasonably continuous, as well as a tolerably thoroughgoing, commitment to party rivalries. In several of these, party conflict had already revived in the later eighteenth century, and the activities and attitudes of patrons and candidates were of vital significance in injecting party appeals and party issues into electoral politics. Bedfordshire inherited strong party traditions from the contested elections of 1774 and 1784. Although too much should not be claimed, party awareness and party identities were well to the fore at the contested elections of 1807, 1820, 1826, and 1831. The well-known party commitments of a series of patrons and candidates kept the party pot simmering at every contest. Much the same can be said of Berkshire and the contested elections of 1796, 1812, 1818, and 1820. The election literature for Berkshire is full of party issues, party loyalties, accusations of party betrayals, and the

---

[83] See above, 330.

[84] S. Lowe, 'Hampshire Elections and Electioneering, 1734–1830', M.Phil. (Southampton, 1972), 123–38, 186. The detailed history of the Hampshire Club can best be reconstructed from the occasional details to be culled from the *Hampshire Chronicle*. For its Foxite loyalties, see edns. of 19 and 28 Dec. 1789, and 15 Feb. 1790.

like.[85] On the whole, the same is true for Durham, which went to the polls in 1790, 1807, and 1820. Perhaps surprisingly, Cambridgeshire falls into this same category. Its candidates frequently imported the parliamentary confrontation between government and opposition into the fairly regular contested elections: after the contest of 1780 Cambridgeshire was contested twice in 1802, in 1826, 1830, and 1831. For much the same reason, however, party was a persistent element in Cambridgeshire county politics, contested election or not.[86] Huntingdonshire conforms closely to this pattern. Uncontested since 1768, the contest of 1807 was followed by further contests in 1807, 1818, 1826, 1830 and 1831. The electoral politics of Surrey and Sussex were similar. The former was contested in 1790, 1806, 1807, 1812, 1813 and 1830. The parliamentary politics of patrons appears to have been decisive both here and in Sussex, which went to the polls in 1807, 1818, 1820 and 1826. Elsewhere, the pattern was rather different. Devon, for example, was a rather special case. The county had not been contested since 1712, but the compromises which had ensured its electoral peace could not survive the intensity of the conflict between William Pitt and Charles James Fox. The contest of 1790 was the result, and this was followed by further contests in 1812, 1816, 1818, 1820, 1826 and 1830. After 1816, the parliamentary ambitions of Lord Ebrington, a notable Whig, ensured that parliamentary politics could not be ignored in Devon elections. Ebrington's tactic was to mobilize latent independent feeling in the county against the existing structure of landlord control and, on this basis, appeal to reformist sentiment. It was a heady mixture. In the years immediately before the Reform Act, Devon must have been one of the most exciting, and politically sophisticated, of English counties.[87]

In some counties, the parliamentary battle between government and opposition, and the alignments and loyalties thus established, were of more direct significance. The politics of Essex turned upon the conflict between government and opposition, a conflict which determined candidatures, organizations, and propaganda. Even the period of *uncontested elections* between 1774 and 1810 was dominated by that conflict and a compromise between the two sides was secured because of their strength rather than their weakness. Contests in 1810, 1812, 1830, and 1831 largely turned upon the same conflict, together

---

[85] See esp. the 76 printed broadsides about county elections in this period to be found in the lib. of Reading Univ.

[86] See the extremely interesting treatment of Cambs. in Thorne, *House of Commons*, ii. 26–30.

[87] Again, the material in Thorne (ibid. ii. 95–9) is extremely valuable. See also, however, *A Synopsis of Elections for Devon, 1812–57*, 51/12/2, Acland MSS, Devon RO.

with powerful admixtures of independence and radicalism. The electoral politics of Hertfordshire were similar. At least, contests in 1784, 1790, 1796, 1802, and 1805 involved senior figures in both government and opposition. Radicalism was a much more potent factor in Middlesex, of course, expecially in a brief yet fiercely contested period between 1802 and 1807 which witnessed no fewer than four contested elections between the supporters of government, opposition, and Sir Francis Burdett. Middlesex was to be contested again in 1820. Furthermore, it was the balance of power between supporters of government and opposition which dominated the politics of Kent. It was upset, and led to contests, in 1790, 1796, 1802, 1806, and 1818.[88]

While there can be no disputing the reality that the structure of electoral politics in the counties was established by patterns of land and property holding, there can be no denying the steadily accumulating influence of party conflict. Although county elections in their inspiration, organization, and financing were conflicts between local families and interests they could, and after 1784, steadily did, come to conform to the alignments established by government and opposition. By the early nineteenth century, very few counties were insulated from the issues and the appeals generated by that conflict. It is true that the rate of contested elections remained low. Nevertheless, partisanship remained a factor. Only 4 counties went to the polls in 1796, but of the 36 which did not no fewer than 15 were compromised between government and opposition.[89] Furthermore, the absence of contested elections does not allow us to conclude that party conflict was absent. Warwickshire was not contested between 1774 and 1820, but organized Whig and Tory groups existed none the less.[90] Party conflict made itself felt in county politics in a number of ways: through the politics of patrons and candidates and the impact of their interests, organization, money, and propaganda; through the power of parliamentary issues to generate enthusiasm and participation; through the existence of local clubs and groups, newspapers and pamphlets, and, no doubt, through the more regular contested elections occurring in boroughs within the county. To these we must now turn.


### THE BOROUGHS

To attempt to measure the strength of party feeling, the power of national party issues and the influence of national party alignments

---

[88]   Thorne, *House of Commons*, ii. 214–15.          [89] Ibid. i. 146–50.
[90]   *VCH Warwickshire*, vii. 293–5.

in the borough constituencies in the last 50 years of the unreformed electoral system is an even more daunting undertaking than it is in the counties. The boroughs differ so much between each other, as well as over time, that any scheme of categorization is bound to appear arbitrary. Individual constituencies move bewilderingly across the spectrum of possible party influence, manifesting at one election many of the characteristics of party political behaviour, such as the existence and awareness of party issues, the perceptions of parliamentary alignments, and the use of party rhetoric, and, at the next, lapsing into a preoccupation with entirely local issues. Idiosyncracies abound, perceived developments come to be aborted, and general patterns are almost impossible to detect. In all this, how should the historian rank and grade the myriad manifestations of party across the differing types of borough constituencies? For what it is worth, the following guide to the varied extent of party influences over electoral behaviour in the boroughs is offered in the hope that it may, at least, provide a preliminary and tentative model for discussion in this most vexed of all areas in Hanoverian historiography.

We can first, and fairly confidently, remove from immediate consideration that large number of borough seats in which party activity, if it had ever existed, had ceased to exist by the later eighteenth century, and in which, to all intents and purposes, it is impossible to trace it thereafter. In short, party is a redundant explanatory category in these places. These seats include 20 venal boroughs,[91] 31 burgage boroughs,[92] 29 of the smaller freeman boroughs,[93] 17 of the scot and

---

[91] The 20 venal boroughs include 5 with a freeman franchise (Bishop's Castle, Bossiney, Dunwich, Grampound, and Launceston), 10 with a scot and lot or freeholder franchise (Arundel, Callington, Cricklade, Mitchell, New Shoreham, St Ives, Shaftesbury, Stockbridge, Wallingford, and Wootton Bassett), and 5 with a householder franchise (Hindon, Honiton, Ilchester, Tregony, and Aylesbury). For the politics of these boroughs, see above, pp. 28–31. The only one where party influences may conceivably be detected is Wootton Bassett; by the late 18th cent. it had become an open borough, and some faint government versus opposition polarity may for a few years be detected . Nevertheless, there can be no doubt that the politics of the borough turned upon a polarity between oligarchy and independence rather than any other. See Thorne, *House of Commons*, ii. 429–30.

[92] The 31 burgage boroughs were: Appleby, Ashburton, Bere Alston, Bletchingley, Boroughbridge, Bramber, Castle Rising, Chippenham, Clitheroe, Cockermouth, Downton, East Grinstead, Great Bedwyn, Heytesbury, Horsham, Knaresborough, Malton, Midhurst, Newport, Newton, Newton (Isle of Wight), Northallerton, Old Sarum, Petersfield, Pontefract, Richmond, Ripon, Thirsk, Weobley, Westbury, and Whitchurch. For the politics of these boroughs see above, pp. 32–38. There are a few hints of party involvement in some of them, usually on account of the parliamentary politics of the occasional candidate; see e.g. the cases of Ashburton, Castle Rising, Chippenham, Downton, and Pontefract, ibid. ii. 100–1, 288, 416, 419, and 457. It is by no means clear in any of these cases, however, that *electoral* behaviour was in the slightest degree affected by these considerations.

[93] The 25 English freeman boroughs were: Aldeburgh, Barnstaple, Bewdley, Camelford, Chipping Wycombe, Dartmouth, East Looe, Guildford, Hedon, Higham Ferrers, Hythe,

lot type of boroughs,[94] and 27 corporation boroughs.[95] In my judgement, therefore, out of the 215 English and Welsh borough seats, a total of 124 may be eliminated from serious consideration when attempting to assess the relevance of party influences (58%). It is in the remaining 91 borough seats (42%) that party influences begin to interest the historian, and the concept of party becomes indispensable to a comprehensive understanding of electoral politics.

There is no obvious way in which the range of party intensity in these constituencies may be simply expressed. The following categorization tries to catch something of the complexity and changeability of different local situations, and thus of the complexity and changeability of party itself, while endeavouring to rank the various levels at which party was experienced.

We may begin with those constituencies in which local considerations remained uppermost, the core of political conflict being the struggle between oligarchy and independence, but in which party rhetoric, party labels, and party issues were intermittently to be heard. Moreover, these constituencies had known something of party early in the eighteenth century and the party distinctions then evident had never entirely disappeared. In these places, then, the recollection of party possibly served some function in defining, and conceivably even intensifying, political conflict in the present. Twenty-five English and six Welsh seats conform to this broad pattern.[96] They range quite widely. At one extreme may be found a seat like Morpeth, where

Liskeard, Lyme Regis, Lymington, New Woodstock, Okehampton, Orford, Plympton Erle, Queenborough, Rye, St Mawes, Totnes, West Looe, Winchester, Winchelsea. The four Welsh boroughs were: Brecon, Haverfordwest, Montgomery, and New Radnor. Occasionally, the party politics of a candidate may be detected, but it is very doubtful if political consciousness in any of these constituencies had gone beyond suport for, or opposition to, local interests. See, however, the cases of Barnstaple, Aldeburgh, and Guildford, ibid. ii, 102–3, 368, 381.

[94] To 12 scot and lot boroughs (Aldborough, Amersham, Bridport, Corfe Castle, Eye, Fowey, Gatton, Milborne Port, Minehead, Seaford, Steyning, and Weymouth and Melcombe Regis) should be added 4 freeholder boroughs (Haslemere, Ludgershall, Reigate, and Tavistock) and one householder borough (St Germans). The many contests at Weymouth and Melcombe Regis should not lead to the assumption that anything other than local interests and issues were at stake (ibid., ii. 143–7). There is a hint, however, of local party consciousness at Bridport and Seaford (ibid. ii. 131–2, 475–9) but it is little more than a hint.

[95] There were 26 English corporation boroughs: Andover, Banbury, Bath, Bodmin, Brackley, Buckingham, Bury St Edmunds, Calne, Christchurch, Devizes, Droitwich, Harwich, Helston, Lostwithiel, Malmesbury, Marlborough, Newport (Isle of Wight), New Romney, Salisbury, Saltash, Scarborough, Thetford, Tiverton, Truro, Wilton, Yarmouth (Isle of Wight). To these should be added the Welsh borough of Beaumaris. Only at Harwich was there some little awareness of parliamentary alignments (ibid. ii. 160–1.)

[96] These seats included Aylesbury (after 1804), Bridgnorth, Cambridge, Cirencester, Cricklade (after 1782), Derby, Dorchester, East Retford, Hastings, King's Lynn, Ludlow, Monmouth, Morpeth, Penryn, Peterborough, Plymouth, Poole, Portsmouth, Stamford, Sudbury, Taunton, Wareham, Warwick, Wells and Wenlock.

overwhelmingly the rhetoric was that of independence versus oligarchy and the issues at stake were essentially local ones. Nevertheless, the contest of 1802 raised a few faint and distant echoes of party awareness. That at King's Lynn in 1826 raised rather stronger echoes. The Whigs and the Tories of the early nineteenth century traced their ancestry continuously back to their predecessors of the early eighteenth.[97] In others, however, the parliamentary loyalties of patrons, members, and candidates acted as a vehicle for reviving faded party inclinations. Cirencester and Sudbury, in their very different ways, experienced fairly regular contests in the last 50 years of the unreformed period in which the politics of patrons, members, and candidates reverberated among the voters.[98] Manifestations of party, however, could appear in some of the more sleepy constituencies which did not experience frequent contests: Bridgnorth, Ludlow, Monmouth, Peterborough, Wareham, Wells, and Wenlock. Stamford had been uncontested since 1734, but what happened at the turn of the century demonstrated what lay beneath the tranquil surface of Hanoverian electoral politics: the rise of an opposition to the Burghley interest, the adoption of party colours, blue against red, after 1809, and finally the adoption of the labels 'Whig' and 'Tory'. At Warwick, the scarcity of election contests—the borough was contested only four times after 1734 (in 1780, 1784, 1792, and 1831)—concealed the steadily building political and religious awareness in the town and the persistent underlying cleavage in local society. Although local alignments did not always coincide with parliamentary divisions, by the later 1820s a Tory corporation faced a Whig, reformist opposition.[99] The Welsh boroughs followed this sort of pattern. Contests were infrequent, but when they occurred they displayed deepening divisions in Welsh urban society, divisions not merely between oligarchs and independents but, as at Cardigan, between Whigs and Tories and, at Denbigh, between Anglicans and Catholics.[100] In yet others (East Retford and

[97] For the marginal case of Morpeth see J. Fewster, 'The Politics and Administration of the Borough of Morpeth in the Late Eighteenth Century', Ph.D. (Newcastle, 1960), 383–404, 534–5; Stoker, 'Elections and Voting Behaviour', Ph.D., 301–2, 334; Thorne *House of Commons*, ii. 311. For King's Lynn see *A Copy of the Poll*, ed. E. Mugridge, 27–8.

[98] For Cirencester and Sudbury see Thorne, *House of Commons*, ii. 173–4, 375–6.

[99] On the politics of Bridgnorth see ibid. ii. 335–6; on Ludlow, ibid. ii. 336; on Monmouth, ibid. ii. 283–4; on Peterborough, ibid. ii. 302–3; on Wareham, ibid. ii. 141; on Wells, ibid ii. 355–6; on Wenlock, ibid. ii. 339–40. On Stamford, see J. Lee, 'Stamford and the Cecils', B.Litt. 110–15. On Warwick, see *VCH Warwickshire*, viii. 502–3.

[100] D. Wager, 'Welsh Politics and Parliamentary Reform, 1780–1835', Ph.D. (Wales, 1972), 135–6; Thorne, *House of Commons*, ii. 487–8. For Denbigh, see ibid. 495; Wager, op. cit. 243–6. For Caernarvon, Cardiff, Flint, and Pembroke, see ibid. 254, 207–8, 122–5, and 148–50, Thorne, op. cit. ii. 485–6, 500–2, 497–9, 508–10. Once again, the impression in Thorne of a settled, parochial aspect to Welsh borough politics is not entirely borne out by reference to other sources.

Cambridge), long-standing patronal vendettas did not allow the divisions of an earlier generation entirely to settle and were responsible for lingering hostilities and confrontations. In Derby, the old Whig–Tory conflict had given way by the middle of the eighteenth century to a preoccupation with local issues concerning the independence of the constituency. Derby was not contested after 1796, but that could not conceal the persisting divisions between Whigs and Tories. In response to the perennial Whiggishness of the Cavendishes, the Tories tried to keep the old patriotic flag flying by organizing themselves into the True Blue Club to honour the memory of Pitt the Younger[101] In some boroughs the presence of a powerful government interest, could itself generate divisions with parliamentary implications.[102] In others, interference and intervention by government and opposition could just as strongly lend a parliamentary aspect to conflicts which were at root essentially local. In a lively constituency like Taunton, there could be no concealing the awareness among the voters of national issues and parliamentary alignments.[103]

In the above constituencies, electoral politics, however, continued to revolve principally around local concerns. Party was an extraneous addition, so far as the voters were concerned, a projection of their immediate interests. In the next group of 20 constituencies,[104] party was a significantly greater ingredient in electoral politics. These constituencies had undergone some experience of party conflict in the earlier eighteenth century. Although these communities had remained seriously divided throughout the eighteenth century, the old party conflicts had given way to a preoccupation with local issues. In the early nineteenth century, a new set of party distinctions was to emerge, superimposed upon the old conflicts between oligarchy and independence and focusing upon the conflict of parties at Westminster. Even now, party was not necessarily the principal determining element in electoral politics but it played a consistent and considerable role

[101] For Cambridge, its hereditary divisions and their extension into the Toryism and Whiggism of the 1820s see D. Cook, 'The Representative History of the County, Town and University of Cambridge, 1689–1832', Ph.D. (Cambridge, 1935), 190–203, For East Retford and the great confrontation between the Newcastle and Fitzwilliam dynasties see J. Moses, 'Elections and Electioneering in the Nottinghamshire Constituencies, 1702–1832', Ph.D. 362–73. For the True Blue Club at Derby see the *Derby Mercury*, 29 July 1813.

[102] The best examples of interests in government boroughs provoking local hostility with some national orientation are Hastings (Thorne, *House of Commons*, ii. 467–8), Plymouth, (ibid. 118–9), and Portsmouth (ibid. 188–9).

[103] For Taunton, see ibid. 354. Other seats of this type include Dorchester (ibid. 133–4), Penryn (ibid. 75–7), and Poole (ibid. 135–8).

[104] These constituencies are: Berwick-upon-Tweed, Beverley, Boston, Carlisle, Carmarthen, Grantham, Grimsby, Hull, Huntingdon, Lancaster, Maldon, Newcastle-upon-Lyme, Northampton, Preston, St Albans, Shrewsbury, Stafford, Tamworth, Tewkesbury, and Wigan.

in rhetoric, perceptions, and issues.[105] In Grantham and Newcastle-under-Lyme the power of local aristocracies remained the most powerful consideration. In Hull, Lancaster, and probably Stafford, the power of the purse determined the course of electoral politics.[106] In all these five seats, however, the role of the candidate and the position he adopted on particular issues remained important. In venal Hull, for example, James Robert Graham, a third man, as was usual came forward in 1818, but by this time, even a third man had to have the right opinions on peace, retrenchment, parliamentary reform, the abolition of slavery, and, of course, Catholic emancipation.[107] In Huntingdon, Tamworth, and Wigan, more settled and more sober patterns of patronal control rendered electoral politics somewhat less frenetic and considerably more dignified but through the dispositions of patrons and Members of Parliament, parliamentary divisions could not but be reflected among the electorate even at the infrequent contests which occurred in these boroughs.[108]

In others of these boroughs, however, more regular contests and a more highly developed sense of politicization served to familiarize the electors with the politics of their MPs and patrons. Consequently, Berwick, Maldon, and Preston, with their very different electoral environments, nevertheless resembled each other in their increasingly frequent contests, their expanding electorates, and the increasing currency of party issues. Party had penetrated the political culture of Preston to such an extent that there were entirely separate social calendars, horse races, and hunts for Whigs, Tories, and Radicals.[109]

[105] Whatever organizational and bureaucratic shortcomings these local party systems might display they were energetic to a fault. I have even traced rival party bull baitings at Grantham (*Storr's Impartial Narrative* (Grantham, 1830), 11. For Grantham see Thorne, ii. 24; for Newcastle see ibid. 361.

[106] For Hull, see Thorne, *House of Commons*, ii. 446–9; for Lancaster, ibid. 224–7; for Stafford, ibid. 362–3.

[107] Barkworth Collection, Election Literature, Hull Pub. Lib.

[108] After 1741, Huntingdon was contested only in 1820 and 1831. After 1741 Tamworth was contested only in 1761, 1774, 1784, and 1818. After 1747 Wigan was only contested in 1763, 1830, and 1831. For these constituencies, see the details in Thorne, *House of Commons*, ii. 213, 365, and 238–40.

[109] For Berwick see Stoker, 'Elections and Voting Behaviour' Ph.D., 303–4, Thorne, *House of Commons*, ii. 308–9. (Berwick was contested 11 times between 1784 and 1831.) For Maldon, see ibid. 161–4 (Maldon was contested 5 times between 1784 and 1831. Party labels appear to have revived there in 1806–7.) The complicated politics of Preston, the coalitions between its Whig and Tory patrons, the Hornby and Horrocks families, and the radical candidatures of Henry Hunt in 1820, 1830 (twice) and 1831 and William Cobbett in 1826 should not lead to any underestimation of the influence of the party press and party clubs of the town (Preston was contested 9 times between 1784 and 1831). See P. Whittle, *History of Preston* (2 vols. (1837), i. 255–7; H. W. Clemsha, *History of Preston in Amounderness* (Manchester, 1912), 208–31; C. Hardwick, *History of the Borough of Preston and its Environs* (Preston, 1858), 333–42. Marks, [?], *The Guild Guide to Preston* (Preston, 1882), 5–3. For an excellent background to electoral politics in Preston and an account of its expanding electorate, see Thorne, *House of Commons*, ii, 236–8.

In at least two of these constituencies, party labels were coming back into use. Continued references to 'the Whig interest' and thus to their 'anti-Whig' opponents did much to define the politics of Beverley, while the currency of the epithet 'Blue' to describe the Foxite Whigs of Carmarthen helped to polarize the language, and thus the practice, of politics there.[110] Finally, in another six of these constituencies, the gradual transformation of parties supporting established interests, on the one hand, and independents on the other, into adherents of one or other of the two parliamentary parties may be observed in the detailed electoral history of Boston, Carlisle, Grimsby, Northampton, St Albans, and Shrewsbury. In Boston the politics of personality and influence which had dominated the borough since the early eighteenth century gave way after 1790 to numerous contests of a political character between the Whig Bertie family and the Tory corporation. The Boston poll books for the early nineteenth century are full of references to national issues and personages.[111] At Carlisle, the struggle between the Whig, John Christian Curwen, MP from 1786 to 1812 and from 1816 to 1820, and his 'Tory' opponents, lifted the electoral struggle there out of a purely local framework.[112] At Grimsby it was less the impact of a charismatic personality than the pressure of issues, the hardening of party feelings, the establishment of party clubs, and the wearing of party colours which tilted partisanship in the direction of Westminster.[113] In mid-eighteenth-century Northampton, elections had been fought overwhelmingly on local issues. By the closing decades of the century, however, the political divisions of Westminster between government and opposition were being reflected there, exacerbated by religious divisions between Anglican and Dissenter and perpetuated by hostility between the prominent Foxite Whig MP, Edward Bouverie, who sat from 1790 to 1810, and Spencer Perceval, MP from 1796 to 1812 and prime minister from 1809 to 1812.[114] At St Albans it was consistent

[110] For Beverley, see Thorne, *House of Commons*, ii. 441–3. (Beverley was contested 12 times between 1784 and 1831.) For the revival of party at Beverley after several decades of preoccupation with parochial affairs see, however, F. Markham, 'Elections and Electioneering in East Yorkshire, 1815–65', Ph.D. (Hull, 1976), 64–7, 109–30. For Carmarthen, see Thorne, op. cit. i. 491–4). (Carmarthen was contested four times between 1784 and 1831.)

[111] *History of the Boston Election* (Boston, 1818); *The Addresses, Squibs and other publications* (Boston, 1820); *The Pool Book . . . together with the Addresses* (Boston, 1826); *A Sketch of the Boston Election* (Boston, 1830). Disappointingly, Thorne does not give these aspects of Boston elections prominent attention; see *House of Commons*, ii. 245–7.

[112] For Carlisle, see Stoker, 'Elections and Voting Behaviour', Ph.D., 302–3; Thorne, *House of Commons*, ii. 92–3.

[113] E. Gillett, *A History of Grimsby* (Oxford, 1970), 170–5, 199–203. See also Thorne, *House of Commons*, ii. 249–53.

[114] See the excellent Collection of Political Handbills, 1790/1, 1796/4, 5, 12, 14, 17. Northampton Public Library. I would endorse Phillips's conclusion, after emphasizing the

patronal rivalry, and the differing (and usually contrasting) politics adopted by the (Whig) Spencer and (Tory) Grimston interests which steadily lent a national political direction to rivalries originally of local concern only. Finally, at Shrewsbury, it was the rapidly expanding electorate together with the political complexion of its candidates which lifted the politics of the Shropshire constituency on to a more than merely local plane.[115] The borough was, however, an unsettled one. Interests did not last for long, and MPs consequently came and went. It is not possible to detect long-term, consistent patterns of support at Shrewsbury in the early nineteenth century, rather two short-lived, local, party systems: those of 1806–14 and those of 1826–31. In both, national issues, and labels, combined with local concerns to brew a potent mix.

A further category of nine English borough and the two university seats[116] may be identified in which party consciousness reflected not merely the interests of patrons, MPs, and candidates, but also the opinions of the voters themselves. These were, for the most part, fairly large, open boroughs whose elections frequently went to a contest. In them, party consciousness was generated more spontaneously than in the constituencies which we have just been considering. Since patronage structures were weaker in these boroughs, and electorates larger, and since party organizations in most of them lacked the self-sufficiency continuously to mobilize the electorate around issues with a national reference, party divisions still tended to be fluid. Local issues, furthermore, continued to play a significant, if declining role, in these places—especially in Chichester, until a sudden rush of four contests in eight years between 1823 and 1831; at Evesham and at Oxford

---

individuality of the Northampton electors, that 'Northampton voters behaved in an impressively partisan manner at the 1796 election in spite of Northampton's political structure and apolitical climate' (J. Phillips, *Electoral Behaviour*, 225; see also 236). The *Northampton Mercury* was fond of noting links between local and national politics. Bouverie was criticized because 'he hath so decidedly disappointed the expectation of a number of his constituents in uniformly and blindly voting in the minority, in every instance however unconstitutional the question might be' (ibid. 14 May 1796). These constituents it defined as 'those conservative of church and state' (ibid. 21 May 1796). The fact that Spencer Perceval was the other MP in these years no doubt emphasized the duality. It was not merely the newspapers, however. A handbill suggested that 'if Mr. Bouverie and other candidates of his parliamentary principles were to succeed, and a majority of that description in consequence constitute the House of Commons, his Lordship [Spencer] must be compelled to abandon that situation [as patron]' (Collection of Political Handbills, 1796/7). It seems entirely signifcant that almost all of the political handbills which have survived for the election of 1796 turn on the question of Bouverie's political principles.

[115] Once again, I find that Thorne's accounts (*House of Commons*, ii. 9, 336–9) while helpful and informative, lack a thorough grasp of the party context of electoral politics. Cf. Lansberry, 'Politics and Government in St Albans', Ph.D., 231–57 on the rival party cultures at St Albans. For both St Albans and Shrewsbury see pp. 220–1, 305.

[116] Canterbury, Chichester, Evesham, Hereford, Hertford, Leominster and Southwark.

University throughout; and, probably on account of its paucity of contests, at Tewkesbury.[117] The power and influence of patrons continued to be a controversial feature of the politics of Hereford and Leominster, the latter of which was contested 11 times between 1784 and 1831.[118] At Cambridge University and Hertford, on the other hand, it was the politics of candidates that attracted attention.[119] The politics of Canterbury and Southwark were perhaps the most tumultuous of any of these boroughs, and in these constituencies the influence of party issues and party organizations is discernible in the election literature evoked by an almost unbroken series of election contests.[120]

In a further group of 22 boroughs, the old party distinctions between Whig and Tory had not completely disappeared when in the 1770s and 1780s new party alignments, reflecting the polarity between government and opposition, began to emerge.[121] This happened in a variety of ways. In eight constituencies, the polarities of party alignment were sustained by the conflict between the corporation and the freemen. In these, the open character of both the corporation and parliamentary franchises together with burgeoning religious antagonisms was the stuff of local party. Regular municipal elections emphasized and expressed party differences. These frequently, though not invariably, coincided with parliamentary alignments. The politics of Norwich was largely mediated by the conflict between the corporation and the anti-corporation party. In the 1770s, however, national issues began to play a part and, as Professor Phillips has demonstrated, by the 1780s, party had come to count for much in the politics of Norwich. Even though party labels were usually eschewed, local parties mobilized candidates who supported government and opposition.[122] By the early nineteenth century, party

[117] For these constituencies, see Thorne, *House of Commons*, ii. 392–3, 432–4, 177–9, 270.
[118] Ibid. 190–2, 199–201.
[119] Ibid. 204–5, 32–6.
[120] Ibid. 216–9, 384–7.
[121] Abingdon, Aylesbury, Bridgwater, Chester, Coventry, Dover, Durham, Exeter, Great Yarmouth, Lewes, Lichfield, Lincoln, Liverpool, Maidstone, New Windsor, Newark, Newcastle-upon-Tyne, Norwich, Oxford, Rochester, Sandwich, Worcester.
[122] J. A. Phillips, *Electoral Behaviour*, 109, 118–9, 215–6, 218–21, 223–6. For local awareness of parliamentary parties see the *Election Magazine* (Norwich, 1784), 16–7, 28–9, 33–4. Old party traditions had fallen into a slumber at Norwich. There were no corporation elections between 1750 and 1786, and only two contested parliamentary elections. The new independents, who began to oppose the corporation in the 1780s, called themseves 'Whigs'. In the 1790s there was a steady increase in the anti-corporation and anti-ministerial vote, culminating in the great opposition victory of 1802 and the defeat of William Windham on account of his support of the war. D. S. O'Sullivan, 'Politics in Norwich, 1701–1835', MA (East Anglia, 1975), 105–6, 121–3, 132–4, 229–30, 235–7. There is a splendid, if brief, account of Norwich in Thorne, *House of Commons*, ii. 292–5.

labels were once again in circulation to describe the two local parties and the competing parliamentary groups which they supported.[123] The pattern at Coventry is comparable. There, a strong vein of popular Toryism among the freemen clashed with the Nonconformity of the Dissenting corporation. For several decades in the middle of the century these lingering tensions were not focused on national issues, but in the 1770s the strains of the American War revived them.[124] At the general election of 1784 there was considerable local excitement over the fate of the India Bill and the coalition.[125] Party had come to stay in Coventry. By the early nineteenth century, elections focused upon the conduct of MPs and their party connections.[126] At Liverpool the traditional focal point of conflict was the struggle between the Anglican corporation and the Dissenting Independent party. The size of the Liverpool electorate (2,000 in 1754, rising to 5,000 on the eve of reform), its political awareness, its regular contests, and its tendency to be represented by national figures (Sir William Meredith, George Canning, William Roscoe, to name just three) lent a competitive national orientation to its politics. Complexity, rather than two-party simplicity, prevailed at Liverpool, however. In 1806 there were three parties: that of the corporation, that of the merchants, and that of the Foxites. Foxite Whiggism, however, made disappointingly little impact in Liverpool, and party labels came quite late to the town.[127] Party was also an element in the politics of Oxford, although by no means the only element. The old distinctions were very slow to die in Oxford, and they were sharply revived by the confrontation between Pitt and Fox in the 1780s.[128] Similarly, at

---

[123] For party labels in early 19th-cent. Norwich see B. Aspinwall, 'William Smith, MP, 1756–1835', MA (Manchester, 1962), 103–4, 111–14.

[124] See, for example, the handbills *To the Worthy Freemen of Coventry who call themselves Whigs*, by An Old Whig, 1780. Sheffield MSS, Coventry City Lib.

[125] *Jopson's Coventry Mercury*, 22 Mar., 5 Apr. 1784; T. W. Whitley, *The Parliamentary Representation of the City of Coventry* (Coventry, 1894), 173–200.

[126] 'Considerations and State of Partys in Coventry at the following periods, 1803, 1811', 1902 Whitbread MSS Beds. RO. See also Thorne, *House of Commons*, ii. 401–4.

[127] Canning has his own Liverpool office, a local secretariat, and clerks who dealt with party affairs on his behalf (bundle 84, Harewood MSS, Leeds Cent. Lib.); see also F. E. Sanderson, 'The Structure of Politics in Liverpool, 1780–1807', *Trans. Hist. Soc. Lancs. and Cheshire* (1977), 66–7, 71–4; *A Compendious and Impartial Account of the Election of 1806* (Wright and Cruickshank, Liverpool, 1806). See also Thorne, *House of Commons*, ii. 228–34 for further discussion of the development of party at Liverpool.

[128] But only with characteristic perversity. For Oxford was one of the few places where independent candidates sided with the government of William Pitt and his successors. The independent, Lockhart, returned in 1807, voted consistently with Portland and Perceval. He was blamed by an opponent some years later: 'You went in free . . . and voluntarily yielded your head to the yoke . . . You have lost the friends of peace, prosperity and happiness and gained the promoters of war, pauperism and misery' (G. A. Oxon. b.15 Papers Relating to the Oxford Borough Election of 1812, Bodleian Lib.) The account in Thorne, *House of Commons*, ii. 325–7 gives little indication of the party context to electoral politics.

Maidstone the local conflict between the corporation and the independents acquired in the 1780s national connotations.[129] And it would be impossible to describe the politics of Exeter without constant reference to the poles of party in which a Tory–Anglican corporation confronted an opposition of Independent Whigs. A similar pattern to this may be observed at Worcester, where the powerful Toryism of the earlier eighteenth century revived in the years of the American War when local Dissenting groups launched a powerful attack on the Tory corporation. At first this attack confined itself to local issues but in the 1780s, as in so many constituencies, parliamentary issues came to count for much. At Great Yarmouth it was a group of Whig Dissenters who contested the hold of the corporation over the town, a contest which it had effectively won by 1784. Thereafter some concern with parliamentary issues could make itself felt.[130]

In four other constituencies, intense rivalry between local families perpetuated the old party distinctions and gave foundation, resources, and structure to the new. At Durham it was the conflict between the Lambton and Tempest families which did so; at Lichfield between Gower and Anson; at Newark between Newcastle and Middleton, and at Newcastle-upon-Tyne between Blackett and Ridley. The patrongage system served as a vehicle for party influences in these constituencies, but it did so slowly. It would be difficult to attribute an enormous awareness of national party issues in them before the early nineteenth century, especially at Lichfield. Even here, however, we find the local Tories organized in their True Blue Club in 1820.[131]

In five further constituencies, ancient conflicts between local patrons and constituency independents began to acquire a parliamentary orientation in the late eighteenth or early nineteenth century. When the Grosvenors became Whigs in the second decade of the nineteenth

---

[129] 'Maidstone politics customarily assumed an Independent/Corporation Ministerial/Anti-Ministerialist vocabulary that served reasonably well for identifying political interests until well into the nineteenth century' (J. A. Phillips, *Electoral Behaviour*, 123). 'Frequent popular participation in local and national elections also marked Maidstone's political structure, and the activities of the Maidstone parties rivalled those of Norwich in every respect except published electoral propaganda') (ibid. 135).

[130] Thorne, *House of Commons*, ii. 107–9, 289–92, 434–5.

[131] 19/1/10–17, Dyott, MSS, Staffs. RO. Of the strength of party at Durham and Newcastle there can be no doubt. See Thorne, *House of Commons*, ii. 151–5, 311–12). There is, admittedly, more room for discussion about Lichfield and Newark (ibid. 316–17, 358–60). In Newark, much of the apparatus of party can be found; not infrequently, there was considerable discussion of political and religious issues among its rapidly expanding electorate, which increased from 1,000 to 1,400 between 1790 and 1830. Nevertheless, it may well be that the real driving force of the politics of Newark was defence of, and hostility to, Newcastle of Clumber. See Moses, 'Elections in Nottinghamshire', Ph.D., 283–303. Significantly, it was through their long traditions of independence that the majority of the Newark electorate came to support parliamentary reform so decisively in 1831.

century and proceeded to emphasize at Chester parliamentary elections their liberal instincts towards Catholics and others, they pushed the local independents in the direction of a popular Toryism, organized in 1817 in the King and Constitution Club. In its turn, this stimulated the formation of a regional Whig Club, serving Cheshire and North Wales. The local press obligingly followed suit: the *Chester Chronicle* supporting the Grosvenors and the liberal cause, the *Chester Courant* that of independence and Toryism. Developments in party terminology matched these interesting party transformations. *The Election Papers Concerning the Election of 1818* describe the opposing sides both as Grosvenors and Independent and as Whig and Tory according to their support of Catholic emancipation, parliamentary reform, and free trade, on the one hand, and of Sidmouth's repressive measures, the suspension of habeas corpus, and support for Liverpool's ministry on the other. For the remainder of the unreformed period the juxtaposition of these two layers of political life combined to define the quality of party activity in Chester.[132] A very similar pattern to this may be discerned at Dover, Rochester, and Sandwich, where earlier conflicts between the government interest and local independents began to align with support for and opposition to government on a national scale. This development may be discerned at Dover and Rochester in the 1780s but at Sandwich it took another twenty years.[133] In New Windsor, the prominene of the monarch in this royal borough tended to generalize the significance of local independency.[134] As at Chester, however, the relatively rare election contests—New Windsor contested only three times after 1727 (in 1780, 1802, and 1806), Chester contested only five times after 1747 (in 1784, 1812, 1818, 1820, and 1826)—should not obscure the intensity of local partisanship.

Finally, among this group of constituencies which experienced continuous party alignments of some significance may be included four fairly open places in which the loyalties of the candidates seems to have been the decisive factor in imposing a government versus opposition axis to electoral politics. This was certainly the case at Bridgwater, Lewes, and Lincoln, constituencies that were too open to permit settled patterns of patronage, and also, arguably, at Aylesbury, which was too venal. In all these four constituencies, powerful patterns of participation enabled issues of

---

[132] *History of the Contested Election (Chester, 1818)*, 11–14, 17; J. Hemingway, *History of the City of Chester*, ii. 415–28; *The Chester Poll Book* (1812), 55–6, 75–6; Thorne, *House of Commons*, ii. 37–40.

[133] P. L. Humphreys, 'Kentish Politics and Public Opinion', D.Phil. (Oxford, 1981), 114–238; Thorne, *House of Commons*, ii. 220–2, 464–6, 473–5.

[134] Thorne, *House of Commons*, ii. 11–13.

national significance to play their part at the frequently contested elections.[135]

In a final group of 12 boroughs the cumulative impact of party continuity, party opinion, and the candidates' (and electors') identification of themselves with the parliamentary parties amounted to a major determining factor at elections. In some of them, the sheer numerical size of the electorates was itself a powerful impetus in the direction of party. At Westminster, rising from 12,000 in 1754 to 17,000 on the eve of reform, no one patron could command. And at London (rising from 7,000 to 12,000), Bristol (5,000 to 7,000), Leicester (2,500 to 5,300), and Nottingham (2,000 to 5,000), the same is true. In these huge places, the loyalties generated by earlier party conflicts lingered long into the eighteenth century, only reluctantly ebbing at mid-century. But by the 1780s the rivalries of the parliamentary parties were being reflected in these boroughs. The Westminster election of 1784, the greatest electoral conflict between the followers of Pitt and Fox, has been endlessly cited, but it should be remembered that Westminster went to a contest at 10 out of 11 general elections between 1774 and 1820. From 1780 onwards, elections there were determined by either or both of two issues: support for government or opposition and radicalism. It is impossible to read the enormous quantities of election literature that has survived without appreciating the sophistication of a vibrant political culture which was as informed as it was partisan.[136] Much of the same can be said about Leicester, where the Dissenting opposition to the Tory corporation openly allied themselves with the Foxite Whigs. Weakened for a time by the war against France, this party alignment emerged stronger than ever in the early nineteenth century.[137] A similar process occurred at Nottingham. Rival clubs, the Whig Society and the Tory White Lion Club, founded in 1774–76, perpetuated the old party distinctions. Regular contested elections focused directly on parliamentary politics.

---

[135] For Lewes, see J. A. Philliips, *Electoral Behaviour*, 123–5, 133–6, 151–2, 159–60, 169–72, 214–16, 218–26, 233–7, 239–44, 247–52. For Aylesbury, see Davis, *Political Change and Continuity*, 43–58. For Lincoln, see Sir F. Hill, *Georgian Lincoln* (Cambridge, 1966), 208–27, 251–2; William Allingham, *A Diary* (Lincoln, 1907), 340–1.

[136] See e.g. the 570 pages of paragraphs and press cuttings in the *History of the Westminster Election* (London, 1784), the 462 pages of the *History of the Westminster and Middlesex Elections* (London, 1806), and the 442 pages of *The Westminster Election of 1819*, all in the Guildhall Library. For the currency of party labels and the prominence of party issues at Bristol at the end of the 18th cent. see M. Vlaeminke, 'Bristol During the French Revolutionary War, 1793–1802', M. Litt. (Bristol, 1981), 69–70.

[137] Temple Patterson, *Radical Leicester*, 27–8, 63, 126–7, 132, 135–6; *VCH Leicestershire*, iv. 126–47, 204–9. The election of 1790 at Leicester seems to have been fought simply on a government versus opposition platform. See the broadsides in the Berridge MSS *A Free Elector* and *A Freeman*, Leicester City Museum. See also Thorne, *House of Commons*, ii. 241–3.

The labels 'Whig' and 'Tory' were in common use not, it should be stressed, merely to define local allegiances but to define local groups as self-conscious supporters of national parties. One of the Nottingham candidates in 1820 declared: 'One word, nay one syllable, would present a faithful picture of his political sentiments, and that syllable was the name of Fox.'[138]

In some of these constituencies, none the less, the structures of electoral patronage acted as the catalyst of party. Party was a reality at York because of the existence of the Rockingham Club and the overwhelming influence of the second Marquis of Rockingham. The Rockingham Club may not have been the same after his death, but at York Whiggism focused upon the Portland–Fox party in Parliament. The York Independents did not organize themselves into a Tory party until the early years of the nineteenth century, but of the strength of local party divisions at York there can be no doubt.[139] Bedford did not go to the polls as frequently as York. Indeed, the borough was contested only once after 1790, in 1830. Nevertheless, the immediate presence of the Russell family gave immediate national significance to local groupings. There was considerable party feeling in the borough and there do seem to have been two organized groups in Bedford, even after 1790.[140] The politics of Southampton similarly revolved around the automatic identification of one local interest, the Admiralty, with the government and, consequently, that of the Independents with the Whigs. Southampton was a fairly open borough of some sophistication. Admiralty influence inevitably made government policy an issue, and there was a regular standing opposition which in the early nineteenth century adopted party nomenclature.[141]

---

[138] *A Brief Review* (Nottingham, 1820), pp. iv, xi. The account of the proceedings and of the politics of the town contained in this pamphlet are essential reading for those who doubt the reality of party in the unreformed period. See also M. Thomis, *Politics and Society in Nottingham, 1785-1835* (Oxford, 1969); Thorne, *House of Commons*, ii. 317-20.

[139] See F. C. Price, 'Parliamentary Elections in York City, 1754-1790', MA (Manchester, 1958), *passim*, but esp. 21-2, 34-5, 221-39. For the development of parties in early 19th cent. York see A. J. Peacock, 'York in the Age of Reform', Ph.D. (York, 1973), 53-74. The labels 'Whig' and 'Tory' were in use again by 1818 at the latest, and in that year a York Whig Club was established. In retaliation the York Tories added to the existing Pitt Club a King and Constitution Club, which had 340 members by the end of 1818. Similarly, the Whig *York Chronicle* confronted the Tory *Yorkshire Gazette* and the radical *York Herald*. See also Thorne, *House of Commons*, ii. 461-4.

[140] Material in the Huw White MSS in the Beds. RO attests to the strength of party feeling in the town in the 1780s. Furthermore, the correspondence of Samuel Whitbread, especially the R-I series in the Beds. RO frequently touches upon party feeling in the town. See also Thorne, *House of Commons*, ii. 4-6.

[141] Southampton Handbills, Cope Collection, vol. i, Southampton Univ. Lib. See also Thorne, *House of Commons*, ii. 189-91.

Within this category, finally, we may notice the quiet and unspectacular development of party awareness and party identification in a number of open boroughs. In Gloucester the old party traditions continued well into the reign of George III and gave birth to new party configurations. The old Tory or High Church party gave way to the 'True Blues' in the 1770s who backed the ministry of North, then that of Pitt, and then the succession of Tory governments of the early years of the new century.[142] At Ipswich after a period of party confusion in the middle years of the century, and when the local Tories had supported the Rockingham ministry of 1765–6, there emerged later in the century a conformity between local Whig groups and the national Whig party of Rockingham and Fox. Throughout, the politics of the town turned on the conflict of labels, Tory Blues versus Whig Yellows.[143] Colchester, in spite of its venality, is an interesting borough, with a large electorate (1,500 falling to 1,300), frequent contests, and strong traditions of party loyalty. At Colchester, however, the Tories maintained their cohesion, and in the early nineteenth century an organized Tory party existed without much coherent opposition until 1831.[144] Party feeling was even stronger at Reading. As early as the 1770s a government-opposition axis had replaced the old Whig–Tory division which had finally expired in the 1750s. The Pitt–Fox conflict found a ready audience here, and after 1800 every one of the six elections at Reading was fought between coherent local Whig and Tory parties, fully aware of the parliamentary implications of their activities, between a Tory corporation and a Whig middle-class opposition of townsmen and traders.[145]

In many of the counties, then, and in the larger and most regularly contesting borough seats, party was steadily becoming a force once more in electoral politics in the closing decades of the unreformed period. Indeed, one of the characteristic features of the unreformed electoral system in its closing years was the revival of party. Just as there was more to parliamentary politics in these years than the conflict of factions or the parliamentary pursuit of self-interest, so there was more to electoral politics than

---

[142] Namier and Brooke, *House of Commons*, i. 291–2; J. A. Cannon, 'The Parliamentary Representation of the City of Gloucester, 1727–1790', *Trans. Bristol and Gloucs. Archaeol. Soc.* 78 (1959), 149 n.; Thorne, *House of Commons*, ii. 174–7.

[143] The life of the town was dominated by party politics. 'Every municipal election accentuated party feeling, and every appointment was conceived in party terms' (Childs, 'Politics and Elections in Suffolk Boroughs', M.Phil., 58). Turnouts at municipal elections were almost as high as they were for general elections. In 1820 the *Morning Chronicle* referred to 'the Blue of Ministerial Party' (24 Mar. 1820). By this time Ipswich elections were being fought on national issues. Few of these elements are dealt with in Thorne's discussion of Ipswich politics (*House of Commons*, ii. 371–4).

[144] M. E. Speight, 'Politics in the Borough of Colchester', Ph.D. (London, 1969), 98–100; Thorne, *House of Commons*, ii. 158–60.

[145] R. C. Bailly, 'The Parliamentary History of Reading 1750–1850', MA (Reading, 1944), 36, 40–1; Thorne, *House of Commons*, ii. 13–15.

the battle of electoral interests for its own sake or the desire to browbeat and corrupt the electors as a matter of course. The electoral politics of almost one-half of the constituencies of England and Wales—and these, it bears repeating, the constituencies where most of the electors were to be found and the contested elections taking place—occured within a local context, a local political community, and a local political culture. One of the great themes of electoral politics in the last 50 years of the unreformed period is the attachment of these local communities and cultures to the great political conflict unfolding at Westminster between successive governments and oppositions, and the political traditions and constitutional legacies to which they were heir. As we have seen, this process of attachment could occur in a variety of ways: through the impact of national issues; through the activities and identities of patrons, members, and candidates; through the exertions of election clubs; and, in places, through the impact and interference of government and opposition themselves. Consequently, the developing party distinctions pioneered by the successive oppositions of the Rockingham, Portland, Foxite, and Grey parties to the governments of North, Pitt, and Liverpool could be, and frequently, were, adopted by the constituencies.

There did not yet exist an automatic, bureaucratic identification between party in its various layers: between 'Whig'- or 'Tory'-inclined electors, between local Whig and Tory constituency parties, and between Whig and Tory parties at Westminster. On none of these layers was party consciousness fully developed and formally defined. In particular, patterns of patronal control lacked that steady commitment to party consistency, and to parties at Westminster, that came later in the nineteenth century. In the early nineteenth century, we stand at the early stages of the development by which this came about. But party sentiment there was in plenty out in the constituencies. Awareness of the parliamentary arena and the doings of its gladiators was commonplace. Indeed, one of the key features of the unreformed electoral system was the readiness to organize and associate in their support among both the patron and voter classes. Before 1832 party attachments may have been less formal and more intermittent than they later became, but they were not noticeably less assertive nor less popular.

Nevertheless, party remained an ideological rather than a terminological force. Party considerations, moreover, did not determine, although they certainly influenced, the structure of constituency politics. Party considerations did not themselves determine the decision to contest a constituency, although, once again, they would certainly influence that decision. Party considerations did not condition and structure the opinions of the mass of the people, although again, they certainly came to influence them. Party descriptions came to be engrafted on to traditional attitudes. How many staunch independents became moderate Whig reformers? How many old patriots found themselves supporting the Tory party of the early nineteenth century?

> Tho' not enlisted amongst the party clan,
> I am, without their badge, a loyal man;
> Ready to join an individual's mite
> To serve the King and guard the people's right;
> Ready t'uphold the great and virtuous cause,
> Of King and church, their government and laws.[146]

What did party mean in practice? To both the patronal and voter classes, party meant an external objective for local action, a widening of horizons, a degree of politicization, and a willingness to pool local endeavour in a common cause. Party meant the imposition of constitutional and parliamentary values upon parochial causes and objectives. Party meant peaceful, constitutional, local participation in action designed to secure national objectives: the securing of peace or victory in war; the defence or reform of the constitution; support for, or opposition to, the government of the day. Party meant the establishment of a national political community, the linking together of local and national issues. For a patron, the language of party might mean an appeal to the electors (and non-electors) to support and vindicate his values, or the values of those like him, an extension of sentiment to and a rallying of sentiment around causes which he held dear. The appeal to party might mean an assertion of patronal control over the voter classes.[147] As the power of patrons over constituencies began to decline in the early nineteenth century,[148] and as the issues and personalities of parliamentary politics came to loom ever-larger in the consciousness of voters through improvements in communications and general education, so the importance of party began significantly to increase and its role and functions to expand. Consequently, it is impossible intelligently to investigate and satisfactorily to analyse the electoral politics of the closing decades of the unreformed period without constant recourse to the concept of party.

---

[146] 'The Guild' by 'A Briton and a Loyal Subject' (Colchester, 1820), Colchester Pub. Lib.

[147] See e.g. the use of party appeals to exercise control over the Norwich voters in the 1790s in M. Weinzierl, 'The Norwich Elections of 1794, 1796 and 1802: Conflict and Consensus', *Parliaments, Estates and Representation*, 6/2 (1986) 167–80.

[148] Thorne, *House of Commons*, i. 53–6.

## RELIGION AND PARTY

In the revival of party distinctions at the constituency level the function of religion can hardly be overestimated. The old Whig historians, notably Trevelyan, regarded religion as the essential, distinguishing characteristic of the Whig and Tory parties and believed that religion furnished these parties with such powerful ideological, organizational, and even personal resources that they enjoyed an unbroken and continuous history from the seventeenth to the nineteenth century.[149] If such a view can no longer be sustained, there can nevertheless be no excuse for failing to recognize the numerous points of contact between religious influences, political behaviour, and party allegiences out in the constituencies. The pulpit was a prime instrument of propaganda, a medium of information, its control and its evaluation. It was also common for the clergy to be used in canvassing.[150] Religious influences, moreover, powerfully moulded the rising humanitarian movements which after the 1780s came to exert such keen ideological pressure upon the constituencies. No account of the role of party in the unreformed electorate which neglected the role of religion could be said to be complete.

While recognizing the importance of the gulf, the widening gulf, between Anglican and Dissenter in electoral behaviour we must not fall into the trap of regarding the Protestant Dissenters as the unvarying agents of liberal progress and reform. After all, Dissenters were a remarkably small percentage of the population. In 1715 they amounted to no more than 6.2% of the population, thereafter rising steadily, but only to 10% by the early nineteenth century.[151] As to their social and occupational structure, urban Dissenters do not seem to have been significantly different from the community as a whole. In the enfranchised towns, the Dissenting voter, like his non-Dissenting counterpart, was drawn overwhelmingly from the economically independent trades and occupations.[152] There is, moreover, no doubt that the overwhelming majority of Protestant Dissenters were quite prepared to accept the Whig oligarchy, with all its indefensible affronts

---

[149] G. M. Trevelyan, *The Two-party System in English Constitutional History* (Oxford, 1926). For the power of religious influences over voters earlier in the 18th cent. see W. A. Speck, *Tory and Whig: The Struggle in the Constituencies, 1701–1715* (London, 1970), 24–5: 'the only predictable blocs of voters were the Anglican clergy and the dissenters'.

[150] E. A. Smith, 'The Election Agent in English Politics, 1734–1782', *Eng. Hist. Rev.* 84 (1969), 13–4. For the activities of the Anglican clergy on nomination days see Thorne, *House of Commons*, i. 16.

[151] Michael Watts, *The Dissenters* (Oxford, 1978), 509; I. R. Christie, *Wars and Revolutions, Britain 1760–1815* (London, 1982), 38.

[152] Watts, *The Dissenters*, 353.

to liberal opinion.[153] They were prepared to accept the fabric of the political system as they found it. We are certainly not entitled to assume that Dissenters automatically and enthusiastically supported every proposal for liberal reform. If they had, why were so many Dissenting areas silent during, for example, the Economical Reform campaign of 1779–85?[154] Still more, why did the Wilkite movement evoke such a disappointing response in most Dissenting areas? Finally, it may even be that Dissenters were so inextricably implicated in the Hanoverian nexus of society and politics that they even neglected to advance their own religious interests. Certainly, the Dissenting laity manifested a noticeable reluctance to champion the movement for the repeal of the Test and Corporation Acts in the 1780s.[155]

By then, of course, political differences did not necessarily coincide with religious differences. The Whigs and Tories of the early eighteenth century, however, had been defined by their religious antagonisms:[156] 'Religious differences had been a primary factor in the initial formulation of party rivalries in local society, and they continued to be of major significance well into the eighteenth century.'[157] As Professor Namier observed, as late as 1754 'whatever genuine popular party feeling there was had a religious colouring'.[158] When mobilized behind a national issue, religious passions could be terrifyingly strong, as Henry Pelham's ministry discovered over the Jewish Naturalization Bill of 1753. But for how long did this last? How far did a religious foundation to electoral behaviour continue to exist, and did it go so far as to effect a noticeable continuity between the party systems of the early and late eighteenth century? The rest of this section is devoted to answering these questions.

[153] The Whig interpretation of 18th-cent. Dissent has only recently been challenged; see J. E. Bradley, 'Whigs and Nonconformists: Presbyterians, Congregationalists and Baptists in English Politics, 1715–1790', Ph.D. (Univ. of Southern California, 1978); id., 'Whigs and Nonconformists: Slumbering Radicalism in English Politics, 1739–1789', *Eighteenth Century Studies*, 8/1 (1975), 1–27. See also J. Seed, 'Gentlemen Dissenters: The Social and Political Meanings of Rational Dissent in the 1770s and 1780s', *Hist. J.* 28/2 (1985), 299–325.

[154] See I. R. Christie, *Wilkes, Wyvill and Reform* (London, 1962), 229.

[155] J. F. Bradley, 'Whigs and Nonconformists', 19 and n. 64. Indeed, the failure of the Dissenters to agitate on this issue during the 50 years since organized attempts were last made in 1737 and 1739 is most significant.

[156] Colley, *In Defiance of Oligarchy*, 108–13: 'Where most Tories deviated from most Whigs was in their insistence that while religious persecution was wrong, giving legislative encouragement to sects outside or alien to the Anglican Church was worse. This was the declared rationale of the Tory opposition to both the Quakers Affirmation Act of 1722 and the Quaker Tithe Bill of 1736 . . . to the Whig-sponsored bills of 1746–47 and 1751 to naturalise foreign Protestants, and of course to the Jew Bill of 1753' (ibid. 112).

[157] Baskerville, 'The Management of the Tory Interest in Lancashire and Cheshire, 1714–1747', D.Phil., 296.

[158] L. B. Namier, *The Structure of Politics at the Ascension of George III* (London, 1929), 90.

Religious distinctions played a significant determining function in about one-tenth of the 269 English and Welsh constituencies in the middle of the eighteenth century. This proportion increased to about one-seventh by the end of the unreformed period. Namier and Brooke list 19 boroughs in which the basis of political differences was the confrontation between Anglican and Dissenter.[159] Bradley has added nine more constituencies to this list.[160] For demographic, social, and economic reasons, a further ten constituencies should be added during the second half of the eighteenth century and the early decades of the nineteenth.[161] According to these calculations, almost one-half of 'party' constituencies had a religious leavening.

In about one-third of these constituencies, Dissenters formed the basis of local groups in more or less permanent opposition to the corporation of the town.[162] At Colchester, where there was no corporation, the Dissenters were the largest and most influential group in opposition to prevailing interests. At Buckingham, Harwich, Portsmouth, and Tiverton, the Dissenters constituted such opposition as there was within the corporation. In the larger householder boroughs the Dissenters found a congenial breeding ground: hence the active political traditions of Cirencester, Hertford, Northampton, Preston, and Taunton. Even in a handful of smaller scot and lot boroughs, opposition politics was synonymous with dissent: as at Abingdon, Aylesbury, Bridgwater, Bridport, and Lewes. In the two county constituencies of Hertfordshire and Northumberland, Dissenters played an active role in independent oppositions. The only constituencies in which the Dissenters can be said to have formed the local oligarchy were Coventry and Nottingham, in both of which they dominated the corporation. In all other constituencies under consideration, Dissenters

[159] Namier and Brooke, *House of Commons*, i. 15, 19, 28, 114–16. Cambridge, Carmarthen, Cirencester, Coventry, Exeter, Great Yarmouth, Hertford, Ipswich, Leicester, Lewes, Liverpool, Maldon, Norwich, Nottingham, Portsmouth, Preston, Taunton, Tiverton, and Worcester.

[160] J. F. Bradley adds nine constituencies to this list: Bridgwater, Ilchester, Bridport, Bristol, Buckingham, Harwich, London, Maidstone, and Wycombe; see 'Whigs and Nonconformists', 15–16, 171, 215, 220, 289, 295, 379, 404, 421.

[161] Changing demographic and economic circumstances surely demand the inclusion of Abingdon, Aylesbury, Beverley, Colchester, Hertfordshire, Hull, Lincoln, Northampton, Northumberland, and Warwick. The historian of Warwick, in fact, concludes: 'The cleavage between Church and Dissent from which the English party system emerged, did not appear in Warwick until the late 1780s' (*VCH Warwickshire*, viii. 502). There is particularly good material on Hull and Beverley, with their rapidly increasing Nonconformist populations in Markham, 'Elections in East Yorkshire', 10–15, 434–8. See also R. W. Ram, 'The Political Activity of Dissenters in the East and West Ridings of Yorkshire, 1815–50', M. A. (Hull, 1964), 67–97.

[162] This was so in the freemen boroughs of Cambridge, Carmarthen, Exeter, Great Yarmouth, Ipswich, Leicester, Lincoln, Liverpool, Maidstone, Maldon, Norwich, Worcester, and Wycombe.

tend to unite with other groups in opposition to the local corporation or to other dominant electoral interests.

The geographical distribution of these constituencies is not without significance. It cuts two swathes: one from the South-west up towards the North-west, comprising Taunton, Exeter, Tiverton, Bridport, Bridgwater, and Bristol, through Carmarthen, Cirencester, and Worcester up towards Liverpool and Preston. The other runs up the eastern side of the country, from Maldon, Hertford, Hertfordshire, Colchester, Harwich, Cambridge, Ipswich, and Great Yarmouth up to the East Midlands and Northampton, Leicester, and Nottingham, and on up to Lincoln. The first of the two swathes was dominated numerically by Presbyterians, the second by Congregationalists and Baptists. These boroughs include a fair representation of commercial and industrial centres which were more open and less easily controlled than some traditional corporate towns. They include Bristol, Coventry, Hertford, Leicester, Northampton, Nottingham, and Tiverton. Distinct from these were a number of smaller market towns that nevertheless stood on excellent lines of communication: Buckingham, Cirencester, Colchester, Lewes, Maidstone, and Taunton. Then there were a number of ports, where there was obviously a regular flow of people and ideas: Bridport, Harwich, Ipswich, Liverpool, and Portsmouth. Finally, there were a number of cathedral cities, whose Anglican establishments bred a countervailing reaction from local Dissenters: Exeter, Lincoln, Norwich, and Worcester. The politics of Dissent were, therefore, by no means purely ideological. Dissenting political and electoral activity rested upon specific geographical and urban foundations, factors which contributed enormously to the strength and continuity of the Dissenting tradition.

The mobilization of Dissenting voters was not confined to these constituencies. In very many of the medium and large freeman boroughs, lingering religious antagonisms could be focused on current issues, especially in a period of religious tension. There had been few signs of religious tension in the electoral history of Chester in the eighteenth century, even though the Grosvenors had customarily relied upon Anglican support and had used Anglican clergy in its canvasses, while the independents enjoyed the support of local Presbyterian congregations. The strong showing of independent candidates at the election of 1812 infuriated the Anglicans, and a first-rate public quarrel broke out in which the Bishop of Chester attacked the Dissenters, their loyalty and their institutions.[163] Similarly, Hampshire was not a

---

[163] G. H. Law, 'Remarks on the Primary Visitation of the Bishop of Chester, July, August and September 1814', in *Sermons, Strictures, etc.* (1814).

county noted for its religious enmities, but as soon as the issue of Catholic emancipation was mooted in 1807 the religious batallions suddenly materialized.[164] In many other constituencies, including Reading, Shrewsbury, and Sudbury, background and incidental evidence suggests that religious traditions and denominational conflict acted as potential sources of electoral mobilization.

Even in the constituencies singled out here for special attention, it would be a mistake to assume that religious considerations were always in the forefront of political concern. As Dr Stoker comments of the four Northern counties: 'common religious attitudes were not reflected at the poll . . . there is no evidence that Dissenters had Whig tendencies or that Angicans had Tory preferences'.[165] Many of these constituencies manifested religious divisions but these sometimes fail to appear in the poll books, or when they appear seem too slight to be taken too seriously. On occasion, the sources are surprisingly silent. For example, Nottingham had a vociferous Dissenting population but at the contested election of 1780 there are no specific references to Dissenters voting. According to the poll book even the Dissenting minister did not vote, although several did vote at a municipal election the following month.[166] Sometimes, the call to religious voting fell on deaf ears. The Bishop of Durham attempted to mobilize 312 freeholders in 1761: only 178 bothered to reply to his letter, and of these only 130 took his advice.[167] The problem is one of fathoming the personal intentions of the voters, to separate the religious from other motivations. For example, Methodism was one of the most coherent of sectarian cultures. If religious batallions of voters are to be found it is surely among Methodist voters. But at Preston in 1807 they showed no overwhelming preference for the coalition or for the independents. The preference they did show—49% gave a party vote for the coalition, 39% a plumper for the independent—was discernible but hardly sensational.[168] In many ways then, religious voting comes to resemble the voting of any other interest, except that it was less frequently mobilized. Indeed, it may be that religious voting, essentially a latent force, and religious mobilization occurred only on exceptional occasions. In normal times, the most important quality of religious

[164] The Anglican clergy supported Sir Richard Worsley in 1779 by 65–54. They proceeded to support Pittite candidates in 1780 and 1805 by 68–31, and 60–51. This is hardly the behaviour of monolithic religious blocs. In 1807, however, they voted 38–9 against a candidate who supported Catholic emancipation (see Lowe, 'Hampshire Elections', M.Phil., 220–5).

[165] Stoker, 'Elections and Voting Behaviour', Ph.D., 210.

[166] *Alphabetical List of the Burgesses* (Nottingham, 1780).

[167] 'Elections and Voting Behaviour', Ph.D. 211–12.

[168] A Register of Methodist Baptism identified 51 names in the 1807 poll book. See *An Alphabetical List of members belonging to the Preston Monthly Meeting, 1798–1868*, Lancs. RO.

divisions, perhaps, was their capacity to inflame the non-electors whenever religious taboos were threatened. So far as the electors were concerned, then, even in the 30–40 seats where the Anglican–Dissent divide dominated politics, the axis offered a general structural and ideological framework for electoral activity rather than a constant set of positive motivations.

Nevertheless, the capacity of Dissenters to vote *en bloc* is most impressive. Their behaviour at Abingdon, one of the very few places for which detailed evidence exists in the middle of the eighteenth century, is interesting. Out of 59 named Anglicans, only 9 opposed the Tories at the general elections of 1754 and 1768: no fewer than 37 voted Tory on *both* occasions. In 1754 not a single Dissenter voted Tory: all 37 voted for the Whig candidate. Only 2 of the 18 Dissenters who voted in both elections voted Tory. By 1774 the Dissenters at Abingdon have moved *as a party* from a position of support for government, supporting Whig candidates, to a position of opposition to government.[169] It is the capacity of Dissenters to behave in this manner, even though it was not always necessary for them to do so, which requires emphasis. We should not exaggerate the power of religious motivations. It is quite likely that some electors voted out of purely religious impulses, but even more likely that on most occasions, most electors voted for a mixture of reasons among which religion was one among several formative influences. It cannot be said that religion always shaped both the issues and fired the rhetoric of electoral politics. While accepting Professor Phillips's conclusion that religion was of greater significance than social resentments in influencing the quality of electoral behaviour, it is not clear that religion was 'the critical element in the political and social perceptions' of voters. Indeed, he only finds conclusive evidence among the Dissenters of two of his four boroughs that political dissent was linked to religious nonconformity.[170]

The conflict between Anglican and Dissenter nevertheless maintained partisanship within local communities long after the old party distinctions between Whig and Tory had been forgotten and generated sentiment among the non-voters, sentiment which could spill over into violence. It may also have widened the political horizons of local groups

---

[169] The behaviour of the Abingdon Dissenters was first noted by Professor Bradley in private correspondence with me. It may be worked out from the poll books of 1754 and 1768, in both of which Dissenters are identified. The paucity of information regarding religious affiliation in most poll books makes it very difficult to estimate how typical this Abingdon phenomenon might have been.

[170] J. A. Phillips, *Electoral Behaviour*, 305. It is surely not enough merely to add, 'their Anglican counterparts should have been affected as well, if somewhat less dramatically'.

by generalizing local divisions onto a national stage. At least, the purely local, anti-corporation, oppositionist tendencies of many groups of Dissenters were slowly being politicized by the Wilkite phenomenon, by the American War, and by the appearance of radical associations after 1779.[171] There is even evidence that local groups of Dissenters were moving into a stance of open hostility to successive governments in the reign of George III. Indeed, in at least 11 constituencies, local Dissenting interests backed successful Rockingham Whig candidates, and in at least 6 others such attempts failed.[172] There are nine other constituencies where the links between local Dissent and the Rockingham party were a contributory rather than a dominant element in electoral politics.[173] The process may be viewed in another way. Of 25 Dissenters who sat in the House of Commons between 1715 and 1760, 22 supported the government rather than the opposition. Of the 15 Dissenters who sat in the House of Commons between 1760 and 1790, only 6 did. Of the 9 oppositionists, 5—possibly 7—were Rockingham Whigs.[174] After 1760, then, the Dissenters were swinging away from their earlier support of the Hanoverian dynasty and towards some connection with opposition groups.

Towards the end of the eighteenth century, religious issues began to play a more central role in politics and such connections became of greater significance. This happened in two ways. The agitation for the abolition of the slave trade after 1787 unquestionably sharpened the politicization of Dissenters through the activities of committees in most large towns and the numerous public meetings that they organized.[175] The Abolitionists decided against using general elections to press their case, but there can be little doubt that 'the politics of conscience' was proceeding apace. The Dissenters were at the same time mobilizing in order to petition Parliament for the removal of the Test and Corporation Acts. Both in 1784 and in 1790 Charles James Fox had promised the assistance of his party in these endeavours. In 1790 the promise paid off, and Dissenters in many constituencies rallied to Fox's banner. At the Hampshire county contest of that year, for

---

[171] For an interesting case study of a local Dissenting opposition undergoing the transition to a nationally conscious, radical party see J. E. Bradley, 'Religion and Reform at the Polls: Nonconformity in Cambridge Politics, 1774–1784', *J. Brit. Studies*, 23/2 (1984), 55–78.

[172] Berwick-upon-Tweed, Bristol, Coventry, Liverpool, London, Maidstone, Maldon, Monmouthshire, Northumberland, Norwich, and Portsmouth. For failed attempts see Abingdon, Cambridge, Great Yarmouth, Morpeth, Nottingham, and Worcester. Bradley, 'Whigs and Nonconformists', Ph.D., 534–40.

[173] Cambridgeshire, Chichester, Essex, Exeter, Hertford, Hertfordshire, Leicester, Leicestershire, and Warwick. Ibid.

[174] Ibid. 540–7.

[175] F. M. Hunt, 'The North of England Agitation for the Abolition of the Slave Trade, 1780–1800', MA (Manchester, 1959), 141–7.

example, numerous pamphlets on the issue deluged the freeholders.[176]
According to Professor Phillips, the local opposition (Whig) party
attracted the support of 80% of Norwich Dissenters in 1780, rising
to 90% by 1802. Whig support among Dissenters, in fact, was
increasing more rapidly than Whig support among the population at
large. At Northampton at the general elections of 1784, 1790, and
1796 Whig support among Dissenters was running twice—and even
three times—as high as their support among others.[177] In the 1790s
there are many indications that the forces of Dissent were rallying
to the party of Charles James Fox. There can be no mistaking the fact,
for example, that the Nottingham Whigs regarded themselves as Foxite
Whigs: 'the Whigs and Radicals made no attempt to deny this
identification of themselves with religious non-conformity but made
it one of the main features of their appeal'.[178] At the election of 1796,
indeed, such identifications were made in at least 17 constituencies.[179]
We would be unwise, however, to make too much of all this. In some
places, Dissenters were seriously divided among themselves. In any
case, the connection between Foxite Whiggism and Dissent was almost
at once to be weakened.

The mobilization of the power of Dissent was matched by the
reassertion of popular prejudices against it, especially in the 1790s
when the French Revolution engendered heightened antipathies
between religious denominations. As early as November 1789 an
Anglican correspondent wrote to a Norwich newspaper, affirming that
the Dissenters 'seek to confound all subordinations, all distinctions
of rank, in democratic equality, and to crumble the temple of the
constitution into vicious anarchy'.[180] The strength of anti-Dissent
opinion, manifested in the Birmingham riots of 1791 and intensifying
with the organization of Reeves societies after November 1792, steadily
eroded the self-confidence of Dissent. Fears of revolution weakened
fatally the connection between Dissent and the party of Charles James
Fox. While his party went into secession between 1797 and 1801,
the Dissenters turned away from national political agitation.[181]
Perhaps, too, they had already achieved such a degree of incorporation
within local ruling élites that they had no wish to endanger that

---

[176] *Hampshire Chronicle*, 12 Apr. 1790.

[177] J. A. Phillips, *Electoral Behaviour*, 166–8, 296–303.

[178] Thomis, *Politics and Society in Nottingham*, 129.

[179] Bridport, Bristol, Cirencester, Coventry, Ipswich, Hertfordshire, Leicester, Liverpool,
London, Maidstone, Maldon, Northampton, Nottingham, Norwich, Preston, Taunton,
Worcester. See D. McAdams, 'Politicians and the Electorate', Ph.D., 223–40.

[180] *Norwich Gazette*, 21 Nov. 1789.

[181] See e.g. the inward focus of Dissent at Leicester. R. W. Greaves, *The Corporation of
Leicester* (Oxford, 1939), 107–8.

status.[182] Furthermore, the enthusiasm with which the Ministry of All the Talents embraced the Catholics' cause was not to their liking. The resignation of the ministry on the issue of Catholic emancipation, moreover, aroused sentiments which flared up ominously at the general election of 1807. One terrified candidate, having abandoned the contest at Bridgwater, gave his reasons: 'I have no desire to increase popular Confusions, nor to enter more deeply in a contest where Religion is falsely and hypocritically introduced into a mere Political Question.'[184] There was no serious disorder at both Bristol and Liverpool. William Roscoe was mobbed at Liverpool and forced to withdraw: 'On Saturday evening a young man with a pink ribbon on his hat: "Roscoe—and King and Constitution"—was assaulted by a man wearing the colours of one of the military candidates. D—n your King and Constitution! No Roscoe: No Papists!'[185] Whig commitment to Catholic emancipation in 1807 diluted the loyalty of Protestant Dissenters to the Whig party of Grey. At the same time, Dissenters were by no means immune to the gusts of patriotism, the rallying of the nation behind the military effort in the concluding years of the Napoleonic War, and the closing of the ranks of the propertied classes behind the forces of law and order in the immediate post-war years. The repeal of the Test and Corporation Acts in 1828 owed more to Wellington's vulnerability and to the opportunism of the Dissenters than to any Whig–Dissent axis.[186]

The strength of the opposition to Repeal may have worried the Dissenters and made them doubt their security under the existing electoral system.[187] What really horrified them enough to drive them into the arms of the Whig party, however, was Catholic emancipation in 1829. Their shock and resentment at emancipation left the Dissenters pledged to the Whigs and the reform of Parliament. They were now

---

[182] See e.g. Seed, 'Gentleman Dissenters', 304–9, 314–15, 320.

[183] 'No Popery' became a general anti-Whig rallying cry in 1807 in at least nine county contests and in many boroughs. See Thorne, *House of Commons*, i. 16, 189–92.

[184] *Oxford Journal*, 9 May 1807.

[185] *Morning Chronicle*, 9 May 1807; *Liverpool Chronicle*, 13 May 1807. Interestingly, this kind of thing did not happen in all constituencies with large Catholic populations. Religion was scarcely an issue at Preston, presumably because of the alliance of the Derby interest, traditionally sympathetic to the Dissenters, and the industrialist Horrocks, supported by the Anglican corporation. Their conspiracy of silence on the religious issue was matched by that of their radical opponents. See Thorne, *House of Commons*, ii. 235–8.

[186] Whig commitment to repeal was much less solid than its commitment to emancipation. It is true that Lord John Russell carried repeal as a Whig measure. The bill was virtually managed by Peel, not by Russell. Repeal was a victory for organized dissent and a recognition of its power and prestige in British society.

[187] G. I. T. Machin, 'Resistance to Repeal of the Test and Corporation Acts, 1828', *Hist. J.* 22 (1979), 115–39; O. Parry, 'The Parliamentary Representation of Wales and Monmouthshire in the Nineteenth Century', MA (Wales, 1924), 127–42.

no longer content to work the existing electoral system as they had for over a century. In 1830 and 1831 Dissenters up and down the country punished MPs who had voted for emancipation.[188] Even the Dissenters of rural Wales, substantial and respectable farmers, not urban radicals, now adopted reform.[189]

Religious distinctions now coincided with parliamentary alignments, and a Whig–Dissenting party confronted a Tory–Anglican one.[190] It was ironic that this match of religious and political loyalties at local and national level was achieved at the cost of threatening to liquidate the existing electoral system in its entirely. In 1831 Dissenting voters were solidly for reform and rallied behind Whig and radical candidates to spearhead the deliberate and calculated destruction of the unreformed electoral system.


## PARTISAN VOTING

One of the most remarkable characteristics of electors in constituencies before 1832 was their capacity to vote in a partisan manner. This could mean either distributing their votes to candidates of the same side, interest or party where two such candidates existed or giving one vote only to a candidate who was standing alone and thus neglecting to use their second vote. Cross-voting between two sides, interests, or parties was much less common. Voters were able to display considerable sophistication in the disposal of their votes. It is not difficult to detect three fairly general reasons why they should wish to vote in a partisan manner. Electors wished to behave—and to be thought to behave—with consistency and honour in their politics. At the same time, they might be pressured, organized, and persuaded to dispose of their votes in a certain way. Finally, they might through their own political choice and will distribute their votes in such a

---

[188] The Reading Dissenters, for example, engineered the defeat of Stephen Lushington in 1830 for his vote on emancipation. A. Aspinall, *Reading Through Seven Centuries* (London, 1962), 92–3. For the strength of Dissenting feeling at Colchester see Speight, 'Politics in Colchester', Ph.D., 253–6. See also G. I. T. Machin, *The Catholic Question in English Politics, 1820 to 1830* (London, 1964), ch. 4.

[189] A. H. Dodd, *The Industrialized Revolution in North Wales*, 2nd edn. (Cardiff, 1951), 166–7.

[190] Vincent has shown that 24 out of 27 votes cast by Dissenting ministers at the elections of 1830 and 1831 in four designated constituencies went to Whig candidates see J. R. Vincent, *Pool Books: How Victorious Voted* (Cambridge, 1967), 67–8. A more recent and much more comprehensive study has shown that in 1831, 76 of the 83 votes cast by Dissenting ministers in 10 designated constituencies went to reform candidates, see Odurkene, 'The British General Elections', B.Litt., 148–50. Anglican ministers voted 1735 to 796 against reform, a nice commentary upon fissures within the Tory party on the reform question.

TABLE 6.1    *Partisan Voting, Selected Constituencies, 1701–1715*

| Constituency | Year | Party Voting (%) |
|---|---|---|
| Bedfordshire | 1715 | 94% |
| Bletchingley | 1710 | 91% |
| Bletchingley | 1713 | 88% |
| Buckinghamshire | 1700 | 80% |
| Buckinghamshire | 1701 | 89% |
| Buckinghamshire | 1705 | 95% |
| Buckinghamshire | 1713 | 95% |
| Huntingdonshire | 1705 | 90% |
| Huntingdonshire | 1710 | 98% |
| Kent | 1713 | 82% |
| London | 1710 | 90% |
| Sussex | 1713 | 82% |
| Westmorland | 1700 | 84% |
| Westmorland | 1701 | 87% |
| Westmorland | 1702 | 92% |
| Average | | 88.9% |

manner. As we shall see, however, it is the scale and extent of partisan voting which is so remarkable.

Such a phenomenon in the early eighteenth century may be related to the 'rage of party', the conflict between parliamentary-based Whig and Tory parties projected out into the constituencies. Almost 90% of all votes cast between 1701 and 1715 at elections in these constituencies studied to date were cast in a partisan manner (see table 6.1).[191] The electorate of the reign of Anne consisted of two vast batallions of voters, one Whig, one Tory, accompanied by a small, albeit significant, minority of 'floating voters'.[192] The same phenomenon has been detected in the age of 'organized' political parties which followed the Reform Act of 1832. For the period 1832–68,

[191] Based on figures in Table 6.1 collected from W. A. Speck, 'A Computer Analysis of Pollbooks: An Initial Report', *Bull. Inst. Hist. Res.* 43 (1970), 105–12; W. A. Speck, W. A. Gray, and, R. A. Hopkinson, 'A Computer Analysis of Poll Books: A Further Report', ibid. 48 (975), 64–90; W. A. Speck and W. A. Gray, 'Londoners at the Polls under Anne and George I', *Guildhall Studies*, 1 (1975), 251–62.

[192] Landau has argued that 'floating voters' float not because of their own independent judgement but because of that of their 'patrons', the government as an employer and the influence of the justices of the peace etc. See N. Landau, 'Independence, Deference, and Voter Participation: The Behaviour of the Electorate in Early Eighteenth Century Kent', *Hist. J.* 22/3 (1979), 561–83. There is nevertheless much in the article that shows 'that the justices possessed relatively little power to persuade voters to change their party allegiance while the fact that voters exercised their right not to vote demonstrate[s] the independence of the electorate' (ibid. 579). The real thrust of Landau's argument is that 'the most striking effect of . . . influence was an increase in the number of voters supporting the candidates favoured by their rules' (ibid. 580).

in the constituencies studied to date no fewer than 82.8% of all votes studied to date were cast in a partisan manner, a figure which would have been ever higher had it not been for the confusion of party alignments both immediately after 1832 and following the repeal of the Corn Laws.[193]

The partisan voting traditions of the early eighteenth century were slow to disappear. At Kent, for example, partisan voting declined slowly, from the impressive 95% at the contest of 1727 down to 91% in 1734 to the still remarkable figure of 82% for the three-cornered contest of 1754.[194] Other remarkable levels of partisan voting can be cited in the mid-eighteenth century: 93% at Hereford in 1741, 98% at Shrewsbury in 1747, 97% at Bristol and 94% at Great Yarmouth in 1754. Voters did not mindlessly dispose of their votes to one side or the other. They were capable of exercising fine levels of discrimination. For example, 85% of the Worcestershire freeholders in 1741 proved themselves capable of distinguishing not merely between government and opposition but between anti-ministerial Whigs and Tories.[195]

The intensity of party voting was conditioned less by the impact of national parties and nationally orchestrated party appeals, although these certainly had an influence, than by the structure and circumstances of the election contest. In four-cornered contests, where two candidates of one party faced two candidates of the other, very few voters split their votes. Newcastle-upon-Tyne had not been contested since 1747, yet in 1774 no fewer than 94% of the freemen used their votes in a partisan manner, exactly the same percentage displayed in Norwich both in 1818 and 1830, after decades of manifestly impressive local party development. Gloucester had only been contested once (at the 1789 by-election) since 1761, when a further by-election in 1816 acted as a dummy run for the contest of 1818. Although only three candidates stood, 95% of voters delivered party votes as defined above. This was higher, even, than was to be attained at the great Leicester contest of 1826 (92%), when there were four candidates, and almost matched the very highest figures for elections to the unreformed Parliament: 97% at York in 1820, 98%

---

[193] I have collected Nossiter's figures from 'Aspects of Electoral Behaviour in English Constituencies, 1832–68', in E. Allardt and S. Rokkan (eds.), *Mass Politics: Studies in Political Sociology* (1970), 164–5. They average as follows: 1832, 74.7%; 1835, 82.0%; 1837, 84.9%; 1841, 91.4%; 1847, 73.7%; 1852, 80.7%, 1857, 84.0%; 1859, 81.5%; 1865, 87.5%, 1868, 87.4%.

[194] Newman, 'Elections in Kent', D.Phil., 173.

[195] Colley, *In Defiance of Oligarchy*, 136–7.

at Nottingham in 1830, 99% at Great Yarmouth in 1820 and 1830, 99% at Ipswich too in 1830.[196]

It may be argued that such suspiciously high figures for partisan voting must be the result of corruption and intimidation. There are, of course, instances of such nefarious practices producing partisan voting, but for the most part such explanations will not suffice.[197] They will not explain why almost every single elector used both his votes at the contests of 1812, 1818, and 1826 at Chester to attain a consistent partisan voting figure of 95%.[198] They will not explain why only 3 out of 1,254 Exeter voters split their votes in 1761, and at Great Yarmouth, with an electorate approaching 1,500, only 21 in 1818, 4 in 1820, and in 1830 only 3.[199] In freeman boroughs with fairly large electorates, what affected partisan voting was a combination of local party consciousness, competitive (and fairly advanced) levels of party organization, the partisan traditions and political sophistication of the electorate, and the divisive potential of national political issues. The competitive mobilization of the electorate and the cultivated intensity of latent political sentiment drove electors into one or other camp. Fence-sitting was hardly possible in the circumstances of a four-cornered contest.

During the century before the Reform Act of 1832, however, three-cornered contests were more common than four-cornered contests, especially in the counties.[200] Partisan voting was not as simply expressed in the former as it was in the latter. By definition, a three-cornered contest demanded single votes (plumpers) for one side or the other. Now, voters might need some persuasion before they agreed

[196] *The Burgesses' Poll at the Late Election* (Newcastle-upon-Tyne, 1774); *An Alphabetical List of the Electors* (Preston, 1807); *Gloucester City Election, 1818. Alphabetical List of the Poll* (Gloucester, 1818); *The Poll for Members* (York, 1820); *An Alphabetical List of the Burgesses* (Nottingham, 1830), *The Poll for Members* (Norwich, 1818 and 1830), *The Poll for Two Members* (Great Yarmouth, 1820 and 1830), *The Poll for the Election*, (Leicester, 1826).

[197] Of course, in smaller places they can. I would not like to argue that the incredible party voting that occurred in Hythe in 1768 had nothing to do with the disgraceful scale of corruption which occurred at that election. See G. Wilks, *The Barons of the Cinque Ports and the Parliamentary Reresentation of Hythe* (Folkestone, 1892). Similarly, I have my suspicions about the Appleby result of 1754, when every one of the 250 votes cast was a party vote. (See B. Bonsall, 23: 'There was not a single instance of a voter dividing his votes between the two parties, an indication of the extent to which the rival families dominated the borough'. At Horsham, according to Albery, not one of the 73 voters split their votes in 1806; see W. Albery, *Parliamentary History of Horsham* (Horsham, 1947), 200–29.

[198] In 1812, 99.3% of voters used both their votes, in 1818, 98.6%, in 1826, 99.5%.

[199] *A List of the Freemen and Freeholders* (Exeter, 1761); Namier and Brooke, *House of Commons*, i. 253; *The Poll for Two Members* (Great Yarmouth, 1818, 1820, and 1830).

[200] Out of 63 county contests between 1790 and 1820 only one was four-cornered. See Thorne, *House of Commons*, i. 5.

TABLE 6.2    *Rates of Partisan and Split Voting in Three-cornered Contests in Five Constituencies, 1768–1831* (%)

|  | Party voting | Split voting |
|---|---|---|
| *Cirencester* | | |
| 1768 | 85.9 | 12.1 |
| 1790 | 65.7 | 33.0 |
| 1802 | 59.1 | 36.8 |
| *Colchester* | | |
| 1790 | 43.0 | 34.4 |
| 1806 | 58.2 | 15.9 |
| 1807 | 50.8 | 29.5 |
| 1812 | 44.7 | 18.5 |
| *St Albans* | | |
| 1820 | 46.2 | 30.3 |
| 1830 | 44.5 | 39.8 |
| 1831 | 67.5 | 29.2 |
| *Shrewsbury* | | |
| 1806 | 64.9 | 32.0 |
| 1807 | 66.1 | 31.6 |
| 1812 | 55.6 | 39.5 |
| 1826 | 56.7 | 38.0 |
| *Southampton* | | |
| 1774 | 71.3 | 22.1 |
| 1790 | 62.2 | 35.0 |
| 1806 | 49.1 | 42.2 |
| 1812 | 48.6 | 38.5 |
| 1818 | 55.2 | 33.3 |
| 1820 | 50.8 | 42.0 |
| 1831 | 83.0 | 13.7 |

*Note*: Figures for individual contests do not add up to 100% because they do not include single votes cast for a party with two candidates.

to plump. They traditionally preferred to use both of their votes. To use one only might involve them in some financial loss; it might require an act of political restraint, or sophistication, of which they might not immediately be themselves capable, especially in those constituencies contested infrequently. To split two votes between two parties might ensure that neither was offended. Consequently, rates of partisan voting at three-cornered contests were markedly lower than at four-cornered contests. Furthermore, rates of split voting (i.e. distributing two votes between two parties) were significantly higher. Table 6.2 summarizes rates for partisan voting at 21 three-cornered contests in five designated constituencies. The mean of partisan voting of these 21 contests is 55.7%, dramatically lower than in the four-cornered contests we observed above. Split voting, at times almost undetectable in four-cornered contests, reached a mean of 30.8% in the examples contained in Table 6.2

Higher rates of partisan voting in three-cornered contests were frequent, especially where religion intervened to impose its own powerful disciplines in a contest. Warwick was rarely contested, yet the three-cornered contest of 1831 yielded partisan voting of 80.6%. Constituencies which normally enjoyed the party discipline of four-cornered contests sometimes carried that discipline over into their occasional three-cornered contests: Canterbury achieved 87% in the three-cornered contest of 1830. Constituencies with strong party traditions might take three-cornered contests in their stride. At York in 1820 only 5% of 2,722 voters, and in 1830 8% of 3,540, split their votes.[201]

Like so much else in electoral history, the motives for splitting votes between parties were varied. Clearly, the anticipation of financial profit was a constant factor. Voters could easily benefit themselves by taking money and treats from both sides. In most cases, voters were not punished for acting in this way. There were other reasons, however, for split voting. Voters may genuinely have liked or disliked a candidate, they may have felt keenly about an issue, and they may have had opinions about the balance of the representation within the constituency. Most commonly, however, tactical considerations lay behind split voting. Candidates and agents actively canvassed for splits as the only, or the desired, means of winning an election. At the Dorset county contest of 1807, the Tory Henry Banks realized that his only hope of victory lay in picking up the second votes of the likely winner, W. M. Pitt. His Whig opponent, E. B. Portman, was likely to obtain more plumpers, and the contest turned on the struggle for Pitt's second votes. Banks did not get quite enough of them and he lost by 10 votes. The representation of Colchester in the early nineteenth century was decided by the destination of the second votes of radical candidates. There was no natural home for them in the opposing camps of Whig and Tory candidates, and the proportion of split votes was consequently high—sometimes even above 30%.[202] Tactical considerations of this type, as much as venality and political indifference, kept the rates of split voting fairly high in most three-cornered contests. On the figures available, I can detect little sign of a gradual decrease in the levels of split voting. The prevalence of three-cornered contests

[201] E. Heathcoate, *Poll of the Burgesses* (Warwick, 1831); *Poll of the Electors* (Canterbury, 1830); *The Poll for Members* (York, 1820).

[202] Speight, 'Politics in Colchester', Ph.D., 113–15.

inhibited the development of partisan electoral behaviour and kept the levels of split voting fairly high. The development of partisan voting within a two-party system required the polarization of electoral politics which four-cornered contests provoked.

In a three-cornered contest, none the less, victory went *either* to the side which could encourage the voters to vote for the two candidates who were running together *or* to the single candidate who could convince his supporters to refrain from using their second votes and thus help his opponents. The extent of 'necessary plumping', as Professor Phillips has aptly termed the latter,[203] is, of course, often a useful further indicator of partisan voting.[204] The most spectacular example is undoubtedly the victory of Lord Milton in Yorkshire contest of 1807. Of his 11,177 votes, no fewer than 9,049 (81%) were plumpers. (Indeed, no less than 52% of all votes cast at this election were plumpers, some indication of the care and selectivity with which voters chose to vote.) At Liverpool in 1818 the Earl of Sefton found that 1,145 of his 1,280 votes were 'necessary' plumpers, an incredible 89%. In view of the unique character of electoral constituencies and the almost limitless variation in the structure of election contests, the relative popularity of particular candidates and issues, and the widely varying efficiency of local organizations it is impossible to generalize with much confidence about the incidence of 'necessary' plumping. Nevertheless, for what it is worth, Table 6.3 summarizes some data drawn from the computerized analysis of three-cornered contests. Clearly, the vast majority of electors preferred to use both of their votes. Only when the lines of party division were tightly drawn—as at Colchester in 1812, Shrewsbury in 1806 and 1807, and in St Albans and Southampton in 1831—did the number of 'necessary' plumps rise to significant proportions. We should be reluctant to seize on generalizations one way or the other. Clearly, split voting was likely to be widespread unless the priorities of party came to obliterate all other priorities. Furthermore, it is difficult to detect clear and unmistakeable tendencies here. 'Necessary' plumping was on the increase over a long period at Southampton and (over a much shorter one) at St Albans. At Cirencester, and with one exception at

[203] 'Necessary in the sense that support for a party renders it necessary to plump. 'Unnecessary' plumping was, when a voter votes for only one or two available candidates. Plumping, in this case, was not 'necessary' (J. A. Phillips, *Electoral Behaviour*, 222–6).

[204] Often but not always. There are examples of strategic plumping which directly repudiate party considerations. At the Bucks. county election of 1831 the Chandos interest persuaded its supporters to give a plumper to the only Tory candidate. When a second Tory appeared they refused to release them from their promises, even though many voters wished to support the two Tory candidates. See Sir. T. Fremantle to John Newman, 19 Dec. 1832, Fremantle MSS, Bucks. RO.

TABLE 6.3 *'Necessary' Plumping in Five Constituencies,*
*1768–1831* (% of voters)

| | Necessary plumping |
|---|---|
| *Colchester* | |
| 1790 | 4.5 |
| 1806 | 8.7 |
| 1807 | 2.7 |
| 1812 | 20.4 |
| 1820 | 4.6 |
| *Cirencester* | |
| 1768 | 31.2 |
| 1790 | 21.9 |
| 1802 | 11.2 |
| *St Albans* | |
| 1820 | 2.5 |
| 1830 | 7.2 |
| 1831 | 17.2 |
| *Shrewsbury* | |
| 1806 | 15.3 |
| 1807 | 19.1 |
| 1812 | 10.3 |
| 1826 | 2.2 |
| *Southampton* | |
| 1774 | 5.0 |
| 1790 | 5.0 |
| 1806 | 3.6 |
| 1812 | 7.7 |
| 1818 | 4.5 |
| 1820 | 13.9 |
| 1831 | 24.5 |

Shrewsbury, it was on the decline. At Colchester, again with one exception, it was noticeably low at the beginning and at the end of the 30 year period in which it was studied. It may be possible to erect confident generalizations about the rise of 'necessary' plumping in three-cornered constituencies[205] when the conditions for it exist, namely: regular contested elections, clearly defined local parties, and some identification with the men and issues of parliamentary politics among the electorate. Where one of these did not exist, the level of 'necessary'

[205] As I suspect J. A. Phillips wanted to do, when he noted 'a marked increase in the willingness of Maidstone and Lewes voters to plump when necessary to support a party' (*Electoral Behaviour*, 224). At Norwich there was a decrease, however, while at Northampton the picture was indeterminate.

TABLE 6.4    *Plumping in Four-cornered Constituencies, 1754–1831*

| | Constituency | Year | % Plumping |
|---|---|---|---|
| Northumberland | County | 1826 | 1.2 |
| Chester | Large freeman | 1812 | 0.9 |
| Chester | Large freeman | 1818 | 1.4 |
| Chester | Large freeman | 1826 | 0.5 |
| Liverpool | Large freeman | 1812 | 3.1 |
| Maidstone | Large freeman | 1831 | 4.6 |
| Newcastle-upon-Tyne | Large freeman | 1774 | 1.8 |
| Shrewsbury | Large freeman | 1831 | 8.6 |
| York | Large freeman | 1784 | 1.1 |
| Sudbury | Medium freeman | 1790 | 1.4 |
| Boston | Small freeman | 1807 | 10.2 |

plumping would be low. Shrewsbury was a lively and thoroughly politicized constituency by 1826 but 'necessary' plumping hardly occurred at the very confused contest of that year, in which no obvious polarities were apparent to the voters.[206] Much the same can be said about Colchester and the election of 1790 in which candidates representing a confusing range of opinion sought support against, and between, each other.[207] At Southampton, on the other hand, 'necessary' plumping was low because the election of 1774 was the first to be contested there since 1741. On top of this, the elections of 1774, 1790, and 1806 did not present the voters with stark choices between the parties. In these circumstances, 'necessary' plumping was low.[208] Everything depends, then, upon the constituency upon which research attention is concentrated and the circumstances of a particular contested election.

Nevertheless, plumping in *four*-cornered constituencies, as we might expect by now, was very rare indeed. The pressures upon voters to use both their votes were all but insuperable. Table 6.4 summarizes some of the available data. Where party lines were closely drawn, plumping would be almost non-existent. Where a more confusing situation obtained, as at Shrewsbury in 1831 when alignments were far from clear, or at Boston, where money and influence mattered, some voters might be persuaded to withhold one of their votes. The number, however, was rarely very large.

[206] The distinction between the ministerialist Corbett and the oppositionist Slaney was fairly clear, but the intervention of an anti-Catholic independent candidate, Boycott, thoroughly confused the situation.
[207] For Colchester in 1790 see Thorne, *House of Commons*, ii. 158.
[208] For Southampton see ibid. 189–91.

An even more rigorous test of partisan voting— perhaps the most rigorous test of partisan voting that can possibly be devised—is the ability of voters to sustain partisan voting over time. Professor Phillips found that in the second half of the eighteenth century between 45% and 65% of Norwich electors who voted in a second election sustained the party choice they had made in the first. At Maidstone the range was 30% to 50%, at Lewes 30% to 55%, and at Northampton 30% to 40%. There seems, in addition, to have been a slight tendency for partisan voting to increase over time, and for split and floating voting to diminish.[209] Other studies have confirmed, and are confirming, that such ranges of partisan voting were not confined to these constituencies. A manual analysis of the York electorate undertaken nearly 30 years ago revealed that 62% of electors who voted in both the elections of 1758 and 1774 (the next election to be contested in the constituency) voted in a consistent manner, a remarkable level of partisan behaviour to be sustained over 16 tumultuous years. When the analysis was projected further forward, examining the voting behaviour of electors who voted both in 1774 and 1784, the date of the next contest, no less than 55% of the electorate was found to have voted in exactly the same manner.[210] Short-term analysis yields still higher levels of consistent partisan voting behaviour. No less than 81.5% of the electors voting in both the Bristol by-election of 1781 and the general election of 1784 supported the same party. At Newcastle-upon-Tyne 75% of the voters who voted in both the general election of 1774 and the by-election of 1777 did so, and of those voting in both the by-election of 1777 and the general election of 1780 the proportion was 72%.[211] Similar figures can be found for the early nineteenth century. Of the Rochester voters who exercised the franchise at the general election of 1826 and of 1830, 64% did so in an identical manner on both occasions.[212] At Preston in the general elections of 1818 and 1820, 59% of the electorate did so, and in 1820 and 1826, 65%.[213]

Clearly, everything depends upon the constituency and the structure of the contest. There seems little point in presenting more instances of partisan voting. What is needed is a close analysis of a large group of voters in order to reveal the complex processes which produce partisan voting. To achieve this I established a database of all 1,575

[209] Ibid. 232–8.
[210] Price, 'Parliamentary Elections in the City of York', MA, 263.
[211] I am grateful indeed to Professor Bradley for this information in advance of the publication of his book, *Religion and Revolution*.
[212] *The Poll of the Electors* (Rochester, 1826, 1830).
[213] *An Alphabetical List of the Freeman* (Preston, 1818, 1820, 1831).

TABLE 6.5 *Partisan Voting at Shrewsbury Elections, 1806–31* (%)

| Year | Partisan voting |
|------|-----------------|
| 1807 | 72.3 |
| 1812 | 53.3 |
| 1814 | 71.9 |
| 1819 | 42.9 |
| 1830 | 76.7 |

electors in the constituency of Shrewsbury who voted at the eight successive elections of 1806, 1807, 1812, 1814, 1819, 1826, 1830, and 1831. Electors were identified by name so that the computer could measure the cumulative voting behaviour of individuals rather than deal in round totals. Table 6.5 summarizes the levels of partisan voting in those elections where reasonably close comparisons can be made across the electorate as a whole. Within these global figures, it is possible to move in a little more closely and to observe the fluxes and continuities within the electorate which collectively created the phenomenon of partisan voting. At the election of 1806 there were three candidates, each of whom superficially represented a distinct political position: Sir William Hill (Tory), Henry Bennet (Whig), and Thomas Jones (Independent). Party lines were weakly drawn at Shrewsbury at this early stage, however, and the electors voted in the three following major patterns of candidates: Hill–Bennet, Hill–Jones and Jones (plumper). Let us trace what happened to these voting patterns at the subsequent elections.

Taking the 354 Hill–Bennet voters first, 292 (82.5%) of them voted again in the following year. No less than 232 (65.5%) opted for the identical combination. Just as remarkable was the fact that of the 209 (59.0%) who also voted in the election of 1812, 145 (69.4%) voted for the same combination. At the by-election of 1814 voters were given the opportunity of voting for a Hill-sponsored candidate. Of the 199 (56.2%) who voted, 84.0% did so.

Partisanship was less emphatically displayed at the other end of the spectrum of Shrewsbury politics. Nevertheless, of the 111 who plumped for the Independent candidate in 1806, 103 (92.8%) voted again in 1807, and fractionally under 60% plumped once again for the Independent. In 1812, 46 (41.4%) voted again, and 58.6% plumped once again for the Independent candidate. In 1814, 49 (44.2%) voted, but on this occasion only 51% plumped for the Independent. The lack of staying power among Independents could not be better illustrated.

Just as interesting, however, is the political behaviour of the 218 split voters, those who divided their votes between Hill and Jones in

1806. Of these, 199 (91.2%) voted again in 1807, and 68.8% of them repeated the split. In 1812, too, when 113 (51.8%) of them survived they split again, but in an interestingly different manner. It is as though the latent contradiction in their position had now become apparent: 35 (30.9%) of them voted Hill–Bennet and 53 of them (49.1%) for Bennet and the Independent candidate. At the next two elections, these split voters stayed split. In 1814, 112 (51.4%) of them remained; on this occasion they voted *against* the Independent candidate by 55.3% to 44.7%. In 1819, however, 61.0% of the 96 who remained (44.1%) voted *for* the Independent.

Even in one of the less party-inclined of the 'party' seats, then, powerful continuities may be discerned, even in three-cornered contests and even with split voters. Where political issues imposed their own disciplines, the continuities became all the greater. In 1831 Shrewsbury was confronted with the reform issue. Jenkins and Boycott were the two anti-reform candidates. Together they received 124 votes. If we test these votes against the election of 1830, eliminating the 13 non-voters in the earlier election, we find that no fewer than 108 out of 111 voters had been distributed in exactly the same manner. On the reform side, the conclusion is the same. It is possible to trace in 1830 the votes of 89 of the 104 voters who supported the reform candidates in 1831. Seventy-six (84.3%) of them had supported exactly the same candidates.

This analysis provides a little more evidence to suggest that voting was essentially partisan. Beneath the surface of electoral politics, strong and consistent tides appear to flow. If the example of the Shrewsbury electors may be generalized—and nobody, surely, would regard the Shrewsbury constituency as the ideal breeding ground for partisan voters—then electoral behaviour can be seen to be consistent and rational rather than random and atomized.

We should not, however, overlook that relatively small yet determined minority of voters who energetically bucked the trend of partisan voting. A voter who, having voted in one manner at an election and who then proceeded to contradict that vote by casting his suffrages in the opposite direction, may be defined as a floating voter. To estimate the number of floating voters is a somewhat arbitrary and artificial proceeding. In a constituency like Shrewsbury, where three-cornered contests abounded, it is, in fact, not at all easy *totally* to contradict the manner of voting from one election to the next, so that the low figures from Shrewsbury tend to lend exaggerated importance to the extent of partisan voting. For what they are worth, then, Table 6.6 assembles the summary data for floating voting in Shrewsbury in the early nineteenth century. These figures nevertheless

TABLE 6.6 *The Floating Vote at Shrewsbury,
1807–1830 (%)*

| Year | Floating vote |
|------|---------------|
| 1807 | 7.4% |
| 1812 | 6.1% |
| 1814 | 9.7% |
| 1819 | 4.2% |
| 1826 | 2.2% |
| 1830 | 7.4% |

confirm independently the cumulative findings of other historians. Professor Phillips found that by 1802 floating voting in all four of his constituencies was running at less than 10%.[214] Dr Stoker calculated a rate of 9% for Westmorland between 1818 and 1820 and again between 1820 and 1826.[215] My own manual calculations yield figures of 11% for Chester between 1820 and 1826 and 9% for Preston beteen 1818 and 1820.[216] At Rochester for the period 1826–30 the figure sinks as low as 4%.[217] All this evidence points to one conclusion: that in early nineteenth century elections, rates of floating voting in excess of 10% seem to have been the exception rather than the rule.

To concentrate exclusively upon the significant extent of partisan voting behaviour and the relative unimportance of floating voting carries with it the danger that we shall ignore and neglect that large minority of electors who fall into neither of these categories. There were several intermediate ways of voting which enabled a voter to avoid both these classifications. Having voted in a partisan manner at one election, he might split his vote, withhold one of his two votes, or not vote at all at the next election. Or he might deliver a partisan vote at a second election having voted in one of these ways in the first. There were many shades of political indifference, confusion, and indeed persuasion and conviction lying between the two poles of partisan voting and floating voting. Depending on local circumstances, perhaps between one-fifth and one-half of all electors might at any election inhabit this somewhat non-descript middle ground (see Table 6.7). Nevertheless, it is important to underscore that of all these separate variations of electoral behaviour on offer to the electors, consistent party voting was by a long way the most popular.

---

[214] J. A. Phillips, *Electoral Behaviour*, 232–7.

[215] Stoker, 'Elections and Voting Behaviour', Ph.D., 206.

[216] Based on *The Poll Book for the General Election* (Chester, 1820); *The Complete Poll Book* (Chester, 1826).

[217] See sources cited in n. 212.

TABLE 6.7 *Non-partisan and Non-floating Voters at Shrewsbury, 1807–1830* (%)

| Year | Non-partisan and non-floating vote |
| --- | --- |
| 1807 | 20.3% |
| 1812 | 40.6% |
| 1814 | 18.4% |
| 1819 | 52.9% |
| 1830 | 15.9% |

The electorate, then, was highly partisan, displaying patterns of impressively solid and consistent partisan voting. It nevertheless contained a small but, in the context of a close contest, significant 'floating vote', together with a somewhat nebulous, inconsequential, and shifting element of the electorate which moved between the parties but without ever sustaining consistent partisanship. Partisanship was prominent but it was not overwhelming. This was, no doubt, because of the inconclusive nature of some contests, but, more generally, because elections enabled social pressures to accompany political pressures, and social accommodations did not require the precision in electoral behaviour that political pressures did. For example, to express courtesy and gratitude towards a landlord or employer might require only one vote, while an expression of faith in the independent cause might require two.

Partisan electoral behaviour of this type was not unique to the unreformed electorate. What came before and after was not dissimilar. Early eighteenth-century voters did not exhibit markedly different patterns of consistent partisan voting behaviour. Less than 25% of county voters seem to have switched their loyalties completely between elections.[218] Over one-half remained totally loyal to the party of their first choice.[219] Voters early in the seventeenth century appear to have unconsciously followed very similar patterns of behaviour. Comparing the voting behaviour of the electors of Wigan between 1628 and 1640, Dr Hirst concludes that 49% of them voted

---

[218] Often considerably less: in Bucks. 13% between 1705 and 1710, 6% between 1710 and 1713; in Hants. 20% between 1705 and 1710, 10% between 1710 and 1713; in Northants. 21% between 1702 and 1705; in Westmorland 20% between 1700 and 1701, 25% between 1700 and 1702. This average of around 16% does not depart significantly from the figures for Shrewsbury. See Speck, Gray and Hopkinson, 'Computer Analysis: A Further Report' Speck, *Tory and Whig*, 23–5.

[219] In Beds. 58% between 1705 and 1715, in Rutland 54% between 1710 and 1713. See Speck and Gray, 'Computer Analysis: A Further Report', 69, 71–2.

in exactly the same manner while 16% defected from their earlier allegiance.[220]

A very similar pattern may be observed with the post-1832 electorate with perhaps one slight exception. The post-1832 electorate appears to have been on occasion capable of slightly higher levels of consistent partisan voting than its predecessor. The figure at Ashford for 1852–7 is only 56%, but at Bath between 1841 and 1847 it rose to an impressive 76% and at Leeds between 1832 and 1835 it rose to 79%.[221] At Cambridge, however, the proportion topped even 80% on occasions between the first two Reform Acts.[222] There seems no doubt, too, that in Professor Phillips' constituencies, voters began to vote in a sustained partisan manner to a degree they had not hitherto achieved.[223] Clearly, the existence of a defined franchise, annually renewable, more frequently contested elections, the presence of registration societies and, ultimately, formally and nationally organized political parties enabled party agents to tighten the screws on the voter and to impose stricter discipline than prevailed before 1832. Levels of split voting were predictably low. At Leeds in the 1830s the extent of cross-party split voting was very small: between 2% and 6%; at Hereford in 1841, 5%.[224] The 'floating vote' at Sunderland between 1865 and 1866 was a fairly high 17%, but at Bath between 1841 and 1847 it was only 8%.[225] These are, of course, straws in the wind, but they do tend to blow in the same general comparative direction.

To what extent is partisan voting party voting? There are several reasons to think that on many occasions we ought to keep these two concepts distinct. The rapid turnover and replacement of electors must have inhibited the steady evolution of party consciousness. The intermittent frequency of formally contested elections made it difficult for electors to develop consistent party attachments. The operation of social influence and of money, especially in some of the smaller constituencies, might have fashioned partisan voting but of a non-political

---

[220] D. Hirst, *The Representative of the People? Voters and Voting in England Under the Early Stuarts* (London, 1975), 125.

[221] M. Drake, 'The Mid-Victorian Victor', in id., *Introduction to Historical Psephology*, Open University Course D301, units 9–12 (Milton Keynes, 1974), 91–3.

[222] J. C. Mitchell and J. Cornford; 'The Political Demography of Cambridge, 1832–1868', *Albion*, 9 (1977), 242–72.

[223] J. A. Phillips, 'The Many Faces of Reform: The Reform Bill and the Electorate', *Parl. Hist. Yrbk.* (1982) 131–2. More frequent contested elections would, of course, have aided the process.

[224] D. Fraser, 'The Fruits of Reform: Leeds Politics in the 1830s', *Northern Hist.* 7 (1972), 105; J. C. Mitchell, 'Electoral Strategy Under Open Voting, 1832–1880', *Public Choice*, 28 (1976), 24; see J. A. Phillips, 'The Many Faces of Reform', 123, for other figures below 10%.

[225] T. J. Nossiter, *Influence, Opinion and Political Idioms in Reformed England: Case Studies from the North-East* (Brighton, 1975), 126; Drake, 'The Mid-Victorian Voter', 93.

character. It is not always easy to be sure, and it is tempting to generalize about *all* electors at a particular date. There can be no questioning the influence of men and money at Callington, Cornwall, a tiny scot and lot borough with only 50 electors. A detailed canvass, unfortunately undated,[226] considers each of 55 voters in turn. As might be expected, many were attached to one or other of the opposing interests by material ligaments: 9 had jobs, 7 had a house, 5 would vote for the highest bidder, and 10 were attached by direct or indirect family connection. Of the remaining 24, however, no fewer than 14 were unknown, 6 were 'true blues', and, of the other 2, 1 was 'supposed Ministerial' and the other was 'a Ministerial Man'. Even in Callington, then, partisan voting could encompass a wide spectrum of motivations, ranging from sheer greed to sophisticated party awareness. It is surely not stretching fancy and optimism too far to believe that some voters, at least, were aware of the political inclinations of the candidates and, perhaps, the political records of the sitting Members. If it is the case that local élites largely dominated local parties, it is by no means unlikely that their politics, as well as their jobs, money, and influence might have been a vital contributory factor to the partisan distributions of votes. Even in venal Sudbury, political issues could contribute to partisan voting. John Pytches had won a seat with 493 votes in 1806. A year later he lost it with a derisory 174. His voters were no less partisan, but he had dramatically fewer of them because of his support for the Talents ministry.[227] In cases like this, partisan voting comes to resemble party voting. In those constituencies where national party influences in electoral politics have been noted—[228] in places like Nottingham, Norwich, Liverpool, and Leicester—there is every reason to believe that votes were determined by something other than purely local considerations. At Ipswich in 1806, only 6 out of 1,083 voters split their votes. Great excitement was generated as national political and religious issues came to obliterate local concerns. As the historian of Suffolk remarks, 'national party issues were clear-cut', and the result 'was a vote for the Whigs'.[229] The day of party, and, indeed, of party, and not merely partisan, voting was dawning.

---

[226] 1262M/Elections 15 Callington n.d. The date is almost certainly 1802. This would fit the number of voters. At the dates of the other contests in this period (1818, 1820 and 1826) the number of voters had declined to under 50.

[227] For the influence of issues at Sudbury, see Thorne, *House of Commons*, ii. 376.

[228] See above pp. 334–58.

[229] Childs, 'Politics and Elections in Suffolk Boroughs', M.Phil., 173–4.

# Conclusion

The unreformed electorate of Hanoverian England has been described from different standpoints in this book, and a variety of conclusions about it has been reached. Fundamental to them all is the assertion that the unreformed electorate is to be taken seriously. This does not, of course, mean that electoral politics before 1832 were unaffected by the oligarchical tendencies of the time. We have found too many indelible marks of these tendencies to persuade us to abandon the concept of electoral oligarchy. Nevertheless, there seems every reason to argue the countervailing case: that the unreformed electorate was no less powerfully influenced by movements and reactions *against* that oligarchy: the rise of extra-parliamentary opinion, the abiding and near-universal phenomena of electoral independence and anti-patronage revolts, the development of radical opinions within the electorate[1] and the elusive and partial, but none the less widespread, growth of the force and influence of parliamentary party. Both the oligarchical tendencies and the anti-oligarchical reactions which they bred need to be kept in mind, though no doubt in different relationships, depending on the nature of a particular constituency. It is their interaction which forms the running theme of electoral politics in this period.

We began with three initial propositions around which much of this book has been designed.[2] The *first* of these was the reality of the control of the electorate by local élites, a control, however, which was exercised at great cost, with great care, with great difficulty, with much effort, and sometimes for no very great return. Throughout, we have sustained and developed this argument with reference to the following realities of the unreformed electoral system. (*a*) The voters required constant care and intensive cultivation. (*b*) In most places, most people behaved as though voters were open to persuasion; they did not

---

[1] It is surprising just how little attention has been devoted to electoral radicalism. Rude's article 'The Middlesex Electors of 1768–69' appeared in the *English Historical Review* in 1960. (Vol. 75, pp. 601–17), but for many years it made little methodological impact upon historians. Even then, interest focused largely upon the (admittedly important) socio-economic status of radical electors.

[2] See above, pp. 7–11.

assume that votes were guaranteed as a consequence of social relationships. (*c*) The attitudes and the behaviour of the voters themselves do not permit us to conclude that they were mindless fodder for venal agents. (*d*) The (surely undeniable) importance of issues and principles in election campaigns strongly suggests that elections concerned much more than purely personal and purely mercenary considerations.[3] (*e*) The worry, indeed, the prickly and fastidious concern, among patrons over observing customary consultation procedures suggests that election campaigns were not simply one-way processes. Certainly, we found that the absence of an election contest usually indicated the satisfactory and acceptable operation of contemporary paternalist practices, not the reduction of the electorate to a state of impending serfdom. (*f*) We saw repeatedly that an integral aspect of electioneering was the involvement of non-electors in some capacity. The election campaign *as a communal event* requires an explanatory framework somewhat broader and more comprehensive than the usual preoccupation with electoral oligarchy normally permits.[4]

The *second* initial proposition follows logically from all this. The electoral system in most places was never dead, never closed. Where there were electors to vote, there were problems of control. With the benefit of hindsight, it is the *weakness* of the patronal classes in their attempts to control the electorate which is so striking. Admittedly, many advantages were stacked, in their favour, but electoral control was often incomplete, tentative, and temporary. The electors had political minds of their own. They did not unprotestingly imbibe the political culture of their superiors. They brought something of their own to electoral politics, and there can be no doubt that many of them saw electoral affairs from their own perspective and in their own way. Electoral independence may have been inchoate and historically unsatisfying, but it nevertheless stands as the psychological base line of electoral opinion upon which everything else had perforce to be erected.

Furthermore, and *thirdly*, the immediate environment of most electors was the local community. Indeed, at their simplest level,

---

[3] Namierite historians have seriously underestimated the role and importance of issues in election campaigns. Certainly, several of the constituency sections in the History of Parliament volumes (L. B. Namier and J. Brooks, *The House of Commons, 1784–1790*, ed. 3 vols. (London, 1964) ), seem to me woefully to neglect this aspect of things (see e.g. Coventry, Leicester, Liverpool). See, too, the neglect of political issues in I. R. Christie, *The End of North's Ministry* (London, 1958), esp. in the open boroughs (pp. 79–88).

[4] Once again, the communal aspects of electioneering have been ignored by most of the standard authorities, a surprising omission in view of the readily available evidence. Interestingly, this aspect was even missed by N. Gash in his influential *Politics in the Age of Peel* (London, 1953).

elections focused attention upon the origin and exercise of power and authority over the community. It is at this point that the socio-economic status of the electorate acquires enormous significance. The electorate in many cases represented local property and local wealth. The attitudes of the electorate towards the dominant local family or families, towards the corporation, the cathedral, or the most powerful local interests, were of real significance whether or not initial canvassing culminated in a contested election. This communal aspect of electioneering was reinforced in 1832. From this point of view, the function of the 1832 Reform Act was to remove the representation from bogus communities but to redefine community loyalties in the remaining constituencies and to endow new and emerging communities with rights of representation.[5] In this lies much of the continuity between electoral politics before and after the 1832 Reform Act.

It follows, then, and it has been implicit as well as explicit throughout this book, that the results of elections were determined not so much by the electors as by the patron or patrons involving themselves in a complex and long-term dialogue with the community, its social and economic requirements, and its leaders and their personal and familial interests. Indeed, the electioneering processes of the campaign could be more significant and more important than the simple result of a contested election. Elections, from this standpoint, were not simply a vital element in the processes of what passed for representative government in the eighteenth and early nineteenth centuries. They may almost be regarded as a form of community action, providing a highly participatory type of social and political framework within which individuals and groups were able to assert their own interests and their own views of the needs of the community. Elections put on public display, and in a very real sense held to public account, the governing élite, their clients, dependants, and supporters. Elections enabled critical voices to be raised, vexed issues to be debated, and, in the last analysis, provided a peaceful means of accommodating difficulties. Elections, then, had a local community reference. Consequently, they had much to do with maintaining and reasserting certain normative criteria by which publicly to weigh the exercise of power and authority over the community, the state of that community, and the provision of adequate resources for it.[6] Most electors appear to have been

---

[5] This aspect of the 1832 Act deserves careful scrutiny. D. C. Moore does discuss the concept of community in the context of the 1867 Reform Act (see *The Politics of Deference* (Hassocks, 1976), 394–8). His insistence of the fundamental importance of the idea of community in mid-19th cent. England does not, however, lead him to explore it in the context of the 1832 Act.

[6] It is my impression that this constitutes the staple diet for election speeches and propaganda. Historians have tended to neglect these sources. Namierite historians were fond

agreed upon the manifest necessity for the upper classes to perform their paternalist duties honestly and decently. In this sense, elections asserted a normative framework within which the landed interest survived and ruled because they expressed certain community values to which all (or most) subscribed. Consequently, elections stabilized the authority of the landed interest and went far towards legitimizing their rule. They did so in a highly participatory manner, however outdated the formal structure of electoral politics and however unrepresentative its personnel were becoming.

There is much to suggest that the electoral system made no little contribution to the political stability of the Hanoverian regime. Unfortunately, historical discussions of political stability have proceeded upon a distressingly narrow and confined basis. Professor Plumb, who pioneered the concept, was content to describe it as 'the acceptance by society of its political institutions, and of those classes of men or officials who control them'.[7] That definition had been available for 14 years before it was noticed that it did not include the word 'religion', a striking omission.[8] In any case, the word 'institutions' is misleadingly narrow and 'society' impossibly vague. At the electoral level, at least, it was the involvement of large numbers of men, electors and non-electors alike, in electoral processes which, as we saw in Chapters 3 and 5, did something to broaden the basis of a dangerously oligarchical regime. It was the recurrence of elections which promoted the universal acceptance of common values towards the community and its leaders, its welfare, and its requirements, as we saw in Chapter 2. It was the achievemet of elections peacefully to secure the (or some) popular and public endorsement of local élites. In this way, an undoubtedly oligarchical electoral regime was rendered less narrow and perhaps less brittle and less unpopular than may otherwise have been the case. What other aspect of the political process could claim as much? It was, however, not merely the function of elections to procure maximum community advantage and thus the considerable enhancement of the material conditions of the inhabitants. Elections offered a stage, and election campaigns a script, for the expression of dissidence and hostility towards local representatives of

---

of recounting patronage structures, to the virtual neglect of other aspects of elections. Some of their successors have been selective in their interests. The easily accessible election speeches and handbills need to be more thoroughly mined than they have hitherto if they are to yield the substance of electoral conflict.

[7] J. H. Plumb, *The Growth of Political Stability in England, 1675–1725* (London, 1967), p. xvi.

[8] In this case, by Professor Holmes. See G. S. Holmes, 'The Achievement of Political Stability: The Social Context of Politics from the 1680s to the Age of Walpole' in J. A. Cannon (ed.), *Colloquies on Hanoverian England The Whig Ascendancy* (London, 1981), p. 180.

the Hanoverian regime and its measures. The expression, but yet the containment, of dissidence was an important element in the political stability of the Hanoverian regime. Patterns of electoral protest appear, on examination, to be just as traditional as, for example, patterns of popular rioting. They were mediated just as much by 'custom, inherited expectations and moral evaluation'.[9] As might be expected, such electoral protest was shot through with restraint, with moderation, with the expectation of practical remedy, and with the unspoken assumption that existing usages would normally achieve the desired goal. Electoral opposition is a sure sign of the health of the Hanoverian electoral system, but this was an electoral opposition which was little inclined to run to extremes or to agitate ambitious schemes of reform. Political stability, then, was achieved less through the imposition of an oligarchical electoral system and its acceptance by 'society' than by the established forms of action within that system and the high degree of public participation which they elicited. Electoral politics were permeated with ideals of restraint and discipline, of service and civic pride, and of conciliation and collaboration with the regime. The functions of such ideals, and the practices which were built upon them, should not be underestimated in an age of unremitting warfare and at a period of rapid demographic and urban as well as agricultural change.

This is entirely unsurprising. After all, very many forms of public and popular expression were inhibited by their powerful commitment to customary procedures. Electoral politics were boisterous and vibrant but they were, at the same time, profoundly defensive in character. Complaint against particular individuals or upon specific issues might be vigorous but it did not carry with it implications of general hostility towards the regime. Electoral politics bears little trace either of republicanism or of fundamental disaffection. On the contrary, elections might blow up a storm of local strong feeling but animosities and rivalries flowed into customary channels for the resolution of communal conflicts, resolutions which were achieved peacefully and accepted by both sides. This is, after all, what a contested election amounted to. Indeed, contested elections, or the threat of them, promoted just those activities and practices whose absence might have seriously endangered the popularity and possibly even the stability of the Hanoverian regime. They encouraged patrons and landlords to reside locally, to concern themselves in the business of the county or town, to attend actively to community interests, to mingle with local people. Elections permitted and encouraged local expressions

[9] R. W. Malcolmson, *Life and Labour in England, 1700–1780* (London, 1981), 121.

of hostility towards nepotism and corruption, partiality, and cruelty. Elections enabled local Dissenting groups to involve themselves in politics at the local level at a time when it was difficult to do so with any regularity at the national level. Elections facilitated the incorporation into political life of the middling orders, rapidly coming to political consciousness. Taken together, these are weighty contributions to the achievement of continued political stability. Indeed, 'the period of the greatest political stability ever known in England' was not the consequence of the force and power of oligarchy,[10] but, as a study of electoral politics suggests, the interaction between the orthodox forces of oligarchy and the countervailing reaction which it created within a sophisticated political society and within a highly participatory electoral system. A stable electoral order bred not apathy but outrage, concern, and criticism. A self-perpetuating cycle of electoral control may, in the last analysis, be perceived, but it was the never-ending stream of political controversy which it bred and the criticism and dissidence which it provoked which did most to render the electoral system as acceptable as it was for as long as it was.

As we saw in Chapter 4, the electorate was a numerically impressive and, for most of this period, steadily increasing entity. It comprised a vast, if somewhat nebulous, electoral pool of fairly wealthy, propertied individuals. Its members participated with commendable frequency in elections whenever the possibilities of such participation were open to them. Many of the constituencies were strongly politicized by the later eighteenth century; even more important, they were *party* politicized. This explains the remarkable extent of the phenomenon of partisan voting. Voting was not a casual and random affair. It was an immensely serious and premeditated activity, influenced and orchestrated from a number of sources. Nevertheless, there can be absolutely no mistaking the partisan nature of electoral behaviour and the partisan inclinations of non-electors, too. There is more to this than a projection of natural competitive instincts. The indelible imprint of the *two-party* conflicts of the late seventeenth and early eighteenth centuries had been quite remarkable. Spokesmen for local groups and interests appealed to party traditions and party sentiment in their endeavours to augment their support. By the end of the eighteenth century they were being drawn into a renewal of partisan activity upon the Westminster stage, the conflict between the governments of North and Pitt, on the one hand, and the oppositions of Rockingham and Fox, on the other. The identification of the patronal classes with the fortunes of government and opposition inevitably filtered down to their agents, canvassers, and committee men, and, thereafter, to the electors.

[10] R. Porter, *English Society in the Eighteenth Century* (London, 1982), 127.

It was the traditional local issues concerned with oligarchy and independence which constituted the stuff of electoral politics until the great political and constitutional issues of the parliamentary classes began to supplement them in the later eighteenth century. It is worth underlining the abiding *political* interests of the electorate. I have encountered little evidence of *serious* economic and social divisions within the electorate. Few traces of socio-economic differences emerge from the study and analysis of occupational groups within the electorate. Even in the rapidly developing large freeman boroughs, few such social and economic differences have been located.[11] There are, of course, exceptions, and further analysis of constituencies like Westminster, Coventry, and Preston may yield evidence of such divisions, but it is remarkable how traditional the politics of towns like Liverpool and Newcastle-upon-Tyne continued to be until a very late date. Professor Phillips asserts that 'the political, religious, and social cleavages that were to become so obvious in later nineteenth-century England were already evident among portions of the populace by the end of the eighteenth century'.[12] This seems to me a slightly rash pronouncement. Some elements of political ancestry may then be discerned, and not a few religious elements, but it is hard to see more than a few distant anticipations of the origins of the social cleavages of the Victorian era within the unreformed electoral system, at least. It may be that these were consequent upon, rather than a causal element in, the emergence of the political and religious fissures which were so characteristic of Victorian society.

The electoral system exhibited flaws and inconsistencies which enabled radical polemicists to wax strong and lyrical. Nevertheless, the 'movement' for securing parliamentary reform had had a peculiarly chequered history, enjoying only infrequent and intermittent periods of genuine popular support and in the 1820s returned to its customary state of tentative apathy. It was not the 'faults' of the electoral system which were responsible for reform in 1831–2 but an unprecedented conjunction of political circumstances.

There may be some significance in the fact that the unreformed electoral system lasted as long as it did, its vitality and adaptability enabling it to retain the confidence of the political nation until the

[11] I very much endorse J. C. D. Clark's surmise: 'It may be that the largest cities, at the very end of the century, especially London, begin to witness slight affects of wealth in influencing voter preference. But it is the tardiness and weakness of any such influence, and the few constituencies in which it was evident, which is remarkable' (J. C. D. Clark, *English Society 1688–1832* (Cambridge, 1985), 370 n. 66).

[12] J. A. Phillips, *Electoral Behavior in Unreformed England, 1761–1802* (Princeton, 1982), 310.

end of the 1820s. When the end came, it came quickly, after the trauma of Catholic emancipation, but it came not a little fortuitously. It did not take long for the moral lesson of the Catholic emancipation crisis to be learned: that only an unrepresentative House could have passed the Emancipation Bill. Nevertheless, as I have remarked,[13] it took a dramatic and unrepeatable conjunction of circumstances actually to transform the electoral system: the passage of Roman Catholic emancipation, the fragmentation of the Tories, the death of George IV and the accession of William IV, the French Revolution of July 1830, the Swing Riots, the activities of the political unions, and, not least, the courage and tactical acumen of the Whig government of Lord Grey. If there is a central element in all this, it must surely be the very widespread recognition among the upper classes of British society that the old electoral system would have to be abandoned. They learned the lesson of Catholic emancipation, and they learned from the French Revolution of 1830 that concession could maintain stability and order, not endanger it. As the Wellingtonian Tories tottered unsteadily to political destruction in the closing months of 1830, a sufficiently large majority of the Hanoverian governing class rallied behind the reforming administration of Charles Grey. Even the ultra-Tories fell into line, terrified by the rioting in the rural districts of the south of England. No fewer than 22 county seats changed hands in 1831, but only 2 fell to the Tories.[14]

In short, the Reform Act of 1832 passed because an unprecedented political crisis could not be resolved without a change in the electoral system. In 1784 a constitutional crisis had been resolved and a political *impasse* broken by an appeal to the electorate made by William Pitt the Younger on behalf of George III. In 1831-2 the fragmentation of the Tories, the removal of the impassable obstacles to parliamentary reform, and the temporary alliance of a Whig government with a highly mobilized public opinion ensured the peaceful achievement of a parliamentary reform which in the mid-1820s had looked almost as unlikely as it had done at any time since the 1790s. In this very real sense, the unreformed electoral system was the sacrificial lamb of 1831-2. Those who fought for it—the Tories, the Anglican Church, and the House of Lords—fought hard for it, but in the last analysis they were not prepared to defy the popular will which the general election of 1831 had aroused.[15] Nevertheless, and as all observers

---

[13] See above pp. 309-14.

[14] J. Odurkene, 'The British General Elections of 1830 and 1831', B.Litt. (Oxford, 1976), 38.

[15] Ibid. 107-11. What has been much underestimated is the enormous popularity of William IV in 1831 and the calculated use of his name to arouse enthusiasm for the Bill. It is doubtful if a Reform Bill could have passed against the stated wishes of the monarch.

agree, the old system was sufficiently like the new to prove, in the end, acceptable to enough elements to make it viable.

After all, the Reform Bill was the brainchild of men who not only knew the unreformed electoral system but who owed their political careers in some measure to its existence. As several commentators have emphasized, their painfully evolved objectives in 1831–2 were to make the new electoral system as much like the old one as possible in many fundamental respects. The routines and the norms of election campaigns were not significantly altered by the Reform Act. Almost all elements of constituency electioneering continued unchanged after 1832. Charles Seymour, indeed, trembled on the brink of indecision before affirming that corruption after 1832 probably worsened.[16] As Palmerston said in 1839: 'I speak it with shame and sorrow, but I verily believe that the extent to which bribery and corruption was carried at the last election, has exceeded anything that has ever been stated within these walls.'[17] It is very difficult to know whether Palmerston was empirically correct in reaching such a judgement. Nevertheless, there can be little doubt that most contemporaries *believed* that to be the case.[18] The men, the money, and the institutions which had contrived to control the unreformed electoral system and to organize its electorate were the same as those which contrived to control and organize its successor. The new party clubs after 1832 were very like the old. The West Kent Conservative Association was established in July 1833 to register voters, to canvass support, to distribute money, and to run the campaign. Apart from registration there was little that was novel here, and even registration was little more than a streamlined means of locating voters.[19]

One electoral system disappeared and gave way, then, to one remarkably like itself. The men, the institutions, the values, and the practices are remarkably similar each side of 1832. It is surely misleading for historians to reduce this similarity to specific matters. Halevy and other writers have pointed to the similarity in the kind of men who sat in Parliament before and after the Reform Act.[20] Professor Cannon, furthermore, is only one in a long line of scholars to note that 'bribery and corruption' continued.[21] No doubt all these

[16] C. Seymour, *Electoral Reform in England and Wales*, (New Haven, 1915), 171.

[17] *Hansard*, xcviii. 1437.

[18] Seymour, *Electoral Reform*, ch. 8.

[19] J. Andrews, 'Political Issues in the County of Kent 1820–1846', M.Phil (London, 1967), 116–22.

[20] See e.g. E. Halevy, *A History of the English People in the Nineteenth Century: iii, The Triumph of Reform* (London, 1924), 62–4.

[21] J. A. Cannon, *Parliamentary Reform 1640–1832* (Cambridge, 1972), 255. See also Gash, *Politics in the Age of Peel*, pp. x–xi.

things are true in their way. What most needs recognition, however, is the strength of the electoral continuities. This is not the same as asserting that everything continued unaffected, for that was not the case.[22] Nor would it be true to say that there were not innovations after 1832. What it does mean is that a characteristic electoral culture, with its own men and organizations, its own institutions and conventions, its own rules and regularities, embracing hundreds of thousands of individuals in hundreds of communities up and down the land, endured down to 1832 until, for political reasons, the forms of that culture, the legalities, and the statutory definitions were remodelled. The electoral forms duly changed through statutory enactment but the substance of electoral life, already participatory, partisan, and popular, continued. Upon that basis was to be erected the representative democracy of the Victorian era.

---

[22] I am not concerned here to speculate on the enormity of the changes ushered in by the Reform Act of 1832 nor to ruminate upon the extent of the collapse of the old regime in England between 1828 and 1832. 'The modern historian of Victorian and twentieth century England sees in 1832 a classic crisis but a viable social order. The eighteenth century historian by contrast sees in the events of 1828–32 a dissolution of the social order with which he is familiar' (J. C. D. Clark, *English Society*, 410). I would only comment that at the electoral level, at least, the continuities are far more apparent than the upheavals.

# APPENDIX 1

## Classification of Occupations Used in this Study

The classification of occupations used in this study are detailed below. A comparison between this classification and that used in earlier studies is given in Appendix 2.

### 1  GENTLEMEN AND PROFESSIONALS

Accountant
Agent
Alderman
Apothecary
Appraiser
Architect
Army officer
Artist
Assessor
Assistant
Attorney
Auctioneer
Banker
Baronet
Barracks master
Barrister
Beadle
Bird stuffer
Book-keeper
Broker
Butler
Captain
Charioteer
Civil engineer
Clergyman
Clerk
Clerk of works
Coach agent
Coach master/proprietor
Coal agent
Collector
Common councillor
Coroner
Councillor

Customs officer
Dentist
Dispenser
Doctor
Drawing master
Editor
Esquire
Estate agent
Exciseman
Fitter's clerk
Gaol governor
Gentleman
Governor of poor house guards
Harbour master
House agent
Keeper of treasury papers
Land agent
Law student
Lawyer
Librarian
Magistrate's clerk
Master mariner
Master of the band
Medical student
Merchant's clerk
Militia sergeant/officer
Minister
Musician
Music teacher/master
Navy officer
Notary Public
Optician

Organist
Owner
Parish clerk
Pensioner
Physician
Pilot
Post master
Professor
Purser
Recorder
RIHM
Schoolmaster
Scrivener
Sculptor
Sergeant
Sergeant-at-law
Sergeant-major
Ship agent
Solicitor
Steward
Stock broker
Student
Surgeon
Surveyor
Teacher
Tide surveyor/waiter
Town clerk
Town porter
Town sergeant
Translator
Veterinary surgeon
Valuer
Verger
Viewer
Writer

## 2 MERCHANTS AND MANUFACTURERS

Auctioneer
Bacon factor
Bacon jobber
Barge owner
Bleacher
Brassfounder
Brewer
Broker
Builder
Carpet manufacturer
Cashier
China dealer
China merchant
Cinder manufacturer
Clock dial
  manufacturer
Cloth dealer
Clothier
Coach contracter
Coach owner
Coach
  manufacturer/
  master
Coach proprietor
Coal fitter
Coal owner
Commission
  merchant/agent
Copper manufacturer
Corn factor
Corn merchant
Cork
  manufacturer
Distiller
Dyer

Earthenware
  manufacturer
Fell monger
Flint manufacturer
Floor cloth
  manufacturer
Flour dealer
Flour merchant
Furniture broker
Glass
  manufacturer/man
Hardware
  manufacturer
Hardware merchant
Hat manufacturer
Hop merchant
Horse dealer
'India House'
Insurance broker
Iron founder
Iron manufacturer
Iron merchant
Lead manufacturer
Maltmill maker/cutter
Maltman
Maltster
Manufacturer
Marine stores dealer
Meal dealer/man
Mercer
Merchant
Merchant Tailor
Miller
Mill owner
Owner

Oyster merchant
Paper-hanging
  manufacturer
Paper Manufacturer
Paper merchant
Plat Dealer
Porter merchant
Provision merchant
Raff merchant
Rag merchant
Renter of baths
Sail cloth
  manufacturer
Ship broker
Ship owner
Silver dealer
Soap manufacturer
Spade manufacturer
Spirit merchant
Stocking manufacturer
Straw hat
  manufacturer
Tea dealer/man
Timber merchant
Toy dealer
Umbrella
  manufacturer
Warehouseman
Watch manufacturer
Wharfinger
Whip manufacturer
Wholesale draper
Wine merchant
Wool Stapler
Worster manufacturer

## 3 RETAILERS

Apothecary
Baker
Barber
Basket seller
Beer shopkeeper

Billiard room keeper
Bookseller
Bootmaker
Butcher
Chandler

Cheesemonger
Chemist
Clubhouse keeper
Coffee house keeper
Confectioner

Dairyman
Draper
Druggist
Eating house
  keeper
Fishmonger
Flesher
Florist
Fruiterer
Greengrocer
Grocer
Haberdasher
Hairdresser
Hardwareman
Horse keeper
Horse manager
Horse master
Horse owner
Hotel keeper
Huckster
Innkeeper
Ironmonger

Jeweller
Laceman
Leather
  seller
Linen draper
Livery stable
  keeper
Meal seller
Milliner
Mugman
Music seller
Newsman
Oilman
Orange dealer
Oyster man
Pawnbroker
Perfumerer
Peruke seller
Pieman
Poulterer
Publican
Quarry keeper

Salesman
Seedsman
Shopkeeper
Shopman
Silversmith
Slopseller
Smockseller
Snuffman
Stable keeper
Stationer
Staymaker
Storemaker
Tailor
Tallow chandler
Tavern keeper
Tobacconist
Toyman
Tripeman
Upholder
Victualler
Woolen
  draper

## 4 CRAFTSMEN

Accoutrement maker
Anchor smith
Artificer
Basket maker
Beamer
Bedstead maker
Blacking maker
Blacksmith
Bleacher
Block, mast and pump
  maker
Boat builder
Book binder
Bootmaker
Bottle maker
Box maker
Brass founder
Brazier
Breeches maker
Bricklayer

Brickmaker
Brushmaker
Builder
Cabinet maker
Cage maker
Calenderer
Calico printer/glazier
Cap maker
Card maker
Cord stripper
Carpenter
Carpet weaver
Canvass dresser
Cartwright
Carver
Chain cable maker
Chain maker
Checker
China rivetter
Chimney sweep

Clicker
Coach maker
Coach printer
Coach smith
Coach spring maker
Clock maker
Clogger
Comber
Coffee roaster
Collar maker
Cook
Cooper
Copper smith
Cordwainer
Cork cutter
Cotton spinner
Crate maker
Currier
Cutler
Dyer

Edge-tool grinder
Engine builder
Engineer
Engine keeper/
  weaver
Engineman
Enginewright
Engraver
Farrier
Fellmonger
Felt maker
Figure maker
File cutter
File smith
Fishing tackle maker
Fishhook maker
Flagger
Flax dresser
Flower maker
Forgeman
Founder
Fringe manu-
  facturer
Furrier
Gaitermaker
Gilder
Glass cutter
Glass engraver
Glass maker/
  stainer/cutter
Glazier
Glover
Goldsmith
Grainer
Grinder
Gunmaker/
  smith
Harness maker
Hat maker
Hatter
Heckle maker
Heckler
Heel maker
Herring curer
Hook maker
Horse breaker
Hosier

Instrument maker
Iron founder
Ivory turner
Japanner
Joiner
Last maker
Leather cutter
Leather dresser
Limner
Linen weaver
Locksmith
'Makers' in general
Machine maker
Machinist
Malster
Maltmill cutter/maker
Mangler
Marble mason
Marine painter
Mason
Mathematical
  instrument maker
Mechanic
Meter
Millwright
Mineral grinder
Mode weaver
Moulder
Moulderer
Mould maker
Nailer
Needle maker
Net maker
Oil crusher
Oil of Vitriol maker
Organ builder
Painter
Paper hanger
Paper maker
Paper stainer
Pastry cook
Pattern maker
Pattern drawer
Pavier
Perfumer
Peruke maker
Pewterer

Pin maker
Pipe maker
Plasterer
Playing card
  maker
Plumber
Potter
Printer
Print cutter
Pump maker
Quill dresser
Rectifier
Ribbon weaver
Roper
Rope maker
Sack maker
Sadler
Sailmaker
Scale maker
Seed crusher
Shipbuilder
Ship carpenter
Shipwright
Shuttle maker
Silk throwster
Shoemaker
Skinner
Slater
Smelter
Smiths
Spinner
Springmaker
Staymaker
Stenciller
Stocking maker
Stone mason
Sugar baker
Sugar refiner
Tanner
Tent maker
Threadmaker/dresser-
  /finisher
Tile maker
Tinman
Tinner
Tinplate
  worker

Tool maker
Trimmer
Trunk maker
Turner
Twine spinner
Umbrella maker
Upholsterer
Vicemaker
Waller

Warper
Watch glass
    cutter
Watch glass-
    maker
Watchmaker
Weaver
Wheeler
Wheelwright

Whip maker
White cooper
Whitesmith
Whiting
    maker
Wine cooper
Working
    jeweller
Yarnmaker

## 5 LABOURERS

Bailiff
Bargeman
Battler
Bay dresser
Bay maker
Beadle
Bellman
Boatman
Brick burner
Car man
Card maker
Carrier
Carter
Cartman
Caulker
Cellar man
Chairman
Chaise driver
Chimney sweep
Cleaner
Clothworker
Coach driver
Coachman
Coal heaver/
    meter/whipper
Collier
Comedian
Common
    carrier
Constable
Corporal
Drayman
Dredger
Drover

Drummer
Ferryman
Fiddler
Fireman
Fisherman
Flatman
Flour dresser
Flyman
Foundryman
Fullman
Gardener
Gatekeeper
Gig driver
Girth web maker
Groom
Guard/guard man
Hallier
Haulier
Hawker
Hemp dresser
Horse patrol
Hospital man
Hostler
Huntsman
Jobber
Journeyman
Keelman
Keeper of prison
Labourer
Landwaiter
Lath-cleaver/
    maker/river
Laundryman
Letter carrier/founder

Lighterman
Lighthouse keeper
Lime burner
Mail guard
Mariner
Marshall
Mayor's sergeant
Militia man/private
Miner
Ostler
Outrider
Overseer
Oyster dredger/meeter
Packer
Park keeper
Pasteboard maker
Pitman
Police officer
Porter
Postman
Private
Proctor
Pump sinker
Quarryman
Rougher
Sailor
Salesman
Sawyer
Seaman
Sergeant at mace
Servant
Sexton
Shearman
Sheriff's officer

Sieve maker
Silk winder
Singing man
Soldier
Starch maker
Steam engine feeder
Stone cutter
Swayer
Sword bearer

Tapster
Tavern waiter
Tollman
Town crier
Traveller
Turnkey
Wagoner
Waiter
Warehouseman

Watchman
Watch superintendent
Waterman
Well digger
Wherryman
Wire worker
Wool comber/carder/
    cardmaker/sorter
Wool sorter

## 6 AGRICULTURE

Castrator
Cattle dealer
Countryman
Cow keeper
    leach
Decoyman
Farmer
Field brieve
Forrester

Gamekeeper
Grazier
Husbandman
Land steward/
    holder
Miller
Mole catcher
Nurseryman
Pig jobber

Poacher
Poulterer
Seedman
Shepherd
Smallholder
Sow gelder
Woodman
Wood warden
Yeoman

# APPENDIX 2

## Analysis of Electorate by Occupational Category

COMPARISON OF OCCUPATIONAL CLASSIFICATION

| Category | Nossiter | Phillips | Stoker | O'Gorman |
|---|---|---|---|---|
| 1. | Gentlemen and professionals | Gentleman and professionals | Gentlemen and professionals | Gentlemen and professionals |
| 2. | Manufacturers and merchants | Merchants and entrepreneurs | Merchants and manufacturers | Merchants and manufacturers |
| 3. | Retail trade | Retailers | Retailers | Retailers |
| 4. | Craft trade | Craftsmen, artisans, skilled workmen | Craftsmen | Skilled craftsmen |
| 5. | Other | Labourers | Unskilled | Semi/unskilled labourers |
| 6. | Farming | Agriculturalists | Agriculture | Agriculturists |
| 7. | Drink | — | — | — |

Source: Nossiter, *Influence, Opinion and Political Idioms*, 211–12; J. A. Phillips, *Electoral Behavior*, 321–2; Stoker, 'Elections and Voting Behaviour', 391–401.

PHILLIPS'S ANALYSIS OF ELECTORATES AT VARIOUS LOCATIONS

| Category | | Norwich | Maidstone | Northampton | Lewes | All |
|---|---|---|---|---|---|---|
| 1. | Gentlemen/ professionals | 11.6 | 9.3 | 6.3 | 15.7 | 10.7 |
| 2. | Merchants/ entrepreneurs | 5.1 | 4.0 | 4.6 | 3.6 | 4.3 |
| 3. | Retailers | 16.3 | 17.9 | 19.5 | 18.6 | 18.1 |
| 4. | Craftsmen, skilled workmen | 60.6 | 52.9 | 54.9 | 44.1 | 53.1 |
| 5. | Labourers | 1.2 | 8.9 | 12.2 | 11.4 | 8.4 |
| 6. | Agriculturalists | 3.3 | 2.9 | 0.7 | 2.6 | 2.3 |
| 7. | Other | 1.9 | 4.1 | 1.8 | 4.0 | 3.1 |

Source: J. A. Phillips, *Electoral Behavior*, 195–7.

STOKER'S ANALYSIS OF ELECTORATES AT VARIOUS LOCATIONS

| Category | | Berwick (1803) | Morpeth (1802) | Newcastle (1832)[a] | Durham (1832)[a] | Carlisle (1786) | All |
|---|---|---|---|---|---|---|---|
| 1. | Gentlemen/ professionals | 11 | 6 | 11 | 7 | 13 | 10 |
| 2. | Merchants/ manufacturers | 3 | 5 | 4 | 1 | 5 | 4 |
| 3. | Retailers | 26 | 31 | 19 | 30 | 31 | 23 |
| 4. | Craftsmen | 41 | 50 | 56 | 49 | 31 | 50 |
| 5. | Unskilled | 14 | 2 | 8 | 9 | 3 | 8 |
| 6. | Agriculture | 5 | 7 | 1 | 3 | 18 | 4 |

*Source*: Stoker, 'Elections and Voting Behavior', *passim*.

[a] Freemen only.

# BIBLIOGRAPHY

PRIMARY SOURCES

*Manuscript Sources*

*Bedfordshire Record Office*
Bedford MSS
Huw White MSS
Lucas MSS
Lyall MSS
Wade MSS
Wells MSS
Whitbread MSS
*Berkshire Record Office*
Abingdon Borough MSS
Hartley Russell MSS
Loveden MSS
Neville MSS
Pleydell Bouverie MSS
Stevens MSS
*University of Birmingham Library*
Notebook of a Citizen of Worcester
*Bodleian Library, Oxford*
Clarendon MSS
Dashwood MSS
Holkham Letter Books
Hughes Hughes MSS
Monk Bretton MSS
Russell of Swallowfield MSS
*Bristol Archives Office*
Bathurst MSS
Hare MSS
Steadfast Society Minutes
*British Library*
Add. MSS
32914 Newcastle Papers
32918-9 Newcastle Papers
32058 Newcastle Papers
33110 Newcastle Papers
35382 Hardwicke Papers

37908 Windham Papers
50240–52 Hodgson Papers
40181 Liverpool Papers
61862 North (Sheffield Park) Papers
*Buckinghamshire Archaeological Society*
Aylesbury MSS
Wendover MSS
*Buckingham Record Office*
Buckingham MSS
Cavendish MSS
Drake MSS
Fremantle MSS
Hartwell MSS
Lee MSS
Verney MSS
*Cambridgeshire Record Office*
Cotton MSS
Evans MSS
Hinchingbrooke MSS
*Cardiff Central Library*
Bute MSS
Jones MSS
Thomas MSS
*Carmarthenshire Record Office*
Cawdor MSS
Dynevor MSS
Plas Llandstephen MSS
*Cheshire Record Office*
Crewe MSS
Egerton MSS
*Chester Record Office*
Grosvenor MSS
*Clwyd County Record Office*
Hanmer MSS
Keene and Kelly
Mostyn MSS
Rhual MSS
*Cornwall Record Office*
Graham MSS
Hawkins MSS
Lostwithiel Election Papers
Luly MSS
Pendarves MSS
Robartes MSS
Whitford MSS
*Coventry Record Office*
Sheffield MSS

*Cumbria Record Office*
Curwen MSS
Hothfield MSS
Howard MSS
Lonsdale MSS
Senhouse MSS
*Derby Borough Library*
Collection of Squibs and Broadsides
*Devon Record Office*
Acland MSS
Bedford MSS
Courtenay MSS
Ebrington MSS
Harrowby-Tiverton MSS
Palk MSS
Quicke MSS
Simcoe MSS
*Dorset Record Office*
Anglesey Estate Papers
Bankes MSS (Fooks Papers)
Calcraft MSS
Ilchester MSS
Rutter MSS
*Durham County Record Office*
Chaytor MSS
Clavering MSS
Londonderry MSS
*Essex Record Office*
Braybrooke MSS
Burgoyne MSS
Cunningham MSS
Lennard MSS
Strutt MSS
*Glamorgan Record Office*
Bute MSS
Kemeys-Tynte MSS
Smyth MSS
Strutt MSS
*Flintshire Record Office*
Keene and Kelly MSS
*Gloucestershire Public Library*
Painswick House Collection
*Gloucestershire Record Office*
Codrington MSS
Estcourt MSS
Guise MSS
Parsons MSS

*Grimsby Central Library*
Charles Tennyson MSS
Skelton MSS
*Guildford Muniment Room*
Loseley MSS
*Gwynedd Record Office*
Caernark MSS
Paget MSS
Poole MSS
Williams MSS
*Hampshire Record Office*
Bolton MSS
Bonham-Carter MSS
Palmerston MSS
Tierney MSS
*Herefordshire Record Office*
Foley MSS
Norfolk MSS
Pilley MSS
*Hertfordshire Record Office*
Baker MSS
Calvert MSS
Grimston MSS
Halsey MSS
Radcliffe MSS
*Hull University Library*
Sykes MSS
*Humberside Record Office*
Bower MSS
Grimston MSS
*Huntingdonshire Record Office*
Hinchingbrooke MSS
Manchester MSS
Sandwich MSS
*Huntington Library, San Marino, California*
Stowe MSS
*Kent Record Office*
Chapman MSS
Delaune MSS
Guildford MSS
Harris MSS
Knatchbull MSS
Sackville MSS
Sandwich Borough MSS
Tufton MSS
*Lancashire Record Office*
Blundell MSS

Cawthorne MSS
Lancashire Evening Post MSS
Stanley MSS
*Leeds Central Library*
Battie-Wrightson MSS
Canning MSS
Harewood MSS
*Leicester City Museum*
Berridge MSS
Braye MSS
*Leicestershire Record Office*
Halford MSS
Paget MSS
Tompkins MSS
*Lincolnshire Record Office*
Ancaster MSS
Brownlow MSS
Cragg MSS
Manson MSS
Tennyson D'Eyncourt MSS
*Liverpool Public Library*
Binns MSS
Roscoe MSS
Williamson Collection
*London University, University College Library*
Brougham MSS
*John Rylands University of Manchester*
Legh of Lyme MSS
*Monmouth County Record Office*
Evans and Evill MSS
Stanbury MSS
*National Library of Wales*
Traherne Scrapbook
Wynnstay MSS
*Newcastle-upon-Tyne University*
Bell-White Collection
Liddell MSS
*Norfolk Record Office*
Folkes MSS
Hobart MSS
Rumbold MSS
Walsingham MSS
*Northampton Public Library*
Collection of Political Handbills
*Northamptonshire Record Office*
Cartwright MSS
Fitzwilliam MSS

Gunning MSS
Langham MSS
*Northumberland Record Office*
Delavall MSS
Newcastle Society of Antiquaries MSS
Ridley MSS
*Nottingham City Library*
Smith MSS
*Nottinghamshire Record Office*
Dowson MSS
Folambe MSS
Copies of Speeches on Repeal of the Triennial Act (D/DA/62/3)
Savile MSS
Smith Godfrey MSS
Tallents MSS
*Nottingham University Library*
Galway MSS
Newcastle (Clumber) MSS
Portland MSS
Savile MSS
*Oxfordshire Record Office*
Thane MSS
*Pembrokeshire Record Office*
Court MSS
*Public Record Office (Northern Ireland)*
Anglesey Papers
Caledon MSS
*Reading University Library*
Broadsides on Berkshire County Elections
*Scarborough Public Library*
Election Posters, Addresses, etc.
*Sheffield Public Library*
Bagshawe MSS
Fitzwilliam MSS
Spencer Stanhope MSS
Wentworth Woodhouse MSS
Wharncliffe MSS
*Shropshire Record Office*
Attingham MSS
Eyton Hall MSS
Forester MSS
Hill MSS
*Somerset Record Office*
Drake MSS
Dunster Castle MSS
Hammet-Beadon MSS
Lethbridge MSS

*Southampton University Library*
Cope Collection
*Spalding Getleman's Society*
Banks Stanhope File 6
Charles Frederick Barber Scrap Book
*Staffordshire Record Office*
Anson MSS
Aqualate MSS
Dyott MSS
Hatherton MSS
Leveson-Gower MSS
Sutherland-Trentham MSS
*Suffolk (East) Record Office*
Barne MSS
Barrington MSS
Betts-Doughty MSS
Edgar MSS
Eye MSS
Lennard MSS
Rous MSS
*Suffolk (West) Record Office*
Bunbury MSS
Coxe-Hippisley MSS
Cullum MSS
Grafton MSS
Hertford MSS
Hervey MSS
*Surrey Record Office*
Bletchingley Voters Papers
Frederick MSS
Loseley MSS
*Sussex (East) Record Office*
Ashburnham MSS
Mont Bretton MSS
Shiffner MSS
*Sussex (West) Record Office*
Barrington MSS
Goodwood MSS
Horsham Museum MSS
Petworth MSS
*University College of North Wales, Bangor*
Plas Newydd MSS
*Wigan Public Library*
Broadsheet Collection
Holt-Leigh MSS
Parliamentary Elections Volume
*Wiltshire Record Office*

Cheswick MSS
Ellett MSS
Godard MSS
Grove MSS
MSS of the Borough of Heytesbury
*Yorkshire Archaeological Society*
Bradfer-Lawrence MSS
Clitheroe MSS
Slingsby MSS
Staveley MSS
*Yorkshire (North) Record Office*
Hickleton MSS
Kirkleatham MSS
Wyvill MSS
*Manuscripts in Private Ownership*
Althorp MSS, Althorp House, Northamptonshire
Blair-Adam MSS, Blair-Adam by Kelty, Kinrosshire
Devonshire MSS, Chatsworth House, Derbyshire

*Contemporary Books, Collections, Pamphlets, etc.*

*Account of the Mandamus Clause (An)* (Shrewsbury, 1806).
*Account of the Grand Dinner in Celebration of the Final Victory of Independence and the Substance of the Speeches Delivered on that Occasion* (Nottingham, 1820).
*Account of the Proceedings at Berkshire, 1818, Speeches at the Nomination* (Windsor, 1818).
*Addresses, Squibs and Other Publications* (Boston, 1820).
ADAMS, J., *An Impartial Collection* (Dublin, n.d.).
*Additional Grenville Papers, 1763–65*, ed. J. Tomlinson (Manchester University Press, 1962).
ANDREWS, W., *An Address to the Public* (Southampton, 1774).
ALLEN, L., *A History of Portsmouth* (Portsmouth, 1817).
*Alphabetical Copy of the Poll* (Newcastle-under-Lyme, 1792).
*Alphabetical Copy of the Poll* (St Albans, 1820).
*Alphabetical Copy of the Poll* (St Albans, 1821).
*Alphabetical Copy of the Poll* (St Albans, 1830).
*Alphabetical Copy of the Poll* (St Albans, 1831).
*Alphabetical List of the Burgesses* (Nottingham, 1780).
*Alphabetical List of the Burgesses* (Nottingham, 1830).
*Alphabetical List of the Burgesses* (Nottingham, 1832).
*Alphabetical List of the Electors.* (Preston, 1807).
*Alphabetical List of the Freemen* (Preston, 1818).
*Alphabetical List of the Freemen* (Preston, 1820).
*Alphabetical List of the Freemen* (Preston, 1831).
*Alphabetical List of the Voters, An* (Southampton, 1794).
*Alphabetical List of the Voters, An* (Southampton, 1802).

*Alphabetical List of the Voters, An* (Southampton, 1812).

*Althorpiana* (Northampton, 1831).

BARFOOT P., and WILKES, J., *The Universal British Directory* (London, 1792).

BELLAMY, J. *The Whig Club, instituted in May 1784* (London, 1792).

*Book of the Poll* (Cirencester, 1790).

*Book of the Poll* (Cirencester, 1802).

*Book of the Poll* (Cirencester, 1812).

*Brief Review*, A (Nottingham, 1820).

*Buckingham and Chandos, 2nd Duke . . . Courts and Cabinets of George III* (London, 1853–55).

*Burgesses' Poll at the Late Election* (Newcastle-upon-Tyne, 1774).

CARPENTER, W., *Peerage for the People* (London, 1841).

*Chester Election, 1818: The Complete Poll Book* (Chester, 1818).

*Chester Election, 1826: The Complete Poll Book* (Chester, 1826).

*Chester Poll Book, Containing the Names of the Voters* (Chester, 1812).

*Circumstantial Account of the Great Contest* (Worcester, 1774).

COBBETT, W., *The Parliamentary History of England*, 36 vols (London, 1806–20).

*Collection of All the Addresses:Squibs* (Grantham, 1831).

*Collection of the Addresses* (Great Grimsby, 1820).

*Collection of the Authentic Papers, Speeches & etc.* (Alnwick, 1826).

*Collection of Handbills, Squibs & etc.* (Winchester, 1780).

*Collection of Papers* (Chester, 1807).

*Compendious and Impartial Account . . .* (Liverpool, 1806).

*Complete Collection of Papers, A* (Newark, 1790).

*Copy of the Poll* (Hull, 1802).

*Copy of the Poll* (Hull, 1826).

*Copy of Poll* (King's Lynn, 1826).

*Copy of the Poll, A* (Newcastle-under-Lyme, 1790).

*Copy of the Poll, A* (Newcastle-under-Lyme, 1807).

*Copy of the Poll, A* (Southampton, 1790).

*Copy of the Poll, A* (Southampton, 1806).

*Copy of the Poll, A* (Southampton, 1812).

*Copy of the Poll, A* (Southampton, 1818).

*Copy of the Poll* (Windsor, 1794).

*Copy of the Poll* (Windsor, 1802).

*Copy of the Poll* (Windsor, 1804).

*Correct Alphabetical List of the Burgesses* (Shrewsbury, 1806).

*Correct Alphabetical List of the Burgesses* (Shrewsbury, 1807).

*Correct Alphabetical List of the Burgesses* (Shrewsbury, 1812).

*Correct Alphabetical List of the Burgesses* Shrewsbury, 1814).

*Correct Alphabetical List of the Burgesses* (Shrewsbury, 1826).

*Correct Alphabetical List of the Burgesses* (Shrewsbury, 1830).

*Correct Alphabetical List of the Burgesses* (Shrewsbury, 1831).

*Correct Copy of the Evidence on the Norwich Petition* (Norwich, 1807).

*Correspondence and Diaries of John Wilson Croker*, ed. L. J. Jennings (London, 1884).

*Correspondence of Edmund Burke, The* gen. ed. T. W. Copeland (London, 1958–78).

*County of Southampton: A True Copy of the Poll Book* (London, 1780).

DEBRETT, J., *Parliamentary Register, 1780–96*. 45 vols. (London, 1781–96).

DEFOE, D., *The Complete English Tradesman* (London, 1726, 1838).

*Election Flights: To the Freeholders of the County of Cambridge* (Cambridge, 1780).

*Election Magazine (The)* (Norwich, 1784).

*Electors' Remembrancer* (London, 1822).

*Farington Diary, 1793–1821*, J. Greig (ed.), (8 Vols. London, 1922–8).

*Five Minutes Good Advice to the Freemen and Freemen Burgesses of Shrewsbury before a General Canvass* (Shrewsbury, 1796).

*Full Report of the Proceedings of the Town Hall, New Windsor, 1831* (Reading, 1831).

*Full View of the British Commons*, 8 vols. (London, 1821).

GISBORNE, T., *An Enquiry into the Duties of Men in the Higher and Middle Classes of Society in Great Britain resulting from their Respective Stations* 2 vols. (London, 1798).

*Gloucester City Election, 1818. Alphabetical List of the Poll* (Gloucester, 1818).

GORE J., *The Poll for the Election . . .* (Liverpool, 1830).

GRIFFITHS, V., *Picture of Parliament or A History of the General Election of 1802* (London, 1803).

HANSARD, T. C., *Cobbett's Parliamentary History of England to 1803* 36 vols. (London, 1806–20).

—— *Cobbett's Parliamentary Debates, 1806–20* 36 vols. (London)

HEATHCOTE, E., *Poll of the Burgesses* (Warwick, 1831).

HEATHCOTE, R., *Memoirs of the Late Contested Election*, (Leicester, 1818).

HEMINGWAY J., *History of the City of Chester* 2 vols. (Chester, 1831).

HEYWOOD, S., *A Digest of the Law Respecting Borough Elections* (London, 1798).

*Historical Manuscripts Commission, Dropmore MSS* 10 vols. (London, 1894–1927).

*History of the Boston Election* (Boston, 1818).

*History of the Contested Election* (Chester, 1818).

*History of the Westminster Election* (London, 1784).

*History of the Westminster and Middlesex Elections* (London, 1806).

*Honest Elector's Proposal for Rendering the Votes of All Constituents Free and Independent* (by C.W.) (1767).

*Journals of the House of Commons.*

*Journals of the House of Lords.*

LAW, G. H., 'Remarks on the Primary Visitation of the Bishop of Chester, July, August and September, 1814' in *Sermons, Structures etc* (1814).

LEWIS, W. G., *A Peep at the Commons* (1820).

*Links of the Lower House* (1821).

*List of the Freemen and Freeholders* (Exeter, 1761).

MARKHAM, J., *The 1820 Parliamentary Election at Hedon* (York, 1821).

MARSHALL, John, *An Alphabetical List of Members of the Commons* (London, 1823).
—— *Analysis of the British House of Commons as at Present Constituted* (London, 1823).
MUGGERIDGE, R., *History of the Late Contest* (Bedford, 1830).
*Narrative of Proceedings* (Stamford, 1809).
*Norfolk Election Budget* (Norwich, 1817).
OLDFIELD, T. H. B., *The History of the Boroughs of Great Britain*, 2 vols. (London, 1794).
—— *History of the Original Constitution of Parliaments* (London, 1797).
—— *Representative History of Great Britain and Ireland* (6 vols. London, 1816).
—— *Key to the House of Commons* (London, 1819).
*Papers and Squibs Relating to the Chester Election of 1784* (Chester, 1784).
PHILLIPS, T., *History and Antiquities of Shrewsbury* (Shrewsbury, 1837).
*Pollbook for Members* (Ipswich, 1832).
*Pollbook, Together with Addresses* (Boston, 1826).
*Pollbook for the General Election* (Chester, 1820).
*Poll for the Borough, The* (Grimsby, 1818).
*Poll for the Borough, The* (Grimsby, 1826).
*Poll for the Borough, The* (Grimsby, 1830).
*Poll of the Borough, The* (Cirencester, 1768).
*Poll of the Burgesses* (Warwick, 1831).
*Poll of the Electorate* (Rochester, 1830).
*Poll of the Electors* (Canterbury, 1830).
*Poll for the County of Lincoln* (Lincoln, 1807).
*Poll for the Election* (Leicester, 1826).
*Poll for the Election* (Wigan, 1830).
*Poll of the Freeholders* (Abingdon, 1812).
*Poll of the Freeholders* (Windsor, 1818).
*Poll for Members, The* (Colchester, 1790).
*Poll for Members, The* (Colchester, 1796).
*Poll for Members, The* (Colchester, 1806).
*Poll for Members, The* (Colchester, 1807).
*Poll for Members, The* (Colchester, 1812).
*Poll for Members, The* (Colchester, 1818).
*Poll for Members, The* (Colchester, 1820).
*Poll for Members, The* (Colchester, 1831).
*Poll for Members* (Norwich, 1818).
*Poll for Members,* (Norwich, 1830).
*Poll for Members, The* (York, 1820).
*Poll for The Election* (Leicester, 1826).
*Poll for The Election . . . Lincolnshire* (Lincoln, 1807).
*Poll for The Election . . . Lincolnshire* (Lincoln, 1824).
*Poll for The Election* (Liverpool, 1807).
*Poll for The Election* (Liverpool, 1812).
*Poll for The Election* (Liverpool, 1830).

*Poll for Two Knights of the Shire The* (Chelmsford, 1830).
*Poll for Two Members* (Great Yarmouth, 1818).
*Poll for Two Members* (Great Yarmouth, 1820).
*Poll for Two Members* (Great Yarmouth, 1830).
*Poll for Two Members The* (Lincoln, 1820).
*Poll of the Electors* (Rochester, 1826).
*Poll of the Electors* (Rochester, 1830).
*Ready and Sure Way to Obtain a Reform in Parliament (London, 1819).*
*Report of the Committee on the Shaftesbury Election Petition* (London, 1775).
*Report of the Committee on the Cricklade Election Petition* (London, 1782).
*Report of the Committee on the Stockbridge Election Petition* (London, 1790).
*Report of the Committee on the Aylesbury Petition* (London, 1804).
*Report of the Commissioners, Appointed to Inquire Concerning Charities and the Education of the Poor in England and Wales* (London, 1836).
*Report of the Society of the Friends of the People on the State of the Representation* (London, 1793).
*Short Review of Proceedings, A* (Nottingham, 1820).
*Sketch of the Boston Election* (Boston, 1830).
STOOKS-SMITH, H., *Register of Parliamentary Contested Elections* (London, 1842).
*Storrs Impartial Narrative . . . 1820* (Grantham, 1820).
*Storr's Impartial Narrative . . . 1830* (Grantham, 1830).
*Survey of Wiltshire during the Election* (Trowbridge, 1818).
SUTTON, C., *Alphabetical List of the Burgesses* (Nottingham, 1803).
*Thoughts of a Lincolnshire Freeholder* (Lincoln, 1795).
*True Copy of the Poll, A* (Southampton, 1774).
WADE, George, *The Extraordinary Black Book* (London, 1820), 2 vols.
*Westminster Election of 1819, The* (London, 1819).
WHITTLE, P., *History of Preston* (Preston, 1837, 2 vols.).
WILSON, JOSHUA, *Biographical Index to the Present House of Commons* (London, 1806).
—— *Biographical Index to the Present House of Lords* (London, 1808).
*Workings of the Borough System, The* (London, 1830).
WRAXALL, N., *Historical Memoirs of My Own Time* (London, 1884).
WYVILL, CHRISTOPHER, *Political Papers*, 6 vols. (London, 1794–1802).

NEWSPAPERS AND PERIODICALS

*Annual Register*
*Berrow's Worcester Journal*
*Blackwoods*
*Chester Chronicle*
*Derby Mercury*
*Durham Chronicle*
*Edinburgh Review*
*General Evening Post*

*Halifax Journal*
*Hampshire Chronicle*
*Jopson's Coventry Mercury*
*Leicester and Nottingham Journal*
*Liverpool Chronicle*
*Liverpool Mercury*
*Morning Chronicle*
*Morning Post*
*Northampton Mercury*
*Norwich Gazette*
*Oxford Journal*
*Preston Chronicle*
*Public Advertiser*
*Reading Mercury*
*Shrewsbury Chronicle*
*Worcester Journal*
*York Gazette*
*York Herald*
*Yorkshire Chronicle*

## SECONDARY SOURCES: BOOKS

ALBERY, W., *Parliamentary History of Horsham* (Horsham, 1947).
ALLINGHAM, W., *A Diary* (Lincoln, 1907).
ARMSTRONG, W. A., 'The Interpretation of the Census Enumerators' Books for Victorian Towns', in H. J. Dyos (ed.), *The Study of Urban History*, (London, 1968).
—— *Stability and Change in an English Country Town* (Cambridge, 1974).
—— 'The Use of Information about Occupations', in E. A. Wrigley (ed.), *Nineteenth Century Society* (Cambridge, 1972).
ASPINALL, A., *Politics and the Press 1780–1850* (London, 1949).
—— (ed.) *The Later Correspondence of George III* (Cambridge, 1962).
—— *Reading Through Seven Centuries* (Reading, 1962).
—— *The Correspondence of George, Prince of Wales* (Cambridge, 1963–71).
—— and SMITH, E. A. (eds.), *English Historical Documents* (London, 1959).
BEALES, D., 'The Independent Member', in R. Robson (ed.), *Ideas and Institutions of Victorian Britain* (London, 1967), 1–19.
BEAN, W. W., *The Parliamentary Representation of the Six Northern Counties, 1603–1886* (Hull, 1886).
BEASTALL, T., *A North Country Estate: The Lumleys and Saundersons as Landowners 1600–1900* (London, 1975).
BEATTIE, A., *English Party Politics* (London, 1970).
BENTLEY, M., *Politics Without Democracy, 1815–1914* (London, 1984).
BEST, G., *Mid-Victorian Britain, 1851–1870* (London, 1971).
BLACK, E. C., *The Association: British Extra-Parliamentary Political Organization* (Cambridge, Mass., 1963).

BLACK, J., *Britain in the Age of Walpole* (London, 1984).

BONSALL, B., *Sir James Lowther and Cumberland and Westmorland Elections, 1754–1775* (Manchester, 1960).

BOUCH, C. M. L., and JONES, G. P., *The Lake Counties, 1500–1830* (Manchester, 1961).

BRADEY, JAMES, E. *Popular Politics and the American Revolution in England: Petitions, The Crown and Public Opinion* (Macon, Georgia, 1986).

BREWER, J., *Party Ideology and Popular Politics at the Accession of George III*, (Cambridge, 1976).

—— *An Ungovernable People: The English and their Law in the Seventeenth and Eighteenth Centuries* (London, 1980).

—— 'Commercialization and Politics', in N. McKendrick (ed.), *The Birth of a Consumer Society* (London, 1982), 197–262.

BROCK, M., *The Great Reform Act* (London, 1973).

BROOKE, J., *The Chatham Administration* (London, 1956).

BURTON, K. G., *The Early Newspaper Press in Berkshire, 1723–1825* (Reading, 1954).

BUTLER, D., and CORNFORD, J., *International Guide to Electoral Statistics* (London, 1968).

BUTLER, J. R. M., *The Passing of the Great Reform Bill* (New York, 1914).

BOURNE, J. (ed.), *Georgian Tiverton: The Political Memoranda of Beavis Wood, 1768–1798*, Devon and Cornwall Record Society, NS 29 (Torquay, 1986).

BUTTERFIELD, H., *George III and the Historians* (London, 1957).

CANNON, J. A., *The Fox–North Coalition: The Crisis of the Constitution 1782–1784* (1969).

—— *Parliamentary Reform, 1640–1832* (Cambridge, 1972).

—— *Aristocratic Century: The Peerage of 18th-century England* (Cambridge, 1984).

—— (ed.), *The Whig Ascendancy: Colloquies on Hanoverian England* (London, 1981).

—— *The Historian at Work* (London, 1982).

CHALKIN, C. W., *The Provincial Towns of Georgian England* (London, 1974).

CHAMBERS, J. D. (ed), 'Population Change in Nottingham, 1700–1800', in L. S. Presnell (ed.), *Studies in the Industrial Revolution Presented to T. S. Ashton* (London, 1960), 97–124.

CHAMBERS, J. D., and MINGAY, G. E., *The Agricultural Revolution* (London, 1966).

CHRISTIE, I. R., *The End of North's Ministry* (London, 1958).

—— *Wilkes, Wyvill and Reform* (London, 1962).

—— *Myth and Reality in Late Eighteenth-century British Politics* (London, 1970).

—— *Wars and Revolutions: Britain, 1760–1815* (London, 1982).

—— *Stress and Stability in Late Eighteenth-century Britain* (Oxford, 1984).

CLARK, J. C. D., *English Society, 1688–1832* (Cambridge, 1985).

CLARKSON, A., *The Pre-industrial Economy in England, 1500–1750* (London, 1971).

CLAY, C. 'Landlords and Estate Management', in J. Thirsk (ed.), *The Agrarian History of England and Wales*, ii (Cambridge, 1985).

CLEMSHA, H. W., *History of Preston in Amounderness* (Manchester, 1912).

CLIFFORD, J. L., *Man versus Society in the Eighteenth Century* (London, 1968).

COLLEY, L., *In Defiance of Oligarchy: The Tory Party, 1714–1760* (Cambridge, 1982).

COOK, C., *British Historical Facts* (London, 1975).

COOOKSON, J., *Lord Liverpool's Administration, 1815–1822* (Edinburgh, 1975).

—— *The Friends of Peace: Anti-war Liberalism in England, 1793–1815* (Cambridge, 1982).

COWHERD, R. G., *The Politics of English Dissent* (New York, 1956).

CRANFIELD, G. A., *The Development of the Provincial Newspaper, 1700–1760* (Oxford, 1962).

—— *The Press and Society: From Caxton to Northcliffe* (London, 1978).

COX, E. W., *Hints to Solicitors for the Conduct of Elections* (London, 1868; Open University edn., Milton Keynes, 1974).

COX, J. C., *Records of Northampton* (Northampton, 1898).

CRUICKSHANKS, E., *Political Untouchables: The Tories and the 1745* (London, 1979).

DARVALL, F. O., *Popular Disturbances and Public Order in Regency England* (Cambridge, 1934).

DAVIS, R. W., *Dissent in Politics, 1780–1832: The Political Life of William Smith MP* (London, 1971).

—— *Political Change and Continuity, 1760–1885: A Buckinghamshire Study* (Newton Abbot, 1972).

DICKINSON, H. T., *Liberty and Property: Political Ideology in Eighteenth-century Britain* (London, 1977).

DILKS, T. B., *Charles James Fox and the Borough of Bridgwater* (Bridgwater, 1907).

DINWIDDY, J., *Christopher Wyvill and Reform, 1790–1820* Borthwick Papers no. 39 (York, 1971).

DOD, C. R., *Electoral Facts From 1832–1852 Impartially Stated* (Brighton, 1972).

DODD, A. H., *The Industrial Revolution in North Wales*, 2nd edn. (Cardiff, 1951).

DOUGLAS, R., and SYKES, R., *The Political Sociology of Guildford and West Surrey in the Nineteenth Century* SSRC Report HR 2611 (London, 1976).

DOZIER, R. B., *For King, Constitution and Country: The English Loyalists and the French Revolution* (Kentucky, 1983).

DRAKE, M., 'The Mid-Victorian Voter', in id., *Introduction to Historical Psephology*, Open University Course D301, units 9–12 (Milton Keynes, 1974).

DYOS, H. J. (ed.), *The Study of Urban History* (London, 1968).

EVANS, E., *The Forging of the Modern State: Early Industrial Britain* (London, 1983).

—— *The Great Reform Act of 1832* (London, 1983).

EVERITT, A., *The Pattern of Rural Dissent* (Leicester, 1972).

—— *Perspectives in English Urban History* (London, 1973).

EVERSLEY D., *An Introduction to English Historical Demography* (London, 1966).

FERGUSON, R. S., *The MPs of Cumberland and Westmorland, 1660–1867* (London, 1871).

FEUCHTWANGER, E. J., *Disraeli, Democracy and the Tory Party* (London, 1963).

FORRESTER, E. G., *Northamptonshire County Elections and Electioneering 1695–1832* (London, 1941).

FORTESCUE, Sir J., *The Correspondence of George III*, 6 vols. (London, 1928).

FOSTER, J., *Class Struggle and the Industrial Revolution* (London, 1974).

FRITZ, P. (ed.), *The Triumph of Culture* (Toronto, 1972).

GARDINER, W., *Music and Friends*, 2 vols. (Leicester, 1938).

GASH, N., *Politics in the Age of Peel* (London, 1953).

—— *Aristocracy and People*, (London, 1979).

GIBBS, R., *Buckinghamshire: Records of Local Occurrences* (Aylesbury, 1879–85).

—— *A History of Aylesbury* (Aylesbury, 1885).

GILLETT, E., *History of Grimsby* (Oxford, 1970).

GINTER, D. E., *Whig Organization in the General Election of 1790* (Berkeley–Los Angeles, 1967).

GLUBB, A. de C. *When Cornwall Had Forty-four MPs* (Truro, 1945).

GOODER, A., *The Parliamentary Representation of Yorkshire* (York, 1938).

GRANT, R., *The Parliamentary History of Glamorgan* (Swansea, 1978).

GRAY, D., *Nottingham: Settlement to City* (Nottingham, 1953).

—— *Spencer Perceval* (Manchester, 1963).

GREAVES, R. W., *The Corporation of Leicester* (Oxford, 1939).

GREGO, J., *History of Parliamentary Elections and Electioneering from the Stuarts to Queen Victoria* (London, 1892).

GREIG, J. (ed.), *The Farington Diary, 1793–1821* (London, 1922–8).

GUNN, J. A. W., *Beyond Liberty and Property* (Ontario, 1983).

GWYN, W. B., *Democracy and the Cost of Politics in Britain* (London, 1962).

HALEVY, E., *A History of the English People in the Nineteenth Century,* iii. *The Triumph of Reform* (London, 1924).

HANHAM, H., *The Reformed Electoral System in Great Britain, 1832–1914* (London, 1968).

—— *Elections and Party Management: Politics in the Time of Disraeli and Gladstone* (London, 1959).

HARVEY, A. D., *Britain in the Early Nineteenth Century* (London, 1978).

HAY, D., *Albion's Fatal Tree: Crime and Society in Eighteenth Century England* (London, 1975).

HILL, B. W., *The Growth of Parliamentary Parties, 1689–1832* (London, 1976).

HILL, B. W., *British Parliamentary Parties, 1742–1832* (London, 1985).

HILL, Sir F., *Georgian Lincoln* (Cambridge, 1966).

HIRST, D., *The Representative of the People? Voters and Voting in England Under the Early Stuarts* (London, 1975).

HOLMES, G., *The Electorate and the National Will in the First Age of Party* (Kendal, 1976).

—— 'The Achievement of Political Stability: The Social Context of Politics from the 1680s to the Age of Walpole' in J. A. Cannon (ed.), *The Whig Ascendancy: Colloquies on Hanoverian England* (London, 1981).

—— *Augustan England: Professions, State and Society, 1680–1730* (London, 1982).

—— and SPECK, W. A., *The Divided Society* (London, 1967).

HONE, J. A., 'Radicalism in London, 1796–1802: Convergences and Continuities', in J. Stevenson (ed.), *London in the Age of Reform* (Oxford, 1977).

HOPPEN, K. T., *Elections, Politics and Society in Ireland, 1832–1885* (Oxford, 1984).

HUGHES, E., 'The Eighteenth century Estate Agent', in *Essays in British and Irish History* ed. H. A. Cronne, T. W. Moody, and D. B. Quinn (eds.), (London, 1949).

—— *North Country Life in the Eighteenth Century* Vol. 1. *The North-East, 1700–1750* (London, 1952); *Cumberland and Westmorland, 1700–1830* (London, 1965).

HUXLEY, G., *Lady Elizabeth and the Grosvenors* (Oxford, 1965).

JACKSON, G., *Hull in the Eighteenth Century* (London, 1972).

JACOB, M., and J. J., *The Origins of Anglo-American Radicalism* (London, 1984).

JENKINS, P., *The Making of a Ruling Class: The Glamorgan Gentry, 1640–1790* (Cambridge, 1983).

JEPHSON, H., *The Platform: Its Rise and Progress* (London, 1892).

JOLLIE, F., *The Political History of Carlisle* (Carlisle, 1820).

JUDD, G. P., *Members of Parliament, 1734–1832* (Yale, 1955).

JUPP, P., *British and Irish Elections, 1784–1831* (Newton Abbot, 1973).

KELLY, J. A., *England and Englishmen in German Literature in the Eighteenth Century* (New York, 1921).

KETTLE, A., 'The Struggle for the Lichfield Interest, 1747–1768' in M. W. Greenslade (ed.), *Essays in Staffordshire History* (Stafford, 1970).

KISHLANSKY, M., *Parliamentary Selection: Social and Political Choice in Early Modern England* (Cambridge, 1986).

LANDAU, N., *The Justices of the Peace, 1679–1760* (London, 1984).

LANGFORD, P., *The First Rockingham Administration, 1765–1766* (London, 1973).

—— *The Excise Crisis* (Oxford, 1975).

—— 'Old Whigs, Old Tories and the American Revolution' in P. Marshall, and G. Williams (eds.), *The British Atlantic Empire before the American Revolution* (London, 1980).

LAPRADE, T. W., *Parliamentary Papers of John Robinson, 1774–1784*, Camden Society, 3rd ser., vol. xxxiii (London, 1922).

LAWSON, P., *George Grenville: A Political Life* (Oxford, 1984).

LAWSON-TANCRED, T., *Records of a Yorkshire Manor* (Aldborough, 1937).

LLOYD, T., *The General Election of 1880* (Oxford, 1968).

LOCKETT, H., *The Relations of French and English Society, 1763–1793* (London, 1920).

MACHIN G. I. T., *The Catholic Question in English Politics, 1820–1830* (London, 1964).

MCKENDRICK, N. (ed.), *The Birth of a Consumer Society* (London, 1982).

MALCOLMSON, R. W., *Life and Labour in England, 1700–1780* (London, 1981).

MARKS, [?], *The Guild Guide to Preston* (Preston, 1882).

MEE, G., *Aristocratic Enterprise: The Fitzwilliam Industrial Undertakings* (Glasgow–London, 1975).

MILLS, W. B. *Parliamentary History of the Borough of Lewes, 1795–1885* (London, 1908).

MINGAY, G. E., *English Landed Society in the Eighteenth Century* (London, 1963).

—— 'The Eighteenth-century Land Steward', in *Land, Labour and Population in the Industrial Revolution*, ed. L. Jones and G. E. Mingay (London, 1967).

—— *The Gentry: Rise and Fall of a Ruling Class* (London, 1976).

—— *The Victorian Countryside* (London, 1981).

MITCHELL, A., *The Whigs in Opposition, 1815–1830* (Oxford, 1967).

MITCHELL, L., *Charles James Fox and the Disintegration of the Whig Party, 1782–1794* (Oxford, 1971).

MONEY, J., *Experience and Identity: Birmingham and the West Midlands, 1760–1800* (Manchester, 1977).

MOORE, D. C., *The Politics of Deference* (Hassocks, 1976).

NAMIER, L. B., *The Structure of Politics at the Accession of George III* (London, 1929).

—— *England in the Age of the American Revolution* (London, 1930).

—— *Monarchy and the Party System* (Oxford, 1952).

—— and BROOKE, J., *The House of Commons, 1754–1790*, 3 vols. (London, 1964).

NEALE, R. S., *Class and Ideology in the Nineteenth Century* (London, 1972).

—— *Bath 1680–1850: A Social History* (London, 1981).

NEUBERG, V. E., *Popular Education in Eighteenth-century England* (London, 1971).

NEW, C., *The Life of Henry Brougham to 1830* (Oxford, 1961).

NOSSITER, T. J., 'Aspects of Electoral Behaviour in English Constituencies', in E. Allardt and S. Rokkan (eds.), *Mass Politics: Studies in Political Sociology* (New York, 1980).

—— (ed.), *Imagination and Precision in the Social Sciences* (London, 1972).

—— *Influence, Opinion and Political Idioms in Reformed England: Case Studies from the North-east* (Brighton, 1975).

OBELKEVICH, J., *Religion and Rural Society: South Lindsey, 1825–1875* (Oxford, 1976).

O'GORMAN, F., *The Whig Party and the French Revolution* (London, 1967).

O'GORMAN, F., *The Rise of Party in England: The Rockingham Whigs, 1760–1782* (London, 1975).

—— 'Party in the Later Eighteenth Century', in J. A. Cannon (ed.), *The Whig Ascendancy: Colloquies on Hanoverian England* (London, 1981), 77–93.

—— *The Emergence of the British Two-party System, 1760–1832* (London, 1982).

O'LEARY, C., *The Elimination of Corrupt Practices in British Elections, 1868–1911* (Oxford, 1962).

OLNEY, R. J., *Lincolnshire Politics, 1832–1885* (Oxford, 1973).

OWEN, J., *The Eighteenth Century; 1714–1815* (London, 1974).

PARKER, A. C., *Coke of Norfolk* (Oxford, 1975).

PELLING, H., *Social Geography of British Elections 1885–1910* (London, 1967).

—— *Popular Politics and Society in Late Victorian England* (London, 1968).

PERKIN, H., *The Origins of Modern English Society, 1780–1880* (London, 1969).

PERRY, T. W., Public Opinion, Propaganda and Politics in Eighteenth-century England (Harvard, 1962).

PETERS, M. *Pitt and Popularity: the Patriot Minister and London Opinion during the Seven Years War* (Oxford, 1980).

PHILBIN, J. H., *Parliamentary Representation 1832: England and Wales* (New Haven, 1965).

PHILLIPS, J. A., *Electoral Behavior in Unreformed England, 1761–1802* (Princeton, 1982).

PHILLIPS, N. C., *Yorkshire and English National Politics* (Christchurch, 1961).

PLUMB, J. H., *The Growth of Political Stability in England, 1675–1725* (London, 1967).

—— 'Political Man', in J. Clifford (ed.), *Man versus Society in the Eighteenth Century* (Cambridge, 1968), 1–21.

POLE, J. R., *Political Representation in England and the Origins of the American Republic* (London, 1966).

PORRITT, E. and A., *The Unreformed House of Commons*, 2 vols. (Cambridge, 1909).

PORTER, R., *English Society in the Eighteenth Century* (London, 1982).

POYNTER, J. R., *Society and Pauperism: English Ideas on Poor Relief 1715–1834* (London, 1969).

PREST, J., *Politics in the Age of Cobden* (London, 1979).

PROTHERO, I., *Artisans and Politics in Early Nineteenth-century London: John Gast and his Times* (Folkestone, 1978).

READ, D., *Press and People, 1790–1850. Opinion in Three English Cities* (London, 1961).

—— *The English Provinces* c. *1760–1960: A Study in Influence* (London, 1964).

REID, R., *Modern Leicester* (London, 1881).

RICHARD, E., 'The Land Agent', in G. E. Mingay (ed.), *The Victorian Countryside*, 2 vols. (London, 1981).

ROBERTS, D., *Paternalism in Early Victorian England* (London, 1979).

ROBSON, R., *The Oxfordshire Election of 1754* (Oxford, 1949).
—— *The Attorney of Eighteenth-century England* (Cambridge, 1959).
—— (ed.), *Ideas and Institutions of Victorian Britain* (London, 1967).
ROGERS N., 'Resistance to Oligarchy': The City Opposition to Walpole and His Successors, 1725–1747', in J. Stevenson (ed.), *London in the Age of Reform* (Oxford, 1977), 1–29.
ROYLE, E., and WALVIN, J., *English Radicals and Reformers* (Hassocks, 1982).
RUDE, G., *Wilkes and Liberty: A Social Study of 1763 to 1774* (Oxford, 1962).
—— *Paris and London in the Eighteenth Century: Studies in Popular Protest* (London, 1973).
SEDGWICK, R. R., *The House of Commons, 1715–1754*, 2 vols. (London, 1970).
SEYMOUR, C., *Electoral Reform in England and Wales* (New Haven, 1915).
SMITH, E. A., *Whig Principles and Party Politics* (Manchester, 1975).
SPECK, W. A., *Tory and Whig: The Struggle in the Constituencies, 1701–1715* (London, 1970).
—— *Stability and Strife: England, 1714–1760* (London, 1977).
SPENCE-WATSON, R., *The National Liberal Federation, 1877–1906* (London, 1907).
SPRING, D., *The English Landed Estate in the Nineteenth Century* (Baltimore, 1963).
STONE, L., *An Open Élite? England 1540–1880* (Oxford, 1984).
TEMPLE PATTERSON, A., *Radical Leicester* (Leicester, 1954).
—— *A History of Southampton 1700–1914* (Southampton, 1966).
THIRSK, J. (ed.) *Agrarian History of England and Wales*, vol. V.ii. (Cambridge, 1985).
THOMAS, P. D. G., *The House of Commons in the Eighteenth Century* (Oxford, 1971).
—— 'Government and Society', in D. Moore (ed.), *Wales in the Eighteenth Century* (Swansea, 1976).
THOMIS, M., *Politics and Society in Nottingham, 1785–1835* (Oxford, 1969).
THOMPSON, E. P., *The Making of the English Working Class* (London, 1963).
THOMPSON, F. M. L., *English Landed Society in the Nineteenth Century* (London, 1963).
—— 'Landownership and Economic Growth in England in the Eighteenth Century', in E. L. Jones and S. Woolf (eds.), *Agrarian Change and Economic Development* (London, 1969).
THORNE, R. G. *The House of Commons, 1790–1820*, 5 vols. (London, 1986).
TREVELYAN, G. M., *Lord Grey of the Reform Bill* (London, 1920).
—— *The Two-party System in English Constitutional History* (Oxford, 1926).

TURBERVILLE, A. S. *The House of Lords in the Eighteenth Century* (Oxford, 1927).
—— *A History of Welbeck Abbey and its Owners*, 2 vols. (London, 1938–9).
VAISEY, D., *The Diary of Thomas Turner, 1754–1765* (London, 1984).
VEITCH, G. S., *The Genesis of Parliamentary Reform* (London, 1913).
*Victoria County History* (*VCH*): *Somerset*, iii– ; *Hampshire*, iv– ; *Berkshire*, ii– ; *Wiltshire*, v– ; *Huntingdonshire*, ii– ; *Leicestershire*, ii, iv; *Warwickshire*, vii, viii.
VINCENT, J. R., *Pollbooks: How Victorians Voted* (Cambridge, 1967).
WARD, W. R., *Religion and Society in England, 1790–1850* (London, 1972).
WATTS, M., *The Dissenters* (Oxford, 1978).
WEYMAN, H. T., 'Ludlow Members of Parliament', *Trans. Salop. Archaeol. Soc.* 2nd ser. 7 (1895), 43.
WHITLEY, T. W., *The Parliamentary Representation of the City of Coventry* (Coventry, 1894).
WHITTINGTON-JONES, B., 'The History of Liverpool Politics' (2 vols. TS, n.d., in Liverpool City Lib.).
WILBERFORCE, R. I., and S., *Life of William Wilberforce* (1839).
WILES, R. M., *Freshest Advices: Early Provincial Newspapers in England* (Columbus, Ohio, 1965).
—— 'Provincial Culture in Early Georgian England', in P. Fritz and D. Williams (eds.), *The Triumph of Culture* (Toronto, 1972), 49–68.
WILKS, G., *Barons of the Cinque Ports and the Parliamentary Representation of Hythe* (Folkestone, 1892).
WILLIAMS, W. R., *The Parliamentary History of Oxfordshire* (Oxford, 1899).
WINSTANLEY M. J., *The Shopkeeper's World* (London, 1982).
WITMER, H. E., *The Property Qualifications of Members of Parliament* (New York, 1943).
WRIGLEY, E. A., *Nineteenth-century Society* (Cambridge, 1972).
—— *Identifying People in the Past* (London, 1973).

*Periodical Literature*

ASPINALL, A., 'English Party Organisation in the 19th Century', *Eng. Hist. Rev.* 41 (1926), 389–411.
BECKETT, J., 'The Making of a Pocket Borough: Cockermouth, 1722–1756', *J. Brit. Studies* (1980), 140–57.
—— 'The Decline of the Small Landowner', *Ag. Hist. Rev.* 30 (1982), 97–111.
BLACK, J., 'The *Cirencester Flying Post and Weekly Miscellany*', *Cirencester Arch. Hist. Soc.* 25 (1985), 5–18.
BLACKMAN, J. 'The Development of the Retail Grocery Trade in the Nineteenth Century', *Business Hist.* 9 (1967), 110–17.

BONEY, K. 'Liverpool Plumper Mug', *Libraries Bulletin,* 3/3 (1954), 39-40.

BRADLEY, J. E. 'Whigs and Nonconformists: Slumbering Radicalism in English Politics, 1739-1789', *Eighteenth-century Studies,* 9 (1975), 1-27.

—— 'Religion and Reform at the Polls: Nonconformity in Cambridge Politics, 1774-1784', *J. Brit. Studies,* 23/2 (1984), 55-78.

BREWER, J. 'Commercialisation in Politics' in *The Birth of a Consumer Society,* ed. N. McKendrick. (London, 1982).

BURNS, W. L., 'Electoral Corruption in the Nineteenth Century', *Parl. Affairs,* 4 (1951), 437-42.

CANNON, J. A., 'The Parliamentary Representation of the City of Gloucester 1727-1790', *Trans. Bristol and Gloucs. Archaeol. Soc.* 78 (1959), 37-52.

—— 'Pollbooks: Short Guides to Records', *History* 47 (1963), 166-9.

—— 'The Wiltshire Election of 1772. An Interpretation', *Wiltshire Arch. Mag.* 58 (1960).

CHRISTIE, I. R., 'The Yorkshire Association, 1780-1784: A Study in Political Organisation', *Hist. J.* 3 (1960), 144-61.

—— 'The Wilkites and the General Election of 1774', *Guildhall Misc.* 1/4 (1963), 155-64; repr. in id. (ed.), *Myth and Reality,* 244-59.

CLARK, J. C. D., 'A General Theory of Party, Opposition and Government, 1688-1832'. *Hist. J.* 23/2 (1980), 295-325.

CLARKE, P. F., 'Electoral Sociology of Modern Britain' *History,* 57 (1972), 31-55.

CLAY, C., 'Marriage, Inheritance and the Rise of Large Estates in England, 1660-1815', *Econ. Hist. Rev.* 21 (1968), 503-18.

—— 'The Greed of Whig Bishops: Church Landlords and their Lessees', *Past and Present,* 87 (1980) 128-57.

—— 'Lifeleaseholds in the Western Counties of England, 1650-1750', *Ag. Hist. Rev.* 29 (1981), 83-96.

COLLEY, L., 'The Loyal Brotherhood and the Cocoa Tree', *Hist. J.* 20 (1977), 77-95.

DAVIES, J., 'The Second Marquess of Bute', in *Glamorgan Historian,* 8 (1972), 3-21.

DAVIS, R. W., 'The Whigs and the Idea of Electoral Deference', *Durham Univ. J.* 67 (1974), 79-91.

—— 'Deference and Aristocracy in the Time of the Great Reform Act', *Am. Hist. Rev.* 81 (1976), 532-9.

—— 'The Mid-Nineteenth Century Electoral Structure', *Albion,* 8 (1976), 142-53.

—— 'Yes', *J. Brit Studies,* 15/2 (1976), 159-61.

DINWIDDY, J. 'Sir Francis Burdett and Burdettite Radicalism', *History,* 65 (1980), 17-31.

DITCHFIELD, G. M., 'The Parliamentary Struggle over the Repeal of the Test and Corporation Acts', *Eng. Hist. Rev.* 352 (1974), 551-77.

—— 'The House of Lords and Parliamentary Reform in the 1780s' *Bull. Inst. Hist. Rev.* 54/130 (1981), 207-25.

DOOLITTLE, I. G., 'Walpole's City Elections Act (1725)', *Eng. Hist. Rev.* 98 (1982), 501–14.

DRAKE, M., 'The Mid-Victorian Voter', *J. Interdiscip. Hist.* 1/3 (1971), 473–90.

EVERITT, A., 'Country, County and Town: Patterns of Regional Evolution in England', *Trans. Royal Hist. Soc.* 5th ser., 29 (1979), 79–108.

FISHER, J. R., 'The Limits of Deference: Agricultural Communities in a Mid-nineteenth-century Election Campaign', *J. Brit. Studies*, 20 (1981), 90–105.

FRASER, D., 'The Fruits of Reform: Leeds Politics in the 1830s', *Northern Hist.* 7 (1972), 89–111.

FRASER, P., 'Party Voting in the House of Commons, 1812–27', *Eng. Hist. Rev.* 98 (1983), 763–84.

GARRARD, J. A., 'Parties, Members and Voters after 1867', *Hist. J.* 20 (1977), 145–63.

GEORGE, M. D., 'Fox's Martyrs', *Trans. Royal Hist. Soc.* 4th ser., 21 (1939), 133-68.

GINTER, D. E., 'The Financing of the Whig Party Organisation, 1783–1793', *Am. Hist. Rev.* 71 (1966), 421–40.

GOLBY, J., 'A Great Electioneer and His Motives', *Hist. J.* 8/2 (1965), 201–18.

GRIGG, D. B., 'Small and Large Farms in England and Wales: Their Size and Distribution', *Geography*, 48 (1963), 268–79.

HABBAKUK, H. J., 'English Landownership, 1680–1740', *Econ. Hist. Rev.* 10 (1940), 2–17.

—— 'Marriage Settlements in the Eighteenth Century', *Trans. Royal Hist. Soc.* 4th ser., 32 (1950), 15–30.

—— 'The Rise and Fall of English Landed Families, 1600–1800', *Trans. Royal Hist. Soc.* 5th ser., 29 (1979), 187–207.

HANHAM, H., 'Some Recent Studies of Voting', *Political Studies* (1955–6), 150–2.

HEESOM, A., '"Legitimate" vs. "Illegitimate" Influences: Aristocratic Electioneering in Mid-Victorian Britain', *Parliamentary History* (forthcoming).

HILL, B. W., 'Executive Monarchy and the Challenge of the Parties, 1689–1832', *Hist. J.* 13 (1970), 379–401.

—— 'Fox and Burke: The Whig Party and the Question of Principle', *Eng. Hist. Rev.* 89 (1974), 1–24.

HOLDERNESS, B. A., 'The English Land Market in the Eighteenth Century', *Econ. Hist. Rev.* 28 (1974), 557–76.

HOLLINGSWORTH, T. W., 'Historical Studies of Migration', *Annales de demographie historique*, 2 (1970), 87–96.

HOPPEN, K. T., 'The Franchise and Electoral Politics in England and Ireland, 1832–1885', *History*, 70 (1985), 202–17.

HUME, T. A., 'Buckinghamshire and Parliament', *Records of Bucks.* 16 (1960), 91–104.

JAGGARD, E., 'The Parliamentary Reform Movement in Cornwall, 1805–1826', *Parl. Hist. Yrbk.* 2 (1983), 113–29.

—— 'Cornwall Politics, 1826–1832: Another Face of Reform', *J. Brit. Studies* 22 (1983), 80–97.

JASPER, R., 'Edward Eliot and Grampound Elections', *Eng. Hist. Rev.* 58 (1943), 475–81.

JENKINS, P., 'Tory Industrialism and Town Politics: Swansea in the Eighteenth Century', *Hist. J.* 28 (1985), 103–23.

JONES, I. G., 'Merioneth Politics in the Mid-nineteenth Century', *The Politics of a Rural Economy, Merioneth, 5/4* (1968), 284–99.

KATZ, M., 'Occupational Classification in History', *J. Interdiscip. Hist.* 3, (1972), 63–88.

KELLY, P., 'Radicalism and Public Opinion in the General Election of 1784', *Bull. Inst. Hist. Res.* 45 (1972), 73–88.

KEMP, B., 'Crewe's Act 1782', *Eng. Hist. Rev.* 68 (1953), 258–63.

KNOX, T. R., 'Popular, Politics and Provincial Radicalism: Newcastle-upon-Tyne, 1769–1785', *Albion*, 11 (1979), 220–39.

—— 'Wilkism and the Newcastle Election of 1774', *Durham Univ. J.* 72 (1979–80), 23–37.

LANDAU, N., 'Independence, Deference and Voter Participation: the Behaviour of the Electorate in Early Eighteenth-Century Kent', *Hist. J.* 22/3 (1979), 561–83.

LANG, R. G., 'Social Origins and Social Aspirations of Jacobean London', *Econ. Hist. Rev.* 2nd ser. 27 (1974), 28–47.

LANGFORD, P., 'William Pitt and Public Opinion, 1757', *Eng. Hist. Rev.* 88 (1973), 54–80.

LAPRADE, W. T., 'Public Opinion and the Election of 1784', *Eng. Hist. Rev.* 31 (1916), 224–37.

LAWSON, P., 'Grenville's Election Act, 1770', *Bull. Inst. Hist. Res.* 53 (1980), 218–28.

LINDERT, P. H., 'English Occupations, 1670–1811', *J. Econ. Hist.* 40 (1980), 685–712.

LLOYD, J. H., 'Dr Wade and the Working Class', *Midland Hist.* 2 (1974), 61–83.

MCADAMS, D., 'Electioneering Techniques in Populous Constituencies, 1784–1796', *Studies in Burke and his Time*, 14 (1972), 23–54.

MACDONALD, H., 'Two Eighteenth-century Parliamentary Elections in Worcester', *Trans. Worcs. Archaeol, Soc.* 22 (1943–5), 61–9.

MCGILL, B., 'Francis Schnadhorst and Liberal Party Organisation', *J. Mod. Hist.* 34 (1962), 19–39.

MACHIN, G. I. T., 'Resistance to the Repeal of the Test and Corporation Acts, 1828', *Hist. J.* 22 (1979), 115–39.

MCINTYRE, S., 'The Scarborough Corporation Quarrel, 1736–1760', *Northern Hist.* 14 (1978), 208–26.

MCQUISTON, J. R., 'Sir Richard Hill, Shropshire Evangelist', *Trans. Salop. Archaeol. Soc.* 58/2 (1961), 170–1.

—— 'Sussex Aristocrats in 1820', *Eng. Hist Rev.* 88 (1973), 534–58.

MAIN, J. M., 'Radical Westminster, 1807–1820', *Hist. Stud. ANZ* 12 (1966), 186–204.

MENZIES, E. M., 'The Freeman Voter in Liverpool, 1802–1835', *Trans. Hist. Soc. Lancs. and Cheshire*, 124 (1973), 83–107.

MILLER N., 'John Cartwright and Radical Parliamentary Reform, 1808–1819', *Eng. Hist. Rev.* 83 (1968), 705–28.

—— 'Major John Cartwright and the Founding of the Hampden Clubs', *Hist. J.* 17 3 (1974), 615–19.

MITCHELL, J. C., 'Electoral Strategy Under Open Voting 1832–1880', *Public Choice* 28 (1976), 17–35.

—— and CORNFORD J., 'The Political Demography of Cambridge, 1832–68', *Albion*, 9 (1977), 242–72.

MITCHELL, S. I. 'Retailing in Eighteenth-century and Early Nineteenth-century Cheshire', *Trans. Hist. Soc. Lancs. and Cheshire*, 130 (1981), 37–60.

MOIR, E., 'The Gloucestershire Movement for Parliamentary Reform, 1780', *Trans. Bristol and Gloucs. Archaeol. Soc.* 75 (1956), 171–91.

MONEY, J., 'Taverns, Coffee Houses and Clubs: Local Politics and Popular Articulacy in the Birmingham Area in the Age of the American Revolution', *Hist. J.* 14 (1971), 15–47.

—— 'Birmingham and the West Midlands, 1760–93: Politics and Regional Identity in the English Provinces in the Later Eighteenth Century', *Midland Hist.* (1971), 1–19.

MOORE, D. C., 'The Other Face of Reform', *Victorian Studies*, 5/1 (1961), 7–34.

—— 'The Matter of the Missing Contests: Towards a Theory of Nineteenth-century English Politics', *Albion*, 6 (1974), 93–119.

—— 'Is the Other Face of Reform in Bucks. an Hallucination?', *J. Brit. Studies*, 15 (1976), 150–61.

—— 'Some Thoughts on Thoroughness and Carefulness Suggested by Comparing the Reports of the Aylesbury Meeting of 24 February 1830 in *The Times and the Bucks. Gazette*', *J. Brit. Studies*, 17/1 (1977), 141–4.

MORRIS, R. J., 'Voluntary Societies and British Urban Elites, 1780–1850: An Analysis', *Hist. J.* 26 (1983), 95–118.

NEALE, R. S., 'Class and Class Consciousness in Early Nineteenth Century England: Three Classes or Five?', *Victorian Studies*, 12 (1968), 5–32.

NEWMARCH, W., 'On the Electoral Statistics of the Counties and Boroughs of England and Wales, 1832–1857', *J. Stats. Soc.* 20 (1857), 169–234.

NOSSITER, T. J., 'Voting Behaviour, 1832–1872', *Political Studies*, 18 (1968), 380–9.

O'GORMAN, F., 'The Chester Election of 1784', *J. Chester Archaeol. Soc.* 57 (1970–71), 41–50.

—— 'Fifty Years After Namier: The Eighteenth Century in British Historical Writing', *The Eighteenth Century*, 20 (1979), 99–120.

—— 'Electoral Deference in Unreformed England, 1760–1832', *J. Mod. Hist.* 56 (1984), 391–429.

O'GORMAN, F., 'The Unreformed Electorate of Hanoverian England: The Mid-18th Century to 1832', *Social Hist.* 11/1 (1986) 33–52.

—— 'Party Politics in the Early Nineteenth Century', *Eng. Hist. Rev.* 102 (1987), 62–83.

PERKINS, J., 'Tenure, Tenant-right and Agricultural Progress in Lindsay, 1780–1850', *Agric. Hist. Rev.* 23 (1975), 1/22.

—— 'Social and Electoral Influence of the Trentham Interest, 1800–1860', *Midland Hist.* 3 (1975–6), 142.

PHILLIPS, J. A., 'The Structure of the Unreformed Electorate', *J. Brit. Studies* 19 (1979), 76–100.

—— 'Popular Politics in Unreformed England', *J. Modern Hist.* 52/4 (1980), 599–625.

—— 'The Many Faces of Reform: The Reform Bill and the Electorate', *Parl. Hist. Yrbk.* (1982), 115–35.

PHILLIPS, N. C., 'Edmund Burke and the County Movement, 1779–1780', *Eng. Hist. Rev.* 76 (1961) 254–78.

PLUMB, J. H., 'The Growth of the Electorate in England, 1600–1715', *Past and Present*, 45 (1969), 90–116.

POCOCK, J. G. A., 'The Classical Theory of Deference', *Am. Hist. Rev.* 81 (1976), 516–23.

PORTER, R. E., 'The Marketing of Agricultural Produce in Cheshire during the Nineteenth Century', *Trans. Hist. Soc. Lancs. and Cheshire*, 126 (1975), 139–55.

QUINAULT, R. E., 'Lord Randolph Churchill and Tory Democracy, 1880–1885', *Hist. J.* 22 (1979), 141–65.

REES, R. D., 'Electioneering Ideals Current in South Wales, 1790–1830', *Welsh Hist. Rev.* 11 (1965), 233–50.

RICHARDS, E., 'The Social and Economic Influence of the Trentham Interest, 1800–60', *Midland Hist.* 3 (1975–6), 117–48.

ROGERS, N., 'Aristocratic Clientage, Trade and Independency: Popular Politics in Pre-Radical Westminster', *Past and Present*, 61 (1973), 70–106.

—— 'The City Elections Act Reconsidered', *Eng. Hist. Rev.* 200 (1985), 604–17.

RUDE, G., 'The Middlesex Electors of 1768–69', *Eng. Hist. Rev.* 75 (1960), 601–17.

SACK, J. J., 'The House of Lords and Parliamentary Patronage, 1802–1832', *Hist. J.* 23 (1980), 913–37.

SANDERSON, F. E., 'The Structure of Politics in Liverpool, 1780–1807', *Trans. Hist. Soc. Lancs. and Cheshire* 127 (1978), 65–90.

SEARLBY, P., 'Paternalism, Disturbance and Parliamentary Reform: Society and Politics in Coventry, 1819–32', *Int. Rev. Soc. Hist.* 22 (1977), 198–208.

SEED, J., 'Gentlemen Dissenters: The Social and Political Meanings of Rational Dissent in the 1770s and 1780s', *Hist. J.* 28 (1985), 299–325.

SMITH, E. A., 'Earl Fitzwilliam and Malton: A Proprietary Borough in the Early Nineteenth Century', *Eng. Hist. Rev.* 81 (1965), 51–69.

SMITH, E. A., 'The Yorkshire Elections of 1806 and 1807', *Northern Hist.* 11 (1967), 69–90.

—— 'The Election Agent in English Politics, 1734–1782', *Eng. Hist. Rev.* 84 (1969), 12–35.

SMITH, R. W., 'Political Organization and Canvassing: Yorkshire Elections before the Great Reform Bill', *Am. Hist. Rev.* 74 (1969), 1538–60.

SPECK, W. A., 'A Computer Analysis of Poll Books: An Initial Report', *Bull. Inst. Hist. Res.* 43 (1970), 105–12.

—— 'Brackley: A Study in the Growth of Oligarchy', *Midland Hist.* 3 (1975), 30–41.

—— and GRAY, W. A., 'Londoners at the Polls Under Anne and George I', *Guildhall Studies* (1975), 251–62.

—— —— and HOPKINSON, R. 'A Computer Analysis of Poll Books: A Further Report', *Bull. Inst. Hist. Res.* 48 (1975), 64–90.

SPRING, D., 'The English Landed Estate in the Age of Coal and Iron, 1830–1880', *J. Econ. Hist.* 11 (1951), 3–24.

—— 'Walter Bagehot and Deference', *Am. Hist. Rev.* 81 (1976), 524–31.

THOMAS, W., 'Whigs and Radicals at the Westminster Election of 1819', *Guildhall Misc.* 3/3 (1970), 174–217.

THOMPSON, E. P., 'Eighteenth Century English Society: Class Struggle Without Class?', *Soc. Hist.* (1978), 133–65.

—— 'Patrician Society and Plebeian Culture', *J. Social Hist.* 7 (1974), 383–405.

THORNE, R. G., 'The Pembrokeshire Elections of 1807 and 1812', *The Pembrokeshire Historian*, 6 (1979), 1–18.

TRATNER, N. L., 'Population and Social Structure in a Bedfordshire Parish in the Cardington List of 1782', *Population Studies*, 21 (1967), 261–82.

VON DEN STEINEN, K., 'The Fabric of Interest in the County: The Bucks. Election of 1784', *Albion*, 4 (1972) 206–18.

VEITCH, G. S., 'Huskisson and Elections at Liskeard', *Trans. Royal Hist. Soc.* 4th ser., 13 (1930), 204–28.

WAGER, D., 'Welsh Politics and Parliamentary Reform, 1780–1832', *Welsh Hist. Rev.* 7 (1975), 427–49.

WEINZIERL, M. 'The Norwich Elections of 1794, 1796 and 1802: Conflict and Consensus', *Parliaments, Estates and Representation* 6, 2 (1986), 167–80.

WEYMAN, H. T., 'Ludlow Members of Parliament', *Trans. Salop. Archeol. Soc.* 2nd ser., 7 (1895), 43.

WHITTINGHAM-JONES, B., 'Electioneering in Lancashire before the Secret Ballot: 11. Liverpool's Political Clubs, 1812–1830', *Trans. Hist. Soc. Lancs. and Cheshire* (1959–60), 117–38.

—— 'Some Unreformed Elections at Liverpool', *Liverpool Dioc. Rev.* 8 (1933).

WILD, M. T., and SHAW, G., 'Locational Behaviour of Urban Retailing during the Nineteenth Century, *Trans. Inst. British Geog.* 61 (1974), 101–18.

WOODLAND, P., 'Benjamin Heath and the Opposition to the 1763 Cider Excise', *Parl. Hist. Yrbk.* 4 (1985), 115–36.

WORDIE, J. A., 'Social Change on the Leveson–Gower Estates, 1714–1832', *Midland Hist.* 4 (1977), 593–607.


*Unpublished Dissertations*

ANDREWS, J. H., 'Political Issues in the County of Kent, 1820–1846', M.Phil. (London, 1967).

ASPINALL, B., 'William Smith MP, 1756–1835', MA (Manchester, 1962).

ASQUITH I., 'James Perry and the Morning Chronicle, 1790–1821', Ph.D. (London, 1973).

BAILLY, R. C., 'The Parliamentary History of Reading, 1750–1850', MA (Reading, 1944).

BALL, E., 'Glamorgan: A Study of the Concerns of the County and the Work of its Members in the House of Commons, 1825–1835', Ph.D. (London, 1965).

BASKERVILLE, S. W., 'The Management of the Tory Interest in Lancashire and Cheshire, 1714–1747', D.Phil. (Oxford, 1976).

BEAMISH, D. F., 'The Parliamentary and Municipal History of the Borough of Poole, *c.*1740–*c.*1840', M.Phil. (Southampton, 1982).

BECKETT, J. V., 'Landownership in Cumbria, 1680–1750', Ph.D. (Lancaster, 1975).

BERRY, D. 'The Social and Economic Development and Organisation of the Lake District', MA (Manchester, 1955).

BRADLEY, C., 'The Parliamentary Representation of the Boroughs of Pontefract, Newark and East Retford 1754–1768', MA (Manchester, 1953).

BRADLEY, JAMES E. 'Whigs and Nonconformists: Presbyterians, Congregationalists and Baptists in English Politics, 1715–1790', Ph.D. (Univ. of Southern California, 1978).

BYRNE, M. J., 'Local Government and Politics in Shrewsbury in the Nineteenth Century', MA (Wales, 1983).

CANNON, J. A., 'The Parliamentary Representation of the Boroughs of Chippenham, Cricklade, Downton, Hindon, Westbury and Wootton Bassett, 1754–1790', Ph.D. (Bristol, 1958).

CHILDS, A. R., 'Politics and Elections in Suffolk Boroughs During the Late Eighteenth Century and Early Nineteenth Century', M.Phil. (Reading, 1973).

CLOSE, D. 'The General Election of 1835 and 1837 in England and Wales' D.Phil. (Oxford, 1966).

COMBER, W. M., 'The Cornish Boroughs and Parliamentary Reform, 1800–1832', MA (Exeter, 1976).

COOK, D., 'The Representative History of the County, Town and University of Cambridge, 1689–1832', Ph.D. (Cambridge, 1935).

CRAMP, M. M., 'Parliamentary Representation of Five Sussex Boroughs: Bramber, Midhurst, Lewes, Rye and Winchelsea', MA (Manchester, 1953).

DAVID, I. W. R., 'Political and Electioneering Activity in South East Wales, 1820–1852', MA (Wales, 1959).

DAYKIN, C. W., 'The History of Parliamentary Representation in the City and County of Durham, 1675–1832', M.Litt (Durham, 1961).

ELVINS, W., 'The Reform Movement and County Politics in Cornwall, 1809–1852', MA (Birmingham, 1959).

FEARN, E., 'Reform Movements in Derby and Derbyshire, 1790–1832', MA (Manchester, 1964).

FEWSTER, J. M., 'The Politics and Administration of the Borough of Morpeth in the Later Eighteenth Century', Ph.D. (Newcastle, 1960).

FRASER, P., 'The Conduct of Public Business in the House of Commons, 1812–1827', Ph.D. (London, 1957).

GADDIS, E. R., 'William Windham and the Conservative Reaction in England, 1790–96: The Making of a Conservative Whig and the Norwich Electoral Response', Ph.D. (Pennsylvania, 1979).

GOLBY, J., 'The Political and Electioneering Influence of the Fourth Duke of Newcastle', MA (Nottingham, 1961).

GUNSTONE, D. P., 'Stewardship and Landed Society: A Study of the Stewards of the Longleat Estate', MA (Essex, 1972).

HAVILL, E., 'The Parliamentary Representation of Monmouthshire and Monmouth Boroughs, 1536–1832' (Wales, 1948).

HAYES, B. D., 'Politics in Norfolk, 1750–1832', Ph.D. (Cambridge 1958).

HINTON, M., 'The General Elections of 1806 and 1807', Ph.D. (Reading, 1959).

HOGARTH, C. E., 'Parliamentary Elections in Derby and Derbyshire, 1832–1865', MA (Manchester, 1957).

HUMPHREYS, P. L., 'Kentish Politics and Public Opinion, 1768–1832', D.Phil (Oxford, 1981).

HUNT, F. M., 'The North of England Agitation for the Abolition of the Slave Trade, 1780–1800', MA (Manchester, 1959).

JONES, L., 'An Edition of the Correspondence of the 1st Marquis of Anglesey relating to the General Elections of 1830, 1831 and 1832', MA (Liverpool, 1956).

KENT, G. B., 'Party Politics in the County of Staffordshire, 1830–1847', MA (Birmingham, 1959).

KERRISON, S. E., 'Coventry and the Municipal Corporations Act', MA (Birmingham, 1939).

LANSBERRY, H. F., 'Politics and Government in St Albans, 1688–1835', Ph.D. (London, 1964).

LEE, J., 'Stamford and the Cecils', B.Litt. (Oxford, 1957).

LOWE, S., 'Hampshire Elections and the Electioneering, 1734–1830', M.Phil. (Southampton, 1972).

MCADAMS, D. R., 'Politicians and the Electorate in the Late Eighteenth Century', Ph.D. (Duke University, North Carolina, 1967).

MARKHAM, J., 'Elections and Electioneering in East Yorkshire, 1815–1865', Ph.D. (Hull, 1976).

MASON, G. C., 'The Radical Bequest: Continuity in English Popular Politics, 1789–1832', Ph.D. (York, 1976).

MITCHELL, J., 'Electoral Change and the Party System in England, 1832–1868', Ph.D. (Yale, 1976).

MOSES, J. H., 'Elections and Electioneering in Nottinghamshire Constituencies, 1702–1832', Ph.D. (Nottingham, 1965).

NEWMAN, A., 'Elections in Kent and Its Parliamentary Representation, 1715–1754', D.Phil. (Oxford, 1957).

NOSSITER, T. J., 'Elections and Political Behaviour in County Durham and Westmorland, 1832–1874', D.Phil. (Oxford, 1968).

ODURKENE, J. N., 'The British General Elections of 1830 and 1831', B.Litt. (Oxford, 1976).

O'SULLIVAN, D. S., 'Politics in Norwich, 1701–1835', MA (East Anglia, 1975).

PARRY, O., 'The Parliamentary Representation of Wales and Monmouthshire in the Nineteenth Century', MA (Wales, 1924).

PEACOCK, A. J., 'York in the Age of Reform', Ph.D. (York, 1973).

PHILLIPS, J. G., 'Electoral Behaviour in Pre-reform England', Ph.D. (Iowa, 1976).

PICKERSGILL, A., 'Parliamentary Elections in Essex, 1761–1784', MA (Manchester, 1953).

PRICE, F. C., 'Parliamentary Elections in York City, 1754–1790', MA (Manchester, 1958).

PRICE, T., 'The Foxite Whigs: A Study of Opposition Politics, 1794–1797' (Manchester, 1981).

RAM, R. W., 'The Political Activity of Dissenters in the East and West Ridings of Yorkshire, 1815–1850', MA (Hull, 1964).

RAYMOND, H. B., 'English Political Parties and Electoral Organization, 1832–1867' (Harvard, 1952).

REES, R. D., 'The Parliamentary Representation of South Wales, 1790–1830', Ph.D., 2 vols. (Reading, 1962).

ROBERTS, K., 'English County MPs, 1784–1832', B.Litt (Oxford, 1974).

SAYER, M. J., 'William Weddell and Yorkshire Politics', B.Litt (Oxford, 1976).

SCHOFIELD, D. A., 'Henry Addington as Speaker of the House of Commons, 1789–1801', MA (Southampton, 1959).

SHRIVER, D. P., 'The Problem of Corruption in British Parliamentary Elections, 1750–1860', Ph.D. (Case Western Reserve University, 1974).

SPEIGHT, M. E., 'Politics in the Borough of Colchester, 1812–1847', Ph.D. (London, 1969).

STOKER, D., 'Elections and Voting Behaviour: A Study of Elections in Northumberland, Durham, Cumberland, and Westmorland, 1760–1832', Ph.D. (Manchester, 1980).

STUART, D. G., 'The Parliamentary History of Tamworth', MA (London, 1958).

SUMNER, L. V., 'The General Election of 1818', Ph.D. (Manchester, 1969).

THOMAS, P. D. G., 'The Parliamentary Representation of North Wales, 1715–1784', MA (Wales, 1953).

THOMAS, R. G., 'Politics in Anglesey and Caernarvonshire, 1826–1852', MA (Wales, 1970).

TUNSIRI, V., 'The Party Politics of the Black Country and Neighbourhood, 1832–1867', MA (Birmingham, 1964).

VLAEMINKE, M. 'Bristol During the French Revolutionary War, 1793–1802', M.Litt. (Bristol, 1981).

VON DEN STEINEN, K., 'The Fabric of an Interest: The First Duke of Dorset and Kentish and Sussex Politics, 1705–1765', Ph.D. (UCLA, 1969).

WAGER, D. A., 'Welsh Politics and Parliamentary Reform, 1780–1835', Ph.D. (Wales, 1972).

WILLIAMS, H. M., 'The Geographic Distribution of Political Opinion in the County of Glamorgan, 1820–1950', MA (Wales, 1951).

# INDEX